WordPerfect 5.2 for Windows

A Professional Approach

Author

Deborah A. Hinkle
Instructor, Microcomputing
Forsyth Technical
Community College

GLENCOE

Macmillan/McGraw-Hill

New York, New York Columbus, Ohio Mission Hills, California Peoria, Illinois

Screens were captured using SnapPRO! from Window Painters, Ltd., Minneapolis, MN.

This program has been prepared with the assistance of Gleason Group, Inc., Norwalk, CT.

Library of Congress Cataloging-in Publication Data

Hinkle, Deborah A.
WordPerfect 5.2 for Windows: a professional approach/Deborah A. Hinkle.
p. cm.
Includes index.
ISBN 0-02-801803-6
1. WordPerfect for Windows (Computer file) 2. Word processing. I. Title
Z52.5.W65H55 1994 92-42253
652.5'5369—dc20 CIP

WordPerfect 5.2 for Windows: A Professional Approach

Send all inquiries to:

Glencoe Division, Macmillan/McGraw-Hill
936 Eastwind Drive
Westerville, OH 43081
ISBN 0-02-801803-6

2 3 4 5 6 7 8 9 POH 97 96 95 94

Contents

A Word to the Student

WordPerfect 5.2 for Windows: A Professional Approach has been written to help you master WordPerfect for Windows. The text is designed to present a WordPerfect concept, then to present a step-by-step procedure that walks you through the actual use of that concept. This "explain and do" format provides you with a chance to practice each important WordPerfect feature before being introduced to the next one.

There are eleven modules in the text. Each module is divided into smaller lessons. Each lesson begins with a list of the lesson's objectives, and includes detailed explanations of WordPerfect concepts and step-by-step procedures that lead you through these concepts. Key terms in the lesson are defined. A list of key terms also is compiled at the end of the lesson for review purposes. Keyboard shortcuts for WordPerfect also are listed at the end of each lesson. Special "Feature Boxes" provide you with tips and hints to increase your efficiency.

To reinforce your understanding, exercises follow each lesson. The exercises provide realistic practice by incorporating documents from a fictional business ("Five Points Realty" located in Atlanta, Georgia). Exercises one and two provide a comprehensive review of the concepts introduced in the lesson. Exercises three and four require more extensive keying and the use of proofreader's marks.

Your instructor may hand out a project to conclude each of the modules. This provides you with a very challenging assignment—to create realistic business documents independently. Procedures and explanations are limited to basic instructions. The project is a "test" of your knowledge of WordPerfect for Windows.

The first two modules are introductory. *Module 0* introduces you to Windows and to the mouse. *Module 1* is designed to give you such basic skills as entering text, editing text, and character formatting.

Module 2 introduces basic formatting. It discusses margins and line formatting, working with tabs, and paragraph formatting. *Module 3* explains how to cut and copy text in the same document or between multiple document windows. The Search and Replace features also are presented in this module.

Module 4 focuses on page formatting. You learn how to control page breaks, apply page numbering, and add headers and footers. *Module 5* emphasizes printing and special printing options and features.

Module 6 discusses advanced character formatting including fonts, type sizes, and special characters. *Module 7* focuses on creating tables and columns.

Module 8 includes the advanced features of styles and macros. *Module 9* contains two other important professional features—merging and sorting. *Module 10* includes working with lines and graphics boxes.

As you read about and practice each concept, illustrations of the screens have been provided to help you follow the instructions. (Don't worry if your screen looks somewhat different from the screen illustration. These differences are the result of varying system and computer configurations.)

The *Appendices* help you become familiar with correct business-document format—business letters, envelopes, and memoranda. Additionally, a *Glossary* provides a definition of all the key terms encountered in the lessons. The Glossary also indicates the lesson in which the term was used first. The inside front and back covers of the text provide a description of the WordPerfect screen, the toolbar, the ribbon, and the keyboard shortcut keys. A WordPerfect keyboard template also is provided.

The data disks contain all the text and graphics used in the lesson and the exercises. The files used in the projects are available from your instructor.

A book like this would be impossible without the help of many people. We would like to thank our reviewers: Rolayne Day, Salt Lake Community College, Salt Lake City, UT; Lynne D. Groves, Mankato Technical College, North Mankato, MN; Gene E. Parker, Lansing Community College, Lansing, MI; and Martha R. Lambert, WordPerfect Certified Resource, Brookfield, CT. They reviewed an incredible amount of material, and we benefited greatly from their suggestions.

Deborah A. Hinkle

Module 0

Basic Windows Skills

Lessons

1: Getting Started
2: Inside Windows
3: Starting Applications and Using Help

Lesson 1

Getting Started

Objectives

- Operate the mouse.
- Start and exit Windows.
- Minimize, maximize, and restore windows.
- Change the active window.
- Rearrange windows.

Before you use WordPerfect for Windows to create and edit documents on your computer, you need to become familiar with another program called Microsoft Windows (or Windows, for short). Windows is an operating environment for IBM and compatible computers. It supplements the computer's operating system, known as DOS (Disk Operating System), by adding a graphical screen display. WordPerfect for Windows and many other graphics-based programs need Windows to operate.

In computer terms, a *window* is a rectangular area on the computer screen with borders that separate it from the rest of the screen. When you open a file in Windows, a window appears on the computer screen with the contents of the file inside it. When you close the file, the window disappears.

Window
A rectangular area on the computer screen with borders that separate it from the rest of the screen.

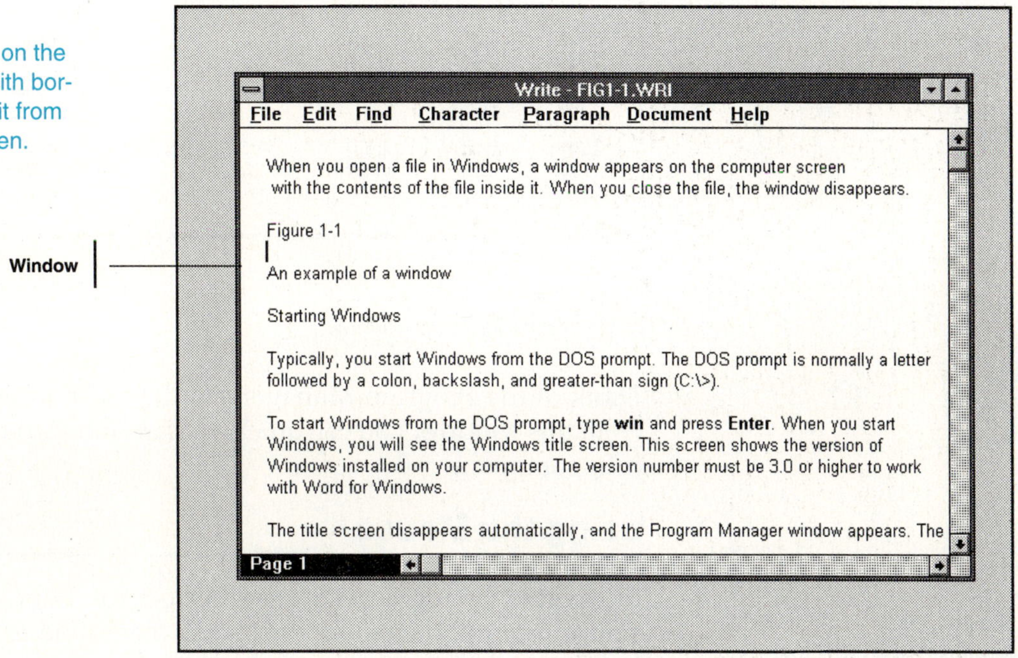

Figure 1-1
An example of a window

Starting Windows

Typically, you start Windows from the DOS prompt. The DOS prompt is normally a letter followed by a colon, backslash, and greater-than sign (**C:\>**).

Note: Your computer may require different startup instructions. If it does, your instructor will provide them.

To start Windows from the DOS prompt, type **win** and press **Enter**. When you start Windows, you will see the Windows title screen. This screen shows the version of Windows installed on your computer. The version number must be 3.0 or higher to work with WordPerfect for Windows.

The title screen disappears automatically, and the Program Manager window appears. The Program Manager window shows you, at a glance, the general categories of programs you have on your hard disk.

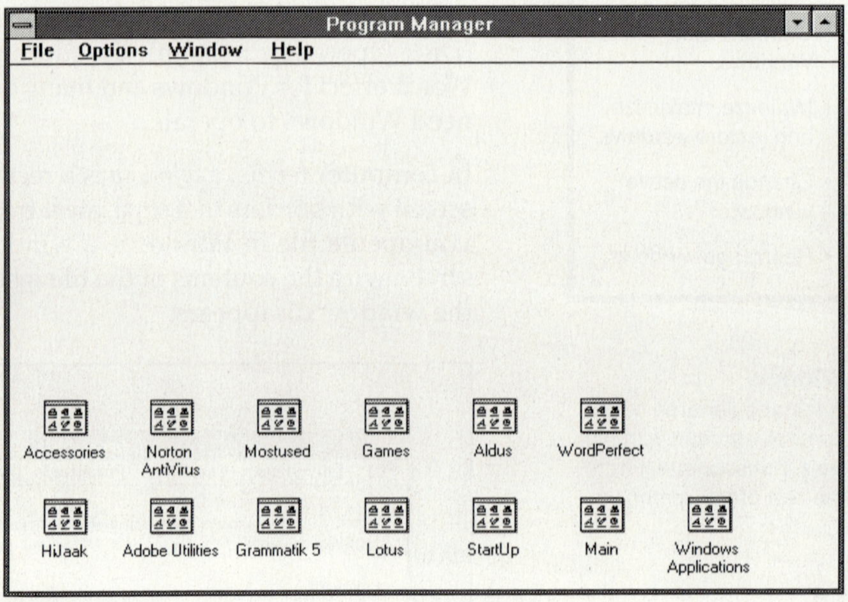

Figure 1-2
The Program Manager window

Think of the Program Manager window as a program organizer. From this window, you can quickly locate and start the programs on your computer.

Using the Mouse

Mouse pad
A small mat on which a mouse may be rolled.

Pointer
A small symbol on the screen that shows the position of the mouse.

To operate Windows and WordPerfect for Windows, you use a mouse. You roll the mouse on a small mat called a *mouse pad* (or on any flat surface, if you do not have a mouse pad). On one type of mouse, a rubber ball on the bottom of the mouse translates your movements to the computer. A *pointer*, a small symbol on the computer screen, shows your on-screen location as you move the mouse.

To select items on the computer screen using a mouse, you press a mouse button. Your mouse may have two or three buttons. Whenever you are told to "click" or "double-click" the mouse button, use

Note: A trackball, which looks like an upside-down mouse, is sometimes used in place of a mouse. It provides the same functions as the mouse.

the left button. In cases where you should use the right button, you will be told to do so.

There are four ways to operate the mouse:

- Point

  When you *point*, you move the mouse until the on-screen pointer is on top of an item on the computer screen.

- Click

  When you *click*, you press the mouse button and then quickly release it.

- Double-click

  When you *double-click*, you quickly press and release the mouse button twice.

- Drag

  When you *drag*, you point to an object, hold down the mouse button, and move the mouse to a new position. Then release the mouse button.

Practicing with the Mouse

Note: If you do not see a moving, arrow-shaped pointer on the computer screen, try moving the mouse farther to the left, right, toward you, or away from you until you see the pointer. Then pick up the mouse so the rubber ball underneath it does not touch the mouse pad or desktop. Move the mouse back to the center of the mouse pad and put it down. The position of the pointer on the computer screen does not change until the ball under the mouse once again touches a flat surface.

Pointer over the word "File"

In Windows (and in WordPerfect for Windows) there are often several ways to accomplish the same task. For example, you will learn three ways to close a window in the following practice session.

1. Place your hand over the mouse in a comfortable position with a finger on the left button, but without pressing the button.
2. Move the mouse around on its mouse pad and watch the computer screen. Look for a moving, arrow-shaped pointer.
3. Move the mouse toward you, away from you, to the left, and to the right, and watch the corresponding movements of the pointer on the computer screen.
4. Use the pointer to point to the word "File". To do this, move the mouse until the tip of the arrow is on top of File.
5. Move the mouse to the right, and stop when the pointer is on the word "Help".
6. Click (press and release) the left mouse button.

   A menu appears on the screen.

7. Point to the empty area to the right of the menu and click.

   The menu disappears.

8. Point to the rectangular symbol directly above the words "Windows Applications" and double-click (quickly press and release the mouse button twice).

   The Windows Applications window opens on the screen.

9. Point to the small, square box at the upper left of the window.

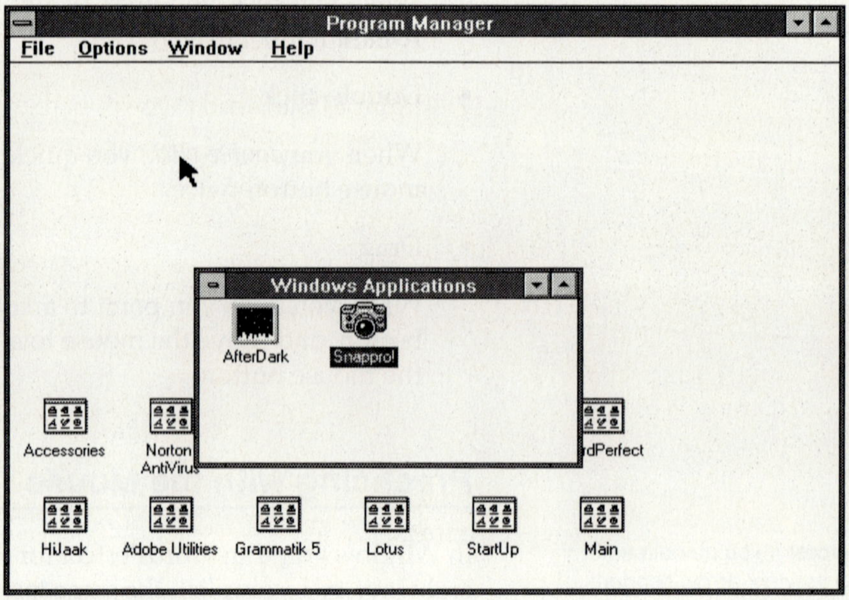

Figure 1-3
Your screen may look different from this screen, depending on the programs included in the Windows Applications window.

10. Drag the mouse, by holding down the mouse button and moving the mouse toward you, until the pointer is on top of the word "Close". Then release the mouse button.

    The window disappears.

11. Point to the rectangular symbol directly above the words "Windows Applications" again, and click once.

    A menu appears above the symbol.

12. Point to the word "Restore" and click.

    The Windows Applications window reopens.

13. Point to the small, square box in the upper left corner of the Windows Applications window and double-click.

    The Windows Applications window closes.

14. Again, point to the rectangular symbol directly above the words "Windows Applications" and click once.

    The menu again appears above the symbol.

15. Point to the empty area to the right of the menu and click.

    The menu disappears.

16. This time, point to the word "File" at the top of the screen and click.

    A menu appears below File.

17. Point to the word "Open" and click.

    The Windows Applications window reopens.

18. Close the window again by double-clicking the small, square box in the upper left corner of the Windows Applications window.

Icons

Icons
Small pictures or symbols on the computer screen representing programs or tools.

Program Manager icon

One feature that makes Windows and programs that work with Windows different from most other computer programs is their use of *icons*. Icons are small pictures or symbols on the computer screen. The symbol above the words "Program Manager" is an example of an icon.

Icons are used to represent many items on the computer screen, such as programs, groups of programs, and tools you use within programs. By getting to know the icons, you will be able to locate and select the programs and tools you need quickly.

To select the Accessories icon in the Program Manager window:

1. Point to the icon above Accessories.

2. Click the left mouse button once.

   A menu appears above the icon. If the word "Accessories" was not already shown with a dark background, the background changes now. That is how you know the icon has been selected.

3. To select the Windows Applications icon, point to the icon, and click the mouse button once.

   The menu above the Accessories icon disappears. The word "Accessories" returns to a light background, indicating that it is no longer selected. The words "Windows Applications" are shown on a dark background, indicating that the Windows Applications icon has now been selected. A menu appears above the icon.

4. Point to an empty area in the window, and click the mouse button once.

   The menu disappears; however, the background of Windows Applications is still dark, indicating that it is still selected.

Parts of a Window

All windows contain several basic elements. The Program Manager window is a good example of a typical window.

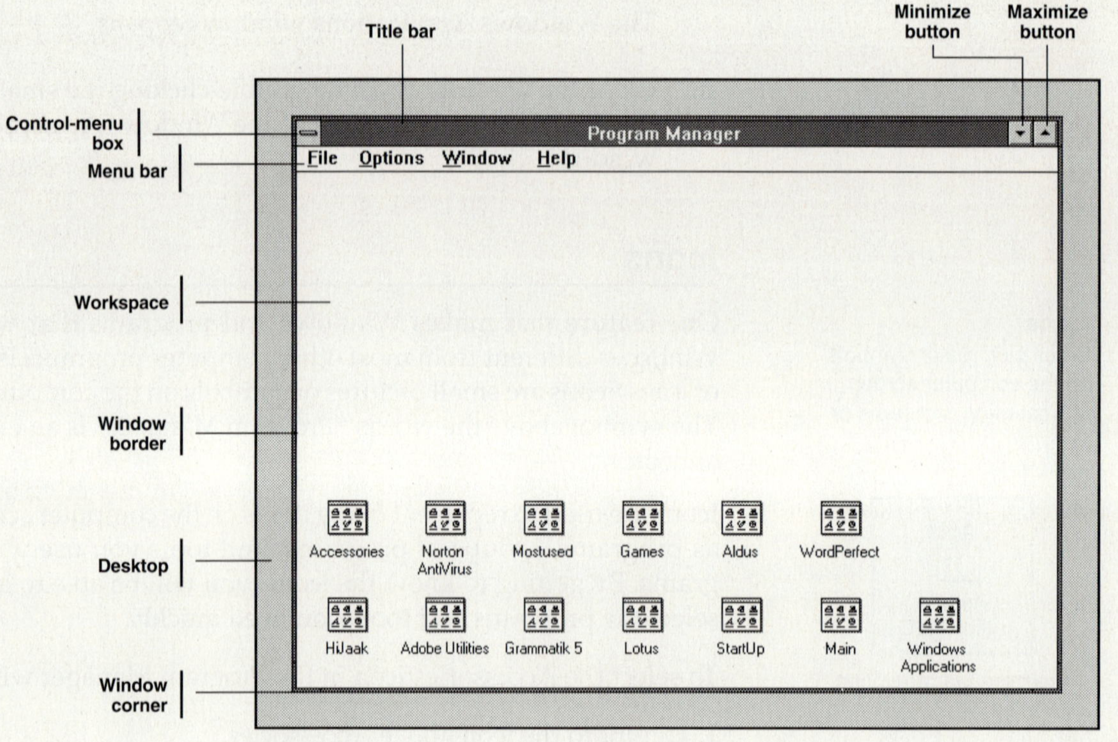

Figure 1-4
The Program Manager window

The common window elements are:

- Window borders

  The *window borders* are the boundary lines surrounding the window.

- Window corners

  The *window corners* are the areas at the four corners of the window border. These corners are used to adjust the size of the window.

- Title bar

  The *title bar* is the shaded bar at the top of the window that displays the name of the window.

- Control-menu box

  The *Control-menu box* is the box in the upper left corner of the window. Clicking this box displays the Control menu, which contains options for manipulating windows.

- Minimize button

  The *Minimize button* is the box in the upper right corner containing a down arrow. Clicking this button shrinks the window to its icon.

- Maximize button

  The *Maximize button* is the box in the upper right corner containing an up arrow. Clicking this button enlarges the window to fill the entire screen.

- Menu bar

  The *menu bar* is the area under the title bar that displays the words File, Options, Window, and Help.

- Workspace

  The *workspace* is the area in the window that displays the contents of the window.

- Desktop

  The *desktop* is the area of the computer screen outside the window borders.

Types of Windows

As you work in Windows, you will notice that there are two types of windows: application windows and document windows.

Application window
A window that contains a running application and has a menu bar.

An *application window* has a menu bar. For example, the Program Manager window and the WordPerfect for Windows window are application windows.

Document window
A window without a menu bar, appearing in the workspace of an application window.

A *document window* does not have a menu bar. It appears in the workspace of an application window. It may contain documents, programs, groups of programs, files, or tools. More than one document window can be open in an application window at one time.

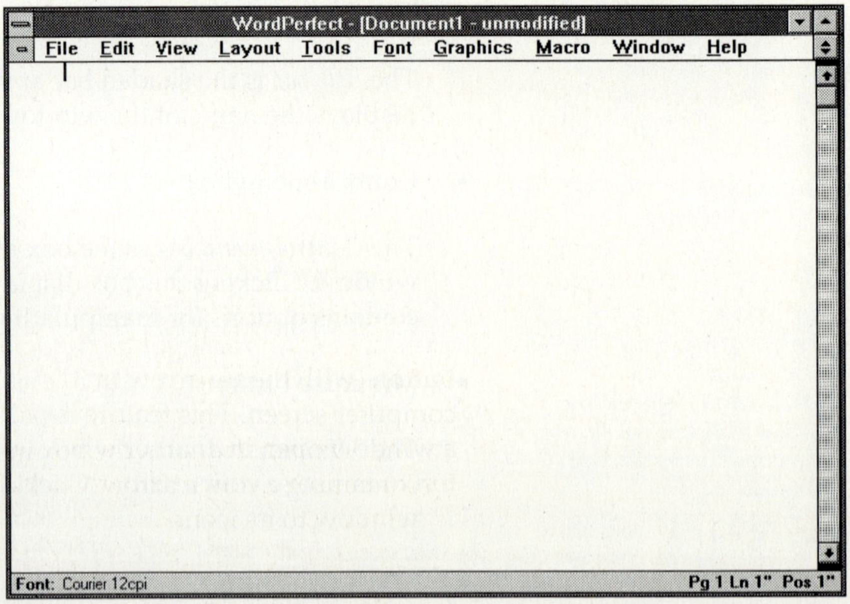

Figure 1-5
The WordPerfect for Windows window

The following example shows two document windows (the Main window and the Accessories window) open in the Program Manager window at one time.

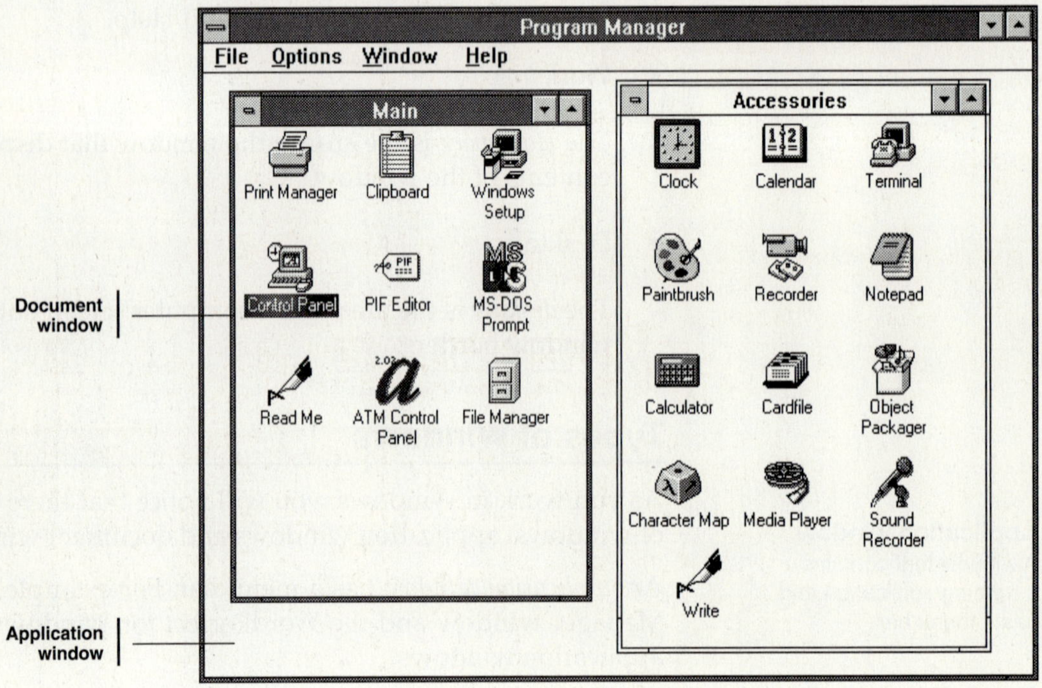

Figure 1-6
Two document windows open in an application window

Active window
The window currently in use on the computer screen.

When more than one window is open on the computer screen, only one of the windows is in use, or *active*. The active window appears in front of all other windows. On some computer screens, its title bar appears in a different color from the other windows. In the previous example, the Main window is active.

Minimizing/Maximizing Windows

Restore button
The box at the right of the title bar containing a double arrow. Returns the window to its original size. Appears after maximizing a window.

Restore button

Note: When you use the Maximize button in a window located within another window, the second window grows to the size of the original window. It will not fill the entire screen unless the original window already does.

The Minimize and Maximize buttons in the upper right corner of a window let you change the window's size quickly. The Maximize button (with the up arrow in it) enlarges a window to fill the entire computer screen. This feature is particularly useful when you have a window open in another window. You can use the Maximize button to improve your ability to see what is in the window. Once you have maximized a window, the Maximize button for that window changes to the *Restore button* containing a double arrow. Clicking the Restore button returns the window to its original size.

The Minimize button (with the down arrow in it) reduces the window to its icon, which typically appears in the lower left corner of the screen.

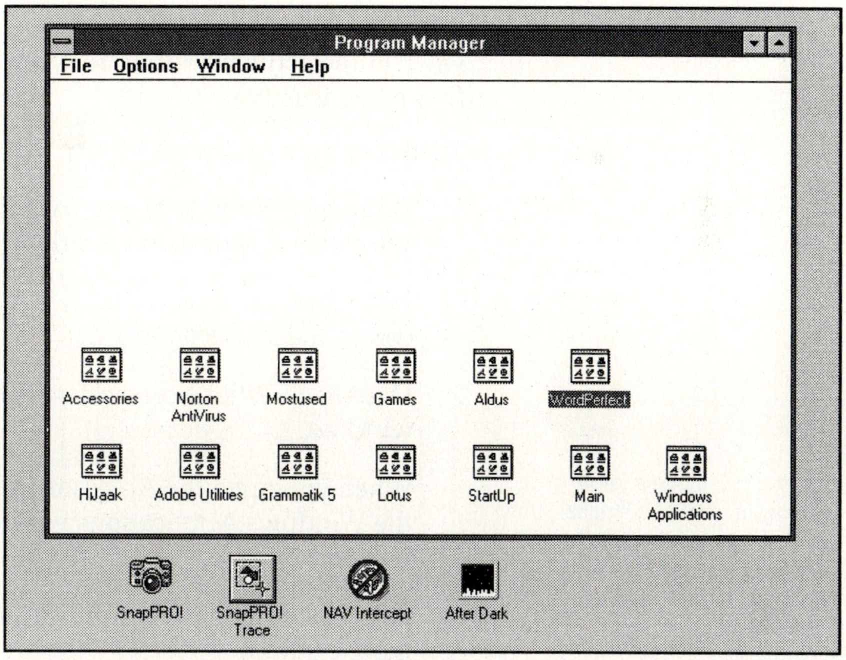

Figure 1-7
A screen showing minimized windows

To maximize a window:

1. Point to the Maximize button in the upper right corner of the Program Manager window.

2. Click the left mouse button.

To restore a window to its original size:

1. Point to the Restore button in the window.
2. Click the left mouse button.

To minimize a window:

1. Point to the Minimize button in the window.
2. Click the left mouse button once.

To restore a window to its original size:

1. Point to the window's icon.
2. Double-click the left mouse button. (After the first click, you may see a menu flash on the screen above the icon. This disappears when the window is restored after your second click.)

Moving Between Windows

When two or more windows are open simultaneously, you can only work in the active window. To work in another window, you must first make it active.

To move to a window and make it active:

1. Double-click the Windows Applications icon to open the Windows Applications window.

   When you open the Windows Applications window, it becomes the active window.

2. Double-click the Accessories icon to open the Accessories window.

   When you open the Accessories window, it moves in front of the Windows Applications window and becomes the active window.

3. Point to the Windows Applications window, and click the left mouse button.

   The Windows Applications window moves in front of the Accessories window and becomes active.

Note: If you move a larger window in front of a smaller one, you will not be able to point to the smaller window when you want to make it active. Instead, you can use the Minimize button in the current active window to reduce the larger window to its icon. Then you will be able to see the smaller window.

Rearranging Windows

When working with several open windows, some windows are hidden behind others. You can rearrange windows so that a part of each one is visible.

Cascading windows
Open windows that are arranged in layers with the title bar of each window visible.

You can layer each window within the Program Manager workspace so that you can see each window's title bar. These are *cascading windows*.

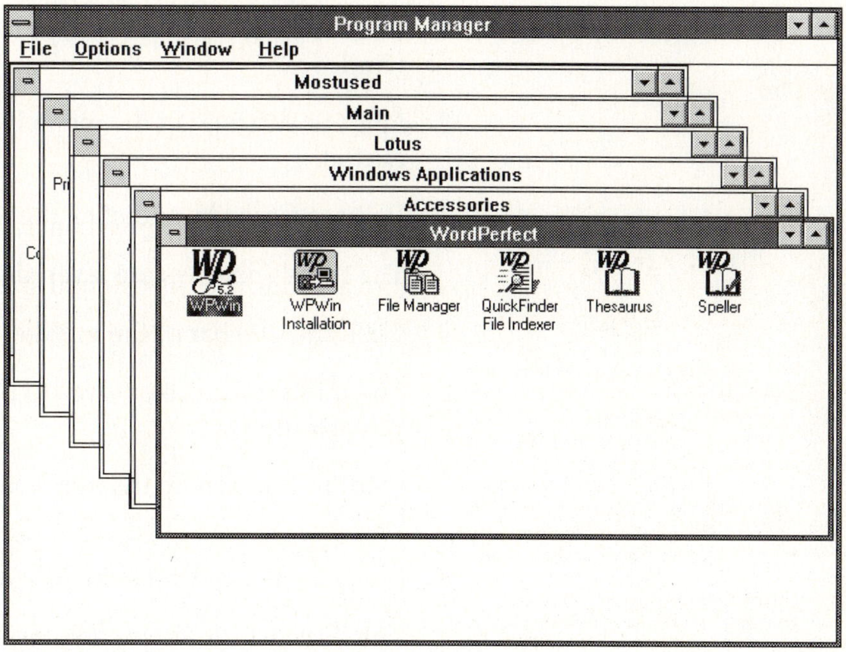

Figure 1-8
Cascading windows within the Program Manager window

Or, you can arrange the windows so that they appear side by side within the Program Manager workspace. These are *tiled windows.*

Tiled windows
Open windows that are resized and arranged side by side on the screen.

Note: Tiled windows are arranged in smaller sizes. Therefore, not all icons may be visible within a tiled window.

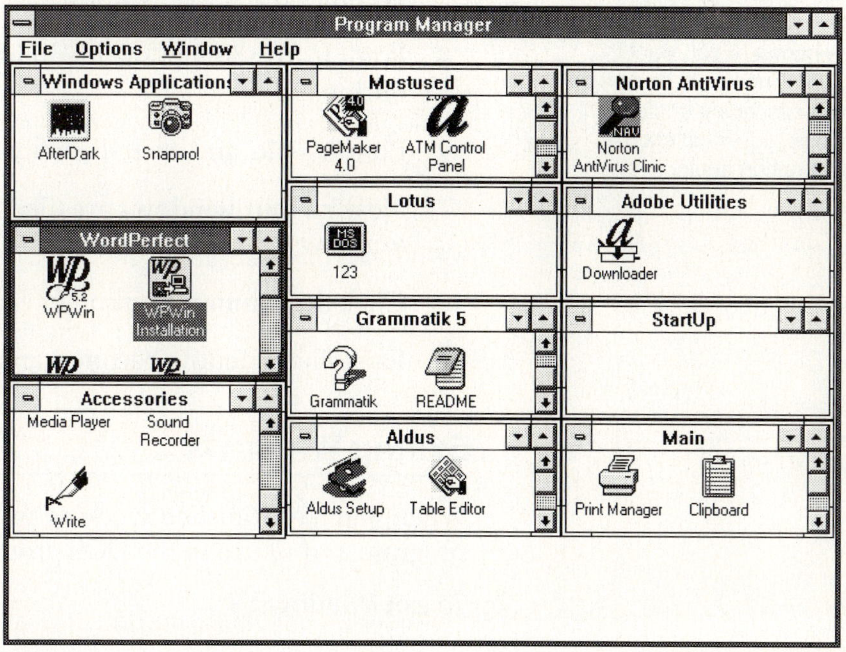

Figure 1-9
Tiled windows within the Program Manager window

Both options are chosen from the Window menu. Menu options are discussed further in the next lesson.

To rearrange windows:

1. Double-click the Main icon so that there are three open windows.

2. Point to Window in the menu bar, and click the left mouse button.

3. Point to Cascade, and click the left mouse button.

   The three windows are layered with their title bars showing.

4. Click the title bar of the middle window.

   The middle window moves to the front and becomes the active window.

5. Point to Window in the menu bar, and click the left mouse button.

6. Point to Tile, and click the left mouse button.

   The three windows are displayed side by side within the Program Manager window.

7. Double-click the Word for Windows icon that appears below the tiled windows.

   Word for Windows overlaps one of the tiled windows and becomes the active window.

8. Point to Window in the menu bar, and click the left mouse button.

9. Point to Tile, and click the left mouse button.

   Now all four windows are tiled within the Program Manager window.

10. Click the Minimize button in each of the tiled windows.

    Each tiled window becomes an icon again.

Note: When you open an additional window after choosing the cascade or tile option, the window overlaps the rearranged windows. If you want the new windows to be part of the cascading or tiled windows, you must choose the option again.

Exiting Windows

When you have finished working in Windows, you should exit the program and return to the DOS prompt.

To exit Windows:

1. Point to File in the menu bar of the Program Manager window, and click the left mouse button.

2. Point to Exit Windows in the menu that appears, and click the left mouse button.

   A box appears prompting you to confirm that you would like to end the Windows session.

3. Point to OK, and click the left mouse button.

   You are returned to the DOS prompt.

Key Terms

Active window
Application window
Cascading windows
Click
Control-menu box
Desktop
Document window
Double-click
Drag
Icons
Maximize button
Menu bar
Minimize button
Mouse pad
Point
Pointer
Restore button
Tiled windows
Title bar
Window
Window borders
Window corners
Workspace

Exercises

Exercise 1.1

1. Turn on the computer and start Windows.
2. Move the mouse until the pointer is in the Program Manager menu bar.
3. Point to File. Then point to Options and Help.
4. With the pointer on Help, click the left mouse button.

   A menu appears.

5. Point to an empty area in the workspace, and click the left mouse button again.

   The menu disappears.

6. Point to the Maximize button, and click the left mouse button.

   The window fills the entire screen.

7. Point to the Restore button, and click the mouse button.

   The window returns to its original size.

8. Point to the Minimize button, and click the left mouse button.

   The window changes to an icon at the bottom of the screen.

9. Point to the Program Manager icon at the bottom of the screen, and double-click the left mouse button.

   The window returns to its original size.

   If you will be doing Exercise 1.2 immediately, skip Steps 10 through 12.

10. Point to File in the menu bar.

11. Hold down the left mouse button, and drag the mouse toward you until the pointer is on top of Exit Windows. Then release the mouse button.

12. Point to OK in the box that appears and click the left mouse button.

Exercise 1.2

1. If necessary, turn on the computer and start Windows.

2. Double-click the Windows Applications icon in the Program Manager window.

   The Windows Applications window opens.

3. Double-click the Non-Windows Applications icon.

   The Non-Windows Applications window opens.

4. Double-click the Accessories icon.

   The Accessories window opens.

5. Point to Window in the menu bar, and click the left mouse button.

6. Point to Cascade, and click the left mouse button.

7. Point to the Minimize button in the Accessories window, and click the left mouse button.

   The Accessories window changes to its icon.

8. Point to the title bar in the Windows Applications window, and click the left mouse button.

   The Windows Applications window becomes active (moves to the front).

9. Point to the Maximize button in the Windows Applications window, and click the left mouse button.

   The Windows Applications window fills the entire Program Manager window.

10. Point to the Restore button (double-headed arrow) in the Windows Applications window, and click the left mouse button.

    The Windows Applications window returns to its original size.

11. Click the Minimize button in each of the open windows.

    The windows all change to icons.

12. Click the Minimize button in the Program Manager window.

    Only the Program Manager is now visible as an icon.

13. Double-click the Program Manager icon.

    The Program Manager window opens.

14. Point to File in the menu bar, and click the left mouse button.

    A menu appears.

15. Point to Exit Windows, and click the left mouse button.

16. Point to OK in the box that appears, and click the left mouse button.

Inside Windows

Objectives

- Select options from menus.
- Respond to dialog box requests.
- Manipulate windows.
- Operate scroll bars.
- Choose a printer.

While you do not need to understand all aspects of Windows to operate WordPerfect for Windows successfully, you will find a basic knowledge of the program's features helpful. Because WordPerfect for Windows is built on the structure of the Windows environment, you will be able to transfer much of what you learn about Windows to WordPerfect for Windows. So learning Windows will make learning WordPerfect for Windows much easier.

Using Menus

To conserve space in Windows, many available program features, or options, are kept in menus that you access from the menu bar. Windows has five menus, containing lists of options.

- File menu

  The File menu contains file-management options, such as Move, Copy, and Delete. It also contains the Exit Windows option for exiting the program.

- Options menu

  The Options menu contains options for arranging and sizing icons.

- Window menu

  The Window menu contains options for arranging windows and icons. It also lists the available windows and allows access to them.

- Help menu

  The Help menu contains options for accessing the Windows Help features.

- Control menu

  This menu appears when you click the Control-menu box located to the left of the title bar. The Control menu contains options for changing the size and location of windows. All applications that work with Windows have a similar Control menu.

Control-menu box

When a menu is closed, you see only its name in the menu bar. When a menu is open, you can view and select menu options.

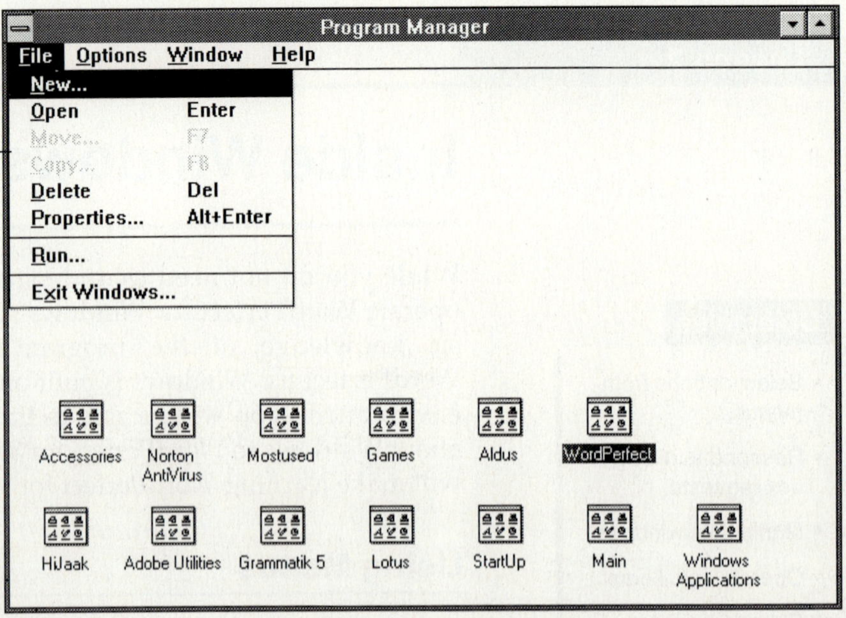

Figure 2-1
On this screen, the File menu is open.

Pull-down menus
Menus that pull down to display a list of options when the name of the menu is clicked. (Also called drop-down menus.)

Note: You can use this drop-down feature to view menu options without making a selection. When you click a menu name, the menu opens, and you can look over the options. When you are ready to close the menu, you can click in an empty part of the workspace, and the menu will close.

Highlighting
To position the pointer on a menu option, causing the option to change to light type on a dark background.

The menus are called *pull-down* or *drop-down menus* to describe the two ways you can open them.

The two ways to open menus and select options are:

- *By clicking the name of the menu in the menu bar.* When you do this, the menu drops down and the menu options appear. Then you can click the name of the option you want.

- *By clicking the menu name and dragging the mouse to pull down the menu.* When the menu is open, you can drag to the option you want and release the mouse button to select it.

More About Menu Options

When you drag the pointer on top of a menu option, the name changes to light type on a dark background. This is called *highlighting*. The option that is highlighted when you release the mouse button is selected.

Some menu options are only available at certain points in the program. When they are not available, they appear gray in the menu, and you are not able to select them.

Some menu options are followed by three dots. These dots let you know that a dialog box appears if you select that option. (Dialog boxes are discussed below.)

To the right of some menu options, you will notice keys (such as **F7** or **Del**) or a combination of keys (such as **Shift+F4** or **Ctrl+Esc**). These are keyboard commands that allow you to select menu options using the keyboard. To use a combination of keys, hold down the first key, press the second key, then release both keys.

Cascading menu
A menu that opens from a command on another menu.

A triangle (▶) at the right side of a menu command indicates that the command leads to a *cascading menu*, which lists additional options that are available.

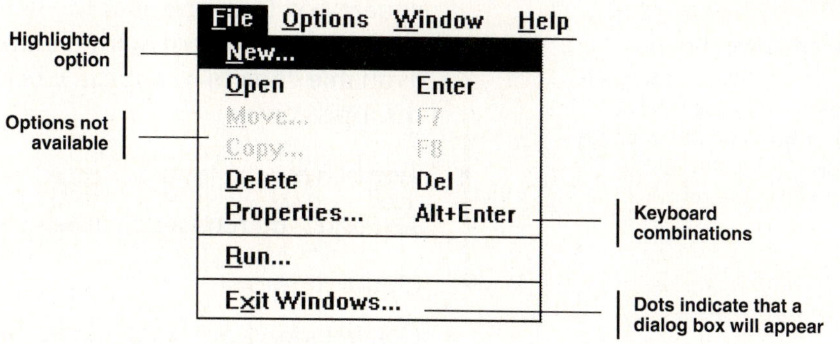

Figure 2-2
Menus provide immediate information about options.

Introduction to Dialog Boxes

Dialog box
A box that displays a question or presents options and asks you to respond.

A good portion of your interaction with Windows and WordPerfect for Windows will involve the use of *dialog boxes*. A dialog box displays a question or presents options and asks you to respond. It gives you a choice in how you want to proceed at certain points in the program.

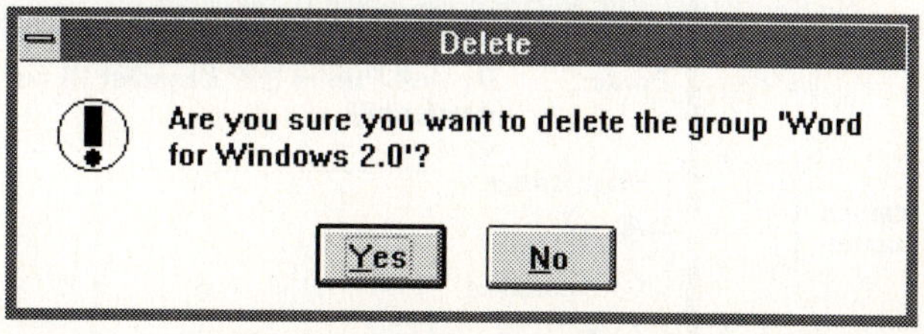

Figure 2-3
The Delete dialog box

Dialog boxes usually contain some or all of these items:

- Title

  The title is the name of the dialog box.

- Command buttons

  Command buttons are small rectangles, sometimes with rounded corners. You click a command button to choose an option.

  Some command buttons contain a word followed by three dots. When you click this type of command button, another dialog box appears offering you additional choices. Another type of command button contains a double chevron (»). Clicking this type of button causes another portion of the current dialog box to appear.

- List boxes

  List boxes contain a list of available choices. An arrow in a square box to the right of the list box indicates a *drop-down list box*. Clicking the box with the down arrow causes a list of available choices to appear. Clicking it again causes it to disappear.

Drop-down list box
A list box that contains additional choices that appear when an arrow on the right side of the list box is clicked.

- Text boxes

  Text boxes are rectangles in which you can type information.

- Option buttons

  Option buttons are small circles that indicate a list of mutually exclusive items. You can select only one item from the list at a time. To change your selection, select a different button. The selected option button contains a black dot.

- Check boxes

  Check boxes are small boxes offering you the chance to switch an option off or on. An **X** in the box indicates a yes response.

  To change the response in a check box, click the box.

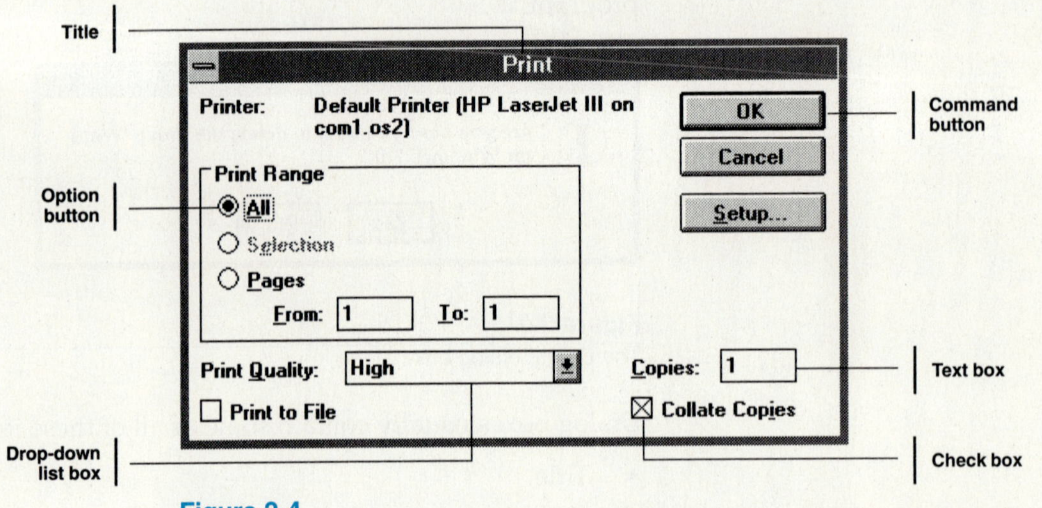

Figure 2-4
Often, you will use one dialog box to make several choices.

Choosing Dialog-Box Options

The method you use to respond to options in a dialog box depends on the information in the box. The simplest dialog boxes have two buttons, representing a yes or no decision. More complex dialog boxes may require you to choose from among several buttons, type a choice in a text box, and select a choice from a list box.

Most dialog boxes use OK to represent a yes decision and Cancel to represent a no decision. In dialog boxes containing several options, clicking OK saves the options you have chosen, while clicking Cancel closes the dialog box without saving your choices.

To choose dialog-box options using command buttons, click the button representing the choice you prefer. The procedure to exit Windows, for example, requires you to respond to a dialog box by clicking the appropriate button.

1. Turn on the computer and start Windows.
2 Click File in the menu bar of the Program Manager window.
3. Click Exit Windows in the File menu.

   The Exit Windows dialog box appears. Notice that this dialog box contains an OK and a Cancel command button.
4. Click the Cancel command button to close the dialog box and remain in Windows.

Moving Windows

You can move windows to new locations on the desktop using the mouse to create whatever desktop arrangement you like.

To move a window:

1. Point to the title bar of the Program Manager window, and hold down the mouse button.
2. Drag the window to a new location on the desktop.
3. Release the mouse button.

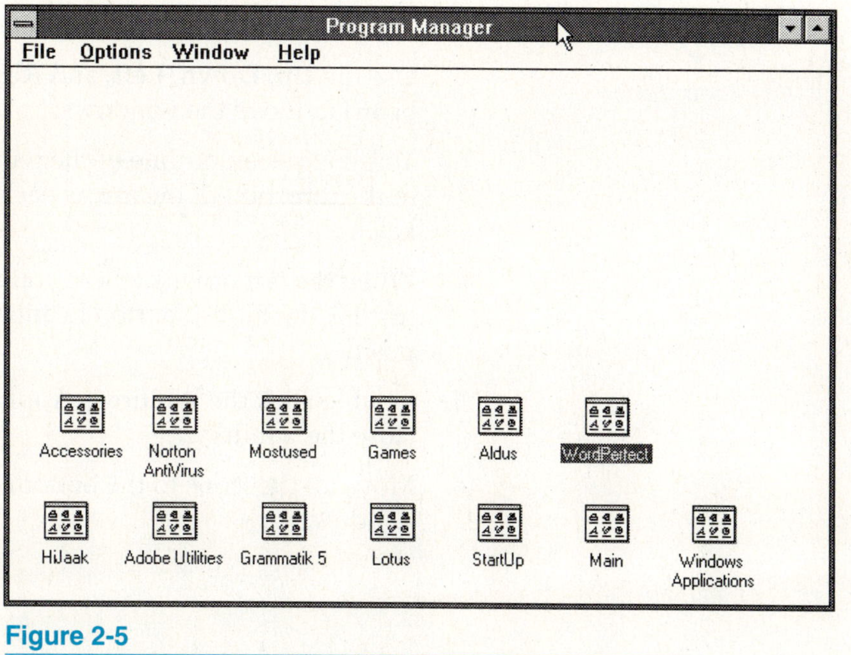

Figure 2-5
Point to the title bar, and drag the window.

Moving Items Within a Window

Items within a window, such as icons, dialog boxes, and other windows, are movable. You can arrange them any way you like. When windows or dialog boxes overlap inside a window, you can move them to see areas they are covering.

Note: Some dialog boxes cannot be moved. You cannot move a window or dialog box outside the window it is in. If you need to see an area behind a window or dialog box and cannot move it out of the way, you can enlarge the original window using the Maximize button and then move it.

To move a window or dialog box within a window:

1. Double-click the Windows Applications icon.
2. Point to the title bar of the Windows Applications window, and hold down the mouse button.
3. Drag the window to a new location while continuing to hold down the mouse button.
4. Release the mouse button.

To move an icon:

1. Point to the Main icon.
2. Drag the icon to a new location while continuing to hold down the mouse button.
3. Release the mouse button.

Note: If the Main icon is hidden by the Windows Applications screen, move the Windows Applications screen to the left or right until you see the Main icon.

Another method is available for moving windows within other windows using the Control menu and the keyboard:

1. Click the Windows Applications window to select it.
2. Click the Windows Applications Control-menu box to open the Control menu. Then select the Move option from the menu.

   The pointer changes to a four-headed arrow.

Four-headed arrow

3. Use the **Up**, **Down**, **Left**, and **Right Arrow** keys on the keyboard to move the windows.

   You will see an outline of the window move a small distance in the direction of the arrow each time you press an **Arrow** key.
4. When the window is where you want it, press the **Enter** key or click the mouse button to anchor the window in its new position.
5. Double-click the Windows Applications' Control-menu box to close the window.
6. Move all the icons to the bottom of the Program Manager window.

Changing the Size of Windows

You can control the size of windows. You can use the Minimize, Maximize, and Restore buttons described in Lesson 1 to adjust a window from the size of its icon to the size of the entire computer screen. But what if you want to make a window a particular size? Windows lets you use the mouse to adjust a window to any size.

To change the size of a window with the mouse:

↔

Double-headed arrow

1. Point to the right border of the window.

   The pointer changes to a double-headed arrow.

2. With the pointer still shaped like a double-headed arrow, hold down the mouse button, and drag the window border toward the center of the window until the window is about 2 inches wide. See Figure 2-6 on page 2-8.

3. Release the mouse button.

4. Now, point to the bottom window border.

   The pointer changes to a double-headed arrow.

5. With the pointer still shaped like a double-headed arrow, hold down the mouse button, and drag the window border up until the window is about 2 inches tall. See Figure 2-7 on page 2-8.

6. Point to the bottom right corner of the reduced window.

   The pointer changes to a diagonal double-headed arrow, which lets you move two adjoining sides at the same time.

7. Hold down the mouse button, and drag outward until the window is slightly wider and taller, but not its original size.

Using the Scroll Bars

Scroll bar
Bars appearing at the right and bottom edges when the contents of the window are not entirely visible.

Scroll box
The box in a scroll bar that represents your approximate position in the window.

With the window reduced from its original size, you can no longer see the icons at the bottom of the window. To allow you to view the hidden areas of the window, *scroll bars* appear along the right and bottom edges. The scroll bars let you scroll up, down, left, and right inside the window. The scroll bars represent the total area of the window, both visible and hidden. The *scroll box* represents your approximate position in the window. (If the scroll bar is very short, a scroll box does not appear on it.)

Figure 2-6
This window has been made narrow using the mouse (as in step 2 on page 2-7).

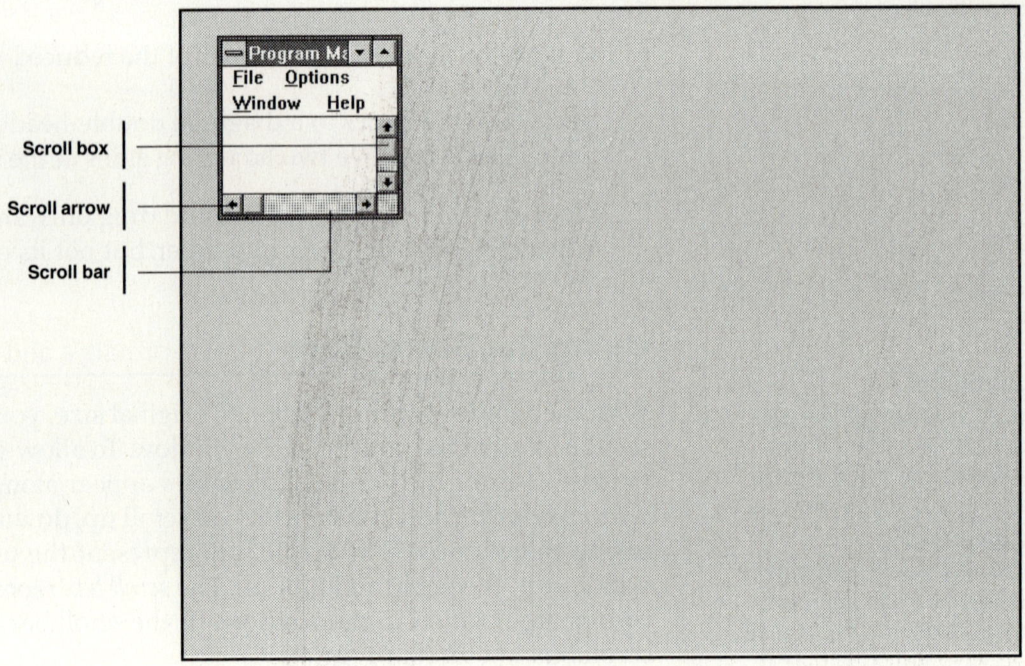

Figure 2-7
Scroll bars appear as you reduce the size of the window (as in step 5 on page 2-7).

Scroll arrow
The arrow at either end of the scroll bar that, when clicked, causes the workspace to move a short distance in the opposite direction of the arrow.

- To move a short distance, click one of the *scroll arrows*.
- To move a longer distance, click the scroll bar above or below the scroll box on the vertical scroll bar, and to the left or right of the scroll box on the horizontal scroll bar.
- To scroll continuously, point to one of the scroll arrows, and hold down the mouse button.
- To scroll to a particular position in the window, drag the scroll box to that position. Scroll bars represent the total area of the window, and the scroll box represents your position in the window. So, for example, if the scroll box is at the top of the vertical scroll bar, you are viewing the top of the window.

To practice using the scroll bars:

1. Point to the down scroll arrow of the vertical scroll bar.
2. Click the mouse button a few times, and watch the workspace shift until the bottom portion of the window containing the icons appears.
3. Point to the right scroll arrow of the horizontal scroll bar.
4. Click the mouse button once and watch the screen.

   The workspace shifts a small distance to the right.
5. Point to the scroll bar to the right of the scroll box on the horizontal scroll bar and click.

   The workspace shifts a greater distance to the right.
6. Point to the scroll box in the horizontal scroll bar, and drag the box left or right along the scroll bar. Then release the mouse button.

   The workspace shifts.

Note: The icons will remain at the top of the window and may be outside the workspace.

7. Click the lower right corner of the window, and drag outward to return the window to its approximate original size.

Choosing a Printer

Before you print from WordPerfect for Windows, you should make sure that Windows and WordPerfect for Windows are set to print to the same printer. Otherwise, you may run into trouble when you try to print. If your computer is currently connected to a printer, someone has probably set up Windows for that printer already. However, we will review the steps to choose a printer, so you can check to make sure your printer is correctly identified in Windows.

Control Panel
A Windows application with controls for adjusting the screen and mouse and for choosing the printer.

Note: You may have to scroll in the window to locate the Main icon.

To choose a printer, you need to use the *Control Panel*. The Control Panel contains controls for adjusting the screen and mouse and for choosing the printer. To access the Control Panel:

1. In the Program Manager window, double-click the Main icon.

   The Main window opens.

2. Double-click the Control Panel icon.

   The Control Panel opens.

3. Double-click the Printers icon.

   The Printers dialog box opens. In the box labeled "Installed Printers" is a list of printers that can be installed on your computer. The printer currently in use is highlighted.

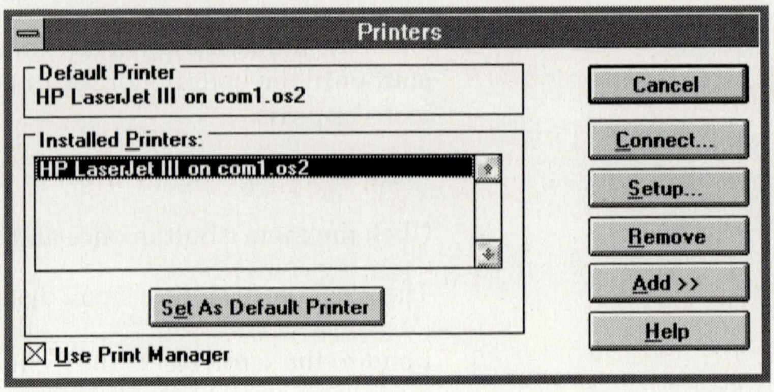

Figure 2-8
Printers dialog box

4. If the highlighted printer is correct, you only need to click the Cancel button. If you need to choose a different printer, click the name of the printer. Click the Set As Default Printer button, then click the Close button.

   If your printer does not appear in the Installed Printers list, it has not been installed on your computer. To install the printer, click the Add button, and choose the printer from the list that appears. Then click the Install button. You will not be able to install a printer unless the software required to run it, known as the *printer driver*, is also installed on your computer.

Printer driver
Software that controls how a computer and printer interact; required to install a printer.

5. When you are finished, close the Control Panel, and arrange the icons in the Program Manager window (by clicking the Arrange Icons option in the Window menu). Then exit Windows (unless you will be doing the following exercises immediately).

Key Terms

- Cascading menu
- Check box
- Command button
- Control Panel
- Dialog box
- Drop-down list box
- Drop-down menus
- Highlighting
- List box
- Option button
- Printer driver
- Pull-down menus
- Scroll arrow
- Scroll bar
- Scroll box
- Text box

Exercises

Exercise 2.1

1. If necessary, turn on the computer and start Windows.
2. Click the Control-menu box in the Program Manager window.

   The Control menu opens.
3. Select Move from the Control menu.

   A four-headed arrow appears.
4. Press the **Right Arrow** key four times to move the Program Manager window slightly to the right.
5. Press the **Down Arrow** key four times to move the Program Manager window slightly downward.
6. Click the mouse to anchor the window into this position.
7. Point to the Program Manager window's title bar, and drag the window to the top of the computer screen. Then release the mouse button.
8. Point to the title bar again, and drag the window to the left. Then release the mouse button.
9. Double-click the Accessories icon.

   The Accessories window opens.
10. Click the Control-menu box of the Accessories window to pull down the Control menu.

11. Click Close on the Control menu.

    The Accessories window closes and returns to its icon.

12. Double-click the Accessories icon again to open it.

    The Accessories window opens.

13. Close the Accessories window using a keyboard combination. Remember: A keyboard combination is a command you select by holding down one key, pressing another key, and then releasing both keys. So, in this case, hold down the **Ctrl** key, and press the **F4** key, then release both keys.

    The Accessories window closes and returns to its icon.

14. Exit Windows (unless you will be doing the following exercise immediately).

Exercise 2.2

1. If necessary, turn on the computer and start Windows.
2. Drag the Windows Applications icon to the top of the Program Manager window just below the menu bar, and release the mouse button.
3. Drag the Non-Windows Applications icon to the top of the Program Manager window, and position it next to the Windows Applications icon. Release the mouse button.

   The Windows Applications icon and the Non-Windows Applications icon are now at the top of the Program Manager window. The other icons remain at the bottom of the Program Manager window.

4. Click Window on the Program Manager's menu bar to open the Window menu.
5. Click Arrange Icons.

   The Windows Applications icon and the Non-Windows Applications icon are arranged neatly with the other icons at the bottom of the Program Manager window.

6. Point to the right border of the Program Manager window until the double-sided arrow appears.
7. Drag the right border toward the center of the window until the border covers an icon in the Program Manager window.
8. Point to the bottom border of the window until the double-sided arrow appears.

9. Drag the bottom border of the window up until it covers the icons at the bottom of the Program Manager window.
10. Click the **Down Arrow** in the vertical scroll bar until the icons are visible.
11. Now, click the **Right Arrow** in the horizontal scroll bar until the last icon is visible.
12. Drag the scroll box in the horizontal scroll bar from one side of the scroll bar to the other.
13. Scroll right and left by clicking with the pointer directly on the scroll bar.
14. Drag the right border outward until all the icons are visible in the Program Manager window.
15. Exit Windows.

Lesson 3

Starting Applications and Using Help

Objectives

- Start and exit applications.
- Locate Help topics using the Help menu.
- Identify the parts of the Help window.
- Search for information on a topic.
- Locate information in the Help Index.

Application
A computer program used to do a particular kind of work, such as word processing.

Applications are programs you use to do your work, such as word-processing programs. Some applications, such as WordPerfect for Windows, use the Windows environment to provide their basic structure; others do not. You can start either type of application from within Windows.

Starting Applications from Within Windows

The Program Manager window contains icons for the two categories of applications you can start from within Windows: the Windows Applications icon and the Non-Windows Applications icon. When you open these icons, you see icons representing the applications installed on your computer. You can start any of these applications.

To start an application from within Windows:

1. Turn on your computer and start Windows.
2. Double-click the Windows Applications icon in the Program Manager window.

   The Windows Applications window opens.

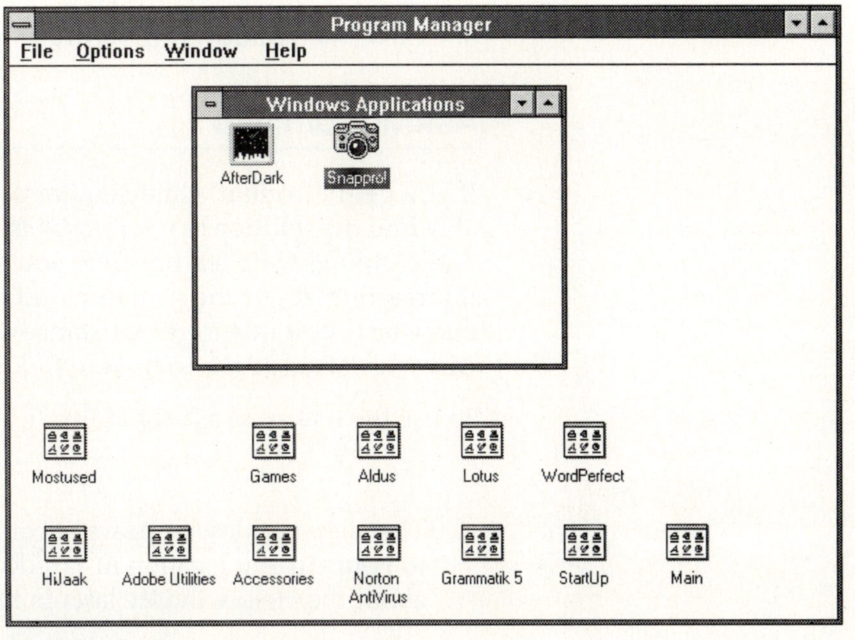

Figure 3-1
The Windows Applications window

3. Double-click an application icon.

   The application starts.

Exiting Applications

When you have finished working with an application, you exit the application and return to Windows. The exit procedure for non-Windows applications will differ depending on how the individual applications are structured. For Windows applications, you usually have three options for exiting.

To exit a Windows application, you could:

- Double-click the window's Control-menu box.
- Click the Control-menu box, and then click Close on the Control menu.
- Click File on the application's menu bar, and then click the Exit option in the File menu (not all applications have menu bars).

When you exit an application, a dialog box may appear asking you if you really want to exit the application. (The exact language will vary slightly from application to application.)

Exit your application:

1. Use any method described above to exit your application.
2. If a dialog box appears, indicate that you want to exit the application.
3. Close the Windows Applications window.

Asking for Help

If you get in trouble while you are using Windows, you can probably find the solution to your problem right on the computer screen. The Windows Help feature gives you immediate access to on-screen information about the program and how it works. This feature is often the fastest way to get assistance when you have a problem. One way to ask for Help is to use the **F1** key.

To use the **F1** key to ask for Help:

1. Press the **F1** key.

   The Help window appears. It contains information that relates to your current location in Windows. (You will learn more about the Help window later in this chapter.)

2. Close the Help window.

The Help Menu

Another way to use the Help available in Windows is the Help menu. When you select a Help menu option, a Help window opens.

Try selecting an option from the Help menu:

1. Click Help on the menu bar in the Program Manager window.

Note: The last option in the About Program Manager menu opens a dialog box containing the Windows version number and some other information about the program.

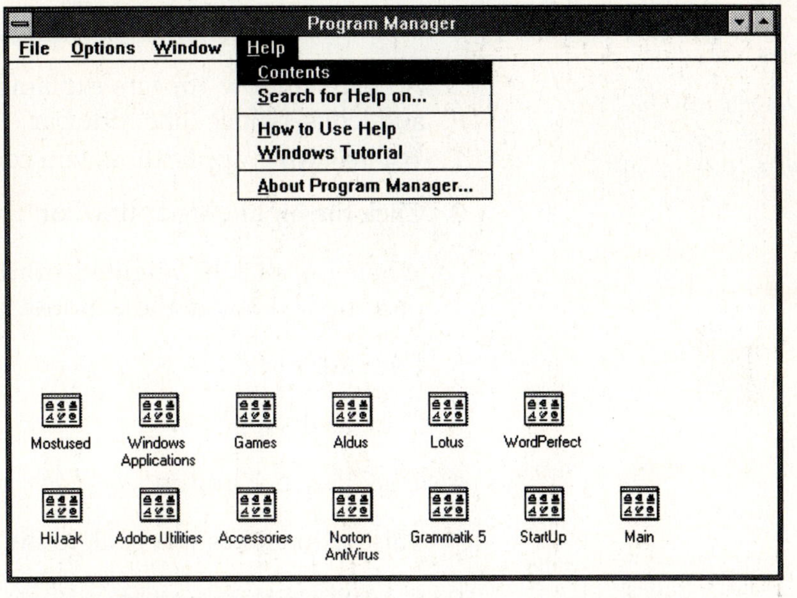

Figure 3-2
The Help menu

2. Choose Contents from the Help menu to view the Help window.

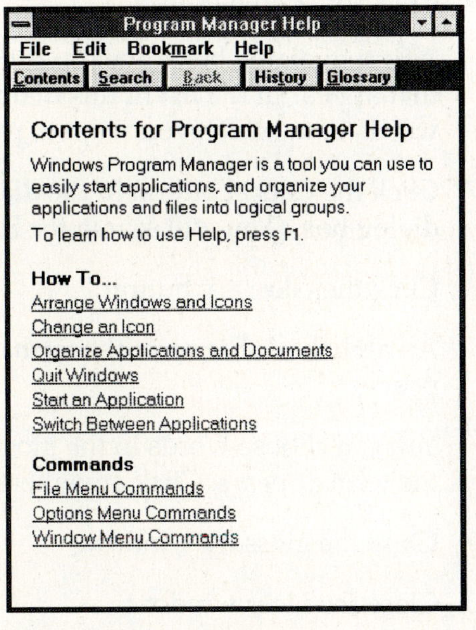

Figure 3-3
A Help window

The Help Window

The Help window looks different from other windows you have seen in Windows. It has a menu bar with buttons underneath. You will use the menus and buttons to move from one Help screen to another. As you move to different screens, they appear in the Help window.

Practice using the Help window:

1. Click the first How To topic, Arrange Windows and Icons.

   A Help window appears explaining how to arrange windows and icons. Notice that "title bar" in the first paragraph is highlighted.

Note: As you move the pointer, it changes to a hand with a pointing finger.

2. Click the highlighted "title bar".

   When you click highlighted words, a definition of the word pops up in a box in the window.

3. Click again.

   The box disappears.

4. Click the Back button.

   This button takes you back to the previous Help topic.

5. Click the History button.

   A list of the Help topics you have viewed in this session appears.

6. Click the Search button.

   A Search dialog box appears. You can search for the topics that appear in the list in this dialog box, or you can type a word about which you want to request Help.

7. Click the Cancel button in the dialog box to close the Search dialog box. (You will search for Help in the next section.)

8. Click the Glossary button.

   An alphabetic listing of the terms used in Windows Help appears.

   You can choose words in the glossary list, and a definition for the term appears. Click anywhere to remove the definition.

9. Close the glossary window.

10. Close the Help window.

The File menu contains a Print Topic option that lets you print the on-screen information about a topic on your printer. The other menus in the Help window provide advanced Help features, which you probably will not use very often, if at all. (For example, you can use the Annotate option in the Edit menu to make your own notations part of Help.)

Searching for Help

When you know the topic you would like to locate, you can let Windows find it for you:

1. Click Help on the menu bar in the Program Manager window.
2. Select Search for Help on from the Help menu.

   The Search dialog box appears.

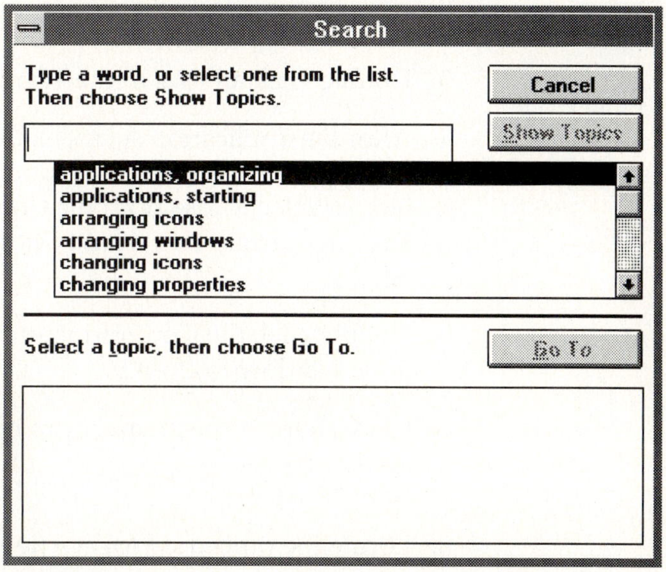

Figure 3-4
The Search dialog box

3. Use the scroll bar to the right of the list of topics in the dialog box to find the topic "applications, starting" in the list.
4. Click "applications, starting" to select it.
5. Click the Show Topics button in the Search dialog box.

   A list of topics appears in the box at the bottom of the dialog box. Each of these topics leads you to information related to starting an application.
6. Click "Starting an Application from a Group".
7. Click the Go To button.

   Information about the topic appears in the Help window.

8. After you have read the Help topic, close the Help window by double-clicking the Control-menu box. Then exit Windows (unless you will be doing the following exercises immediately).

Key Term

Application

Exercises

Exercise 3.1

1. If necessary, turn on your computer and start Windows.
2. Double-click the Windows Applications icon.
3. Double-click an icon in the Windows Applications window.
4. After the application starts, exit it (you can select Exit from the application's File menu, double-click the Control-menu box, or select Close from the Control menu). (You may also have to indicate you want to exit the application in a dialog box.)
5. Double-click the Control-menu box in the Windows Applications window to close it.
6. Click Help on the menu bar to open the Help menu.
7. Choose Search for Help on from the Help menu.
8. Locate the procedure for starting applications.
9. Click "applications, starting".
10. Click the Show Topics button.
11. Click "Starting an Application from a Group".
12. Click the Go To button.
13. Click "group" in the first line.

    The definition of "group" appears.
14. Click anywhere to remove the definition.
15. Close the Help window.
16. Exit Windows (unless you will be doing the following exercise immediately).

Exercise 3.2

1. If necessary, turn on your computer and start Windows.
2. Click Help on the menu bar to open it.
3. Choose Contents from the Help menu.
4. Click Window Menu Commands. (It is near the bottom of the window.)
5. Click "scroll bar" in the first line.

   The definition of "scroll bar" appears.
6. Click anywhere to remove the definition.
7. Click the Back button.

   You are returned to the first Help screen.
8. Click the History button.

   A list of the Help topics you have viewed in this session appears.
9. Close the Windows Help History window.
10. Click the Glossary button.
11. Scroll to the term "command button".
12. Click the term "command button".

    A definition of "command button" appears.
13. Click anywhere to remove the definition.
14. Close the Glossary window.
15. Close the Help window.
16. Exit Windows.

Module 1

Basic WordPerfect for Windows Skills

Lessons

A Guided Tour

Objectives

- Learn what you need to operate WordPerfect.
- Become familiar with the WordPerfect screen.
- Open a new file.
- Key and edit text.
- Name and save a document.
- Use WordPerfect Help.
- Print a document.
- Close a document and exit WordPerfect.

This module introduces the basic features of WordPerfect for Windows. WordPerfect is a versatile, easy-to-use program. Using it is very different from typing on a typewriter. Although it is more sophisticated than traditional word-processing programs, you will become a productive WordPerfect user quickly.

Lesson 4 begins with an overview of what the WordPerfect screen looks like. Windows skills will help you navigate through the program. This lesson will teach the steps involved in creating a document, including keying, simple editing, naming, saving, and closing the document. It also will explain the use of WordPerfect Help. Different methods for performing tasks will be taught, using both the keyboard and the mouse. As you become more familiar with the program, you will use the method that you find most comfortable.

What You Need to Operate WordPerfect for Windows

The minimum software and hardware requirements needed to run WordPerfect are:

- A personal computer with an 80386sx or higher microprocessor
- A hard-disk drive and a floppy-disk drive
- 4 MB of RAM
- An EGA (enhanced graphics adapter), VGA (video graphics adapter), 8514/A, or Hercules monitor
- Microsoft Windows version 3.0 or later
- A mouse or pointing device (While this is recommended to operate WordPerfect, it is required for the purpose of this course.)

Starting WordPerfect

Before beginning WordPerfect, the program must be loaded into the computer's memory from Windows. First, open Windows, if you have not already done so. To start WordPerfect:

1. Open Windows by keying **win** at the DOS prompt c:\ and pressing **Enter**.

The WordPerfect icon

2. At the Program Manager window, double-click the WordPerfect icon.

   The WordPerfect window appears.

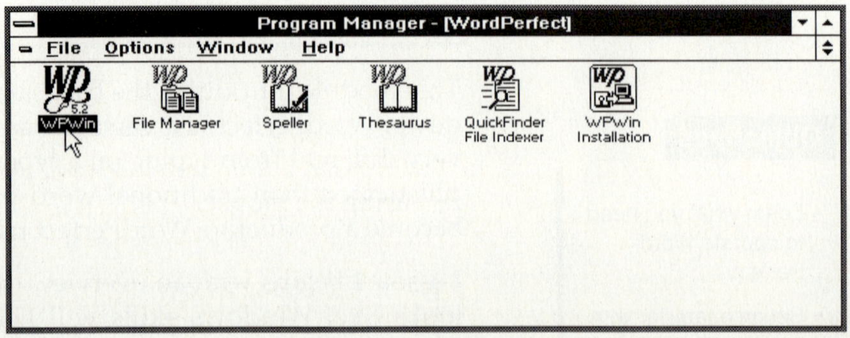

Figure 4-1
The WordPerfect window

3. Double-click the WPWin icon.

   In a few seconds, the program is loaded, and the opening WordPerfect screen appears.

Figure 4-2 is an illustration of the opening WordPerfect screen, or desktop. You have seen parts of the screen in Windows, such as the Minimize and Maximize buttons, the scroll bars and arrows, and the Control-menu boxes.

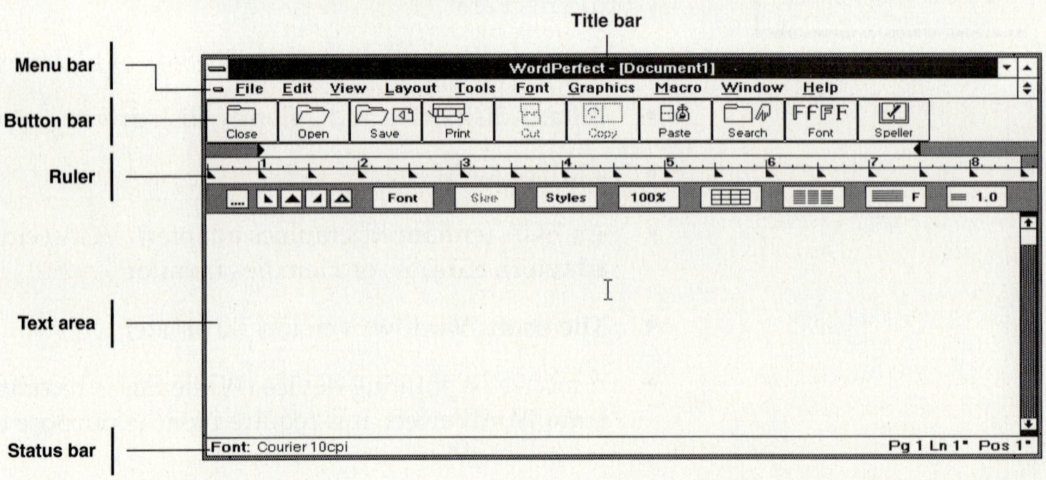

Figure 4-2
The opening WordPerfect screen

Some of the important parts of the WordPerfect screen are:

- The title bar

  The program name, "WordPerfect", and the name of the document appear in the top center of the screen. The opening screen of WordPerfect is always a blank document called "Document1".

- The menu bar

  The WordPerfect menu bar displays the names of the menus from which you can select options to perform various tasks. The menus are File, Edit, View, Layout, Tools, Font, Graphics, Macro, Window, and Help. Menus are accessed with the mouse or the keyboard.

- The Button Bar

  The Button Bar is a row of buttons. The buttons allow instant access to commands that are used frequently. Access buttons using the mouse.

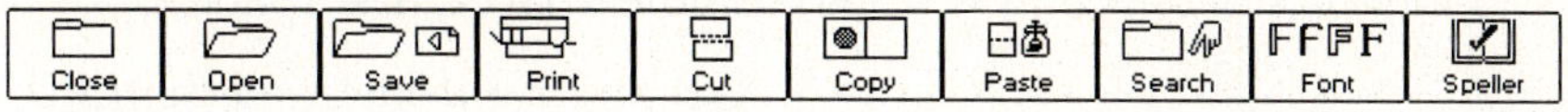

Figure 4-3
The Button Bar

- The Ruler

  The buttons on the Ruler allow you to change the appearance of text quickly. The Ruler also allows you to convert text into a desired format quickly by changing margins and tabs. The Ruler is accessed with the mouse.

- The text area

  The main, rectangular section of the screen that displays text and graphics is called the text area. This is where you view a document.

- Scroll bars

  The scroll bars operate the same way in WordPerfect as they do in Windows. The scroll arrows and scroll boxes are used with the mouse to move right or left and up or down through a document.

Note: The Button Bar, Ruler, and horizontal scroll bar each can be taken off the screen to make more room for your document. Using the View menu on the menu bar, you can click any of these features to uncheck them and hide them from view.

- The status bar

  At the bottom of the screen, the status bar displays important information about a document. The left side displays information about how the text in a document looks. During certain operations, the text information is replaced by messages, such as "Please Wait". The right side of the status bar shows the page, line number, and position in a document.

Creating a New Document

When you start WordPerfect, a new file called "Document1" opens automatically. This is the document's name until you name it and save it.

You also can open a new file by opening the File menu and choosing New. The keyboard shortcut for opening a new file is **Shift+F4**. Each time you open a new file, WordPerfect gives it the next new document name, such as "Document2".

Default settings
Settings predefined by WordPerfect. The user can change default settings to customize documents.

New files are created automatically using WordPerfect's *default settings*. This means that a new file is created automatically with the following settings:

- Standard 8½" x 11" paper
- 1-inch left and right margins
- 1-inch top and bottom margins
- Single-spaced line spacing
- Left and right-justified margins
- .5-inch tab settings
- No hyphenation

Future lessons will explain how to change default settings to customize a document.

To open a new file:

1. Move the mouse pointer to the menu bar (notice the arrow shape of the pointer when it is outside the text area). Choose File to open the File menu.

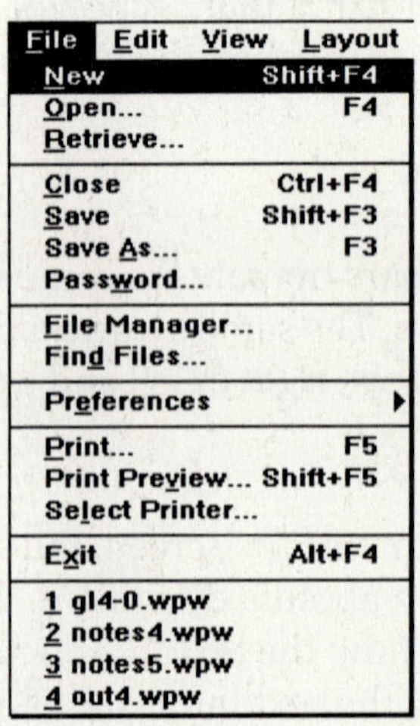

Figure 4-4
The File menu

2. Choose New, which is the top menu option.

   WordPerfect opens a new file named Document2.

Keying Text

The WordPerfect screen contains symbols that are important to your keying actions.

The point where you begin keying text is the *insertion point*. This is indicated by the vertical blinking bar in the upper left corner of the text area. The mouse pointer takes on different shapes, depending on where it is moved. When you point in the text area, the pointer is in the shape of an I-beam. When you point to areas of the screen outside the text area, the pointer is in the shape of an arrow. When you click the mouse in different areas of text, you move the insertion point.

Insertion point
A vertical blinking bar on the WordPerfect screen that shows the current location and determines where an action will begin.

To begin the document and understand these symbols:

1. Key **Five Points Realty**.

   Notice the insertion point moved as you keyed, so it is now at the last letter keyed.

Note: Insert only one space after punctuation between sentences.

2. Continue keying:

   is a large real estate agency located in downtown Atlanta.

   Notice how the text moved to the beginning of the next line when it reached the end of the line. This is known as *wordwrap*, and it marks an important difference between word-processing and typing. With a typewriter, you must press the Return key at the end of each line. In WordPerfect, you only need to press the **Enter** key to start a new paragraph or to insert a blank line.

Wordwrap
The automatic placement of text on the next line.

Note: In addition to not pressing **Enter** at the end of each line, you should not press the **Spacebar** to move the insertion point through the text. Instead, use the Arrow keys or click the mouse to the desired location in the text. The **Spacebar** is used to insert a space in the text.

3. Continue by keying the following:

   It was started in 1975 by Harold Porter. While working for a real estate agency, Mr. Porter came to the conclusion that the downtown Atlanta business area was about to explode. He quit his job, started Five Points Realty, and the rest is history.

   This is now a one-paragraph document. Notice that the insertion point is at the end of the paragraph.

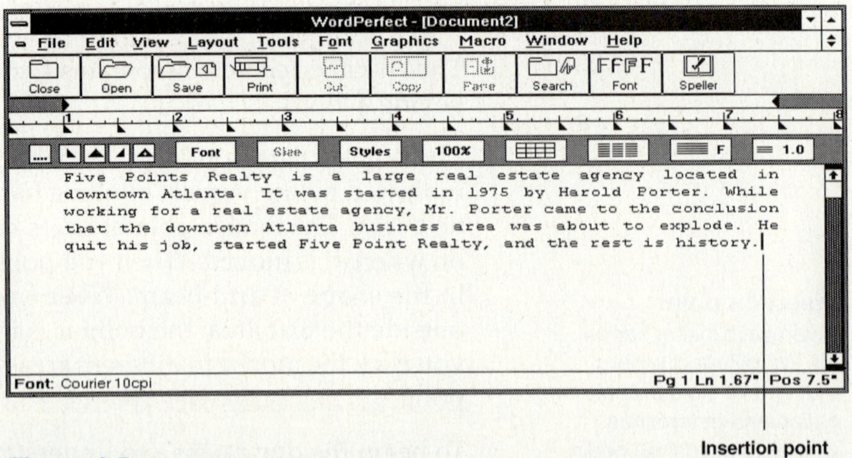

Figure 4-5

The WordPerfect screen with keyed text

Editing Text

In WordPerfect, it is very easy to edit text. This lesson reviews the methods of deleting, revising, and inserting text using the following keys:

- **Delete** key

  Deletes characters to the right of the insertion point

- **Backspace** key

  Deletes characters to the left of the insertion point

- **Insert** key

  Toggles between insert mode and typeover mode. When you want to insert or add text, use insert mode. When you want to key over text, use typeover mode. Typeover mode is indicated on the left side of the status bar.

Note: Always check to make sure you are not in typeover mode when you want to insert text. Accidentally having typeover mode turned on can cause you to lose text as you key.

To insert text in the document:

1. Look at the status bar to make sure the typeover mode is not on. If it is, press the **Insert** key once. This will return you to insert mode.

2. Position the insertion point to the left of the word "real" in the third sentence. (Use the mouse to move the I-beam into place, then click the mouse.)

3. Key **downtown**, and press the **Spacebar** once to leave a space between the two words.

   The text now reads "downtown real estate agency".

To create two paragraphs:

1. Position the insertion point to the left of the word "It" at the start of the second sentence.
2. Press **Enter** once to start a new paragraph. Press **Enter** again to create a blank line between the two paragraphs.

To revise text using the **Backspace** key:

1. Position the insertion point to the right of the word "It" in the second paragraph.
2. Press the **Backspace** key twice to delete the word.
3. Key **Five Points Realty**.

   The second paragraph now begins "Five Points Realty was started in 1975 by Harold Porter."

To revise text using the **Delete** key:

1. Position the insertion point to the left of the "7" in the date "1975" in the second paragraph.
2. Press the **Delete** key twice to delete "75".
3. Key **53**.

If your keyboard has a numeric keypad, usually to the right of the regular keyboard, you can key numbers there by pressing the **Num Lock** key. This activates the keypad as number keys and disables their other functions.

To change the words "Five Points Realty" to all uppercase letters using the **Caps Lock** key and the typeover mode:

1. Position the insertion point at the beginning of the document, to the left of "Five".

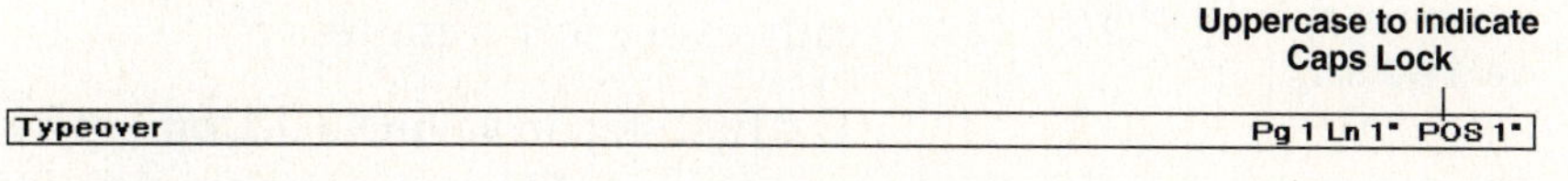

Figure 4-6
The status bar

2. Press the **Insert** key to switch to the typeover mode.

   "Typeover" appears on the left side of the status bar.

3. Press the **Caps Lock** key.

   The insertion-point-position indicator, "Pos", on the right side of the status bar changes to uppercase, "POS", indicating Caps Lock mode.

4. Key **FIVE POINTS REALTY**. Press the **Caps Lock** key to turn off the Caps Lock mode. Press the **Insert** key to turn off the typeover mode.

   "FIVE POINTS REALTY" is now in uppercase letters. Repeat the process for "Five Points Realty" at the beginning of the second paragraph.

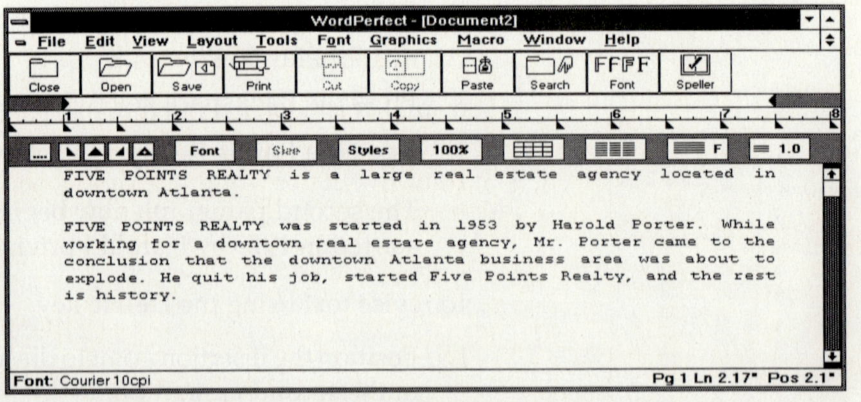

Figure 4-7
The edited document

Note: If you are not used to working on a computer, it is easy to forget that documents must be saved. If you do forget, WordPerfect reminds you. When you try to close a document or exit the program, WordPerfect asks if you want to save the document(s) on which you were working.

Filename
The unique name given to a document that is saved in WordPerfect.

File
A document that has been created and saved under a unique filename.

Naming and Saving a Document

The document on which you are working, called "Document2," is a temporary document that is stored in the computer's temporary memory. Until you name it and save it to disk, it can be lost due to a power failure or to a computer hardware or software problem. That is why it is always a good idea to save your work frequently. Lesson 5 teaches how WordPerfect can backup your documents automatically every few minutes.

The first step in saving a document for future use is to name it. When you name a document, you are giving it a *filename*. In WordPerfect, a document is referred to as a *file*.

Filenames can be one to eight characters long, and generally are followed by a period and a one-to-three character extension. You can use filename extensions to distinguish different types of files.

Throughout the lessons and exercises in this course, when you save a document, the document name will consist of three parts:

- *[Your three-letter identifier]*, which may be your initials or the identifier your instructor asks you to use, such as RST
- The number of the document, such as 4-1

  RST4-1

Save commands

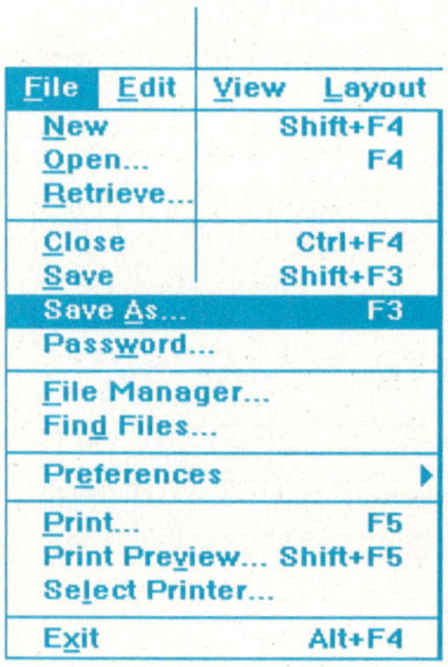

The File menu

- The extension .wpw to indicate the document is a WordPerfect for Windows document

  RST4-1.WPW

A document can be saved using either the Save command or the Save As command. Both commands are available from the File menu. Use the Save As command to name and save a document for the first time. The Save command is used to save an existing document as you key and edit. The keyboard shortcut for Save is **Shift+F3**, and the keyboard shortcut for Save As is **F3**.

You also can save a document by clicking the Save button on the Button Bar. When you are saving a document for the first time, the button will execute the Save As command. When you use the Save button for a document that has been saved already, it will execute the Save command and update the document with your most recent changes.

Before you save a new document, it is important to determine where you plan to save it. WordPerfect will save a document in the current drive and directory, which is the default drive and directory, unless you specify otherwise. If you do not want to save a document to the current drive and directory, which is most likely c:\wpwin, but wish to save it to a floppy disk, you need to change the default drive to either a: or b:, whichever is appropriate for your computer. Your instructor will advise you on the proper drive and directory.

To name and save the document created in this lesson:

1. Choose File to open the File menu.

2. Choose Save As.

   The Save As dialog box appears.

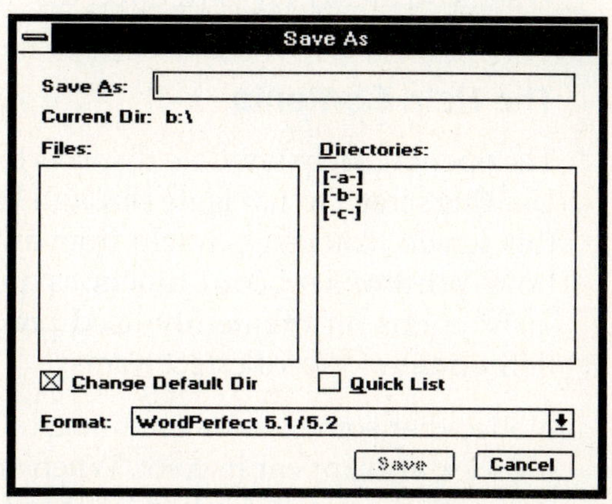

Figure 4-8
The Save As dialog box

3. In the Filename text box, key ***[your three-letter identifier]*4-0.wpw**.

   If you make a mistake while keying the filename, use the **Right Arrow** or **Left Arrow** key or the **Backspace** key to correct mistakes.

4. Click Save if you are saving the document to the current drive and directory.

   When saving a document to a floppy disk, make sure you have a formatted disk in the floppy-disk drive. Click the appropriate drive in the Directories list box. WordPerfect reads the disk in the floppy drive and is ready to save the file to it. Click Save.

   The document is named *[your three-letter identifier]*4-0.wpw and is saved for future use. Notice that the filename in the title bar changed from "Document2" to "*[your three-letter identifier]*4-0.wpw".

Using WordPerfect Help

WordPerfect Help is very similar to Windows Help. While working in WordPerfect, use Help to:

- Explain the procedures for a task you are performing
- Find a definition for a term you do not understand
- Learn about a WordPerfect command or area of the screen

WordPerfect Help and Windows Help are accessed in similar ways. The easiest way to access WordPerfect Help is to press the **F1** key. When you press **F1**, WordPerfect displays the opening Help window.

The Help Contents

The opening Help window displays the WordPerfect Help Contents. Use this screen to navigate through Help screens and menus. From this screen, you can get help from an alphabetized index of operations, a list of keyboard functions and combinations, step-by-step instructions on frequently used procedures, and a glossary with definitions of WordPerfect terms.

Jump term
A Help topic that is linked to other Help topics or to more information, usually identified by an underline and a color.

Notice that some words are underlined. If you have a color monitor, they also appear in color. When you click on a word with a dotted underline, a definition of that term appears in a box in the window. When you click on a word with a solid underline, you can move quickly around the Help system, going from one term to a cross-reference term. These are called *jump terms*.

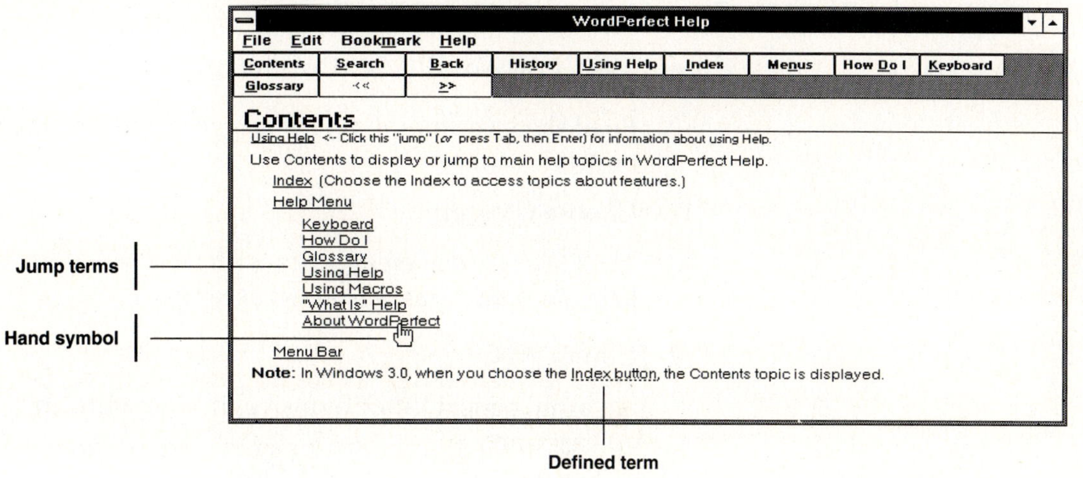

Figure 4-9
The opening Help window

To access Help and navigate the Help Contents:

1. Press **F1**.

   The opening Help window appears.

2. Using the mouse, point to How Do I in the Help Menu section.

   The pointer changes to a hand symbol.

3. Choose How Do I by clicking on it.

   A new Help screen, How Do I, appears.

   Notice that choosing a solid underline jump term opens a new Help screen.

4. At the new screen, choose Basics.

   Help displays a new screen, How Do I: Basics.

5. Choose Save.

   Help displays a full description of the Save As command.

6. Click Contents from the Button Bar near the top of the screen.

   The Contents screen reappears.

7. Choose Index.

   The Help Index screen appears. The screen contains letters. Each letter brings up an alphabetical list of topics. Click C for an alphabetical list of topics beginning with "c".

8. Using the vertical scroll bar, scroll through the list until you find Close File.

   If the vertical scroll bar is hidden, drag the window's title bar to move the window until the scroll bar appears.

9. Choose Close File.

   The Close WordPerfect Document screen appears.

10. Read the information on the screen, then click the Contents button.

11. Choose Glossary.

    The Glossary screen appears with a list of letters. Each letter brings up an alphabetical list of terms.

12. Choose M-O.

    An alphabetical list of terms beginning with "m," "n," and "o" appears.

13. Choose menu bar.

    Notice that choosing a dotted underline jump term displays a definition.

14. Click anywhere to clear the definition, and click the Contents button to return to the Help Contents screen.

The Search Feature

When you know the topic you want to locate, use the Search feature to find it. The Search feature in WordPerfect Help and Windows Help operates the same way. You can find a specific topic either by keying in a word or phrase, or by scrolling through a list of topics.

To use the Search feature:

1. Click the Search button.

   The Search dialog box appears. Notice the similarity between this dialog box and the Search dialog box in Windows.

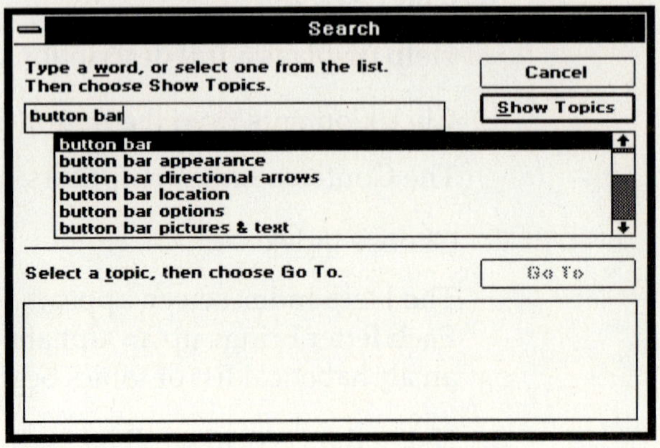

Figure 4-10
The Search dialog box

2. Key **button bar** in the text box.

   Notice that the phrase appears in the search list before you finish keying the phrase.

3. Click the Show Topics button.

   A list of related Help topics concerning the Button Bar appears. You can select from any of the topics by highlighting the topic and clicking Go To, or by double-clicking the topic.

4. Click Close to return to the Help Contents.

5. To close Help, choose Exit from the File menu.

Context-Sensitive Help

While working in WordPerfect, you may come to a command, a key, a dialog box, or even an area of the screen about which you have a question. WordPerfect Help is context-sensitive. This means that it provides help on an as-needed basis: while you are performing a procedure or before you begin a procedure.

This can be done two ways. To get help on a menu item or a dialog box, display the item or dialog box and press **F1**. Help goes directly to that subject with an explanation. For example:

1. Choose Save As from the File menu.

   The Save As dialog box appears.

2. Press **F1**.

   Help displays information about the Save As command.

3. Exit Help.

The Help pointer with a question mark

To get help on a command, a key, or a screen region, press **Shift+F1**. A question mark appears with the pointer. Press the key or command, or point to the area in question. Help goes directly to that topic.

To get help on a command:

1. Press **Shift+F1**.

   The pointer changes to a question mark.

2. Move the pointer to the Save button on the Button Bar and click.

   A Help screen about saving documents appears.

3. Exit Help.

Bookmarks and Annotations

WordPerfect's Help allows you to mark topics that you use frequently with a bookmark for quick reference. To mark a topic, choose Bookmark from the Help menu bar and identify a topic. Choose the topic from the Bookmark menu to go to a marked topic. Help then will display information on that topic.

You can use Help's annotation feature to add your own comments to Help topics. These annotations, or comments, are like reminder notes. To create an annotation, choose Annotate from the Edit menu. Write your reminder and click Save. Help displays annotations on the screen in the form of a paper-clip symbol. Just click the paper-clip symbol to display the annotation.

Printing a Document

Once you have created a document, it is easy to print it.

You can use the Print command by:

- Choosing Print from the File menu
- Clicking the Print button on the Button Bar
- Pressing **F5**

When you perform any of the above actions, WordPerfect displays the Print dialog box. The dialog box contains WordPerfect's default print settings. You can make changes in the dialog box, but, for now, use the default settings.

To print the document:

1. Choose Print from the File menu.

   WordPerfect displays the Print dialog box containing the print default settings.

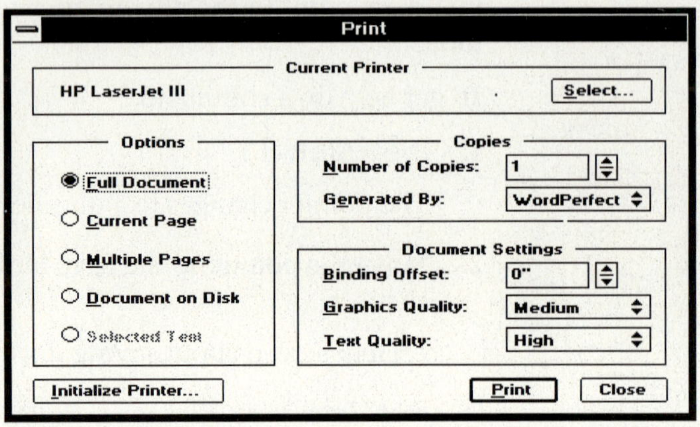

Figure 4-11
The Print dialog box

2. Click the Print button or press **Enter**.

   WordPerfect displays a message that tells you the document is being printed. You can click the Cancel Print Job button or press **Esc** if you need to stop printing.

Closing a Document and Quitting WordPerfect

Control-menu boxes

When you are finished working on a document and have saved it, you can close it and open another, or quit the program. In WordPerfect, a document does not have to be closed to open another. In the Windows environment, you can open several documents, or files, and keep them open throughout the WordPerfect session.

You can close a document by:

- Choosing Close from the File menu
- Double-clicking the document Control-menu box in the upper left corner of the document window or choosing Close from the document Control-menu box
- Pressing **Ctrl+F4**
- Clicking the Close button on the Button Bar

You can quit WordPerfect by:

- Choosing Exit from the File menu
- Double-clicking the application Control-menu box or choosing Close from the application Control-menu
- Pressing **Alt+F4**

To close the document and quit WordPerfect:

1. Double-click the document Control-menu box.

   WordPerfect closes the document.

2. Choose Exit from the File menu.

   WordPerfect closes and the Windows opening screen appears.

Table 4-1: Keyboard Shortcuts for Introductory WordPerfect Skills

Keyboard Shortcut	Action
Shift+F4	Open a new file
Shift+F3	Save
F3	Save As
F1	Open Help
Shift+F1	Open context-sensitive Help
F5	Print a document
Ctrl+F4	Close a document
Alt+F4	Quit WordPerfect

Key Terms

Default settings	Insertion point
File	Jump term
Filename	Wordwrap

Exercises

Exercise 4.1

1. Start WordPerfect:
   - A. At the DOS prompt c:\, key **win** and press **Enter** to open Windows.
   - B. At the Windows Program Manager screen, double-click the WordPerfect icon.
   - C. At the WordPerfect window, double-click the WPWin icon.
2. Key Document 4-1, which appears at the end of this exercise.
3. Position the insertion point to the right of "Mart" at the end of the first sentence.
4. Make sure the typeover mode is not turned on.
5. Press the **Spacebar**, and key **and Apparel Mart**.
6. Position the insertion point to the left of "greater" in the last sentence.
7. Use the **Delete** key to delete "greater".
8. Position the insertion point to the right of "1970s" in the first sentence.
9. Key **,** (the comma).
10. Change "1940s" to "1960s" using typeover mode:
    - A. Position the insertion point to the left of the "4" in "1940s".
    - B. Press the **Insert** key to switch to typeover mode.
    - C. Key **6** over "4".
    - D. Press the **Insert** key again to switch back to insert mode.
11. Save the document as *[your three-letter identifier]*4-1.wpw:
    - A. From the File menu, choose Save As.
    - B. In the Save As dialog box, key the name of the document and click Save.

12. Print the document:

    A. Choose Print from the File menu.

    B. In the Print dialog box, click Print.

13. Before closing the document, look up the Close document command in Help using the context-sensitive feature:

    A. Press **Shift+F1**.

    B. Click the Close button on the Button Bar.

14. After reviewing the information, close Help by double-clicking the Control-menu box.

15. Close the document and exit WordPerfect using the File menu:

    A. Choose Close from the File menu.

    B. Choose Exit from the File menu.

Document 4-1

```
In the 1940s and 1970s Five Points Realty was instrumental in the
development of many of the hotel and office complexes that sprang up
around Atlanta's Merchandise Mart. This was the period that Five Points
Realty grew to become one of the major real estate agencies in the greater
Atlanta area.
```

Exercise 4.2

1. Start WordPerfect.
2. Open a new document by choosing New from the File menu.
3. Key Document 4-2, which appears at the end of this exercise.
4. Position the insertion point to the left of the "P" in "Peachtree" in the first sentence.
5. Press **Insert** to switch to typeover mode.
6. Key **Wall and Peachtree**.
7. Switch back to insert mode, and position the insertion point to the right of "It" in the second sentence.
8. Use the **Backspace** key to delete "It" and key **Five Points**.
9. In the last sentence, key **original** before "location".
10. Save the document as *[your three-letter identifier]*4-2.wpw.

11. Print the document using the Print button on the Button Bar:
    A. Click the Print button on the Button Bar.
    B. In the Print dialog box, click Print.
12. Use the Help Index command to get information on quitting WordPerfect:
    A. Press **F1**.
    B. Choose Index.
    C. Choose E.
    D. Scroll down to Exit (move the window by dragging its title bar if the scroll bar is hidden) and choose it.
13. Read the information about exiting WordPerfect, then close Help.
14. Close the document and quit WordPerfect using the keyboard shortcuts (unless you will be doing the following exercises immediately):
    A. Press **Ctrl+F4** to close the document.
    B. Press **Alt+F4** to quit WordPerfect.

Document 4-2

Five Points Realty was originally located at the corner of Peachtree and Wall Streets. It moved to its current address when the Metropolitan Atlanta Rapid Transit Authority (MARTA) was created in the mid-1970s. MARTA purchased Five Point's location and built its Five Points Station on the site.

Exercise 4.3

1. Start WordPerfect, if necessary.
2. Key Document 4-3, which appears at the end of this exercise.
3. Key **municipal and** before the word "civic" in the second sentence.
4. In the last sentence, delete the phrase "in the 1960s".
5. Delete "helped" in the third sentence and key **assisted**.
6. Save the document as *[your three letter identifier]*4-3.wpw.
7. Use the Help Search feature to get information on typeover mode. (Press **F1** and choose Search from the Help menu bar.)
8. Exit Help.
9. Print the document.

10. Close the document.
11. Exit WordPerfect (unless you will be doing the following exercises immediately).

Document 4-3

Harold Porter, the founder of Five Points Realty, is a long-time Atlanta resident. He has served on many civic boards. Because of Mr. Porter, Five Points Realty has helped in some of Atlanta's most significant civic development projects. For example, Five Points was one of the early real estate pioneers of Underground Atlanta in the 1960s.

Exercise 4.4

1. Start WordPerfect, if necessary.
2. Open a new document.
3. Key Document 4-4, which appears at the end of this exercise.
4. Insert the word "Porter" near the beginning of the first sentence so it reads "Harold Porter's son".
5. Delete "Porter" after the word "Chester" in the first sentence.
6. Key **"Bud",** (include the quotation marks and comma) after "Chester" in the first sentence.
7. Change "1985" in the first sentence to "1987" using the typeover mode.
8. Delete "followed" in the second sentence and key **continued**.
9. Save the document as *[your three-letter identifier]*4-4.wpw.
10. Print the document.
11. Close the document.
12. Exit WordPerfect (unless you will be doing the following exercise immediately.)

Document 4-4

Harold's son, Chester Porter has run the company since his father retired in 1985. Bud Porter has followed his father's tradition of being involved with Atlanta's booming downtown business area. He was very involved with the recent "rediscovery" of Underground Atlanta after it had been closed down in 1981 due to subway construction and other problems.

Exercise 4.5

1. Start WordPerfect, if necessary.
2. Get information from Help about opening a new file by pressing **Shift+F1** and choosing New from the File menu.
3. At the File New Help screen, choose the jump term <u>Open</u>.
4. Scroll to the bottom of the screen and choose <u>Save As</u>.
5. After reviewing the information, close Help.
6. Key Document 4-5, which appears at the end of this exercise.
7. Key **commercial** before the words "real estate" near the beginning of the paragraph.
8. Create two paragraphs by pressing **Enter** after "offices:".
9. Insert a blank line between the paragraphs by pressing **Enter**.
10. Delete the space at the beginning of the second paragraph, and change the "t" in "the" to uppercase.
11. Delete the "," (the comma) at the end of the first line in the second paragraph.
12. Press **Enter** at the end of the first line in the second paragraph to create a third paragraph.
13. Create a fourth paragraph for the last satellite office.
14. Delete any blank spaces from the beginning of each paragraph, and delete "and" from the beginning of the last paragraph. Change the "t" at the beginning of the third and fourth paragraphs to uppercase.
15. Remove punctuation from the end of the paragraphs.
16. Save the document as *[your three-letter identifier]*4-5.wpw.
17. Print the document.
18. Close the document.
19. Exit WordPerfect.

Document 4-5

```
While the downtown office continues to focus on real estate, Five Points
Realty now has three satellite offices: the Marietta Office (located in a
northwest suburb of Atlanta), the Buckhead Office (located in the Buckhead
section of Atlanta), and the Midtown Office (located in Midtown Atlanta).
```

Lesson 5

Revising Text

Objectives

- Open and retrieve an existing document.
- Merge and split paragraphs.
- Move within a document.
- Use the Undo and Undelete commands.
- Select text.
- Delete and replace selected text.
- Learn more about saving documents.

Now that you are familiar with the basics of WordPerfect for Windows, you will learn how easy it is to revise text in a document. This lesson teaches how to move through a document quickly, make changes to a document, undo changes, and save a revised document using several different save options.

Opening an Existing Document

When the WordPerfect program starts, a new document window is opened automatically. However, an existing document can be opened from WordPerfect. To open an existing document, you can use one of three methods:

- Choose Open from the File menu.
- Click the Open button on the Button Bar.
- Press **F4** (the keyboard shortcut).

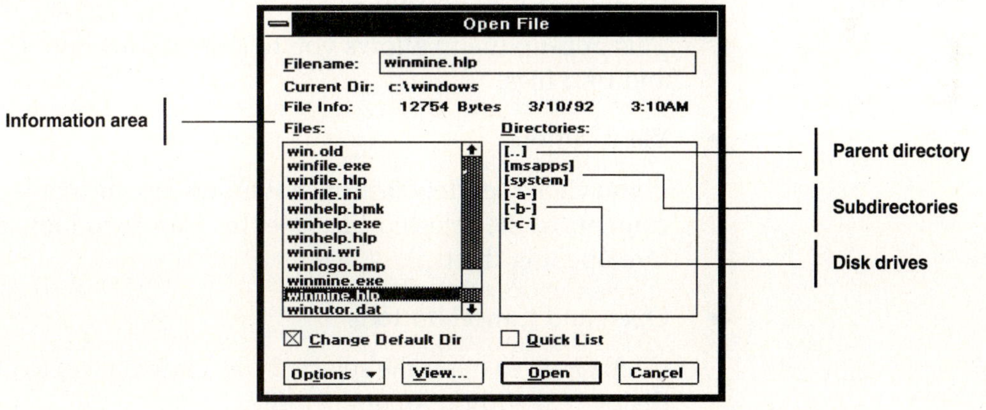

Figure 5-1
The Open File dialog box

The Open button

With each of these methods, WordPerfect displays the Open File dialog box with these features:

- Filename text box

  If you know the full name of the file, key its path and name here. If you select a file from the Files list box, its name appears here automatically.

- Information area

  The area just below the Filename text box displays the current directory and information about the currently selected file or directory.

- Files list box

  This area displays the names of all the files in the current directory. If the list is long, a scroll bar appears.

- Directories list box

  Use this area to choose a specific fixed disk or a directory on the fixed disk or to change to a floppy drive. The list displays icons representing the parent directory [..], subdirectories, and disk drives ([-a-], [-c-], etc.).

- Change Default Dir check box

  If this box is checked, WordPerfect "remembers" the directory to which you change and displays it as the current directory the next time you open or save a file.

- Quick List check box

  If this box is checked, the Quick List list box is displayed in place of the Directories list box. This list contains descriptive names representing frequently used drives and directories.

The Options pop-up menu

- Options pop-up button

  This pop-up menu allows you to delete, copy, move, rename, and find files.

- View button

  If you click the View button, a window opens displaying the contents of the selected file. Use this feature to look at files before opening them.

- Open and Cancel buttons

  Click Open to open the selected file; click Cancel to close the dialog box without opening a file.

From the Open File dialog box, you can select a file listed in the current directory or key the name of the file, including the path. You can change the directory, the drive, and the type of file, if necessary, to locate a file.

Follow your instructor's directions as to the disk drive and directory of the files you will open in this lesson and in future lessons.

To open the file 5-0a.wpw:

1. Start WordPerfect.

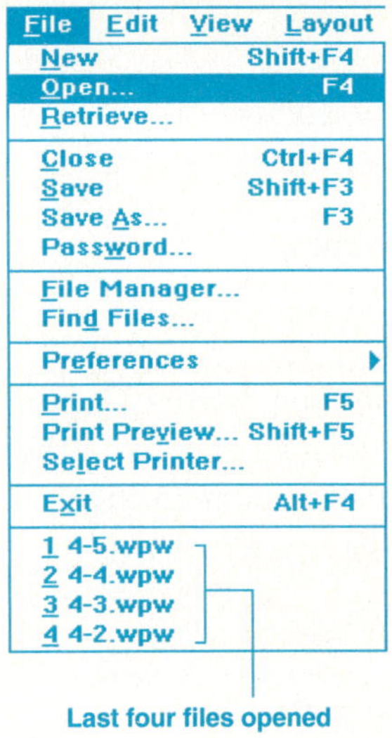

The File drop-down menu

Note: When the Change Default Dir check box in the Open File dialog box is checked, WordPerfect remembers the last directory you chose. The next time you open or save a document, the directory you were working in will be current. You will not need to choose one again (unless you wish to work in a different directory).

2. From the menu bar, choose File to open the File menu.

   Notice the list of filenames at the bottom of the File menu. This list represents the last four files opened. When the file you are looking for is listed, select it from this list.

3. Choose Open from the File menu.

   The Open File dialog box appears.

4. If necessary, check the Change Default Dir check box, so the drive and directory you choose now appears every time you open or save a file.

5. In the Directories list box, choose the appropriate drive for your computer, according to your instructor's directions. If you are using a floppy disk, make sure a disk is in the floppy-disk drive.

   Click the scroll arrow in the Directories list box, if necessary. The drives are at the bottom of the list.

   Click the appropriate drive, and then click the Open command button (or double-click the drive).

6. If your instructor has directed you to open a specific directory, click the appropriate directory in the Directories list box and then click Open.

   The path you chose appears in the information area of the dialog box.

7. From the Files list box, select the file 5-0a.wpw.

   The file size, date saved, and time saved appear in the information area of the dialog box.

8. Click Open. You also can double-click the filename to open the file.

   The file appears in the document window, and the filename is displayed on the title bar.

Now, use the Button Bar to close the file:

1. From the menu bar, choose View to open the View menu.

   If the Button Bar option is not checked, choose Button Bar. The Button Bar appears below the menu bar.

   If the Button Bar option is checked, choose View again to close the View menu.

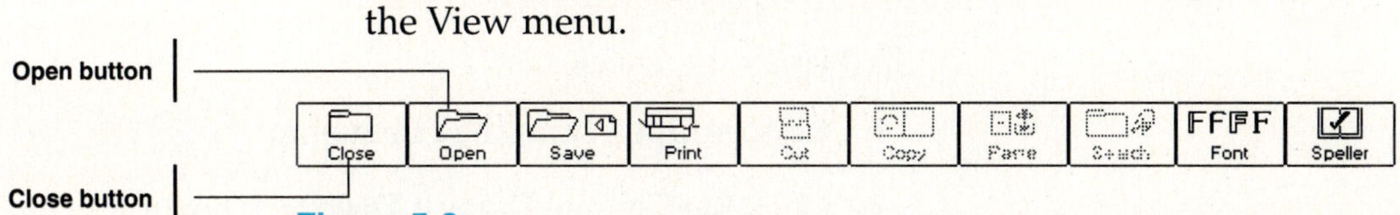

Figure 5-2
The Button Bar

2. Click the Close button on the Button Bar.

   The on-screen document closes, and a new document window appears, ready for you to create a new document.

Open the file again, and explore the View option:

1. Click the Open button on the Button Bar.

   The Open File dialog box appears. Because the Change Default Dir box is checked, the path that you chose is displayed in the information area, and the class-exercise files appear in the Files list box.

2. Choose file 5-0a.wpw from the Files list box.

3. Click the View button at the bottom of the dialog box.

   The View window opens, displaying text from the selected file.

4. Click the Open button.

Using Quick List

Quick List
In the Open File dialog box, a list of descriptive names that allow you to move quickly to frequently used paths and filenames.

When you check the *Quick List* check box, the Directories list box is replaced with the Quick List list box. This is a list of descriptive names for frequently used directories and files. You can change a path or choose a filename quickly with Quick List.

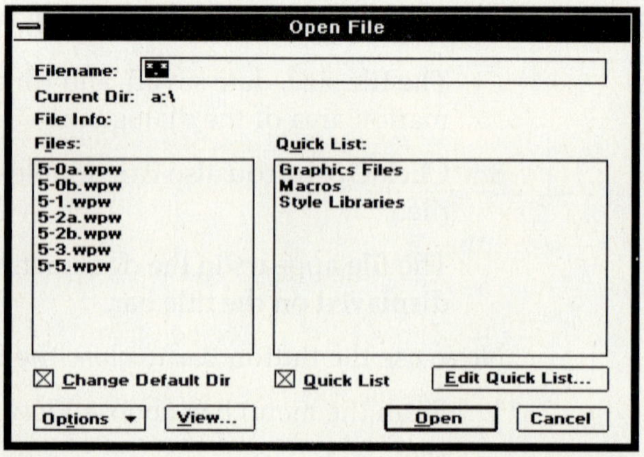

Figure 5-3
The Open File dialog box with Quick List displayed

To display the Quick List:

1. Choose Open from the File menu.

2. Click the Change Default Dir check box to uncheck it (there should be no "X" in the check box).

Note: Unchecking the Change Default Dir check box is an important step in this procedure. If this option is checked, the newly opened directory will become the current directory. The next time you try to open or save a file, you may have a difficult time returning to the drive or directory where your class-exercise files are stored.

3. Check the Quick List check box.

   The Quick List list box replaces the Directories list box.

4. Choose Graphics Files in the Quick List, and then click Open or double-click Graphics Files.

   The information area of the dialog box shows that the current directory is c:\wpwin\graphics.

5. Choose auto.wpg from the Files list box.

6. Click the View button.

   The View window appears and displays the graphic file auto.wpg. The View command allows you to see the contents of a file before you open or retrieve it. Working with graphics is discussed in "Module 10: Lines and Graphics".

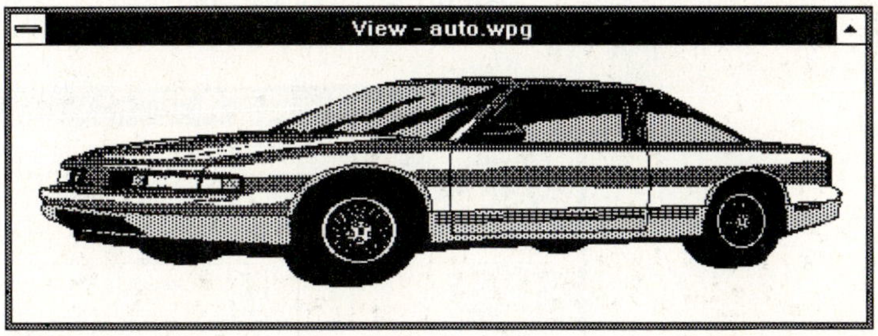

Figure 5-4
The View window displaying a graphics file

7. Click Quick List in the Open File dialog box to uncheck it.

8. Click Cancel to close the Open File dialog box without opening a file.

   The document 5-0a.wpw is still displayed.

9. Press **F4** to open the Open File dialog box again.

10. Check the Change Default Dir check box.

Open vs. Retrieve

Retrieve is similar to Open, but has some important differences. If the current document window is empty, choosing Retrieve has the same effect as choosing Open.

If, however, the current document window contains text, the Retrieve command will place the contents of the selected file at the insertion point in the existing document. For example, if the insertion point is at the beginning of the second paragraph of the on-screen document, the retrieved file will be inserted between the first and second paragraphs of that document. The Retrieve command can save time when assembling documents that contain standard paragraphs. You also can use it for closing paragraphs and signature blocks.

If a file is opened rather than retrieved, a new document window will open, and the document that was displayed previously will remain open. Up to nine documents can be open at one time, but, in general, you should save and close one document window before opening a new one. Working with multiple documents is covered in Lesson 12.

To retrieve a file into the current document:

1. Press **Ctrl+End** to move the insertion point to the bottom of the document.
2. Choose Retrieve from the File menu.

   The Retrieve File dialog box opens. It is very similar to the Open File dialog box.

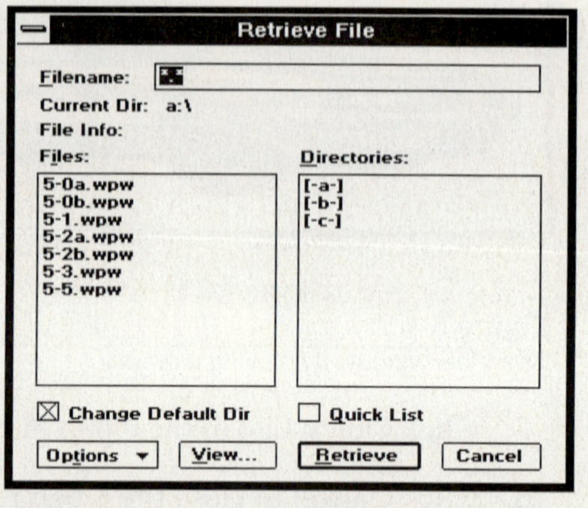

Figure 5-5
The Retrieve File dialog box

3. Double-click the file 5-0b.wpw.

   A question box appears, asking if you want to insert the file you selected into the current document.
4. Click Yes.

   The contents of document 5-0b.wpw are inserted at the end of the on-screen document, at the insertion-point position.

Word, Sentence, Paragraph: Some Definitions

Although you are very familiar with words, sentences, and paragraphs from a writer's point of view, these document elements have very specific structural definitions as they apply to word processing.

Word
The characters that make up a word, plus any spaces that follow it.

Sentence
Any text ending with a period or other end-of-sentence punctuation and at least one space.

Hard return
A non-printing character, created by pressing the **Enter** key, that creates a new line.

Paragraph
Any part of a document that ends with a hard return, and the blank lines that follow it.

A *word* is a group of characters that are not separated by spaces, plus any spaces that follow that group of characters. A word does not include the punctuation that sometimes follows a word, such as a period or comma.

A *sentence* is a group of words ending with a period or other end-of-sentence punctuation and at least one space. The spaces following a sentence are part of it. WordPerfect requires at least one space between sentences to recognize them correctly.

A *hard return* is a nonprinting character that causes text following it to move to the beginning of the next line. A hard return is inserted each time the **Enter** key is pressed. Any text following a hard return is placed on a new line. If no text follows the hard return, a blank line is created.

Normally, the term "paragraph" refers to a group of related sentences. In word-processor terminology, however, a *paragraph* is any group of words ending with a hard return. By this definition, the salutation line of a business letter is a paragraph, and so is the first line of an inside address. In WordPerfect, any blank lines at the end of a paragraph are treated as part of that paragraph.

Merging and Splitting Paragraphs

In the last lesson, you practiced creating new paragraphs. Now that you know the definition of a paragraph and a hard return, you can practice revising a document by merging and splitting paragraphs.

To merge paragraphs:

1. Move the insertion point to the beginning of the second paragraph.
2. Press the **Backspace** key twice.

   The paragraphs are merged. However, there is no space between the sentences at the point of the merge.
3. Press the **Spacebar**.

To split the merged paragraph:

1. Move the insertion point to the left of the word "In".
2. Press **Enter** twice.

Moving Within a Document

As explained in the previous lesson, when you key text, it is inserted at the insertion point. As you continue keying text, WordPerfect automatically scrolls through the document, keeping the section in which you are working visible.

You can move to different parts of the document using the following methods:

- Move the insertion point using the mouse.

  To move the insertion point (the blinking vertical bar), position the I-beam with the mouse and click. This is the easiest way to move around the portion of the document displayed in the document window.

- Move the insertion point using the keyboard.

  Certain keys on the keyboard move the insertion point. The Arrow keys, for example, move the insertion point up or down one line, or one character to the left or to the right. Table 5-1 lists other keys and key combinations that can move the insertion point to specified locations in the document quickly.

Table 5-1: Keys to Move the Insertion Point

To move:	Use:
One word to the left	**Ctrl+Left Arrow**
One word to the right	**Ctrl+Right Arrow**
To the beginning of the line	**Home**
To the end of the line	**End**
Up one paragraph	**Ctrl+Up Arrow**
Down one paragraph	**Ctrl+Down Arrow**
Up one screen	**PgUp**
Down one screen	**PgDn**
Up one page	**Alt+PgUp**
Down one page	**Alt+PgDn**
Shift screen left	**Ctrl+PgUp**
Shift screen right	**Ctrl+PgDn**
To the beginning of the document	**Ctrl+Home**
To the end of the document	**Ctrl+End**

- Scroll through the document.

  You can use the vertical scroll bar to the right of the document window to move through a document. The position of the scroll box indicates the approximate location of the on-screen text in the document, which is particularly helpful in long documents.

  To view and move through a document that is wider than the document window, use the horizontal scroll bar at the bottom of the document window. If the horizontal scroll bar is not showing, display it by choosing Horizontal Scroll from the

Note: Remember that scrolling through a document does not move the insertion point. It moves only the portion of the document you currently are viewing in the document window.

View menu. Table 5-2 lists additional ways to scroll through a document.

Table 5-2: Scrolling Through a Document

To move:	You can:
Up five lines	Click the up scroll arrow
Down five lines	Click the down scroll arrow
Up one screen	Click the scroll bar above the scroll box
Down one screen	Click the scroll bar below the scroll box
To any relative position	Drag the scroll box up or down
To the right	Click the right scroll arrow on the horizontal scroll bar

To practice moving the insertion point in document 5-0a.wpw:

1. Make sure the insertion point is at the beginning of the document. Press the **End** key to move to the end of the line.
2. Press **Ctrl+End** to move to the end of the document.
3. Press **Page Up** twice to move up two screens.
4. Press **Ctrl+Right Arrow** several times to move to the right one word at a time.
5. Press **Ctrl+UpArrow** several times to move up in the document.

To practice scrolling within the document:

1. Click below the vertical scroll box to move down one screen.
2. Drag the scroll box down to within 1 inch of the bottom of the scroll bar.
3. Click above the scroll box to move up one screen.

   Notice the position of the scroll box.
4. Click above the scroll box to move up one more screen.
5. Click the down scroll arrow twice to move down ten lines.
6. Drag the scroll box to the top of the scroll bar.

   Notice that throughout this scrolling procedure, the insertion point remained in the same place, at the top of the document.

The Undo and Undelete Commands

When inserting and deleting text in a document, the Undo and Undelete commands are two very helpful WordPerfect features that can save time and correct errors.

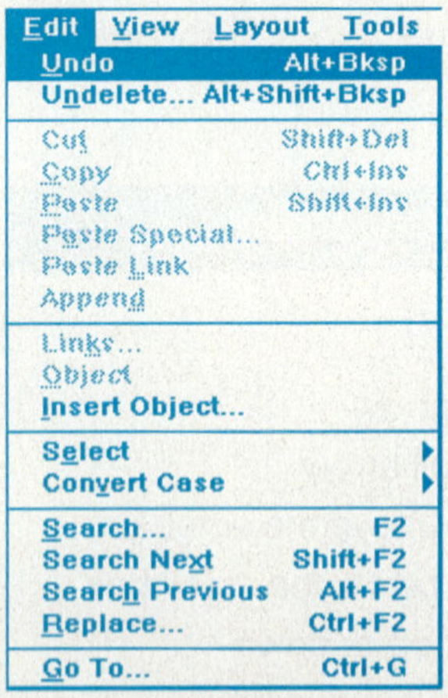

The Edit menu

The Undo Command

If you delete some text accidentally or change your mind about a particular revision, use the Undo command. This command cancels your most recent action and restores the document to the form it was in before you took the action.

The Undo command can be issued three ways:

- By choosing Undo from the Edit menu
- By pressing **Alt+Backspace**
- By pressing **Ctrl+Z**

To practice using the Undo command:

1. Move the insertion point to the left of the first word in the document, "Five".
2. Press the **Delete** key five times to delete "Five" and the space following it.
3. Choose Undo from the Edit menu. (Notice the reminder for the Undo keyboard shortcut, **Alt+Backspace**.)

   The word "Five" is restored on the on-screen document.
4. Move the insertion point to the left of the word "downtown", near the end of the first sentence in the document.
5. Key **busy**, and press the **Spacebar** once.

   The text now reads "in busy downtown Atlanta".
6. Press **Alt+Backspace** (the keyboard shortcut for Undo).

   The word "busy" is deleted.

The Undelete Command

Note: If you remove text using the Undo command, Undelete cannot restore it. Undelete restores only text that was removed from a document using the **Delete** key, **Ctrl+Delete**, or **Ctrl+Backspace**.

In the section above, you learned that you can undo your most recent editing action, which, in some cases, restores text that you deleted. Sometimes, you need to restore text that was deleted prior to your last editing action. In this case, the Undelete command can help.

When you choose Undelete from the Edit menu, two things happen:

- The most recently deleted text appears, highlighted, at the insertion point, which is not necessarily the original location of the text.
- The Undelete dialog box opens.

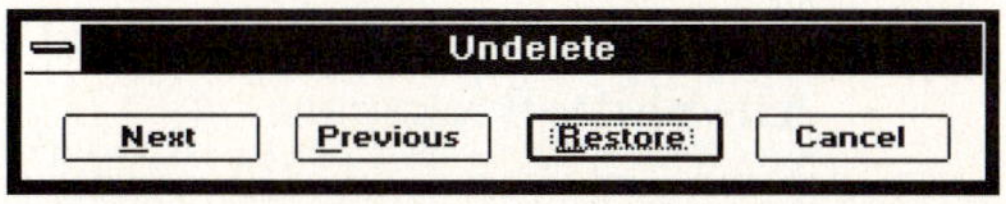

Figure 5-6
The Undelete dialog box

Undelete can restore any of the last three deletions you made. Click the Next or Previous button to cycle through these choices. When the text you want to restore appears, click the Restore button. Click the Cancel button if you decide not to restore any of the choices.

The amount of text included in a deletion is determined by insertion-point movement. All the text deleted from the time you position the insertion point until you move it again is one deletion. For example, pressing the **Delete** key five times and then pressing **Ctrl+Backspace** twice is one deletion, as long as you did not move the insertion point between actions.

Practice deleting and undeleting text:

1. On the first line of the third paragraph, position the insertion point to the left of the word "located".
2. Press the **Delete** key eight times to delete the word "located" and the space following it.
3. Open the Edit menu and choose Undelete.

   The Undelete dialog box opens, and the word "located" appears, highlighted, at the insertion point.
4. Click the Restore button.

   The dialog box closes, and the word "located" is no longer highlighted.
5. Position the insertion point anywhere on the word "Merchandise" in the third line of the second paragraph.
6. Press **Ctrl+Backspace** three times to delete "Merchandise" and the next two words.

   The text now reads "Atlanta's Apparel Mart".
7. On the next line, position the insertion point just to the left of the word "major".
8. Press **Ctrl+Delete** to delete to the end of the line.

   The words "major real estate" are deleted.
9. Position the insertion point just to the left of the word "Apparel" on the third line of the second paragraph.

10. Choose Undelete from the Edit menu, or press **Alt+Shift+Backspace**.

    The Undelete dialog box appears, but it may be hiding the highlighted text.

11. If necessary, move the dialog box to the lower right corner of the window by dragging its title bar. (Almost any dialog box can be moved to see what is underneath it.)

    The text from the last deletion, "major real estate", appears, but it is not the correct text for this location.

Previously deleted text

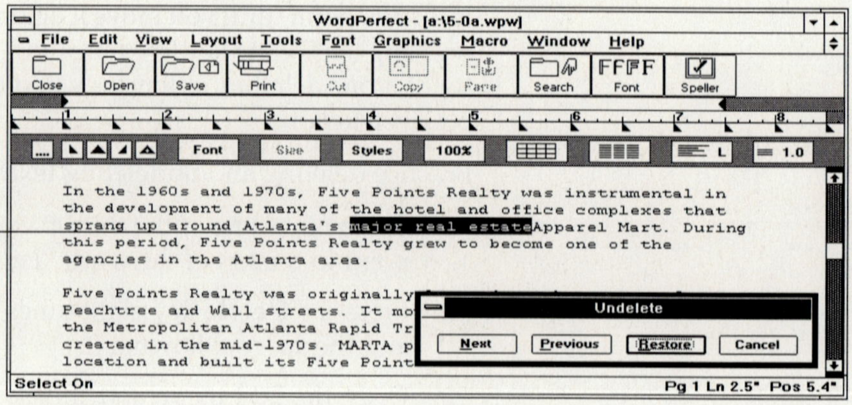

Figure 5-7
The Undelete dialog box moved to reveal highlighted text

12. Click the Previous button in the dialog box.

    The highlighted words "Merchandise Mart and " appear in place of "major real estate".

13. Click the Restore button.

14. Position the insertion point at the end of the fourth line of the second paragraph, one space to the right of "the".

15. Choose Undelete from the Edit menu.

    The highlighted words "major real estate" appear at the insertion point.

16. Click Restore.

Undo vs. Undelete

You can think of Undo as the "panic button". If you catch yourself panicking because of a revision, issue the Undo command immediately, before you do anything else. Undo reverses your very last action only. For example, if you delete a word and then key a word, Undo will remove the keyed word, but will not bring back the deleted word. It can remove and restore formatting as well as text, but some actions cannot be undone. You cannot, for example, unsave or unscroll.

Undelete is used only with text. It is important to understand that undeleted text appears at the insertion point when it is restored. If you delete a sentence at the beginning of a document, move the insertion point to the end of the document, and then undelete it, the sentence will be restored at the wrong location, unless you are using Undelete as a way of moving the sentence.

Selecting Text

Selecting text is an important, basic technique that adds speed and ease to revising documents. Future lessons will discuss moving, copying, saving, and printing a selected portion of a document. In this lesson, you will delete and replace selected text.

There are many different methods for selecting text, using both the keyboard and the mouse. As you work more in WordPerfect, the method best suited to the task will become apparent.

Selection
The selected portion of a document (or the whole document) that appears highlighted on the screen.

When selecting text, that area of the document, called the *selection*, is highlighted on the screen. The selected text remains highlighted until you cancel the selection.

Selecting with the Mouse

You can choose from several methods of text selection using the mouse, depending on the size of the area to be selected.

- Drag-selecting

Drag-select
To select text by holding down the mouse button while moving the mouse.

  The standard method of selection is called *drag-selecting*. This is done by placing the mouse pointer at one end of the area you want to select, holding down the left mouse button, and dragging the I-beam to the end of the selection.

- **Shift**+click

  With this method of selection, you position the pointer and click at one end of the desired selection, such as the beginning of a sentence. Then you hold down the **Shift** key (on the keyboard) while clicking at the other end.

- Multiple clicking

  You can double-click to select a word, triple-click to select a sentence, and quadruple-click to select a paragraph.

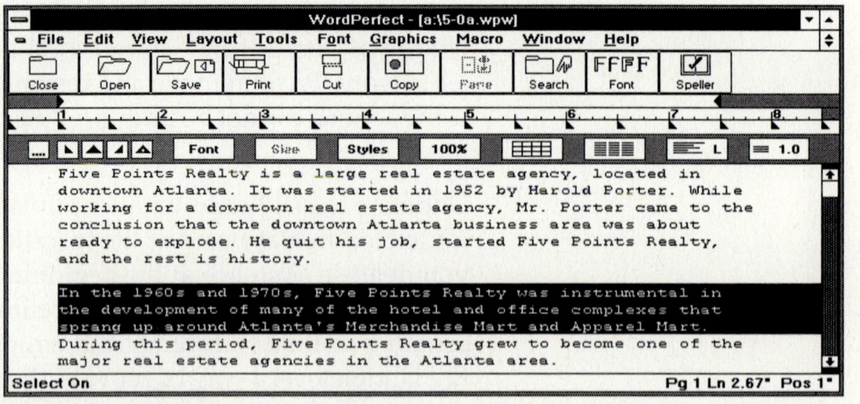

Figure 5-8
Document 5-0a.wpw with selected text

Table 5-3 reviews all methods of mouse selection.

Table 5-3: Mouse Selection Methods

To select:	Use the mouse to:
A series of characters	Click and drag, or click at one end of the series, and then click the other end while holding down the **Shift** key.
A word	Double-click anywhere in the word.
A sentence	Triple-click anywhere in the sentence.
A line of text	Click in the left margin of the line and drag down. To select multiple lines, drag up or down in the left margin.
A paragraph	Quadruple-click anywhere in the paragraph.
The entire document	Position the insertion point at the beginning of the document, and then drag the scroll box to the bottom of the scroll bar. **Shift**+click at the end of the document.

Once you make a selection, you can adjust the amount of text selected or cancel the selection.

To adjust a mouse selection:

- Hold down the **Shift** key, and click where you want the selection to end, either beyond the highlighted area to lengthen the selection, or within the highlighted area to shorten the selection.

- Hold down the **Shift** key, and press any Arrow key to lengthen or shorten the selection.

To cancel a mouse selection:

- Click anywhere in the document.
- Press an Arrow key.

To practice mouse selection:

1. Select the first word in the document by double-clicking it.

   Notice that the space following the word also is selected.

2. Cancel the selection by clicking anywhere in the document.
3. Position the insertion point at the beginning of the sentence and click.
4. Press the left mouse button, and drag to the end of the sentence.
5. Release the mouse button.
6. Adjust the selection to include the second sentence by holding down the **Shift** key, moving the pointer to the end of the second sentence, and clicking.
7. Press any Arrow key to clear the selection. If you use an Arrow key from the numeric keypad, make sure **Num Lock** is not on.
8. Select the second paragraph by placing the mouse pointer anywhere in the second paragraph and quadruple-clicking.

   Notice that the blank line following the paragraph also is selected.

9. Position the insertion point at the beginning of the document, and drag the scroll box to approximately 1 inch from the bottom of the scroll bar. Be careful not to click in the document area while doing this.
10. **Shift**+click at the end of the last sentence in the document.

    The entire document is highlighted.

11. Click the scroll bar above the scroll box several times to see the highlighting.
12. Click anywhere in the document window to deselect the document.

Selecting with the Keyboard

You can use a variety of keyboard commands to select text. Most of these selections use the **Shift** key. Table 5-4 lists some of these keyboard commands.

Table 5-4: Keyboard Selection

To select:	Press:
One character to the right or left	**Shift+Right Arrow** or **Shift+Left Arrow**
To the end of a word	**Ctrl+Shift+Right Arrow**
To the beginning of a word	**Ctrl+Shift+Left Arrow**
To the end of a line	**Shift+End**
To the beginning of a line	**Shift+Home**
One line up or down	**Shift+Up Arrow** or **Shift+Down Arrow**
To the beginning of a paragraph	**Ctrl+Shift+Up Arrow**
To the end of a paragraph	**Ctrl+Shift+Down Arrow**
To the bottom of the screen	**Shift+Page Down**
To the top of the screen	**Shift+Page Up**
To the end of a document	**Ctrl+Shift+End**
To the beginning of a document	**Ctrl+Shift+Home**

Select Mode

When you press **F8**, the words "Select Mode" appear on the left side of the status bar, indicating that select mode is active. When select mode is active, pressing the Arrow keys will extend or shrink the selection from the insertion point. Pressing any character key will extend the selection to the next occurrence of that character.

To cancel select mode, press **F8** again, or click the mouse pointer anywhere.

Practice using Select Mode:

1. Position the insertion point at the beginning of the second paragraph.
2. Press **F8**.
3. Press the **Right Arrow** key several times.

   Several characters are selected.
4. Press **Ctrl+Right Arrow** several times to extend the selection a word at a time.
5. Key an uppercase **M**.

   The selection extends to the first occurrence of an uppercase "M".

6. Press **Enter** to extend the selection to the end of the paragraph.
7. Press **Ctrl+Left Arrow** twice to shrink the selection by two words.
8. Press **F8** to cancel the selection.

   The text is no longer highlighted, and the status bar no longer displays the Select Mode indicator.

Deleting and Replacing a Selection

Note: While this is an excellent editing feature, it is sometimes the cause of accidental deletions. Remember, when text is selected in a document (or even in a dialog box), and you begin keying text, WordPerfect deletes all the selected text with your first keystroke. If you key text without realizing that a portion of the document is selected, use the Undo or Undelete command to restore the text.

Once text is selected, you can delete it by pressing the **Delete** key. You also can replace it simply by keying over the selected text. Unlike using the typeover mode, when you key over selected text, the keyed text can be longer or shorter than the selection. Whatever the length, WordPerfect will replace the selected text with the newly keyed text.

To practice deleting and replacing selected text:

1. Select the first sentence of the second paragraph by triple-clicking.
2. Press the **Delete** key.
3. Choose Undo from the Edit menu.
4. In the fourth paragraph, which begins "Harold Porter, the founder", drag-select "resident of Atlanta" at the end of the first sentence.
5. Key **long-time Atlanta resident**.

   The selected text is replaced with the new text.

More Ways to Save a Document

In the last lesson, you named and saved a new document. In this lesson, after revising an existing document, you will save it, close it, and rename it. WordPerfect's additional save options also will be reviewed.

Saving a Revised Document

Saving a revised document is as easy as saving a new one. You can either click the Save button on the Button Bar or choose Save from the File menu. This command will save the document with all the changes made to it automatically, replacing the old file with the revised file.

Timed Document Backup

Timed Document Backup is a WordPerfect safety feature that makes a copy of each open document automatically at the interval you specify. While WordPerfect performs the backup, a message appears on the status bar for a few seconds.

If you exit WordPerfect correctly by closing all documents and choosing the Exit command, the timed backup files are deleted. In the event of a power outage or a system failure, you can retrieve documents from the backup file. Backup files are named wp{wp}.bk*n*, where "n" is the number of the document window. Your instructor will explain the location of the backup files.

Backup files contain all your work up to the point of the last backup. Consider this when deciding the backup interval you want to set. The longer the backup interval, the greater the chance of losing work if a power or system failure occurs.

See your instructor to learn how to turn on the Timed Document Backup feature.

The Save As Command

You may wish to save the revised document under a new name and retain the original document without the revisions. This can be done using the Save As command. When you use this command, you actually are renaming the document with the revisions. The original document remains unchanged. There are now two documents that may be very similar in content, but have distinct file names.

To use the Save As command on the document you have revised:

1. Choose Save As from the File menu (or press **F3**).

   The Save As dialog box appears.

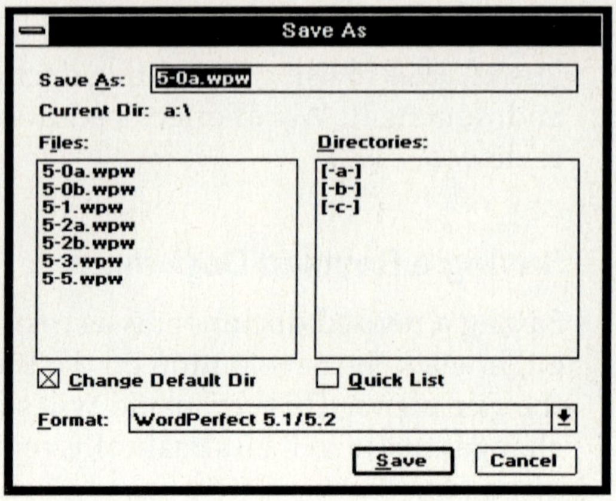

Figure 5-9
The Save As dialog box

2. In the Filename text box, move the insertion point to the left of "5-0a" and key *[your three-letter identifier]*.

3. Click the Save command button.

   The revised document is saved as *[your three-letter identifier]*5-0a.wpw. Notice the change in the title bar at the top of the screen. The original document file is closed automatically, and the revised document file with the new name remains open.

The document 5-0a.wpw has been revised, and the revisions have been saved as a new version of the document. The original document remains unchanged.

Saving Selected Text

You can save part of a document as a separate file. If some of the text in the current document, such as the closing paragraph or signature block, can be used again in another document, you can save time by selecting it and then choosing the Save command. Later, when you create another document, you can use the Retrieve command to insert the saved text into the new document.

Saving vs. Closing a Document

Closing is different from saving. When you are finished working on a document, you save it. Then you close it so that it does not take up unnecessary memory, especially when working with several opened documents. It is best to close all open documents before exiting WordPerfect.

If you attempt to close a document with changes that have not been saved, the Save Changes question box appears. Click Yes if you want to save the changes, No if you do not want to save the changes, and Cancel if you clicked the Close button accidentally.

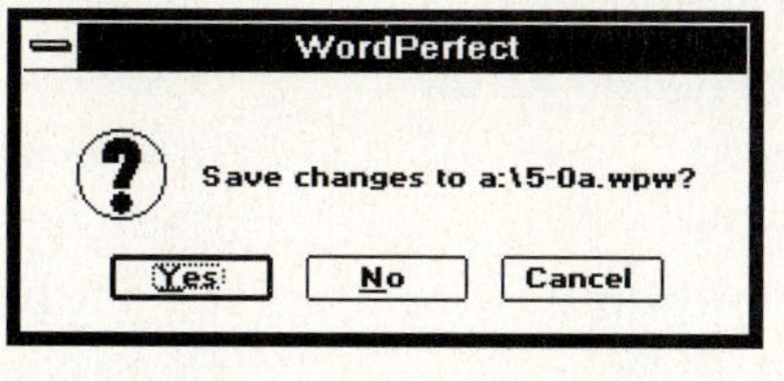

Figure 5-10
The Save Changes question box

Make changes to the document and close it:

1. Select the acronym "FPR" in the first line of the fourth paragraph.

2. Key **Five Points Realty.**

3. Click the Close button on the Button Bar.

   The Save Changes question box appears.

4. Click Yes.

   The document *[your three-letter identifier]*5-0a.wpw is saved again with the latest changes.

5. Exit WordPerfect (unless you will be doing the following exercises immediately).

Table 5-5: Keyboard Shortcuts for Revising Text

Keyboard Shortcut	Action
F4	Open
Shift+F3	Save
F3	Save As
Shift+F4	New document
Ctrl+Shift+F4	Close document and open a new one
Alt+Backspace	Undo
Ctrl+Z	Undo
Alt+Shift+Backspace	Undelete
F8	Select mode on/off

Keyboard Shortcut	To Move the Insertion Point:
Ctrl+Left Arrow	One word to the left
Ctrl+Right Arrow	One word to the right
Home	To the beginning of the line
End	To the end of the line
Ctrl+Up Arrow	Up one paragraph
Ctrl+Down Arrow	Down one paragraph
PgUp	Up one screen
PgDn	Down one screen
Alt+PgUp	Up one page
Alt+PgDn	Down one page
Ctrl+PgUp	Shift screen left
Ctrl+PgDn	Shift screen right
Ctrl+Home	To the beginning of the document
Ctrl+End	To the end of the document

Table 5-5—Continued

Keyboard Shortcut	To Select Text:
Shift+Right or **Left Arrow**	One character to the right or left
Ctrl+Shift+Right Arrow	To the end of a word
Ctrl+Shift+Left Arrow	To the beginning of a word
Shift+End	To the end of a line
Shift+Home	To the beginning of a line
Shift+Up or **Down Arrow**	One line up or down
Ctrl+Shift+Up Arrow	To the beginning of a paragraph
Ctrl+Shift+Down Arrow	To the end of a paragraph
Shift+Page Down	To the bottom of the screen
Shift+Page Up	To the top of the screen
Ctrl+Shift+End	To the end of a document
Ctrl+Shift+Home	To the beginning of a document

Key Terms

Drag-select
Hard return
Paragraph
Quick List
Selection
Sentence
Word

Exercises

Exercise 5-1

1. Start WordPerfect, if necessary.
2. Open the file 5-1.wpw:
   A. Choose Open from the File menu.
   B. From the Directories list box, double-click the drive and directory appropriate for your computer, as directed by your instructor.
   C. Double-click the file 5-1.wpw in the Files list box.
3. Replace the word "agency's" in the first sentence with "Five Points Realty":
   A. Select the word "agency's" by dragging the mouse.
   B. Key **Five Points Realty**.

4. Move the insertion point to the beginning of the second sentence in the second paragraph, and key the sentence **It specializes in executive relocation.** Then press the **Spacebar**.

5. Select the next sentence, which begins "The newest and smallest", by positioning the insertion point anywhere on the sentence and triple-clicking it.

6. Press the **Delete** key to delete the selected sentence.

7. Replace the phrase "making it possible for" with the word "enabling" using the Select mode:

   A. Position the insertion point to the left of "making".

   B. Press **F8**.

   C. Press **Ctrl+Right Arrow** four times to extend the selection to the word "for".

   D. Key **enabling**.

8. Save the document as *[your three-letter identifier]*5-1.wpw:

   A. Choose Save As from the File menu.

   B. Key *[your three-letter identifier]* to the left of "5-1.wpw" in the Filename text box.

   C. Click the Save button.

9. Print the document.

10. Close the document.

11. Exit WordPerfect (unless you will be doing the following exercises immediately.)

Exercise 5.2

1. Start WordPerfect, if necessary.

2. Open the file 5-2a.wpw.

3. Position the insertion point just to the left of the word "office" in the second sentence of the second paragraph.

4. Key **satellite** and press the **Spacebar**.

5. Move the insertion point to the end of the first paragraph, just to the right of "Area."

6. Press the **Spacebar**, and then key the sentence:

   The Marietta office also focuses on the increasing demand for retirement homes.

7. In the first sentence of the first paragraph, delete the word "satellite" by double-clicking it and pressing the **Delete** key.

8. In the first line of the second paragraph, select the phrase "(in the Piedmont Park area of Atlanta)" and delete it.

9. Use the Undelete command to restore the phrase deleted in the previous step:

   A. Position the insertion point on the first line of the second paragraph, to the right of the space following the word "office".

   B. Choose Undelete from the Edit menu.

   C. If the Undelete dialog box covers the highlighted phrase in the document window, move the dialog box to the bottom of the screen by dragging its title bar.

   D. Click the Restore command button in the dialog box.

10. Undelete the word "satellite" in the first sentence of the first paragraph:

    A. Move the insertion point to the left of the word "office".

    B. Choose Undelete from the Edit menu.

    C. Click the Previous button.

    D. Click Restore.

11. Split the last sentence of the second paragraph into a separate paragraph:

    A. Position the insertion point to the left of the word "It" at the beginning of the last sentence.

    B. Press **Enter** twice.

12. Merge the last sentence back into the second paragraph:

    A. If necessary, position the insertion point at the beginning of the third paragraph, to the left of the word "It".

    B. Press the **Backspace** key twice.

13. Insert the file 5-2b.wpw between the two paragraphs using the Retrieve command:

    A. Move the insertion point to the beginning of the second paragraph, just to the left of the word "The".

    B. Choose Retrieve from the File menu.

    C. Double-click the file 5-2b.wpw.

    D. Click Yes when the question box appears.

14. Choose Undo from the Edit menu to remove the retrieved paragraph.

15. Choose Undo again to reinsert the paragraph.

16. Save the document as *[your three-letter identifier]*5-2a.wpw.

17. Print the document.

18. Close the document.

19. Exit WordPerfect (unless you will be doing the following exercises immediately.)

Exercise 5.3

1. Start WordPerfect, if necessary.

2. Open the file 5-3.wpw.

3. Revise the first sentence of the document so it reads "The G&H Building at the corner of Techwood and Luckie Streets is a $7.2 million building".

4. At the end of the second sentence, change "soft drinks" to "the soft drink market".

5. Add the phrase "six months ago" to the end of the last sentence in the first paragraph. The sentence should read "relocated to Charlotte, NC six months ago".

6. In the third line of the second paragraph, key the word **computer** to the left of the word "graphics".

7. In the second line of the second paragraph, change the acronym "AMI" to the company name "Actron Multimedia, Inc."

8. Merge the second and third paragraphs. Be sure to add a space between the two sentences at the merge location.

9. Split the last sentence in the second paragraph into a separate paragraph.

10. Save the document as *[your three-letter identifier]*5-3.wpw.

11. Print the document.

12. Close the document.

13. Exit WordPerfect (unless you will be doing the following exercises immediately.)

Exercise 5.4

1. Start WordPerfect, if necessary.
2. Key document 5-4, which appears at the end of this exercise.
3. Key the words **real estate** in the first line, between the words "Atlanta" and "agency".
4. In the fourth line of the first paragraph, change "Bud Porter" to 'Chester "Bud" Porter'.
5. In the first sentence of the second paragraph, change "Bud" to "Mr. Porter", so the sentence reads "In his acceptance speech, Mr. Porter".
6. In the same sentence, key the word **and** after "INFORUM" so it reads "INFORUM, and Georgia".
7. In the second line of the second paragraph, key **one of** before the phrase "the hottest".
8. Split the first paragraph at the sentence that begins "At a recent Atlanta".
9. Merge the second and third paragraphs.
10. Delete the last sentence in the second paragraph, which begins "We're all very proud".
11. Save the document as *[your three-letter identifier]*5-4.wpw.
12. Print the document.
13. Close the document.
14. Exit WordPerfect (unless you will be doing the following exercise immediately.)

Document 5-4

Five Points Realty, a leading Atlanta agency, has been responsible for the relocation of many high tech bus inesses to the area around cnn, the Omni Center, and Georgia Tech. At a recent Atlanta Realtors luncheon, Bud Porter, the presdient of Five Points Realty and son of the founder, was honored, as the "Commercial Realtor of the Year."

In his acceptance speech, Bud said that with CNN, INFORUM, Georgia Tech, Atlanta has become the hottest "high-tech havens in the United States".

We're all very proud of Bud and think he's a really super guy!

Exercise 5.5

1. Start WordPerfect, if necessary.

2. Open the file 5-5.wpw.

3. In the first line, delete the words "fabulous downtown".

4. At the end of the first paragraph, select the last sentence by triple-clicking and delete it.

5. In the fourth paragraph, key **Johnny** to the left of "Mercer Room", so the sentence reads "in the Johnny Mercer Room".

6. Split the first paragraph at the beginning of the sentence that begins "Float down the Chattahoochee".

7. Merge the third and fourth paragraphs, which begin "Tour Ted Turner's" and "Visit the theater where".

8. Select the second paragraph, which begins "Float down the Chattahoochee", by quadruple-clicking and delete it.

9. Quadruple-click the last paragraph and delete it.

10. Use the Undo command to cancel the last deletion.

11. Use the Undelete command to restore the paragraph that begins "Float down the Chattahoochee" to its original position after the first paragraph.

12. Save the document as *[your three-letter identifier]*5-5.wpw.

13. Print the document.

14. Close the document.

15. Exit WordPerfect.

Lesson 6

Character Formatting

The previous lessons have taught the fundamentals of operating Windows and using WordPerfect to create and revise documents. So far, though, you have keyed only standard text. This lesson is an introduction to creating text with different character attributes, such as bold, italic, and underline.

Objectives

- Learn about character formatting.
- Apply character attributes.
- Change character attributes.
- Case conversion (uppercase and lowercase).
- Learn about WordPerfect's hidden codes.
- Learn about hard spaces and the dash character.

Using Character Attributes

A *character attribute* is an option that determines the appearance of the characters that make up a word or block of text. Suppose you want to emphasize a word in a paragraph. You can do this by giving the word a different character attribute than the other text in the paragraph. For example, you can apply the bold attribute to the word.

Character attribute
A formatting option, such as bold, italic, or underline, that determines the appearance of text.

This lesson shows how to apply the following character attributes to text:

- Bold
- Italic
- Underline
- Uppercase/lowercase

It also shows how to turn off these attributes to create normal text. Lesson 20 covers additional character attributes, such as double underline, shadow, and color.

Table 6-1 shows the character-attribute options this lesson discusses:

Table 6-1: Character-Attribute Options

Attribute	Example	Comments
Normal text	This is a sample.	Normal text uses the standard character attributes.
Bold	**This is a sample.**	Bold text is darker and heavier than normal text.
Italic	*This is a sample.*	Italic text is slanted to the right and is somewhat lighter than normal text.
Underline	<u>This is a sample</u>.	Underlined text is underscored with one continuous line.

Character format
The combined character attributes of text.

Character attributes often are combined. For example, text can be both bold and underlined. All the character attributes you apply to text make up the text's *character format*. Table 6-2 shows examples of character formats with multiple optional attributes:

Table 6-2: Character Formats with Multiple Character Attributes

Attributes	Example
Bold, italic, and uppercase	***THIS IS A SAMPLE.***
Bold and underlined	**This is a sample.**
Italic and underlined	*This is a sample.*
Bold and italic	***This is a sample.***

Note: Character formats also can be specified from the Font dialog box, but this method requires more steps. Use the Font dialog box when you need to change the font and size of type.

You can specify character attributes from the Font drop-down menu or with keyboard shortcuts. Using either method, you can apply attributes as you key new text or to text that has been keyed previously. As you gain experience with WordPerfect, the most convenient method for your work will become apparent.

Applying Character Attributes from the Font Menu

You can choose the most commonly used character attributes from the Font drop-down menu. To apply these attributes as you key text, choose the attribute once to turn it on, key the text, and then choose the same attribute again to turn it off.

To specify character attributes for new text as you type using the Font menu:

1. Start WordPerfect.
2. Open the file 6-0.wpw.
3. Press **Ctrl+End** to move to the end of the document.
4. Press **Enter** twice to start a new paragraph.
5. Key **The** and press the **Spacebar**.
6. Choose Font from the menu bar.

   The Font menu drops down. The Normal attribute is checked. Notice the keyboard shortcut reminders on the right side of the menu.
7. Choose Italic from the Font menu.

   The Font menu closes. The sample text on the left side of the status bar is displayed in italic.
8. Key **most**.

   The word "most" appears in italic.

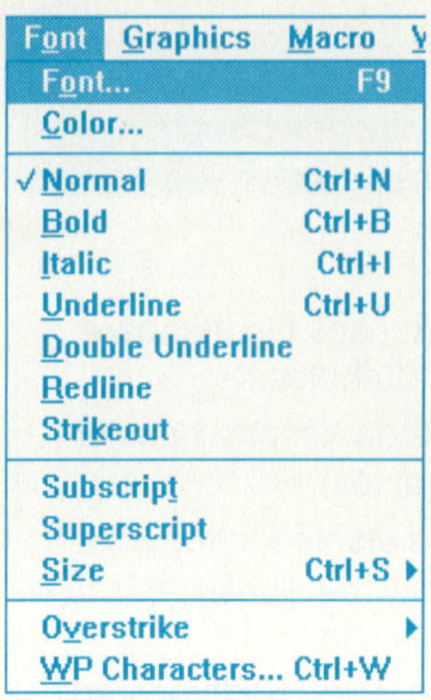

The Font menu

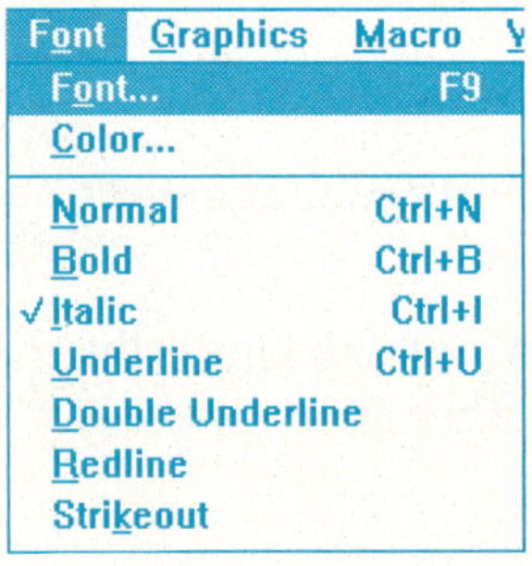

Italic selected

9. Choose Font from the menu bar.

   Italic is checked.

10. Choose Italic to turn off the italic attribute.

11. Press the **Spacebar**, and then key **important task of the property manager is**.

    The remainder of the sentence will be completed later in the lesson.

You also can change the character attributes of existing text using the Font menu. To do this, first select the text to be changed, and then apply the attribute.

1. Position the insertion point at the beginning of the document, and select the title "Five Points' Property Management Group" using the drag method.

2. Choose Bold from the Font menu.

3. Press the **Left Arrow** once to deselect the text.

   Now you can see that the text is bold.

Dragging is often the best method to select text for applying character attributes. If you double, triple, or quadruple-click text, the blank spaces and lines following the text will be selected. These blanks will receive any character attributes that are applied. For example, if you double-click a word and then underline it, the space following the word will be underlined.

Using Keyboard Shortcuts

The keyboard shortcuts for Bold, Underline, Italic, and Normal are very easy to remember, and, because you can keep your hands on the keyboard, they are convenient to use while you are keying text. Table 6-3 lists the keyboard shortcuts for these character options:

Table 6-3: Character-Option Keyboard Shortcuts

Keyboard Shortcut	Action
Ctrl+N	Normal
Ctrl+B	Bold
Ctrl+I	Italic
Ctrl+U	Underline

To apply character attributes using keyboard shortcuts:

1. Press **Ctrl+End** to move to the end of the document, and position the insertion point before the last word, "is".

2. Press the **Spacebar**, and then press **Ctrl+B** to turn Bold on.

3. Key **preservation**.
4. Press **Ctrl+B** to turn Bold off.
5. Press the **Spacebar** and then key:

   of property values. The Five Points property-management group

6. Press the **Spacebar**, and then press **Ctrl+U** to turn Underline on. (Remember, you can check to see whether an attribute is on or off by looking at the status bar.)
7. Key **exercises careful supervision of tenants**.
8. Press **Ctrl+U**, and then type a period.

Combining Character Attributes

It is easy to combine two or more character attributes in the text. To apply combined attributes to new and existing text:

1. Press the **Spacebar** and key:

   Careful review of the prospective tenant's application and a

2. Press the **Spacebar.**
3. Press **Ctrl+U** to turn Underline on.
4. Press **Ctrl+B** to turn Bold on.

   Both attributes are displayed on the sample text in the status bar.

5. Key:

   personal interview and review of references

6. Press **Ctrl+N** to turn off both attributes and return to normal text. (Alternatively, you can press **Ctrl+B** and then **Ctrl+U** to turn the attributes off one at a time.)
7. Press the **Spacebar** and then key:

   aids in the process.

8. Select the words "property manager" in the first line of the first paragraph at the top of the document.
9. Choose Italic from the Font menu.

   Italics has been applied; the text remains selected.

Font attributes displayed

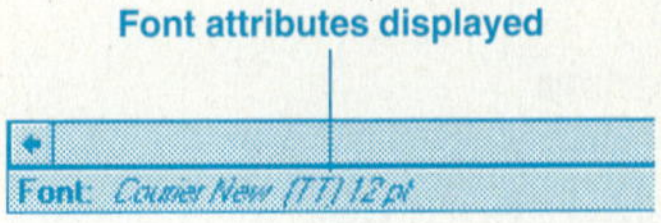

Status bar

10. Choose Bold from the Font menu.

    The text is now both bold and italic.

11. Select the words "investment property" at the end of the first line.
12. Press **Ctrl+B** and then press **Ctrl+I**.

Removing Character Attributes from Existing Text

If you change your mind about the format of some text, you can turn a character attribute off by selecting the text and then choosing the attribute from the Font menu, or by pressing its keyboard shortcut. If text has more than one attribute applied, you can remove all of them by choosing Normal or by pressing **Ctrl+N**.

To remove character attributes:

1. Select the underlined words "exercises careful supervision of tenants." in the second paragraph.
2. Choose Underline from the Font menu.

   The selection is no longer underlined.
3. Select "***investment property***" in the first line of the first paragraph.
4. Press **Ctrl+I**.

   The italic attribute is removed, but the text is still bold.
5. Press **Ctrl+B**.
6. Select "***property manager***" at the beginning of the first line.
7. Choose Font from the menu bar.

   Bold and Italic are checked.
8. Choose Normal.

   All character attributes are removed when you choose Normal.

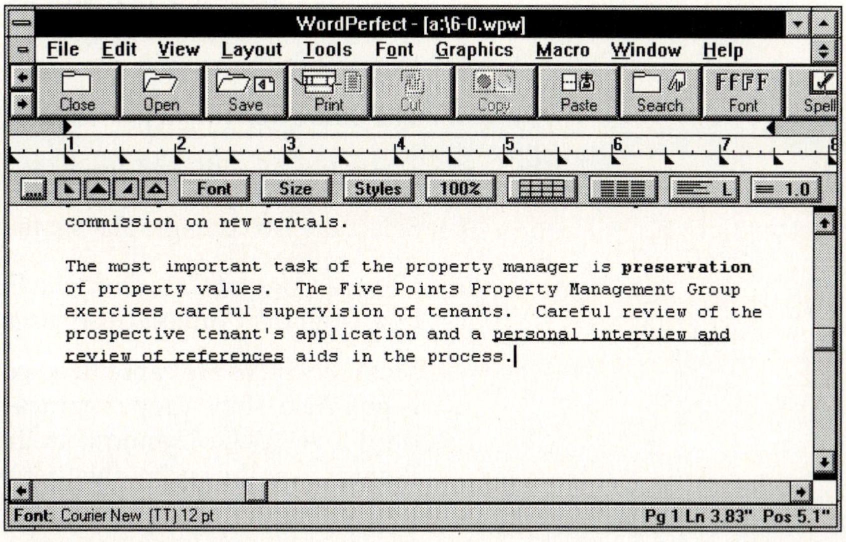

Figure 6-1
Document 6-0.wpw with character formatting

Case Conversion (Uppercase and Lowercase)

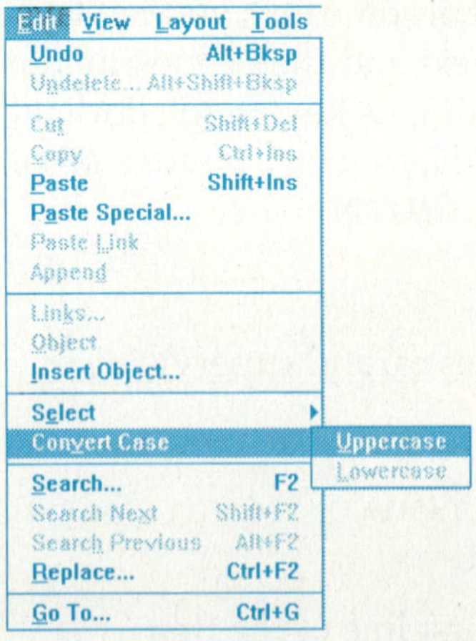

The Edit menu with the Convert Case cascading menu

Note: WordPerfect uses the punctuation at the end of the previous sentence to determine that a new sentence has started and therefore needs an initial capital. If you convert a group of paragraphs to lowercase, the first word in the selection must be capitalized manually.

You already know how to capitalize text as you key it, but suppose you just completed keying the text for a lengthy speech, and then found out it was supposed to have been keyed in uppercase! WordPerfect allows you to convert it quickly and easily. Select the text, choose Convert from the Edit menu, and then choose Uppercase from the Convert cascading menu.

You also can convert from uppercase to lowercase. WordPerfect will make an attempt to capitalize the first word in each sentence, but you must proofread carefully and be prepared to add initial capital letters manually where necessary.

To change text to uppercase:

1. Select the title "Five Points' Property Management Group" at the beginning of the document.
2. Choose Convert Case from the Edit menu.
3. Choose Uppercase from the Convert Case cascading menu.
4. Deselect the text.

To change the entire document to uppercase:

1. Move the insertion point to the beginning of the first paragraph.
2. Drag down the left margin to the end of the document.

   The two paragraphs are selected.
3. Choose Convert Case from the Edit menu, and then choose Uppercase from the Convert Case cascading menu.
4. Deselect the text.

   The entire document is in uppercase.

Convert the two paragraphs to lowercase:

1. Select the two paragraphs again.
2. Choose Convert Case from the Edit menu, and choose Lowercase from the Convert Case cascading menu.

   Most sentences are capitalized correctly, but the first sentence is not. Also, some proper names—"Five Points Realty" in the third line, "Della Crandon" in the fourth line, and "Five Points" near the end of the first paragraph—are not capitalized correctly.
3. Proofread the entire document and correct the capitalization. (Delete the incorrectly capitalized character and rekey it.)

Reveal Codes

As you key text and apply character attributes, WordPerfect displays your work on the screen the way it will appear when printed. WordPerfect also inserts hidden codes that control the ends of lines, turn on and off character attributes, and control advanced formatting features (which are covered in later lessons).

The Reveal Codes feature allows you to view and edit these hidden codes. Viewing the codes is very helpful when your document does not display or print correctly. There are three ways to turn on Reveal Codes:

- Choose Reveal Codes from the View menu.
- Press **Alt+F3**, the keyboard shortcut.
- Drag the Reveal Codes Bar.

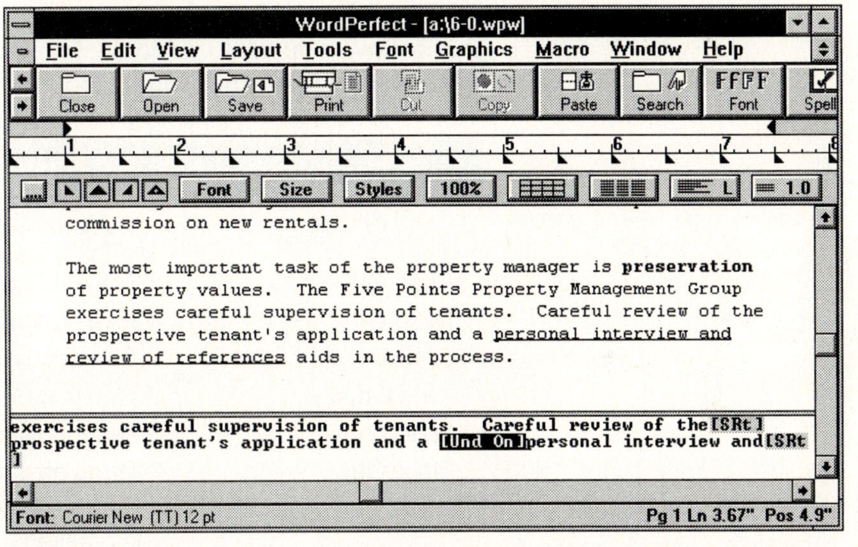

Figure 6-2
The WordPerfect screen with the Reveal Codes space displayed

To view the hidden codes:

1. Choose Reveal Codes from the View menu (or press **Alt+F3**).

   The screen splits. The top is the document window; the bottom is the Reveal Codes space.

2. Press **Ctrl+Home** to move to the top of the document.

   Notice that the first character of the title is highlighted in the Reveal Codes space. The highlight is red if you have a color monitor.

3. Press the **Left Arrow**.

Now the [Bold On] code is highlighted. If you look at the document window, you will see that the insertion point is still to the left of "Five".

4. Press the **End** key.

   Notice the [Bold Off] and [HRt] codes.

5. Choose Reveal Codes from the View menu (or press **Alt+F3**) to turn off Reveal Codes.

Many of the codes you see in the Reveal Codes space were inserted when you applied the character attributes earlier in this lesson. Their names, such as [Bold On], are easy to recognize. Other codes that you see control line breaks. An [HRt] code (hard return) is inserted each time you press the **Enter** key, and an [SRt] code (soft return) is inserted automatically each time WordPerfect wraps text to a new line. When you insert or delete text, WordPerfect automatically adjusts the position of the [SRt] code.

Table 6-4 shows the codes that are used in this lesson. In the lessons that follow, you will use codes for more advanced formatting features, such as margins, fonts, and headers.

Table 6-4: Some Basic Hidden Codes

Hidden Code	Action
[Bold On]	Turns on bold
[Bold Off]	Turns off bold
[Und On]	Turns on underlining
[Und Off]	Turns off underlining
[Italic On]	Turns on italic
[Italic Off]	Turns off italic
[HRt]	Hard return (inserted when the **Enter** key is pressed; starts a new line)
[SRt]	Soft return (inserted when WordPerfect wraps text to a new line)

Navigating the Reveal Codes Space

When Reveal Codes are displayed, every movement of the insertion point in the document window is mirrored by the highlight in the Reveal Codes space. This may not appear to be the case, however, because lines do not wrap at the same point in the Reveal Codes space as they do in the document window. This is because codes take up space, making a line wider than the corresponding line in the document window. The easiest way to navigate the codes is to (1) move the document-window insertion point to the character closest to the codes you need to see, and (2) look in the Reveal Codes space and move to the code. You can use either the mouse or the arrow keys in the Reveal Codes space.

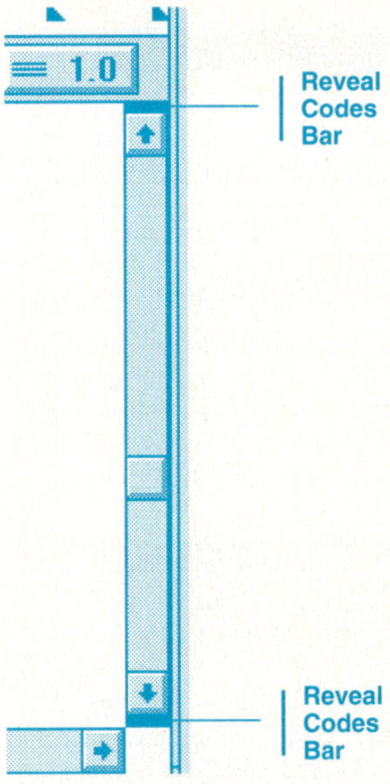

The Reveal Codes Bars

Practice moving in the Reveal Codes space:

1. Move the mouse pointer onto the small, black rectangle just below the Down scroll arrow. This is the Reveal Codes Bar.

2. Adjust the mouse pointer position until you see a small, double-pointed arrow on top of the black rectangle.

3. Hold down the left mouse button, and drag the Reveal Codes Bar up approximately 1½ inches.

   The Reveal Codes space appears. You also can open the Reveal Codes space by dragging the black rectangle located above the Up scroll arrow.

4. In the document window, move the insertion point to the beginning of the second paragraph.

   The Reveal Codes space automatically scrolls to the area corresponding to the insertion-point position.

5. Press the **Right Arrow** four times.

   The code [Italic On] is highlighted. Observe the word "*most*" between the [Italic On] and [Italic Off] codes. Notice that the highlight's movements correspond to the insertion-point position.

6. Press **Ctrl+Right Arrow** several times, until the insertion point is just to the left of the word "**preservation**."

   The insertion point is at the beginning of the word, near the end of the line, but the Reveal Codes highlight is on the character "p" at the beginning of the next line.

7. Press the **Left Arrow** once.

   Now the highlight is on the [Bold On] code, but the insertion point did not move. When the Reveal Codes space is displayed, the insertion point in the document window remains stationary when the highlight moves across the codes.

8. Press the **Left Arrow** once again.

   Now observe that the document-window insertion point is to the left of the space before "**preservation**", and the Reveal Codes highlight is on the space.

Using the Reveal Codes Sizing Bar

You can change the size of the Reveal Codes space by dragging the Reveal Codes sizing bar. The sizing bar is the gray, horizontal border that separates the Reveal Codes space and the document window. You can close the Reveal Codes space by dragging the sizing bar all the way up or all the way down.

Sizing bar

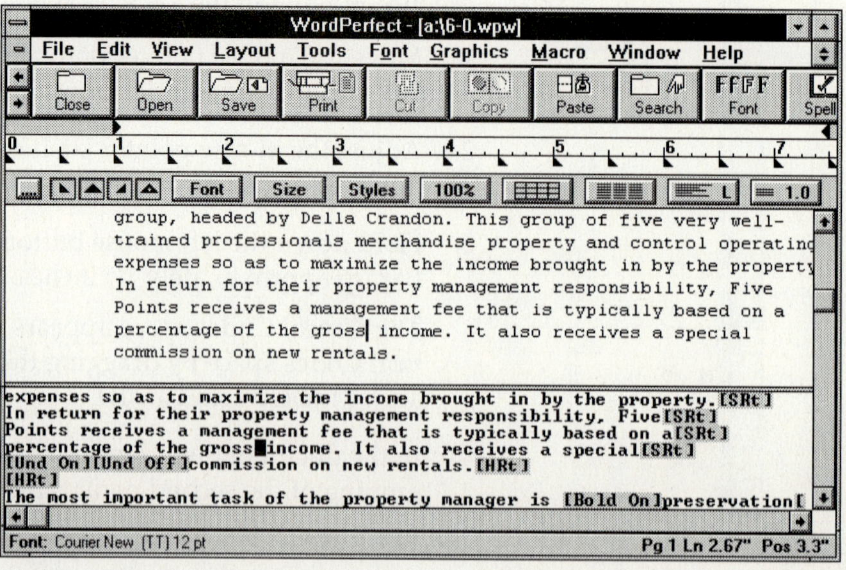

Figure 6-3
The Reveal Codes space sizing bar

Practice sizing, closing, and opening the Reveal Codes space:

1. Position the I-beam pointer on the sizing bar.
2. Slowly move the I-beam up and down across the sizing bar, until the I-beam changes to a double-headed arrow.
3. Drag the double-headed arrow (and the sizing bar) halfway up the screen.
4. Release the mouse button.
5. Close the Reveal Codes space by dragging the sizing bar to the top of the screen.
6. Open the Reveal Codes space by dragging down on the Reveal Codes Bar just above the Up scroll arrow.
7. Close the Reveal Codes space by dragging the sizing bar all the way down to the bottom of the screen.

Reveal Codes Preferences

The default size of the Reveal Codes space is 25% of the WordPerfect screen. The default color for the Reveal Codes text is black; for the codes, it is gray; for the cursor, it is red.

To change these defaults, choose Preferences from the File menu and then choose Display. In the Display dialog box, you can set the size of the Reveal Codes space to a different percentage than the default.

Also in the Display dialog box, click Reveal Codes Colors to display a dialog box in which you can change the colors of the text, code, and cursor.

Paired Codes

Paired codes
A set of codes to turn an attribute on and off.

When you apply character attributes to text, WordPerfect inserts a set of codes, one to turn on the attribute, and another to turn it off. Whenever an "on" code exists in a document, a corresponding "off" code also exists. For example, for each [Bold On] code, there is a [Bold Off] code. These often are called *paired codes*. In later lessons, you will learn about codes that do not come in pairs, such as font, margin, and tab-setting codes. These are called open codes.

Deleting Codes

As you know by now, any commands that you issue happen at the insertion-point (or selection) position in the document window. This is also true in the Reveal Codes space, but Reveal Codes uses a highlight instead of an insertion point. The highlight and the insertion point behave in slightly different ways:

- In the document window, an insertion point always rests between two characters, but the Reveal Codes highlight rests on a character or code.
- In the document window, the **Delete** key deletes the character to the right of the insertion point, but, in the Reveal Codes space, it deletes the character or code on which the highlight is resting.
- In the document window, the **Backspace** key deletes the character to the left of the insertion point. In the Reveal Codes space, it deletes the character or code to the left of the highlight.

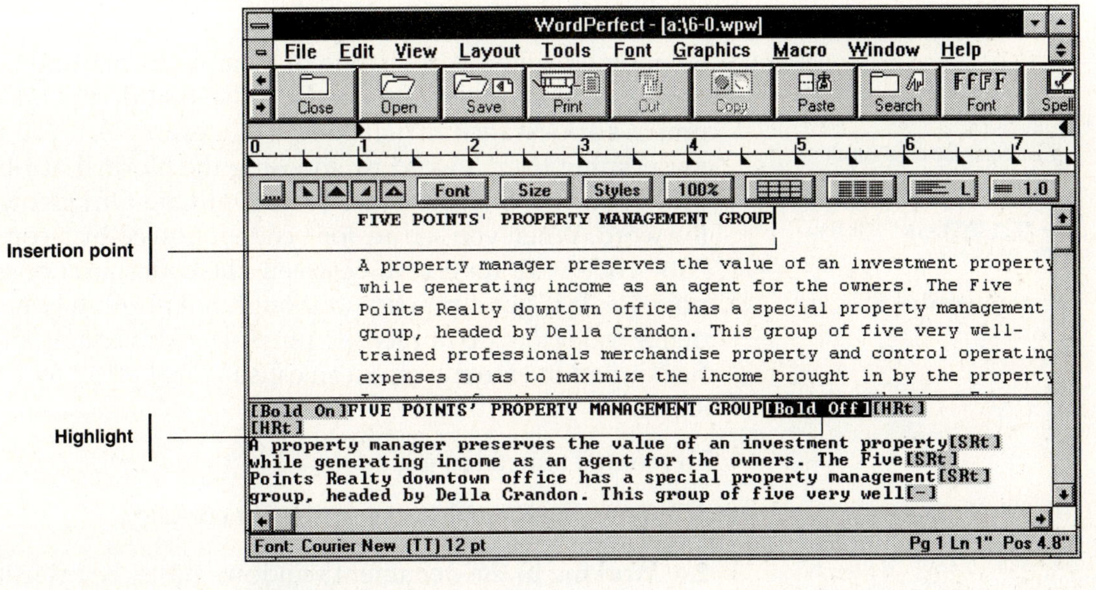

Figure 6-4
Insertion point and Reveal Codes highlight

Practice deleting and inserting codes:

1. Choose Reveal Codes from the View menu.
2. Adjust the size of the Reveal Codes space, so that it fills the bottom 25% of the screen.
3. Working in the document window, move the insertion point to the left of the word "*most*" at the beginning of the second paragraph.
4. Working in the Reveal Codes space, position the highlight on the character "*m*" in "*most*", if necessary, using the Arrow keys or the mouse.
5. Press the **Backspace** key.

   The word "most" is no longer italicized, the [Italic On] code is deleted, and the [Italic Off] code is also deleted. Deleting an "on" code automatically deletes its corresponding "off" code.
6. Working in the document window, move the insertion point just to the right of the word "**references**" in the last line of the second paragraph.
7. Working in the Reveal Codes space, position the highlight on the [Bold Off] code just to the right of "**references**".
8. Press the **Delete** key.

   The [Bold Off] code is deleted, the corresponding [Bold On] code is deleted, and the phrase "personal interview and review of references" is no longer bold, although it still is underlined.

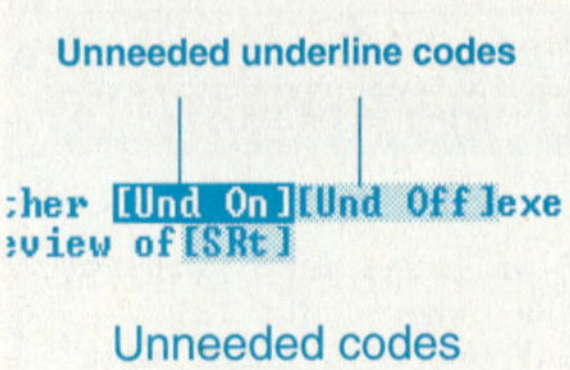

Sometimes, when you change or remove formatting using menu or keyboard-shortcut commands, codes that do not affect the document's appearance are left behind. For example, if you remove the underlining from a word by choosing the Normal attribute, sometimes you will find the codes [Und On][Und Off] just to the left of the word. When you see an "on" code followed by a corresponding "off" code with no text in between, the codes are not serving any purpose. It is good practice (although not absolutely necessary) to delete codes that do not serve a purpose. Extra codes can cause confusion, and in extreme cases can cause WordPerfect to respond very slowly.

To remove unneeded codes:

1. Open the Reveal Codes space, if necessary.
2. Working in the document window, move the insertion point to the left of the word "commission" in the last line of the first paragraph.

Notice the [Und On][Und Off] code combination to the left of "commission".

3. Position the Reveal Codes highlight on the [Und On] code.

4. Press the **Delete** key.

   The "on" and "off" codes are deleted, but there is no change to the document window.

Special Characters

When WordPerfect wraps text, it breaks a line between words or at a hyphen. Sometimes, you need to make sure that a group of words stay together on the same line. For example, the name "Ms. Smith-Jones" should always appear on the same line. You can control this by using a nonbreaking space, called a hard space, or a nonbreaking hyphen, called a dash character, between words that must stay together.

You can insert hard spaces and dash characters in one of two ways:

- Open the Insert Special Codes dialog box.

  Choose Line from the Layout menu, and then choose Special Codes from the Line cascading menu. Choose Hard Space or Dash Character from the dialog box, and then click the Insert button.

- Use the keyboard shortcuts.

  Press **Ctrl+Spacebar** to insert a hard space.

  Press **Ctrl+Hyphen** to insert a dash character.

Hard Space code

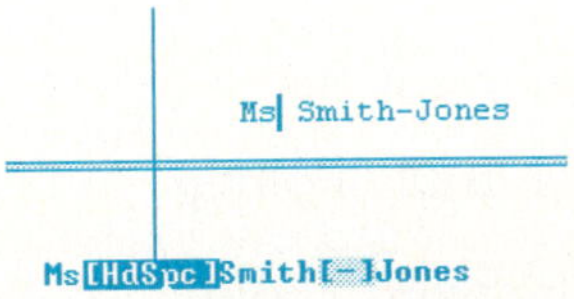

[HdSpc] code

The normal space character has the same appearance in the document window and in the Reveal Codes space. When you insert a hard space, a [HdSpc] code appears in the Reveal Codes space. In the document window, the [HdSpc] code looks exactly like a normal space character.

Keying a normal hyphen inserts a [-] code. A line break can occur at a [-], separating the two parts of a hyphenated word. When you insert a dash character instead, a character, not a code, is inserted. In other words, there are no brackets around the "-" dash character in the Reveal Codes space.

Practice inserting dash characters:

1. Turn on the Reveal Codes space, if necessary.

2. Move the insertion point to the end of the first paragraph.

3. Press the **Spacebar**, and key **For helpful information, call 404/553**

4. Press **Ctrl+Hyphen** and then key **3347**.

   The entire phone number wraps to a new line.

5. Move the insertion point to the end of the fourth line in the first paragraph, after the word "well".

   "well-trained" is broken by a new line. The Reveal Codes space shows a [-] code to the right of "well".

6. Press the **Delete** key.

   The hyphen is deleted, and the insertion point is between "well" and "trained".

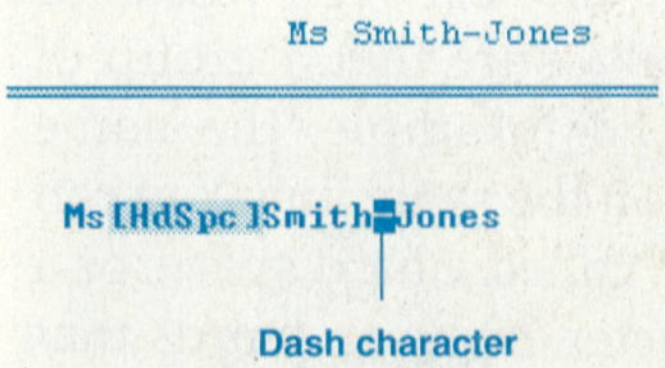

A dash character

7. Press **Ctrl+Hyphen**.

   Now "well-trained" is hyphenated again, but both words are together on the new line.

Practice inserting hard spaces:

1. Working in the document window, position the insertion point at the end of the second line, just to the right of "Five".

   The [SRt] code is highlighted in the Reveal Codes space.

2. Press the **Delete** key.

   The [SRt] code is now to the right of the word "The". "Five" and "Points" are one word, with the insertion point in between.

3. Press **Ctrl+Spacebar**.

   A [HdSpc] code is inserted between "Five" and "Points."

4. Move the insertion point to the right of the word "Points".

5. Press the **Delete** key to delete the space between "Points" and "Realty."

6. Choose Line from the Layout menu, and then Choose Special Codes from the Line cascading menu.

   The Insert Special Codes dialog box opens.

7. Choose Hard Space from the Other Codes section of the dialog box and then choose Insert.

   A [HdSpc] code is inserted.

8. Save the document as *[your three-letter identifier]*6-0.wpw.

9. Close the document.
10. Exit WordPerfect (unless you will be doing the following exercises immediately).

Table 6-5: Keyboard Shortcuts

Shortcut	Description
Alt+F3	Reveal Codes On/Off
Ctrl+Spacebar	Hard space (Non-breaking space)
Ctrl+Hyphen	Dash character (Non-breaking hyphen)

Key Terms

Character attribute
Character format
Paired codes

Exercises

Exercise 6.1

1. Start WordPerfect, if necessary.
2. Open the file 6-1.wpw.
3. Create a new paragraph at the end of the document:
   A. Move to the end of the document, and press **Enter** twice to begin a new paragraph.
   B. Choose Italic from the Font menu, and then key **For more information**.
   C. Choose Italic from the Font menu to turn off italic.
   D. Press the **Spacebar,** key **contact**, and press the **Spacebar** again.
   E. Press **Ctrl+B**, key **Susan Ellis**, and then press **Ctrl+B** again.
   F. Press the **Spacebar**, and then key **in Bud Porter's office at 555-4598**.
4. Merge the first and second paragraphs.
5. Remove the underlining at the beginning of the first paragraph:
   A. Select "Basketball season".
   B. Press **Ctrl+U**.

6. Remove the bold attribute from "**eligible**" using Reveal Codes:
   A. Press **Alt+F3** to view the Reveal Codes space.
   B. Working in the document window, position the insertion point to the left of "**eligible**" in the third line of the first paragraph.
   C. Working in the Reveal Codes space, click the [Bold On] code to the left of "**eligible**" to highlight it, and then press the **Delete** key.
7. Insert two blank lines at the beginning of the document.
8. On the first line, key the title **Atlanta Hawks Ticket Discounts**.
9. Convert the title to uppercase and make it bold:
   A. Select the title.
   B. Choose Convert Case from the Edit menu, and then choose Uppercase from the Convert Case cascading menu.
   C. Press **Ctrl+B**.
   D. Deselect the text.
10. Save the document as *[your three-letter identifier]*6-1.wpw.
11. Close the document
12. Exit WordPerfect (unless you will be doing the following exercises immediately).

Exercise 6.2

1. Start WordPerfect, if necessary.
2. Open the file 6-2.wpw.
3. Apply the bold and italic attributes to the title, and convert it to uppercase:
   A. Select the title "Atlanta's Gardens".
   B. Press **Ctrl+B** and then press **Ctrl+I**.
   C. Choose Convert Case from the Edit menu, and then choose Uppercase from the Convert Case cascading menu.
4. Remove all character formatting from the second sentence:
   A. Select "**Walking, driving, and biking tours**".
   B. Press **Ctrl+N**.
   C. Remove extra codes.

5. Select "LARGE ELEGANT HOMES" near the end of the first paragraph, and convert it to lowercase.
6. Open the Reveal Codes space by dragging the Reveal Codes Bar:
    A. Position the mouse pointer on the Reveal Codes Bar below the Down scroll arrow.
    B. Adjust the pointer position until you see the double-headed arrow.
    C. Drag the double-headed arrow up approximately 1½ inches.
7. Remove the bold and underline attributes from "**greenery and blossoms**" in the second paragraph by deleting the codes:
    A. Working in the document window, move the insertion point to the left of "**greenery**".
    B. Working in the Reveal Codes space, click the "g" in greenery to highlight it, if necessary.
    C. Press the **Backspace** key twice to delete [Bold On] and [Und On].
8. Insert a hard space between "Piedmont" and "Park" at the end of the second line of the second paragraph:
    A. Move the insertion point to the right of "Piedmont", and press the **Delete** key.
    B. Press **Ctrl+Spacebar**.
9. Insert a hard space between "Fuqua" and "Conservatory" near the end of the second paragraph.
10. Move to the end of the document and press **Enter** twice.
11. Key **For more information on tours of Atlanta's Gardens, call 404/554**.
12. Press **Ctrl+Hyphen** to insert a dash character and then key **1700**.
13. Save the document as *[your three-letter identifier]*6-2.wpw.
14. Close the document.
15. Exit WordPerfect (unless you will be doing the following exercises immediately).

Exercise 6.3

1. Start WordPerfect, if necessary.
2. Open the file 6-3.wpw.

3. Move to the blank line between the first and second paragraphs, above the line that begins "We are always improving".
4. Press **Enter** to insert a blank line.
5. Turn on the bold and italic attributes, and key in uppercase **IMPROVING THE PROPERTY**.
6. Split the third paragraph at the end of the sentence that begins "Providing for adequate insurance" so that it is a paragraph heading. Delete the period and the extra blank spaces.
7. Format the paragraph heading so that it matches the second paragraph heading; make it bold, italic, and uppercase.
8. Format the first sentence of each remaining paragraph as a paragraph heading in the same manner.
9. Apply uppercase, bold, and italic to the title at the top of the document.
10. The first paragraph contains many extra codes that serve no purpose. Open the Reveal Codes space and delete these codes.
11. Save the document as *[your three-letter identifier]*6-3.wpw.
12. Close the document.
13. Exit WordPerfect (unless you will be doing the following exercises immediately).

Exercise 6.4

1. Start WordPerfect, if necessary.
2. Key the document found at the end of this exercise, applying the bold, underline, and italic attributes as shown in the document. As you are keying the document, insert hard spaces between the words making up the following company names:

   Five Points Realty
   Actron Multimedia, Inc.
   Par Excellence

3. Remove the italics formatting from "*five-year contract*" in the last sentence of the first paragraph, and make it bold instead.
4. Insert a dash character between the words "**five**" and "**year**".

5. In the second paragraph, remove the underlining from "Par Excellence" and "Renee and David".
6. Remove all the bold formatting from the last paragraph.
7. Convert the heading at the top of the document that begins "Press release" to uppercase and make it bold.
8. Convert the subheading that begins "Five Points Realty Makes" to uppercase, and make it bold and italic.
9. View the codes for the entire document, deleting any extra codes, if necessary.
10. Save the document as *[your three-letter identifier]*6-4.wpw.
11. Close the document.
12. Exit WordPerfect (unless you will be doing the following exercise immediately).

Document 6-4

Press release for immediate release

Five Points Realty Makes Actron Multimedia Feel Welcome

Five Points Realty, a well-known real estate agency based in downtown Atlanta, recently hosted a dinner for the newest member of the Atlanta-area business community, **Actron Multimedia, Inc**. The dinner was held at **Actron Multimedia's** new home, the G&H Building at Techwood and Luckie Streets. Actron signed a *five-year contract* with Five Points Realty for the lease of this property.

The dinner was attended by several of the most influential businesspeople in the Atlanta area, as well as many local politicians. Following a four-course dinner catered by **Par Excellence**, guests *danced the night away* to the jazz sounds of **Renee and David**.

Five Points Realty's main office is located at 233 Peachtree St. NE, Atlanta. They also have offices at 1472 Spring St., 108 W. Paces Ferry Rd., and Marietta Square, Marietta.

Exercise 6.5

1. Start WordPerfect, if necessary.
2. Open the file 6-5.wpw.
3. Convert the heading "Fall Announcement" to uppercase and make it bold.
4. In the first sentence, make the phrase "fall schedule of realty courses" bold.
5. Italicize the phrase "discount rates" on the fourth line of the first paragraph.
6. Remove all the bold and underline attributes in the second paragraph.
7. "abr" appears in the first sentence of the second, third, and fourth paragraphs. Convert each occurrence of "abr" to uppercase.
8. Underline "Minimum class enrollment is 20" at the end of the third paragraph.
9. In the fifth paragraph, convert "Make checks payable to" to lowercase, and correct capitalization, if necessary.
10. At the end of the fifth paragraph, make "Atlanta Board of Realtors" bold.
11. Move to the end of the document. Start a new paragraph, and turn on the italic attribute.
12. Key "Registration by" and press the **Spacebar**.
13. Turn on the bold attribute and key "FAX".
14. Turn off the bold attribute (italic should still be on) and press the **Spacebar.**
15. Key **is acceptable up to 48 hours prior to class.**
16. View the hidden codes for the entire document, and remove any extra codes, if necessary.
17. Save the document as *[your three-letter identifier]*6-5.wpw.
18. Close the document.
19. Exit WordPerfect.

Lesson 7

Speller/Thesaurus/Grammar

Objectives

- Understand proofing tools.
- Check spelling.
- Check grammar and writing style.
- Use the Thesaurus.
- Check the word count of a document.

This lesson focuses on the three important tools that WordPerfect provides to help proof documents: the Speller, the grammar checker (called Grammatik), and the Thesaurus. These proofing tools allow you to find and correct many common errors quickly.

What is the Speller?

The Speller is a valuable word-processing tool that should become a routine step in proofing documents. It can be used while working on or after completing a document. The Speller compares the spelling in a document with the spelling in WordPerfect's internal dictionary. If a word in the document does not match a word in the dictionary, WordPerfect brings it to your attention. Using the Speller dialog box, you can choose from among several actions to take for the word. For example, you can:

- Select from a list of words that may be suggested for the correct spelling, and instruct WordPerfect to make the change.
- Leave the word unchanged by instructing WordPerfect to skip it.
- Add the word to a supplementary dictionary that can be created for special words (including names and abbreviations) not contained in WordPerfect's dictionary.

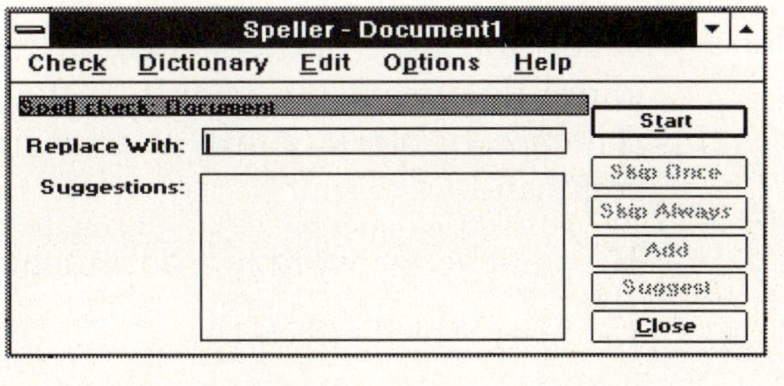

Figure 7-1
The Speller dialog box

What the Speller Can and Cannot Do

The Speller can find many mistakes and provide useful suggestions. However, it is important to understand what it can and cannot do.

Along with finding regular misspellings, the Speller can find:

- Repeated words, such as "the the" in a sentence
- Words with unusual capitalization, such as "THeir" or "vAcation"

The Speller cannot find:

- A word that is spelled correctly but used incorrectly

  For example, if you use the word "then" instead of "than" or "your" instead of "you're", the Speller will not catch it. The Speller is a valuable aid, but proofreading still is essential.

- Special words, such as proper names, technical terms, acronyms, or abbreviations, that are not in WordPerfect's dictionary

  This means that every one of these unfamiliar words will be questioned during the spell-checking process. To minimize this, you can add the words to a supplementary dictionary, which is discussed later in this lesson.

Using the Speller

The Speller can confirm the spelling of a single word, a group of words, or all the words in a document. There are three ways to issue the Speller command:

- Choose Speller from the Tools menu.
- Click the Speller button on the Button Bar.
- Press the keyboard shortcut, **Ctrl+F1**.

The Speller button

When you issue the Speller command, WordPerfect will check the entire document by default. If you want to check just a word, sentence, or block of text, select it first, and then issue the Speller command.

To spell-check a word in a document:

1. Start WordPerfect.
2. Open the file 7-0.wpw.
3. Double-click the misspelled word "trule" in the second line.
4. Choose Speller from the Tools menu (or click the Speller button on the Button Bar).

   The Speller dialog box opens.
5. Click the Start command button.

When you click the Start button, several things happen:

- The Start button becomes the Replace button.
- The Replace With text box shows the word "truce", WordPerfect's best guess.
- The Suggestions list box shows several words that might be correct.

6. Choose "truly", the third word in the Suggestions box.

   "Truly" appears in the Replace With text box.

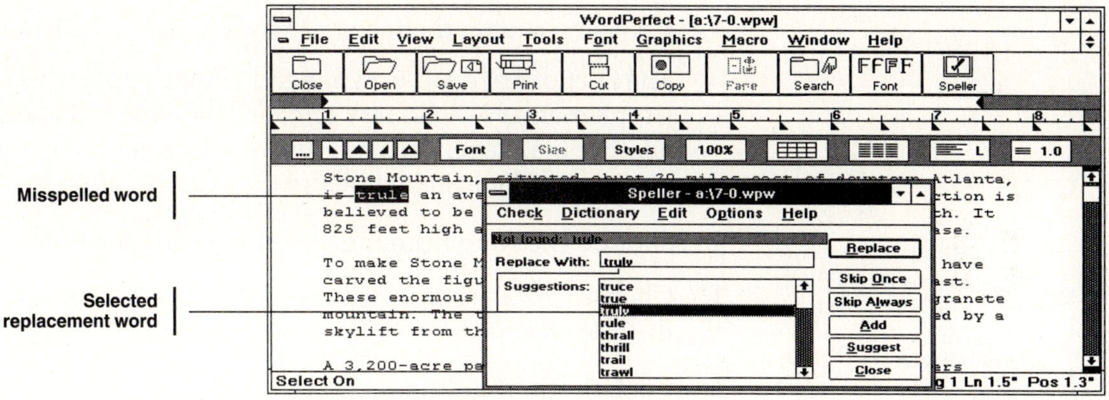

Figure 7-2
A suggested word chosen to replace a misspelled word

7. Click the Replace button. (Alternatively, you could have double-clicked "truly" in the previous step, eliminating the need for this step.)

   The misspelled word is corrected, and a question box appears asking if you are finished using the Speller.

8. Click the Yes button.

You also can check spelling from the insertion point to the end of the page or to the end of the document:

1. Move the insertion point to the beginning of the third paragraph, which begins "A 3,200-acre park".
2. Click the Speller button on the Button Bar.

   The Speller dialog box opens. The information area displays the message "Spell check: Document".

From the Speller dialog box, you can control the way the Speller works by:

- Defining what part of the document will be checked

  By default, WordPerfect checks the entire document. If text is selected before opening the Speller dialog box, only that text is checked. If you open the drop-down Check menu, you can choose to check from the insertion point to the end of the document or to the end of the page. You also can check the page the insertion point is on only.

- Choosing what kind of errors to check

  WordPerfect always checks for words that are not in its dictionary. By default, it also checks for duplicate words, such as "the the"; irregular capitalization; and words with numbers, such as "21st". The Options drop-down menu allows you to turn these off or back on again.

- Choosing a main dictionary or supplementary dictionary

  The Dictionary drop-down menu allows you to choose a supplementary dictionary or change the main dictionary to another language, such as French or German. (Foreign dictionaries must be installed before they can be chosen).

To continue checking from the insertion-point position:

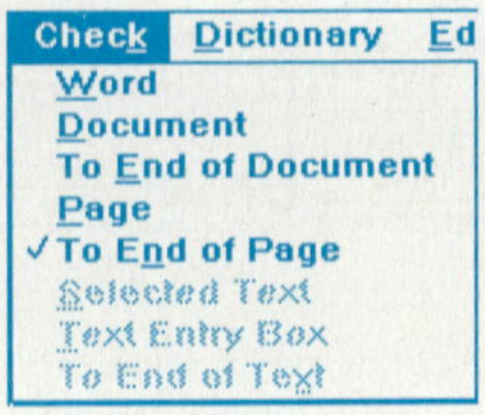

Speller Check menu

1. Choose Check from the Speller menu bar, and then choose To the End of Page.

2. Click the Start button.

   The misspelled word "surounding" is highlighted in the document. The information area displays the message "Not found: surounding". The correct spelling is displayed in the Replace With text box.

3. Click the Replace button.

   The Duplicate Words Found dialog box appears. The Speller has found "a a".

4. Click Delete 2nd.

   The Speller highlights "MAgnolia", and the Irregular Capitalization Found box appears.

5. Click Replace to correct the capitalization.

6. Continue clicking Replace each time an error is found, until "MARTA" is highlighted.

   "MARTA" is an acronym for Metropolitan Atlanta Rapid Transit Authority.

7. Click the Skip Always button to accept "MARTA" as a valid word.

   If you click Skip Always, all other occurrences of "MARTA" will be accepted as correct for the rest of the spell-check session (unless "MARTA" is keyed incorrectly).

8. Click Replace to correct the capitalization of "ATlanta".
9. Click Yes to close the Speller.

There are two other ways to correct a misspelled word. One is to key the corrections in the Replace With text box, and the other is to key the corrections directly in the document window. Practice both methods while checking the first paragraph:

1. Quadruple-click anywhere in the first paragraph to select it.
2. Press the keyboard shortcut **Ctrl+F1** to open the Speller dialog box.
3. Click Start.

   The word "abuot" is highlighted. The Speller incorrectly suggests replacing it with "abbot".
4. Position the insertion point in the Replace With text box between the two "b" characters in "abbot", and press the **Delete** key twice.
5. Key **ou**.

   Notice that the Suggestions box shows only one word now.

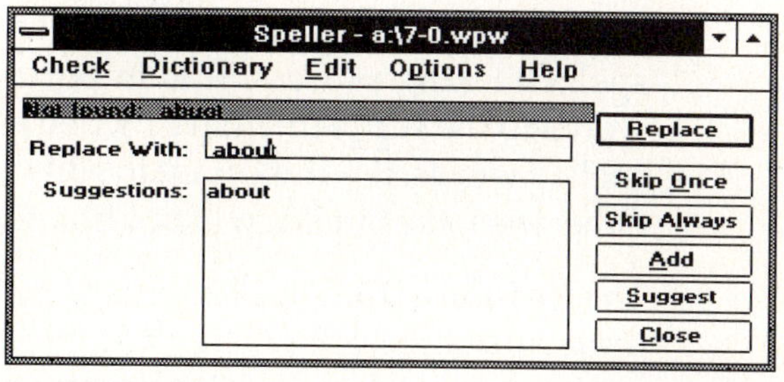

Figure 7-3
Keying corrections in the Replace With text box

6. Click Replace.

   Now "milesin" is highlighted.
7. Click in the document window.

   Notice the changes in the appearance of the dialog box and the document window.
8. Position the insertion point between the "s" and "i".
9. Press the **Spacebar**.
10. Click Resume in the Speller dialog box to continue checking the document.

    The Speller question box appears.

11. Click Yes to close the Speller.

If you need to check the entire document, the insertion-point position is not important. Just make sure no text is selected when you open the Speller dialog box.

1. Press **Ctrl+F1** (or click the Speller button on the Button Bar).
2. Click Start.
3. Click the appropriate command button each time the Speller finds an error. When the Speller highlights the words "skylift" and "MARTA", click Skip Once.
4. When the Speller question box appears, click Yes to close the Speller.
5. Save the document as *[your three-letter identifier]*7-0.wpw.

Using the Supplementary Dictionary

WordPerfect uses a standard dictionary that may not contain the special words, names, or abbreviations you commonly use. By adding these words to a supplementary dictionary, WordPerfect will not question them during spell-checks.

WordPerfect has set up a supplementary dictionary for you called wp{wp}us.sup. You can add words to this dictionary throughout the spell-checking process. It is important to be careful when adding words to the supplementary dictionary. If you accidentally add misspelled words, it is important to edit your dictionary to remove them. Otherwise, the Speller will not find those misspellings in the future.

The location of the supplementary dictionary file should be set to the drive and directory where your practice files are stored. If this has not been done already, follow your instructor's directions to do this.

Practice adding words to the supplementary dictionary:

1. Click Speller on the Button Bar to open the Speller dialog box.
2. Click Start.

   The word "skylift" is highlighted.
3. Click Add.

   "Skylift" is added to the supplementary dictionary and "MARTA" is highlighted.
4. Click Add again to add "MARTA" to the supplementary dictionary.

   "MARTA" is added to the supplementary dictionary.
5. Click Yes to close the Speller.
6. Run the Speller again.

No spelling errors are found, because "skylift" and "MARTA" are in the supplementary dictionary.

7. Click Yes to close the Speller.

Sometimes, words get into the supplementary dictionary accidentally. You can edit the dictionary just as you edit a document, deleting words that should not be there and adding words, such as acronyms and proper names, that you use regularly.

To edit the supplementary dictionary:

1. Choose Open from the File menu.
2. Choose the file wp{wp}us.sup and click Open. This file will be near the bottom of the Files list box.

   The file opens. It contains the words "skylift" and "marta". It may contain other words, if you accidentally clicked the Add button earlier in this lesson.

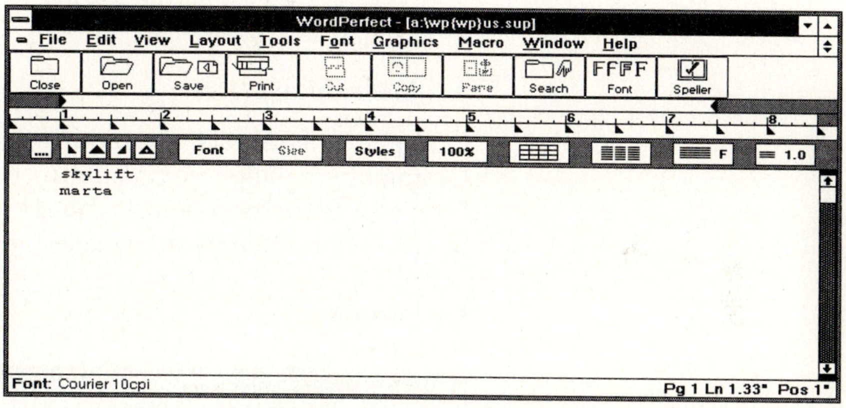

Figure 7-4
Supplementary dictionary document containing two words

3. Delete all the words in the document.
4. Choose Save (not Save As) from the File menu to update the file (or click Save on the Button Bar).

   The supplementary dictionary has no words in it now.

5. Choose Close from the File menu (or click Close on the Button Bar).

   The supplementary dictionary file closes and document 7-0.wpw reappears.

When you spell-check the document again, the Speller will stop on "skylift" and "MARTA", because they are no longer in the supplementary dictionary.

Speller Edit Menu

The Speller Edit menu allows you to manipulate the text in the Replace With text box. For example, if you make a mistake when keying a word in the Replace With text box, you can undo your last editing change by choosing the Undo command in the Edit menu.

The Edit menu also contains options for cutting, copying, and pasting between the Replace With text box and the Clipboard. The Select All option selects all the text currently in the Replace With text box. These options are helpful when you correct words with similar constructions, but that are not in the dictionaries.

What is Grammatik?

Grammatik is a valuable tool that can improve the quality of a document. Grammatik 5 is a separate software application provided as part of the WordPerfect package. It checks sentences for:

- Grammatical errors
- Stylistic errors
- Mechanical errors

Grammatik suggests corrections, just like the Speller. From the Grammatik 5 dialog box, you can choose the correction from a list box and change the sentence. You also can ignore the suggestion, find out more about the error, or make changes directly in the document.

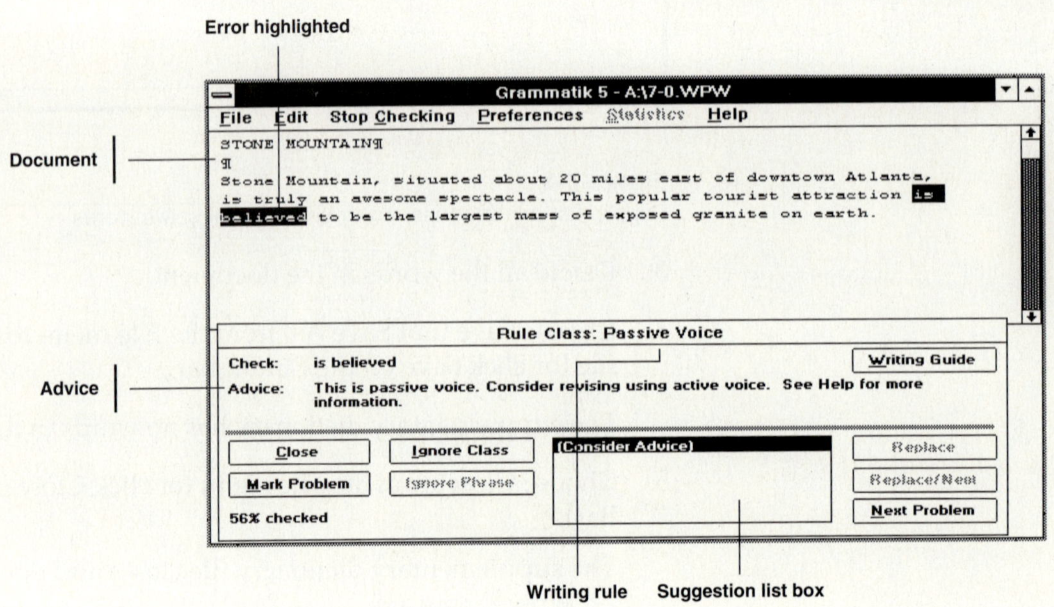

Figure 7-5
The Grammatik 5 window with error found

Grammatik has its own spell-checker. You can check spelling either with the WordPerfect Speller or with Grammatik.

Like the WordPerfect Speller, Grammatik has a menu bar with various options to customize the way it works. From the Preferences menu, you can choose a particular writing style (Formality Level) against which your document is checked.

Using Grammatik

You can use Grammatik to check a single word, a selected block of text, or the entire document. To check the entire document, choose Grammatik from the Tools menu.

To start Grammatik:

1. Choose Grammatik from the Tools menu (the insertion-point position is not important).

   The Grammatik application window opens on top of the WordPerfect window. The first sentence in the first paragraph is highlighted, and Grammatik advises that the sentence may be an incomplete sentence.

2. Choose Writing Style from the Preferences menu.

   The Writing Style dialog box allows you to choose a style against which your writing is checked. Informal styles allow more flexibility and have fewer rules applied to them. Formal styles strictly follow all grammatical rules.

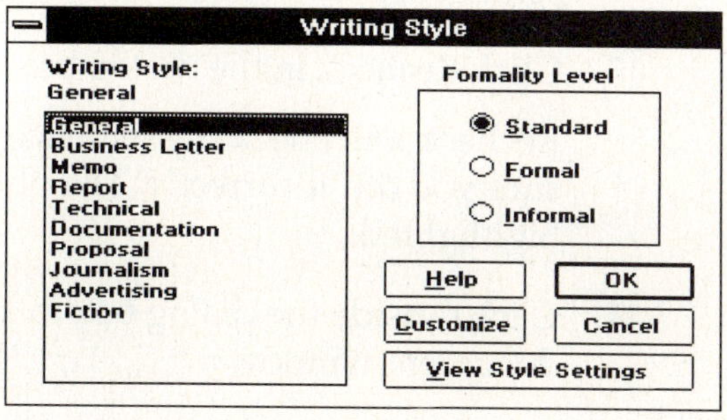

Figure 7-6
The Writing Style dialog box

3. Choose Technical from the Writing Style list box.

   The Formality Level changes to Formal.

4. Choose General to set the Formality Level to Standard and click OK.

   The Writing Style dialog box closes.

5. Click Next Problem to ignore Grammatik's advice, because the sentence is complete.

   The words "is believed" in the first paragraph are highlighted, and Grammatik advises that the sentence is constructed in the passive voice.

6. Click the Writing Guide command button.

   The Writing Guide Topics dialog box opens. Passive Voice is highlighted in the list box.

7. Click Help.

   The Grammatik Help window opens with an explanation of passive voice.

8. Read about passive voice, and then choose Exit from the File menu to close the Help window.

9. Click Ignore Class to tell Grammatik to stop checking for passive-voice construction.

   An incomplete sentence is highlighted.

10. Click outside the dialog box to activate the Grammatik document window.

11. Position the insertion point at the beginning of the highlighted text and deselect it. Position the insertion point between "It" and "825".

12. Key **is**, and press the **Spacebar**, if necessary. The corrected sentence should read "It is 825 feet".

13. Click Recheck in the dialog box.

    Recheck will check the sentence you just changed to make sure you did it correctly. The phrase "granite mountain" is highlighted.

14. Click outside the dialog box to activate the Grammatik document window.

15. Position the insertion point before "granite" and key **the**.

16. Click Recheck in the dialog box.

    "Skylift" is highlighted as a spelling error.

17. Click Next Problem to ignore the "skylift" error and move on.

    Grammatik highlights the phrase "a wide variety of" and suggests that you simplify this phrase. The list box shows possible substitutions for the phrase. "Many" is selected.

18. Click Replace/Next to replace the phrase with "many" and move to the next problem.

    Grammatik detects a one-sentence paragraph, which usually should be avoided.

19. Click Next Problem.

    Grammatik advises that the grammar-check is complete.

20. Click Save (do not click Save As).

    A prompt asks you if you want to save a custom writing style. Because you turned off passive-voice checking, Grammatik is giving you the opportunity to make that change permanent.

21. Click No and then click Exit.

    The grammar-checked document appears in the WordPerfect window.

What is the Thesaurus?

The Thesaurus is a tool that can add interest and variety to your writing. Use the Thesaurus to look up a synonym (a word with a similar meaning) for a selected word. The Thesaurus will offer several different meanings of the word, such as the word's noun and verb meanings, as well as a list of synonyms from which to choose. Sometimes, the Thesaurus also displays antonyms (words with the opposite meaning). You then can replace the selected word with one of the suggested words. The list of alternative words is arranged according to headwords, references, and subgroups.

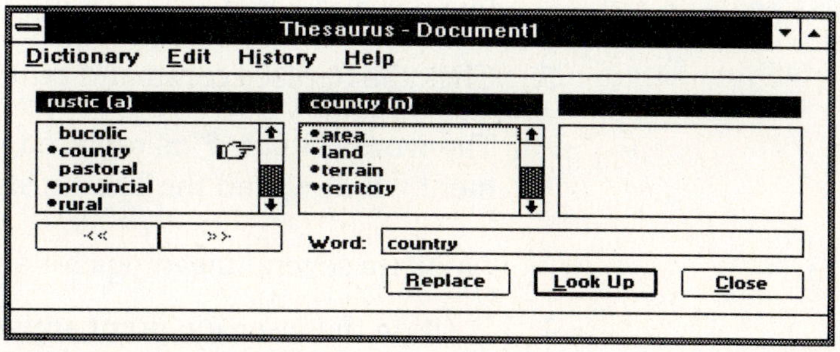

Figure 7-7
Thesaurus dialog box

Headword
A word that can be looked up in the Thesaurus.

A *headword* is a word that can be looked up in the Thesaurus. The synonyms and antonyms that are found for a particular headword are called *references*. The list of references is divided into groups of nouns, verbs, adjectives, and antonyms. These are further divided

References
The synonyms and antonyms that are found for a particular headword in the Thesaurus.

into subgroups that correspond to different meanings of the headword. A reference word that has a bullet in front of it is also a headword. You can look up headwords to get more word ideas.

Using the Thesaurus

The Thesaurus applies to individual words in a document. To look up a word, position the insertion point anywhere on the word, and open the Thesaurus dialog box. The Thesaurus dialog box can be opened in two ways:

- Choose Thesaurus from the Tools menu.
- Press the keyboard shortcut **Alt+F1**.

To replace a word in the on-screen document:

1. Position the insertion point anywhere on the word "situated" in the first sentence.
2. Choose Thesaurus from the Tools menu.

   The Thesaurus dialog box opens. The word "situated" is displayed in the Word text box, and a list of words is displayed in the first list box area. The headword "situate" is displayed above the list box.
3. Choose "locate" from the list box.

   The word "locate" is displayed in the Word text box. "Locate" is not the correct form of the word needed to replace "situated". You can edit the text in the Word text box.
4. Position the insertion point at the end of "locate" in the Word text box and key **d**.
5. Click the Replace command button.

   The word "situated" is replaced with "located" in the document window, and the Thesaurus dialog box closes.

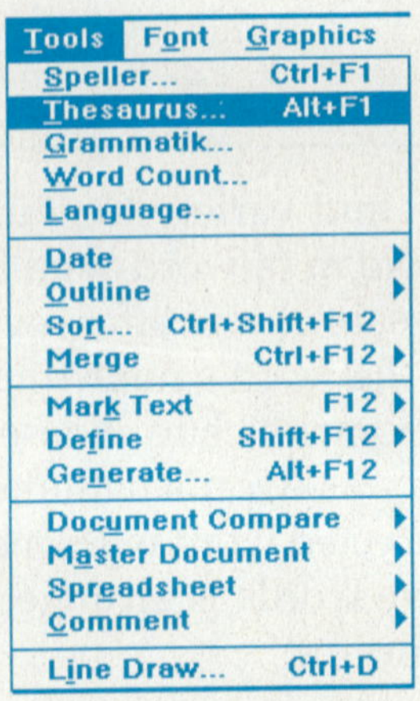

The Tools menu

Now look up several meanings for a word:

1. Position the insertion point anywhere on the word "unforgettable" in the first line of the second paragraph.
2. Press **Alt+F1**, the keyboard shortcut for Thesaurus.
3. Double-click "memorable" in the list box.

   The second list box displays synonyms and antonyms for "memorable".

4. Double-click "impressive" in the second list box.

   The Thesaurus displays a third list of words.

5. Click "awe-inspiring" once in the third list box.

   The word "awe-inspiring" appears in the Word text box.

6. Click the Replace command button.

   The Thesaurus replaces "unforgettable" with "awe-inspiring" in the on-screen document.

Using Word Count

If you ever have an assignment to write a memo or report of a specified number of words, you can let WordPerfect do the counting for you. To count the words in the on-screen document:

1. Choose Word Count from the Tools menu.

   The Word Count dialog box appears displaying the number of words in the document.

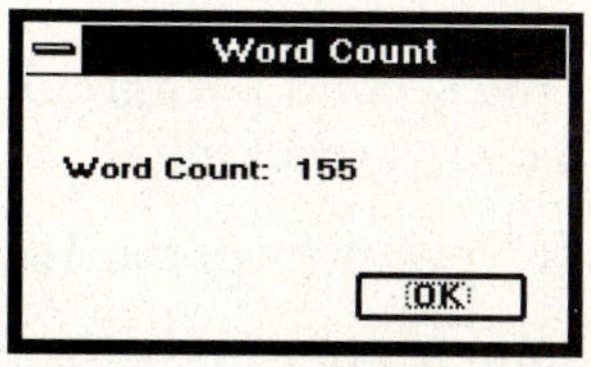

Figure 7-8
Word Count dialog box

2. Read the word count and click OK.

You also can count the words in a selected text block:

1. Quadruple-click the third paragraph.
2. Choose Word Count from the Tools menu.
3. Read the word count and click OK.
4. Save the document.
5. Print the document.
6. Close the document.
7. Exit WordPerfect (unless you will be doing the following exercises immediately).

Table 7-1: Keyboard Shortcuts for the Speller and Thesaurus

Keyboard Shortcut	Action
Ctrl+F1	Speller
Alt+F1	Thesaurus

Key Terms

Headword
References

Exercises

Exercise 7.1

1. Start WordPerfect, if necessary.
2. Open the file 7-1.wpw.
3. Spell-check the second paragraph:
   A. Select the second paragraph, which begins "In the 1920s", by quadruple-clicking it.
   B. Choose Speller from the Tools menu and click Start.
   C. When the Speller finds the first misspelling, choose Skip Once to accept "1920s".
   D. At the next misspelling, choose "tracks", the second word in the Suggestions list box, to correct "traks". Then click Replace.
   E. Click Delete 2nd to change "at at" to "at".
   F. Replace "storry" with "story", the fourth word in the Suggestions list.
   G. When the Speller question box appears, click Yes to close the Speller.
4. Spell-check a word:
   A. In the first line of the third paragraph, double-click the word "merchents".
   B. Press **Ctrl+F1** and click Start.
   C. Click Replace to correct the spelling, and then click Yes to close the Speller.

5. Spell-check to the end of the document:

   A. Position the insertion point at the beginning of the second sentence in the third paragraph, if necessary (just after the word you checked in the previous step).

   B. Click Speller on the Button Bar.

   C. Choose To End of Document from the Check menu in the Speller dialog box.

   D. Click Start.

   E. Skip "1960s", and correct "bulidings" and "the the", as you did with previous errors in the steps above.

   F. When the Speller finds "nitelife", key **nightl** to change the text in the Replace With text box.

   G. Double-click "nightlife" in the Suggestions list box.

   H. Click Replace to correct the capitalization of "ATlanta".

   I. Click Yes to close the Speller.

6. Spell-check the entire document:

   A. Click Speller on the Button Bar.

   B. Prevent the Speller from checking words with numbers by choosing the Words With Numbers command in the Options drop-down menu.

   C. Click Start.

   D. Check the document using the steps outlined above, and then close the Speller.

      The Speller finds "aTlanta".

7. Correct a word that the Speller missed:

   A. Read the last paragraph in the document.

      The word "from" is correctly spelled, but it is the wrong word.

   B. Select "from" in the last paragraph.

   C. Key **form**, and then press the **Spacebar**, if necessary.

8. Save the document as *[your three-letter identifier]*7-1.wpw.

9. Print the document.

10. Close the document.

11. Exit WordPerfect (unless you will be doing the following exercises immediately).

Exercise 7.2

1. Start WordPerfect, if necessary.
2. Open the file 7-2.wpw.
3. Spell-check the document:
   A. Open the Speller dialog box and click Start.
   B. Replace "succeded" with "seceded", the third word in the Suggestions box.
   C. Change "ofthe" to "of the" by moving the insertion point to the incorrect word in the document window and adding the space where needed.
   D. Click Resume in the Speller dialog box to continue checking.
   E. Key **Rebuild** in the Replace With dialog box, and then double-click the second word in the suggestions box, "Rebuilding", to correct "Rebuildining".
   F. Click Add to add "Hartsfield" to the supplementary dictionary.
   G. Click Yes to close the Speller.
4. Spell-check the document again. This time, no errors are found.
5. Edit the supplementary dictionary:
   A. Open the file wp{wp}us.sup at the bottom of the Files list box.
   B. Add the word "skylift" on a separate line.
   C. Save and close the file.
6. Use the Thesaurus to find replacements for "center" and "confluence":
   A. Select "center" in the phrase "and transportation center" near the end of the first paragraph.
   B. Press **Alt+F1** to open the Thesaurus dialog box.
   C. Choose "hub" from the references in the list box.
   D. Click Replace.
   E. Replace "confluence" in the third line of the last paragraph with "crossroads". (Double-click "junction" in the first list box, and then choose "crossroads" from the second list.)
7. Save the document as *[your three-letter identifier]*7-2.wpw.

8. Grammar-check the document:

   A. Choose Grammatik from the Tools menu.

   B. Choose "influence" from the list box, and then click Replace/Next to replace the overused word "impact" and move to the next problem.

   C. Click Next Problem to skip over the passive-voice warning.

   D. Click Replace/Next to replace "Atlanta become" with "Atlanta becomes" and move to the next problem.

   E. Click Replace/Next to simplify "once again".

   F. Click Ignore Class to ignore "Hartsfield" and stop spell-checking.

   G. Move the insertion point to the document window, change "second busiest" to "second-busiest", and then click Recheck to recheck the sentence and move to the next problem.

   H. Click Replace/Next to change "Atlanta continue" to "Atlanta continues" and move to the next problem.

   I. When the Grammatik 5 dialog box opens, click Save.

   J. Click No when prompted to save a custom writing style.

   K. Click Exit to close Grammatik and return to the WordPerfect document window.

9. Count the words in the document:

   A. Choose Word Count from the Tools menu.

   B. Read the Word Count dialog box and click OK.

10. Rekey "influence" in the title so it is uppercase.

11. Choose Save to update the disk file. (Do not choose Save As, because you already saved the file as *[your three-letter identifier]*7-2.wpw).

12. Print the document.

13. Close the document.

14. Exit WordPerfect (unless you will be doing the following exercises immediately).

Exercise 7.3

1. Start WordPerfect, if necessary.

2. Open the file 7-3.wpw.

3. Spell-check the document. Add "chitlins", "Buckhead", "Theatre", "Piedmont", "Fulton", and "Omni" to the supplementary dictionary when the Speller finds them. Skip "Ritz-Carlton".

4. In the second paragraph, use the Thesaurus to replace "wonderful" with "splendid", "appreciate" with "prize", and "liberal" with "generous".

5. Remove "omni" from the supplementary dictionary.

6. Save the supplementary dictionary and close it.

7. Count the words in the document.

8. Save the document as *[your three-letter identifier]*7-3.wpw.

9. Print the document.

10. Close the document.

11. Exit WordPerfect (unless you will be doing the following exercises immediately).

Exercise 7.4

1. Start WordPerfect, if necessary.

2. Open the file 7-4.wpw.

3. At the end of the document, key in the paragraphs that appear in Figure 7-9, which appears at the end of this exercise. Include the corrections.

4. Spell-check the document. Click Skip Always when the Speller finds "Chattahoochee". Click Skip Once when the Speller finds "1960s". Add "CNN" and "Ebenezer" to the supplementary dictionary.

5. Use the Thesaurus to change "hired" to "rented" in the second paragraph. Be sure to add the "ed" to "rent".

6. In the paragraph that begins "Visit Auburn Avenue", replace "community" with "neighborhood" using the Thesaurus.

7. Count the words in the document.

8. Save the document as *[your three-letter identifier]*7-4.wpw.

9. Print the document.

10. Close the document.

11. Exit WordPerfect (unless you will be doing the following exercise immediately).

Figure 7-9

```
Visit Auburn Avenue, the community in which 1960s civil rights leader
Martin Luther King, Jr., as born and buried. An eternal flame marks his
tomb next door tothe Ebenezer Baptist Church, where three generztions of
his family preached. The King Center has a collection of artifacts, a
lirbary, and comunity educational programs that honor Martin Luther King,
Jr.

Explore the neighborhood near underground atlanta. There, the new Georgia
Rairload offers trips to Stone Mountain and guided tours.
```

Exercise 7.5

1. Start WordPerfect, if necessary.
2. Open the file 7-5.wpw.
3. Spell-check the document, adding "Fuqua" to the supplementary dictionary (there are no misspellings).
4. Use the Thesaurus to change "abundance" to "profusion" in the second paragraph.
5. In the phrase "The Botanical Garden contains five acres" in the second paragraph, use the Thesaurus to replace "contains" with "includes".
6. Save the document as *[your three-letter identifier]*7-5.wpw.
7. Grammar-check the document.
8. When "plantings" is highlighted as a spelling error, turn off spell-checking.
9. Replace "are" with "is" for the next two problems.
10. Ignore the passive-voice problem.
11. When the Grammatik 5 question box opens, click Save.
12. Click No when prompted to save a custom writing style.
13. Click Exit to close Grammatik and return to the WordPerfect document window.
14. Count the words in the document.

15. Open the supplementary dictionary file, and check the list of words.

16. Add or delete words as necessary, so only the following words are in the dictionary:

    buckhead

    chitlins

    cnn

    ebenezer

    fulton

    fuqua

    hartsfield

    marietta

    piedmont

    theatre

17. Save and close the dictionary document.

18. Save the document.

19. Print the document.

20. Close the document (there is no need to save it again).

21. Exit WordPerfect.

Module 2

Basic Formatting

Lessons

Lesson 8

Margins and Line Formatting

Objectives

- View default margin settings.
- Change margins.
- Center, align, and justify text.
- Adjust line spacing.
- Use hyphenation options.
- Explain Auto Code Placement options.
- Insert the date in a document.
- Create a Document Summary.

Margin
The white space between the text and the edge of the printed page.

In WordPerfect, there are many ways to make a document more professional looking and more readable. One way is to vary the placement of text on a page by changing margins. A *margin* is the white space between the text and the edge of the printed page.

Default Settings for Margins

WordPerfect's default setting for margins is 1 inch on all four sides: top, bottom, left, and right. Margins settings are independent of the size of the paper you use.

With 1-inch margins all around, an 8½ x 11 inch page would have a text area of 6½ x 9 inches. If you use stationery that is 7¼ inches wide, the line length would be 5.25 inches using the default margin settings (7.25 minus 1 inch on each side).

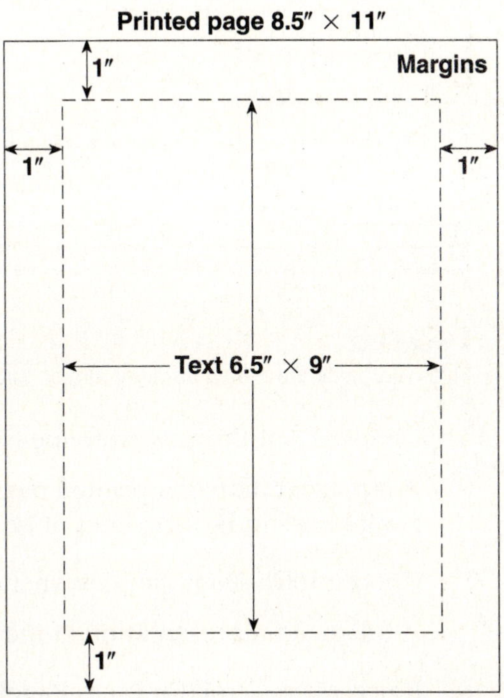

Figure 8-1
Margins are measured from the edge of the paper.

Margin marker
A ruler icon that marks and sets the boundary between the text and the margin.

Margin markers on the ruler indicate the position of the left and right margin in inches. Moving a margin marker repositions that margin at the insertion point.

To see the default margin settings:

1. Start WordPerfect.

2. Open the file 8-0a.wpw.

3. Choose Ruler and Reveal Codes from the View menu.

   The Ruler appears above the document. Tab settings are marked below the ruler. Above the Ruler, margin markers show the left margin at 1 inch and the right margin at 7.5 inches. Each margin is one inch from the edge of the page.

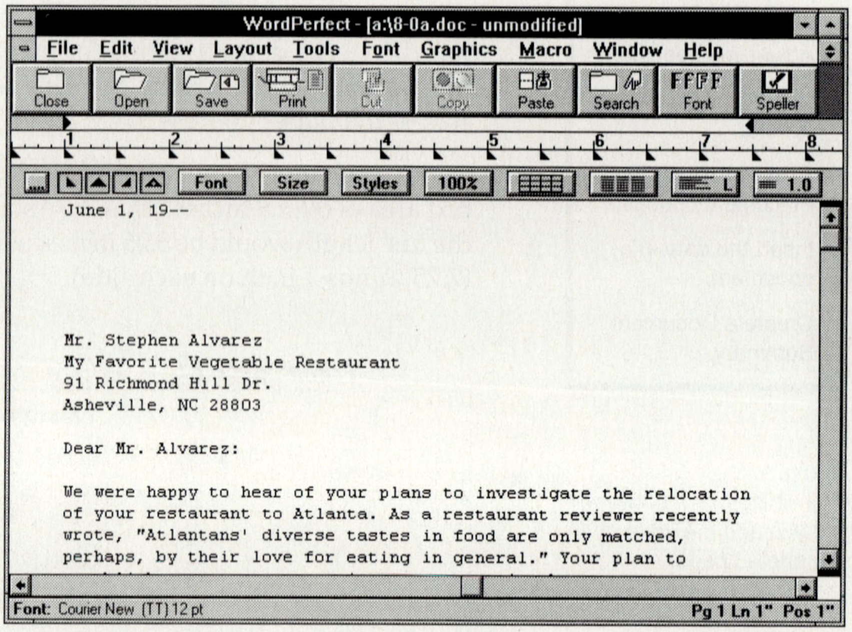

Figure 8-2
This letter uses the 1-inch default margins that are shown on the Ruler.

4. Choose Print Preview from the File menu.

   A representation of a printed page appears, with solid horizontal lines indicating lines of type.

5. Choose 100% from the View menu.

   A full-sized representation of the text appears.

6. If necessary, scroll (or press **PageUp** and **PageDown**) to see the entire page.

   Notice that the margins are 1 inch on each side.

7. Choose Close from the File menu to close the Print Preview window and return to the document.

Changing Margins

Note: If a business letter has more than one page, the continuation pages should have a top margin of one inch.

To change margins, insert a code in the text at the point where the change should take place. You also may select a block of text and apply a new margin setting. To change any of the four margin settings, you can use the Margins dialog box. To change a left or right margin, you also may use the margin markers on the Ruler.

Margin changes help conform to standard formats, like modified-block style for a business letter.

The Margins Dialog Box

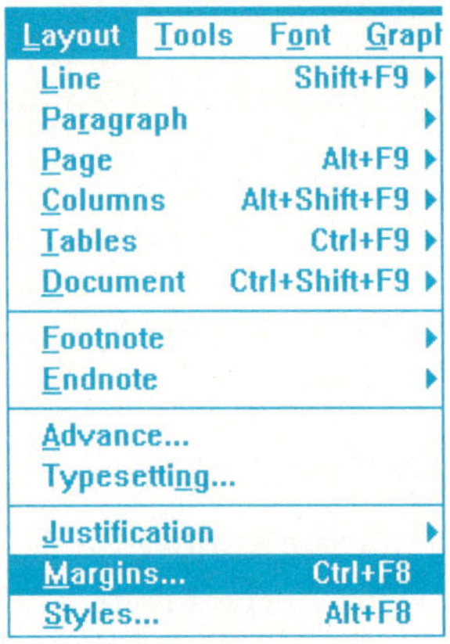

The Layout menu

You can define any margin code by using the Margins option on the Layout menu.

To practice changing margins:

1. Position the insertion point within the complimentary closing, "Sincerely yours".

2. Choose Margins from the Layout menu.

   The Margins dialog box appears with the default settings shown. The left margin value of 1 inch is highlighted.

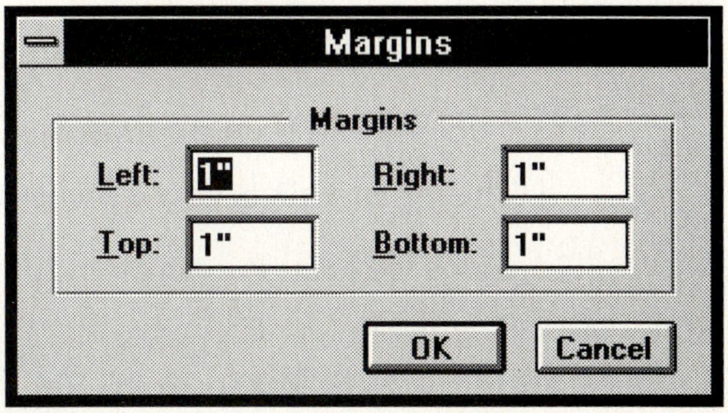

Figure 8-3
The Margins dialog box (with 1-inch default settings)

3. Key **4.25** to change the left margin to 4.25 inches, the center of the 8½-inch page.

4. Click OK.

   A [L/R Mar:4.25",1"] code begins the paragraph "Sincerely yours". WordPerfect normally places a side margin code at the beginning of the paragraph containing the insertion point.

(This will be explained further in the section "Auto Code Placement" later in this lesson.)

The text following the margin change aligns with the 4.25-inch measure.With the insertion point in the complimentary-closing text, the left margin marker on the Ruler is at the 4.25-inch measure. Before this code, however, the text still aligns on the left margin.

5. Position the insertion point in the paragraph above the complimentary closing.

   The left margin marker moves back to the 1-inch margin.

6. Position the insertion point within the reference initials "dah".

7. Press **Ctrl+F8**.

   The Margins dialog box appears.

8. Change the left margin to 1 inch.

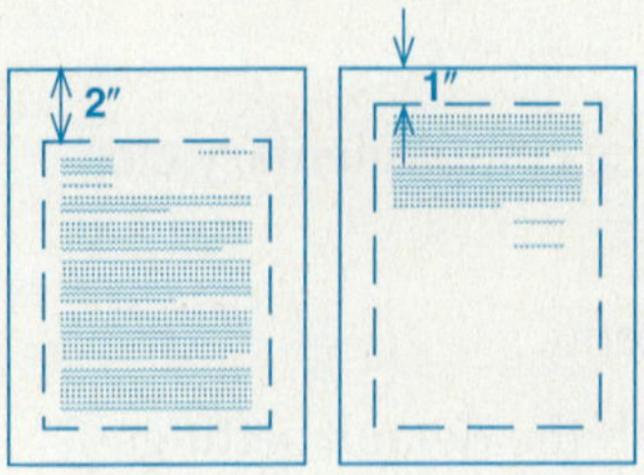

Top margin settings for first page and continuation pages in business letters

9. Press the **Tab** key twice to highlight the Top margin text box. Then key **2** and click OK.

   A [L/R Mar:1",1"] code appears at the beginning of the paragraph, which now aligns at the 1-inch measure.

10. Press **Ctrl+Home** to move to the top of the document.

    A [T/B Mar:2",1"] code indicates the top margin is now 2 inches and the bottom margin is 1 inch. WordPerfect normally places top and bottom margin codes at the top of the page containing the insertion point.

11. Choose Print Preview from the File menu.

    The top margin is now 2 inches from the top of the page.

12. Close the Print Preview window.

Adjusting Side Margins on the Ruler

You can change the left or right margin by moving a margin marker on the Ruler. Codes are placed normally. If you select text before changing the margin, a code is placed before and after the selection.

To practice changing side margins using margin markers:

1. Triple-click in the date at the top of the page to select that text.

2. Drag the left margin marker to 4.25 inches. Then deselect the paragraph.

   A [L/R Mar:4.25",1"] code precedes the date, making the date align on the 4.25-inch measure.

Note: When changing margins for selected text, WordPerfect inserts an extra [HRt] after the second margin code.

After this paragraph, WordPerfect inserts another margin code, [L/R Mar:1",1"], to maintain previous margin settings for the rest of the text.

3. Delete the [HRt] code between the date and inside address, if necessary, to conform to modified-block style for this business letter. (For more information on modified-block style, see Appendix B.)

Centering Text

Center
To align text with equal distance from the left and right margins.

One way to call attention to the information in a short line of text is to *center* it between the left and right margins. You can center text before or after you key it. You also can center one or more words within a line of text.

Centering As You Key Text

You can insert the [Center] code before you key the text. A hard return [HRt] will turn off line centering. Also, if the text you key is longer than one line, line centering ends, and the remaining text wraps to the left margin of the next line.

To center as you key text:

1. Position the insertion point at the end of the second paragraph, after "a high-traffic area".

2. Press **Enter** twice to start a new paragraph, and key:

   To help you select your ideal location, we at Five Points Realty can coordinate a full range of services, including:

3. Press **Enter** twice to start a new paragraph.

4. Choose Line from the Layout menu, and then choose Center (or press **Shift+F7**).

   A [Center] code is placed at the insertion point. The insertion point moves to the center of the line.

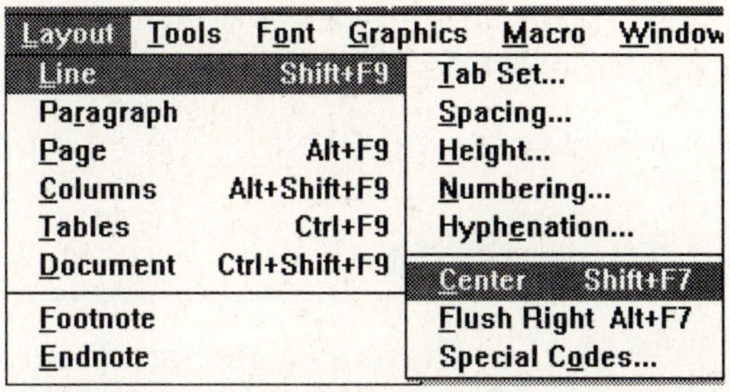

Figure 8-4
The Line cascading menu

5. Key **traffic-pattern analysis.**

   WordPerfect centers the text as you key each character.

6. Press **Enter**.

   The insertion point returns to the left margin.

Centering Existing Text

You also can center text after it has been keyed.

To center existing text:

1. Key the following lines of text, pressing **Enter** after each one:

   zoning and regulation review
   city master-plan review
   contract negotiation
   relocation
   financing
   remodeling

2. Select the text you just keyed and press **Shift+F7**.

   Each line of the selected text is centered.

3. Position the insertion point at the beginning of the selection to deselect the text.

   A [Just:Center] code appears before the selection. (Justification will be discussed more fully later in this lesson.)

4. Position the insertion point at the end of the list.

   A [Just:Left] code and a [HRt] code appear after the text that had been selected.

Centering Words Within a Line of Text

You also can center a numeral, word, or phrase within a line of text. This is done commonly when identifying a page in a document. (In Lesson 15, you will learn to create headers and footers for this purpose.) For instance, you can create the following line using the [Center] code:

My Favorite Vegetable   page 2   June 1, 199-

Flush Right

Flush Right
To align text at the right margin.

Flush Right aligns a single line of text with the right margin. You can insert a [Flsh Rgt] code before you key the text. The flush-right condition ends when you insert a hard return [HRt]. It also ends when the text you key is longer than one line.

To align text flush right:

1. Position the insertion point at the end of the first paragraph, after "is quite exciting".
2. Press **Enter** three times to add space and start a new paragraph.
3. Choose Line from the Layout menu, and then choose Flush Right (or press **Alt+F7**).

   A [Flsh Rgt] code is placed in the Reveal Codes space, and the insertion point moves to the right margin.
4. Key **NEIGHBORHOOD BACKGROUND** as a heading for the next paragraph.
5. Position the insertion point at the end of the next paragraph, after "a high-traffic area".
6. Press **Enter** twice, and then press the **Down Arrow** key to move to the next blank line.
7. Key **AVAILABLE SERVICES** as a heading for the next paragraph.

   The text is aligned at the left margin.
8. Select the new heading, and then press **Alt+F7** (or choose Line from the Layout menu, and then choose Flush Right).

   The selected text is aligned at the right margin. In this case, however, a [Just:Right] code is inserted before the selected text and a [Just:Left] and a [HRt] code are inserted after it.

Justification

Justification
The alignment of text in relation to the side margins.

Justification is the alignment of text in relation to the side margins. As you have seen, the [Center] and [Flsh Rgt] codes affect justification within a single line.

Text can be justified four ways: left, right, center, or full. The default setting is left-justified.

Ragged
Uneven, as the edge of text that is not aligned with a margin.

Left justification aligns text along the left margin, with an uneven or *ragged* right margin.

Right justification is the mirror image of left justification. Words are aligned along the right margin, and uneven lines produce a ragged left margin.

Center justification aligns text at the midpoint between the left and right margins, resulting in both ragged right and ragged left margins.

Full justification aligns text on both the left and right margins, eliminating ragged margins. To make the text span the entire line, however, the spaces between words may be expanded or compressed.

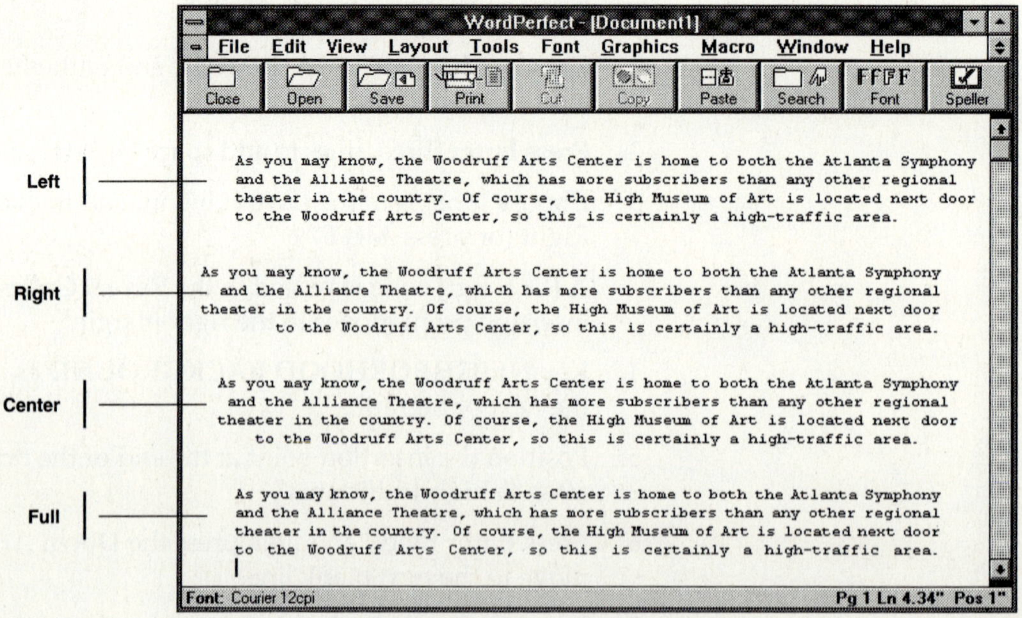

Figure 8-5
Text may be justified left, right, center, or full.

You can change justification in a document in three ways:

- Position the insertion point at the beginning of a new paragraph, and choose a justification option. All text following the change is affected until the end of the document or until the next justification code is chosen.

- Position the insertion point anywhere in an existing paragraph, and choose a justification option. Justification will change at the beginning of that paragraph. All text following the change is affected until the end of the document or until the next justification code is chosen.

- Select text, and choose a justification option. Only selected paragraphs are affected. WordPerfect inserts justification codes as needed to maintain the format of the remaining text.

  For instance, you may select and center-justify text in a document that is otherwise full-justified. A [Just:Center] code will appear before the selected text, and a [Just:Full] and a [HRt] code will appear after it.

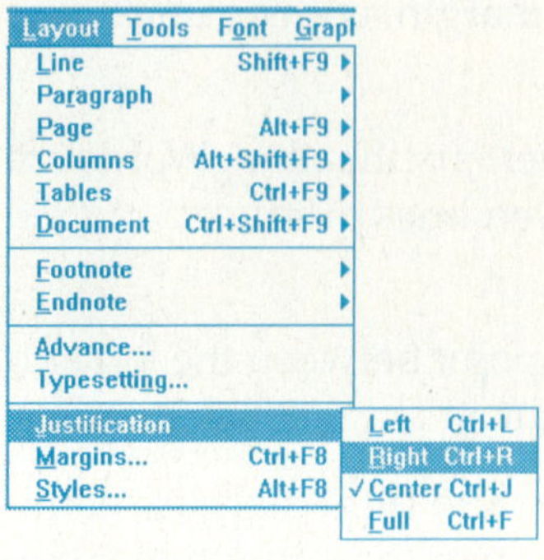

The Justification cascading menu

You can choose a justification option in three ways:

- From the Justification menu in the Layout menu

- By using the keyboard shortcuts **Ctrl+L** (left), **Ctrl+R** (right), **Ctrl+J** (center), **Ctrl+F** (full)

- From the Justification button on the Ruler

To change justification:

1. Position the insertion point anywhere in the first paragraph, which begins "We were happy".

2. Choose Justification from the Layout menu. Then choose Full.

   A [Just:Full] code begins the paragraph, and the following text is aligned at the left and right margins, until WordPerfect encounters a different justification code.

3. Position the insertion point within the text "NEIGHBORHOOD BACKGROUND".

   A [Flsh Rgt] code begins this line, so it is aligned on the right margin. Full justification is still in effect, however, so the next paragraph (which begins "As you may know") is also full-justified.

4. Position the insertion point within the text "AVAILABLE SERVICES".

   A [Just:Right] code begins this line, so full justification stops.

5. Select the paragraph that begins "To help you select". Remember, you may quadruple-click within a paragraph to select it.

The Ruler's justification pop-up menu

6. Choose Full on the Justification pop-up list from the Justification button on the Ruler. (Click and hold the button, and then drag to highlight Full on the pop-up list.)

   The paragraph is full-justified.

   Notice that the last line of a full-justified paragraph often is short. Default settings for typesetting options prevent WordPerfect from excessively expanding or compressing the spaces between words. (For more information, see Lesson 19.)

7. Position the insertion point within the paragraph that begins "Please let us". Press **Ctrl+F** to full-justify the remainder of the letter.

8. Position the insertion point at the [HRt] code before the [Just:Full] code at the beginning of this paragraph.

9. Press **Enter** to add space. Press **Ctrl+R** to move the insertion point to the right margin.

10. Key **NEXT STEPS** and then press **Enter**.

The [Just:Right] code affects only this new text, because a [Just:Full] code immediately follows.

Line Spacing

Line spacing
The amount of space from the bottom of one line to the bottom of the next line.

Line spacing is the space from the bottom of one line to the bottom of the next line. Single spacing is WordPerfect's default setting.

Like justification, line spacing can be changed at the insertion point or for selected text. For selected text, line spacing will apply only to the paragraphs containing selected text. If no text is selected, the change will affect all text up to the next line-spacing code.

You can specify a line-spacing change in the Line Spacing dialog box, or you can use the Spacing button on the Ruler. The Spacing button, however, only offers the three most common options: 1.0, 1.5, and 2.0.

To change line spacing:

1. Select the list of services from "traffic-pattern analysis" to "remodeling".

2. Choose Line from the Layout menu and then choose Spacing.

   The Line Spacing dialog box appears.

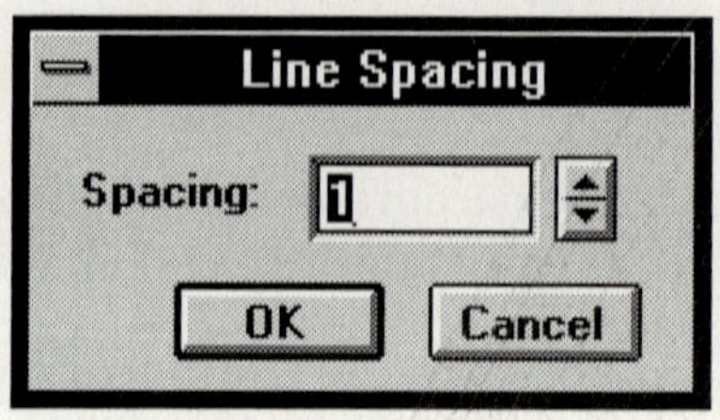

Figure 8-6
The Line Spacing dialog box

3. Key **3** to specify triple spacing (or press the **Up Arrow** until 3 appears). Click OK.

   The list of services is triple-spaced. A [Ln Spacing:3] code appears at the beginning of the selected text, and a [Ln Spacing:1] code appears at the end. Only the selected text is affected.

4. Without deselecting the text, choose the Spacing button on the Ruler and then choose 1.5. (Click and hold the button, and then drag to highlight your choice.)

   The line spacing changes to 1.5.

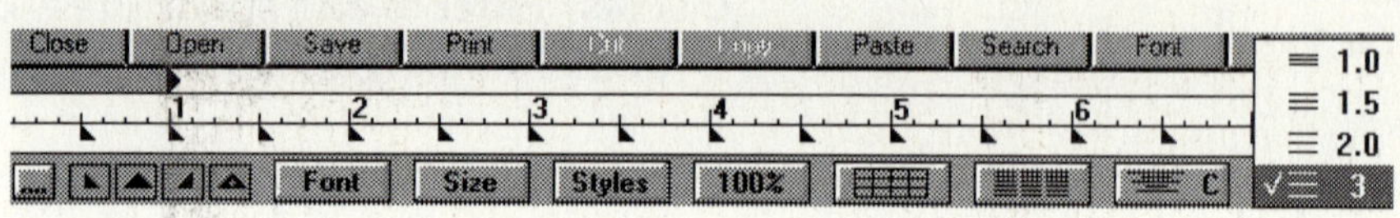

Figure 8-7
The Ruler with Spacing button menu

5. Without deselecting the text, choose Line from the Layout menu and then choose Spacing.

6. Key **0.5** to specify half-line spacing in the Line Spacing dialog box, click OK, and press **End** to deselect the text.

   The list appears to be single-spaced on the screen, but it is not.

7. Choose Print Preview in the File menu. If necessary, choose 100%, and scroll to the list of services.

   The lines overlap, since too little space was specified between them.

8. Close Print Preview.

9. Select the list of services again, choose 2.0 from the Spacing button, and deselect the list.

10. Position the insertion point within the paragraph that begins "We were happy".

11. Choose Line from the Layout menu and then choose Spacing.

12. Key **3** to specify triple-spacing in the Line Spacing dialog box, and click OK.

    The body of the letter is triple-spaced until the [Ln Spacing:2.0] code that starts the list of services appears.

13. Delete the [Ln Spacing:3] code.

    The letter is single-spaced again, except for the double-spaced list.

14. Save the file as *[your three-letter identifier]*8-0a.wpw.

15. Print the document.

16. Close the document.

Hyphenation

Hyphenation
The division of words, usually with a hyphen (-).

Hyphenation is the division of words that extend into the right margin, usually with a hyphen (-). WordPerfect's default setting for Hyphenation is "off." Normally, when a complete word extends into the right margin, the text wraps to a new line.

Hyphenation provides a more uniform look. The ragged right margin in left-justified text will be a little more even, and full-justified text will have fewer compressed or expanded spaces between words. (You cannot use Hyphenation with center-justified or right-justified text.)

Hyphenation Zone

WordPerfect hyphenates a word when it enters a small zone near the right margin.

Words that end within the zone stay on the same line. Words that start within the zone are wrapped to the next line. You can change the size of the zone if you prefer. Figure 8-7 shows the default settings for the hyphenation zone.

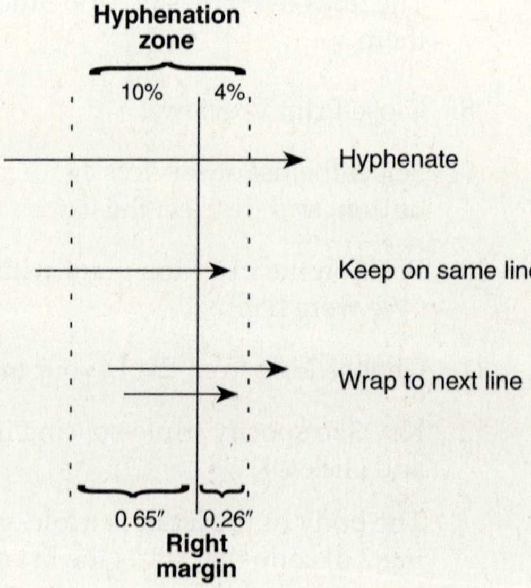

Figure 8-8
The default hyphenation zone for a 6.5-inch line

Dividing Words

There are several ways to divide words when hyphenating text. The regular hyphen is a [-] code (the "minus sign" key) that always displays and prints. This code also divides a word when it crosses the hyphenation zone. Hyphens typically connect words like "father-in-law" or "well-known".

A soft hyphen is like a regular hyphen, but it appears and prints only when a word needs to be divided at the end of a line. WordPerfect uses soft hyphens to break words when Hyphenation is on. (You also can insert a soft hyphen by pressing **Ctrl+Shift+**the minus key.)

A Hyphenation Soft Return is another code, [HyphSRt], that divides a word that crosses the hyphenation zone. The [HyphSRt] does not insert a hyphen, however. It just breaks the word. It is useful for words connected by slashes, such as "either/or". You can choose a Hyphenation Soft Return when you are prompted by the Position Hyphen dialog box.

Note: In this activity, words presented for hyphenation may vary depending on your printer and the typeface you are using.

To use Hyphenation:

1. Open the file 8-0b.wpw, and choose Reveal Codes from the View menu, if necessary.

2. Choose Preferences from the File menu and then choose Environment.

   The Environment Settings dialog box appears. Hyphenation is affected by choices in three sections of this box.

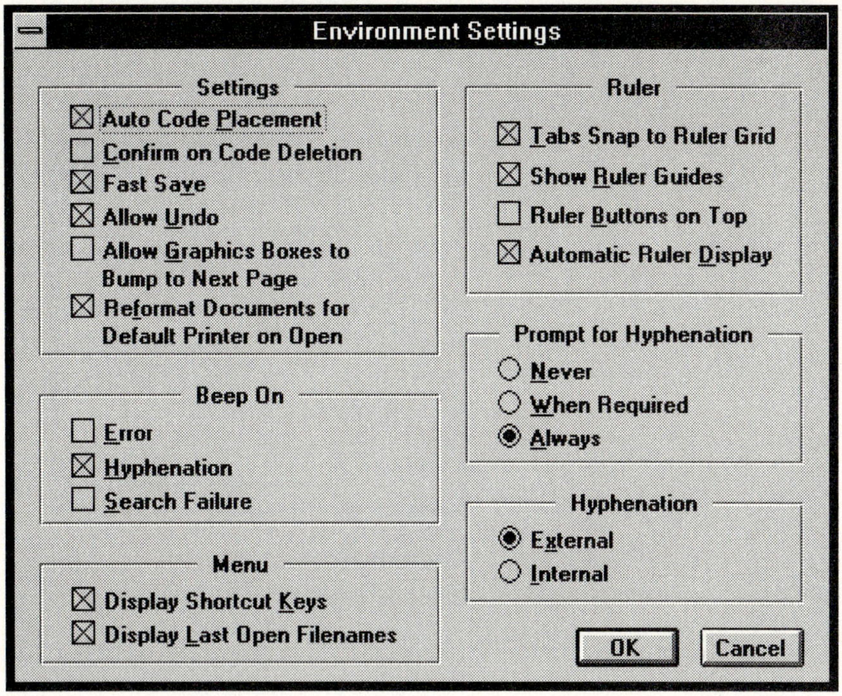

Figure 8-9
The Environment Settings dialog box

3. In the Hyphenation section, choose External, if necessary.

   WordPerfect will use its larger External dictionary to determine syllable breaks for hyphenation. (A smaller Internal dictionary is built into WordPerfect, in case an External dictionary is not available.)

4. In the Prompt for Hyphenation section, choose Always.

   When you choose Always, you will be prompted for every hyphenation decision.

   If you choose Never, you will not be prompted. WordPerfect will use its rules and the selected dictionary to hyphenate words. It will wrap words that are not in this dictionary.

If you choose When Required, WordPerfect will prompt you only when it cannot find a word in the dictionary.

5. In the Beep On section, select Hyphenation, if necessary.

   WordPerfect will beep whenever it prompts you to hyphenate a word.

6. Click OK.

7. Press **Ctrl+Home** to move to the top of the document.

8. Choose Line from the Layout menu. Then choose Hyphenation.

   The Line Hyphenation dialog box appears.

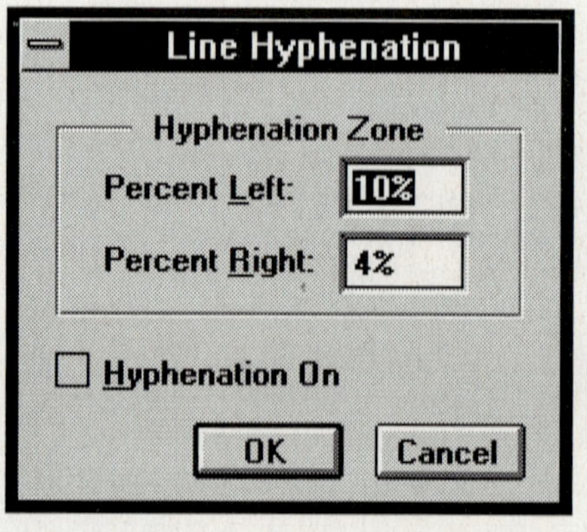

Figure 8-10
The Line Hyphenation dialog box

9. For the Hyphenation Zone, change both the Percent Left and the Percent Right to 0.

   WordPerfect will prompt you for every word that extends into the right margin.

Note: Follow the basic rules and preferred practices for word division. See the Feature Box "Guidance for Word Division" at the end of this section or *The Gregg Reference Manual.*

10. Check the Hyphenation On box and click OK.

    The Position Hyphen dialog box presents the suggested hyphenation of the word "per-haps".

    In the Position Hyphen dialog box, you may reposition the hyphen with the mouse or arrow keys. The hyphenation zone determines how far left or right the hyphen will go. See Figure 8-11 on page 8-15.

11. Click the Insert Hyphen button to accept the suggested word division.

    WordPerfect inserts a Soft Hyphen in per-haps. It then presents "estab-lish" in the Position Hyphen dialog box.

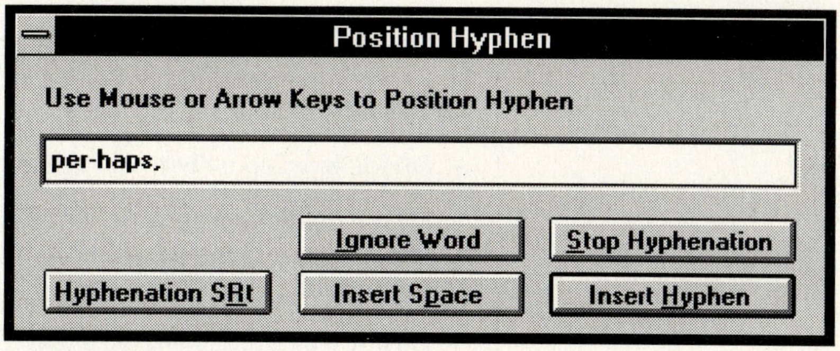

Figure 8-11
The Position Hyphen dialog box (as in step 10 on page 8-14)

12. Click the Insert Hyphen button.

    WordPerfect presents "sub-scribers" in the Position Hyphen dialog box.

13. Click the Insert Hyphen button.

    WordPerfect presents "Wood-ruff" in the Position Hyphen dialog box.

14. Click Ignore Word.

    Since Woodruff is a proper name, you prefer to keep it unbroken.

    WordPerfect marks the word with a [Hyph Ign Wrd] code, so it will not be hyphenated in the future.

15. In the Reveal Codes space, click the Soft Hyphen (-) code that divides establish. Press **Delete**.

    The Position Hyphen dialog box appears. When Hyphenation is on, you can change any code with the help of this box. If you remove the [Hyph On] code, you can delete hyphenation codes.

Note: You may prefer to use hyphenation after a document is otherwise complete. If you use hyphenation last, other operations, such as spell-checking, are not interrupted by the hyphenation procedure.

16. Click the Ignore Word button.

    You may prefer not to end two consecutive lines with a hyphen.

17. Choose Line from the Layout menu, and then choose Hyphenation.

18. Check the Hyphenation On box to deselect hyphenation.

Guidance for Word Division

Basic Rules

- Divide words only between syllables.
- Do not divide one-syllable words. Even when *ed* is added to some words, they still remain one-syllable words and cannot be divided (for instance: *stressed*, not *stres-sed*).
- Do not separate a one-letter syllable at the beginning or the end of a word (for instance: *amaze*, not *a-maze*).
- Do not divide a word unless you can leave a syllable of at least three characters (the last of which can be a hyphen) on the upper line, and you can carry a syllable of at least three characters (the last of which may be a punctuation mark) to the next line (for instance, these are both correct: *ad-* mit, happil- *ly.*).
- Do not divide abbreviations (for instance: *UNICEF*, *assoc.*).
- Do not divide contractions (for instance: *o'clock*, *shouldn't*).

Preferred Practices

- Divide words to avoid confusion and preserve meaning.
- Try not to end more than two consecutive lines in hyphens.
- Divide a solid compound word between the elements of the compound (for instance: *eye- witness*).
- Divide a hyphenated compound word at the point of the hyphen (for instance: *self- confidence*).
- Divide a word after a prefix or before a suffix, rather than within the prefix or suffix.

Table 8-1: Hyphenation with Prefixes and Suffices

Acceptable	Preferred
in- troduce	intro- duce
in- ternational	inter- national
comprehensi- ble	comprehen- sible
Confusing	**Better**
coin- cide	co- incide
extra- neous	ex- traneous

Auto Code Placement

Auto Code Placement
The automatic placement of codes in their proper place in a page or paragraph.

Some WordPerfect codes are designed to be inserted at the beginning of a paragraph. Others are meant for the beginning of a page. When *Auto Code Placement* is on, WordPerfect automatically places a code in the appropriate place. With Auto Code Placement on, even if you insert a formatting code in the middle of a paragraph or the middle of a page, WordPerfect moves the code to the beginning of the paragraph or page. Auto Code Placement on is the default setting. Table 8-2, Auto Code Placement, summarizes the codes affected by automatic placement.

Table 8-2: Auto Code Placement

Formatting Code	Beginning of Paragraph	Beginning of Page
Columns	x	
Hyphenation Zone	x	
Justification	x	
Line Spacing	x	
Margins, Left and Right	x	
Margins Top and Bottom		x
Page, Center		x
Page Numbering		x
Page, Size		x
Paragraph Numbering	x	
Tab Set	x	

Inserting the Date and Time

Note: To change your computer's calendar or clock, use Windows' Date/Time utility, which usually is found in the Control Panel group within the Main group.

If the date and time on your computer's clock are correct, you can use Date options to insert the date or time into documents.

Date Text

Inserting the current date as text is convenient for saving keystrokes and for ensuring accuracy and consistent format. Use Date Text in correspondence to identify the original date of a letter. Once inserted, Date Text does not change with the computer's calendar.

To insert a date as text:

1. At the beginning of the file, triple-click to select "June 1, 199-".
2. Choose Date from the Tools menu, and then choose Text.

   The current date replaces the selected text. In the Reveal Codes area, notice that this date is inserted as normal text.
3. Choose Undo from the Edit menu to restore the original text.

Date Codes

You also can insert a date code that will change whenever you open, retrieve, or print a document. Form letters or periodic reports always will show the current date. After it is inserted, a Date Code always represents the current date.

To insert a Date Code:

1. At the beginning of the file, triple-click to select "June 1, 199-".

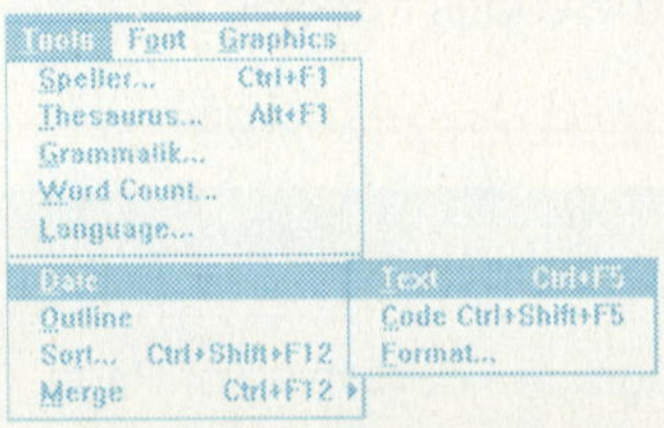

The Date cascading menu

2. Choose Date from the Tools menu and then choose Code.

   Again, the current date replaces the selected text. In the Reveal Codes space, however, a date code has been inserted: [Date:Month DayOfMon, Yr(4)].

3. Click the date code and press **Delete**. Then key the original date, June 1, 199-.

Date Format

You can specify the information, sequence, and format in the date code with the Date Format option. This is also how you specify time of day.

To define a date and time format:

1. Choose Date from the Tools menu and then choose Format.

   The Document Date/Time Format dialog box appears. The default format is shown in the Edit Date Format text box: [Month] [Day #], [Year ####]. This translates as: "Month Name (space) Day Number (comma) (space) Four-Digit Year".

   The Date Preview shows how the date will appear when inserted in a document (for instance: June 1, 1993).

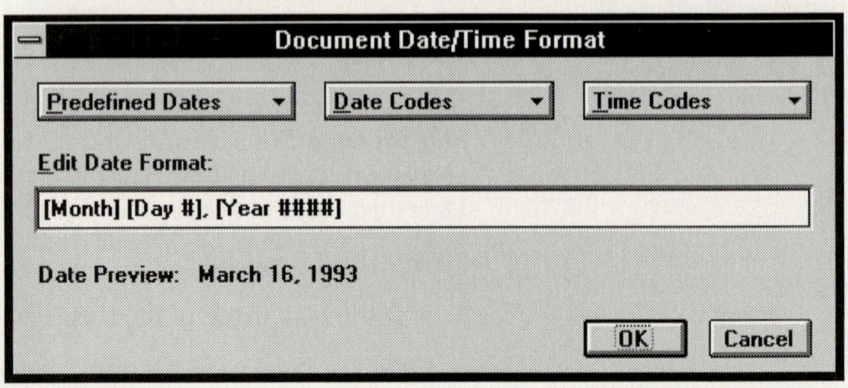

Figure 8-12
The Document Date/Time Format dialog box

2. Choose the last format from the Predefined Dates pop-up list (3/4/92).

   The Edit Date Format and Date Preview fields change correspondingly.

3. Press **E** to edit the format.

   The format is highlighted. To create a new format, you will choose codes from the Date Codes and Time Codes pop-up lists and insert punctuation and spacing from the keyboard.

4. From the Date Codes pop-up list, choose the following:

   - [Day #]
   - [Month]
   - [Year ##]

5. From the Time Codes pop-up list, choose the following:

   - [Hour(12)#]
   - [Minute 0#]
   - [AM/PM]

   The Date Preview shows the date and time information run together.

6. Click in the Edit Date Format text box. Use the Arrow keys to position the insertion point between codes and insert spaces and punctuation as follows:

   - one space between [Day #] and [Month]
   - one space between [Month] and [Year ##]
   - two spaces between [Year ##] and [Hour(12)#]
   - a colon (:) between [Hour(12)#] and [Minute 0#]

7. Click OK to return to the document.

8. Press **Ctrl+End** to move to the end of the document. If necessary, press **Enter** to start a new line after the reference initials, "dah".

Note: You inserted the date and time at the end of this letter for practice only. This is not a standard procedure.

9. Choose Date from the Tools menu and then choose Code.

   The newly formatted date and time is inserted.

10. Return the date-code format to the default setting. (The default setting is the first one listed in Predefined Dates.)

Document Summary

Document summary
A formal document description including reference information.

Abstract
A narrative summary of a document.

A *document summary* helps you to organize and then locate your documents quickly. The summary gives you a brief on-screen synopsis of each document, listing the author, typist, and a brief description of the file's contents. You also can write an *abstract*, or narrative summary, of the document.

To practice creating a document summary:

1. Choose Document from the Layout menu and then choose Summary.

   The Document Summary dialog box appears.

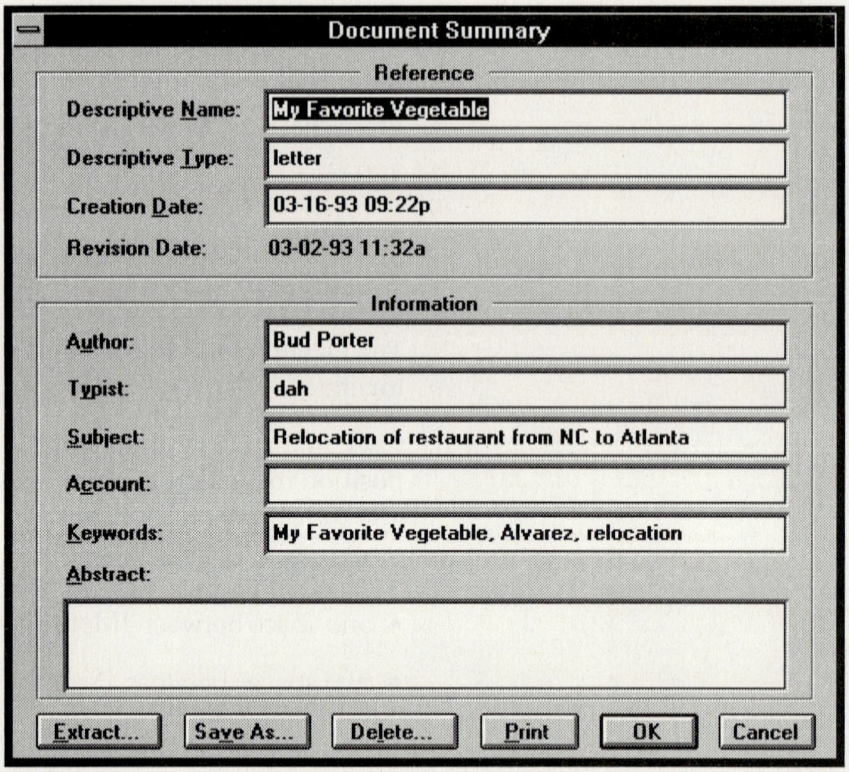

Figure 8-13
The Document Summary dialog box

2. Fill in the fields in this dialog box. (Skip the Abstract field for now.)

   To fill in dialog box fields:

   Press the **Tab** key to move to the next field.

   Press **Shift+Tab** to move to the previous field.

   Position the insertion point anywhere in the box.

3. Position the insertion point in the Abstract field.

4. Click the Extract button.

   A confirm dialog box appears asking, "Extract Document Summary Fields?"

5. Click Yes.

   WordPerfect retrieves information from the document to act as a summary. This summary is not satisfactory, so you will write your own.

6. Select all the text in the Abstract field and press **Delete**.

7. Key the following:

   Letter of encouragement to Stephen Alvarez of My Favorite Vegetable vegetarian restaurant. Alvarez is considering relocating from Asheville, NC, to the Woodruff Arts Center area.

8. Print the document summary by clicking Print.

9. Save the document as *[your three-letter identifier]*8-0b.wpw.

10. Print the document.

11. Close the document and exit WordPerfect (unless you will be doing the following exercises immediately).

Table 8-3: Margins and Line Formatting

Keyboard Shortcut	Action
Ctrl+F8	Open Margins dialog box
Shift+F7	Center text
Alt+F7	Right-align text
Ctrl+L	Left-justify text
Ctrl+R	Right-justify text
Ctrl+J	Center-justify text
Ctrl+F	Full-justify text
Ctrl+Shift+[-]	Insert a Soft Hyphen

Key Terms

Abstract
Auto Code Placement
Center
Document summary
Flush right
Hyphenation
Justification
Line spacing
Margin
Margin marker
Ragged

Exercises

Exercise 8.1

1. Start WordPerfect, if necessary.
2. Open the file 8-1.wpw.
3. If necessary, position the insertion point at the top of the document, and turn on the Ruler.
4. Change the top margin to 2 inches and the right margin to 4 inches:

   A. Choose Margins from the Layout menu.

   B. Double-click the Right-margin text box and key **4**.

   C. Double-click the Top-margin text box and key **2**.

   D. Click OK.
5. Change line spacing to 1.5:

   A. Choose Line from the Layout menu and then choose Spacing.

   B. Key **1.5** in the Spacing box and click OK.
6. Full-justify the document by choosing that option from the Ruler's Justification button pop-up list.
7. Immediately before the word "Five" in the first-line, key **AT-LANTA.** Then press the **Spacebar** twice.
8. Insert the date code followed by a period and a space:

   A. Choose Date from the Tools menu.

   B. Choose Code.

   C. Key a period and add a space.
9. Above the first paragraph, centered on its own line, key **FOR IMMEDIATE RELEASE**:

   A. Press **Home** to move to the beginning of the line.

   B. Press **Enter** twice to add space. Then position the insertion point at the top blank line.

   C. Press **Shift+F7**, and key **FOR IMMEDIATE RELEASE** to center the text as you key it.
10. On the blank line at the bottom of page 1, key **(continued)** at the right margin:

    A. Position the insertion point in the blank line.

    B. Choose Line from the Layout menu, and then choose Flush Right.

C. Key **(continued)**.

11. Spell-check the document.
12. Save the document as *[your three-letter identifier]*8-1.wpw.
13. Print the document.
14. Close the document and exit WordPerfect (unless you will be doing the following exercises immediately).

Exercise 8.2

1. Start WordPerfect, if necessary.
2. Open the file 8-2.wpw.
3. Position the insertion point at the beginning of the document, if necessary.
4. Turn Hyphenation on with the default hyphenation zone:

   A. Choose Line from the Layout menu and then choose Hyphenation.

   B. If necessary, set Percent Left to 10% and Percent Right to 4%.

   C. Check the Hyphenation On check box and click OK.
5. Follow the basic rules and preferred practices for word division when you are prompted by the Position Hyphen dialog box.
6. Position the insertion point at the end of the document, and key **END** centered on its own line.
7. Change the top margin to 1 inch for the second page.
8. Create a document summary for this document using the information given in Figure 8-14 at the end of this exercise. Use the Extract option to create the Abstract:

   A. Choose Document from the Layout menu and then choose Summary.

   B. Key the information in Figure 8-14 on the proper lines in the summary.

   C. Click the Extract button, and then click Yes in the confirming dialog box to create an abstract.
9. Click the print button to print the document summary.
10. Spell-check the document.
11. Save the document as *[your three-letter identifier]*8-2.wpw.
12. Print the document.
13. Close the document and exit WordPerfect (unless you will be doing the following exercises immediately).

Figure 8-14

```
Descriptive Name:        Rigdon Direct Announcement

Descriptive Type:        Press Release

Author:                  Mary Rigdon

Typist:                  [Your initials]
```

Exercise 8.3

1. Start WordPerfect, if necessary.
2. Open the file 8-3.wpw.
3. Refer to Figure 8-15 at the end of this exercise, the document with Ann Delbridge's notes.
4. Format the document as a modified-block style letter with 1.25-inch side margins. Use appropriate top and bottom margins for first and continuation pages.
5. Full-justify and single-space, except for the list of first-floor features.
6. Break the list of first-floor features into separate lines with 1.5-line spacing, center-justified.
7. Edit the content of the letter, as shown in Figure 8-15.
8. Include your reference initials, enclosure notation, delivery notation, and the cc to Bud Porter.
9. Turn Hyphenation on. Follow the basic rules and preferred practices for word division.
10. Create and print a document summary.
11. Spell-check the document.
12. Save the document as *[your three-letter identifier]*8-3.wpw.
13. Print the document.
14. Close the document and exit WordPerfect (unless you will be doing the following exercises immediately).

Figure 8-15

We here at Five Points Realty are delighted to assist you and Felton Electronics in your move to Atlanta. In fact,

Dear Jack and Lisa:

the city

I found a strong candidate for your "dream house" north of ~~Atlanta~~. It offers privacy and space, and it is ideal for entertaining and for seclusion from the stresses of business life.

The home was build in the 1950s in an antebellum style on four private acres surrounded by woodlands. It borders a nature preserve on two sides and another private estate on the third side. The property borders a six-acre lake that extends into the preserve. The recreation area includes a dock, boathouse, and cabana. An in-ground pool and patio are surrounded by formal gardens, separating them from the tennis court.

leads you

~~The entrance of the main house takes you through~~ a six-pillared portico into a two-story atrium with a double, curving staircase. The first floor includes a marble-floored ballroom, panelled library, dining room with crystal chandelier, parlor/family room, gourmet kitchen, with pantry, ~~and~~ servant's quarters.

Center list, 1 1/2 line space

The second floor features a master suite with sitting room, bed chamber, and luxury spa. Five additional bedrooms, each with a private bath, will accomodate your three children and leave room for house guests.

bf

I enclose photographs and a data sheet.

I believe we could get the property for under $1 million.

Shall I arrange a visit during your next trip to Atlanta?

- 1 1/2" side margins
- Full Justify
- Modified block style
- Hyphenate
- Enclose photos and data sheet
- Mail today Rush!
- Copy to Bud Porter

Sincerely, yours

FIVE POINTS REALTY

Ann Delbridge

Address: Jack and Lisa Felton
9 Pueblo Canyon
Elko, NV 89801

Exercise 8.4

1. Start WordPerfect, if necessary.
2. Open a new file, and key in the document in Figure 8-16 using 2.5-inch side margins.
3. Format the first line of each listing uppercase and bold.
4. Align the phrases "NEW LISTING" and "INSIDE 285" flush right.
5. Format the last line of each listing italic, upper- and lowercase. Align the phone numbers flush right.
6. Center-align the prices and make them bold.
7. Full-justify the document and turn Hyphenation on.
8. Set the line spacing of the main paragraphs at 1.25 lines.
9. Spell-check the document.
10. Save the document as *[your three-letter identifier]*8-4.wpw.
11. Print the document.
12. Close the document and exit WordPerfect (unless you will be doing the following exercise immediately).

Figure 8-16

BUCKHEAD NEW LISTING

Extraordinary 5,700 sq. ft. Antebellum Mansion on three private acres surrounded by woodlands. A dramatic 30-ft. entry introduces the living room with marble fireplace opening to a 60-ft. flagstone terrace. Upstairs: airy master bedroom with marble bath/spa. In addition: three family bedrooms, three baths, and a two-bedroom guest wing.

$890,000

Ann Delbridge 555-1789

```
DUNWOODY    INSIDE 285

Outside the city, but in easy commuting distance! Fabulous Williamsburg
with three to four bedrooms and five baths. Separate living room, dining
room, and recreation room. Three fireplaces. In-ground pool and
professional landscaping set this one-acre lot apart.
$725,000
Mary Rigdon      555-3421
```

Exercise 8.5

1. Start WordPerfect, if necessary.
2. Open the file 8-5.wpw, and refer to Figure 8-17, the author's edited copy of this document.
3. Format the document as a memo from Ann Delbridge to Bud Porter, Della Crandon, Mary Rigdon, and John Soloman according to the style in Appendix C. (Use the **Tab** key to align text after the guidewords in the memo heading.)
4. Insert the date as text.
5. For the SUBJECT, key **450 Wood Valley Road**.
6. Edit the document as indicated in Figure 8-17.
   - Break the description into three paragraphs and single-space that text.
   - Set both side margins for the Tipsheet material to 2.5 inches.
   - Capitalize, bold, and center the word "Tipsheet".
   - Format the guidewords in the Tipsheet as bold with initial caps.
   - Set line spacing for the Tipsheet to 1.5, except for the list of amenities.
7. For the list of amenities:
   - Put the six items on this list on separate lines, right-justified.
   - Single-space the list.
   - Set the right margin of the list to 3½ inches.
8. Key **AD** (for Ann Delbridge) as the writer's initials, and key your own reference initials.

9. Create and print a document summary.
10. Spell-check the document.
11. Save the document as *[your three-letter identifier]*8-5.wpw.
12. Print the document.
13. Close the document and exit WordPerfect.

Figure 8-17

SS

I am pleased to provide you with a description of a unique new listing in Buckhead. 450 Wood Valley Road features an unusual open-arched entry with tiled floor that highlights this five-bedroom colonial. Built in 1935, the property is offered at $419,000 through the Rorden Agency. Oak French doors open off the center hall to a living room and dining room that includes built-in cabinets, shelving, and a china closet. The bright family room is accessed through French doors flanking the living room's fireplace, and a carpeted den adjoins the dining room and oak-cabineted eat-in kitchen. The second floor landing is brightened by a grand window, and wide multi-paned landing windows light the way to the bedroom/study.

This home

1½ space

Tipsheet

bf

Address: 450 Wood Valley Road

bf

Asking price: $419,000

Bedrooms: 5

bf

Baths: 3.5

bf

amenities: living-room fireplace, built-in cabinets, oak cabinets in kitchen, self-cleaning oven, smoke alarm

bf

heating/cooling: oil, steam

bf

listing agency: Rorden Agency, Buckhead, 555-0990

bf

Please format as a memo
To: Bud Porter, Della Crandon
Mary Rigdon, John Soloman

AD

Lesson 9

Tabs and Tabbed Columns

Tabs are a used to align text vertically on the page. With tabs, you can create documents, such as a memo or a business letter, using a specific format. You also can create lists of information in columns.

Objectives

- Set tabs.
- Clear tab settings.
- Set tabbed columns.
- Set dot leaders.
- Set evenly spaced tabs.
- Use the tab-align option.
- Set a hard tab.

What Is a Tab?

Tabs are used to align text at a specified distance from the left margin or the left edge of the paper. A *tab* is a code that advances the insertion point to the next tab setting. The **Tab** key inserts a [Tab] code. A *tab setting* is the specified distance that is marked by a triangular *tab marker* on the Ruler.

Tab
A code that advances the insertion point a set distance from the left.

Tab setting
The set distance where a tab stops.

Tab marker
A triangle that marks a tab setting on the Ruler.

Note: You cannot simulate a tab by pressing the **Spacebar**, as you might on a typewriter. Characters and spaces do not necessarily occupy the same amount of space on a line. Tabs must be used to align text properly in a printed document.

WordPerfect specifies tab settings every 0.5 inches as the default.

To insert a tab code in a document:

1. Start WordPerfect.
2. Choose Ruler and Reveal Codes from the View menu.
3. At a new document screen, key **Five Points Realty**, and press the **Tab** key.

   The insertion point advances to the right. A [Tab] code is inserted in the code window.

4. Click and hold the tab marker on the Ruler above the insertion point.

   A dotted vertical line extends through the document, passing through the insertion point. The position shown on the status bar matches the tab setting.

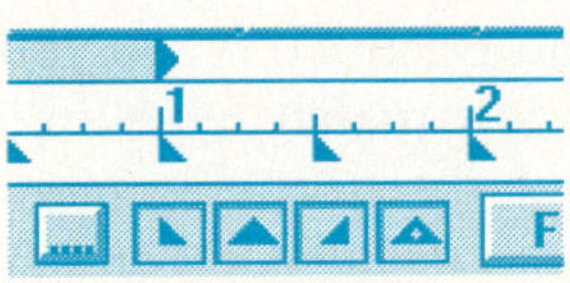

Tab markers

Note: If you accidentally drag a tab marker, choose Undo from the Edit menu.

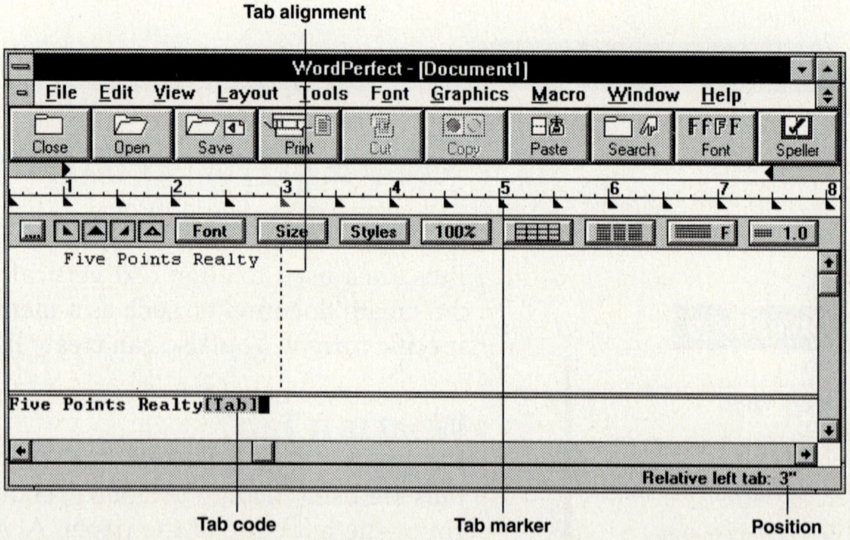

Figure 9-1
Tab alignment matches the position shown on the status bar.

5. Release the mouse button, and press the **Tab** key again.

   The insertion point advances to the next tab setting to the right.

6. Close this document without saving it.

Default Tabs

WordPerfect's default tab setting is every 0.5 inches, from the left edge of the paper to the 14″ measure on the Ruler. With the default left margin of 1 inch, the default Tab Set code is [Tab Set: Rel: -1″, every 0.5″].

You can change the default tab settings by clearing them and then creating your own tab settings. You can create four different types of tabs in WordPerfect documents.

Types of Tab Alignment

Text lines up with a tab setting according to the type of tab you set. WordPerfect's default alignment for tabs is Left. You can set four different types of tabs: Left, Right, Center, and Decimal. When you press the **Tab** key, WordPerfect inserts a tab code to match the setting. The tab codes align text with a tab setting similarly to the alignment of text with the margins by justification codes. The tab codes are:

- Left [Tab]

  The left edge of the text lines up with the tab setting.

- Right [Rgt Tab]

  The right edge of the text lines up with the tab setting.

- Center [Cntr Tab]

  The text is centered at the tab setting.

- Decimal [Dec Tab]

  The text lines up at the first decimal point. If no decimal point is present, the text lines up at the last character. (It will appear to be right-aligned.)

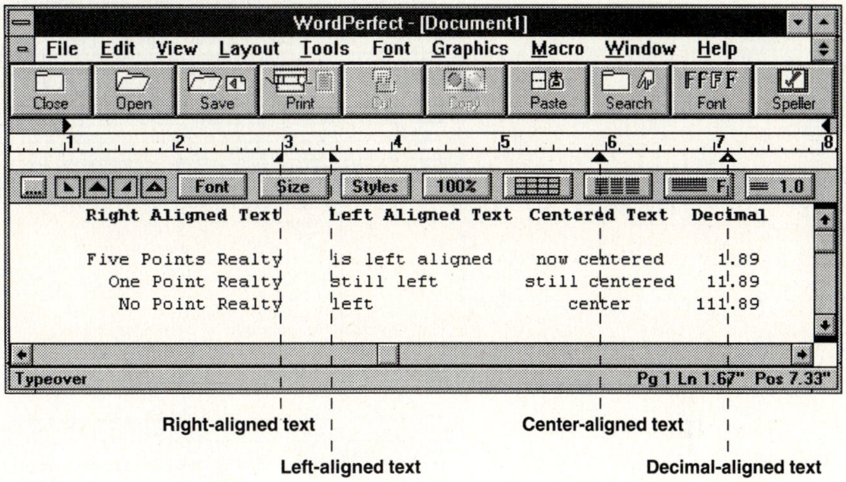

Figure 9-2
Tabs can align text in four ways.

Absolute and Relative Tabs

Absolute tab
A tab measured from the left edge of the paper.

Relative tab
A tab measured from the left margin.

In WordPerfect, you can set an *absolute tab* from the left edge of the paper or a *relative tab* from the left margin. WordPerfect's default is the relative tab.

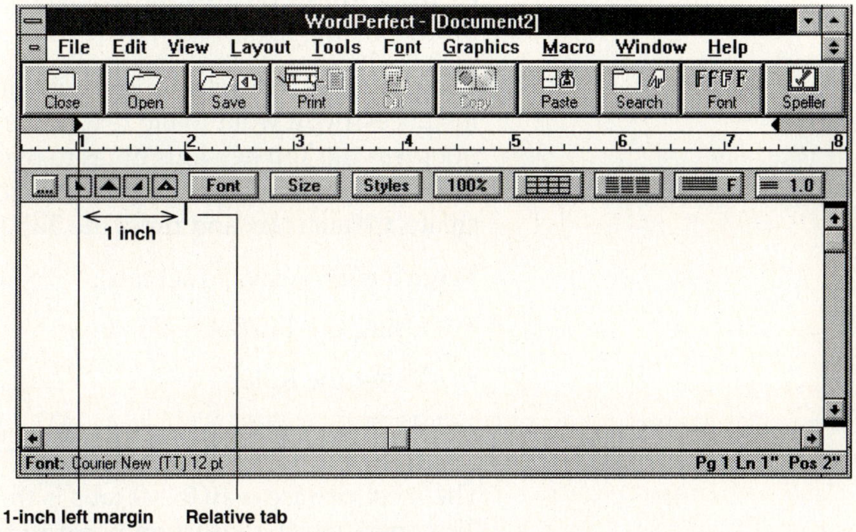

Figure 9-3
The relative tab is set 1 inch from the left margin.

Absolute tab settings are positioned from the left edge of the paper. They stay the same, even if you change the left margin. This is useful for positioning text on preprinted forms.

Relative tab settings are positioned from the left margin. This is useful in text you key entirely. If you change the left margin, the relative tab settings adjust accordingly.

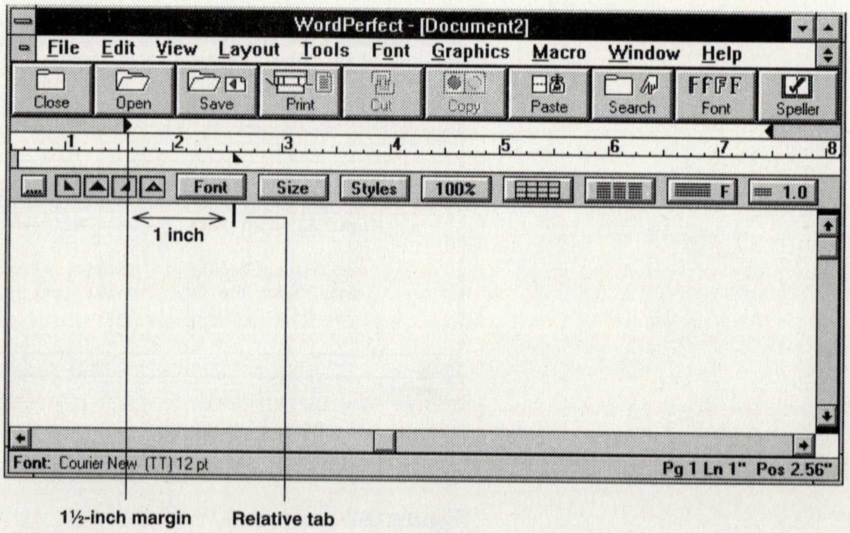

Figure 9-4
When the margin changes, the relative tab changes.

Setting Tabs

When you set tabs in a document, the settings remain in effect for each line, until you reset the tabs. You can set tabs before you key text or for existing text.

You should set up a document with only the settings you need. For instance, if you want to tab text to the 2-inch mark on the Ruler, do not press the **Tab** key four times to reach the 2-inch default tab stop. This inserts extraneous tab codes that clutter the document. Instead, create a 2-inch tab, and press the **Tab** key once.

There are two ways to set tabs:

- Using the Tab Set dialog box
- Using the Ruler

Setting Tabs Using the Tab Set Dialog Box

The most precise way to set tabs is through the Tab Set dialog box. First, position the insertion point in the line where the tab-setting change is to take place. Be sure Auto Code Placement is on, so

WordPerfect will place a [Tab Set] code at the beginning of a paragraph.

You also may select text and then apply tab settings.

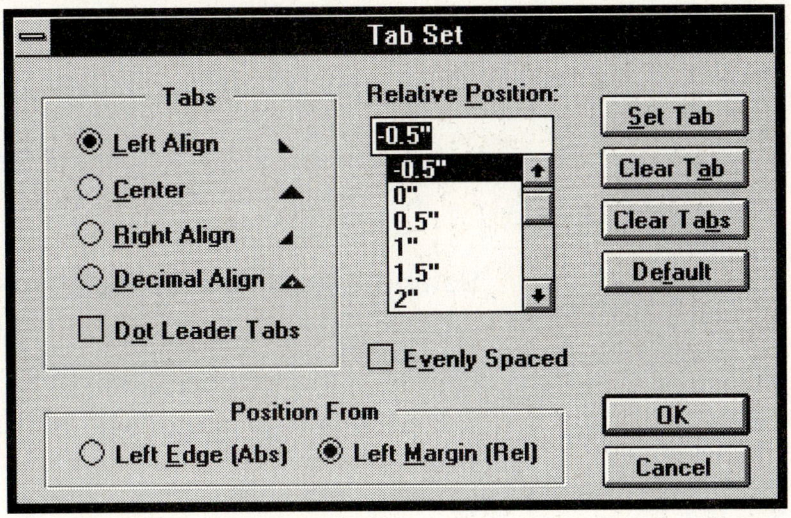

Figure 9-5
The Tab Set dialog box

To set tabs using the Tab Set dialog box:

1. Open the file 9-0a.wpw.
2. Position the insertion point to the beginning of the document, if necessary.
3. Press **Enter** twice to insert space, and press **Ctrl+Home** to return to the beginning of the document.
4. Choose Line from the Layout menu. Then choose Tab Set.

   The Tab Set dialog box appears.

5. Choose Clear Tabs to clear all tabs at the insertion point.
6. Choose Left Align under Tabs, if necessary.
7. Choose Left Margin (Rel) in the Position From group, if necessary.
8. Key **2** in the Relative Position text box and click OK.

   A [Tab Set:Rel: +2(] code is inserted, and a left tab marker appears 2 inches to the right of the left margin (at the 3-inch measure) on the Ruler.

9. Now, key the following as the memo heading:

   MEMO TO:[Tab]Bud Porter[HRt]
   [HRt]
   FROM:[Tab]Ann Delbridge[HRt]
   [HRt]
   DATE:[Tab]June 9, 199-[HRt]
   [HRt]
   SUBJECT:[Tab]New Properties[HRt]

   After each tab, the left edge of the text aligns with the tab stop, 2 inches past the left margin.

Setting Tabs Using the Ruler

If you have a mouse, you can set a tab directly on the Ruler. Ruler settings have the same effect as those made in the Tab Set dialog box.

Tab buttons
Ruler buttons for setting left, center, right, and decimal tabs.

Tab markers show tab settings. *Tab buttons* represent the four alignment options.

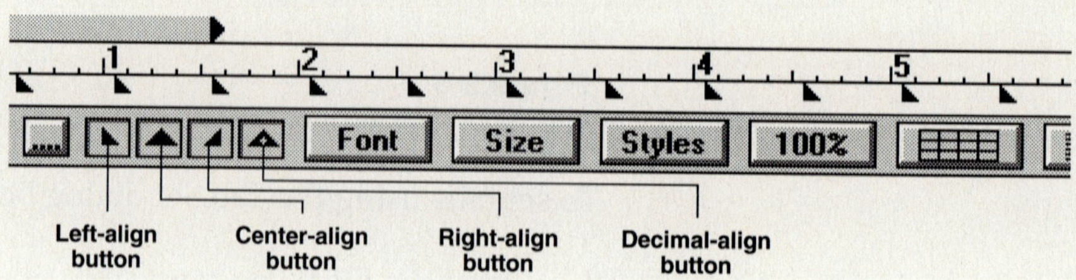

Figure 9-6
Ruler with Tab buttons

The chief advantage to using the Ruler to set tabs is that you can see your result immediately. No dialog box blocks your view. Furthermore, there are fewer steps involved when setting tabs from the Ruler.

To set tabs on the Ruler:

1. Position the insertion point to the right of "May 1:" and press **Enter** twice.

2. Drag a Left Tab button to the 2-inch measure on the Ruler, and drag another one to the 4.5-inch measure. The Ruler now shows three tab markers.

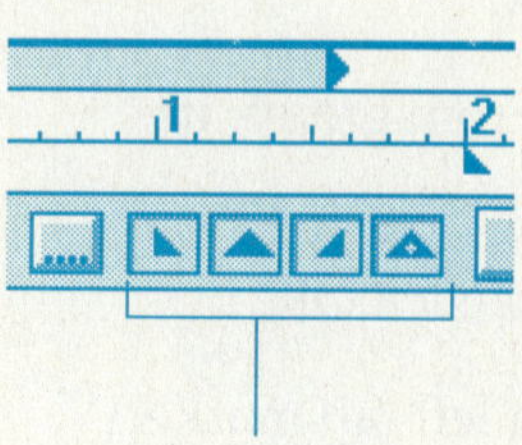

To set a tab, drag a Tab button on the Ruler

3. Key the following, pressing the **Tab** key before each word:

   Number   Location   List Price

   WordPerfect aligns the text, which is a table heading, at the 2-inch, 3-inch, and 4.5-inch tab stops.

Using the Ruler to Set Tabs

You can use the Ruler to set tabs easily. First, position the cursor or select the text to be affected. Then delete, move, or copy tabs on the Ruler:

- To copy a tab, press and hold the **Ctrl** key while you drag the tab to a new position.
- To delete any individual tab setting, drag it off the Ruler.
- To move any existing tab setting, drag it to a new position. If you drag one tab on top of another, the new tab replaces the old tab.
- To select a group of tabs, drag across those tabs, creating a gray ribbon. Then drag to delete, move, or copy the selection.
- To replace a group of tabs, press and hold the **Shift** key while you drag a group of tabs. When you release these tabs, they replace the tabs in the covered area.
- To add a group of tabs to another location, just drag and release the group of tabs.
- To deselect a group of tabs, click anywhere.
- To open the Tab Set dialog box, double-click on a tab on the Ruler.

Clearing Tab Settings

You can clear any tabs inserted in a document. When tabs are cleared, no tab settings are in effect. If you press the **Tab** key, nothing happens. You can restore the default settings after you clear tabs.

To clear all tab settings:

1. Position the insertion point before the word "MEMO".
2. Choose Line from the Layout menu. Then choose Tab Set.

   The Tab Set dialog box appears.

   The tab setting in the Relative Position list box indicates the distance of each tab from the left margin. The setting (2″) represents the 2-inch mark to the right of the left margin. It is 2 inches relative to the left margin.
3. Choose Clear Tabs and click OK.

   The Position list box is empty, and the tab marker no longer appears on the Ruler. A [Tab Set:No Tabs] code is inserted before the line in the Reveal Codes window. The [Tab] code remains in the line.
4. Press the **Tab** key.

   Nothing happens. No tab code is inserted. The insertion point does not move. You cannot insert a tab code without a tab setting.

You can reinsert default tab settings by using the Default tab command.

To reinsert default tab settings:

1. Open the Tab Set dialog box again by choosing Line from the Layout menu and then choosing Tab Set.
2. Choose Default and click OK.

   The default tab settings reappear. The memo header text moves back to the nearest default tab setting, at 2 inches.

You can clear individual tab settings by using the Clear Tab command or by dragging a tab marker off the Ruler.

To clear individual tab settings:

1. Open the Tab Set dialog box again by double-clicking a tab marker on the Ruler.
2. Choose the tab setting 0.5" in the Relative Position list box. This is the first tab setting to right of the left margin.
3. Choose Clear Tab.

   The 0.5-inch setting and the tab marker both disappear. The next tab to the right (1") appears in the Relative Position text box.
4. Choose Clear Tab.

   The 1-inch setting and tab marker disappear.
5. Click OK.

   The tabular material moves to the 2.5-inch measure. A new Tab Set code is inserted in the Reveal Codes window. This code is very complex, listing all the tab settings that remain on the Ruler.

To clear a tab using the Ruler:

1. Drag the tab at the 2.5-inch measure off the Ruler.

   The memo header text moves right to the next tab setting.
2. Select the tab setting at 3 inches, and drag it off the Ruler. Then drag the 3.5 inch tab off the Ruler.

   The tabular material shifts further right as tab settings are removed.

You also can clear a tab by deleting Tab Set codes.

To delete a Tab Set code:

1. Click the [Tab Set] code in the code window.
2. Press the **Delete** key.

   The default tab settings reappear. Default tabs are in effect when no other Tab Set code is present.

Setting Tabbed Columns

Tabs can be used to create tabbed columns or side-by-side vertical lists of information. Information in a columnar format, separate from the body text, often is easier to read.

Based on *The Gregg Reference Manual*, the general rules for setting up a table are:

Note: To set up large tables of columnar information, it generally is easier to use the Table feature, which is discussed in Lessons 21 and 22. The Table feature allows for more precisely centered columns.

- The table should be centered horizontally within the margins.
- Columns within the table should be spaced attractively, usually between six to ten spaces apart. A minimum of two spaces is required between columns.
- The width of a table should not exceed the width of the document's body text.
- There should be at least one blank line separating the body text of the document and the top and the bottom of the table.

The standard procedure for centering tabbed columns horizontally is provided in *The Gregg Reference Manual*, under the heading "Centering Tables Horizontally". This method, derived from typing, can be used in WordPerfect. However, the following method takes advantage of the visual and interactive qualities of WordPerfect for Windows:

- Create a guide line.

  Above the table, key a line made up of the longest item in each column. Key six spaces between each item to represent the approximate space between columns.

- Center the guide line.
- Set the tabs.

  Clear all tabs. Then, to set a left-aligned tab, drag the left tab marker to the point on the Ruler above the first character in each column in the guide line. To set a center-aligned tab, drag the center tab marker to the point on the Ruler above the center character in the column. To set a right-aligned tab, drag the right tab marker to the point on the Ruler above the last character in the column. To set a decimal tab, drag a decimal tab marker to a point on the Ruler that will allow for the alignment of the decimal point and the numbers to the right and left of it.

- Key the rest of the table.
- Delete the guide line. Be careful not to delete needed codes.

80886	Hillbrooke	79,000
97558	Alpharetta	565,000
34490	Parsons Station	94,000
76121	Dunwoody	240,000

Figure 9-7
Tabular material for Document 9-0a.wpw

To set up a table using tabbed columns:

1. Position the insertion point before the table heading "Number".

2. In the Reveal Codes space, delete the Tab Set code for this line.

3. Press **Enter**, and position the insertion point at the blank line above the table heading.

4. Begin creating the guide line. Key the longest item in each column in Figure 9-7, and insert six empty spaces between each item:

   80886   Parsons Station   565,000

Note: Positioning will depend on the typeface used.

5. Press **Home** to move the insertion point to the beginning of the guide line. Then center the guide line by pressing **Shift+F7**.

6. Open the Tab Set dialog box, choose Clear Tabs, and click OK.

7. Set three left-aligned tabs:

   Drag the Left Tab button to the point on the Ruler just above the first 8 in "80886". The dotted vertical line helps you set the tab in the correct location.

   Drag the Left Tab button to the point on the Ruler just above the first character in "Parsons".

   Drag the Left Tab button to the point on the Ruler just above the first 5 in "565,000".

8. Delete the [Center] code in the guide line.

9. The guide line, which does not include any [Tab] codes, moves back to the left margin. The table-heading line, which includes the three [Tab] codes, now is lined up on the three centered tab settings.

10. Press **Enter**, position the insertion point at the end of the table-heading line, and press **Enter** twice.

11. Key the text in Figure 9-7, pressing the **Tab** key before each item.

12. Delete the guide line and any extra [HRt] codes, being careful not to delete any Tab Set codes.

13. Save the document as *[your three-letter identifier]*9-0a.wpw.

14. Close the document.

Setting Dot Leaders

Dot leader
A series of periods before a tab or text.

Dot leaders are a series of periods that precede text or a tab. They are used commonly to guide the eye between segments of text that are widely separated on a line. You can assign dot leaders to any tab setting in the Tab Set dialog box or on the Ruler. The Ruler displays a Dot Leader button next to the tab buttons. You can turn dot leaders on and off by clicking this button.

To insert dot leaders:

1. Open the file 9-0b.wpw.

2. Choose Ruler and Reveal Codes from the View menu, if necessary.

3. Position the insertion point at the first line of the table body text, "80886".

4. Open the Tab Set dialog box.

5. Select 5" in the Relative Position list box, and check the Dot Leader Tabs box.

6. Choose Set Tab and click OK.

   Dots lead from the second to the third column.

7. Position the insertion point below the last line of the table, and key the following text, pressing the **Tab** key between each word:

45987	**Monitor**	**390,000**	**4/15**
89793	**Dunwoody**	**234,000**	**5/7**

   The dot leader tab between columns two and three is still in effect.

To set dot leader tabs on the Ruler:

1. Position the insertion point before the number "80886" in the first line of the table body.

2. Drag the 7" tab off the Ruler.

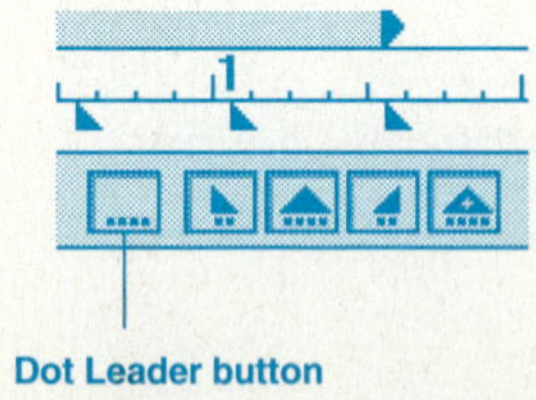

The Dot Leader button

3. Click the Dot Leader button.

   Dots appear on the tab buttons.

4. Drag the Right Tab button, which now has dot leaders, to the Ruler. Position that marker at the 7-inch measure.

   Dot leaders connect the third and fourth tabular columns.

5. Save the document as *[your three-letter identifier]*9-0b.wpw.

6. Close the document.

Evenly Spaced Tabs

Default tabs are spaced every half inch. The half-inch interval can be changed by creating evenly spaced tab settings. Use the Evenly Spaced option in the Set Tabs dialog box, and set the starting point for the beginning tab and interval.

For example, if you want tabs to begin 2 inches from the left margin and continue every 2 inches, the starting-point value would be 2, and the interval value would be 2. You also may choose the type of tab (relative or absolute; left, right, center, or decimal).

To set evenly spaced tabs:

1. Open a new file, and choose Ruler and Reveal Codes from the View menu, if necessary.

2. With the insertion point at the beginning of the document, open the Tab Set dialog box.

3. Click Clear Tabs.

4. Click Left Margin (Rel), if it is not selected.

5. Click Right Align.

6. Click Evenly Spaced.

   The Repeat Every text box appears.

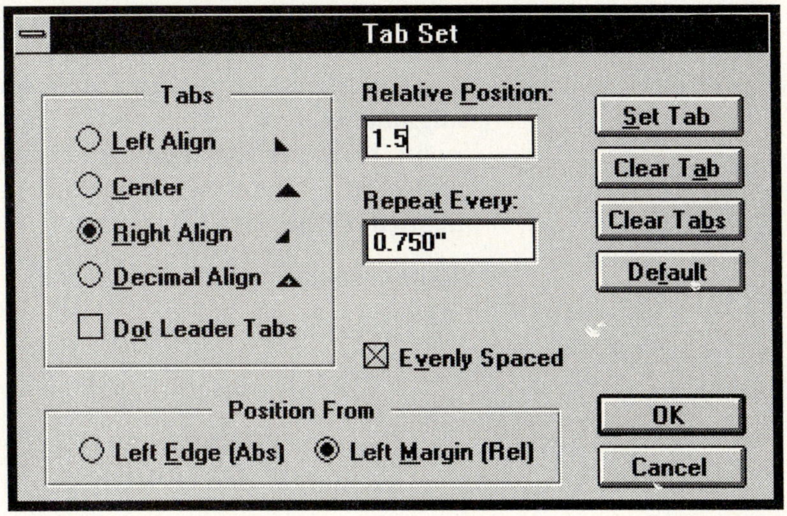

Figure 9-8
The Tab Set dialog box with the Repeat Every text box

7. Key **1.5** in the Relative Position text box, so the first tab will be 1.5 inches from the left margin (at the 2.5-inch measure).
8. Key **0.75** in the Repeat Every text box.
9. Click Set Tab.

   Tab settings appear in the Relative Position text and list boxes. Tab markers appear on the Ruler.
10. Click OK.

    You are returned to the document window, and a [Tab Set] code appears in the code window.
11. Key the text shown in Figure 9-9. Capitalize and apply bold as shown.

NEW LISTINGS BY OFFICE

	Jan	**Feb**	**Mar**	**Apr**	**May**
Buckhead	4	5	7	9	4
Downtown	6	8	9	11	13
Marietta	3	5	8	12	15
Midtown	5	7	9	11	13

Figure 9-9
Evenly spaced tabs

12. Proofread the document.
13. Save the document as *[your three-letter identifier]*9-0c.wpw.

Tab Align (The Decimal Align Character)

The Tab Align feature aligns text using a decimal tab setting and an alignment character you specify. The default character is the decimal point. However, the alignment character can be changed to a colon and used to align memo headings or clock times. Dates may be aligned on the slash (/) character.

To insert a decimal-align character:

1. Open the file 9-0d.wpw.
2. Position the insertion point after "List Price".
3. Open the Tab Set dialog box, set a Right tab 6 inches from the left margin, and click OK.
4. Press the **Tab** key, and key **Date** as a fourth column heading.
5. Position the insertion point after "79,000".
6. Choose Line from the Layout menu. Then choose Special Codes.

   The Insert Special Codes dialog box appears.

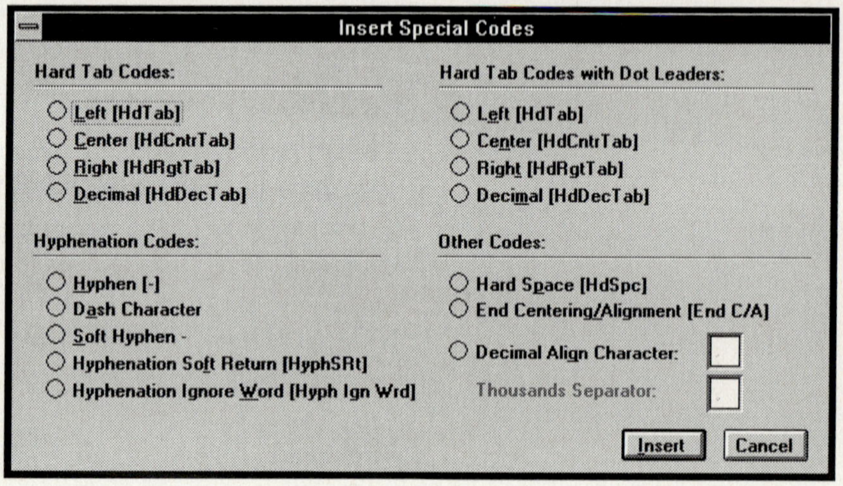

Figure 9-10
The Insert Special Codes dialog box

7. Click the Decimal Align Character button.
8. Press the **Tab** key to highlight the text box, and key / (the slash character).
9. Click Insert.
10. Drag a decimal-aligned tab (without dot leaders) to the Ruler at the 6.75 inch measure.

11. At the end of each row in the table body, insert a [Tab] code, and key the following dates:

    5/17

    5/29

    6/1

    6/7

    The dates in the fourth column now align on the slash. They are right-aligned under the "Date" heading.

Hard Tabs

When you want to change the type of one tab within a single line, use a hard tab. For instance, you may want the next tab to be center-aligned, without changing that tab setting itself. Or you may want dot leaders on one line only. A hard tab will:

- move to the next tab setting
- change the alignment of the tab in that line only, according to the type of hard tab you select: Left [HdTab], Right [HdRgtTab], Center [HdCntrTab], Decimal [HdDecTab], or each of the previous tabs with dot leaders.

To insert a hard tab:

1. Delete the second date (5/29), and key **?** in its place.

   "?" lines up under the 5.

2. Position the insertion point on the [Dec Tab] code before "?".

3. Choose Line from the Layout menu. Then choose Special Codes.

4. In the Insert Special Codes dialog box, click Left [HdTab] in the Hard Tab Codes group.

   If you choose from the Hard Tab Codes with Dot Leaders group, dot leaders will accompany the next [Tab] code.

5. Click Insert.

   A [HdTab] code is inserted. "?" lines up under the slash, as if the tab setting were a left tab. No other tabs are affected.

6. Position the insertion point after the last date in the table, and press **Enter** twice to start a new paragraph. Then key the following to explain the unknown date:

   The Alpharetta listing was signed in late May (the listing sheet is currently with the agent).

7. Save the document as *[your three-letter identifier]*9-0d.wpw.
8. Print the document.
9. Close the document and exit WordPerfect (unless you will be doing the following exercises immediately).

Key Terms

Absolute tab	Tab buttons
Dot leader	Tab setting
Relative tab	Tab marker
Tab	

Exercises

Exercise 9.1

1. Start WordPerfect, if necessary.
2. Open a new file, key the following two-line title, and center it:

   Allatoona Resorts and Condominiums
   Introductory Rates

   Triple-space after the heading by pressing **Enter** three times.
3. Use the Tab Set dialog box to set column-heading tabs, using 3- and 5-inch center tabs:
   A. Open the Tab Set dialog box by double-clicking a tab marker on the Ruler.
   B. Choose Clear Tabs.
   C. Choose Center alignment and Left Margin (Rel).
   D. Key **3** in the Position text box and choose Set Tab.
   E. Key **5** in the Position text box, choose Set Tab, and click OK.
4. Key the following two-line column headings, pressing the **Tab** key once before each part:

3 nights,	**Single add-on**
double occupancy	**per night**

5. Double-space after the column headings, and key the following text, pressing the **Tab** key before each dollar amount:

North Beach Towers	**$378**	**$36.75**
Plantation Parlor Suites	**$432**	**$42**
Buck Island Cottages	**$455**	**$43.75**
Country Club Homes	**$519**	**$49**

6. Change the tab settings for the dollar amounts to decimal alignment with dot leaders:
   A. Position the insertion point before the word "North".
   B. Open the Tab Set dialog box.
   C. Select 3" in the Position list box.
   D. Check Dot Leader Tabs and Decimal Align and choose Set Tab.
   E. Select 5" in the Position list box.
   F. Check Dot Leader Tabs and Decimal Align and choose Set Tab.
   G. Click OK.
7. Save the document as *[your three-letter identifier]*9-1.wpw.
8. Print the document.
9. Close the document and exit WordPerfect (unless you will be doing the following exercises immediately).

Exercise 9.2

1. Start WordPerfect, if necessary.
2. Open the file 9-2.wpw, and choose Ruler and Reveal Codes from the View menu.
3. Refer to Figure 9-11 at the end of this exercise, and key a guide line for the tabular material, starting two lines above the last paragraph. (Remember to place six spaces between each element in the guide line.)

   Bank of the South   8.375   Points

4. Center the guide line by pressing **Shift+F7**.
5. Scroll until the guide line is just below the Ruler. Position the insertion point at the beginning of the guide line.
6. Open the Tab Set dialog box and choose Clear Tabs.
7. Using the Ruler, set three tabs for the table:
   A. Drag the Left Tab button to the Ruler, just above "Bank" (near the 2.25-inch measure).
   B. Drag the Center Tab button to the Ruler, just right of the "3" in "8.375" (near the 5-inch measure).
   C. Drag the Center Tab button to the Ruler, just right of the "i" in "Points" (near the 6-inch measure).

8. In the Tab Set dialog box, check Left Edge (Abs) to align the tabs from the left edge of the paper.

9. Key the tabular material in Figure 9-11, pressing the **Tab** key before each word.

10. Delete the guide line and the [Center] code, making sure not to delete the [Tab Set] code.

11. Add a line space between the column headings and the body of the table.

12. Change this letter to modified-block style:

    A. Select the date code.

    B. In the Tab Set dialog box, click Clear Tabs and specify an absolute left-aligned tab. Key **4.25** in the Absolute Position text box (the center of the page). Choose Set Tab and click OK.

    C. Insert a [Tab] code before the date code.

    D. Position the insertion point at the end of the document.

    E. Delete the center tabs from the Ruler. Drag the left tab to the middle of the page (the 4¼-inch measure).

    F. Following the style in Appendix B, key the following closing:

    Sincerely,
    FIVE POINTS REALTY

    Bud Porter
    President
    [your initials]

13. Adjust the alignment in the body of the table:

    A. Select the body of the table (from the [Tab] code before "First" through the "0" in the last line).

    B. Drag a Decimal Tab button to each of the Center tab markers on the Ruler.

    C. Position the insertion point at the [Dec Tab] code before the "n" in "neg".

    D. Open the Insert Special Codes dialog box.

    E. Check the Right box in the Hard Tab Codes group and choose Insert.

14. At the beginning of the document, change the side margins to 1½ inches.

The absolute tabs controlling the table, date, and closing will not change.

15. Proofread the document.

16. Save the document as *[your three-letter identifier]*9-2.wpw.

17. Print the document.

18. Close the document and exit WordPerfect (unless you will be doing the following exercises immediately).

Figure 9-11

Bank	Rate	Points
First Georgia	8.5	3
Home Fidelity	8.375	3.5
Bank of the South	8.75	neg
Marietta Savings	9.0	0

Exercise 9.3

1. Start WordPerfect, if necessary.
2. Open the file 9-3.wpw, and choose Ruler and Reveal Codes from the View menu.
3. Format the document as a memo from Bud Porter to Della Crandon, Ann Delbridge, Mary Rigdon, and John Solomon, dated today.
4. Set evenly spaced right-aligned tabs, repeated every ½ inch, to accomodate the temperature table in Figure 9-12 at the end of this exercise.
5. Key the temperature data in Figure 9-12 in tabular columns, beginning the heading in column 2.
6. Underline column headings, apply bold to the average daily high temperatures, and apply italics to the average daily lows. Apply bold to the table title.
7. Proofread the document.
8. Save the document as *[your three-letter identifier]*9-3.wpw.

9. Print the document.
10. Close the document and exit WordPerfect (unless you will be doing the following exercises immediately).

Figure 9-12

AVERAGE DAILY TEMPERATURE (F)

ATLANTA

	Jan	Feb	Mar	Apr	May	June	July	Aug	Sep	Oct	Nov	Dec
High	**52**	**54**	**63**	**72**	**79**	**86**	**88**	**86**	**83**	**72**	**61**	**52**
Low	36	38	43	52	61	67	70	70	65	54	43	38

Exercise 9.4

1. Start WordPerfect, if necessary.
2. Open a new file, and choose Ruler and Reveal Codes from the View menu.
3. Key the memo in Figure 9-13 at the end of this exercise, following the style shown in Appendix C.
4. Center the table horizontally.
5. Align the column headings as shown in Figure 9-13.

   The first column heading is left-aligned.

   The second through fourth column headings are centered.
6. Align the columns in the body of the table as shown in Figure 9-13.

   Column one is left-aligned.

   Column two is centered.

   Column three is right-aligned with dot leader tabs.

   Column four is decimal-aligned with dot leaders.
7. Format the column headings and columns one and four in bold.
8. Spell-check and proofread the document.

9. Create a document summary.
10. Save the document as *[your three-letter identifier]*9-4.wpw.
11. Print the document.
12. Close the document and exit WordPerfect (unless you will be doing the following exercise immediately).

Figure 9-13

MEMO TO: ~~File~~ Della Crandon, Ann Delbridge, Mary Rigdon, John Soloman

FROM: Bud Porter

DATE: ~~December 17, 199-~~

SUBJECT: 12-month Sales and Commissions

The following list represents the last fiscal year's sales ~~of~~ for our seven full-time sales agents~~ during the last 12 months~~.

Agent	**Units**	**Dollar Sales**	**Commissions (3%)**
G. Crane	12	1,890,756	**56,722.68**
A. Delbridge	16	2,521,008	**75,630.24**
M. Washington	11	1,733,193	**51,995.79**
H. Smith	13	2,048,319	**61,449.57**
I. Hightower	24	3,781,512	**113,445.36**
R. Porter	28	4,411,764	**132,352.92**
J. Solomon	22	3,466,386	**103,991.58**

Exercise 9.5

1. Start WordPerfect, if necessary.
2. Open a new file, and choose Ruler and Reveal Codes from the View menu.
3. Key Document 9-5 at the end of this exercise as shown, following the style shown in Appendix C.
4. Center the table horizontally, making the first column right-aligned and the second column left-aligned.
5. Apply bold, italic, and underlining to column headings.
6. Full-justify the memo.
7. Set the heads, "**PRIZES!!**", and "**HIGHER COMMISSIONS!!**" flush right.
8. Center-align and apply bold to the last line, which begins "We wish you".
9. Set left and right margins to 1¼ inches.
10. Spell-check and proofread the document.
11. Turn hyphenation on.
12. Create a document summary. Write your own abstract. Then print the document summary.
13. Save the document as *[your three-letter identifier]*9-5.wpw.
14. Print the document.
15. Close the document and exit WordPerfect.

Document 9-5

MEMO TO: Sales Associates

FROM: Bud Porter

DATE: December 17, 19–

SUBJECT: Sales Incentives

I am pleased to announce a sales incentive program that will prove to be fun and profitable for successful sales associates.

PRIZES!!

Five Points Realty will award prizes to associates whose closing sales between January 1 and June 30 next year reach the goals listed below. Closing totals include the actual selling prices of properties you have listed or sold.

Sales Goal	**Prize**
$500,000	Theater Tickets
$750,000	Resort Weekend
$1,000,000	Resort Week

Theater prizes include a pair of tickets to any performance at the Atlanta Civic Center.

Resort prizes include lodging for two at Allatoona Lake Resorts. The Weekend prize includes three days and two nights. The Week prize includes seven days and six nights.

HIGHER COMMISSIONS!!

In addition, we will increase sales commissions for our most successful associates. As you know, sales associates normally are paid fifty percent of the commission earned by a transaction they have listed or sold. For the first half of next year, commissions will be as follows:

Sales Level	***% of Commission***
to $500,000	50%
$500,000 +	52%
$750,000 +	55%
$1,000,000 +	60%

Sales up to $500,000 will earn 50% of the transaction commission. Sales between $500,000 and $750,000 will earn 52%. Sales between $750,000 and $1,000,000 will earn 55%. Sales over $1,000,000 will earn 60% of the commission due our agency.

We wish you a Happy and Lucrative New Year!!

Lesson 10

Paragraph Formatting

Indents, like margins, tabs, and line spacing, are a paragraph-formatting feature. An *indent* is the distance between the sides of a paragraph and the margins. Indents are used to emphasize or separate paragraphs in a document.

Objectives

- Describe different types of indentation.
- Use first-line indents.
- Use left indents.
- Use double indents.
- Use hanging indents.
- Use the margin-release code.

Indenting

Indent
The distance between the sides of a paragraph and the margins.

You may format existing paragraphs or key new paragraphs using four indentation options. These options depend on the insertion-point position, text justification, and tab settings.

In WordPerfect, indenting takes effect at the insertion point. WordPerfect does not move an indentation code to the beginning of a paragraph automatically. This means that you should position the insertion point at the beginning of a paragraph and then choose an indentation option.

Indenting works only when text is left- or full-justified, because indenting left-aligns every line of a paragraph along the same tab stop. Right- or center-justified text creates a ragged left edge. In WordPerfect, indenting has no effect on right- or center-justified text.

Regardless of the indentation you use, the distance the text is indented from the left depends on the tab settings. You can change this distance by changing the tabs. You even can use multiple indentation codes to indent text more than one tab.

Keying Text after Indenting

When you have not yet keyed the text you want to indent, you can choose an indentation option and then key the text. When you press **Enter,** the indentation will end, and the insertion point will return to the left margin.

Methods of Indenting

There are five ways to indent text. With the insertion point at the beginning of a paragraph:

- A tab ([Tab]) indents the first line of a paragraph to the next tab setting. The rest of the paragraph aligns with the left margin.
- A left indent ([Indent]) indents all the lines of a paragraph from the left margin to the next tab setting.

- A double indent ([Dbl Indent]) indents all the lines of a paragraph from both margins.
- A hanging indent ([Indent][MarRel]) keeps the first line at the left margin, but indents the rest of the paragraph to the next tab setting.
- A Margin Release ([MarRel]) moves the first line one tab stop left of the left margin, creating an indent for the rest of the paragraph.

These paragraphs were created with 1" left and right margins, default tab settings (every 0.5"), and full justification. This first paragraph is not indented.

This paragraph has a first-line indent. Simply begin the paragraph with a Tab. The rest of the lines are aligned flush left.

This paragraph is left indented. All you need to do is begin the paragraph with a left-indent code [Indent]. Either choose Paragraph from the Layout menu and then choose Indent, or press **F7**. Every line of the paragraph is aligned at the first tab setting.

This paragraph is double indented. Notice that every line is one tab setting from both left and right margins. Double indenting is used commonly to set off long quotations from the rest of a discussion.

This is a paragraph with a hanging indent. The first line is flush left, but the rest of the lines are indented one tab. Hanging indents are used commonly in bibliographies and references.

This is a paragraph with a margin release. The first line is moved into the left margin, and the rest of the lines are flush left. Margin releases are used commonly to create a side-by-side text heading for a paragraph of text.

Figure 10-1
Methods of indenting

First-Line Indent

A first-line indent clearly marks the beginning of a paragraph. Some writers prefer this style. To make text seem more unified, you can use first-line indents without blank lines between paragraphs.

To indent the first lines of paragraphs:

1. Start WordPerfect, and open the file 10-0.wpw.

2. Turn on the Ruler, and choose Reveal Codes from the View menu.

3. Position the insertion point at the beginning of the paragraph that begins "Basically". Remember, to move up or down one paragraph, press **Ctrl+UpArrow** or **Crtl+DownArrow**.

4. Press the **Tab** key.

   WordPerfect inserts a [Tab] code. The first line of the paragraph is indented. The rest of the paragraph aligns at the left margin.

5. Repeat steps 3 and 4 for the paragraphs that begin "In the court case", "[The court] is unwilling", and "Under".

Left Indent

A left-indented paragraph has a wider left margin than normal paragraphs. Left indenting often is used to emphasize special material.

To left-indent one paragraph:

1. Position the insertion point at the [Tab] code before the paragraph that begins "Basically".

2. Choose Paragraph from the Layout menu and then choose Indent.

   The paragraph shifts to the right, as if the left margin was moved to the next tab setting.

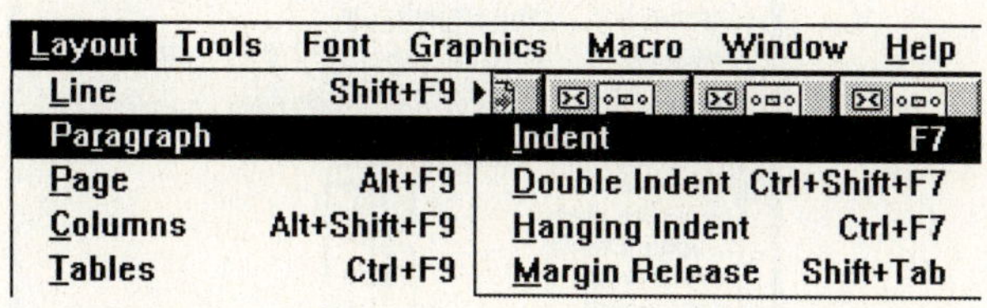

Figure 10-2
The Paragraph cascading menu

3. Position the insertion point at the [Tab] code before the paragraph that begins "In the court".

4. Press **F7** to indent this paragraph one tab from the left.

   In the Reveal Codes space, each of the two paragraphs begins with an [Indent] code.

5. Delete the [HRt] between these two paragraphs.

Left-Indenting List Items

Left indents are used commonly in creating list items. Typically, paragraphs in lists are numbered or bulleted. The indent separates the text from its number or bullet.

Numbered List
A series of numbered items treated as separate paragraphs.

In a *numbered list*, each numbered item is treated as a separate paragraph. Numbered lists are used when the sequence of items is important, or when you need to refer to items by number. The procedures in this textbook are examples of numbered lists. The text of each step is left-indented from the step number.

Bulleted List
A series of bulleted items treated as separate paragraphs.

Bullet
A special character (such as a bold dot) that calls attention to an item.

A *bulleted list* is similar to a numbered list, but items begin with bullets instead of numbers. A *bullet* is a special character, such as a star (*), dash (–), or bold dot (•), that helps call attention to an item. Bulleted lists are used when the sequence of the items is not important. For instance, the list of the five different methods of indenting on pages 10-1 and 10-2 is a bulleted list.

The quickest way to create a bulleted list is to use the Bullet button on the Features Button Bar. In WordPerfect, you can display different Button Bars. Just as you choose commands from the default Button Bar for spell-checking, copying or pasting, you can choose Bullet from a different Button Bar, and WordPerfect makes the selected text into a bulleted list item.

To create a bulleted list using the Bullet button:

1. Choose Button Bar Setup from the View menu and then choose Select.

   The Select Button Bar dialog box appears.

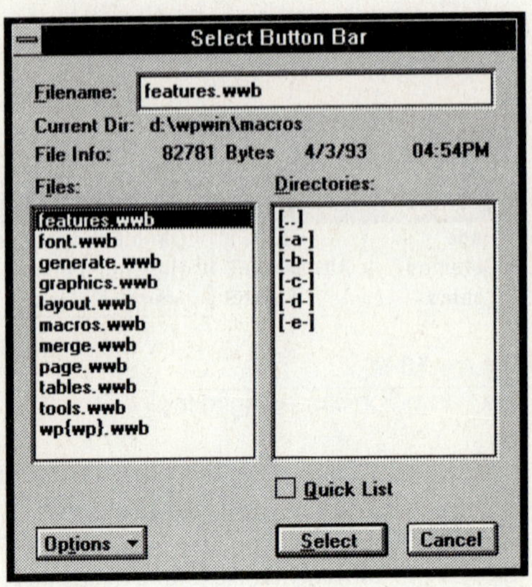

Figure 10-3
The Select Button Bar dialog box

2. Double-click on features.wwb.

   The Button Bar now contains a Bullet button.

Figure 10-4
Features Button Bar

3. Move to the paragraph that begins "As you know". Then:

   - Replace the comma after "Therefore" with a colon.
   - Capitalize the A in "ask".
   - With the insertion point immediately before "Ask", press **Enter** twice to start the first list item.

4. Click the Bullet on the Button Bar.

   A bullet is inserted, and the list item is indented.

5. Position the insertion point before the word "Make", press **Enter** twice, and click Bullet.

   A second bulleted item is formed.

6. Position the insertion point before the word "Once", press **Enter** twice, and click Bullet.

   A third bulleted item is formed.

7. Position the insertion point between the words "buyer," and "and". Then:

   - Delete the comma, and key a period after "buyer".
   - Delete "and".
   - Capitalize "should".

8. Position the insertion point before "Should", press **Enter** twice, and click Bullet.

   The last bulleted item is formed. The left-indent code [Indent] separates the text of each item from its bullet.

9. Restore the default Button Bar by repeating Steps 1 and 2, selecting wp{wp}.wwb.

> **Choosing Special Bullets**
>
> The Bullet button on the Features Button Bar inserts a standard bullet (•) at the beginning of a list item. The BulletDf button lets you choose another symbol, such as a diamond (◆) or an arrow (➨), instead of the standard bullet. When you click BulletDf, an Insert Bullet dialog box is opened from which you can select a new bullet symbol. After you select the new symbol, WordPerfect uses it whenever you click Bullet.
>
> Depending on the fonts installed on your computer or printer, you will have a variety of symbols for use in bulleted lists.

Double Indent

When you choose Double Indent, a paragraph is indented one tab setting from the left margin. It also is indented 0.5 inches from the right margin.

A double indent is used commonly to set off long quotations. These quotations (sometimes called extracts) often are set in smaller type, as well.

To double-indent:

1. If necessary, full-justify the document.
2. Position the insertion point at the [Tab] code in the paragraph that begins "[The court] is unwilling".
3. Choose Paragraph from the Layout menu, and then choose Double Indent.

   The paragraph (a quotation from the court decision) is double indented. A [Dbl Indent] code appears in the Reveal Codes space.
4. Position the insertion point at the [Tab] code that begins the next paragraph, and press **Ctrl+Shift+F7**.

   The paragraph is double indented using a keyboard shortcut.

   Notice that the right edge of the double-indented paragraphs are 0.5 inches from the right margin.
5. Delete the blank line ([HRt]) between the two double-indented paragraphs.

Hanging Indent

A hanging indent keeps the first line in a paragraph at the left margin (or at the current tab setting). The remaining lines of the paragraph are indented to the next tab setting.

Hanging indents are used commonly in bibliography entries and source references.

To format text with a hanging indent:

1. Position the insertion point before the last paragraph, which begins "Information".

2. Choose Paragraph from the Layout menu, and then choose Hanging Indent.

   The paragraph is formatted with a hanging indent. In the Reveal Codes space, two codes are inserted: [Indent] and [Mar Rel].

3. Delete both the [Indent] and [Mar Rel] codes and press **Ctrl+F7**.

   The paragraph is formatted with a hanging indent again. The [Indent] code shifts the entire paragraph one tab setting from the left. Then the [Mar Rel] code (margin release) moves the text of the first line one tab setting back to the left. Together, the two codes produce the hanging indent.

Margin Release

Margin Release is like a reverse tab. It moves the insertion point and accompanying text one tab stop to the left, sometimes even beyond the left margin.

Margin Release can be used in a number of ways:

- A hanging indent uses [Indent] and [Margin Release] codes together.
- When text is keyed in a narrow column, Margin Release can be used to move headings into the left margin.
- Margin Release can be used instead of deleting a [Tab] or [Indent].

To practice using Margin Release:

1. Position the insertion point before the last paragraph, which begins "Information".

2. Delete the [Indent] and [Mar Rel] codes.

3. Choose Paragraph from the Layout menu, and then choose Margin Release.

   The first line of the paragraph is moved into the left margin one tab stop.

4. Delete the [Mar Rel] code and press **Shift+Tab**.

   Shift+Tab is the keyboard shortcut for inserting the [Mar Rel] code.

5. Position the insertion point at the [Mar Rel] code.

6. Choose Paragraph from the Layout menu and then choose Indent (or press **F7**).

   You just created a hanging indent at the left margin.

7. Examine the document.

   The second page begins within the bulleted list.

8. To keep the bulleted list and its introductory paragraph together:

   - Position the insertion point before the paragraph that begins "As you know".
   - Press **Crtl+Enter** to insert a [HPg] code (hard page) that will start a new page.
   - Change the top margin of the second page to 1 inch.

9. Save the document as *[your three-letter identifier]*10-0.wpw.

10. Print the document.

11. Close the document and exit WordPerfect (unless you will be doing the following exercises immediately).

Table 10-1: Keyboard Shortcuts for Indenting (Paragraph Formatting)

Keyboard Shortcut	Action
F7	Left Indent
Ctrl+Shift+F7	Double Indent
Crtl+F7	Hanging Indent
Shift+Tab	Margin Release

Key Terms

Bullet	Indent
Bulleted list	Numbered list

Exercises

Exercise 10.1

1. Start WordPerfect, if necessary.
2. Open the file 10-1.wpw, which begins "DIRECTIONS TO FIVE POINTS' OFFICES".
3. Full-justify the document.
4. Left-indent the four paragraphs that describe each office's role ("The Downtown office", "The Marietta office", "The Buckhead office", and "The Midtown office"):
   A. Position the insertion point at the beginning of a paragraph.
   B. Press **F7**.
5. For each of the four paragraphs that gives directions to an office, double-indent twice and first-line-indent, as well:
   A. Position the insertion point at the beginning of a paragraph.
   B. Press **Ctrl+Shift+F7** twice.
   C. Press the **Tab** key.
6. Spell-check the document.
7. Save the document as *[your three-letter identifier]*10-1.wpw.
8. Print the document.
9. Close the document and exit WordPerfect (unless you will be doing the following exercises immediately).

Exercise 10.2

1. Start WordPerfect, if necessary.
2. Open the file 10-2.wpw, which begins "OUR ROLE".
3. Center the title, "OUR ROLE", and format it as bold.
4. Indent the first line of the first paragraph:
   A. Position the insertion point before the word "Five".
   B. Press the **Tab** key.
5. Format the second, third, and fourth paragraphs which begin *"Improving"*, *"Providing"*, and *"Improving"*, respectively, with hanging indents:

A. Position the insertion point at the beginning of a paragraph.

B. Choose Paragraph from the Layout menu, and then choose Hanging Indent (or press **Ctrl+F7**).

6. Add the two paragraphs in Figure 10-5, which appears at the end of this exercise, to document 10-2.wpw. Begin each paragraph with an [Indent] and [Mar Rel] code:

   A. At the end of the document, press **Enter** twice, if necessary, to start a new paragraph.

   B. Press **F7**, and then press **Shift+Tab**.

   C. Key the paragraph that begins *"Tracking"*.

   D. Repeat steps A and B. Then key the paragraph that begins *"Adjusting"*.

7. Spell-check the document.

8. Save the document as *[your three-letter identifier]*10-2.wpw.

9. Print the document.

10. Close the document and exit WordPerfect (unless you will be doing the following exercises immediately).

Figure 10-5

Tracking all expenditures. We constantly check all expenditures to make sure that your costs are as low as possible, and we ensure that all necessary and budgeted expenditures are made.

Adjusting the rental fee. We adjust the rental fee as expenses and the market dictate to produce the highest level of income for you from your property.

Exercise 10.3

1. Start WordPerfect, if necessary.

2. Open the file 10-3.wpw, which begins "OUR RESPONSIBILITIES".

3. Full-justify the document.

4. Center the title, and format it as bold and italic.

5. Format the five numbered paragraphs as bold. Also, left-indent to separate the text from its number. (Be sure to delete the spaces that now follow each number.)

6. Double-indent each paragraph that follows a numbered paragraph.

7. Position the insertion point at the end of the document, key the two paragraphs in Figure 10-6 (which appears at the end of this exercise), and format the paragraphs you keyed to match the rest of the document. Adjust line spacing as needed.

8. Spell-check the document.

9. Save the document as *[your three-letter identifier]*10-3.wpw.

10. Print the document.

11. Close the document and exit WordPerfect (unless you will be doing the following exercises immediately).

Figure 10-6

```
6.    We keep appropriate accounts and provide monthly reports for each
piece of property Five Points manages.

Again, through our networked database, we always have accurate and
appropriate records. Our detailed monthly reports provide you with all the
information you need to ensure that your property is managed profitably
and effectively.
```

Exercise 10.4

1. Start WordPerfect, if necessary.

2. Open the file 10-4.wpw, which begins "ATLANTA GUIDE-BOOKS".

3. Center the title, and format it as underlined.

4. Format the last three paragraphs with hanging indents. These paragraphs are bibliographic references and begin "Bulkin", "*Fodors's*", and "*Mobil*".

5. Position the insertion point at the end of the document, key Figure 10-7, which appears at the end of this exercise, and format it to match the other bibliographic references.
6. Spell-check the document.
7. Create a document summary and print it.
8. Save the document as *[your three-letter identifier]*10-4.wpw.
9. Print the document.
10. Close the document and exit WordPerfect (unless you will be doing the following exercise immediately).

Figure 10-7

`Schemmel, William, ` *`Georgia: Off the Beaten Track`*`, The Globe Pequot Press, Chester, CT, 1989.`

Exercise 10.5

1. Start WordPerfect, if necessary.
2. Open the file 10-5.wpw, which is a letter to Mrs. Danielle Lawson.
3. Format this letter in modified-block style according to Appendix B. Use a 2-inch top margin on the first page and a 1-inch top margin on the continuing page.
4. Clear all tabs. Then set absolute left-aligned tabs at the 4¼-inch measure for the date and closing.
5. Insert date text.
6. Set relative left-aligned tabs at the 1-inch, 1½-inch, and 2-inch measures for the rest of the document (0", 0.5", and 1" from the left margin).
7. Full-justify the document.
8. Double-indent the long quotation, which is the third body paragraph.
9. Format the last paragraph, which begins *"Number"*, with a hanging indent.
10. Position the insertion point at the end of the document, and key the paragraphs in Figure 10-8, which appears at the end of this exercise.

- Format the first two of these paragraphs, which begin "*Student/teacher*" and "*Teacher*", with hanging indents.
- Format the next paragraph, which begins "We hope", as a normal body paragraph.

11. Format the closing of the letter in modified-block style (see step 3, above).
12. First-line-indent each body paragraph, but do not change the hanging indents.
13. Spell-check the document.
14. Turn Hyphenation on for the document. Use the default hyphenation zone.
15. Save the document as *[your three-letter identifier]*10-5.wpw.
16. Print the document.
17. Close the document and exit WordPerfect.

Figure 10-8

Student/teacher ratio: grades K-3, 21.5:1; grades 4-6, 26:1; grades 7-12, 23:1.

Teacher salaries: minimum, $21,000; maximum, $41,304.

We hope this information helps. We have also enclosed some information on specific areas in the greater Atlanta metropolitan area. I will be calling you within the next few days to begin working toward a smooth transition to your new home.

Module 3

Working with Text and Documents

Lessons

Lesson 11

Moving and Copying Text

Objectives

- Use the Clipboard.
- Cut, copy, and paste text.
- Move and copy text with the mouse.
- Move, copy, and delete tabular columns.
- Append text to the Clipboard.

One of the most useful features of word processing is the ability to move text from one part of a document to another, and to copy text from one part of a document to another, without having to rekey the entire document. In WordPerfect, there are several ways to move and copy text quickly. This lesson introduces the Cut, Copy, and Paste commands, as well as a special Windows feature–the Clipboard.

The Clipboard

Clipboard
A temporary electronic holding area, or buffer, in the computer memory that stores text or graphics for later use.

The *Clipboard* is a temporary electronic holding area, or buffer, in the computer memory that stores text or graphics. You send information to the Clipboard with the Cut or Copy commands. Information stored on the Clipboard can be retrieved and inserted anywhere in the on-screen document. It remains on the Clipboard and can be used again and again to insert additional copies in other locations or in other documents.

The contents of the Clipboard remain unchanged until you do one of the following:

- Perform a new cut or copy procedure.
- Exit Windows.
- Turn off the computer's power.

Information stored on the Clipboard is not lost, however, if you exit WordPerfect or switch to another Windows application while WordPerfect is running. This feature allows the transfer of information from a WordPerfect document to another application or from another application into a WordPerfect document. For example, you can copy numbers from a spreadsheet (such as Lotus 1-2-3 or Excel) and paste them into a report you are creating in WordPerfect.

Copy
To store a copy of selected text or graphics on the Clipboard for future use.

Cut
To delete selected text or graphics and store it on the Clipboard.

Paste
To insert a copy of the Clipboard's contents at the insertion point.

Cut, Copy, and Paste

The Cut and Paste commands are the computer equivalents of using scissors and tape to rearrange text in a document. In WordPerfect and other Windows applications, the Cut and Copy commands transfer information to the Clipboard. When you *copy* selected text, that text is duplicated on the Clipboard but is not deleted from the document. When you *cut* selected text, it is removed from the document and stored on the Clipboard. When you *paste* text, you insert a copy of

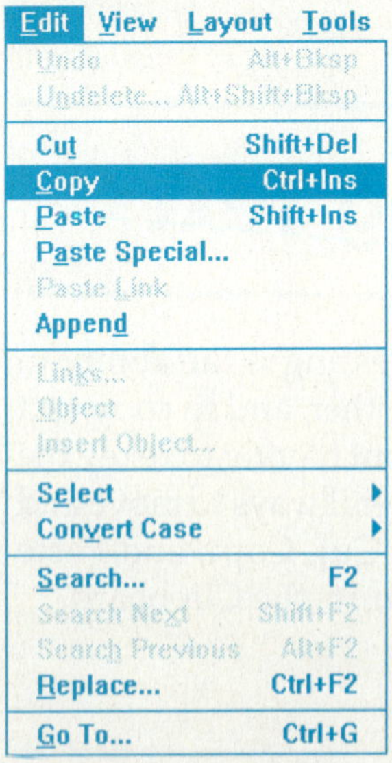

The Edit menu

the Clipboard's contents at the insertion point in the current document. Use the Paste command to complete a copy or move procedure.

Selecting Text to Copy or Move

"Lesson 5: Revising Text" explains how to select text. When you select text to be copied or moved, be sure to include the blank space after a word or sentence or the blank line at the end of a paragraph to preserve the correct spacing of the document after the move. If you neglect to select the space or line at the end of the selection, you will need to go back to the place where the block came from and manually delete it. Likewise, when you paste the selection in a new place, you will need to add the extra line or space. Although inserting and deleting extra spaces and lines is not a big job on small documents, it can become tedious when revising long documents.

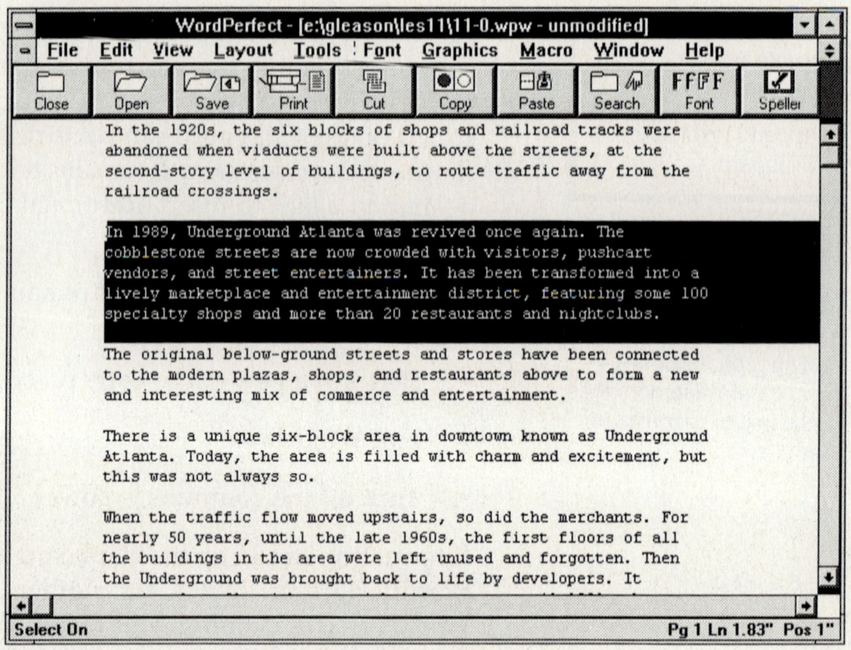

Figure 11-1
A selected paragraph

If you use double-click to select a word, triple-click to select a sentence, and quadruple-click to select a paragraph, the extra space or line is selected along with the text automatically. If you are selecting blocks of more than one word, sentence, or paragraph, you will need to make sure that the selection block includes the extra space or line.

Selecting Formatting Codes

If you need to copy or move a paragraph or sentence that has been formatted in a special way, be sure to include the formatting codes as part of the selected block. For example, if you want to move a table that contains tabular columns, you need to make sure the Tab Set code is included in the selection. If it is not included, the columns will be formatted incorrectly after the move.

To include formatting codes when copying or moving selected text, turn on Reveal Codes, click the beginning code, and then, while holding down the **Shift** key, position the insertion point at the end of the block. In the Reveal Codes space, you will see the code [Select] at the beginning of the selection and a highlighted block at the end of the selection.

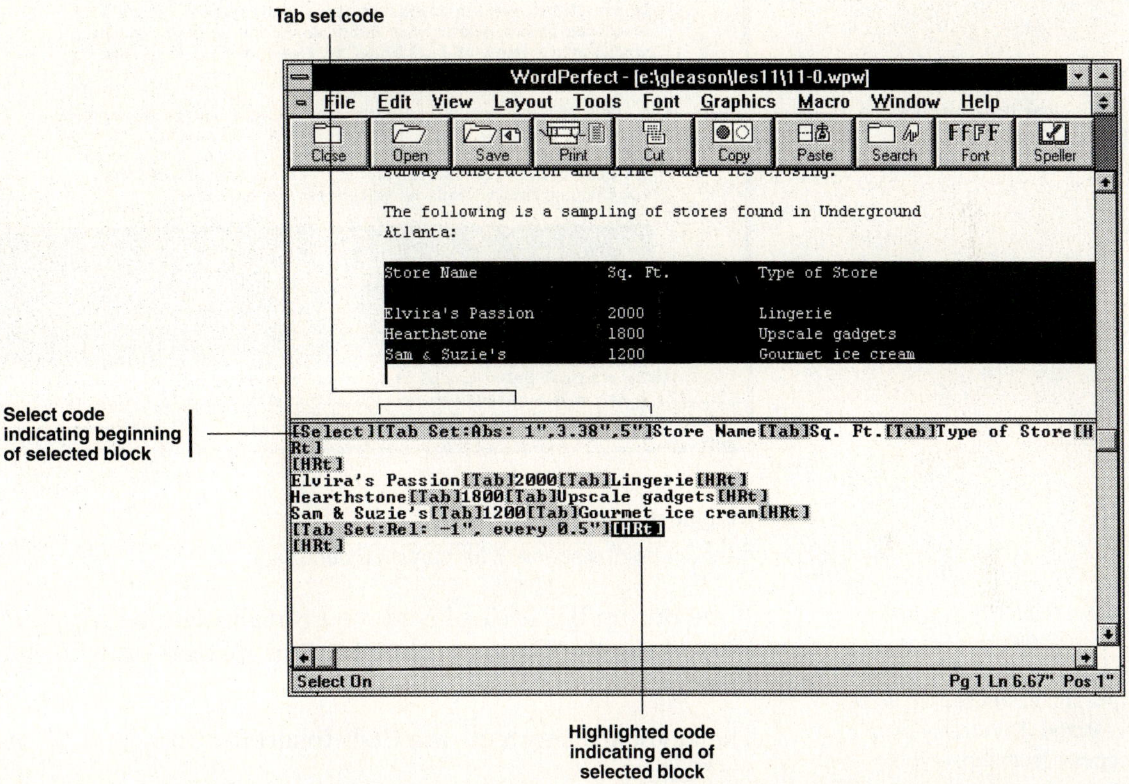

Figure 11-2
The Reveal Codes space

Copying a Block of Text

To copy a block of text (a few words, a sentence, or an entire page), select it as described above, choose Copy from the Edit menu to place a copy of the selected text on the Clipboard, position the insertion point at the location where you want the copy to appear, and choose Paste from the Edit menu.

When you paste text, position the insertion point immediately in front of the first word that follows the place where the text will go. If you position the insertion point on a blank line or in front of a space, the pasted text will be positioned incorrectly, making it necessary for you to add a space or line before the text manually, and delete a space or line after the text. An exception is if you are pasting text at the end of a document. You normally will need to adjust the spacing manually in this case.

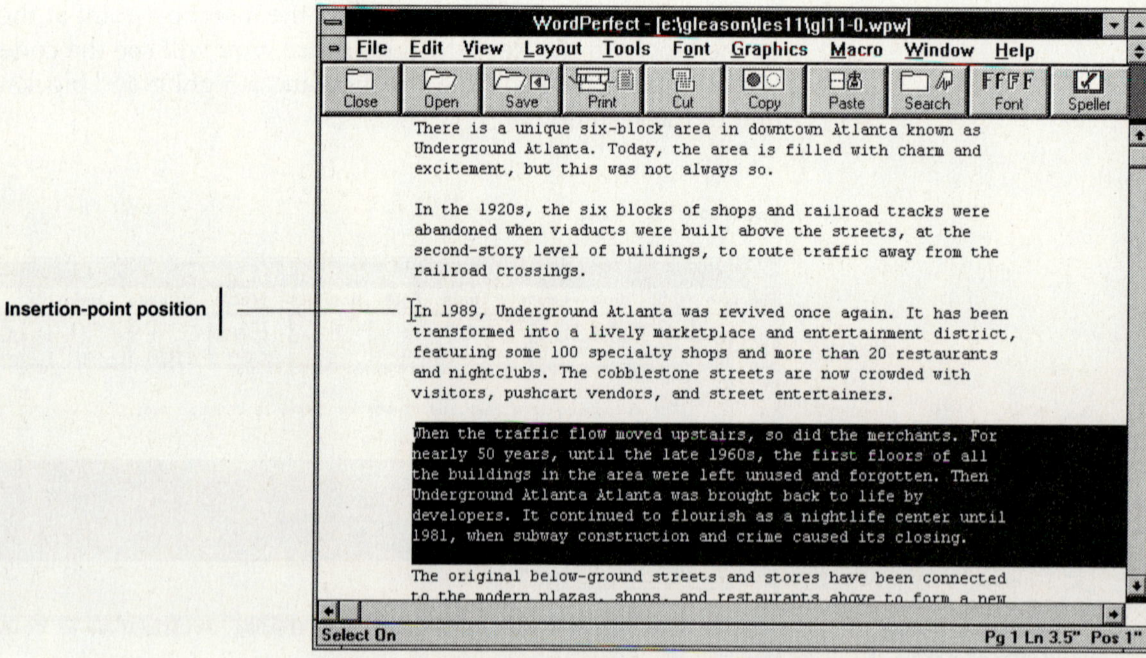

Figure 11-3
Insertion-point placement for pasting a paragraph

Note: If the Paste command is dimmed when you try to choose it, some text in your document is selected. To remedy this, reposition the insertion point where you want the text to go, and choose the Paste command again.

If the Button Bar is displayed, you can shorten the copy procedure by clicking the Copy or Paste buttons instead of using the menu commands.

The keyboard shortcuts are **Ctrl+Insert** for Copy and **Shift+Insert** for Paste.

To copy a block of text:

1. Start WordPerfect, if necessary.

2. Open the file 11-0.wpw.

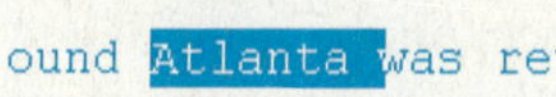

A selected word

3. Double-click the word "Atlanta" in the second paragraph on the first line.

   Notice that the blank space following "Atlanta" is included in the selection.

The Copy button

4. Choose Copy from the Edit menu.

   If the Button Bar is displayed, you can click the Copy button instead.

5. In the fourth paragraph, position the insertion point to the left of the word "known" in the phrase "six-block area in downtown known".

   There should be a space between "downtown" and the insertion point.

The Paste button

6. Choose Paste from the Edit menu (or click Paste on the Button Bar).

   "Atlanta" is inserted after "downtown". If you positioned the insertion point correctly, "Atlanta" has one space before it and one space after it. If not, correct the spacing.

7. Position the insertion point on the fourth line of the fifth paragraph (which begins "When traffic flow moved upstairs"), to the left of "was".

8. Press **Shift+Insert** to paste "Atlanta" again. (**Shift+Insert** is the keyboard shortcut for the Paste command.)

   "Atlanta" is pasted a second time. You can paste the contents of the clipboard as many times as desired.

Moving a Block of Text

Moving a block of text is very similar to copying it. The only difference is that you choose Cut instead of Copy in the second step. Cut removes the selected text from your document and stores it on the Clipboard.

To move a sentence:

1. Triple-click anywhere on the sentence in the second paragraph that begins "The cobblestone streets".

   The entire sentence, including the blank space after it, is selected.

The Cut button

2. Choose Cut from the Edit menu (or press **Shift+Delete**, the keyboard shortcut).

   The selected text is removed from the document and stored on the Clipboard.

3. Position the insertion point after the period at the end of the second paragraph.

4. Press the **Spacebar** once to insert a space at the end of the sentence.

5. Choose Paste from the Edit menu (or click the Paste button on the Button Bar).

   The sentence appears at the end of the paragraph.

To move a paragraph:

1. Quadruple-click the fourth paragraph, which begins "There is a unique six-block area".

   Notice that the blank line below the paragraph is included in the selection.

2. Choose Cut from the Edit menu (or click the Cut button on the Button Bar).

3. Position the insertion point at the beginning of the first paragraph, which begins "In the 1920s".

   The insertion point should be on the same line as the paragraph. Do not insert a blank line above it.

4. Choose Paste from the Edit menu (or click Paste on the Button Bar). If necessary, insert a blank line at the end of the paragraph.

   The paragraph you moved now should be at the top of the document with a blank line separating it from the second paragraph.

Alternate Cut and Paste Shortcut Keys

There is an alternate set of **Control**-key combinations for Undo, Cut, Copy, and Paste that is very convenient to use. The combinations are:

Ctrl+Z to Undo

Ctrl+X to Cut

Ctrl+C to Copy

Ctrl+V to Paste

Although these key combinations may not be easy to remember at first, they are conveniently located at the lower left corner of the keyboard. When revising text by moving or copying, you can "drive" the mouse with your right hand, and, with practically no left-hand movement, use your left pinkie on the **Control** key, and use the other fingers of your left hand to press **Z**, **X**, **C**, or **V**.

(You can find out about other **Ctrl+***letter* combinations by choosing Keyboard from the Help menu, then choosing **Ctrl+A** through **Ctrl+Z**.)

Drag and Drop

Drag and Drop
To move or copy selected text by dragging it with the mouse.

Note: Drag and Drop does not copy text to the Clipboard, and Drag and Drop cannot be used to transfer information between documents or between applications.

Drag and Drop is a shortcut for moving or copying text within the current document. When you press and hold the mouse button on selected text, the pointer changes to the Drag and Drop pointer. This pointer is an arrow with a small rectangle attached to its end. When this special pointer is displayed, dragging your mouse will move the pointer and the insertion point. When you release the mouse button, the selected text will be moved to the insertion-point position. You can copy text with the Drag and Drop pointer if you hold down the **Ctrl** key while you are dragging.

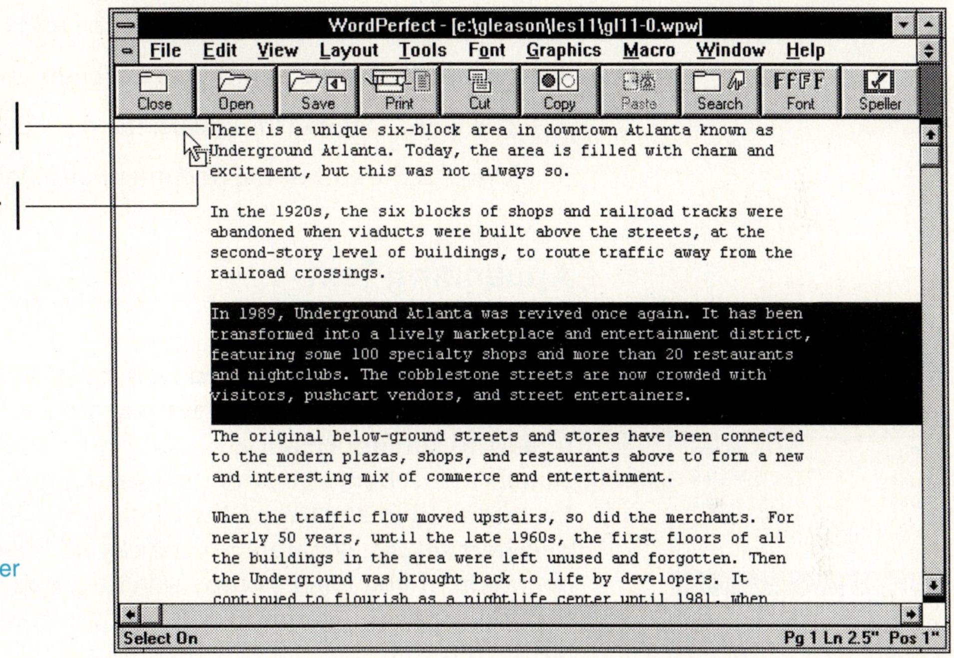

The Drag and Drop pointer

Figure 11-4
Dragging a block of text

To move a paragraph using Drag and Drop:

1. Select the third paragraph, which begins "In 1989, Underground Atlanta", by quadruple-clicking it.

2. Point anywhere in the selected paragraph, and then press and hold down the left mouse button.

   The mouse pointer changes to the Drag and Drop pointer.

3. While pressing the left mouse button, move the Drag and Drop pointer to the beginning of the first paragraph. The insertion point should be in front of the word "There".

4. Release the mouse button.

   The selected paragraph moves to the beginning of the document.

To copy text using Drag and Drop:

1. Select the word "Atlanta" on the first line in the first paragraph by double-clicking it.
2. Press and hold the **Ctrl** key.
3. While pressing the **Ctrl** key, point to the selected text with the mouse, and drag the pointer to the end of the document.

   The word "Atlanta" is copied to the end of the document.

4. Press **Ctrl+Home** to move to the beginning of the document.

   The word "Atlanta" is still on the first line.

5. Move to the end of the document and delete "Atlanta".

Appending Text

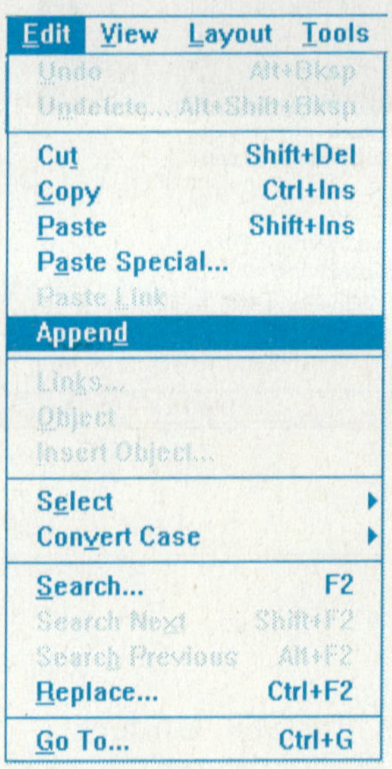

The Edit menu

Append
To add text or graphics to the contents of the Clipboard.

With most Windows applications, when you Cut or Copy a new selection, the information previously stored on the Clipboard is cleared. In WordPerfect, however, you can use the Append command to add to the information already on the Clipboard. When you *Append* a selection, a copy of the selected text is added to the end of the information already on the Clipboard. This is a convenient way to collect several separate text blocks and paste all of them in one operation. If you need to copy several paragraphs to another location, one append operation will take the place of several copy and paste procedures.

When you Append a selection, remember that the previous Clipboard contents are not erased. Therefore, the first selection to be collected on the Clipboard should be either Cut or Copied, not Appended. After the first selection is on the Clipboard, all additions to the Clipboard should be Appended.

To Append a paragraph to the Clipboard:

1. Quadruple-click the first paragraph, which begins "In 1989, Underground Atlanta".
2. Choose Cut from the Edit menu. (In an Append procedure, the first item must be Cut or Copied.)
3. Quadruple-click on the third paragraph, which begins "The original below-ground streets".
4. Choose Append from the Edit menu. (There is no keyboard shortcut for Append).

5. Position the insertion point at the beginning of the first line of the last paragraph, which begins "The following is a sampling of stores".
6. Choose Paste from the Edit menu.

   Both paragraphs appear on the screen at the insertion point.
7. Press **Ctrl+Home** to move to the beginning of the document.

   Notice that the third paragraph is a duplicate of the sixth paragraph. When you Append selected text, the original is not removed from the document.
8. Quadruple-click the third paragraph, which begins "The original below-ground streets".
9. Press the **Delete** key.

   The duplicate paragraph is removed.

Moving and Copying Tabular Columns

Lesson 9 discussed methods for creating tables with tabular columns. In this section, you will learn how to move and copy a tabular column to a new location.

Whenever you move or copy text, you select the text, choose either the Cut or Copy command, position the insertion point on the destination location, and choose the Paste command. The trick to moving tabular columns lies in the way you select the text. The best way to select a tabular column is to position the insertion point on the first line of the column, in the center of a word in that column. Then drag the insertion point down the center of the column, ending in the center of the column on the last line. When your selection is completed, it will have an irregular shape.

At first, when you attempt to block a column, you will select all the columns in the table. To refine the selection, choose Select from the Edit menu. Then choose Tabular Column from the Select cascading menu. Now the selection includes just the column and its tab codes.

To select a tabular column:

1. Scroll to the table at the end of document 11-0.wpw.
2. Using the mouse, point to the space between "Sq." and "Ft." in the second column on the first line of the table.
3. Click and drag down the center of the column, ending in the center of the last number in the column.

   The selection should be irregular, highlighting the end of the first line, the beginning of the last line, and all the lines in between.

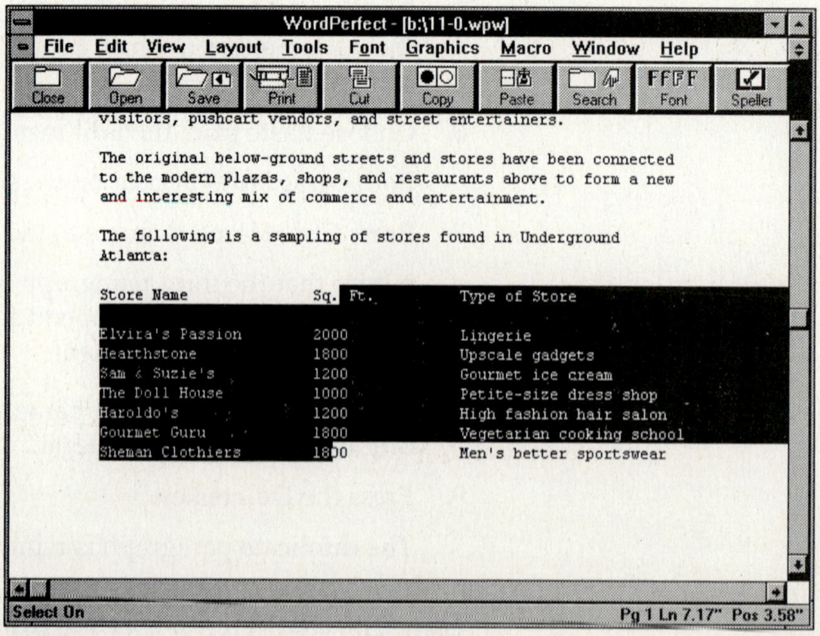

Figure 11-5
Preliminary text selection for moving a tabular column

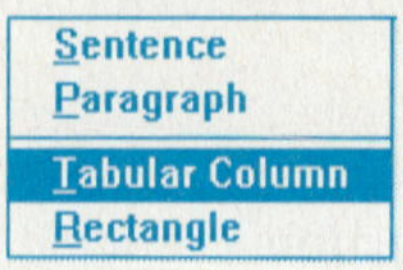

The Select cascading menu

4. Choose Select from the Edit menu, and then choose Tabular Column from the Select cascading menu.

   The shape of the highlighted selection has changed. The text in the second tabular column and the tab codes preceding each item in that column are selected, while the remaining columns are not selected.

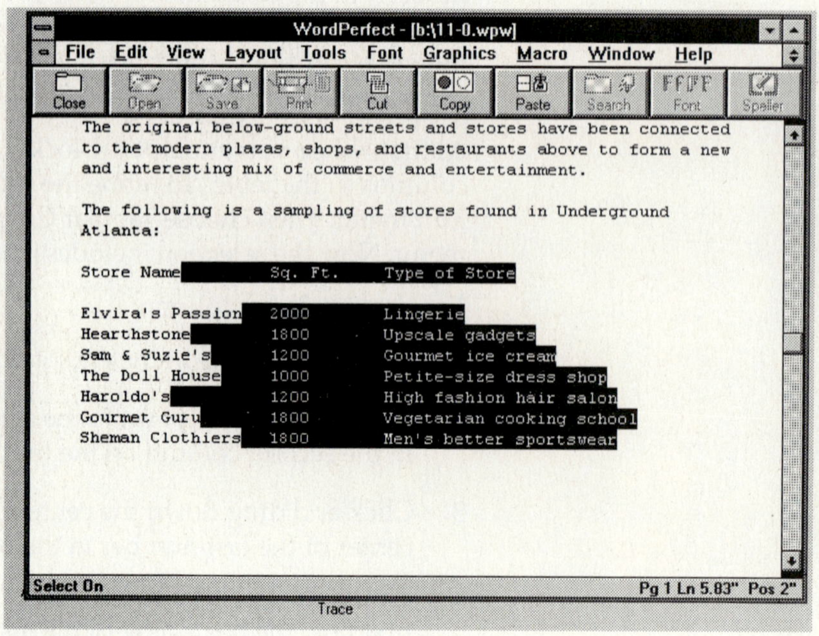

Figure 11-6
Completed tabular-column selection

To move a selected tabular column:

1. Choose Cut from the Edit menu (or use the keyboard or Button Bar equivalents).
2. Position the insertion point at the end of the first line of the table, to the right of "Type of Store".
3. Choose Paste from the Edit menu (or use the keyboard or Button Bar equivalents).

   The column has moved, but the tab settings need to be adjusted.
4. Choose Ruler from the View menu to display the Ruler, if necessary.
5. Position the insertion point anywhere on the first line of the table, if necessary.
6. Point to the tab marker at the 4-inch mark, and drag it to 5.5 inches.

To copy a tabular column:

1. Position the insertion point on the first line of the table, if necessary.
2. Set a left-aligned tab at the 6.5-inch mark on the Ruler.
3. Position the insertion point on the space between "Sq." and "Ft." in the last column, and drag down the center of the column to the last number.
4. Choose Select from the Edit menu, and choose Tabular Column from the Select cascading menu.
5. Choose Copy from the Edit menu (or use the keyboard or Button Bar equivalents).
6. Position the insertion point at the end of the first line of the table.
7. Choose Paste from the Edit menu (or use the keyboard or Button Bar equivalents).

   A second copy of the "Sq. Ft." column appears.

Deleting Tabular Columns

To delete a tabular column, select it using the selection methods described above, and press the **Delete** key.

To delete a tabular column:

1. Using the methods outlined above, select the third column with the heading "Sq. Ft."
2. Press the **Delete** key.

   The extra "Sq. Ft." column is deleted.
3. Spell-check the document.
4. Save the document as *[your three-letter identifier]*11-0.wpw.
5. Print the document.
6. Close the document and exit WordPerfect (unless you will be doing the following exercises immediately).

Table 11-1: Keyboard Shortcuts for Cutting and Pasting

Keyboard Shortcut	Action
Ctrl+Insert	Copies selected text to the Clipboard
Shift+Insert	Pastes the Clipboard contents at the insertion point
Shift+Delete	Cuts selected text and stores it on the Clipboard

Key Terms

Append
Clipboard
Copy
Cut
Drag and Drop
Paste

Exercises

Exercise 11.1

1. Start WordPerfect, if necessary.
2. Open the file 11-1.wpw.
3. The historical events in this document need to be arranged in chronological order. Begin by moving the last paragraph to the first paragraph position using the Cut and Paste method:

   A. Quadruple-click the last paragraph, which begins "1845".

   B. Choose Cut from the Edit menu (or click Cut on the Button Bar).

C. Position the insertion point at the beginning of the first paragraph, to the left of "1881".

D. Choose Paste from the Edit menu (or click Paste on the Button Bar).

Remember, you can access the Copy, Cut, and Paste commands from the Button Bar or the Edit menu. You also can use the keyboard shortcuts **Ctrl+Insert** for Copy, **Shift+Delete** for Cut, and **Shift+Insert** for Paste.

E. Press **Enter** to insert a line after the first paragraph. (This usually is necessary only when you are moving the last paragraph in a document).

4. Move the third paragraph to the second paragraph position using the Drag and Drop method:

   A. Quadruple-click the paragraph that begins with "1860".

   B. Point to the selected text. Press and hold the mouse button. (You should see the Drag and Drop mouse pointer).

   C. While pressing the mouse button, move the Drag and Drop insertion point to the beginning of the second paragraph, to the left of "1881".

   D. Release the mouse button.

5. Arrange the remaining paragraphs in chronological order using either the Drag and Drop or the Cut and Paste method.

6. In the last paragraph, which begins "1895", position the insertion point in the first sentence, between the words "International Exposition" and the period. Press the **Spacebar**, and key **is held in Atlanta**.

7. Copy " is held in Atlanta" (including the space before "is") to the end of the sentence that begins with "1881". Use the Copy and Paste method:

   A. Select the words " is held in Atlanta" that you keyed in step 6. Be sure to include the blank space before the word "is".

   B. Choose Copy from the Edit menu (or click Copy on the Button Bar).

   C. At the end of the line that begins with "1881", position the insertion point between the word "Exposition" and the period.

   D. Choose Paste from the Edit menu, or click Paste on the Button Bar.

8. Copy " is held in Atlanta" (including the space before "is") to the end of the sentence that begins with "1887". Use the Drag and Drop method:

   A. Select the words " is held in Atlanta" that you copied in step 7.

   B. While pressing the **Ctrl** key, point to the selected text, and hold down the mouse button so that you see the Drag and Drop pointer. (Remember, the Drag and Drop pointer has a small rectangle on the end of the arrow).

   C. Position the Drag and Drop insertion point at the end of the sentence that begins with "1887", between the word "Exposition" and the period.

   D. Release the mouse button.

9. Spell-check the document.

10. Save the document as *[your three-letter identifier]*11-1.wpw.

11. Print the document.

12. Close the document and exit WordPerfect (unless you will be doing the following exercises immediately).

Exercise 11.2

1. Start WordPerfect, if necessary.

2. Key Document 11.2, which appears at the end of this exercise. When formatting the tabular table, set left-aligned absolute tab markers at 1.5, 2.5, 4.5, and 6.25 inches.

3. Move the tabbed table above the second paragraph in the memo. Remember, when selecting the table, be sure to include the Tab Set codes, [Tab Set], at the beginning and end of the table:

   A. Display Reveal Codes.

   B. Working in the Reveal Codes space, click the Tab Set code, [Tab Set], at the beginning of the table.

   C. While pressing the **Shift** key, click the Hard Return code, [HRt], at the end of the table, just after the Tab Set code.

      The entire table, including its codes, is selected.

   D. Choose Cut from the Edit menu (or click Cut on the Button Bar).

   E. Position the insertion point at the beginning of the second paragraph, to the left of the word "By".

F. Choose Paste from the Edit menu (or click Paste on the Button Bar).

G. If necessary, press the **Enter** key to insert a blank line at the end of the table.

H. Close the Reveal Codes space.

4. Move the tabular column with the heading "Agent" to the left of the "Location" column:

A. Position the insertion point in the center of the word "Agent", and drag down to the center of the word "Delbridge" at the bottom of the "Agent" column.

B. Choose Select from the Edit menu and Tabular Column from the Select cascading menu.

C. Choose Cut from the Edit menu (or click Cut on the Button Bar).

D. Position the insertion point on the first heading line of the table, to the left of the word "Location".

E. Choose Paste from the Edit menu (or click Paste on the Button Bar).

The "Agent" column is moved, but the table formatting may need to be adjusted.

F. Display the ruler, if necessary, and drag the tab markers as necessary to adjust the column spacing.

G. To format the heading, select the entire heading row, and apply the bold attribute.

5. Using the Append command, create a list of the locations represented in the tabular table:

A. Select "North Fulton" on the second line of the table under the "Location" heading.

B. Choose Copy from the Edit menu. (Remember, you must start an append procedure with Copy or Cut.)

C. Select "Parsons Station" from the "Location" column.

D. Choose Append from the Edit menu.

E. Using Steps C and D above as a guide, append Roswell, Litchfield, Martins Landing, Dunwoody, Hillbrooke, and Alpharetta.

F. Position the insertion point at the end of the document.

G. Choose Paste from the Edit menu (or click Paste on the Button Bar).

H. Format the list so that each location is on a separate line.

6. Spell-check the document.
7. Save the document as *[your three-letter identifier]*11-2.wpw.
8. Print the document.
9. Close the document and exit WordPerfect (unless you will be doing the following exercises immediately).

Document 11-2

MEMO TO: Bud Porter

FROM: Ann Delbridge

DATE: June 9, 199-

SUBJECT: New Properties

The following properties have been listed with the Buckhead office since May 1:

By the way, I have been in touch with John, and he has assured me that his tally of new listings for Marietta and Midtown will be in your hands by Wednesday morning.

Prop #	Location	Agent	Price
23145	North Fulton	G. Crane	229,000
34490	Parsons Station	G. Crane	144,900
51234	Roswell	A. Delbridge	799,000
56790	Roswell	G. Crane	298,900
67840	Litchfield	A. Delbridge	524,900
67890	Martins Landing	M. Washington	152,900
76121	Dunwoody	M. Washington	240,000
80886	Hillbrooke	G. Crane	179,900
88788	Dunwoody	M. Washington	350,000
97558	Alpharetta	A. Delbridge	565,000

Exercise 11-3

1. Start WordPerfect, if necessary.

2. Open the file 11-3.wpw.

3. Rearrange the paragraphs with bold headings, so that they are in the following order: "**Restaurants**", "**Nightlife**", "**Performing Arts**", "**Sports**".

4. Using the Append command, create a list of all the bold paragraph headings, and insert it below the first paragraph. If necessary, format the list so that each heading is on a separate line. (Hint: If you use the quadruple-click method to select the headings, they will be appended on separate lines).

5. Indent the list created in step 4, and remove the bold attribute.

6. Key the text **Leisure Activities:** at the beginning of the heading "Restaurants".

7. Copy the text "Leisure Activities: " (including the space after the colon) to the beginning of the headings "Nightlife", "Performing Arts", and "Sports". Use the Copy and Paste method.

8. Reapply the bold attribute to all the headings that begin with "Leisure Activities", if necessary.

9. Format the document as a memo to Ann Delbridge from Bud Porter, dated July 2, 199-, with the subject "Guide to Atlanta Project".

10. Spell-check the document.

11. Save the document as *[your three-letter identifier]*11-3.wpw.

12. Print the document.

13. Save the document and exit WordPerfect (unless you will be doing the following exercises immediately).

Exercise 11-4

1. Start WordPerfect, if necessary.

2. Open the file 11-4.wpw.

3. Position the insertion point at the beginning of the document, and key Figure 11-7, which appears at the end of this exercise. Include the indicated corrections.

4. Format the document as a standard business letter to:

   Mr. Daniel Lawson
   Suite 5
   1094 Eleventh St., SE
   Calgary, Alberta
   Canada T2G 3G2

   From:
   Della Crandon, Office Manager.

   Dated:
   April 14, 199-

5. In the third paragraph, move the last sentence (which begins "Please review") to the beginning of the paragraph.

6. Move the entire third paragraph to the end of the document.

7. Move the second paragraph, which begins "Five Points Realty", to the end of the first paragraph. Correct the paragraph and sentence spacing.

8. Rearrange the paragraphs with bold headings in the following order:

   Improving the property:

   Providing for adequate insurance:

   Improving the neighborhood:

   Tracking all expenditures:

   Adjusting the rental fee:

9. If necessary, reapply the bold attribute to all the headings.

10. Indent all the paragraphs and headings referred to in step 7.

11. Spell-check the document.

12. Save the document as *[your three-letter identifier]*11-4.wpw.

13. Print the document.

14. Close the document and exit WordPerfect (unless you will be doing the following exercise immediately).

Figure 11-7

```
Thank you for your inquiry regarding the property in Marietta.

Five Points Realty has an entire department for managing your kind of
property.

I will call answer any other questions you might have shortly. Please
review the enclosed brochure describing our property-management services
in detail.

Along with the normal services you'd expect from a top-notch property-
management group, we pay particular attention to the following services:
```

(Handwritten corrections: "residential apartment" inserted before "property"; "you own" inserted after "property"; "your kind of property" replaced by "properties" and "such as yours." added; "you in one week to" inserted after "call"; "other" replaced by "further"; "might" replaced by "may"; "shortly" deleted; "'d" deleted; "top-notch" replaced by "first-rate"; "designed to maintain and enhance the value of your property" inserted after "services".)

Exercise 11-5

1. Start WordPerfect, if necessary.
2. Open the file 11-5.wpw.
3. Format the document as a memo to Staff from Bud Porter, dated July 3, 199-, with the subject: Tour of "Things to do in Atlanta" scheduled.
4. Move the first sentence in the second paragraph (which begins "Please dress") to the end of the paragraph.
5. Move the entire second paragraph, which begins "Note:", below the table.
6. Move the fourth line of the table, beginning with "Chattahoochee", to the sixth line, between "Johnny Mercer" and "Botanical Gardens". (Hint: Be sure to include all the codes on the line with the selected text.)
7. Move the "Date" column of the table to the left of the "Tour Leader" column.
8. Adjust the table's column spacing as necessary.
9. Correct the table-heading format by reapplying the bold and underline attributes.
10. Rearrange the tour-description paragraphs at the end of the document so that they are in the same order as in the table.

11. Key **Things to do in Atlanta:** at the beginning of the heading "Cable News Network (CNN) Center".
12. Copy the text keyed in step 11 to all the tour-description paragraph headings.
13. Underline all the tour-description paragraph headings.
14. Spell-check the document.
15. Save the document as *[your three-letter identifier]*11-5.wpw.
16. Print the document.
17. Close the document and exit WordPerfect.

Lesson 12

Working with Multiple Document Windows

Objectives

- Open multiple document windows.
- Change the size of windows.
- Switch between document windows.
- Copy text from one document to another.
- Add comments to a document.

Up to now, you have worked with one document at a time. You created a new document or opened a document from a disk. When you completed an exercise, you saved and closed the document before starting a new one. If you open a new document without closing the one you are working on first, both documents will be available to work on at the same time. This is convenient if you need to transfer text from one document to another. WordPerfect for Windows allows you to have open as many as nine document windows at one time (depending on how much memory your computer has).

Opening Multiple Document Windows

Each time you choose New from the File menu, WordPerfect opens a new document window. You can think of this as placing a new sheet of paper on top of the work already on your desk. If you open a document when other documents are open, that document will appear on top of all the other layers. This allows you to work with your computer document files in the same way as you now work with the papers on your desk.

To open multiple document windows:

1. Start WordPerfect, if necessary.
2. Open the file 5-1.wpw (remember, **F4** is the keyboard shortcut for Open).
3. While document 5-1.wpw is displayed, open the file 6-0.wpw. (Remember, do not close document 5-1.wpw.)

   Once document 6-0.wpw is displayed, you will not be able to see document 5-1.wpw. It is underneath the newly opened document.

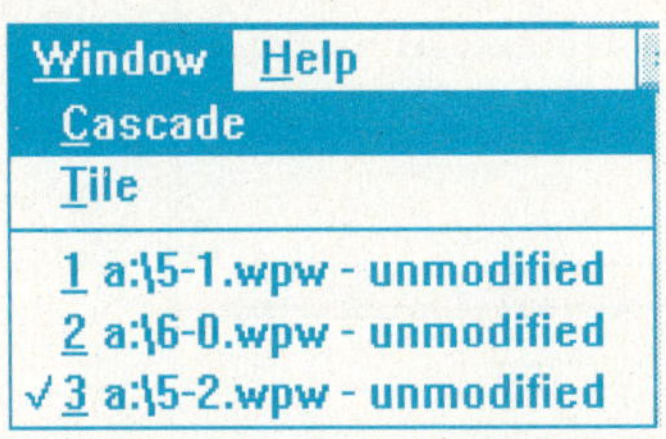

The Window menu showing the list of open files

4. Open the file 5-2.wpw.
5. Choose Window on the menu bar.

   The three open files are listed at the bottom of the drop-down menu. (If you closed one of the files by mistake, open it again now).
6. Close the Window drop-down menu.

Adjusting the Size of Windows

You can change the size of each open document, so you can see a portion of all the open documents at one time. "Lesson 2: Inside Windows" introduced the Cascade and Tile options on the Window menu. That lesson also discussed the Maximize, Restore, and Minimize buttons in the upper right corner of document windows. These tools are used to work with multiple document windows.

Cascading Windows

The best way to see all the open documents at one time is to choose Cascade from the Window menu. Each window changes to its restored, or "normal," size and is arranged one on top of the other, so that all the title bars show. When you choose Cascade, the current window appears on the top layer and has a highlighted title bar.

Note: The actual color of the title bars depends on whether you are using a color or monochrome monitor and on the color scheme chosen in the Windows Control panel. In most cases, the active window title bar will be a more intense color than the inactive title bar.

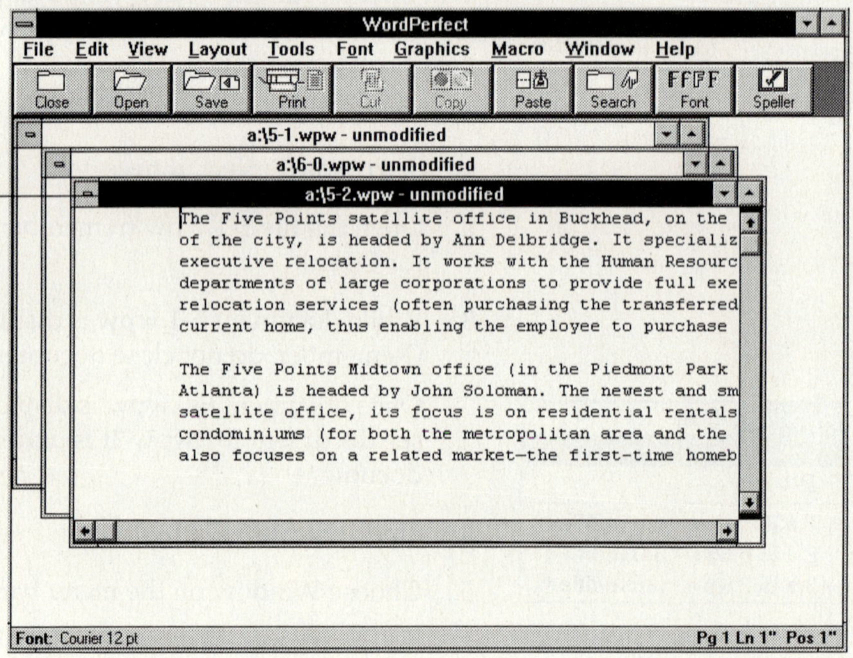

Figure 12-1
Cascading document windows

To cascade the open document windows:

Maximize button

The Maximize button

1. Choose Cascade from the Window menu.

   The three open document windows are displayed, one on top of the other. The title bar of the active document is colored or highlighted, and the other title bars are white or pale in color.

2. Click the 5-2.wpw document window's Maximize button.

   Document 5-2.wpw is displayed in full-screen size, its window frame is no longer showing, and the other windows cannot be seen.

Tiling Windows

Another way to see all the open document windows is to choose Tile from the Window menu. When Tile is chosen, a portion of each document is displayed, edge to edge, so that there is no overlapping.

To Tile the open document windows:

1. Choose Tile from the Window menu.

   All the open windows are arranged edge to edge, filling the entire screen.

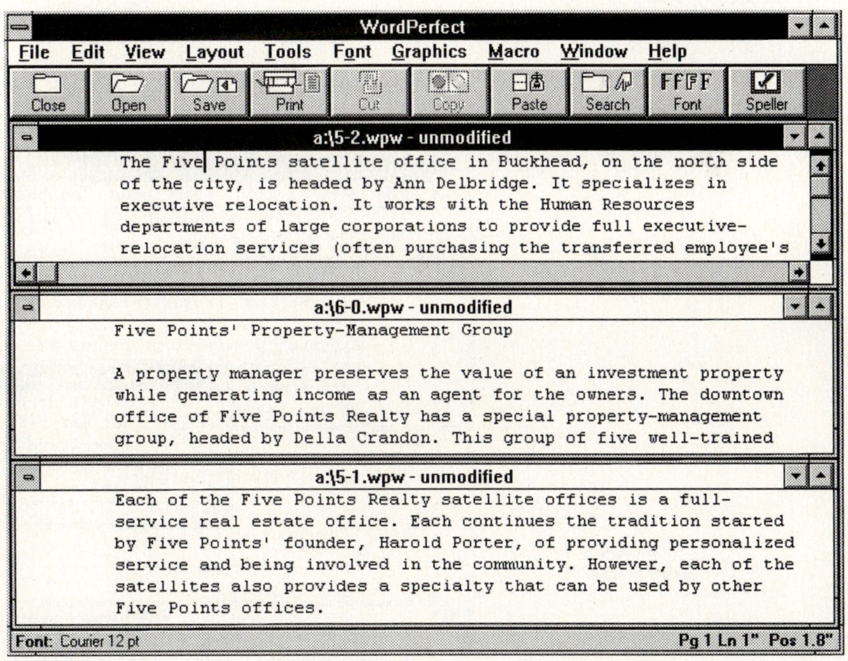

Figure 12-2
Tiled document windows

2. Click anywhere in the 6-0.wpw document window to make it active.

The 6-0.wpw title bar is highlighted.

3. Click the active window's Maximize button to return it to full-screen size.

Dragging the Window Frame

When a document window's frame is displayed, you can change the size of it by pointing to the frame and dragging it. (See "Lesson 2: Inside Windows" for a complete discussion of changing the size of a window.)

To change a window's size by dragging its frame:

1. Choose Cascade from the Window menu.
2. Choose Tile from the Window menu.
3. Click anywhere on the center window to select it.

   The title bar is highlighted, indicating that it is the active window.

4. Click and drag the left window frame 2 inches towards the center of the screen.

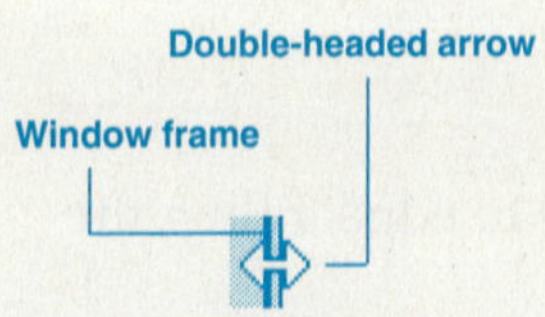

The double-headed arrow pointer

   The mouse pointer must change to a double-headed arrow to drag the frame.

5. Drag the right window frame toward the center.
6. Point to the active document's title bar, and drag it up 1 inch.

   The entire window is repositioned.

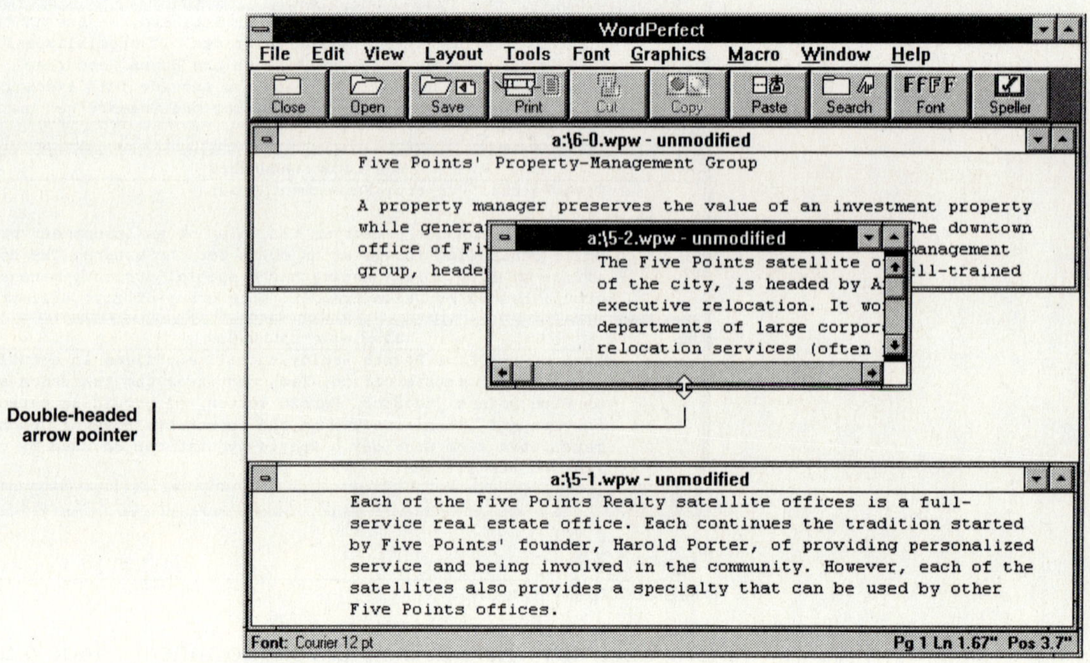

Figure 12-3
The resized window

7. To return to the document's full-screen size, click the active document's Maximize button.

Using the Restore Button

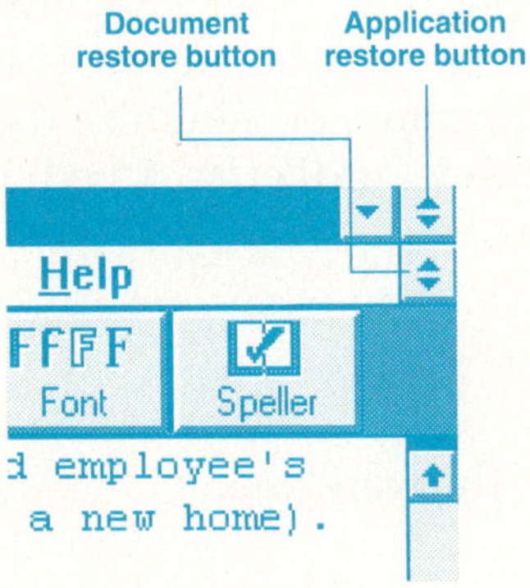

The Restore button

Another way to see all the open windows is to click the current document window's Restore button. (Remember, use the document Restore button on the Menu bar, not the application Restore button on the Title bar.) If you click the Restore button before you change the size of any windows, the result will be the same as if you choose Cascade from the Window menu. If you previously changed the size of any windows by tiling, cascading, minimizing, or dragging the window frames, the Restore button will return these windows to their previous window-frame size.

To restore the open document windows to their previous size:

1. Click the Restore button for the active document.

   Your screen should look the same as it did when you completed the resizing procedure above (refer to Figure 12-3). Documents 5-1.wpw, 5-2.wpw, and 6-0.wpw should be displayed.

2. Click the Maximize button on the 6-0.wpw document window to display it in full-screen size.

3. Click the active document's Restore button.

Using the Minimize Buttons

If several windows are open, but you want to display only two or three, tile them, click the Minimize buttons on the windows you do not want to see, and then tile them again. When you minimize a window, you may not see its resulting icon, because it is hidden behind another window. The icons always go to the lowest layer in the lower left corner of the application window. To see the document icons, make the window that occupies the lower left corner smaller, or drag it to a different location.

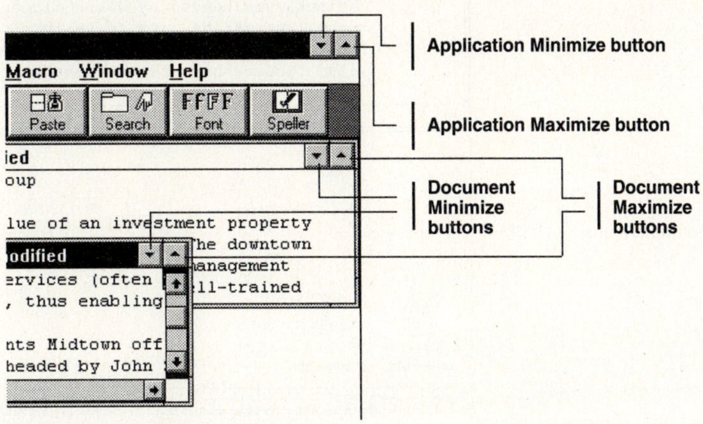

Figure 12-4
The Maximize and Minimize buttons

When you minimize a document window, be sure to click the document Minimize button and not the application Minimize button. If you click the application Minimize button by mistake, the entire WordPerfect application will shrink to an icon. Just double-click it to maximize it again. All your documents will remain as they were before you accidentally minimized the application. If other applications are running when the WordPerfect window is minimized, you might not see the icon. In this case, either restore or minimize the other application windows until you see the WordPerfect icon (or press **Ctrl+Esc** to open the Task List dialog box).

To minimize a document window:

1. Choose Tile from the Window menu.

   All three documents are resized to fill the work area completely.

2. Click the Minimize button on the top document window to turn this window into an icon.

   You cannot see the minimized icon, because it is hidden behind the bottom document window.

3. Choose Tile from the Window menu.

   The two remaining document windows fill the entire screen.

4. Click the Minimize button for the bottom document window to shrink it to an icon.

   Now you can see two document icons in the lower left corner.

Document icons

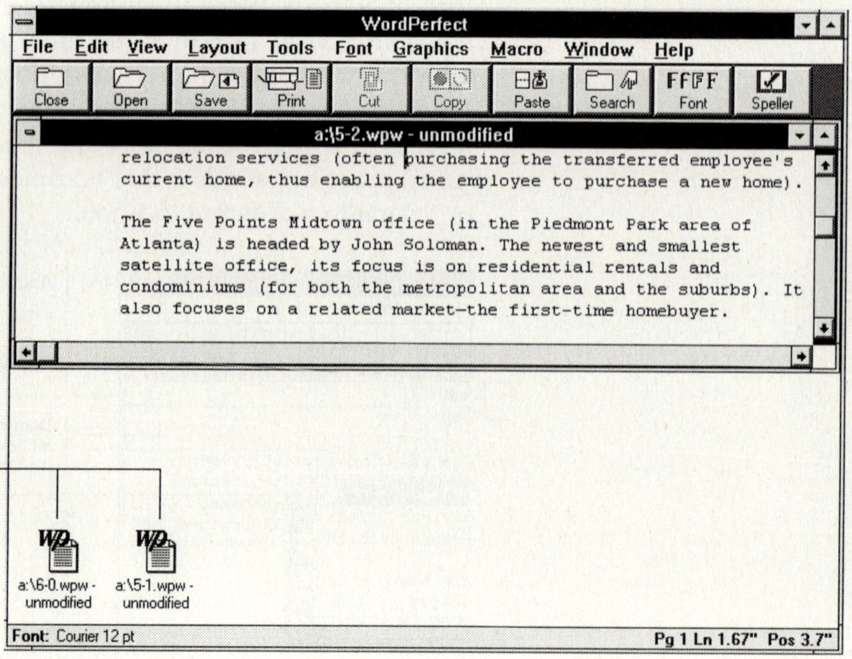

Figure 12-5
Minimized document icons

5. Double-click one of the icons to restore it to window size.

6. Double-click the other document icon. (If you cannot see it, resize or move the window that is on top of it.)

   You now should see three windows, but they may be overlapping.

7. Choose Tile from the Window menu to display the documents edge to edge.

Switching Between Document Windows

The ability to have several document windows open at the same time is convenient if you want to copy or move text from one document to another, or if you need to look at information in another document. There are several ways to move from one document window to another.

If you can see more than one document window on your screen, the easiest way to switch from one to another is simply to click anywhere on another document. If, when switching document windows, you click the title bar, the previous insertion-point position will be preserved. If you click anywhere else, the insertion point will appear approximately where you clicked. It will not be exactly where you clicked, because when you are switching windows you are pointing with the arrow pointer, not the I-beam. Remember, the active document is the one that has an insertion point and a highlighted or colored title bar.

When more than one window is displayed, menu commands that you choose will affect only the active window. For example, if you click Save on the Button Bar, the file in the active window will be saved, but the files in inactive windows will not.

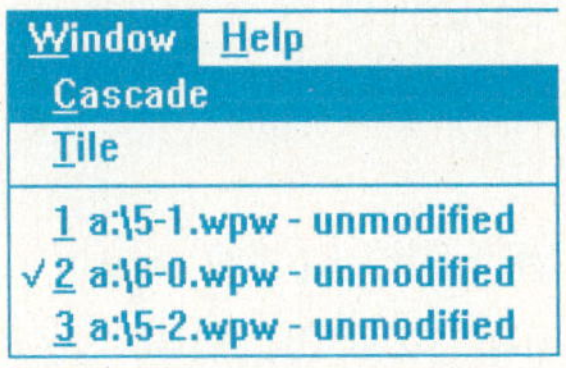

The Window menu

If the active document window is maximized so that you cannot see other open documents, you can switch to another document by choosing its file name from the Window menu. When you open the Window menu, a list of all open documents appears at the bottom of the menu. The active document is indicated by a check mark.

The keyboard shortcuts for moving between documents are **Ctrl+F6** to switch to the next document and **Ctrl+Shift+F6** to switch to the previous document. Pressing **Ctrl+F6** or **Ctrl+Shift+F6** repeatedly will cycle through all open documents.

To switch document windows:

1. Click the word "Five" on the first line of document 5-1.wpw. If necessary, move the insertion point to the beginning of the word "Five".

2. Click the word "manager" on the second line of document 6-0.wpw.

   The insertion point and highlighted title bar have switched to the new active window.

3. Click the title bar of document 5-1.wpw.

   Notice that the insertion point remains in front of the word "Five".

4. Maximize document 5-1.wpw by clicking its Maximize button.

5. Choose document 6-0.wpw from the Window menu.

   The document is full-screen size. The insertion point remains in the position it had the last time the window was active.

Copying Text to Another Document

In "Lesson 11: Moving and Copying Text," you learned to move and copy text to another location within a document. The same commands are used to transfer text to another document window. After you cut or copy a selection to the Clipboard, switch documents using any method described above, position the insertion point where you want the text to go, and choose the Paste command.

To copy information from one document to another:

1. Choose Cascade from the Window menu.
2. Minimize the 5-2.wpw document window.
3. Choose Tile from the Window menu.

   Documents 5-1.wpw and 6-0.wpw are displayed. If you see other document windows, minimize them, and then choose Tile again.

4. Select the second and third sentences in document 6-0.wpw, beginning with "The downtown office" and ending with "by the property." Use the click and drag method. See Figure 12–6 on page 12–9.

5. Choose Copy from the Edit menu.

6. Position the insertion point at the end of the last line in the first paragraph of document 5-1.wpw (the other document window).

7. Press **Enter** twice to make room for a new paragraph.

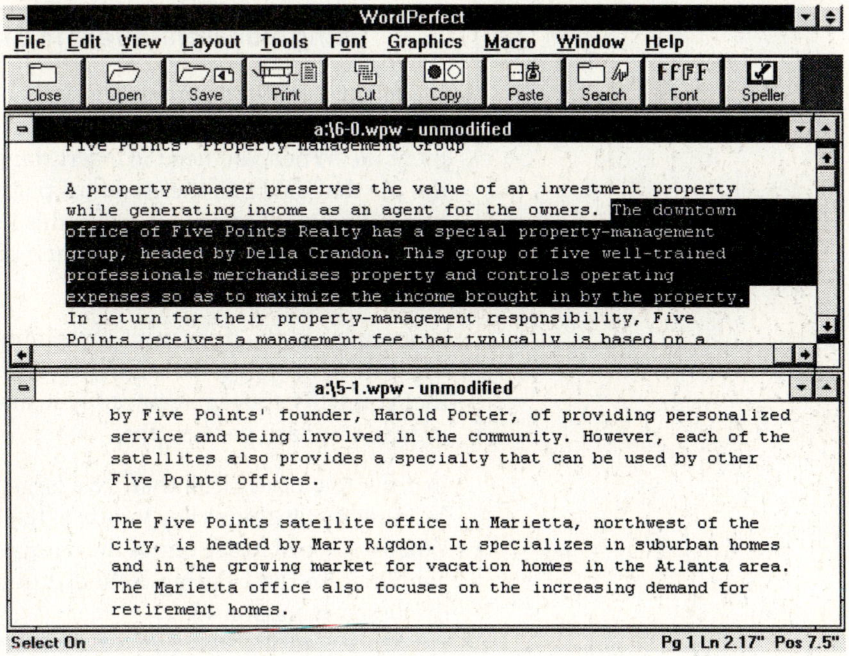

Figure 12-6

Documents 5-1.wpw and 6-0.wpw with text selected (as in step 4 on page 12-8)

8. Choose Paste from the Edit menu.

   The two sentences copied from document 6-0.wpw are pasted into a separate paragraph in document 5-1.wpw.

9. Choose document 5-2.wpw from the Window menu.

10. Maximize the 5-2.wpw document window.

11. Position the insertion point at the beginning of the first line of the first paragraph, and drag to the end of the second paragraph.

    Both paragraphs are selected.

12. Choose Copy from the Edit menu.

13. Choose document 5-1.wpw from the Window menu.

14. Press **Ctrl+End** to position the insertion point at the end of the document.

15. Choose Paste from the Edit menu.

    Document 5-1.wpw now contains paragraphs copied from documents 5-2.wpw and 6-0.wpw.

16. Save the current document as *[your three-letter identifier]*12-0a.wpw and close it.

17. Close all open files.

Using Boilerplate Text in Standard Documents

If you have standard paragraphs that you key repeatedly, you can save time and insure accuracy if you collect those paragraphs in one document file. When you need to insert standard text in a document, open the file that contains the standard paragraphs, and copy the needed text. Using methods described in this lesson, switch to the document on which you are working, and then paste the text at the desired location.

You can build the document containing standard paragraphs by using the above suggestions in reverse. Each time you key a paragraph that you will be using again, copy it, and paste it into the file containing the standard paragraphs.

In order to work efficiently with a large file, insert a short, descriptive heading that includes key words at the beginning of each paragraph. When you need to use one of the paragraphs, search for the key words contained in the heading to find it quickly. Search and Replace are discussed in Lesson 13.

Adding Document Comments

Document comment
A note within a document that is displayed on the screen, but that does not print.

WordPerfect *document comments* are notes that can be inserted in a document. They appear as gray shaded boxes and do not print. Document comments can indicate the purpose of the document, explain why you put certain information into a document, how you arrived at a conclusion, or from where certain numbers came. They can indicate information that needs to be added or revised. Comments are useful in forms to tell someone how to use the form and what information to insert.

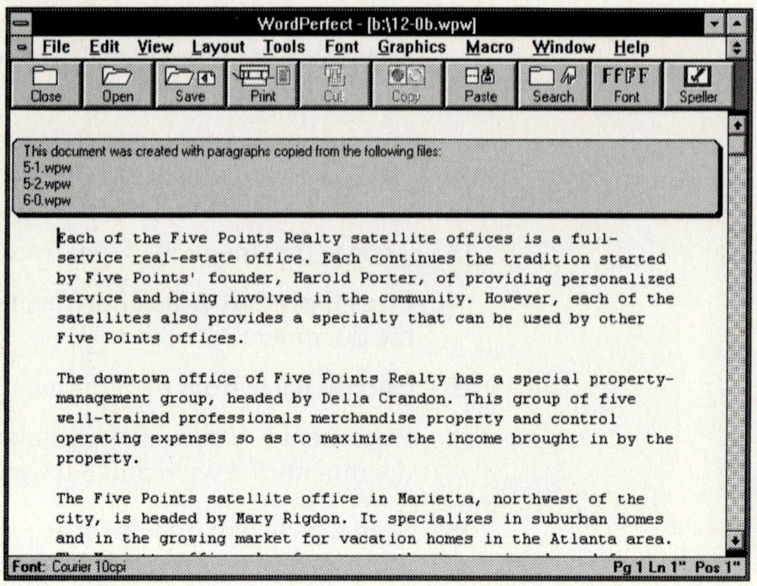

Figure 12-7
A comment displayed in a document

How to Put Comments in a Document

To add a comment, position the insertion point where you want the comment to go, choose Comment from the Tools menu, and choose Create from the Comment cascading menu. The Create Comment dialog box will open. This box has a window with an insertion point, ready for you to key your note. When you finish keying the note, click OK, and the comment will appear in the document at the insertion-point position. If you look at Reveal Codes, you will see the code [Comment] placed at the insertion point.

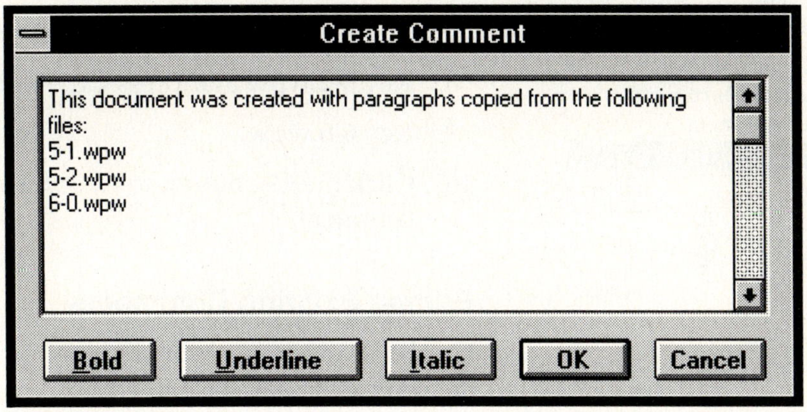

Figure 12-8
The Create Comment dialog box

Editing capabilities are limited when keying comments. You can select text to delete it, but you cannot cut, copy, or paste it. You can apply the attributes bold, underline, or italics, but you cannot use the **Ctrl** keyboard shortcuts. Instead, you must click the Bold, Underline, or Italics buttons at the bottom of the Create Comment dialog box. You cannot change the font or type size of a comment. To start a new line, you must press **Ctrl+Enter**. If you press **Enter** without the **Ctrl** key pressed, the comment box will close. If this happens by mistake, you can open the comment window again to continue keying by choosing Comment from the Tools menu and Edit from the Comment menu. A quicker way to get back to the comment dialog box is to point to the comment and double-click it.

To create a comment:

1. Close all open documents, if necessary, and open the file 12-0b.wpw.

2. Open the View menu. If Comment is checked, close the View menu. If not, choose Comment.

3. Position the insertion point at the beginning of the document, if necessary.

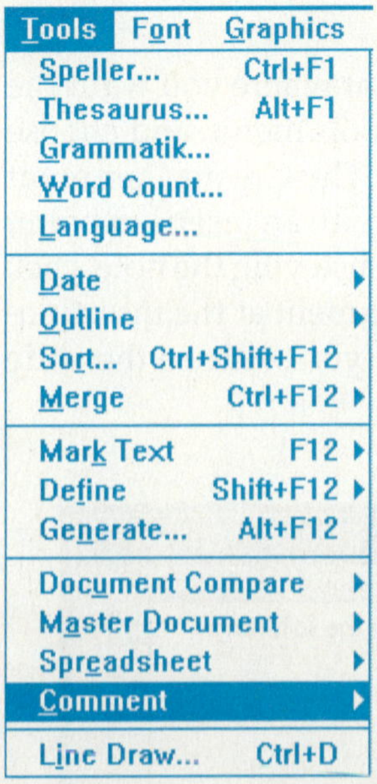

The Tools menu

4. Choose Comment from the Tools menu and Create from the Comment cascading menu.

   The Create Comment dialog box opens.

5. Key **This document was created with paragraphs copied from the following files:**.

6. Press **Ctrl+Enter** to start a new line.

   If you press **Enter** without first pressing **Ctrl**, the Create Comment dialog box will close. If this happens, double-click the comment to reopen the dialog box.

7. Key **5-1.wpw** and press **Ctrl+Enter**.

8. Key **5-2.wpw** and press **Ctrl+Enter**.

9. Key **6-0.wpw**.

10. Click the OK button to close the dialog box and display the comment.

Editing Existing Comments

To edit an existing comment, position the insertion point just after the comment you want to edit but before the next comment in the document. Choose Comment from the Tools menu and Edit from the Comment menu. The Edit Comment dialog box looks just like the Create Comment dialog box, and you use the same techniques for editing text as in the Create Comment process.

It is important to position the insertion point carefully before editing a comment. The Comment Edit command always works on the comment immediately preceding the insertion point. If there are no comments before the insertion point, it works on the first comment following the insertion point.

To edit a document comment:

1. Position the insertion point at the beginning of the first paragraph.

   This will position the insertion point just after the code [Comment].

2. Display Reveal Codes (**Alt+F3**) to check that the insertion point is positioned correctly.

3. Choose Comment from the Tools menu and Edit from the Comment cascading menu.

   The Edit Comment dialog box opens.

4. In the first line of the comment, double-click "created" to select it.

5. Click the Bold button.

6. Click the OK button.

   The Edit Comment dialog box closes, and the document comment is displayed again, this time with "created" in bold.

7. Close the Reveal Codes space.

Converting Text to Comments

A form letter may contain a paragraph that is needed only in special cases. You can convert that paragraph to a comment, then, when it is needed, convert it to text, print the letter, and convert the paragraph back to a comment.

To convert text into a comment:

1. Select the third paragraph, which begins "The Five Points satellite office in Marietta". Use the click and drag method, and be sure to include the blank line under the comment.

Note: When selecting a paragraph adjacent to a comment, do not use the quadruple-click method. Doing so will cause the comment to be included as part of the selection.

2. Choose Comment from the Tools menu and Create from the Comment menu.

   The paragraph is displayed now as a comment.

3. Select the fourth paragraph, including the blank line after it, using the click and drag method. Convert the selection into a comment as in step 2.

4. Convert the fifth paragraph into a comment.

Converting Document Comments to Text

Note: Do not be tempted to delete the code [Comment] when you convert the comment to text. Deleting the comment code will cause all text in the comment to be lost.

Sometimes, you may place information in a comment to remind you that it needs to be revised. After it has been changed, you can convert it to text, so that it will appear when you print the document. To convert a comment to text, position the insertion point just after the comment, and choose Comment from the Tools menu and Convert to Text from the Comment menu.

To convert a document comment to text:

1. Position the insertion point between the first and second comments.

The Comment cascading menu

2. Choose Comment from the Tools menu and Convert to Text from the Comment menu.

   The paragraph preceding the insertion point is converted back to text.

Deleting Comments

To delete a comment, display Reveal Codes, highlight the [Comment] code, and press the **Delete** key. Deleting the comment code deletes the comment text.

To delete a comment:

1. Position the insertion point at the beginning of the first line of the first paragraph, to the left of "Each of the Five".
2. Choose Reveal Codes from the View menu (or press **Alt+F3**).
3. Click the code [Comment] in the Reveal Codes space to select it.

   [Comment] is highlighted.
4. Press the **Delete** key.

   The Comment code and the comment are deleted. All text that was in the comment box also is deleted.
5. Choose Undo from the Edit menu to restore the comment.

Note: To restore a deleted comment, be sure to choose Undo before performing any other action. If Undo is not successful, use the Undelete command.

Hiding Comments

If you have several comments in a document, you may find it distracting to have them displayed when you do not need to see them. You can hide them temporarily by choosing Comment from the View menu. To make your comments reappear, choose Comment from the View menu again.

To hide and then redisplay comments:

1. If necessary, scroll through the document until the two comments at the bottom of the document (formerly paragraphs four and five) are visible.
2. Click the View menu, and verify that there is a check mark in front of the Comments option.

   The check mark indicates that comments are being displayed.
3. Choose Comments from the View menu.

   Choosing Comments removes the check mark, and the comments are no longer displayed.
4. Choose Comments from the View menu again; the comments are displayed.
5. Spell-check the document.
6. Save the document as *[your three-letter identifier]*12-0b.wpw.

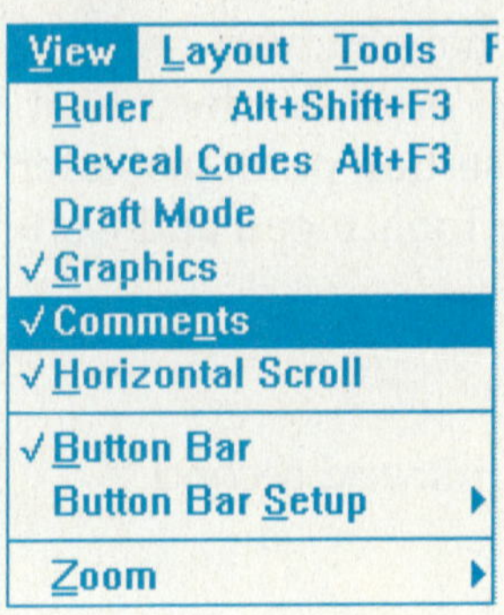

The View menu

7. Print the document.

   Notice that the comments do not print.

8. Close all open document windows and exit WordPerfect (unless you will be doing the following exercises immediately).

Table 12-1: Keyboard Shortcuts for Multiple Document Windows

Keyboard Shortcut	Action
Ctrl+Esc	Open the Task List dialog box
Ctrl+F6	Next document
Ctrl+Shift+F6	Previous document

Key Term

Document comment

Exercises

Exercise 12.1

1. Start WordPerfect, if necessary.
2. Open the file 12-1a.wpw.
3. Open the files 12-1b.wpw and 12-1c.wpw.

   Three documents are open, but only 12-1c.wpw is visible.

4. Create a new document window by choosing New from the File menu.
5. Display all four document windows at one time, first by using the Cascade command and then by using the Tile command:

   A. Choose Cascade from the Window menu.

   B. Choose Tile from the Window menu.

6. Keeping all windows open, arrange them so that only the new, untitled document window and document 12-1a.wpw are displayed:

   A. Minimize documents 12-1b.wpw and 12-1c.wpw by clicking their Minimize buttons in the upper right corner of the document windows.

   B. Choose Tile from the Window menu.

7. Copy the first paragraph in document 12-1a.wpw (beginning with the heading "Downtown") to the new, untitled document:

   A. Position the insertion point in document 12-1a.wpw at the beginning of the heading "Downtown".

   B. Select the first paragraph, its heading, and the blank line below it.

   C. Choose Copy from the Edit menu.

   D. Position the insertion point in the untitled document, and choose Paste from the Edit menu.

   E. Minimize document 12-1a.wpw.

8. Copy the first paragraph in document 12-1b.wpw (beginning with the heading "Directions to Downtown Office") to the untitled document:

   A. Double-click the document 12-1b.wpw icon.

   B. Choose Tile from the Window menu.

   C. Select and then copy the directions to the Downtown office. (Include the heading and the blank line after the paragraph.)

   D. Position the insertion point at the end of the untitled document, and choose Paste from the Edit menu.

9. Copy the Downtown office address, phone number, and office manager information from document 12-1c.wpw into the untitled document. Work with maximized windows, and use the Window drop-down menu to switch documents:

   A. Choose the document 12-1c.wpw from the Window menu and maximize it.

   B. Select the Downtown office information. Include the heading before and the blank line after the information.

   C. Choose Copy from the Edit menu.

   D. Choose the untitled document from the Window menu.

   E. Position the insertion point at the end of the document, and choose Paste from the Edit menu.

10. Copy all the information for the Midtown, Buckhead, and Marietta offices from documents 12-1a.wpw, 12-1b.wpw, and 12-1c.wpw into the untitled document. Follow steps 7 through 9 for each office.

11. Spell-check the document.

12. Save the document as *[your three-letter identifier]*12-1d.wpw.

13. Print the document and then close it.

14. Close all open documents.

15. Exit WordPerfect (unless you will be doing the following exercises immediately).

Exercise 12.2

1. Start WordPerfect, if necessary.

2. Open a new file, and key Figure 12-9, which appears at the end of this exercise. Format it as a standard block-style business letter.

3. Insert the table found in file 12-2a.wpw into the business letter created in step 2 above:

   A. Open the file 12-2a.wpw.

   B. Select the sentence above the table, the table, and the blank line below the table.

   C. Choose Copy from the Edit menu.

   D. Choose the untitled document from the Window menu.

   E. Position the insertion point at the beginning of the paragraph that begins "I suggest that we", and choose Paste from the Edit menu.

   F. Correct the spacing between paragraphs, if necessary.

4. Convert the paragraph above the table to a comment:

   A. Select the paragraph that begins "These are comparisons".

   B. Choose Comment from the Tools menu and Create from the Comment cascading menu.

5. Insert the text found in file 12-2b.wpw at the end of the letter. This file contains standard closing paragraphs for Five Points Realty:

   A. Open the file 12-2b.wpw.

   B. Select all the text in the file, including the first paragraph, and choose Copy from the Edit menu.

   C. Switch to the untitled document.

   D. At the end of the document, position the insertion point to the left of "Sincerely," and choose Paste from the Edit menu.

   E. Convert the line "Closing paragraphs for comparisons letter." and the two blank lines below it to a comment.

F. Correct the paragraph spacing, if necessary.

6. Spell-check the untitled document.

7. Save the untitled document as *[your three-letter identifier]*12-2c.wpw. Do not save 12-2a.wpw or 12-2b.wpw.

8. Print the current document, and then close all open documents.

9. Exit WordPerfect (unless you will be doing the following exercises immediately).

Figure 12-9

July 10, 199-

Mr. & Mrs. Steven Smaha

234 Crescent Hill Lane

Roswell, GA 30076

Dear Mr. & Mrs. Smaha:

Thank you for contacting me about the sale of your lovely home on Crescent Hill Lane. The following table lists the comparisons on homes that have sold recently in your area:

I suggest that we list your home at $165,900. The selling price most likely will be about $162,000. If you list at $165,900, I am quite confident that your home will be sold within three months.

Sincerely,

Ronnie Palmer

Sales Associate

Exercise 12.3

1. Start WordPerfect, if necessary.
2. Open the file 12-3a.wpw.
3. Format it as a memo to Mary Rigdon from Bud Porter, dated July 29, 199-, with the subject "Defects in Listed Property".
4. Copy all of the text in file 12-3b.wpw, and paste it at the end of the memo, after the paragraph that begins "The following is a copy".
5. Spell-check the document.
6. Save the document as *[your three-letter identifier]*12-3a.wpw and print it.
7. Open the file 12-3c.wpw.
8. Format document 12-3c.wpw as a business letter addressed to Mr. & Mrs. Robert Waters, 7 Mountain View Lane, Stone Mountain, GA 30331; from Mary Rigdon, Office Manager; dated July 31, 199-. Use the standard block style.
9. Copy the fifth and sixth paragraphs from document 12-3b.wpw, beginning with "[The Court]".
10. Paste the paragraphs into the document 12-3a.wpw before the fourth paragraph, which begins "I always make every effort".
11. Double-indent the two paragraphs copied in step 9.
12. Spell-check the document.
13. Save the document as *[your three-letter identifier]*12-3c.wpw.
14. Print the document.
15. Close all open document windows and exit WordPerfect (unless you will be doing the following exercises immediately).

Exercise 12.4

1. Start WordPerfect, if necessary.
2. Create a new document, and format it as a standard business letter dated August 31, 199-.
3. Open the file 12-4a.wpw.
4. Copy the name and address for Angela Jacoby from document 12-4a.wpw, and paste it to the inside address area of the document created in step 2.

5. Insert an appropriate salutation.
6. For the body of the letter, key Figure 12-10, which follows this exercise. Include the corrections indicated.
7. Open the file 12-4b.wpw.
8. Copy the two paragraphs and heading for "Real Estate Principles and Practices", and paste them above the paragraph that begins "Remember, the fall semester".
9. Underline the course-description heading, if necessary.
10. Insert an appropriate signature block from Mary Trant, Coordinator.
11. Spell-check the document.
12. Save the document as *[your three-letter identifier]*12-4c.wpw.
13. Print the document, but do not close it.
14. Delete the inside address and salutation.
15. Copy Gideon Fraser's name and address from document 12-4a.wpw.
16. Insert a salutation for Mr. Fraser.
17. Delete the course description.
18. Insert the course description for "Real Estate Finance" from document 12-4b.wpw. Underline the course heading, if necessary.
19. Save the document as *[your three-letter identifier]*12-4d.wpw.
20. Print the document.
21. Close all open document windows, and exit WordPerfect (unless you will be doing the following exercise immediately).

Figure 12-10

This letter *acknowledges receipt of* ~~is to let you know that we received~~ your check for $150~~.00~~,

and confirms ~~that~~ your registration ~~is all set~~ *for the following courses:*

Remember ~~Don't forget~~, the Fall semester begins on Monday, September 13, and,

unless otherwise noted runs for six weeks, in the course description.

Exercise 12.5

1. Start WordPerfect, if necessary.

2. Open a new document window, and key Figure 12-11, which appears at the end of this exercise. Format the tabulation so that it is attractively spaced. Set separate tabs for the dollar signs. Dollar signs should appear only on the first line, but should be aligned to the left of the largest number in the column.

3. Save the document keyed in step 2 as *[your three-letter identifier]*12-5a.wpw. Do not close it.

4. Open a second new document window, and key Figure 12-12, which appears at the end of this exercise.

5. Save the document keyed in step 4 as *[your three-letter identifier]*12-5b.wpw. Do not close it.

6. Open the file 12-5c.wpw.

7. Copy all the information from document *[your three-letter identifier]*12-5a.wpw to the end of document 12-5c.wpw.

8. Copy all the information from document *[your three-letter identifier]*12-5b.wpw to the end of document 12-5c.wpw.

9. Working in document 12-5c.wpw, in the Marietta tabulation, move the line with P. Golden's figures above R. Palmer's figures.

10. Spell-check the document.

11. Convert the two notes in the document to comments.

12. Save the current document as *[your three-letter identifier]*12-5c.wpw.

13. Print the document, but do not close it.

14. Convert the comments to text, and save the document as *[your three-letter identifier]*12-5d.wpw.

15. Print the document again, and close all open documents.

16. Exit WordPerfect.

Figure 12-11

Note: These are preliminary figures supplied by A. Delbridge and are subject to change.

Buckhead	Qtr 1	Qtr 2
A. Delbridge	$ 452,000	$ 548,000
R. Denton	625,000	510,000
R. Mercer	710,000	540,000
C. Morton	647,000	472,000
W. Reston	450,000	420,000

Figure 12-12

Note: These are preliminary figures supplied by M. Rigdon and are subject to change.

Marietta	Qtr 1	Qtr 2
D. Feingold	$ n/a	$ 450,000
R. Palmer	445,000	572,000
M. Rigdon	1,200,000	1,157,000
P. Golden	437,000	489,000
G. Swain	642,000	597,000

Lesson 13

Search and Replace

Objectives

- Search for words and phrases in a document.
- Search for formatting codes.
- Use strings and wildcards.
- Search for strings and replace them with new strings.

Search and Replace are extremely valuable timesavers for revising text. They make it easy to find words or phrases in long documents and make changes to them. Suppose you printed the first draft of a contract, and then used your red pen to edit the document. With the Search option, you can move to words or phrases that need to be corrected quickly. The Replace feature allows you to search a document for a word or phrase that may appear several times and to replace each occurrence with new text. For instance, if the name "A. R. Smith, Inc." appears many times, and you realize that the correct name is "The Smith Corporation," you can use Search and Replace to find the incorrect company name and make the corrections quickly and accurately.

Searching for Text

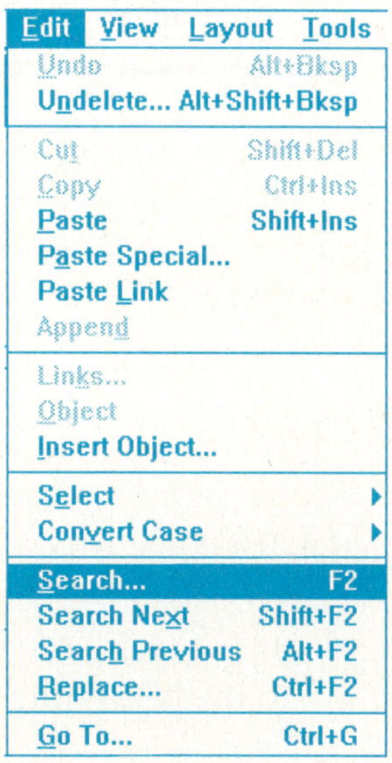

The Edit menu

Note: When you close the Search dialog box, the text in the Search For text box is remembered. The next time you open the Search dialog box, the text used in the previous search will appear.

To search for text, open the Search dialog box by choosing Search from the Edit menu. Key a word or phrase in the Search For text box, and click the Search command button. The Search dialog box will close, and the insertion point will move to the left of the first occurrence of the Search For text in the document.

If the text is not found, the message "String not found" will appear briefly on the status bar in the lower left corner of the screen. In this case, the insertion point will remain where it was before you opened the Search dialog box.

The Search Dialog Box

When you open the Search dialog box by choosing Search from the Edit menu, you will see the following options:

- The Search For text box

  An insertion point or selected text will appear in this box. Key the word or phrase to be searched.

- The Search Document Body Only check box

  By default, WordPerfect searches all text in a document, including headers, footers, footnotes, and other text that is not part of the document body. To eliminate this text from your search, put a check mark in this box.

- The Direction pop-up button

  WordPerfect always starts a search at the insertion-point position and searches forward or backward, depending on the direction you choose.

- The Codes command button

  Choosing the Codes button opens a dialog box allowing you to search for format codes, such as underline, bold, and hard return.

- The Search command button

  The Search command button is equivalent to an OK button in other dialog boxes, and should be clicked after all search options are selected.

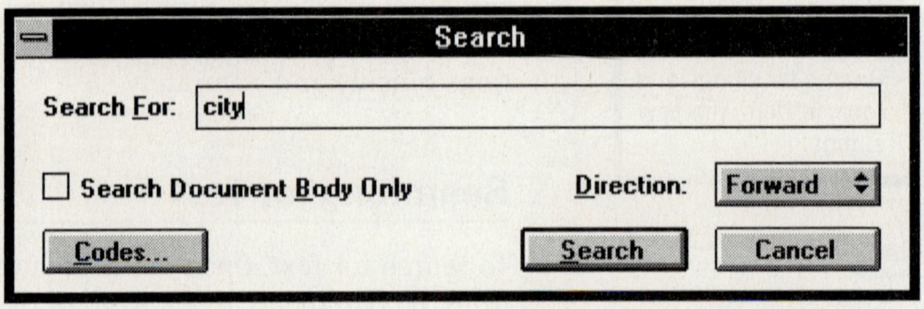

Figure 13-1
The Search dialog box

Searching for a Word

Search for a word by keying it in the Search For text box, and then clicking the Search command button.

1. Start WordPerfect, if necessary.

2. Open the file 13-0.wpw.

3. Press **Ctrl+Home** to move the insertion point to the beginning of the document, if necessary.

   WordPerfect always starts a search from the insertion-point position. If the insertion point is in the second paragraph, words in the first paragraph will not be found, unless you search backwards.

The Search button

4. Choose Search from the Edit menu (or click the Search button if the Button Bar is displayed).

   The Search dialog box opens, showing either an insertion point or selected text in the Search For text box.

5. Key **city**.
6. Click the Search command button to start the search.

   The Search dialog box closes. WordPerfect finds "city" in the second line of the document. The insertion point moves to the right of the last character in the word that was found.

To find the next occurrence of the word "city":

1. Choose Search from the Edit menu (or press the keyboard shortcut **F2**) to open the Search dialog box.

   Notice that the word "city" is displayed already in the Search For text box.

2. Click the Search command button.

   The word "city" is found again in the third line.

A faster way to find the next occurrence is to choose Search Next from the Edit menu:

1. Choose Search Next from the Edit menu (or use the keyboard shortcut **Shift+F2**).

   The dialog box does not open, but the next occurrence of "city" is found in the second paragraph.

2. Choose Search Next from the Edit menu again.

   This time, the insertion point does not move. WordPerfect displays a message in the status bar telling you that it cannot find any more occurrences of the word "city" in this document.

To go back to a previous occurrence of "city", you can search backwards:

1. Choose Search Previous from the Edit menu (or press **Alt+F2**).

   The insertion point moves back to the first paragraph and finds "city" on line three.

The Direction pop-up button

2. Choose Search from the Edit menu.

   The Search dialog box opens. The Direction button indicates Backward.

3. Choose Cancel to close the Search dialog box.

Searching for a Phrase

You can search for a phrase by keying the words in the Search text box. You must be careful to key the words exactly as they appear in the document, including the spacing between words and any punctuation.

To search for the phrase "of the city":

1. Press **Ctrl+Home** to move the insertion point to the beginning of the document.
2. Open the Search dialog box by choosing Search from the Edit menu or pressing **F2**.
3. Key **of the city** in the Search For text box.
4. Choose Forward by clicking and dragging up on the Direction pop-up button.

   The Direction pop-up button was set to Backward when you chose Search Previous in the last procedure.
5. Click the Search button.

   The phrase "of the city" is found in the second line of the first paragraph.
6. Choose Search Next (or press **Shift+F2**) to find the next occurrence of the phrase.

   The phrase "of the city" is found again, this time on the third line.
7. Press **Shift+F2** to find a third occurrence in the second paragraph.

Note: If a Search command is unsuccessful, check to be sure you are searching in the correct direction. Remember, WordPerfect searches from the insertion-point position in the direction indicated by the Direction pop-up button.

Searching for Codes

You can search for formatting codes such as [Indent] or [HRt]. To insert a code in the Search For text box, click the Codes command button in the Search dialog box. The Codes dialog box will open with a list of codes from which to choose. Codes must be chosen from this dialog box; they cannot be keyed in the Search For text box.

Characters keyed to search for the HRt code

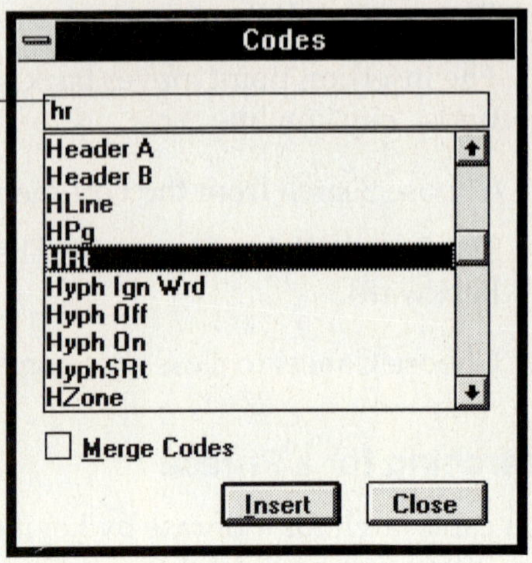

Figure 13-2
The Codes dialog box

The on-screen document has an incorrect hard return in the first paragraph. You can search for this code and then delete it. To search for the code:

1. Press **Ctrl+Home** to move the insertion point to the beginning of the document.
2. Choose Reveal Codes from the View menu (or press **Alt+F3**), so that you can see the results of the search.
3. Open the Search dialog box.
4. Click the Codes command button.

   The Codes dialog box opens, and the Search dialog box remains open.
5. Select the code HRt from the list box. If you know the spelling of a code, you can key the first few characters instead of using the scroll bar to find it on the list. The characters you key appear at the top of the list.

   Notice that the codes are arranged alphabetically.
6. Choose the Insert command button. (You also can double-click the code.)

   The selected code is inserted into the Search For text box in the Search dialog box.
7. Choose Close to close the Codes dialog box.
8. Click the Search command button in the Search dialog box.

   The insertion point moves to the first position after the code [HRt] in the middle of the first paragraph, before the words "perform the covenants".
9. Press the **Backspace** key to delete the [HRt] code.
10. Close the Reveal Codes space by choosing Reveal Codes from the View menu (or pressing **Alt+F3**).

Using Strings

String
A series of any combination of characters, punctuation marks, spaces, format codes, or wildcards.

When you choose the Search command, WordPerfect searches for exactly the characters you keyed in the Search For text box (the search string). A *string* can be any combination of characters, spaces, formatting codes, or wildcards that represent part of a word or phrase you are searching for or want to replace.

If you misspelled a word in a document, but spelled it correctly in the Search For text box, the word will not be found, because the search string in the Search For text box does not match the string of characters in the document. If you suspect that a word is misspelled, you can search for part of the string. For example, the string "doc" will find "document" and also will find the misspelled "documnet."

If you search for "the", WordPerfect will find "the", "other", and "their", because the three-character string is found in each of these words. If you want to find only "the", and not characters that are part of a larger word, insert a space before and after the word. For example, key the five character string "<space>the<space>" to find "the" and not "other", and key "<space>he<space>" to find "he" and not "she" or "help".

Search for the word "the":

1. Position the insertion point at the beginning of the second paragraph, which begins "Lot 23A, Block 3".
2. Open the Search dialog box.
3. Key **the** in the Search For text box.
4. Click the Search button.

   The word "the" is found.

5. Find the next occurrence of "the". (Remember, you can press **Shift+F2** to Search Next.)

   The word "Northeast" is found.

6. Position the insertion point at the beginning of the second paragraph.
7. Open the Search dialog box.
8. Press the **Spacebar**, key **the,** and press the **Spacebar** again.
9. Click the Search button.

   The cursor moves to the word "the".

10. Press **Shift+F2** to find the next occurrence.

    This time, WordPerfect skips over "Northeast".

Using Wildcards

Wildcard
A character or code representing an unknown character. In WordPerfect, the code [Any Char] represents one unknown character in a search string.

Sometimes, you need to find a string that has unknown characters. You can insert a *wildcard* to represent an unknown character in a search string. The code [Any Char] represents a wildcard in search strings. To insert the code [Any Char], choose Codes from the Search dialog box. You must include one [Any Char] code for each unknown character in the string.

For example, suppose the document contains some numbers, and you need to ensure that they are correct. You know that all the numbers start with the characters "PN", have three digits, and end with the character "X". You can use the wildcard string

"PN[Any Char][Any Char][Any Char]X"

to find PN123X, PN763X, and PN901X. The example string will not find PN12X or PN1234X, because the number of characters do not match the search string.

To search for a wildcard string:

1. Press **Ctrl+Home** to move the insertion point to the beginning of the document.

A search string with the wildcard [Any Char]

2. Choose Search from the Edit menu (or press **F2**).
3. Press the **Spacebar** and then key **i**. (Make sure "i" is lowercase.)
4. Choose Codes to open the Codes dialog box.
5. Choose Any Char from the Codes list box.
6. Choose Insert to insert the code [Any Char] in the Search For text box (or double-click the code).
7. Press the **Spacebar**.

Note: It is not necessary to close the Codes dialog box before starting the search.

8. Click the Search button.

   WordPerfect finds the word "if".

9. Choose Search Next from the Edit menu.

   The word "in" is found.

10. Choose Search Next two more times (or press **Shift+F2**).

    The words "in" and "if" are found again. (The words "is" and "it" also would have been found if they were in the document.)

Capitalization

Lowercase characters in a search string will find uppercase and lowercase characters. Uppercase characters in the search string will find only an exact uppercase character match. For example, the search string "five star" will find "five star" and "Five Star", but the string "Five Star" will find only "Five Star". To find each sentence that starts with the word "The", key "The" and not "the" in the Search For text box.

To see how capitalization affects a search string:

1. Press **Ctrl+Home** to move the insertion point to the beginning of the document.

2. Open the Search dialog box and key **payments**.

3. Click the Search button.

   The string "payments" is found.

4. Press **Ctrl+Home** to move the insertion point to the beginning of the document.

5. Open the Search dialog box, and change the lowercase "p" in "payments" to uppercase.

6. Click the Search button.

   This time, the message "String not found" is displayed on the status bar, because there are no occurrences of the string "Payments" (with an uppercase "P") in the document.

7. Press **Ctrl+Home** to move the insertion point to the beginning of the document, if necessary.

8. Search for "atlanta" (lowercase "a").

9. "Atlanta" is found, because lowercase characters find both lowercase and uppercase characters.

Table 13-1: Examples of Strings

String	Represents
the	the, The, northeast
<space>the<space>	the, The
The	The, Their, Then, but not the, their, or then
Warranty Deed	Warranty Deed
qtr[any char]	Qtr1, qtr2, qtrs, Qtrx, etc.
<space>replace.	the word "replace" only at the end of a sentence

Using Search and Replace

The Replace option on the Edit menu will allow you to search for all occurrences of a string in a document and replace it with another string. For example, if you misspelled the name of a city in several places, you can use Search and Replace to correct all occurrences of the name.

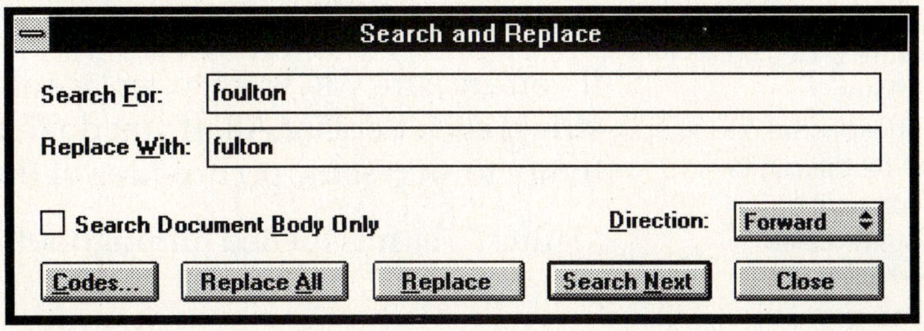

Figure 13-3
The Search and Replace dialog box

Choosing Replace from the Edit menu will open the Search and Replace dialog box. (The keyboard shortcut key for Replace is **Ctrl+F2**.) This dialog box has many of the same features as the Search dialog box. In addition, it has the Replace With text box and three command buttons: Replace All, Replace, and Search Next.

There are two ways to use Search and Replace. Click Search Next to decide whether or not to replace each string as it is found. Click Replace All to change all occurrences of the string without making individual decisions.

Replacing Selectively

If you are not sure what the results of a search-and-replace procedure will be, you can have WordPerfect stop each time it finds the string. Then you can make individual decisions for each occurrence. Click Search Next in the Search and Replace dialog box to find the first occurrence of the search string. If you want it replaced with the Replace string, click Replace. WordPerfect will replace it and move to the next occurrence of the search string. If you do not want to replace the string, click Search Next.

Searching for Space Characters

A simple and helpful use of Search and Replace is to look for extraneous space characters. It is not always easy to spot two consecutive space characters, especially in a long document, until after you print the document. If you are working with proportionally spaced fonts and full justification, they are almost impossible to find.

To search for two consecutive space characters, open the Search dialog box, and press the **Spacebar** twice to insert two space characters. You will not see the space characters in the Search For text box, but the insertion point will move two spaces to the right, indicating that you have entered the spaces. When you click Search, WordPerfect will search for two consecutive spaces.

The quickest way to eliminate two consecutive space characters in a document is to use the Replace command. In the Search For text box, press the **Spacebar** twice. In the Replace With text box, press the **Spacebar** once. Then click Replace All, and all occurrences will be replaced with one space character.

Note: Always save the document before choosing Replace All. Sometimes, you will get unexpected results that can be difficult to undo. If you saved the document before replacing, you can close it without saving, and open the original document again.

Replacing All Occurrences

If you are sure you want to replace all occurrences of the Search For string, click Replace All. If you do this, you will not have an opportunity to skip some occurrences of the search string.

"Fulton" is misspelled throughout the on-screen document. To correct it:

1. Press **Ctrl+Home** to move the insertion point to the beginning of the document, if necessary.
2. Choose Replace from the Edit menu.
3. Key **Foulton** in the Search For text box.
4. Press the **Tab** key to move the insertion point to the Replace With text box.
5. Key **Fulton**.
6. Click Replace All.

   All occurrences are found and replaced. The dialog box remains open.
7. Click Close to complete the operation and close the dialog box.

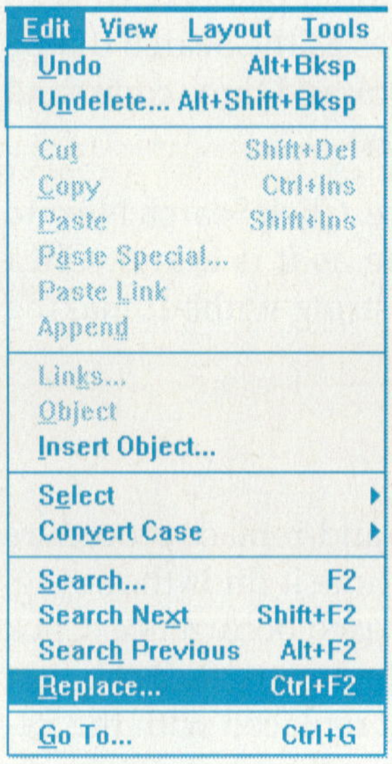

The Edit menu

Several phrases are underlined in this document. To remove all underlines:

1. Press **Ctrl+Home** to move the insertion point to the beginning of the document.
2. Choose Replace from the Edit menu.
3. Choose Codes to open the Codes dialog box.
4. Double-click Und On in the Codes list box.

   The code [Und On] is inserted in the Search For text box.
5. Press the **Tab** key.

   The insertion point moves to the Replace With text box.
6. Press **Delete** to remove any string that might be in the Replace With text box, if necessary.

   You are replacing the [Und On] code with nothing. The Replace With text box must be empty.
7. Click Replace All.

   All the [Und On] codes are removed. Since [Und On] is a paired code, removing it automatically removes its related code, [Und Off].
8. Close the dialog box.

In the on-screen document, the word "state" should be capitalized whenever the phrase "State of Georgia" appears. It is lowercase now. To change "state" to "State":

1. Press **Ctrl+Home** to move the insertion point to the beginning of the document, if necessary.
2. Choose Replace from the Edit menu.
3. Key **state** in the Search For text box.
4. Press the **Tab** key to move to the Replace With text box.
5. Key **State** (uppercase "S").
6. Click Search Next.

   The word "state" is found on the second line.
7. Click Replace.

   "state" is replaced with "State", and the next occurrence is found.
8. Click Replace again.

   The second occurrence of "state" is replaced with "State", and then the word "stated" is found.
9. Click Search Next, to bypass "stated".

   The word "estate" is found.
10. Click Search Next, and continue making individual decisions until the last string "state" is found.
11. Click Close to end the procedure.
12. Save the document as *[your three-letter identifier]*13-0.wpw and print it.
13. Close the document.
14. Exit WordPerfect (unless you will be doing the following exercises immediately).

Table 13-2: Keyboard Shortcuts for Search and Replace

Keyboard Shortcut	Action
F2	Search
Shift+F2	Search Next
Alt+F2	Search Previous
Ctrl+F2	Replace

Key Terms

String
Wildcard

Exercises

Exercise 13.1

1. Start WordPerfect, if necessary.
2. Open the file 13-1.wpw.
3. Replace all occurrences of "GCBR" with "ABR":
   A. Choose Replace from the Edit menu (or press **Ctrl+F2**).
   B. Key **GCBR** in the Search For text box.
   C. Key **ABR** in the Replace With text box.
   D. Click the Replace All button. (Do not close the Search and Replace dialog box.)
4. Replace all occurrences of "Chicago" with "Atlanta":
   A. While the Search and Replace dialog box is open, click anywhere in the document, and then press **Ctrl+Home** to move the insertion point to the beginning of the document.
   B. Double-click "GCBR" in the Search For text box to select it and key **Chicago.**
   C. Press the **Tab** key to move to the Replace With text box and key **Atlanta**.
   D. Click the Replace All button.
5. All evening classes will end at 9:15. Use wildcards to do a selective search and replace of class ending times:
   A. Position the insertion point at the beginning of the document.
   B. Open the Search and Replace dialog box, if necessary.
   C. Key **9:** (including the colon) in the search for text box.
   D. Click the Codes command button.
   E. Choose the Any Char code from the list box.
   F. Click Insert to put the code in the Search for text box.
   G. Click Insert again to put a second Any Char code in the text box.

H. Key **9:15** in the Replace With text box.

I. Click Search Next, and go through the document, making sure you replace only the evening ending times and not the Saturday starting times.

6. Using a wildcard search, change all the evening starting times to 6:15.

7. Indent a list of seminars:

   A. Search for "Fair Housing".

   B. Select the list of seminars, starting with the blank line above "Fair Housing & Ethical Practices" and including "Real Estate Taxes".

   C. Open the Search and Replace dialog box.

   D. Insert the code [HRt] in the Search For text box.

   E. Insert the codes [HRt][Tab] in the Replace With text box.

   F. Click Replace All.

8. Using Search and Replace, indent the list that starts with "Buyers' Brokerage".

9. Use Search and Replace to find all occurrences of "Instructor:" and apply the bold attribute to them. (The Replace With string should be "[Bold On]Instructor:[Bold Off].")

10. Spell-check the document and print it.

11. Save the document as *[your three-letter identifier]*13-1.wpw.

12. Close the document and exit WordPerfect (unless you will be doing the following exercises immediately).

Exercise 13.2

1. Start WordPerfect, if necessary.

2. Open the file 13-2.wpw.

3. Format the document as a standard block-style business letter dated July 17, 199-, from Bud Porter, addressed to Mrs. Dorothy Harris, Chairperson, Atlanta Board of Realtors, 45 Peachtree Street, Atlanta, GA 30303. Use the salutation "Dear Dorothy:".

4. Replace all occurrences of the acronym "ABR" with the phrase "Atlanta Board of Realtors":

   A. Position the insertion point at the beginning of the document.

B. Open the Search and Replace dialog box.

C. Key **ABR** in the Search For text box.

D. Key **Atlanta Board of Realtors** in the Replace With text box.

E. Click Replace All.

5. Search backwards for all occurrences of "ABR" to verify that all occurrences were changed.

6. Capitalize "realtor" where needed:

   A. Position the insertion point at the beginning of the document.

   B. Open the Search and Replace dialog box.

   C. Key **realtor** in the Search For text box.

   D. Key **Realtor** in the Replace With text box.

   E. Selectively replace "realtor" only when it should be capitalized.

7. Search for "The luncheon was extremely well done."

8. Manually delete the words "well done" and key **effective.**

9. Spell-check the document and print it.

10. Save the document as *[your three-letter identifier]*13-2.wpw.

11. Close the document and exit WordPerfect (unless you will be doing the following exercises immediately).

Exercise 13.3

1. Start WordPerfect, if necessary.

2. Open the file 13-3a.wpw.

3. Format the document as a memo to Rick Slaney from Bud Porter, dated July 6, 199-, with the subject "Board of Realtors Courses".

4. Open the file 13-3b.wpw (without closing document 13-3a.wpw), and copy all the text to the end of document 13-3a.wpw.

5. Working in document 13-3a.wpw, replace all occurrences of "Greater Chicago" with "Atlanta".

6. Replace "GCBR" with "ABR".

7. Replace some occurrences of "Chicago" with "Atlanta". Use the context of the surrounding text to determine when "Chicago" should not be changed.

8. Find "194 Illinois Ave.", and manually change the address to "45 Peachtree St., Atlanta, GA 30303".

9. In the next paragraph, which begins "Registration by FAX", manually change the FAX number from "555-2133" to "555-0562".

10. Change Sheila Baldwin's phone number from "555-2323" to "555-0701". Use the Search command to find it in the document, if necessary.

11. Center the title "Fall Announcement".

12. Use Search and Replace to indent the list of payment forms after the fifth paragraph. Each item in the list begins with an asterisk.

13. Spell-check the document and print it.

14. Save the document as *[your three-letter identifier]*13-3a.wpw.

15. Close the document and exit WordPerfect (unless you will be doing the following exercises immediately).

Exercise 13.4

1. Start WordPerfect, if necessary.

2. Open a new file, and key document 13-4, which appears at the end of this exercise, including the corrections indicated.

3. Search for "FPR".

4. Repeat the search for "FPR" six times. (Use the **Shift+F2** keyboard shortcut.)

5. Replace all occurrences of "FPR" with "Five Points Realty".

6. Search backwards for all occurrences of "FPR" to verify that the changes were made.

7. Change all occurrences of "down town" to "downtown".

8. Use search and replace to remove all underlining from the document. (Hint: Search for the [Und On] code. The Replace With text box should be empty.)

9. Move the third paragraph, which begins "Five Points Realty is a large", to the beginning of the document, just after the by-line.

10. Center the title "FIVE POINTS REALTY: GROWING WITH ATLANTA" and make it bold.

11. Right-justify "by Ann Delbridge" and italicize it.

12. Spell-check the document and print it.

13. Save the document as *[your three-letter identifier]*13-4.wpw.

14. Close the document and exit WordPerfect (unless you will be doing the following exercise immediately).

Document 13-4

FIVE POINTS REALTY: GROWING WITH ATLANTA

by Ann Delbridge

In the 1960s and 1970s, FPR was instrumental in the development of many of the hotel and offices complexes that sprang up around Atlanta's Merchandise Mart and Apparel Mart. It was during this period that FPR grew to become one of the ~~greatest~~ major real estate agencies in the Atlanta ~~region~~ area.

FPR originally was located ~~on~~ at the ~~crossroads~~ corner of Peachtree and Wall streets. It ~~was~~ moved in the mid-1970s to its current address when the Metropolitan Atlanta Rapid Transit Authority (MARTA) was created. MARTA purchased Five Point's original location and built its Five Points Station on ~~it~~ the site.

FPR is a large real estate agency in down town Atlanta. It was started in 1952 by Harold Porter. While working for a down town real estate agency, Mr. Porter came to the conclusion that the down town Atlanta business area was about ready to explode. He quit his job, started FPR, and the rest is history.

Harold Porter, the founder of FPR, is a long-time Atlanta resident. He has served on many municipal and civic boards. Because of Mr. Porter, FPR has assisted in some of Atlanta's most significant civic development projects. For example, Five Points was one of the early real-estate pioneers of Underground Atlanta in the 1960s.

~~When his father, Harold, retired in 1987,~~ *Harold's son* Chester "Bud" Porter has run the company *since his father retired in 1987* ~~ever since~~. Bud Porter has followed his father's tradition of being involved with Atlanta's booming down town business area. He was very involved with the recent "rediscovery" of Underground Atlanta after it had been closed down in 1981 due to subway construction and other problems.

Exercise 13.5

1. Start WordPerfect, if necessary.
2. Open the file 13-5.wpw.
3. Use Search and Replace to capitalize all occurrences of "purchaser" and "seller".
4. Remove the bold attribute from all occurrences of "Purchaser".
5. Remove the underline attribute from all occurrences of "Seller".
6. Use the Replace All option of Search and Replace to change the acronym "EOC" to "execution of this contract".
7. All the paragraphs in this document are numbered. Two paragraphs are out of order. Use Cut and Paste or Drag and Drop to rearrange all paragraphs in numerical order.
8. Using Search and Replace and wildcard strings, remove all paragraph numbers, including the lines on which they are found. All paragraph numbers are four characters long, begin with "P", and end with "C".
9. Spell-check the document and print it.
10. Save the document as *[your three-letter identifier]*13-5.wpw.
11. Close the document and exit WordPerfect.

Module 4

Page Formatting

Lessons

Lesson 14

Controlling Page Breaks

In WordPerfect, text flows automatically from the end of one page to the next, just as text wraps automatically from the end of one line to the next. This lesson focuses on the techniques for controlling and customizing this process, particularly in long documents.

This lesson also teaches special techniques for controlling precisely where on a page text and other document elements are placed. For example, a paragraph, graph, or table can be centered vertically on a page automatically. With the Advance command, you can place document elements by specifying a measurement from the edge of the page or from another document element.

Objectives

- Insert hard page breaks.
- Prevent widows and orphans.
- Use Conditional End of Page and Block Protect.
- Use the Advance command.
- Center text vertically on a page.
- Use the Go To command.
- Understand Auto Code Placement.

Soft and Hard Page Breaks

Soft page break
A page break automatically placed by WordPerfect, which is adjusted automatically to reflect changes in the document.

As you work on a document, WordPerfect constantly is calculating the amount of space available on the page. Page length is determined by the size of the paper and the top and bottom margin settings. For example, using standard-size paper and default margins, page length is nine inches. When a document exceeds this size, either through continuous keying, pasting of text, or changes in formatting, WordPerfect inserts a *soft page break*. This is an automatic page break that continually adjusts as text is added or deleted. It appears as a horizontal line on the screen. In the Reveal Codes space, the code [SPg] indicates the position of a soft page break.

To observe the automatic adjustment of a soft page break:

1. Start WordPerfect, if necessary.

2. Open the file 14-0.wpw.

3. Scroll to the bottom of page 1.

   Notice the soft page break in the middle of the last paragraph on the page.

4. At the end of the second-to-last paragraph, position the insertion point after "in the Atlanta area."

5. Press the **Spacebar,** and key the following sentence: **The Marietta office also focuses on the increasing demand for retirement homes.**

   Notice the adjustment of the soft page break.

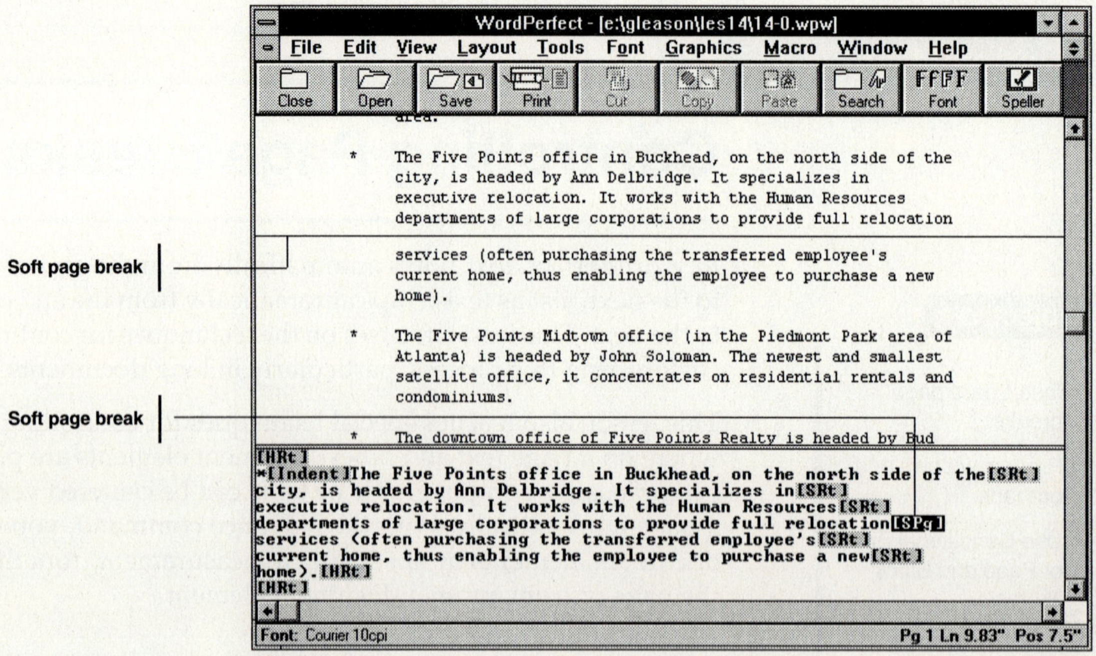

Figure 14-1
Moving a soft page break

6. To see the soft page breaks move again, move to the beginning of the document, and set the line spacing to 2.
7. Scroll to the bottom of the first page.

   Notice that the soft page break is in a new place.

A soft-page-break code cannot be deleted. It can be moved only by adding or deleting text on a page, changing the document's margins, or changing paragraph or line formatting.

Inserting Hard Page Breaks

Hard page break
A page break that is inserted manually and does not move, regardless of changes in the document.

You can control where a page breaks by inserting a *hard page break* manually. A hard page break does not move as the document is changed, and it can only be adjusted by you.

There are many reasons to insert a hard page break. You may want a certain document element to appear at the top of a new page, or the document may contain text, such as a table, that you do not want WordPerfect to break between two pages. A hard page break appears as a double horizontal line. When you create a hard page break, the code [HPg] appears in the Reveal Codes space.

There are two ways to insert a hard page break:

- Choose Page from the Layout menu, and then choose Page Break from the Page cascading menu.
- Use the keyboard shortcut **Ctrl+Enter**.

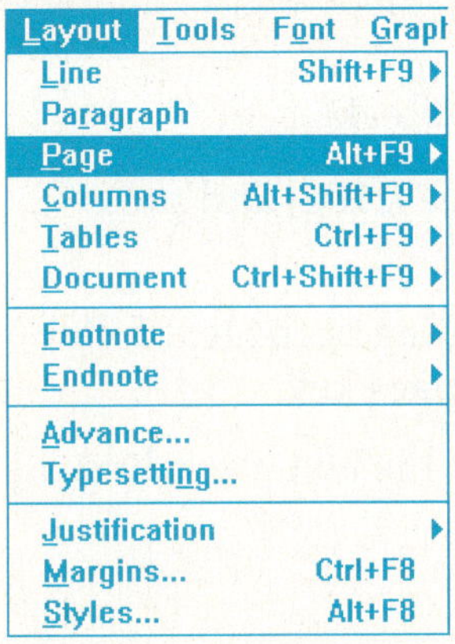

The Layout menu

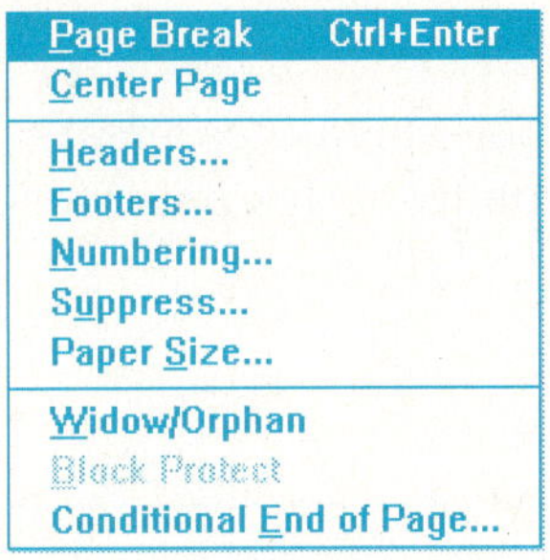

The Page cascading menu

To insert page breaks using both methods:

1. Position the insertion point to the left of the heading "A HISTORY OF SERVICE" on page 1.

2. Choose Page from the Layout menu, and then choose Page Break from the Page cascading menu.

   WordPerfect inserts a hard page break, displayed as a horizontal double line, and the heading moves to the top of the new page. Pagination is adjusted in the document from this point forward.

3. Position the insertion point to the left of the asterisk at the beginning of the last paragraph on page 3, which begins "The downtown office".

4. Press **Ctrl+Enter**.

   WordPerfect inserts a hard page break. The paragraph is no longer split by a soft page break.

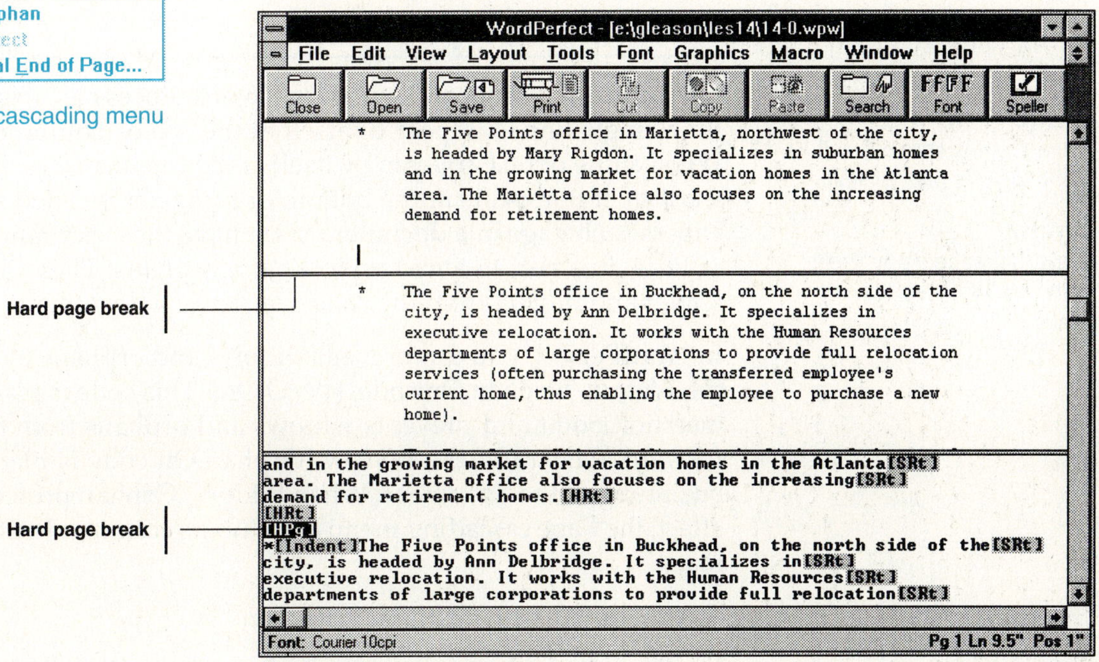

Figure 14-2
A hard page break

5. Display the Reveal Codes space.

   Notice the Hard Page Break code [HPg].

6. Close the Reveal Codes space.

Removing Hard Page Breaks

There are three ways to remove a hard page break:

- In the Reveal Codes space, select the code [HPg] and press **Delete.**
- Position the insertion point at the beginning of the text following the page break, and press the **Backspace** key.
- Position the insertion point at the end of the text preceding the page break, and press the **Delete** key.

To remove the last page break inserted:

1. Position the insertion point to the left of the asterisk at the top of page 4, if necessary.
2. Press the **Backspace** key.

   The hard page break is removed. A soft page break reappears in the middle of the paragraph. Pagination from this point forward is readjusted.

Widows and Orphans

Widow
A line that appears by itself at the top of a page of text.

Orphan
A line that appears by itself at the bottom of a page of text.

In traditional typing, and with many word processors, it is common for a single line to appear by itself at the top or bottom of a page. When a line of text appears by itself at the top of a page, it is called a *widow*. If it appears at the bottom of a page, it is called an *orphan*. Unless each page in a document must have the exact same number of lines, it is best to avoid widows and orphans. They distract the reader and detract from the cohesiveness of a document.

In WordPerfect, you can prevent widows and orphans by inserting the Widow/Orphan On code, [W/O On]. This code is placed at the insertion point and prevents widows and orphans from that point forward. Generally, the Widow/Orphan On code is placed at the beginning of the document. When Widow/Orphan protection is in effect, the Page cascading menu displays its command with a check mark.

To turn on Widow/Orphan protection:

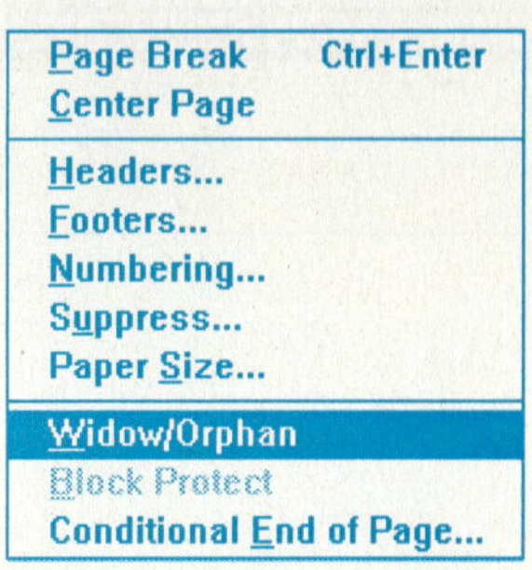

The Page cascading menu

1. Scroll to the bottom of page 3, if necessary. Observe the orphaned line. See Figure 14-3 on page 14-5.
2. Position the insertion point at the beginning of the document.
3. Choose Page from the Layout menu, and then choose Widow/Orphan from the Page cascading menu.
4. Scroll back to the bottom of page 3.

   The orphaned line has moved to the beginning of page 4.

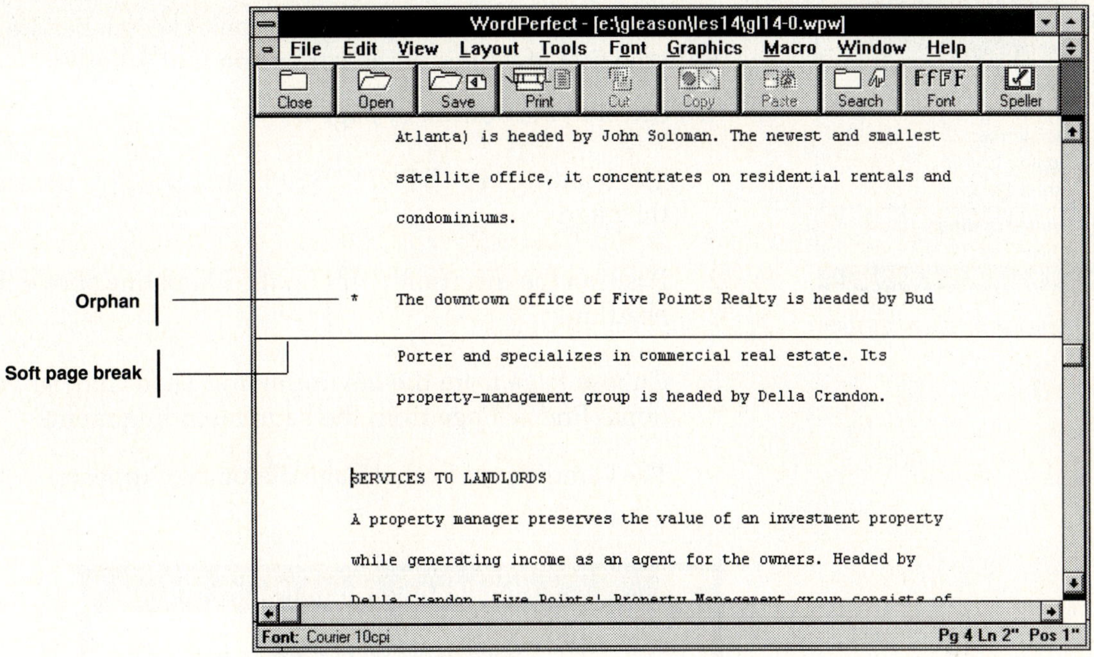

Figure 14-3
An orphaned line of text (as in step 1 on page 14-4)

You can turn off Widow/Orphan protection in two ways:

- Delete the Widow/Orphan On code
- Choose Widow/Orphan from the Page cascading menu to insert the Widow/Orphan Off code. Any text between the codes [W/O On] and [W/O Off] will be protected.

Additional Ways to Control Page Breaks

You also can control the position of soft page breaks by using the following commands:

- Conditional End of Page

  Use this command to keep a heading line together with a few lines of the paragraph following it. You can specify the number of lines that should be kept together.

- Block Protect

  Use this command to prevent a page break in the middle of a document element, such as a table or a list.

Note: When specifying how many lines to keep together, take into account the line spacing in the document. If the document is double-spaced, count the blank lines as well as the lines of text in calculating how many lines to keep together.

Conditional End of Page

To use the Conditional End of Page command, move the insertion point to the first line above the group of lines to be kept together. For example, move the insertion point to the line above a paragraph heading.

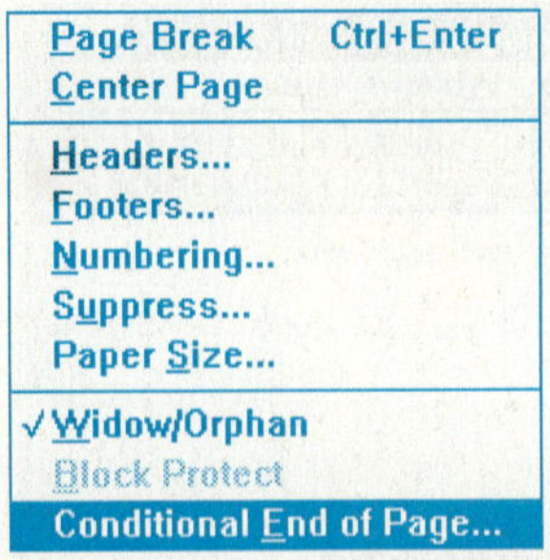

The Page cascading menu

Use the Conditional End of Page option to keep a heading together with the first few lines of the paragraph that follows:

1. Scroll to the bottom of page 2.

   The heading "FIVE POINTS SPECIALIZES" is the last line on the page.

2. Position the insertion point on the blank line above the heading.

3. Choose Page from the Layout menu. Then Choose Conditional End of Page from the Page cascading menu.

   The Conditional End of Page dialog box appears.

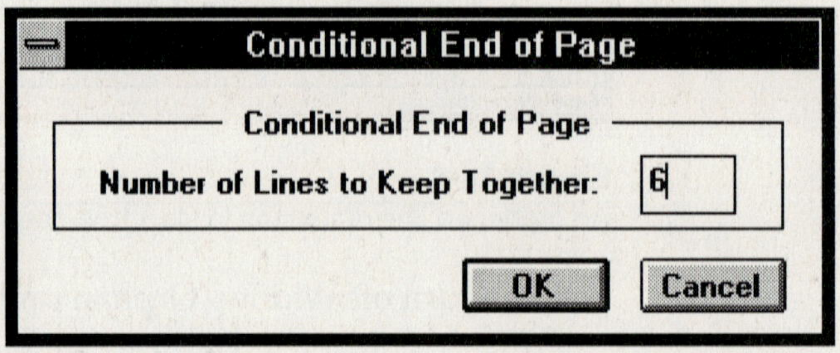

Figure 14-4
The Conditional End of Page dialog box

4. Key **6** in the Number of Lines to Keep Together text box and click OK.

   The heading moves to the top of the next page.

5. Display the Reveal Codes space, if necessary.

   The code [Cndl EOP:6] appears on the line before the heading.

Block Protect

To keep a soft page break from occurring in the middle of a block of text, select the block of text, and choose Block Protect from the Page cascading menu. WordPerfect inserts the code [Block Pro:On] at the beginning of the selected block and inserts the code [Block Pro:Off] at the end of the block.

Use Block Protect to keep a telephone list on one page:

1. Scroll to the bottom of page 4.

2. Select the entire list of phone numbers, including the heading that begins "BRANCH".

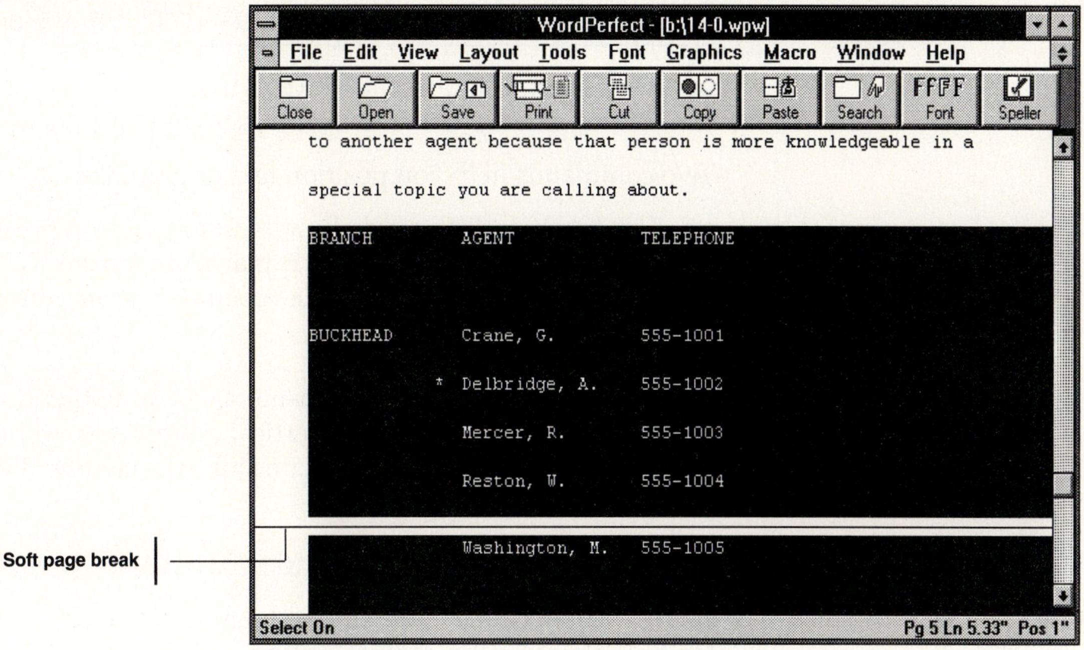

Figure 14-5
The telephone list selected for block protection

3. Choose Page from the Layout menu, and choose Block Protect from the Page cascading menu.

   The entire telephone list moves to page 5. The Block Protect command is available only when text is selected.

4. Deselect the telephone list.

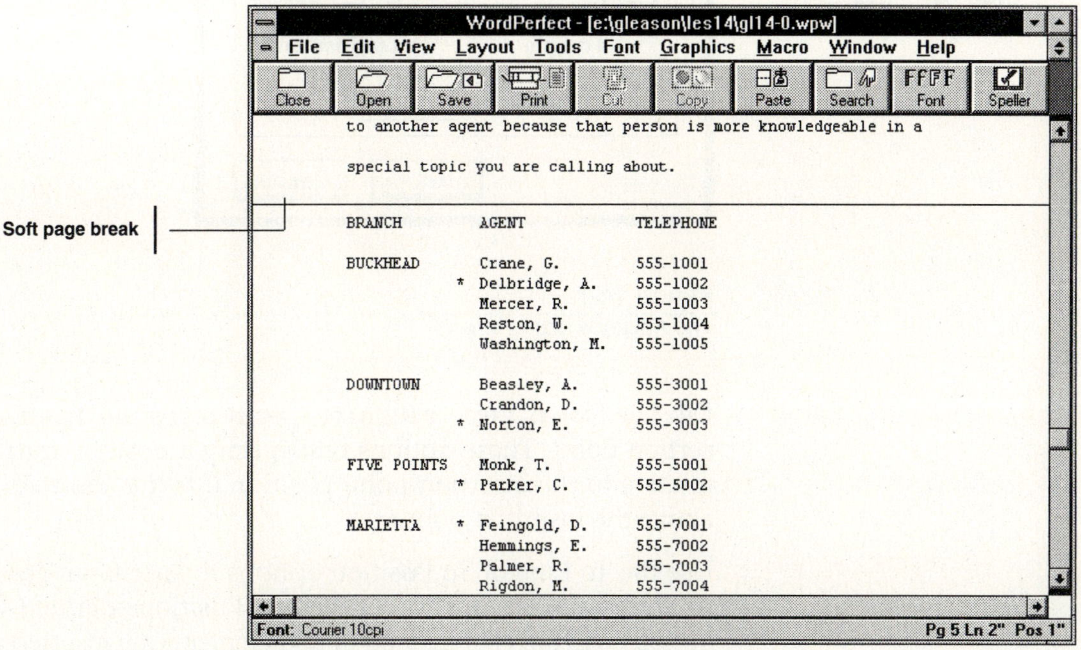

Figure 14-6
The telephone list after block protection is applied

Controlling the Placement of Text on a Page

In WordPerfect, you can center text vertically on a page, and you also can control where a document item is placed on a page.

Two commands help you position text or graphics:

- The Advance command allows you to specify a precise position where a document item is placed on a page. The position can be measured from another document item or from the edge of the page.

- The Center Page command centers text and other document items vertically on a page. Vertical centering is useful for a title page or a page that contains just one table or illustration.

Using the Advance Command

Choose Advance from the Layout menu to open the Advance dialog box. There are six options arranged in two columns in the Advance dialog box. The Up, Down, and To Line options in the left column specify vertical positions. The Left, Right, and Position options in the right column specify horizontal positions.

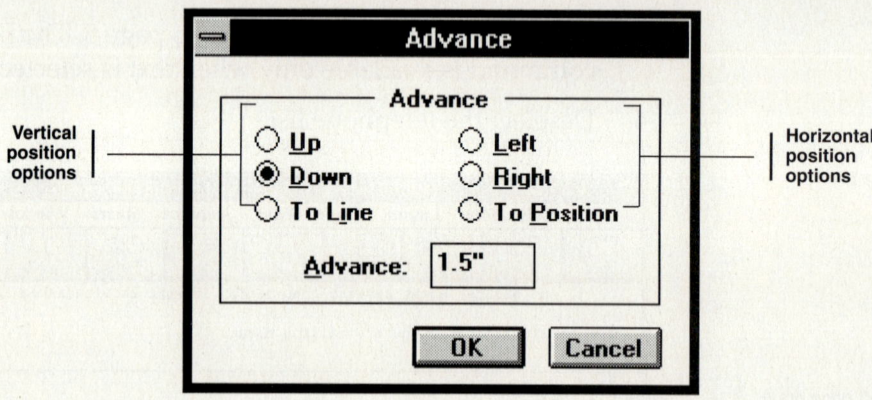

Figure 14-7
The Advance dialog box

Use Up, Down, Left, or Right to specify a position relative to the insertion point. These options will specify a position that will move relative to the insertion-point position if text is inserted or deleted above the insertion point.

Use the To Line or To Position options to specify an absolute position measured from the page edge. Positions defined with these options will not change if other text elements are inserted or deleted.

To use the Advance command:

1. Move to the left of the heading "FIVE POINTS REALTY - TELEPHONE CONTACT LIST" near the bottom of page 4, and press **Ctrl+Enter** to insert a hard page break.
2. Move to the beginning of the first paragraph, which begins "An asterisk signifies".
3. Choose Advance from the Layout menu.

   The Advance dialog box opens.
4. Choose the Down option, and key **0.5"** in the Advance text box.

   The code [AdvDn:0.5"] is inserted, and the paragraph moves down 0.5 inches.
5. Display the Reveal Codes space to see the Advance code.
6. Position the insertion point at the beginning of the telephone list, to the left of "BRANCH".
7. Choose Advance from the Layout menu.
8. In the Advance dialog box, choose To Line.
9. Key **4"** in the Advance text box and click OK.

   The code [AdvToLn:4.5"] is inserted, and the telephone-list heading moves down to the position 4.5 inches from the top edge of the page.
10. Press the **Up Arrow** key once. Watch the line indicator on the status line.

    As the insertion point moves up one line, the line indicator on the status line changes from 4" to 3.17", the position of the previous line.

Inserting or deleting lines above the telephone list will have no effect on the telephone-list position. In fact, if you add enough lines, some lines will overlap the telephone list.

To observe the effect of inserting lines above the telephone list:

1. Scroll to page 5 of the on-screen document, if necessary.
2. Choose Print Preview from the File menu, and observe the placement of text on the page.
3. Close the Print Preview window.
4. Move to the heading at the top of page 5 that begins "FIVE POINTS REALTY".

5. Press **Enter** ten times.
6. Choose Print Preview from the File menu.

   The paragraph that was above the telephone list now overlaps it.

Note: The Advance command will not advance the insertion point past a page break.

7. Close the Print Preview window.
8. Delete the ten hard returns inserted in step 5 above.

Using the Advance Command to Fill in Preprinted Forms

With the help of the Advance command, you can use WordPerfect and a laser printer to fill in the blanks on preprinted forms. To place text at a specific location on a form, measure the distance to that location from the top of the form and from the left edge of the form. Be sure to measure the vertical distance to the top of the text, not to the baseline.

In a blank document window, open the Advance dialog box, choose the To Line option, key the vertical distance in the Advance text box, and click OK. Open the Advance dialog box again to specify the horizontal distance. This time, choose the To Position option, and key the measurement from the left edge of the form. Two Advance codes are inserted—one for the horizontal distance and one for the vertical distance. Now key the information requested for the specified location.

Repeat this process for each blank on the form. When the document is completed, first print it on plain paper to check the alignment, and then feed the form into the laser and print the document again.

If you have a form that gets filled in on a regular basis, create a document with the appropriate advance codes, and key text that prompts for the information needed on the form. It may take a few attempts to get the document right, but the end result will be well worth the effort.

Centering Text Vertically

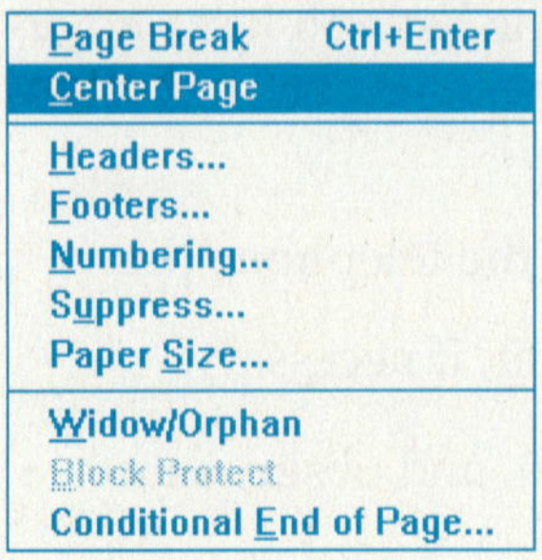

The Page cascading menu

Sometimes, you want text to appear centered vertically on a page, so that there is an equal amount of space above and below it. For example, you may want to center the text on the title page of a report. With WordPerfect, you can do this automatically using the Center Page command. This command centers text only on the current page. To center text on another page, you must move to that page and choose Center Page again. Usually, you will use this command on a page that contains only a small amount of text.

To center the text on page 1 of the on-screen document:

1. Position the insertion point at the beginning of the first page.
2. Horizontally center the first two lines of text, the title.
3. Choose Page from the Layout menu, and choose Center Page to center all the text vertically.

The code [Center Pg] is inserted at the top of the page, but you cannot see the results on the editing screen.

4. Choose Print Preview to see the results.

   The text on page 1 is centered.

Figure 14-8
Text centered vertically on a page

5. Close the Print Preview window.

Using the Go To Command

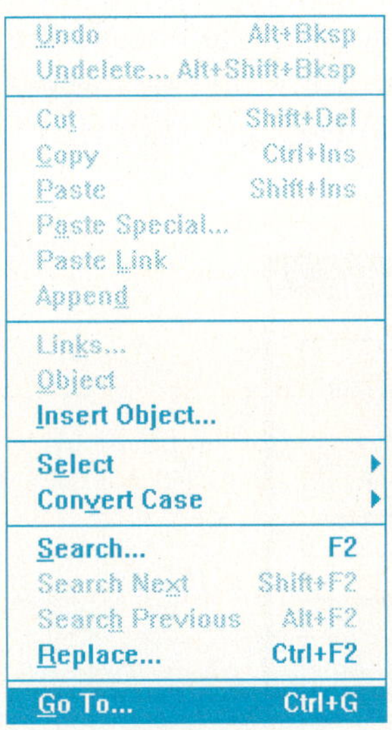

The Edit menu

WordPerfect offers several ways to move through a document quickly. The Search command, the scroll bar, and keyboard shortcuts are all methods that have been discussed in previous lessons. Another method, the Go To command, lets you move to a specific page of a document.

To use the Go To command, select Go To from the Edit menu, or use the keyboard shortcut **Ctrl+G**. In the Go To dialog box, key the appropriate page number. You also can use the Go To dialog box to move to the last insertion-point position, or to go to the top or bottom of the current page.

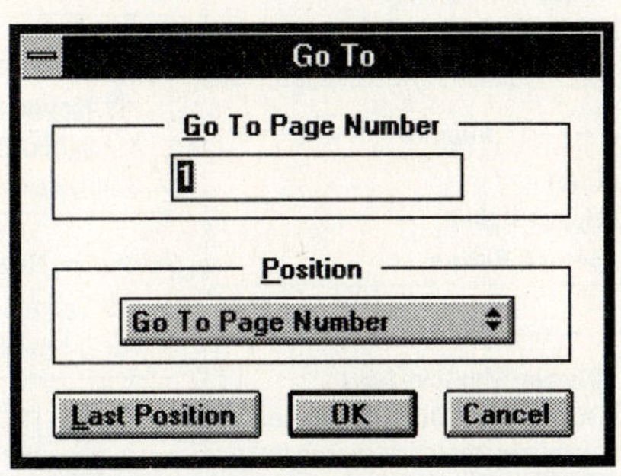

Figure 14-9
The Go To dialog box

The Position pop-up list

Note: If you open the Go To dialog box when text is selected, two additional options will be available on the Position pop-up list: Beginning of Selection and Reselect Text.

Practice using the Go To command:

1. Choose Go To from the Edit menu.

   The Go To dialog box opens.

2. Key **3** in the Go To Page Number text box and click OK.

   The insertion point moves to the top of page 3.

3. Press **Ctrl+G** to open the Go To dialog box again.

4. Click Last Position.

   The insertion point moves back to its previous position.

5. Press **Ctrl+G**.

6. Choose Bottom of Current Page from the Position pop-up list and click OK.

   The insertion point moves to the bottom of the current page.

Auto Code Placement and Page Formatting

Auto Code Placement insures that page-formatting codes will be placed at the beginning of the current page regardless of insertion-point position when the command is chosen. Likewise, it insures the proper placement of paragraph-formatting codes. When you install WordPerfect, Auto Code Placement is turned on by default.

You can turn off Auto Code Placement if you have a special formatting need. To turn off Auto Code Placement, choose Preferences from the File menu, and then choose Environment from the Preferences cascading menu. If Auto Code Placement is checked, it is in effect. Uncheck Auto Code Placement to turn it off.

The Auto Code Placement option

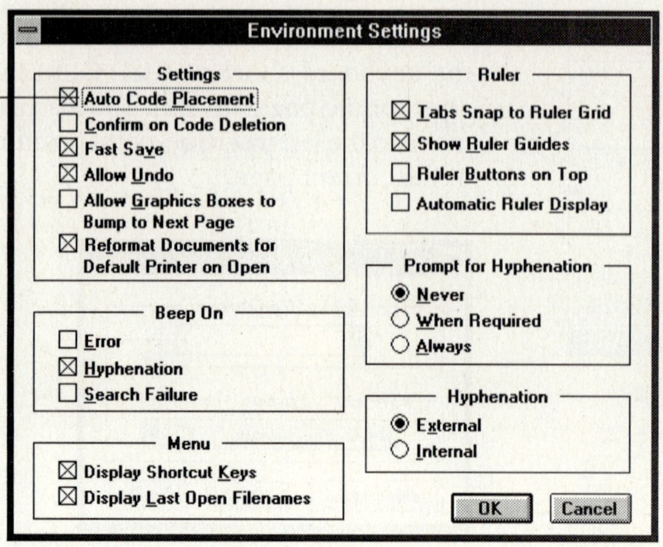

Figure 14-10
The Environment dialog box

To experiment with Auto Code Placement:

1. Move to Page 1, if necessary, and position the insertion point at the beginning of the second sentence in the first paragraph, which begins "While working for".
2. Choose Preferences from the File menu.
3. Choose Environment from the Preferences cascading menu.
4. Click the Auto Code Placement check box to clear it.
5. Click OK.

   Auto Code Placement is turned off.
6. Set a left margin of 2 inches.

   A hard return is inserted at the insertion point, and the balance of the paragraph has a 2-inch left margin.
7. Display the Reveal Codes space, if necessary.

   The code [L/R Mar:2",1"] is inserted at the insertion point.
8. Press **Backspace** to delete the margin code, and press **Backspace** again to delete the hard return code.
9. Open the Environment dialog box again, and click Auto Code Placement to turn it on again. Click OK.
10. With the insertion point still at the beginning of the second line, set a 2-inch left margin.

    This time, the whole paragraph has a 2-inch left margin. The margin code is placed at the beginning of the paragraph, not at the insertion point.
11. Delete the margin code.
12. Save the document as *[your three-letter identifier]*14-0.wpw.
13. Print the document.
14. Close the document and exit WordPerfect (unless you will be doing the following exercises immediately).

Table 14-1: Codes Used in This Lesson

Command	Code
Advance	[Adv]
Block Protect	[Block Pro]
Center Page Top to Bottom	[Center Pg]
Conditional End of Page	[Cndl EOP]
Hard Page Break	[HPg]
Soft Page Break	[SPg]
Widow/Orphan Off	[W/O Off]
Widow/Orphan On	[W/O On]

Table 14-2: Keyboard Shortcuts

Keyboard Shortcut	Description
Ctrl+Enter	Hard page break
Ctrl+G	Go To command

Key Terms

Hard page break
Soft page break
Orphan
Widow

Exercises

Exercise 14-1

1. Start WordPerfect, if necessary.
2. Open the file 14-1.wpw.
3. Insert some text to cause a soft page break to move:
   A. Position the insertion point at the beginning of the last paragraph on page 1, to the left of "The newest and smallest".
   B. Key the sentence **The Five Points Midtown office (in the Piedmont Park area of Atlanta) is headed by John Soloman.** Be sure to insert a space after the sentence.
   C. Observe that the soft page break has moved, and that there is a widow at the top of the second page.
4. Apply Widow/Orphan protection to the entire document:
   A. Position the insertion point at the beginning of the document.
   B. Choose Page from the Layout menu, and then choose Widow/Orphan from the Page cascading menu.
   C. Scroll to the top of page 2, and observe that there is no longer a widow line.
5. Insert a hard page break:
   A. Position the insertion point to the left of the heading "FIVE POINTS OFFICE SPECIALIZATION" in the middle of page 1.
   B. Choose Page from the Layout menu, and then choose Page Break from the Page cascading menu (or press **Ctrl+Enter**).

6. Use the Go To command to go to the top of page 3:

   A. Choose Go To from the Edit menu (or press **Ctrl+G**).

   B. Key **3** in the Go To Page Number text box and click OK.

7. Use Conditional End of Page to keep the line at the bottom of page 2 with the directions at the top of page 3:

   A. Move up two lines, so that the insertion point is at the bottom of page 2, on the blank line above "The Buckhead office".

   B. Choose Page from the Layout menu, and then choose Conditional End of Page from the Page cascading menu.

   C. Key **3** in the text box and click OK.

8. Position the insertion point in the middle of page 2, at the beginning of the heading "DIRECTIONS TO FIVE POINTS' OFFICES", and insert a hard page break.

9. Set a 1-inch top margin at the beginning of page 2.

10. Vertically center the text on page 2:

    A. Position the insertion point at the beginning of page 2.

    B. Choose Page from the Layout menu, and then choose Center Page from the Page cascading menu.

    C. Use Print Preview to see that the text on page 2 is centered, and then close the Print Preview window.

11. Horizontally center the heading on page 2.

12. Vertically center the text on page 3, and horizontally center the heading on page 3.

13. Spell-check the document.

14. Save the document as *[your three-letter identifier]*14-1.wpw.

15. Print the document.

16. Close the document and exit WordPerfect (unless you will be doing the following exercises immediately).

Exercise 14-2

1. Start WordPerfect, if necessary.

2. Open the file 14-2.wpw.

3. Scroll to the beginning of page 2.

4. Press the **Backspace** key to remove the hard page break.
5. Use the Block Protect command to keep the paragraph that is split at the bottom of page 2 on one page:
   A. Position the insertion point at the bottom of page 1, at the beginning of the heading "Underground Atlanta".
   B. Select the heading and the following paragraph, which ends at the top of page 2.
   C. Choose Page from the Layout menu, and then choose Block Protect from the Page cascading menu.
6. Use the Advance command to insert more space before the tabulation on page 1:
   A. Position the insertion point at the beginning of the tabulation heading, at the beginning of the line that starts "Activity". (Press the **Home** key twice to be sure the insertion point is at the very beginning of the line.)
   B. Choose Advance from the Layout menu.
   C. Click Down in the Advance dialog box.
   D. Key **0.5"** in the Advance text box and click OK.
7. Use the Advance command to move the note down 0.5 inches below the bottom of the tabulation.
8. Use Block Protect to keep all the lines and the heading of the "Ebenezer Baptist Church" paragraph together.
9. Insert a hard page break near the bottom of page 1, at the beginning of the sentence that begins "The following is a brief description".
10. Set a 1-inch top margin at the beginning of page 2.
11. Spell-check the document.
12. Save the document as *[your three-letter identifier]*14-2.wpw.
13. Print the document.
14. Close the document and exit WordPerfect (unless you will be doing the following exercises immediately).

Exercise 14-3

1. Start WordPerfect, if necessary.
2. Open the file 14-3.wpw.
3. Block Protect the table at the end of the document. Include the heading "New Properties Listed" and the paragraph below it in the block.

4. Horizontally center the first two lines in the document. Then apply the bold attribute, and convert the text to uppercase.
5. Use the Advance command to position the newly formatted heading 2.5 inches from the top of the page.
6. Scroll to the bottom of page 1, and observe that there is an orphaned line.
7. Apply Widow/Orphan protection to the entire document.
8. Horizontally center each of the four article headings, and apply the bold attribute to them.
9. Use the Advance command to move each article heading down 0.5 inches from the preceding paragraph.
10. Use the Conditional End of Page command to keep each article heading together with the first three lines of the paragraph following it. (Be sure to include three extra lines to account for the space inserted by the advance command.)
11. Spell-check the document.
12. Save the document as *[your three-letter identifier]*14-3.wpw.
13. Print the document.
14. Close the document and exit WordPerfect (unless you will be doing the following exercises immediately).

Exercise 14-4

1. Start WordPerfect, if necessary.
2. Open the file 14-4.wpw.
3. Block Protect the table at the bottom of the first page. Include the paragraph above the tabulation in the block.
4. Use the Advance command to position the first line of the memo heading 2 inches from the top of the page.
5. Move to the line below the list of contributors, and key the figure that appears at the end of this exercise. Include the corrections indicated.
6. Insert a blank line below the list of contributors, if necessary.
7. Apply Widow/Orphan protection to the entire document.
8. Insert a hard page break near the end of page 2, at the beginning of the paragraph that begins "The following is a list of properties".

9. Vertically center the text on page 3.
10. Use the Advance command to move the table on page 3 down 0.5 inches.
11. Spell-check the document.
12. Save the document as *[your three-letter identifier]*14-4.wpw.
13. Print the document.
14. Close the document and exit WordPerfect (unless you will be doing the following exercise immediately).

Figure 14-11

These generous donations *be used to*

~~All this money~~ will ~~go towards the~~ purchase ~~of~~ the following items for the buildings being refurbished by the Help the Homeless ~~crew~~ *volunteers*:

Air Conditioning Units

Carpeting

Computers

Art Work

Furniture

Heating System

Lighting Fixtures

Kitchen Fixtures

Phone Systems

Reference Materials

Televisions

VCRs

Exercise 14-5

1. Start WordPerfect, if necessary.
2. Open the file 14-5.wpw.
3. Apply Widow/Orphan protection to the entire document.
4. Use the Conditional End of Page command to specify that at least four lines be kept with each bold heading in the document.

5. Insert a hard page break at the beginning of the document.
6. On the new first page, key the following two-line heading:

   Real Estate Curriculum

   12-hour courses

7. Center both heading lines horizontally. Convert the first line to uppercase and make it bold.
8. Use the Advance command to move the second line of the heading down 0.5 inches.
9. Vertically center the text on the title page.
10. Insert a hard page break near the bottom of page 2, at the beginning of the heading line "Real Estate Finance".
11. Spell-check the document.
12. Save the document as *[your three-letter identifier]*14-5.wpw.
13. Print the document.
14. Close the document and exit WordPerfect.

Lesson 15

Page Numbering

Numbering pages is a useful feature in WordPerfect that is applicable to all types of documents, particularly long documents. WordPerfect can number the pages in a document automatically, then update the numbering as the document is edited or formatted. This lesson focuses on using the numbering command to apply and customize page numbering. The next lesson, "Headers and Footers," discusses inserting page numbers, along with other information, in headers and footers.

Objectives

- Add page numbers to a document.
- Change page-numbering options.
- Use different types of numbers and accompanying text.
- Force odd or even pages.
- Insert page numbers into the document body.
- Discontinue or suppress page numbering.

Adding Page Numbers

The pages of a document are always numbered as you work in WordPerfect—the status bar serves as a constant indicator of page numbers. Every time text is added, deleted, or formatted, WordPerfect adjusts page breaks and page numbers. This is an automatic process that is always working in the background.

Although WordPerfect is always keeping track of page numbers, they do not appear in a printed document unless you specify that they do. Also, you cannot see page numbers in the document window. Use print preview to check page numbering before printing a document.

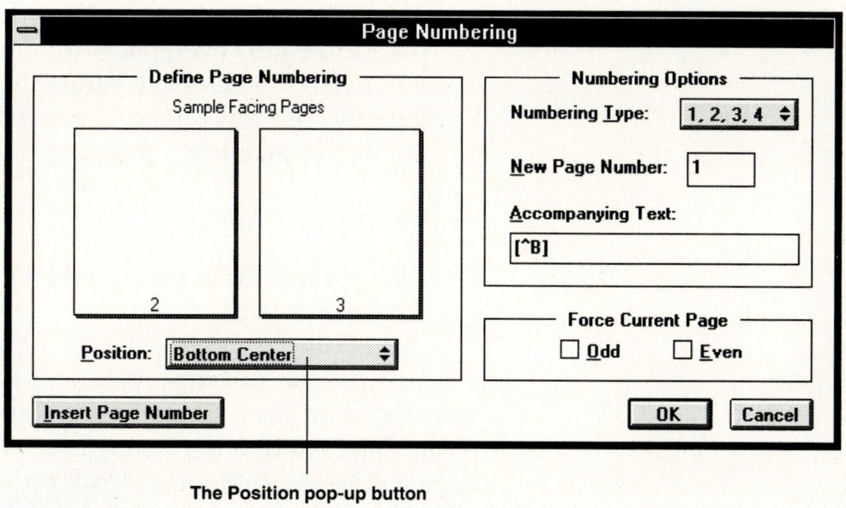

Figure 15-1
The Page Numbering dialog box

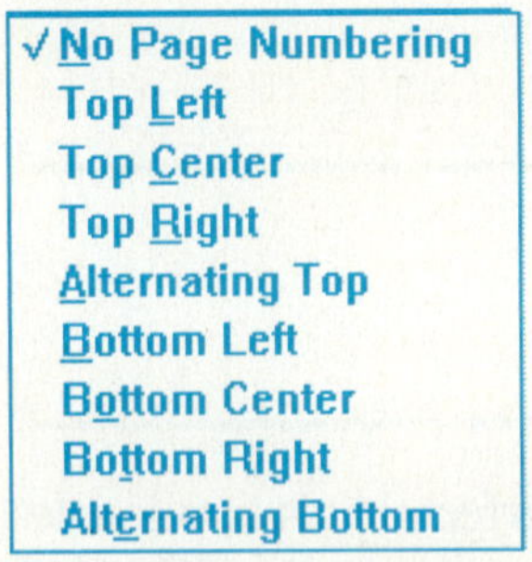

The Position pop-up list

The Numbering Type pop-up list

To insert page numbers, choose Page from the Layout menu, and then choose Numbering to open the Page Numbering dialog box. From the Page Numbering dialog box, you can set the following types of options:

- Position

  The Position pop-up button allows you to choose where on the page the number will appear (for example, the top right corner, or centered at the bottom of the page).

- Numbering Type

  The Numbering Type pop-up button allows you to choose Arabic numerals, uppercase Roman numerals, or lowercase Roman numerals.

- New Page Number

  This option allows you to change the page number for the current page. For example, you can change the numbering on the third and subsequent pages of a document to start at page 10.

- Accompanying Text

  The WordPerfect code for page number is [^B]. Any text that you key in the text box will appear along with the page number on the printed document. For example, if the text box contains "- [^B] -", the number on page 3 of the document will appear as "- 3 -".

- Force Current Page

  This option allows you to force the current page to be the next odd or the next even page number. If necessary, WordPerfect will insert a blank page before the current page to make this happen. Use this option to place the first page of a new section or chapter on an odd page.

- Insert Page Number

  This option allows you to insert the current page number anywhere on a page.

As you choose options, you will see the page-number format previewed on the Sample Facing Pages, displayed on the left side of the Page Numbering dialog box. When you click OK, a separate code will be inserted for each option you selected or changed. Table 15-1 lists examples of codes that the page-numbering command can insert.

Table 15-1: Examples of Page-Numbering Codes

Code	Function
[Pg Numbering:Top Right]	Positions the page number
[Pg Num:4]	Sets the current page number, defines number type
[Pg Num Style: Page ^B]	Defines text to accompany page number
[Force:Odd]	Sets current page to the next odd or even number
[Insert Pg Num:Page ^B]	Inserts page number with accompanying text one time at the insertion point

As with many WordPerfect commands, the insertion-point position is important when adding page numbers. WordPerfect places the page-numbering code on the page where the insertion point is located. If Auto Code Placement is in effect, the code will be placed at the top of the current page. If it is not in effect, the code will be placed at the insertion-point position. If the page-numbering code is not at the very beginning of the page, page numbering will not appear on the current page, but will start on the following page.

To insert basic page numbers:

1. Start WordPerfect, if necessary.

2. Open the file 15-0.wpw.

3. With the insertion point on the first page, choose Page from the Layout menu, and then choose Numbering from the Page cascading menu.

   The Page Numbering dialog box opens.

4. Point to the Position pop-up button. The text on the button should read "No Page Numbering".

5. Click and hold down the left mouse button.

   The Position pop-up list appears.

6. While holding the mouse button, drag down to the Bottom Center option, and release the mouse button.

   The pop-up list closes, and the Position pop-up button now reads "Bottom Center". The numerals 2 and 3 appear at the bottom of the Sample Facing Pages in the Define Page Numbering options box.

7. Click OK.

8. Open the Reveal Codes space.

   The code [Pg Numbering:Bottom Center] is inserted at the top of the page. You cannot see page numbers in the document window.

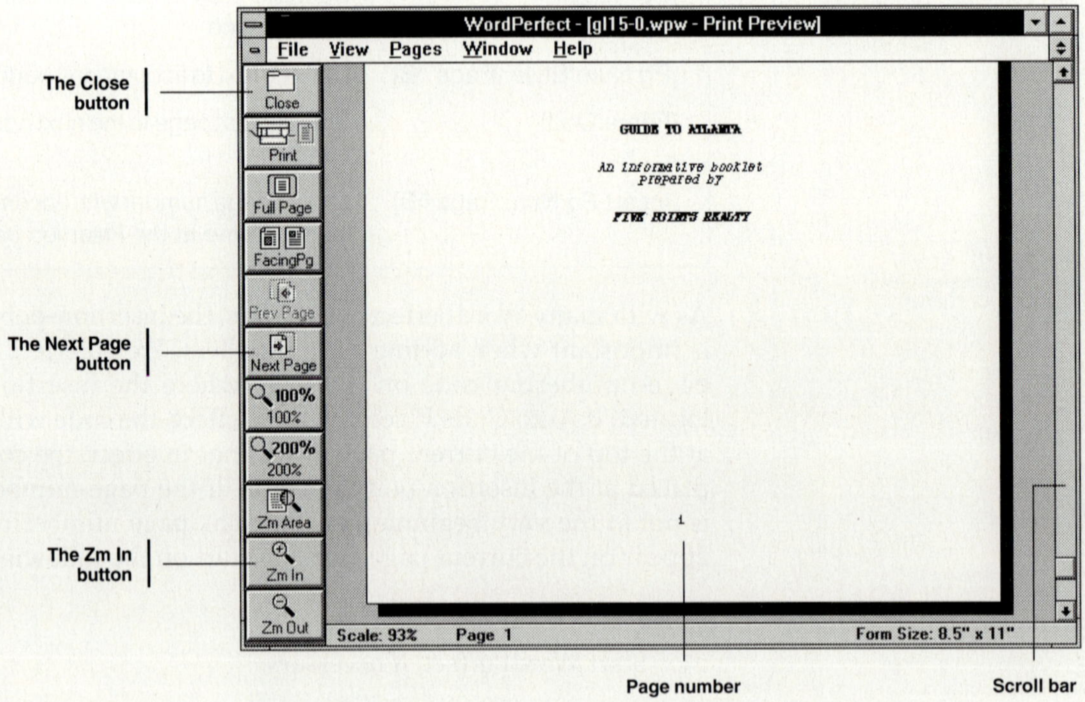

Figure 15-2
The Print Preview window

9. Choose Print Preview from the File menu to see that a page number appears at the bottom of the page.

10. Click the Zm In button to enlarge the display, and then use the scroll bar to move to the bottom of the page.

11. Click the Next Page button to see page 2.

12. Click the Close button to close the Print Preview window.

To remove page numbering, delete the page-numbering code, or choose No Page Numbering from the Position pop-up list in the Page Number dialog box. If you choose the second method, be sure that the insertion point is on the page where the numbering starts when you open the dialog box.

To remove the page numbers inserted above:

1. Position the insertion point at the beginning of the document, and open the Reveal Codes space, if necessary.

2. Click the code [Pg Numbering:Bottom Center] to select it.

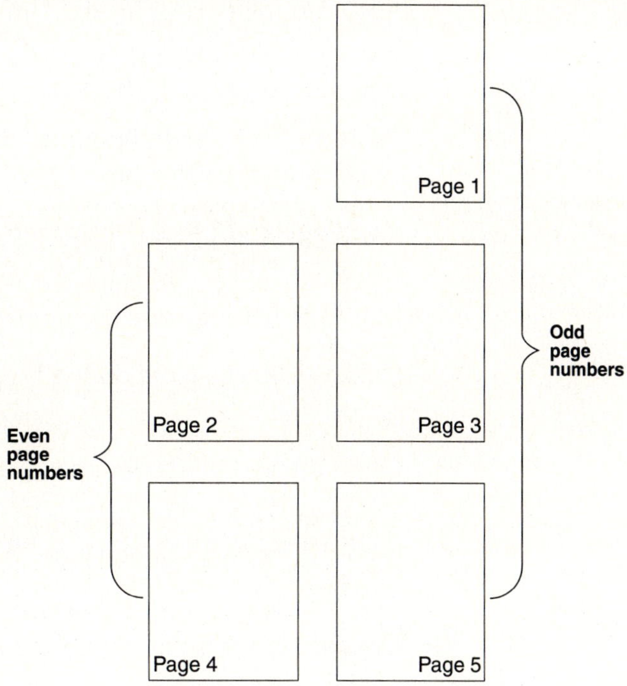

Figure 15-3
Alternating Bottom page numbers

3. Press the **Delete** key.
4. Open the Print Preview window.

   The page number no longer appears at the bottom of the page.
5. Close the Print Preview window.

Setting Page-Number Options

By choosing various options in the Page Numbering dialog box, you can control the starting page number, the type of numbers printed, and the text or other characters that appear along with the page number. As is true with most WordPerfect commands, it is important to place the insertion point on the page where the page-numbering commands are to take effect. Page-numbering codes take effect from the point where they are inserted forward through the document, until the code is overridden by a new code.

To insert customized Roman-numeral page numbers, starting on page 2:

1. Position the insertion point anywhere on page 2.
2. Choose Page from the Layout menu, and then choose Numbering from the Page cascading menu.

3. From the Position pop-up list, choose Alternating Bottom.
4. From the Numbering Type pop-up list, choose uppercase Roman numerals (I, II, III, IV).
5. Position the insertion point to the left of the code [^B] in the Accompanying Text box.
6. Key **Page** and press the **Spacebar**. The text box should include the text "Page [^B]".

   The code [^B] represents the page number.
7. Click OK to close the dialog box and insert the appropriate codes.
8. Open the Reveal Codes space, if necessary.

   The three codes [Pg Numbering:Bottom Alternating][Pg Num:II][Pg Num Style:Page ^B] are inserted at the beginning of page 2.
9. Choose Print Preview from the File menu.

   "Page II" appears at the bottom left side of page 2.
10. Click the Next Page button.

    "Page III" appears at the bottom right side of page 3. Alternating Bottom places odd page numbers at the lower right and even numbers at the lower left of a page. Alternating Top and Alternating Bottom are appropriate to use when you intend to print a document on both sides of the page.
11. Click the Prev Page button twice.

    Page 1, the title page, appears. There is no page number on this page, because the page-numbering codes were inserted on page 2.
12. Close the Print Preview window.

Sometimes, documents have a title page, table of contents, and other front matter. When this is the case, page numbering usually starts on the first page that contains the document text. To place the page number "1" on the second page of the document:

1. Position the insertion point anywhere on the second page of the document, and open the Reveal Codes space, if necessary. Make sure that the reveal codes cursor is placed after the existing page-numbering codes.
2. Open the Page Numbering dialog box.
3. Choose Arabic numerals (1, 2, 3, 4) from the Numbering Type pop-up list.

4. In the New Page Number text box, delete the number 2, and then key the number **1**.

5. Click OK to close the Page Numbering dialog box.

6. Open the Print Preview window.

   The second page of the document appears with "Page 1" in the lower right corner of the page.

7. Click the Prev Page button.

   The document's title page appears. It has no page number.

8. Close the Print Preview window.

When Are Page-Number Options Used?

WordPerfect provides many ways to vary the appearance of page numbers in a document. If you are working with a short report, page numbering is straightforward, but, when you work with long documents, the extra control that the many numbering options provide is very useful. The following are some ways to use page numbering in a long document:

- Front Matter
  The front matter of a book usually contains a title page and a table of contents, and sometimes contains lists of figures or illustrations. These pages usually are numbered with lowercase Roman numerals.

- Document
  Page numbering starts at page 1 again on the first page of the document body. The numbering style for the body pages is usually Arabic numerals.

- Suppressing Page Numbers
  Page numbers often are suppressed on the title page of a document and on the first page of each chapter. Page numbers also may be suppressed on other pages if, because of the page content, the number appears out of place. For example, page numbers may be suppressed on pages with tables or illustrations.

- Chapter Numbers
  Book pages can be numbered in sequence from the first body page to the last index page, or numbering can restart with each new chapter. In the latter case, pages often are numbered 1-1, 1-2, 1-3, for chapter 1; 2-1, 2-2, 2-3 for chapter 2; and so forth. This can be accomplished easily by keying the appropriate chapter number in the Accompanying Text box in the Page Numbering dialog box. Insert an appropriate numbering code at the beginning of each chapter.

Forcing Odd or Even Page Numbering

In an open book, the two pages that are visible at one time are called facing pages. When facing pages are numbered, the left pages are even-numbered and the right pages are odd-numbered. If a book is organized in chapters, each new chapter usually starts on a right (odd-numbered) page. When you create a document that will be printed on both sides of a page, such as a lengthy report or a book, you may want to insure that certain text appears on either a right or a left page.

In the Page Numbering dialog box, you can force the current page to be either odd or even numbered by clicking the Odd or Even check box in the Force Current Page options box. If necessary, WordPerfect will insert a blank page before the current page to force it to be odd or even as directed. For example, if a new chapter starts on page 10, and it contains a Force Odd code, WordPerfect will insert a blank page 10 to force the chapter to begin on page 11. If, however, the new chapter starts on page 11, and that page contains the force Odd code, no action is required of WordPerfect.

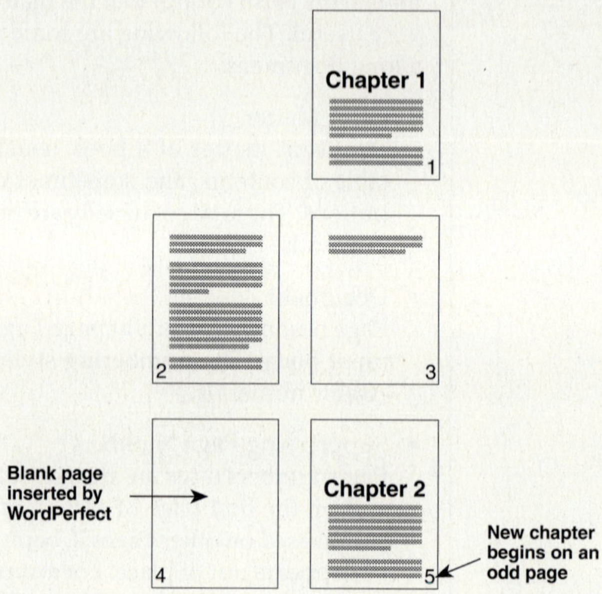

Figure 15-4
Forcing an odd page

It is good practice to insert the Force Odd or Force Even code on each page that requires Odd or Even placement, even when the page is placed correctly already. If later editing or formatting revisions cause page breaks to change, WordPerfect will be able to insert or remove blank pages automatically to insure that odd and even page placement will be correct.

Inserting Page Numbers in the Document Body

The Insert Page Number button

You can insert the current page number anywhere in the body of the current document. If you click the Insert Page Number button in the Page numbering dialog box instead of clicking OK, the code [^B] will appear at the insertion-point position in the document. When the document is printed or you view it with Print Preview, you will see the current page number in place of the [^B] code. If the document pagination changes, the new page number will appear on the page the next time you print or preview the page.

The Insert Page Number command formats the page number with the text that appears in the Accompanying Text text box in the Page Numbering dialog box. The Insert Pg Num code is always placed at the insertion-point position, regardless of the Auto Code Placement setting.

To insert a page number on the last page of the document:

1. Press **Ctrl+End** to position the insertion point at the end of the document.

2. Press **Enter** twice to insert two blank lines.

3. On the last line of the document, apply the italics attribute, key ***This document contains***, and press the **Spacebar**.

4. Open the Page Numbering dialog box.

5. Delete the text in the Accompanying Text text box.

   The code [^B] will remain. It cannot be deleted.

6. Click the Insert Page Number button.

   The dialog box closes, and the code [^B], representing the current page number, appears at the insertion point.

7. Press the **Spacebar,** and then key ***pages, not including the title page.***

8. Open the Print Preview window to check the page number inserted in the last sentence. If necessary, click the Zm In button, and scroll to the last sentence in the document.

9. Close the Print Preview window.

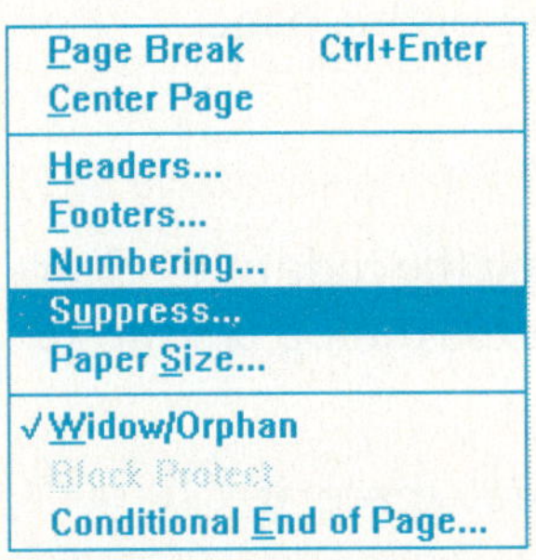

The Page cascading menu

Suppressing Page Numbering

You can keep a page number from printing on one page without disturbing the page numbering of the balance of the document by using the Suppress command.

To suppress page numbering on page 2:

1. Position the insertion point anywhere on page 2 (the page with the heading "THINGS TO DO IN ATLANTA").
2. Choose Page from the Layout menu, and then choose Suppress from the Page cascading menu.

   The Suppress dialog box opens.

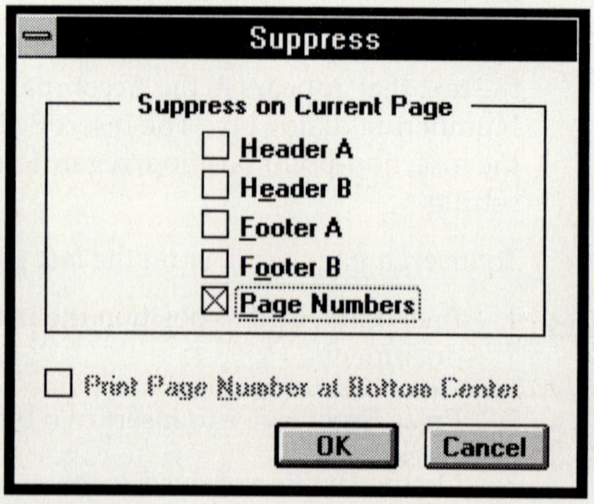

Figure 15-5
The Suppress dialog box

3. Click the Page Numbers check box and then click OK.
4. If necessary, open the Reveal Codes space.

   The code [Suppress:PgNum] appears at the top of page 2.

5. Open the Print Preview window, and move to the bottom page 2.

   No page number appears on this page.

6. Click the Next Page button.

   "Page 3" appears in the lower right corner of this page.

7. Close the Print Preview window.

You can clear the Suppress command by deleting the code or by clearing the Page Numbers check box in the Suppress dialog box. To reinstate page numbering on page 2:

1. Move to page 2, and open the Reveal Codes space, if necessary.

2. Click the code [Suppress:PgNum] to select it.

3. Press the **Delete** key.

4. Open the Print Preview window.

5. Move to the bottom of page 2, if necessary.

   "Page 2" appears in the lower left corner of the page.

6. Close the Print Preview window.

Discontinuing Page Numbering

Position pop-up button

Page Numbering can be discontinued on any page in a document. To discontinue page numbering, position the insertion point anywhere on the page where numbering is to stop, and choose the No Page Numbering option from the Position pop-up list in the Page Numbering dialog box.

To discontinue page numbering:

1. Position the insertion point anywhere on page 4 of the document.

2. Open the Page Numbering dialog box.

3. Choose No Page Numbering from the Position pop-up list.

4. Open the Print Preview window, and move to the bottom of page 4, if necessary.

   There is no page number.

5. Close the Print Preview window.

6. Position the insertion point at the top of page 4, and display the Reveal Codes space, if necessary.

   The code [Pg Numbering:No page number] appears at the top of the page. Page numbers appear on all pages between a [Pg Numbering:Location] code and a [Pg Numbering:No page number] codes.

7. Spell-check the document.

8. Save the document as *[your three-letter identifier]*15-0.wpw.

9. Print the document.

10. Close the document and exit WordPerfect (unless you will be doing the following exercises immediately).

Exercises

Exercise 15-1

1. Start WordPerfect, if necessary.
2. Open the file 15-1.wpw.
3. Insert page numbers at the bottom center position of each page:
   A. Position the insertion point anywhere on the first page of the document, if necessary.
   B. Choose Page from the Layout menu, and then choose Numbering from the Page cascading menu.
   C. Choose Bottom Center from the Position pop-up list.
   D. Click OK.
4. Preview the page numbers:
   A. Choose Print Preview from the File menu.
   B. Click the Zm-In button, and then scroll to the bottom of the page to view the page number.
   C. Using the Next Page button, move to each page of the document, and examine the page numbers.
   D. Click the Close button to return to the document window.
5. Position the insertion point to the left of the first line of the first address, and insert a hard page break.
6. Vertically center the text on the newly created first page.
7. Suppress page numbering on the first page:
   A. Position the insertion point anywhere on the first page, if necessary.
   B. Choose Page from the Layout menu, and then choose Suppress from the Page cascading menu.
   C. Check the Page Numbers check box and click OK.
   D. Open the Print Preview window to make sure a page number does not appear on page 1, but appears on all other pages.
   E. Close the Print Preview window.
8. Change the number on page 2 so that it becomes page 1:
   A. Position the insertion point anywhere on page 2.
   B. Open the Page Numbering dialog box.

C. Delete the text in the New Page Number text box and key **1**.

D. Click OK.

9. Change the appearance of the page numbers so that the numbers are preceded and followed by a hyphen:

A. Open the Page Numbering dialog box.

B. Position the insertion point to the left of the code [^B] in the Accompanying Text text box.

C. Key **-** (the hyphen character) and press the **Spacebar**.

D. Position the insertion point to the right of the code [^B], press the **Spacebar**, and key **-** (the hyphen character).

E. Click OK.

F. Use the Print Preview feature to examine the page numbers, and then close the Print Preview window.

10. Apply block protection where needed to prevent addresses from being split by page breaks.
11. Spell-check the document.
12. Save the document as *[your three-letter identifier]*15-1.wpw.
13. Print the document.
14. Close the document and exit WordPerfect (unless you will be doing the following exercises immediately).

Exercise 15-2

1. Start WordPerfect, if necessary.
2. Open the file 15-2.wpw.
3. Center the first two lines of text horizontally.
4. Convert the first line, "The Five Points Reporter", to uppercase and make it bold.
5. Use the Advance command to position the first line 2 inches from the top of the page.
6. Apply the italics attribute to the line "Newsworthy articles for our agents".
7. Set page numbers so they appear in the upper right corner of every page, formatted as lowercase Roman numerals :

A. Position the insertion point anywhere on page 1, if necessary.

B. Open the Page Numbering dialog box.

C. Choose Top Right from the Position pop-up list.

D. Choose lowercase Roman numerals (i, ii, iii, iv) from the Number Type pop-up list.

E. Click OK.

F. Open the Print Preview window, examine the page numbers, and then close the Print Preview window.

8. Suppress page numbers on the first page.

9. Change the page numbers so that they appear as Arabic numerals with the text "Page" to the left of each page number.

10. Apply the underline attribute to each heading in the document.

11. Apply Widow/Orphan protection to the entire document.

12. Set a conditional end of page where necessary, so that each heading is kept together with at least three lines of the paragraph following it.

13. Spell-check the document.

14. Save the document as *[your three-letter identifier]*15-2.wpw.

15. Print the document.

16. Close the document and exit WordPerfect (unless you will be doing the following exercises immediately).

Exercise 15-3

1. Start WordPerfect, if necessary.

2. Open the file 15-3.wpw.

3. Set uppercase Roman-numeral page numbering for the entire document. Position the page numbers in the lower right corner of the document.

4. Use Print Preview to inspect the page numbers, and then close the Print Preview window.

5. Insert a blank page at the beginning of the document.

6. Key the following text on the new first page, centered both vertically and horizontally:

WEEKLY NEW PROPERTIES LIST
October 15, 199-

7. Change the page numbering so that numbering starts on the title page and is centered at the bottom of the page. Change the number format so that it uses Arabic numerals and appears as the following example:

   *** 1 ***

8. Remove the underlining from all property-description headings, and make them bold instead.

9. Apply block protection where necessary, so that property descriptions and their headings are never split by a page break.

10. Spell-check the document.

11. Save the document as *[your three-letter identifier]*15-3.wpw.

12. Print the document.

13. Close the document and exit WordPerfect (unless you will be doing the following exercises immediately).

Exercise 15-4

1. Start WordPerfect, if necessary.

2. In a new document window, key the document that appears at the end of this exercise, including the corrections indicated. Use the Advance command to force the first line of the memo heading to start 2 inches from the top of the page. Format the document in the standard memo style.

3. Insert a hard page break at the end of the memo.

4. At the beginning of the new page, retrieve the document 15-4.wpw so that it is appended to the memo.

5. Horizontally center the first two heading lines at the top of page 2 and make them bold.

6. Insert a hard page break before the heading "REAL ESTATE CURRICULUM" at the bottom of page 2.

7. Horizontally center the first two heading lines at the top of page 3 and make them bold.

8. Beginning on page 3, add page numbers with the following attributes:

Position:	Top left
Number type:	Arabic numerals
New page number:	1
Accompanying text:	Curriculum, page [^B]

9. Suppress page numbering on the first page of the real estate curriculum.
10. Apply Widow/Orphan protection to the entire document.
11. Apply block protection where needed so that each complete course description stays together on one page.
12. Spell-check the document.
13. Save the document as *[your three-letter identifier]*15-4.wpw.
14. Print the document.
15. Close the document and exit WordPerfect (unless you will be doing the following exercise immediately).

Document 15-4

MEMO TO: Distribution

FROM: Ann Delbridge

DATE: July 16, 199-

SUBJECT: Board of Realtors Course Announcwement

The attached pages include ~~Please find enclosed~~ the new *fall* course announcement *and curriculum*. I know many of you are working towards *earning your state licenses* ~~board certification~~. *I suggest that you* ~~You really need to~~ register *early,* ~~immediately~~ because the courses *fill up quickly* ~~get more and more popular all the time~~.

Distribution:

K. Barnes

K. Jackson

R. Boyle

D. Feingold

J. McKnight

W. Reston

P. Silvers

R. Smith

B. Smith

M. Wood

Exercise 15-5

1. Start WordPerfect, if necessary.
2. Open the file 15-5.wpw.
3. Key the following text, centered horizontally and vertically, as a title page at the beginning of the document:

   Supplementary Materials
   for
   REAL ESTATE EXAM REVIEW

   Instructors: Marilyn and Mike Montefiore

4. Horizontally center the heading "Sample Purchase Agreement" at the top of the second page, make it bold, and convert it to uppercase.
5. Beginning on the second page, set page numbering with the following attributes:

Position:	Top center
Number type:	Arabic numerals
New page number:	1
Accompanying text:	Sample Agreement, page [^B]

6. Suppress page numbering on the new page 1 (originally the second page).
7. Use the Print Preview feature to examine the numbering on all pages of the document, and then close the Print Preview window.
8. Near the top of page 3, insert a hard page break at the beginning of the heading "Real Estate Terms".
9. Discontinue page numbering on page 4 and for the remainder of the document. At this point, only the second and third pages of the sample agreement should have page numbers.
10. Format the heading "Real Estate Terms" at the beginning of page 4 so that it is bold, horizontally centered, and uppercase.
11. Underline all the defined terms, starting on page 4 and continuing to the end of the document.
12. Apply Widow/Orphan protection to the entire document.
13. Apply block protect where necessary to prevent defined terms from being split by page breaks.

14. Spell-check the document.
15. Save the document as *[your three-letter identifier]*15-5.wpw.
16. Print the document.
17. Close the document and exit WordPerfect.

Lesson 16

Headers and Footers

Lesson 15 introduced page numbering. Page numbers placed at the top or bottom of pages are special types of headers and footers. This lesson focuses on the different kinds of descriptive information headers and footers can contain, such as the date, document title, and author's name. It also explains the many ways header and footer text can be formatted and positioned on the printed page.

Objectives

- Understand headers and footers.
- Create headers and footers.
- Insert page numbers in headers and footers.
- Use the placement option.
- Edit headers and footers.
- Suppress and discontinue headers and footers.

Header
Text that is repeated at the top of a series of document pages.

Footer
Text that is repeated at the bottom of a series of document pages.

Understanding Headers and Footers

Text that is repeated at the top of a series of pages is called a *header*. Text that is repeated at the bottom of a series of pages is called a *footer.* In WordPerfect, headers and footers are placed inside the page margins. The document text is separated from headers and footers automatically by one blank line.

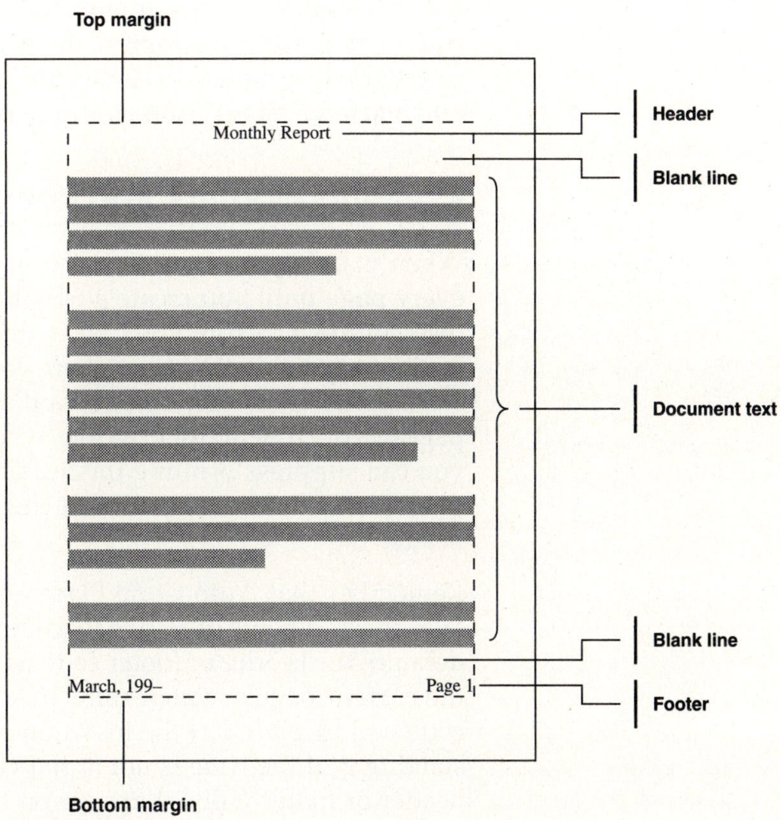

Figure 16-1
Header and footer placement on a page

Headers and footers are used commonly in documents to show such information as:

- the name of the document or chapter
- the page or chapter numbers
- the date the document was created or revised
- the name of the author
- a graphic, such as a company logo
- the draft or revision number

The descriptive text in headers and footers can appear in many different combinations. For example, the second page of a business letter typically contains a header with the name of the addressee, the page number, and the date. A report may contain a footer with the report name and a header with the page number and chapter name. A newsletter may contain a header with the title and logo on the first page and a footer with the title and page number on the pages that follow.

As is true with page numbering, you can change the header or footer text anywhere in a document (for example, when a new chapter starts). You also can suppress the printing of a header or footer on selected pages, and you can create different headers or footers for odd and even pages. These options are discussed later in the lesson.

Creating Headers and Footers

When you create a header or footer, it will continue to appear on every page until you create a new header or footer, suppress it, or discontinue it. Before you create a header or a footer, position the insertion point on the page where you want the header or footer to start. Sometimes, you do not want a header to appear on the first page of a document (for example, when it is a title page). In this case, you can suppress printing the header on the first page, or you can position the insertion point on the next page when creating the header.

Remember that Auto Code Placement controls where commands take effect. When Auto Code Placement is in effect (the WordPerfect default), the header or footer code will be placed at the beginning of the current page automatically. If Auto Code Placement is off, the code will be placed at the insertion point. It is important to understand that, if the code is not at the very beginning of the page, the header or footer will not appear on the current page, but will start on the following page instead.

How Soft Page Breaks Affect Headers and Footers

When placing a header or footer code on a page that begins with a soft page break, inserting or deleting text or changing formatting may change the position of the header or footer code. Auto Code Placement insures that the code is placed properly when the code is created. It does not insure that the code remains in the proper place after editing text. To ensure that header and footer codes (and other page-formatting codes) do not move to an inappropriate location, place them on a page that begins with a hard page break.

Hard page breaks are appropriate at the beginning of chapters and at the beginning of pages that contain special document elements, such as tables or graphics. Hard page breaks usually are not appropriate on the second page of a letter, the second page of a chapter, or other locations where the document flow continues past the break. This is because, when text is inserted or deleted on previous pages, the hard page break position will no longer be correct.

There are times when you want headers and footers to start on the second page of a chapter or section. If you place the code on the second page, after a soft page break, and then insert text on the first page, the code will no longer be at the top of the page, causing the header or footer to appear for the first time on the third page instead. A better way is to insert the header or footer code on the first page of a document or chapter and then use the suppress command to keep it from printing on that page.

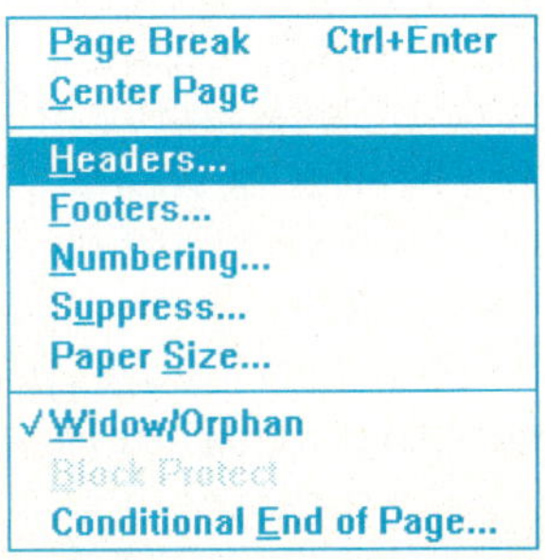

The Page cascading menu

Headers and footers are created by choosing Page from the Layout menu and then choosing either Headers or Footers from the Page cascading menu. Both commands open dialog boxes that are identical except for the title.

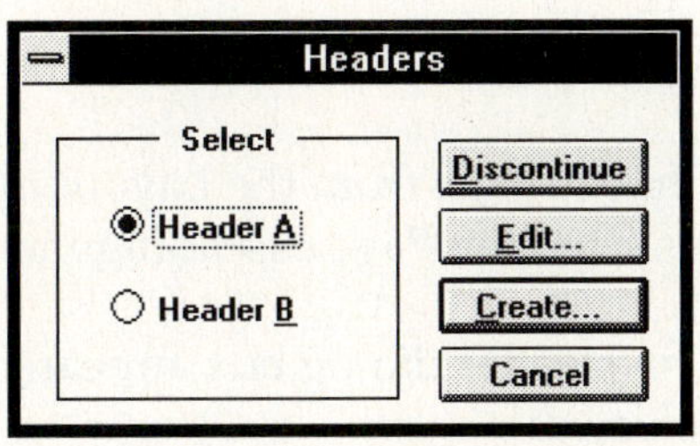

Figure 16-2
The Headers dialog box

Each dialog box has a Select option box, allowing you to choose between Header A and Header B (or Footer A and Footer B). Having two alternative headers and footers, A and B, allows you to specify two independent header or footer formats. For example, you can use

Header A on odd-numbered pages and Header B on even-numbered pages, or you can use both headers or footers on the same page.

When two headers or footers print on the same page, they will print on top of one another. This is a useful feature if, for example, Header A prints left-aligned text, and Header B prints right-aligned text.

The following command buttons allow you to control headers and footers:

- Create
  The Create button opens the header or footer window, where you can key the text and set formatting for new headers or footers. Key text and apply formatting in the same way as in a document window. If a header or footer of the same type (A or B) already exists in the document, the new one created with this command will take effect at the current page.

- Edit
  The Edit button opens the header or footer window, allowing you to change the text or formatting of existing headers or footers. This command will affect the most recent preceding header or footer code of the same type (A or B), even if the insertion point is not on the same page as the header or footer code.

- Discontinue
  The Discontinue button ends the printing of the header or footer specified (A or B) from the current page forward.

To create a basic header that will appear on all pages of a document:

1. Start WordPerfect, if necessary.

2. Open the file 15-0.wpw.

3. Choose Page from the Layout menu, and then choose Headers from the Page cascading menu.

   The Header dialog box appears, with the Header A option selected.

4. Click the Create button.

   The Header A window opens. Enter and format text in this window just as you do in a document window. Headers and footers can have multiple lines. The number of lines available for a header or footer is limited only by the size of the document page.

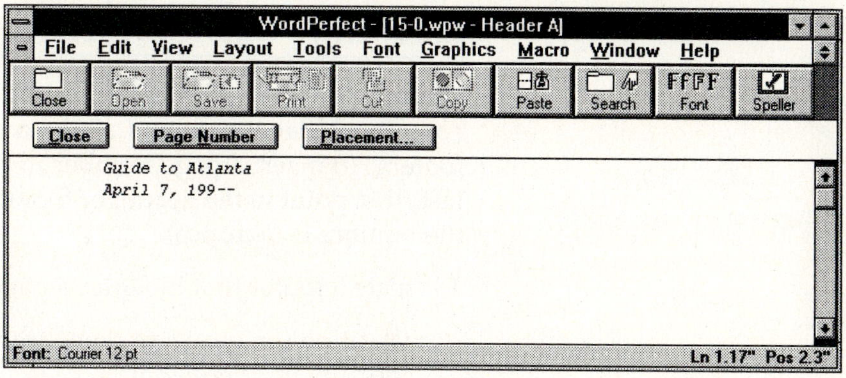

Figure 16-3
The Header A window

5. Apply the italics attribute, and then key the following text:

   Guide to Atlanta

6. Press the **Enter** key. Then choose Date from the Tools menu, and choose Code from the Date cascading menu.

7. Click the Close button in the upper left corner of the header window.

   The document window appears, but the header is not displayed.

8. Choose Print Preview from the File menu.

9. Click the Zm In button, and scroll to the top of the page to view the header, if necessary.

10. Click the Next Page button several times to see the header on other pages of the document.

11. Close the Print Preview window.

You may want the header or footer to change later in the document (for example, at the start of a new chapter). To create a new header or footer, position the insertion point on the page where you want it to appear. Then choose Create from the Header dialog box or the Footer dialog box, and key the new header text.

If you are changing Header A, be sure that Header A is selected in the Headers dialog box. If Header A already exists, and you choose Header B, Header A will continue to print on the following pages, and Header B will print on top of it.

Inserting Page Numbers in Headers and Footers

The Page Number button

Lesson 15 discussed adding page numbers using the numbering command. Page numbers also may be included in headers and footers. To insert a page number in a header or footer, position the insertion point in the header or footer window at the location where the number is to appear.

To create a footer that includes a page number:

1. Position the insertion point anywhere on the first page of the document, if necessary.

2. Choose Page from the Layout menu, and then choose Footers from the Page cascading menu.

   The Footer dialog box appears.

3. Choose Footer A, if necessary, and then click Create.

   The Footer A window opens.

4. Key **Five Points Realty**.

5. Press **Shift+F7** to insert the center code, and then key the phone number **(404) 555-1234**.

6. Press **Alt+F7** to insert the flush-right code, and then key **Page** and press the **Spacebar**.

7. Click the Page Number button at the top of the footer window.

   The code [^B], representing the page number, appears at the insertion point.

8. Click the Close button.

   The document window reappears.

9. Open the Print Preview window. Click the Zm In button, and use the scroll bar to view the footer, if necessary.

10. Click Next Page several times to view the footer on other pages.

11. Close the Print Preview window.

Editing Headers and Footers

To make changes to existing headers or footers, position the insertion point anywhere on the page that contains the header or footer code, open the Header or Footer dialog box, choose the appropriate

The Edit button

header or footer letter (A or B), and then click the Edit button. The header or footer window opens, displaying the text and formatting that currently is in effect for that header or footer. Edit header and footer text the same way that you edit document text.

When editing a header or footer, the insertion-point position is not important if there is only one header or footer code in the document. If, for example, there is more than one Header A code in the document, when you choose Edit, WordPerfect opens the window for the first Header A code preceding the insertion point. If the insertion point precedes all Header A codes, WordPerfect opens the window for the first Header A code following the insertion point.

To edit Footer A:

1. Position the insertion point anywhere on the first page of the document, if necessary.

2. Choose Page from the Layout menu, and then choose Footers from the Page cascading menu.

3. Choose Footer A, if necessary, and then click the Edit button.

   The Footer A window opens.

4. Position the insertion point to the right of "Five Points Realty", and press the **Enter** key.

   The phone number and page number move to the second line.

5. Display the Reveal Codes space, and delete the center code at the beginning of the second line.

6. Click the Close button to close the footer window.

7. Open the Print Preview window, and view the footer on several pages.

8. Close the Print Preview window.

Using the Placement Option

The Placement button

Facing pages were introduced in Lesson 15 under the heading "Forcing Odd or Even Page Numbering." If you are working on a long document that will be printed on both sides of the page, you may want to create one set of headers and footers for even pages and another set for odd pages. For example, Header A can appear on odd-numbered pages and contain a right-aligned chapter title. Header B can appear on even numbered pages and contain a left-aligned report title. Footer A can contain a right-aligned page number, and Footer B can contain a left-aligned page number.

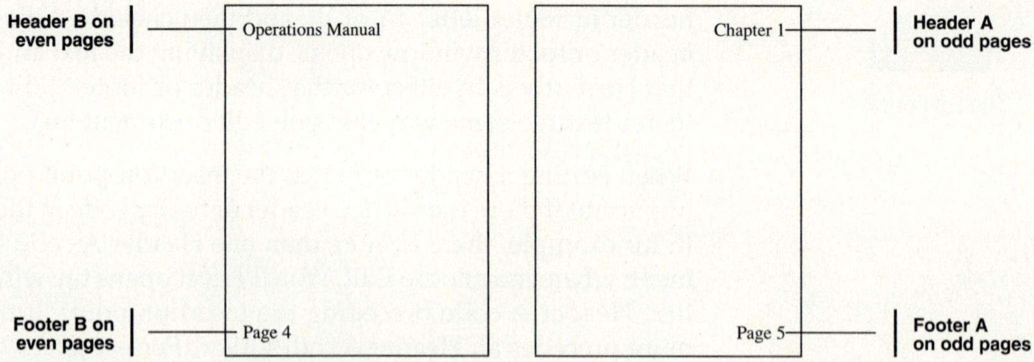

Figure 16-4
Headers and footers for odd and even pages

The Placement command button in the header and footer windows allows you to choose on which pages to place the header or footer that is displayed. The Placement command is available when you are creating new headers and footers or editing existing ones. There are three placement options—Every Page, Odd (right) Pages, and Even (left) Pages. The default is Every Page.

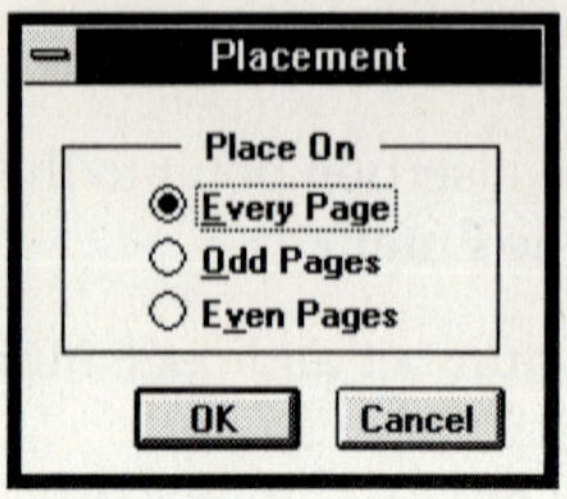

Figure 16-5
The Placement dialog box

Edit Header A and Footer A so that they appear only on odd pages:

1. Position the insertion point on the first page of the document, if necessary.
2. Choose Page from the Layout menu, and then choose Headers from the Page cascading menu.
3. Click Edit.

   The Header A window opens.
4. Click the Placement button.

   The Placement dialog box opens.
5. Choose Odd Pages and click OK.

6. In the Header A window, format the text to be right-aligned.
7. Close the Header A window.
8. Open the Footers dialog box, choose Footer A, if necessary, and click Edit.

   The Footer A window opens.
9. Click the Placement button.
10. Choose Odd Pages from the Placement dialog box and click OK.
11. Click Close.

    The document window reappears.

To create a header and footer for even pages:

1. Position the insertion point anywhere on the first page of the document.
2. Open the Headers dialog box, choose Header B, and click Create.

   The Header B window opens.
3. Click the Placement button.
4. Choose Even Pages from the Placement dialog box and click OK.
5. In the Header B window, key **Chapter 1**, and then press the **Enter** key.

   An extra blank is inserted, because Header A contains two lines. This will keep the document text balanced on facing pages.
6. Close the Header B window.
7. Open the Footers dialog box, choose Footer B, and click Create.
8. Click the Placement button, choose Even Pages, and click OK.
9. Press the **Enter** key, key **Page**, press the **Spacebar**, and click the Page Numbers button.
10. Close the Footer B window.
11. Open the Print Preview window, and view the headers and footers on odd and even pages.

Changing Headers and Footers

Headers and footers often need to convey new information at a certain point in a document. For example, if Header A contains the text "Chapter 1", it must change to "Chapter 2" when the second chapter begins. To change the header or footer text, create a new header on the page where the new text is needed.

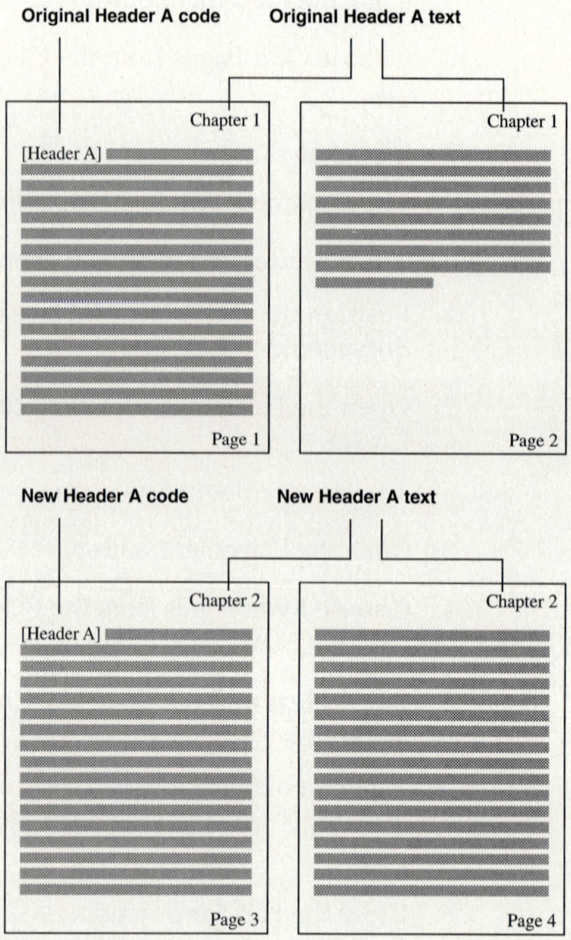

Figure 16-6
Changing header text

To create a new Header A:

1. Position the insertion point anywhere on page 4 of the current document.
2. Open the Headers dialog box.
3. Choose Header A and click Create.

   A blank Header A window opens.
4. Press **Alt+F7** to set right-alignment, apply the italics attribute, and key ***Things To Do in Atlanta***.

5. On the second header line, insert an italicized, right-aligned date code.
6. Choose Odd Pages from the Placement dialog box.
7. Close the Header A window.
8. Open the Print Preview window, and view the headers on page 1 and page 3.
9. Close the Print Preview window.

Suppressing Headers and Footers

The Suppress command was introduced in Lesson 15 to control the printing of page numbers. Using the Suppress command, you also can keep headers and footers from printing on a particular page.

To suppress headers and footers from printing on the first page:

1. Position the insertion point anywhere on the first page of the document.
2. Choose Page from the Layout menu, and then choose Suppress from the Page cascading menu.

   The Suppress dialog box opens.

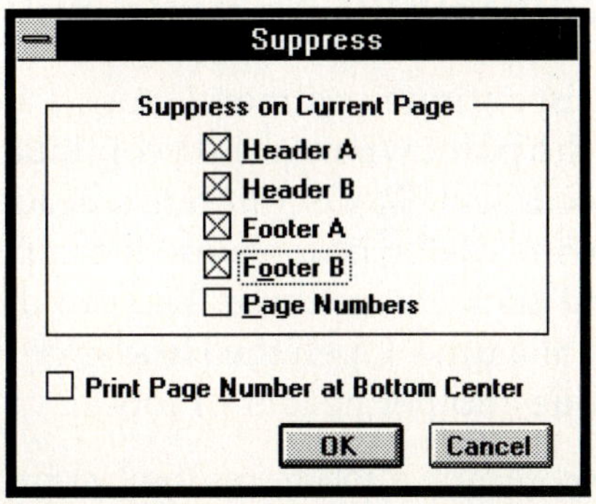

Figure 16-7
The Suppress dialog box

3. Check the Header A, Header B, Footer A, and Footer B check boxes to suppress all headers and footers on the first page.
4. Click OK.

Setting New Page Numbers

The Page Numbering dialog box controls the options available for page numbers appearing in headers and footers just as it does for page numbers created with the Numbering command. When setting options for page numbers appearing in headers and footers, be sure the Position pop-up button indicates No Page Numbering. Otherwise, two page numbers may appear on the same page, one created by the Numbering command, and the other created as part of a header or footer.

To set a new page number on the second page:

1. Position the insertion point anywhere on page 2.
2. Choose Page from the Layout menu and Numbering from the Page cascading menu to open the Page Numbering dialog box.
3. Change the number in the New Page Number text box to 1.
4. Make sure that the Position pop-up button indicates No Page Numbering and click OK.
5. Use Print Preview to verify that page numbering starts at page 1 on the second page.

If changing the page number results in odd pages becoming even pages, headers and footers set for odd and even pages will change appropriately.

Discontinuing Headers and Footers

The Discontinue command stops a header or footer from printing from the point where the discontinue code is inserted to the end of the document. To discontinue a header or footer, open the Headers or Footers dialog box, choose the appropriate header or footer (A or B), and click Discontinue. You can discontinue only one header or footer at a time. Open the Header or Footer dialog box again to discontinue another header or footer.

To discontinue a footer on the last page of the document:

1. Position the insertion point anywhere on the last page of the document.
2. Open the Footers dialog box.
3. Choose Footer A and click Discontinue.

Because editing changes may change a page from odd to even, discontinue Footer B, as well:

1. Position the insertion point anywhere on the last page, if necessary.
2. Open the Footers dialog box.

3. Choose Footer B and click Discontinue.

4. Use Print Preview to verify that footers do not appear on the last page of the document, and close the Print Preview window.

5. Spell-check the document.

   WordPerfect automatically spell-checks headers and footers along with document text.

6. Save the document as *[your three-letter identifier]*16-0.wpw.

7. Print the document.

8. Close the document and exit WordPerfect (unless you will be doing the following exercises immediately).

Key Terms

Footer
Header

Exercises

Exercise 16.1

1. Start WordPerfect, if necessary.
2. Open the file 15-5.wpw.
3. Create a header that includes text and a page number:
   A. Choose Page from the Layout menu, and then choose Headers from the Page cascading menu.
   B. Click Create.
   C. Apply the bold attribute, and key **Sample Purchase Agreement**.
   D. Press **Alt+F7** to insert the flush-right code, key **Page**, and press the **Spacebar**.
   E. Click the Page Number button.
   F. Press the **Enter** key to insert an extra line between the header and the document body.
   G. Click Close.
4. In the document window, at the top of the first page, delete the heading "Sample Purchase Agreement" and the blank line following it.

5. Create a three-line footer:

   A. Choose Page from the Layout menu, and then choose Footers from the Page cascading menu.

   B. Click Create.

   C. Press the **Enter** key to insert an extra blank line between the footer and the document body.

   D. Key the following three lines, centered and italicized:

      Real Estate Exam Review
      Supplementary Materials
      Fall, 199-

   E. Click Close.

6. Change the header and the page number on page 4:

   A. Scroll to the middle of page 3.

   B. Position the insertion point to the left of the heading "Real Estate Terms", and insert a hard page break.

   C. Position the insertion point anywhere on page 4, if necessary.

   D. Open the Headers dialog box, choose Header A, if necessary, and click Create.

   E. Apply the bold attribute, and key **Real Estate Terms**.

   F. On the same line, add a right-aligned page number preceded by the word "Page". The word "Page" and the number should be bold.

   G. Press **Enter** to insert an extra blank line.

   H. Click Close.

   I. With the insertion point anywhere on page 4, choose Page from the Layout menu, and then choose Numbering from the Page cascading menu.

   J. Delete the number in the New Page Number text box, key the number **1**, and click OK.

7. View the headers and footers:

   A. Choose Print Preview from the File menu.

   B. Click Zoom In.

   C. Scroll to the top of the page, if necessary, and click Next Page several times to view all the headers.

   D. Scroll to the bottom of the page, and click Previous Page several times to view all the footers.

8. Spell-check the document.

9. Save the document as *[your three-letter identifier]*16-1.wpw.
10. Print the document.
11. Close the document and exit WordPerfect (unless you will be doing the following exercises immediately).

Exercise 16.2

1. Start WordPerfect, if necessary.
2. Open the file 15-2.wpw.
3. Cut the heading "The Five Points Reporter", and paste it into the Header A window:
   A. Select the heading "The Five Points Reporter", and choose the Cut command.
   B. Open the Headers dialog box, choose Header A, and click Create.
   C. Choose the Paste command.
   D. Using Reveal Codes, check to see if there is a hard return code at the end of the header text. If not, insert one. (There should be only one hard return code.)
   E. Make the header text bold and right-aligned.
   F. Click Placement.
   G. Click Odd Pages and click OK.
   H. Click Close.
4. Cut the subheading "Newsworthy articles for our agents", and paste it into the Header B window:
   A. Cut the heading "Newsworthy articles for our agents".
   B. Open the Headers dialog box, choose Header B, if necessary, and click Create.
   C. Choose the Paste command.
   D. Using Reveal Codes, check to see if there is a hard return code at the end of the header text. If not, insert one. (There should be only one hard return code.)
   E. Italicize the header text.
   F. Click Placement.
   G. Click Even Pages and click OK.
   H. Click Close.
5. On the first page of the document window, delete all the blank lines that precede the heading "Atlanta Hawks Ticket Discounts".

6. Apply Widow/Orphan protection to the entire document and block protection where needed, if necessary.
7. Spell-check the document.
8. Save the document as *[your three-letter identifier]*16-2.wpw.
9. Print the document.
10. Close the document and exit WordPerfect (unless you will be doing the following exercises immediately).

Exercise 16.3

1. Start WordPerfect, if necessary.
2. Open the file 15-3.wpw.
3. Create the following centered heading on the first document page:

   Weekly New Properties List
   October 15, 199-

4. View the header in the Print Preview window. Notice that the column headings "#", "Location", and "Description" appear on page 1 only.
5. Edit the header created above so that the text is bold. Insert three blank lines at the bottom of the header. Do not close the header window.
6. On the third blank line, clear all the tabs, and then set relative tabs at 1 inch and 3 inches.
7. Apply the bold attribute, if necessary, and then key **#**, press the **Tab** key, key **Location**, press the **Tab** key, and then key **Description**.
8. Click Close to return to the document window.
9. Working in the Reveal Codes space, delete all the text and hard return codes above the first property description, beginning with "95156". Be careful not to delete the tab set code. If the tab set code is deleted, set new relative left-aligned tabs at 1 inch and 3 inches.
10. Create a centered footer with a page number of the form - 1 -.
11. Use Block Protect to prevent page breaks from splitting property descriptions between two pages, where necessary.
12. Open the Print Preview window, check the headers and footers, and then close the Print Preview window.
13. Spell-check the document.
14. Save the document as *[your three-letter identifier]*16-3.wpw.

15. Print the document.
16. Close the document and exit WordPerfect (unless you will be doing the following exercises immediately).

Exercise 16.4

1. Start WordPerfect, if necessary.
2. Open the file 14-4.wpw.
3. Delete the memo heading, and then insert the date **June 22, 199-** at the top of the page.
4. Use the Advance command to position the first line 2 inches down from the top of the page. (Keep the top margin at the default 1-inch setting.)
5. Format the document as a standard block-style business letter. Address it to:

   Mrs. Dorothy Harris
   Chairperson
   Atlanta Board of Realtors
   45 Peachtree Street
   Atlanta, GA 30303

   The salutation should be:

   Dear Dorothy:

6. At the end of the document, key the following closing paragraph:

   Again, thank you for your continued interest.

7. Insert an appropriate signature block from Bud Porter.
8 Create an opening paragraph, using the text found in the figure that appears at the end of this exercise. Include the corrections indicated.
9. On the first page of the letter, create a one-line header with the following information:

   Mrs. Dorothy Harris (left aligned)
   [page-number code] (centered)
   June 22, 199- (right-aligned)

   Insert a blank line below the text in the header.

10. Suppress the printing of the header on the first page.
11. Apply Widow/Orphan protection to the entire document, and apply block protect where needed, if necessary.

12. Spell-check the document.
13. Save the document as *[your three-letter identifier]*16-4.wpw.
14. Print the document.
15. Close the document and exit WordPerfect (unless you will be doing the following exercise immediately).

Figure 16-8

I want to / your continued / of / we continue to receive donations from

Thank you ~~so much~~ for ~~the faithful~~ support ~~you give to~~ my pet project, The Help the Homeless volunteers. Through your tireless efforts, the contacts you make ~~are always sending us donations~~.

Exercise 16.5

1. Start WordPerfect, if necessary.
2. Open the file 12-3c.wpw.
3. Format the document as a standard block-style business letter. Use the Advance command instead of the Margins command to position the first line 2 inches from the top of the page. Use the following information:

To:	**Mr. and Mrs. Robert Waters** **7 Mountain View Lane** **Stone Mountain, GA 30331**
From:	**Mary Rigdon, Office Manager**
Date:	**July 31, 199-**

4. Insert an appropriate salutation and signature block.
5. Without closing document 12-3c.wpw, open the file 12-3b.wpw.
6. Select the third through sixth paragraphs, beginning "In the court case" and ending with the blank line following "not liable for damages."
7. Copy the selection to the Clipboard.
8. Switch to the document 12-3c.wpw window, and position the insertion point at the beginning of the paragraph that begins "I always make every effort".
9. Paste the text from the Clipboard.

10. Move the fourth paragraph, which begins "In the court case prompting", below the seventh paragraph, which begins "Under the consumer-protection".

11. On the first page of the letter, create a continuation-page header consisting of the addressee, left-aligned; the page number, centered; and the date, right-aligned. Insert a blank line in the header to provide space between the header and body of the document.

12. Suppress printing of the header on the first page of the letter.

13. Apply Widow/Orphan protection to the entire document. If necessary, apply block protection where needed.

14. Spell-check the document.

15. Save the document as *[your three-letter identifier]*16-5.wpw.

16. Print the document.

17. Close all open documents and exit WordPerfect.

Module 5

Printing

Lessons

Lesson 17

Printing Options

WordPerfect works with a wide variety of printers and provides you with many printing options. You can print all or part of a document. You can print single or multiple copies. You even can print a document from a disk without opening it.

Objectives

- Explain how WordPerfect and Windows work together to print.
- Cancel a print job.
- Troubleshoot printer problems.
- Print single- and multiple-page documents.
- Print multiple copies of a document.
- Print different portions of a document.
- Print a document from disk.
- Print a Document Summary.

How WordPerfect Prints

Since you printed documents in earlier lessons, your printer has been selected already. The *printer definition* includes the *printer driver*, a file that contains the codes to control the printer, and other information, such as the printer name, the port (interface plug) on your computer that leads to the printer, and the location of files containing special fonts. (Fonts are typefaces, which are discussed in Lesson 19.)

Printer definition
A technical definition of a printer, including its driver and connections.

Printer driver
A file that contains codes to control a printer.

When you instruct WordPerfect to print a document, it first processes the document according to the printer definition you are using. It then passes the processed file to a printer-management program, such as the Windows Print Manager, that sends it to the printer. If the printer's memory cannot accept the entire file at once, the printer manager sends the file in parts until the print job is done.

Canceling a Print Job

In the course of a print job, you may discover something is wrong. Perhaps you are printing the wrong file, or you are using the wrong paper. Depending on your equipment, short print jobs may be done before you know it. But you generally can save time and paper by canceling a long print job.

You may cancel a print job that has been received already by your printer-manager program. You also may cancel it before it is sent.

Note: The following procedure uses Windows Print Manager. If you use a different printer-management program, ask your instructor for directions. Also, note that some systems include data-switching utilities that eliminate Print Manager's error messages.

To cancel a print job that has been received by the Windows Print Manager program:

1. Start WordPerfect, and open the file 17-0a.wpw.

2. Either turn off the power to your printer, or take your printer off-line, or deselect it.

   This will ensure an error message and an opportunity to cancel the print job in Windows' Print Manager.

3. Choose Print from the File menu.

   The Print dialog box appears. Your printer is named as the Current Printer.

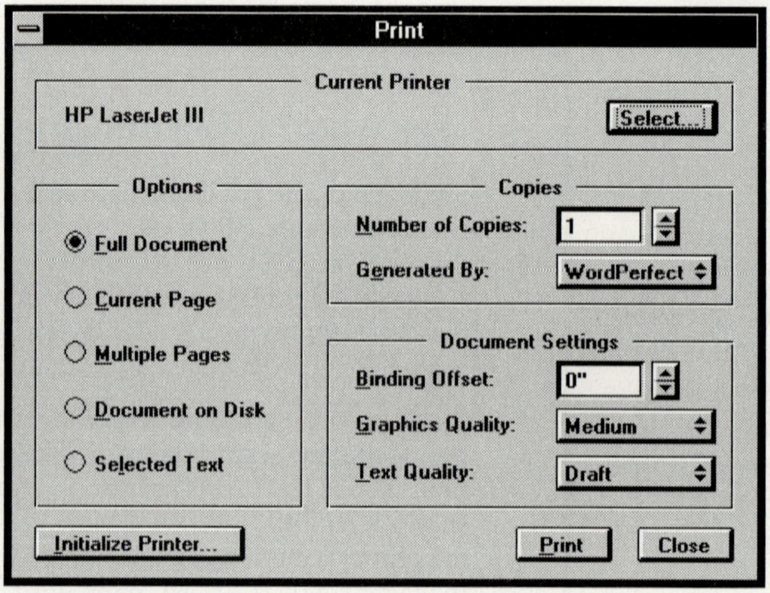

Figure 17-1
The Print dialog box

4. Click Print.

   The Current Print Job dialog box appears. The status message will change as WordPerfect processes your file, as will the page number.

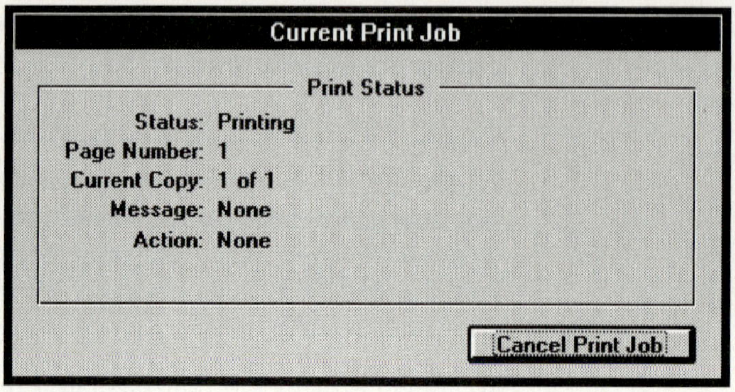

Figure 17-2
The Current Print Job dialog box

After the job is processed, the Current Print Job dialog box disappears. After a short while, a Windows Print Manager STOP message appears, asking you to fix your printer and try again. (On some systems, this message will not appear. If this message does not appear, continue to step 6.)

5. Click Cancel.

   The print job is still in the Windows Print Manager queue. A queue is a waiting line. Print jobs wait in the queue until the printer is ready to take them.

6. Minimize WordPerfect.

   You are returned to the Windows desktop.

7. Double-click the Print Manager icon. (It looks like a printer.)

   Windows' Print Manager dialog box appears.

8. Click "WordPerfect - 17-0a.wpw" to highlight it in the queue.

9. Click Delete. Then confirm that choice.

   Now the print job is gone. (You could have corrected the printer's condition and chosen Resume, instead.)

10. Close the Print Manager dialog box.

11. Press **Ctrl+Esc** to open the Task List. Then select WordPerfect - 17-0a.wpw and choose Switch To.

    You are returned to the document window.

To cancel a print job before WordPerfect sends it to the Print Manager:

1. Choose Print from the File menu (or press **F5**).

   Be ready to press **Enter** as soon as the Current Print Job dialog box appears.

2. Click Print.

3. Press **Enter** when the Current Print Job dialog box appears (or click Cancel Print Job).

   The current print job is cancelled, and you are returned to the document window.

Note: Depending on the length of your document and the speed of your computer's processor, you may not be able to cancel a print job in time. You could turn off your printer (if that is permitted) and then delete the print job from the printer manager's queue.

Troubleshooting

Usually, you will not create printer errors on purpose. Nonetheless, they may occur. Ask the obvious questions first, and then seek advice from documentation or from experts. Table 17-1 lists some common questions that are easy to answer without outside assistance.

Table 17-1: Printer Troubleshooting Questions

Ask Yourself:	Check:
• Is the printer plugged in and the power turned on?	The power-indicator light should be on.
• Is the printer online (selected to accept data)?	The "Select" or "OnLine" indicator light should be on.
• Is the paper supply adequate and feeding correctly?	Check the paper.
• Is the printer connected to the computer?	Check both ends of the connection. Note the name of the connecting plug (the printer port) on the back of the computer.
• Is your printer correctly defined and selected in WordPerfect?	See the topics "Select Printer" and "Printer Setup" at the end of this lesson.

Print Preview

You can see what a document will look like when printed by using the Print Preview option. The Preview Screen Area displays a document in the way that it will be seen using the selected printer driver. (Graphics will display in the Print Preview window, even if you selected a nongraphics printer.)

1. Position the insertion point anywhere in the first page of document 17-0a.wpw.

   This is the cover memo for the document used in Lesson 16. The document has three parts, each starting with its own page 1.

2. Choose Print Preview from the File menu.

   The Print Preview window appears with the current page in the Preview Screen Area. The appearance of this image depends on the options you choose.

3. Choose Button Bar from View in the Print Preview menu bar, if necessary.

   The Button Bar is displayed, usually to the left of the Print Preview image. The buttons are shortcuts to commands available in the menus. See Figure 17-3 on page 17-5.

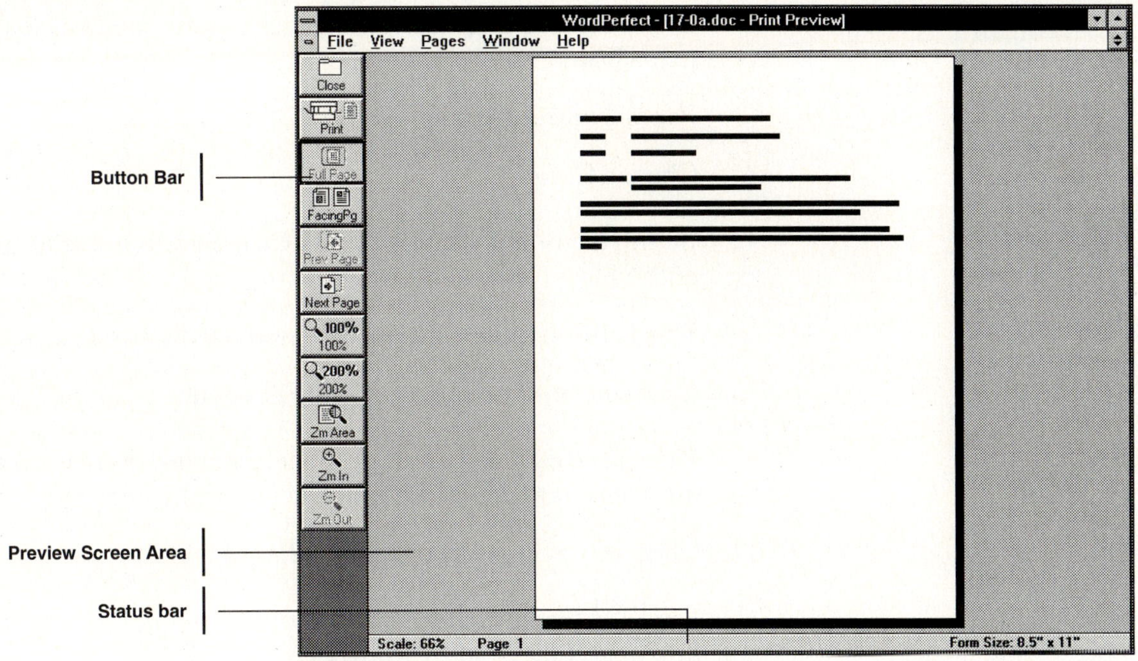

Figure 17-3
Print Preview window with Button Bar (as in step 3 on page 17-4)

4. Click the Full Page button, or choose Full Page from the Pages menu, if necessary. Then move the mouse pointer into the Preview Screen Area.

   A complete view of page 1 is displayed. Unless you have a large screen, the lines of type are represented as solid lines. The status bar at the bottom shows the scale (a percent of the printed size), the document page number, and the form size.

5. Choose Close from the Button Bar or from the File menu.

   You are returned to the document window.

6. In the document window, use the Go To command (**Ctrl+G**) to move to page 3.

7. Choose Print Preview from the File menu or press **Shift+F5**.

8. Choose Facing Pg from the Button Bar, or choose Facing Pages from the Pages menu.

   Images of pages 2 and 3 appear side-by-side. Facing Pages displays a spread, consisting of an even, or left, page and the following odd, or right, page. You can readily check the overall layout of pages as they would appear in a book. Of course, the scale is smaller than it was for Full Page.

9. Choose Next Page from the Button Bar, or choose Next Page from the Pages menu.

   The next spread appears, displaying pages 4 and 5.

10. Choose Go To Page from the Pages menu. Then key **3** and press **Enter**.

    Pages 2 and 3 are displayed.

11. Choose Close.

12. In the document window, press **Ctrl+End** to move to the end of the file.

    This is the sample contract that was used in Lesson 16.

13. Choose Print Preview from the File menu.

    Page 2 is displayed alone at the left. If a last page is even, Facing Pages displays it alone at the left of the window.

14. Choose Previous Page from the Pages menu.

    Page 1 is displayed alone at the right. Facing Pages displays any page 1 alone at the right of the window.

15. Choose 100% from the Button Bar or from the View menu.

    The top half of the page is displayed as it will print.

16. Press **PageDown**.

    The bottom half of the page is displayed as it will print.

17. Choose Previous Page from the Pages menu.

    The bottom half of the previous page is displayed as it will print. (This is the last page of the revised *Guide to Atlanta*, page 11.)

18. Press **PageUp** to see the header, including the page number.

19. Press **Ctrl+Home**.

    In Print Preview, **Ctrl+Home** acts like Go To Page 1, moving to the first page of the current numbering sequence (in this case, the Chapter 2 title page, which contains a [Pg Num:1] code).

20. Choose Previous Page from the Pages menu to move to the first page of the document, the cover memo.

21. Page through the document using Next Page from the Pages menu to review all the headers and page numbers.

    Print Preview at 100% is a convenient mode for reviewing headers, footers, and page numbering.

22. When you reach the last page, choose 200% from the Button Bar or from the View menu.

    The text in the upper left of the page is enlarged. In the status bar, the scale is 200%. This mode is useful for reviewing graphics and special characters.

23. Click in the Preview Screen Area.

    A miniature page image appears in the middle of the screen, including a red location box marking the enlarged area on the page. The cursor changes to a four-headed arrow within this mini-page.

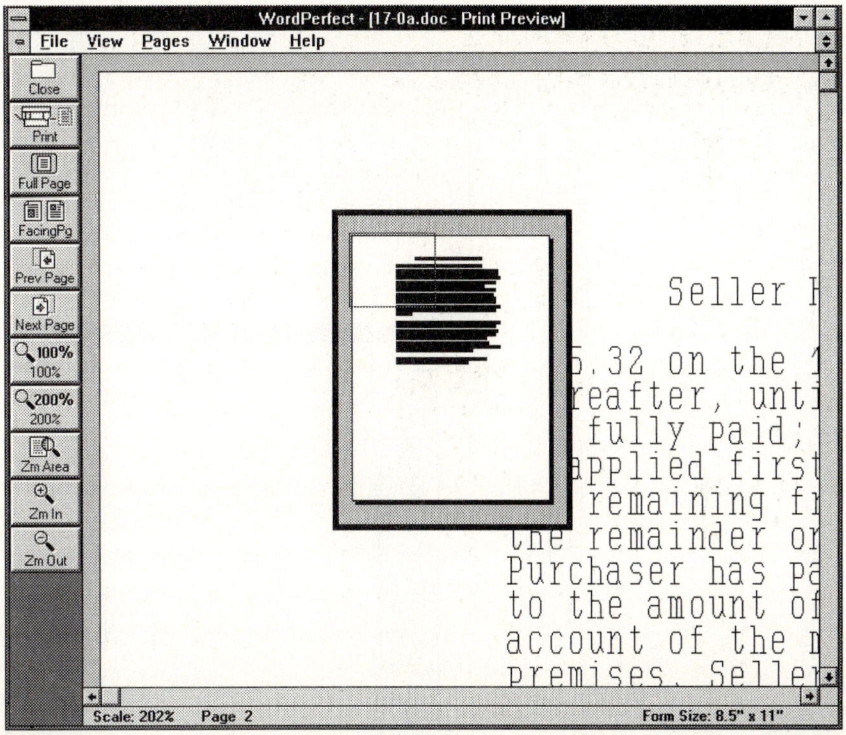

Figure 17-4
Print Preview window at 202%

24. Drag the red location box to another place on the mini-page, and release the mouse button.

    The mini-page vanishes, and the area you marked is enlarged on the screen.

25. Choose Close from the Button Bar or from the File menu.

    WordPerfect returns you to the document window on the page that you viewed last in Print Preview.

Zoom Commands

The Zoom commands in Print Preview allow you to change the magnification of the Preview Screen Area. You can create the level of detail suited to your editing and viewing needs, down to Full Page view and up to 400 percent of the original.

Choose Zoom Out (or press **Ctrl+Up Arrow**) to shrink the viewing size. You will see less detail, but more of the whole page. This option reduces the image in steps of 25 percent of the original. For instance, starting at 200%, Zoom Out will reduce the scale to 175% and then 150%. You can Zoom Out until the image is displayed as in Full Page view.

Choose Zoom In (or press **Ctrl+Down Arrow**) to expand the viewing size of displayed text by 25 percent. You will see more detail, but less of the whole page. The scale can be increased to 400 percent (so text appears four times its original size).

Choose the Zoom Area command to mark the area to expand. Vertical and horizontal guide lines accompany the mouse pointer. Position the pointer at the edge of the area you want to view. Then drag the mouse to form a box surrounding the area of interest. When you release the left mouse button, the area will be resized to fill the Preview Screen Area (up to 400 percent magnification).

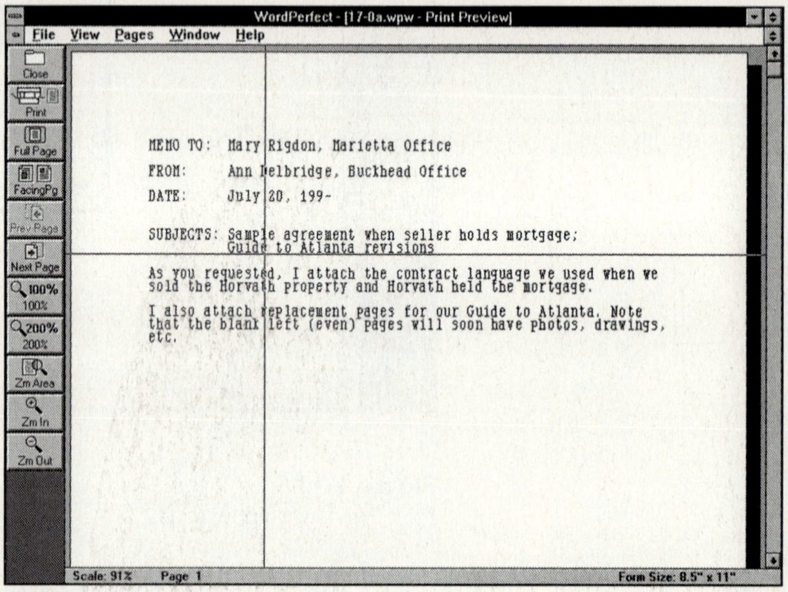

Figure 17-5
Zoom Area guide lines

The Reset command from the View menu returns to the scale that was set when you last closed the Print Preview window.

Whenever the scale is greater than 100 percent, the location box will appear when you click in the Preview Screen Area (see Figure 17-4). You can see other portions of a page by dragging this box.

Printing

In WordPerfect, you can print all or part of a document, and you can choose the quality of the output, as well. The Print dialog box is available from the document window and from the Print Preview window. Choose Print from the File menu or from the Button Bar.

Text Quality

In general, high-quality printing is slower than draft-mode printing. Draft mode produces lower quality output, but at higher speeds than medium- or high-quality modes.

To choose text quality:

1. Open the file 17-0b.wpw.

   This is the memo that began document 17-0a.wpw.

2. Choose Print from the File menu.

   The Print dialog box appears.

3. Click and hold the Text Quality button in the Document Settings group.

   The Text Quality list box appears.

The Text Quality pop-up list

4. Choose Draft.

5. If necessary, choose Full Document in the Options group.

6. Follow your instructor's directions to print this document.

   If you choose Print, the document will print in draft mode. If you then choose High Text Quality and choose Print again, the document will print in high quality (which sometimes is called "letter quality").

You then may compare output speed and quality for your printer.

Printing the Current Page

In longer documents, you may want to print or reprint a single page.

To print the current page of a document:

1. Choose document 17.0a.wpw from the Window menu.

2. Position the insertion point anywhere in page 3, which begins with the heading "Leisure Activities in Atlanta".

3. Choose Print from the File menu.

4. Choose Current Page in the Options group of the Print dialog box.

5. Follow your instructor's directions to print this document.

   Consider choosing draft mode to speed printing. If you choose Print, only page 3 will be printed.

Printing Multiple Pages

You may want to print several pages from a long document. You can specify which pages to print in the Range text box.

To specify a series of single pages, key them in order, separated by commas or by spaces. Thus, **1,2,9** or **1 2 9** in the Range text box will print pages 1, 2, and 9.

You may specify a range of pages by using a hyphen. Thus, **3-5** in the Range text box will print pages 3, 4, and 5.

Some documents, like 17-0a.wpw, are divided into sections by page-numbering changes. To specify a page in a section of a document, use a colon. Thus, **2:3-6** in the Range text box will print pages 3 through 6 from section 2 of a document.

You also may specify several ranges to print within a document. Thus **2:3-6,3:1** in the Range text box will print pages 3 through 6 from section 2 and page 1 from section 3.

The following table summarizes the rules for printing a range of pages:

Table 17-2: Multiple Page Range Text Box Specifications

Key	To Print
p	Page p
p,q,r	Pages p, q, and r
p q	Pages p and q
-p	The beginning of the document through page p
p-	Page p through the end of the document
p-r	Pages p through r
a:p-r	Pages p through r of section a
a:p-r b:p-r	Pages p through r of section a and pages p through r of section b

Note: Key page numbers as Roman (uppercase or lowercase) or as Arabic, depending on how you created them.

In Table 17-2, a & b are section numbers, and p, q, and r are page numbers.

To print multiple pages from a document:

1. Choose 17-0a.wpw from the Window menu, if necessary.

2. Choose Print from the File menu.

3. Choose Multiple Pages in the Options group of the Print dialog box.

4. Click Print.

   The Multiple Pages dialog box appears.

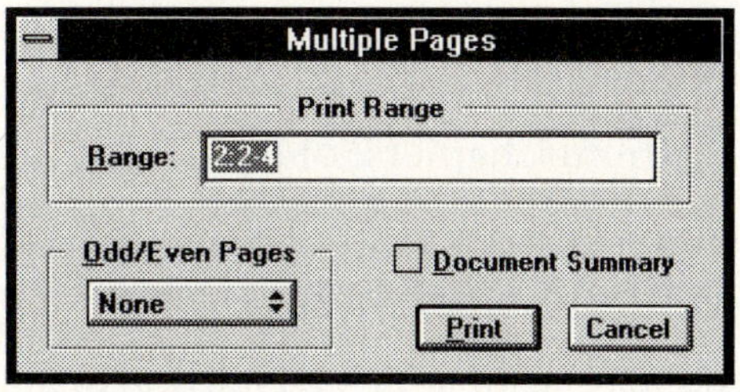

Figure 17-6
Multiple Page dialog box

5. In the Range text box, key **2:2-4**.

6. Follow your instructor's directions to print.

   Consider choosing draft mode to speed printing. If you choose Print, only pages 2 though 4 of section 2 will be printed (part of Chapter 2 of the *Guide to Atlanta*).

Printing Odd/Even Pages

You may want to print only the odd or even pages in a document. For instance, in Chapter 2 of the *Guide to Atlanta* in 17-0a.wpw, the even pages are reserved for art, and the odd pages have text. To circulate a copy of the text portion, you could print only the even pages in that section.

To print odd or even pages:

1. Choose 17-0a.wpw from the Window menu, if necessary.

2. Choose Print from the File menu.

3. Choose Multiple Pages in the Print dialog box.

4. Click Print.

5. In the Range text box, key **2:1-5**.

   This specifies all the pages in section 2, Chapter 2 of the *Guide to Atlanta*.

6. Click and hold the button under Odd/Even Pages.

   The Odd/Even Pages pop-up list appears.

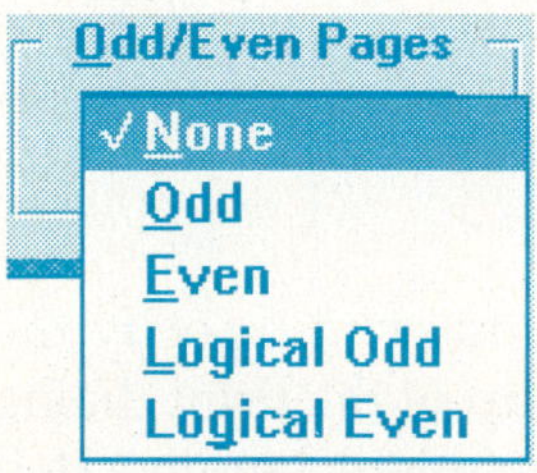

The Odd/Even Pages pop-up list

7. Choose Logical Odd.

   Logical Odd pages are those that are numbered odd. (The actual odd pages in a document are the first, third, fifth pages, and so on, regardless of page numbering.)

8. Follow your instructor's directions to print.

   Consider choosing draft mode to speed printing. If you choose Print, only pages 1, 3, and 5 of section 2 will be printed (from Chapter 2 of the *Guide to Atlanta*).

Printing Selected Text

You may want to print a portion of text that you select. To print with the Select Text option, you must select the text or graphic in the document before choosing Print.

The selected text will be printed on the page in the same format as in the document. Thus, if you print selected text that begins 4 inches from the top of the page in the document, that is where it will be printed. If a text selection begins in the middle of a line, however, it will begin printing at the left margin. Headers, footers, and page numbers associated with the selected material also will be printed.

To print selected text:

1. Choose 17-0a.wpw in the Window menu, if necessary.

2. Press **Ctrl+End** to move to the end of the file.

3. Select the paragraph that begins "Purchaser further agrees to pay".

4. Choose Print from the File menu.

   The Print dialog box appears with Selected Text chosen in the Options group.

5. Follow your instructor's directions to print this selection.

   Consider choosing draft mode to speed printing. If you choose Print, the selected paragraph will be printed about 3.67" from the top margin on a page with its page number and accompanying text.

Printing Multiple Copies

You may print multiple copies of anything you print. Specify the number of copies you want in the Copies group of the Print dialog box. Then specify the device by which those copies will be generated (WordPerfect or your printer).

Note: If you are using a dot-matrix printer, which is slow and noisy, and have access to a photocopier, think twice before printing multiple copies.

If WordPerfect generates each copy of a multiple-page document, processing time may be longer, but the copies will come out collated. If your printer generates the copies, you will get multiple copies of each page, uncollated.

To practice printing multiple copies:

1. Choose 17-0b.wpw (the cover memo) from the Window menu.
2. Choose Print from the File menu.
3. Key **2** in the Number of Copies text box, or click the up arrow, so 2 appears in that box.

   The text box will accept positive values up to 99,999 to accommodate high-volume printing.
4. Follow your instructor's directions to print this document.

   Consider choosing draft mode to speed printing. If you choose Print, two copies of the document will be printed.

Printing from Disk

You may print a document (or any part of it) directly from a disk without opening the file.

To print from disk:

1. Close document 17-0b.wpw without saving it.
2. Choose Print from the File Menu.
3. Click Document on Disk. Then click Print.

   The Document on Disk dialog box appears.

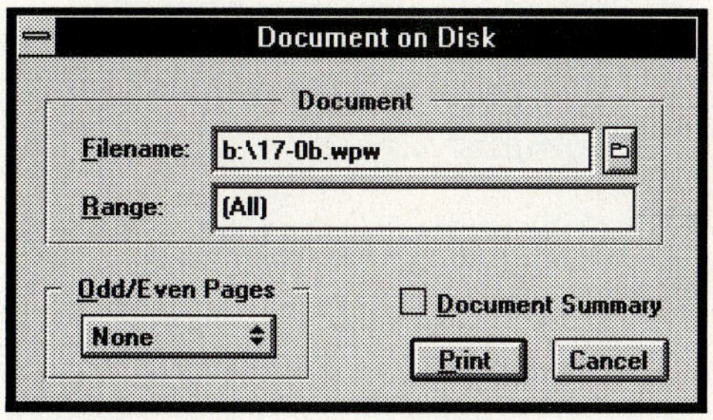

Figure 17-7
The Document on Disk dialog box

4. Key the path of the file you will print (probably **a:** or **b:**) in the Filename text box. Then key the filename, **17-0b.wpw**.

Note: If you do not know the filename you want to print, click the File Folder button to the right of the filename text box, and the Select File dialog box appears. You may change drives and directories to find the file. You may use View to verify the contents of the file you highlight.

As in the Multiple Pages dialog box, you may specify a range and Odd/Even Pages options. Those choices do not suit this file, however.

5. Follow your instructor's directions to print this document.

   If you choose Print, WordPerfect will print 17-0b.wpw from the disk where it is stored.

Printing Document Summaries

A Document Summary contains information identifying, locating, and summarizing a document. You may want to attach a printed copy of a Document Summary to a long document.

To print a Document Summary from a document on disk:

1. Open the file 17-0b.wpw.
2. Choose Document from the Layout menu and then choose Summary.
3. Create a document summary. Name it logically. Specify Ann Delbridge as Author. Use *[your three-letter identifier]* for Typist. Extract the Abstract. Then click OK.
4. Save the document as *[your three-letter identifier]*17-0b.wpw. Then close the document.
5. Choose Print from the File menu.
6. Select Document on Disk. Then Choose Print.

   The Document on Disk dialog box appears.
7. Key the path of the file you will print (probably **a:** or **b:**) in the Filename text box. Then key the filename, **17-0b.wpw**.
8. Select Document Summary.
9. Key **none** in the Range text field (to print only the Document Summary).
10. Follow your instructor's directions to print this document.

    If you choose Print, WordPerfect will print the Document Summary for 17-0b.wpw from the disk where it is stored.

You also may print the document summary from the Multiple Pages dialog box:

1. Choose 17-0a.wpw from the Window menu, if necessary.
2. Choose Document from the Layout menu and then choose Summary.

3. Create a document summary. Name it logically. Specify Ann Delbridge as Author. Use *[your three-letter identifier]* for Typist. Extract the Abstract. Then click OK.
4. Save the document as *[your three-letter identifier]*17-0a.wpw.
5. Choose Print from the File menu.
6. Select Multiple Pages. Then Choose Print.
7. Click Document Summary in the Multiple Pages dialog box.
8. Key **none** in the Range text box to print only the Document Summary.
9. Follow your instructor's directions to print this Document Summary.

   If you choose Print, WordPerfect will print the Document Summary for 17-0a.wpw from the disk where it is stored.
10. Close the document and exit WordPerfect (unless you will be doing the following exercises immediately).

Selecting Another Printer

Some office systems are networked to share resources, such as printers. When one printer is busy or unsuitable to a particular task, you may want to send a print job to another printer. To use a different printer, you need to select a different printer definition.

The Select Printer dialog box is available from the File menu or from the Print dialog box. In this dialog box, you may choose a new printer definition from the Available Printers list.

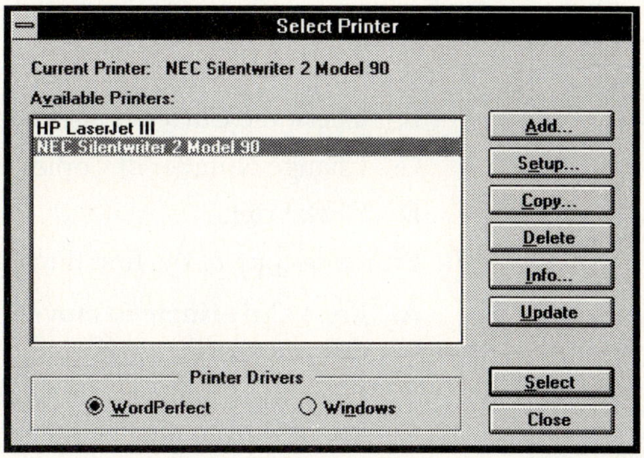

Figure 17-8
Select Printer dialog box

Table 17-3: Keyboard Shortcut for Printing	
Keyboard Shortcut	Action
F5	Open the Print dialog box
Shift+F5	Open the Print Preview window

Key Terms

Printer definition

Printer driver

Exercises

Exercise 17.1

1. Start WordPerfect, if necessary.
2. Open the file 17-1.wpw.
3. Position the insertion point in the last page, which includes part of a listing of seminars.
4. View the last two pages in Print Preview:
   A. Press **Shift+F5**.
   B. Choose Previous Page from the Button Bar.
   C. Choose Close.
5. Insert a hard page break before the heading "**Non-Credit Enrichment Seminars.**"
6. Print two copies of that new last page alone using the Current Page print option:
   A. Press **F5** to open the Print dialog box.
   B. Check the Current Page box.
   C. Change Number of Copies to **2**.
   D. Click Print.
7. Print one copy of the first three pages of the course listings:
   A. Press **Ctrl+Home** to move to the beginning of the document.
   B. Open the Print Preview window by choosing Print Preview from the File menu.
   C. Choose 100% from the Button Bar or from the View menu, if necessary.
   D. Choose Next Page to see the next page. Move the pointer to the preview window, and note its page number in the status bar.

E. Repeat step D to preview the entire document and locate the section and page numbers to be printed.

F. Choose Print from the Button Bar or from the File menu.

G. Check the Multiple Pages option and choose Print.

H. In the Multiple Pages dialog box, key **2:1-3** in the Print Range text box.

I. Choose Print.

8. Print the document summary:

   A. Choose Print from the File menu. Then check the Multiple Pages box and choose Print.

   B. In the Multiple Pages dialog, check the Document Summary box, key **none** in the Range text box, and then choose Print.

9. Save the document as *[your three-letter identifier]*17-1.wpw.

10. Close the document and exit WordPerfect (unless you will be doing the following exercises immediately).

Exercise 17.2

1. Start WordPerfect, if necessary.

2. Print the file 17-2a.wpw from your student disk:

   A. Choose Print from the File menu (or press **F5**).

   B. Check the Document on Disk option and choose Print.

   C. Click the File button beside the Filename text box, and use the Select File dialog box to highlight 17-2a.wpw on your student disk (in drive a: or b:).

   D. Choose View to verify that this is the memo to Mary Trant. Then choose Select.

   E. Choose Print in the Document on Disk dialog box.

3. Print the odd pages of the first section of 17-2b.wpw from your student disk:

   A. Press **F5**, check Document on Disk, and choose Print.

   B. Key ***[your student disk drive]*17-2b.wpw** in the Filename text box.

   C. Key **1:1-5** in the Range text box.

   D. Choose Odd from the Odd/Even Pages pop-up list. Then choose Print.

4. Exit WordPerfect (unless you will be doing the following exercises immediately).

Exercise 17.3

1. Start WordPerfect, if necessary.
2. Open the file 17-3.wpw.
3. Make the changes shown in Figure 17-8.
4. Format the memo following the style in Appendix C.
5. Include Bud Porter's initials (BP), your reference intitials, and a cc to Rick Slaney.
6. Spell-check the document.
7. Save the document as *[your three-letter identifier]*17-3.wpw.
8. Print three copies. Then put a check mark beside "Rick Slaney" on his copy, initial (BP) the copy to Mary Trant, and put a check mark beside "Bud Porter" on the file copy.
9. Close the document and exit WordPerfect (unless you will be doing the following exercises immediately).

Figure 17-9

MEMO TO:
Mary Trant, Atlanta Board of Realtors

FROM:
Bud Porter, Five Points Realty

DATE:
July 16, 199-

SUBJECT:
Board of Realtors Courses Announcement

You really worked hard to arrange these new offerings!

Here is the edited Course Announcement. ¶ My thanks also go to our Rick Slaney for his profesional eye to detail and layout.

Please paste in the Calendar and Regestration Form on pages ii and iv, respectively.

As we agreed, printing and distribution falls to you.

Call if you have any questions.

Exercise 17.4

1. Start WordPerfect, if necessary.
2. Open the file 17-4.wpw.
3. Look over the course-listings section in Print Preview.

4. For each course, format the indented material using a 1 1/2-inch margin. Delete the [Tab] codes that are used currently to indent the day and time of meeting, starting date, location, and instructor information.
5. Use Replace to spell out the word "Instructor", which is now generally abbreviated.
6. Key in the course description shown in Figure 17-9. Format this material like the other course material.
7. Spell-check the document.
8. Full-justify the document, and turn Hyphenation On using a 4% left and right hyphenation zone. Position hyphens appropriately.
9. Check the page layout in Print Preview. Delete any blank pages.
10. Save the document as *[your three-letter identifier]*17-4.wpw.
11. Print the second section of the document (the course listings).
12. Close the document and exit WordPerfect (unless you will be doing the following exercise immediately).

Figure 17-10

Review for Real Estate Exam

This course offers an intensive review for those who failed the license exam, need a refresher course, or are licensed in another state. Sample exams, study tips, and test-taking techniques are included. This is a non-credit course.

1 Session.
Non-Member Fee: $50. Member Fee: $25.
Handout materials included.

Sat. 10/16 (9:00 a.m.-1:00 p.m.)

Downtown Continuing Education Center

Instructors: Marilyn and Mike Montefiore, formerly on the faculty of Buckhead Community College, are seasoned real estate professionals.

Exercise 17.5

1. Start WordPerfect, if necessary.
2. Open the file 17-5.wpw.

   You will adjust the format of this version of the "ATLANTA BOARD OF REALTORS FALL COURSE ANNOUNCEMENT" and print it as a two-sided document.
3. Eliminate page numbering and the page-numbering style beginning on the title page of the course-listings section (section 2).
4. For section 2, define a Footer A, and position it on odd pages:

   Fall 199- **[page number]**
5. For section 2, define a Footer B, and position it on even pages:

   [page number] **Fall 199-**
6. Suppress footers on the title page of the course-listings section.
7. Spell-check the document.
8. Full-justify the document.
9. Turn hyphenation on and position hyphens appropriately.
10. Create a document summary using Figure 17-11 as a model. Write your own abstract.

Figure 17-11

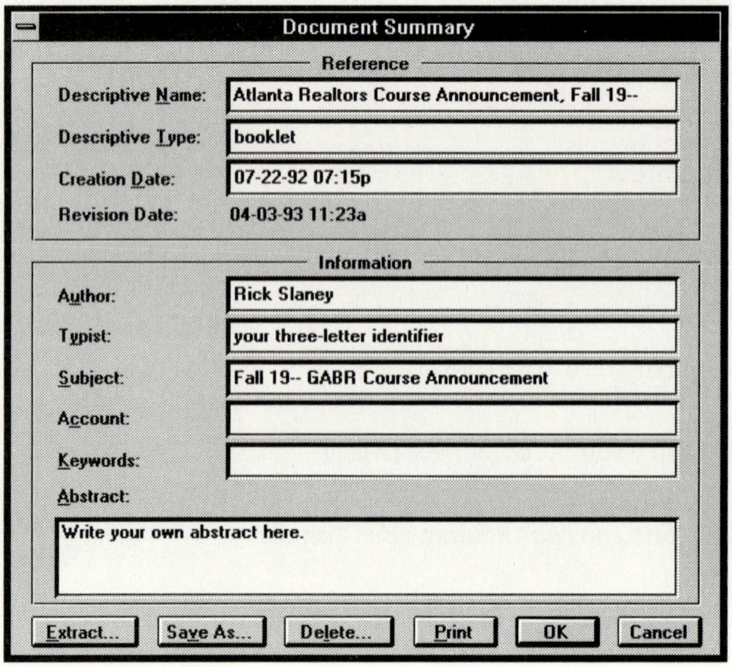

11. Review the document in Page Preview.
12. Save the document as *[your three-letter identifier]*17-5a.wpw.
13. Print the logical odd pages of the document.
14. Set aside page "v," since nothing should print on its back.
15. Feed the other odd pages into your printer, so the logical even pages will print on their backs.
16. Print the logical even pages of the document. Then insert page "v" in its proper place.
17. Close the document.
18. Open a new document.
19. Using the style shown in Appendix C, key the material in Figure 17-12 as a cover memo. Spell-check this document, and save it as *[your three-letter identifier]*17-5b.wpw.
20. Print copies of the memo for each recipient and for the sender.
21. Print copies of the document summary from the file on your student disk to attach to each cover memo.
22. Close the document and exit WordPerfect.

Figure 17-12

from Rick Slaney

to Ann Delbridge, Mary Rigdon, Bud Porter, John Soloman

today's date

subject: GABR Course Announcement Booklet

We will be circulating a copy of the GABR Course Announcement Booklet for your review. Please initial your comments on this copy, so I can call to clarify your concerns. Then pass the copy to the next person on the list.

Please complete your review and pass on the document according to this schedule:

Reviewer	**Day**
Ann	Monday
Mary	Wednesday
John	Friday
Bud	Tuesday

Thanks for your help.

RS

enclosure: Document Summary

Lesson 18

Special Printing Features

Depending on your printer, you can print on different-sized paper, envelopes, and labels. You also can choose the orientation of the paper and print with either the long or short side at the top. This flexibility allows you to create professional-looking documents in a variety of formats.

In order to change paper size or orientation, you need to change the paper definition.

Objectives

- Print on different paper sizes.
- Print in landscape orientation.
- Print envelopes.
- Print labels.

Paper Definitions

Paper Definition
A description, including paper dimensions and orientation, used to format and print documents.

WordPerfect uses a *paper definition* to format and print documents. A paper definition includes a paper type (the name of the paper), paper size (the dimensions of the paper), printing orientation, and other elements. WordPerfect comes with preset paper definitions for each printer.

The default paper definition varies among printers, but includes the following elements: standard paper type, 8½″ x 11″ paper size, and portrait orientation (which prints with the shorter edge at the top).

The descriptions in this lesson assume that Auto Code Placement is on. (To set Auto Code Placement, choose Preferences from the File menu and then choose Environment.)

When Auto Code Placement is on, WordPerfect places a paper-definition code at the beginning of the current page. The paper definition affects all following pages, until the next paper definition appears. A paper definition affects only the current document and is saved with the document.

The Paper Size Dialog Box

The Paper Size dialog box lists the preset paper definitions for your printer in a list through which you can scroll. The current definition is highlighted. The current printer is listed at the top of this dialog box.

Each paper definition includes a paper type, paper size, orientation, location, prompt indicator, double-sided indicator, and label indicator.

To see the paper definitions for your printer:

1. Start WordPerfect.

2. Choose Page from the Layout menu, and then choose Paper Size.

   The Paper Size dialog box appears with the current definition highlighted. If you have more than four paper definitions, a scroll bar is displayed.

3. Scroll through the list.

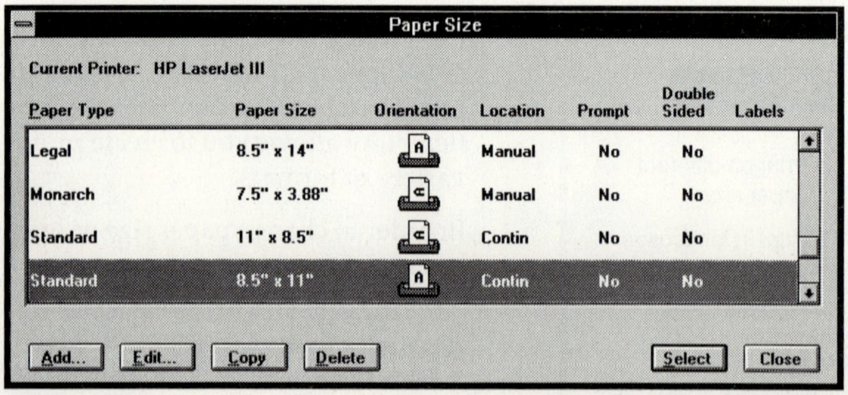

Figure 18-1
The Paper Size dialog box

4. Click Close to return to the document window without selecting a new definition.

Paper Type

A paper type helps identify the use of a paper definition. For instance, "Envelope," "Label," "Standard" and "Legal" are logical names for paper definitions. Of course, if you use several kinds of envelopes, you could create several definitions for that paper type. "Standard" is the default paper type.

If you are editing or adding a paper definition, you should select a paper type, or name, that reflects the dimensions or kind of paper involved. The Add Paper Size and Edit Paper Size dialog boxes include a pop-up list for Paper Type. Table 18-1 lists the paper types that WordPerfect provides.

Table 18-1: Commonly Available Paper Types

Paper Type	Typical Dimensions	Typical Stock
Bond	varies	bond paper
Cardstock	varies	cardstock
Envelope	varies	envelope
Label	varies	label
Legal	8½″ × 14″	varies
Letterhead	8½″ × 11″	preprinted paper
Monarch	7¼″ × 10½″	bond paper
Standard	8½″ × 11″	varies
Transparency	8½″ × 11″	acetate

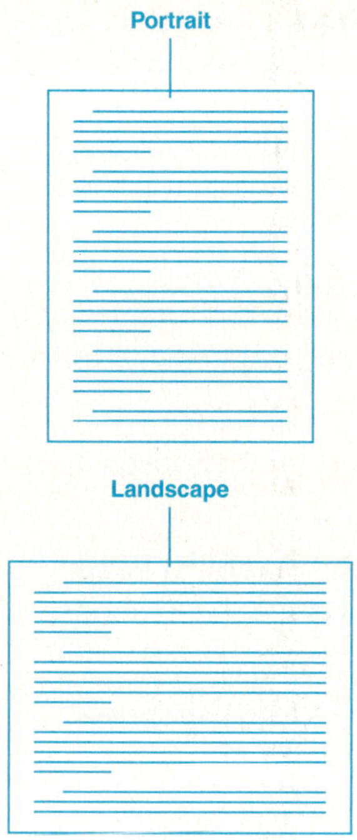

A portrait page and a landscape page

Portrait Orientation
Printing parallel to the short edge of the paper.

Landscape Orientation
Printing parallel to the long edge of the paper.

Paper location
The source of the paper being fed into the printer: Continuous, Bin #, or Manual.

Paper Size

In the U.S. version of WordPerfect, the default paper size is 8½″ x 11″. Other common paper sizes include legal size (8½″ x 14″) and a variety of envelopes and mailing labels.

The Add Paper Size and Edit Paper Size dialog boxes include a pop-up list for Paper Size.

Orientation

Depending on your printer, you may be able to print documents parallel to the short or long edge of the paper. The terms "portrait" and "landscape" were borrowed from fine art to describe these orientations. *Portrait orientation,* which is the default, means printing across the short edge. (Most portrait paintings are oriented with the shorter edge up.) *Landscape orientation* means printing across the longer edge of the paper. (Most fine-art landscapes are painted "sideways," with the longer edge up.)

While portrait orientation is used with most documents, landscape orientation suits envelopes and wide tables.

In WordPerfect dialog boxes, orientation is indicated by the direction of an uppercase "A" on an icon of a printing page.

Other Paper Definition Elements

Each paper definition includes other information, as well.

Paper location describes the source of the paper being fed into the printer. "Continuous" is the source for tractor-fed paper (for dot-matrix and daisy-wheel printers) or for laser printers with one paper cassette or sheet feeder. A "Bin" and "Bin Number" identify the source of paper for laser printers with more than one paper cassette or sheet feeder. "Manual" means paper is fed into the printer one page at a time.

A paper definition may include a "yes" for Prompt, which causes the computer to pause and signal the user to load paper before printing.

If your printer is capable of duplex printing (printing two sides of a page at once), a paper definition may include a "yes" for the Double Sided option.

Paper definitions that include Labels indicate the number of rows and columns of labels on each page (3x10, for instance).

Selecting a Paper Definition

To select a different existing paper definition, simply highlight it in the Paper Size dialog box and then choose Select.

To choose a new paper size in a paper definition:

1. Open the file 18-0a.wpw.

   Notice that this table is crowded. The office locations are abbreviated, and there is little white space between numbers.

2. Choose Ruler from the View menu.
3. Position the insertion point at the top of the document. Then scroll left and right, if necessary, to see the paper-edge markers at 0″ and 8.5″.
4. Choose Page from the Layout menu, and then choose Paper Size.
5. In the Paper Size dialog box, highlight the Standard Paper Type with a landscape orientation (11″ x 8½″). Then choose Select.
6. Scroll right, if necessary, to see that the right paper-edge marker has changed in the Ruler to 11″.
7. Choose Print Preview from the File menu. If necessary, choose Full Page in the Print Preview window.

   The table fits on the page vertically, but there is more horizontal room to adjust the layout. You could make the tabular columns wider, spell out the office names, and make the data easier to read.

8. Close the Print Preview window.
9. Move the insertion point to the beginning of the document, if necessary. Then make both the left and right margins 2.25 inches from the paper edge. (Press **Ctrl+F8**, key **2.25** for the left and right margin, and click OK.)
10. Open the Print Preview window.

    The table and its title are centered on the landscape page.

11. Close the Print Preview window.
12. Save the document as *[your three-letter identifier]* 18-0a.wpw.
13. Print the document.

As you can see, decisions about paper size should come before other layout considerations. Margins and other layout decisions may be influenced by the paper size you use.

Printing Envelopes

To print on envelopes, select an envelope paper definition. Then format your text appropriately, and check your document in Print Preview. Finally, prepare your printer to accept your envelopes, and send the print job.

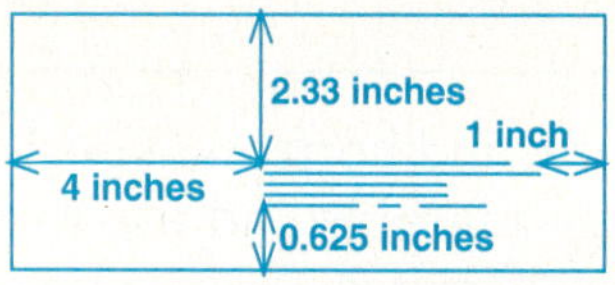

Mailing-address position on a #10 envelope

For a Number 10 business envelope (9.5″ x 4″) with a preprinted return address, use the following margins:

- 4-inch left margin
- 2.33-inch top margin (the equivalent of 14 lines)
- 1-inch right margin
- 0.625-inch bottom margin (⅝ inches)

To print envelopes:

1. Open the file 18-0b.wpw.

   Two addresses appear on one page.

2. Choose Page from the Layout menu, and then choose Paper Size.

Note: If you do not have an envelope paper definition, see "Adding and Editing Paper Definitions" below.

3. In the Paper Size dialog box, select the 9.5″ x 4″ Envelope definition. Then choose Select.

4. Press **Alt+F3** to open the Reveal Codes space.

   Notice the paper-size code at the top of the page.

5. Position the insertion point at the beginning of the second address. Press **Ctrl+Enter** to force a page break between addresses.

6. Press **Shift+F5** to open the Print Preview window, and choose Full Page, if necessary.

   An image of an envelope appears with the address in the upper left of the page. The 1-inch default margins are in effect.

7. Close the Print Preview window.

8. Position the insertion point at the top of the document, if necessary. Change the margins as follows:

Left:	4 inches
Right:	1 inch
Top:	2.33 inches
Bottom:	0.625 inches

9. Open the Print Preview window and examine both pages.

   The addresses are centered appropriately on each envelope.

10. Close the Print Preview window.

11. Save the document as *[your three-letter identifier]*18-0b.wpw.

12. Prepare your printer and load envelopes, if necessary.

13. Print the envelopes.

Formatting Return Addresses

A return address appears in a different vertical and horizontal position from a mailing address. You can change margins and use the Advance To Line feature to position text appropriately.

To print both a return and mailing address on a Number 10 envelope:

- For the return address, use ½-inch left and top margins (Top 0.5″, Left 0.5″).
- Use bottom and right margins as described above (Right 1.00″, Bottom 0.625″).
- After the return address and at the beginning of the mailing address, change the left margin to 4 inches.
- To position the mailing address vertically, click Advance from the layout menu, check To Line, and key **2.33"** in the text box. Then click OK.

Table 18-2 summarizes the positioning of addresses on two common kinds of envelope.

Table 18-2: Positioning Addresses on Envelopes

	Left Margin	Right Margin	Top Margin	Bottom Margin
Return Address	0.5″	NA	0.5"	NA
Mailing Address Number 10 (9″ x 4″)	4.0″	1.0″	(Advance to Line) 2.33″	0.625″
Mailing Address Number 6¾ (6½″ x 3⅝″)	2.5″	1.0″	(Advance to Line) 2.17″	0.625″

To format an envelope with a return address:

1. Open the file 18-0c.wpw, and open the Reveal Codes space, if necessary.
2. Move the insertion point to the [L/R Mar:4″,1″] code before the first mailing address.
3. Key the return address:

   FIVE POINTS REALTY[HRt]
   233 Peachtree Street, NE[HRt]
   Atlanta, GA 30303[HRt]

   It is formatted with default margins.

4. Move the insertion point to the beginning of the return address, and change the Left and Top margins to ½ inch.

5. To position the mailing address vertically, choose Advance from the Layout menu, check To Line, and key **2.33** in the text box. Then click OK.

6. Repeat steps 3, 4, and 5 for the second envelope (or copy the return address and all the margin and advance codes).

7. Look at the envelopes in the Print Preview window. Close the window, and make corrections as needed.

8. When the Print Preview image is acceptable, save the document as *[your three-letter identifier]* 18-0c.wpw.

9. Prepare your printer and print the envelopes.

The WordPerfect Envelope Macro

A macro is a shortcut that performs a series of actions. WordPerfect for Windows 5.2 includes a macro designed to take the address from the letter in the active document window and print it on an envelope automatically.

To use this macro, choose Play from the Macro menu, and then choose envelope.wcm from the Files list in the Play Macro dialog box. The WordPerfect Envelope Macro dialog box appears.

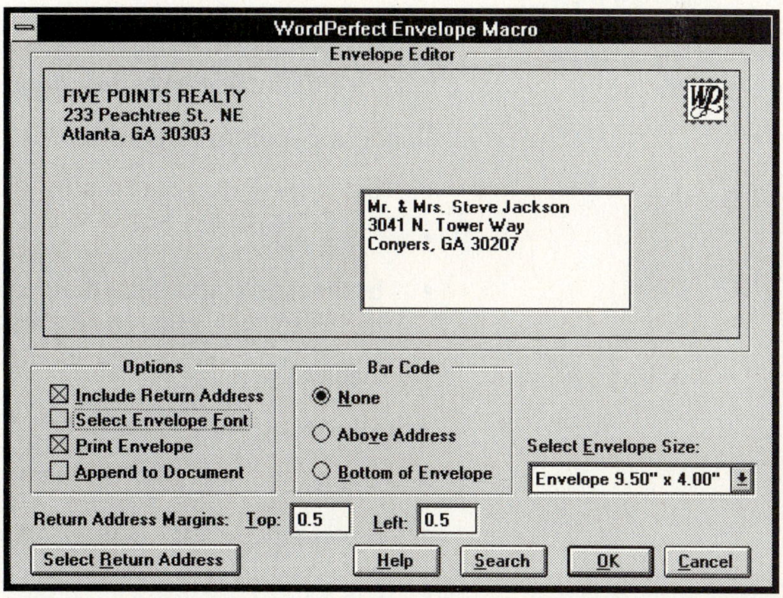

Figure 18-2
The WordPerfect Envelope Macro dialog box

The WordPerfect Envelope Macro (continued)

You can edit both the return address and the mailing address. WordPerfect uses the last return address you specified. To change the return address, just click the return address, or choose Select Return Address. You then can define up to three return addresses to use in the future.

To edit the mailing address, just move the insertion point to that text box. You also can use the search command to find the next block of text that is formatted like an address.

Envelope Macro Options let you print the envelope immediately or append the envelope to the end of the active document.

You even can select another envelope size from available paper-size definitions.

For details about each feature of the Envelope Macro, click the Help button.

For more information on macros, see "Lesson 26: Macros".

Adding or Editing Paper Definitions

Note: For the convenience of others using your computer, at the end of your session, delete any paper definitions that you added. Do not edit any preset paper definitions.

You can add new paper definitions or change existing paper definitions. For instance, your envelopes may not match your printer's preset definition. If you do not expect to use the current envelope definition, you could edit it to suit your envelopes. If, on the other hand, you will print on more than one size of envelope, you could add a definition for each kind. Definitions that you add or edit will appear on the Paper Size list each time you open the dialog box. You may delete unnecessary definitions.

To add a paper-size definition:

- Open the Paper Size dialog box.
- Click Add.
- In the Add Paper Size dialog box, select the necessary elements to customize the default settings.
- Click OK.

To edit a paper-size definition:

- Open the Paper Size dialog box.
- Select a paper-size definition to edit.
- Click Edit.
- In the Edit Paper Size dialog box, change the elements of the existing definition.
- Click OK.

Note: For the following procedure, determine the paper location to use for printing Number 6¾ envelopes on your printer.

For instance, if you printed on Number 6¾ envelopes, you could add a paper definition, or you could edit an existing one.

To add a paper definition:

1. Open the file 18-0d.wpw.
2. Choose Page from the Layout menu, and then choose Paper Size.
3. In the Paper Size dialog box, click Add.

   The Add Paper Size dialog box appears.

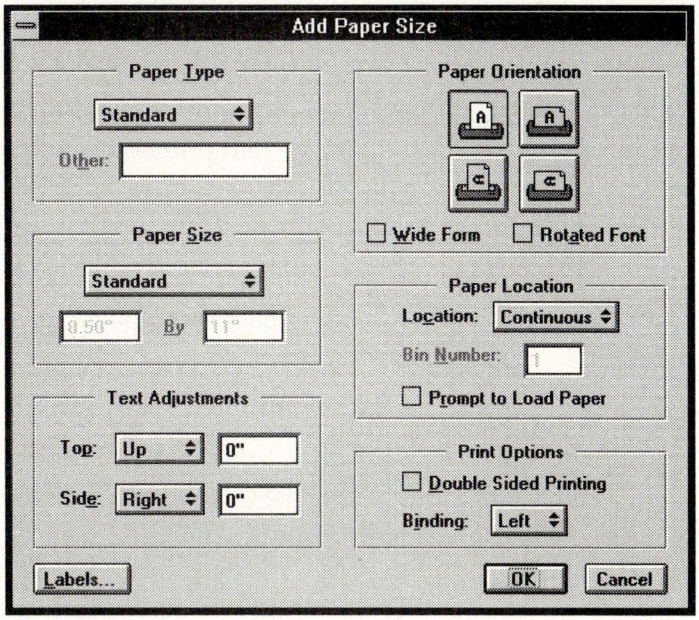

Figure 18-3
The Add Paper Size dialog box

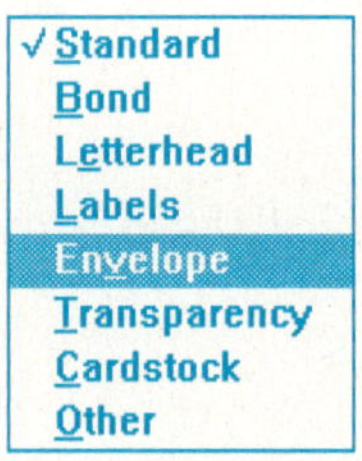

The Paper Type pop-up list

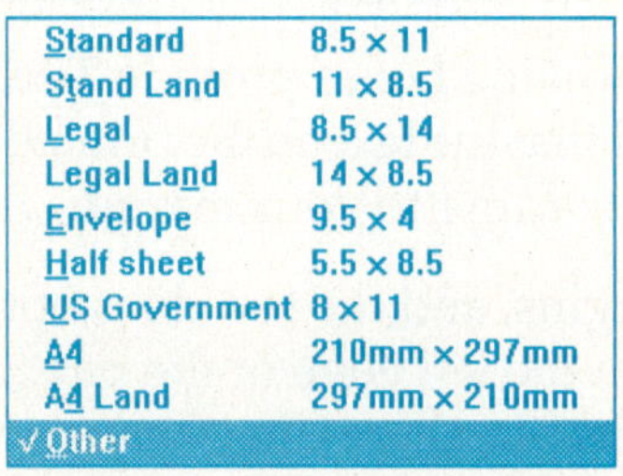

The Paper Size pop-up list

4. From the Paper Type pop-up list, choose Envelope.
5. From the Paper Size pop-up list, choose Other. (Or choose User Defined Size, if you are using a Windows printer.)

   The Paper Size text boxes become active.

6. Tab to the first text box and key **6.5**. Tab to the second text box and key **3.63**.
7. In the Paper Orientation group, choose the icon that best illustrates how you will feed this envelope into your printer and how you want the text to print.

   - If you will feed the short edge of these envelopes, choose the lower left icon.

     Rotated Font will be selected. Text will print sideways on the envelope.

- If you will feed the wide edge of these envelopes, choose the upper right icon.

  Wide Form will be selected.

The Paper Location pop-up list

8. From the Paper Location pop-up list, choose Manual, or choose the paper source that your instructor indicates. If you choose "Bin," you also should key the appropriate number in the Bin Number text box.
9. Check the Prompt to Load Paper box.
10. Click OK.

    You are returned to the Paper Size dialog box, where the new paper definition is highlighted.
11. Click Select to choose this new highlighted definition.

    You are returned to the document window. Notice that a paper-size definition code was inserted at the top of the current page.
12. Press **Alt, F, V** to open the Print Preview window, and choose Full page, if necessary.

    A mailing address appears on an image of a Number 6¾ envelope.
13. Close the Print Preview window.
14. Move the insertion point to the beginning of the document. Then change the margins as follows:

    Left: 2.5 inches
    Right: 1.0 inch
    Top: 2.17 inches
    Bottom: 0.625 inches
15. Proofread and check the format of the envelopes in the Print Preview window.
16. Save the document as *[your-three-letter identifier]*18-0d.wpw.
17. Prepare your printer and print the envelopes.

Text Adjustments

The Add Paper Size and Edit Paper Size dialog boxes provide Text Adjustments options. Use these if you find that the text on the printed page is not located where it should be according to your margins.

For instance, if you are using default margins, and the text does not begin 1 inch from the top and 1 inch from the left edge of the page, you can adjust printing. Printing problems like these can be caused by your printer's feed mechanism.

Specify either Up or Down, and key the distance from the Top adjustment. Then specify Right or Left, and key the distance for the Side adjustment. Always key a positive number for the distance you want the text moved.

Note: Text adjustment will not show up in the Print Preview window.

Deleting Paper Definitions

The Delete command button in the Paper Size dialog box removes a highlighted paper definition from the list box.

Note: If you are sharing equipment with others, please remove any paper definition that you create. Other users will want to create their own.

To delete a paper definition:

1. Press **Alt, L, P, S** to open the Paper Size dialog box.
2. Highlight the envelope definition you just created (6.5″ x 3.63″).
3. Click Delete.

   A confirming dialog asks, "Delete highlighted paper definition?"
4. Click Yes.

   The paper definition is removed permanently from the list box. To use that definition again, you must redefine it using the Add command.

Printing Labels

You can use paper-size definitions to define formats for mailing labels. Labels for laser printers often come on 8½″ x 11″ sheets. You can define the number, size, and position of these labels using the Edit Labels dialog box. You also can define the margins within each label and the starting position of the first label on the sheet.

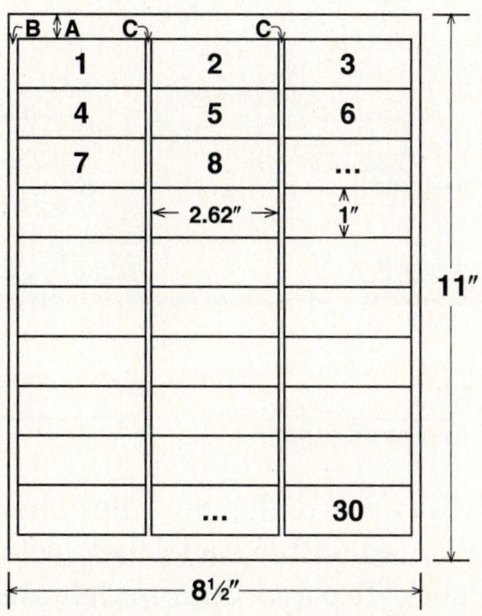

Figure 18-4
A sheet of 30 labels

As seen in Figure 18-4, WordPerfect's default settings describe a standard sheet of 30 labels on an 8½″ x 11″ physical page. Each label (or "logical page") is 2.62″ wide and 1″ high. The position of (1) the Top Left Label is (A) 0.5″ from the Top Edge and (B) 0.187″ from the Left Edge of the physical page.

Logical page
A single label within a paper-size definition.

Default labels are arranged in three columns and ten rows. The default distance between columns is (C) 0.125″. The default distance between rows is 0″.

Logical pages are sequenced left to right, top to bottom. The label in the third row and second column is logical page number 8.

Each label is considered a *logical page,* so a Hard Page Break [HPg] separates labels in a file. This feature also is helpful if you want to print selected labels from a file. You can do so by printing multiple pages and specifying which logical pages to print.

Many logical pages can be put on one *physical page,* the actual sheet that holds the labels. When the printer executes a form feed, the next physical page is moved into position. The physical page in Figure 18-4 contains 30 logical pages.

Physical page
A sheet to be fed into the printer. A physical page may contain one or more labels (logical pages).

The Edit Label dialog box lets you control the specifications for labels on a physical page.

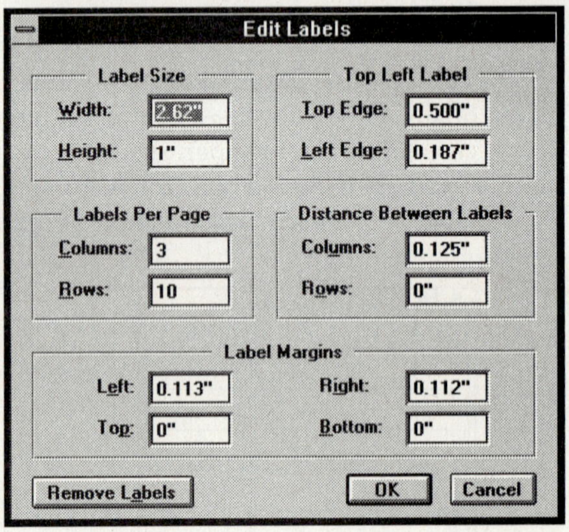

Figure 18-5
The Edit Labels dialog box

In the Edit Labels dialog box, the Label Margins determine where text will be printed within each label. Default Left and Right margins are 0.112 inches. Top and Bottom defaults are 0 inches.

If you want to edit a paper definition so that it no longer includes labels, you can use the Remove Labels command.

To define a sheet of labels:

1. Open the file 18-0e.wpw. Choose Reveal Codes from the View menu, if necessary.
2. Choose Page from the Layout menu, and then choose Paper Size.
3. Click Add.

   The Add Paper Size dialog box appears.
4. In the Paper Type pop-up list, select Labels.

   Our sheet of labels is 8½″ x 11″, so you do not change the paper size. Likewise, do not change the paper orientation, since this sheet of labels is printed in portrait orientation.
5. In the Paper Location pop-up list, select Manual.
6. Select the Prompt to Load check box.

   When you print, WordPerfect will prompt you to load the appropriate paper.
7. Click the Labels button.

   The Edit Labels dialog box appears.
8. Click OK to close the Edit Labels dialog box and accept the default settings.
9. Click OK again to close the Add Paper Size dialog box.
10. Be sure the Labels definition is highlighted in the Paper Size dialog box. Then choose Select.

    You are returned to the document window. In the Reveal Codes space, the page-size code for the label you just defined now begins the address list.

    Each address was on its own page already, separated by [HPg] codes. WordPerfect treats each label as a logical page as it prints. The entire 8½″ x 11″ sheet is considered the physical page for the purpose of form feeding.

    Each address already contained a [Center Pg] code to center it vertically on the label.
11. Choose Print Preview from the File menu. Then choose 100 percent, if necessary.

    Notice that the labels will be printed in sequence from left to right across the rows. For example, the second label in the second row is label number 5.
12. Close the Print Preview window.

13. Save the document as *[your three-letter identifier]*18-0e.wpw.

14. Follow your instructor's directions to print these labels.

15. Delete this label definition.

16. Close the document and exit WordPerfect (unless you will be doing the following exercises immediately).

Key Terms

Landscape orientation	Paper location
Logical page	Physical page
Paper definition	Portrait orientation

Exercises

Exercise 18.1

1. Start WordPerfect, if necessary.

2. Open the file 18-1.wpw.

3. Select Envelope 9½″ x 4″ landscape orientation as the paper size:

   A. Open the Paper Size dialog box.

   B. Select the appropriate Envelope definition.

   C. Click Select.

4. Format the first envelope to print with a return address according to Appendix D:

   A. Set the left and top margins at 0.5 inches and the right margin at 1 inch, if necessary.

   B. Key the following return address above the mailing address:

   FIVE POINTS REALTY
   233 Peachtree St., NE
   Atlanta, GA 30303

   C. Move the insertion point to the beginning of the mailing address, and set the left margin at 4 inches and the bottom margin at 0.625 inches.

   D. Choose Advance from the Layout menu. Then click To Line, key **2.33** in the text box, and click OK.

E. Proofread the first envelope in the Print Preview window, and make any necessary corrections.

5. Repeat steps B, C, and D, or copy the return address and the Margin and Advance To codes, for the second and third envelopes.

6. Proofread the first three envelopes in the Print Preview window.

7. Save the document as *[your three-letter identifier]*18-1.wpw.

8. Prepare your printer, if necessary.

9. Print the first three envelopes only. (Remember, to print the first three pages of a document, check Multiple Pages in the Print dialog box, choose Print, key **1-3** in the Range text box, and choose Print.)

10. Close the document and exit WordPerfect (unless you will be doing the following exercises immediately).

Exercise 18.2

1. Start WordPerfect, if necessary.

2. Open the file 18-2.wpw.

3. Add a paper-size definition to print these addresses on labels as follows:

   A. Choose Page from the Layout menu, and then choose Paper Size.

   B. Click the Add command in the Paper Size dialog box.

   C. Choose Labels from the Paper Type pop-up list.

   D. Choose the Labels command.

   E. Specify the following in the Edit Labels dialog box and click OK:

   Label Size
   Width: 2.62
   Height: 1.5

   Labels Per Page
   Columns: 3
   Rows: 6

   Distance Between Labels
   Column: 0.125
   Row: 0.167

4. Click OK in the Add Paper Size dialog box. Then click Select in the Paper Size dialog box to accept the new paper definition.

5. Insert a center-page code at the beginning of each label:

    A. Search for [HPg] and replace it with [HPg][Center Pg].

    B. Insert the [Center Pg] code for the first label.

6. Save the document as *[your three-letter identifier]*18-2.wpw.

7. On the same physical page, print the first and last label only.

8. Close the document and exit WordPerfect (unless you will be doing the following exercises immediately).

Exercise 18.3

1. Start WordPerfect, if necessary.

2. Open the file 18-3.wpw.

3. At the beginning of the document, insert a cover memo on the subject of "Review of Draft Document" from Bud Porter to Mary Rigdon and John Soloman. Use the current date. Format this memo according to Appendix C. Include an attachment reference. As the body of this memo, key:

    Please review the attached draft, and write your comments in the left margin. Sign and date your review. I'll need your review by Friday.

4. Separate the cover memo from the draft document with a [HPg].

5. Use standard paper size (8½" x 11", portrait) for the memo. Use legal paper size (8½" x 14", portrait) for the draft document. If necessary, add a paper definition that suits your printer.

6. At the top of the draft document, key the following identification line:

    Reviewed by: ________________ Date: _________

7. Change the left margin of the draft document to 2 inches.

8. Spell-check the entire document.

9. Save the document as *[your three-letter identifier]*18-3.wpw.

10. Print two copies of the memo and the draft document.

11. Delete any new paper definition you may have added.

12. Close the document and exit WordPerfect (unless you will be doing the following exercises immediately).

Exercise 18.4

1. Start WordPerfect, if necessary.
2. Open the file 18-4.wpw.
3. Open the Print Preview window to see that the table nearly fills the width of the page.
4. At the beginning of the document, insert a cover memo on the subject of "Review of Sales, Year-to-Date" from Bud Porter to Distribution. Use the current date. Format this memo according to Appendix C. Include an enclosure reference and a distribution list of the agents in the table. As the body of this memo, key:

   Our records show your sales as follows. Please review this material and bring any errors to our attention by next Thursday.

   As you know, sales-incentive awards are based on these figures, so we all want this record to be accurate.

   Thanks for your cooperation.
5. Separate the table from the memo with a [HPg].
6. Use a landscape paper definition (standard 11" x 8½" landscape) for the page with the table.
7. Change the margins so the table is centered horizontally.
8. Insert the necessary space, and key **Quarterly and Year-to-Date Sales Totals** as a title for the table. Center this title above the table.
9. Center the page vertically.
10. Save the document as *[your three-letter identifier]* 18-4.wpw.
11. Print the document.
12. Close the document and exit WordPerfect (unless you will be doing the following exercise immediately).

Exercise 18.5

1. Start WordPerfect, if necessary.
2. Open the file 18-5.wpw.

3. Add and select a paper definition to print the speech on 6″ x 4″ index cards:

Paper Type:	Cardstock
Paper Size:	6″ 4″
Paper Orientation:	landscape, to suit your printer
Paper Location:	to suit your printer

4. Change all four margins to 0.5 inches.
5. Key the following footer with 1-inch left and right margins:

   7/28-- [Center] Atlanta Rotarians [Flsh Right] [Insert Page Number]

6. Double-space the document.
7. Force page breaks after each paragraph. Delete extra [HRt] codes.
8. Spell-check the document.
9. Print the document on 6″ x 4″ cardstock or paper.
10. Save the document as *[your three-letter identifier]*18-5.wpw.
11. Delete the paper definition that you just added.
12. Close the document and exit WordPerfect.

Module 6

Advanced Character Formatting

Lessons

Lesson 19

Fonts and Type Sizes

The appearance of characters on the printed page can affect the legibility of a document, as well as its length and its overall look. In this lesson, you will format text by changing the size and appearance of characters. You also will adjust the spacing between words, letters, and lines to better control the appearance of text.

Objectives

- Change initial fonts.
- Change fonts in a document.
- Change type size.
- Adjust word spacing.
- Adjust letter spacing.
- Adjust kerning.
- Adjust leading.

What Are Fonts and Type Sizes?

A *font* is a type design applied to an entire set of characters, including all the letters of the alphabet, numerals, punctuation marks, and other symbols, such as # and @. Three common typefaces are Courier, CG Times, and Univers.

Font
A set of letters, numbers, and special characters with a consistent design.

ABCDEFGHIJKLMNOPQRSTUVWXYZ
abcdefghijklmnopqrstuvwxyz — Courier
1234567890!@#$%^&*()

ABCDEFGHIJKLMNOPQRSTUVWXYZ
abcdefghijklmnopqrstuvwxyz — Times
1234567890!@#$%^&*()

ABCDEFGHIJKLMNOPQRSTUVWXYZ
abcdefghijklmnopqrstuvwxyz — Univers
1234567890!@#$%^&*()

ABCDEFGHIJKLMNOPQRSTUVWXYZ
abcdefghijklmnopqrstuvwxyz — Nuptial Script
1234567890!@#$%^&()*

Figure 19-1
Examples of fonts

Differences in Fonts

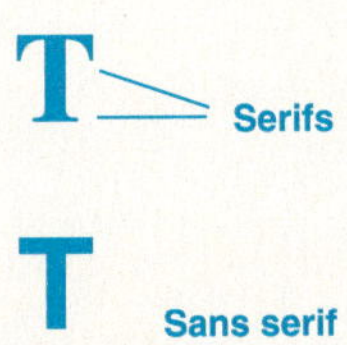

Serif vs. sans serif

As Figure 19-1 shows, the appearance of characters can change dramatically from font to font. Letter spacing is not the same in all fonts. For example, Courier resembles traditional typewriter type, and each character has the same width. A Courier uppercase M occupies the same horizontal space as its lowercase i. In contrast, CG Times and Univers are proportional fonts. Each character has its own width.

Serifs
Small projections at the top and bottom of a letter.

Serif fonts
Fonts with serifs.

Sans serif fonts
Fonts without serifs.

Fonts like Courier and CG Times have small projections, called *serifs*, on the ends of many their characters. *Serif fonts* are used commonly in books and newspapers for the body of text. In contrast, Univers is a *sans serif font* (sans means "without"). Sans serif fonts often are used for headlines, and many people prefer their simpler look for the body of a document.

Script fonts are designed to look like handwriting, with lowercase characters appearing linked. They are used in special documents, such as formal invitations. Script, especially all-uppercase script, is harder to read than other fonts, however.

Note: The fonts and type sizes you can use with WordPerfect depend on the printer, its font cartridges, and the software installed with the computer system. Each printer definition includes a set of fonts.

Table 19-1: Common Serif and Sans Serif Fonts

Serif	Sans Serif
Bookman	Arial
CG Times	Avant Garde
Palatino	Helvetica
Times New Roman	Univers
Times Roman	

Type Size

Scalable font
A font that is defined mathematically, so its size can be changed.

Point (pt)
A measure of type height equal to 1/72 of an inch.

Many fonts are *scalable*, which means that they are defined mathematically, so their size can vary. For these fonts, type size is measured in vertical points. A *point* (abbreviated *pt*) is a very small unit of measurement—1/72 of an inch. Put another way, there are 72 points in 1 inch. Type size is measured from the top of the highest letter to the bottom of the lowest. So, in the word "Jump", the type size of the font is measured from the top of the capital J to the bottom of the lowercase p. The text of most newspapers is set in 9-point or 10-point type.

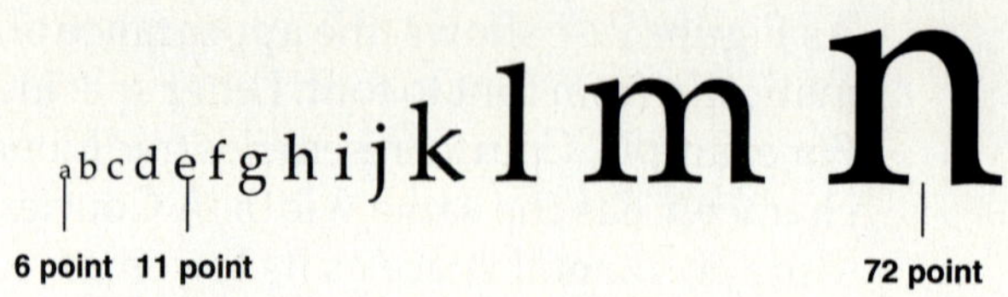

Figure 19-2
Type sizes normally used in publications

cpi
Abbreviation for characters per inch.

Pitch
The horizontal measurement of a font in characters per inch.

For nonscalable fonts, type size is measured horizontally in characters per inch (*cpi*). For instance, in the Courier 10cpi font, 10 characters can be keyed per horizontal inch. This also is known as 10 *pitch*. Courier 12cpi is a narrower font, in which 12 characters can be keyed per inch (12 pitch). Courier 17cpi is a compressed font.

Note: Too many different fonts and type sizes can make a document hard to read. In this lesson, unless otherwise directed, use only one serif font (CG Times, if it is available from your printer), and one sans serif font (Univers, if it is available from your printer).

Setting an Initial Font

Initial font
A font that is set as the default for a printer or document.

An *initial font* is a font that is set as the default for the text of a document, including features such as headers, equations, and footnotes. There are two types of initial fonts: printer initial fonts and document initial fonts.

Note: The codes for initial fonts do not appear in the Reveal Codes space.

Printer Initial Font

Printer initial font
The default font for a particular printer.

A *printer initial font* is a default font set for a particular printer. When you select a font in the Printer Initial Font dialog box, all new documents printed from that printer will default to the specified font.

You can set a printer initial font either while working within an existing document or with all documents closed. The setting will apply automatically to each new document. You can override this default, however, with a document initial font or with fonts selected with the Font dialog box.

To view the printer initial font options:

1. Start WordPerfect.
2. Choose Ruler and Reveal Codes from the View menu, if necessary.
3. Choose Select Printer from the File menu and then choose Setup.
4. Choose Initial Font in the Printer Setup dialog box.

The Printer Initial Font dialog box appears. The Fonts list shows available fonts. The Point Size list is active only for scalable fonts. The sample box shows how text will be formatted.

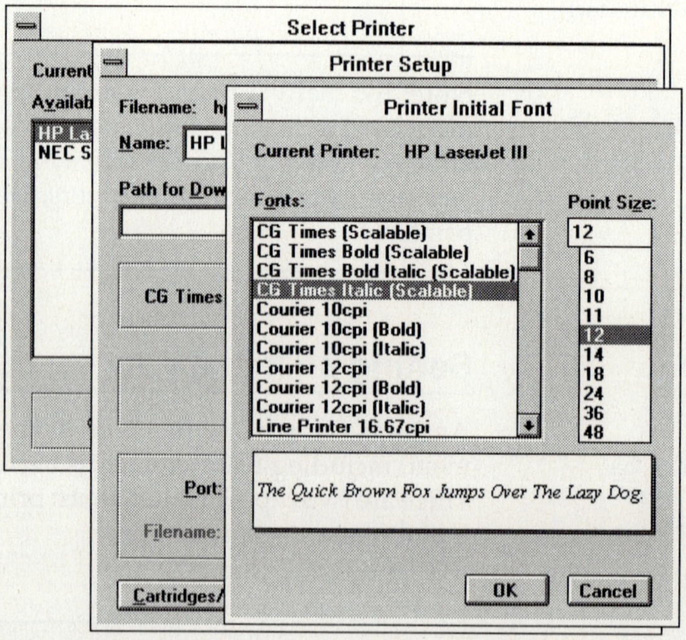

Figure 19-3
The Printer Initial Font dialog box

5. Use the up scroll arrow or down scroll arrow to highlight different fonts. Stop at a scalable font. (The Point Size list will become active.)

6. Choose a new point size from the list.

   The point size you choose also appears in the text box above the list. A sample of the font at the selected size appears in the sample box.

7. Key **20** in the Point Size text box.

   A sample of the font appears. You may specify a size that does not appear in the Point Size list box.

8. Click Cancel to close the Printer Initial Font dialog box without changing fonts.

   If you had clicked OK, the initial font would have changed for the selected printer.

9. Click Cancel to close the Printer Setup dialog box.

10. Choose Close to exit the Select Printer dialog box.

Document Initial Font

Document initial font
A default font for a specific document.

You can set a *document initial font* to serve as the default font for the current document. When you set a document initial font, the document initial font setting overrides the printer initial font setting. The initial font associated with your document, unlike the printer initial font, affects only the current document.

To practice changing the document initial font, you will use a document containing text for a newspaper ad:

1. Open the file 19-0.wpw.
2. Choose Document from the Layout menu, and then choose Initial Font.

   The Document Initial Font dialog box appears. It looks the same as the Printer Initial Font dialog box.
3. Make a note of the current initial font, which is highlighted in the list box. Also note its size.

   For the HP LaserJet III, the default font is Courier 10cpi.
4. Choose CG Times (or another scalable font) from the list box.

   The Point Size box will be active.
5. Choose 18 from the Point Size list.
6. Click OK to accept your change and return to the document window.

   The text is displayed in a much larger size.
7. Choose Print Preview from the File menu.

   The larger size of the typeface is displayed here, as well.
8. Close the Print Preview window.
9. Choose Document from the Layout menu again and choose Initial Font.
10. Choose the original initial font at its original size and click OK.

Changing Fonts Within a Document

When you choose a font within a document, WordPerfect inserts a font code in the text. This code affects all the text following the insertion point to the end of the document or to the next font code. The font code overrides both the printer initial font and the document initial font settings.

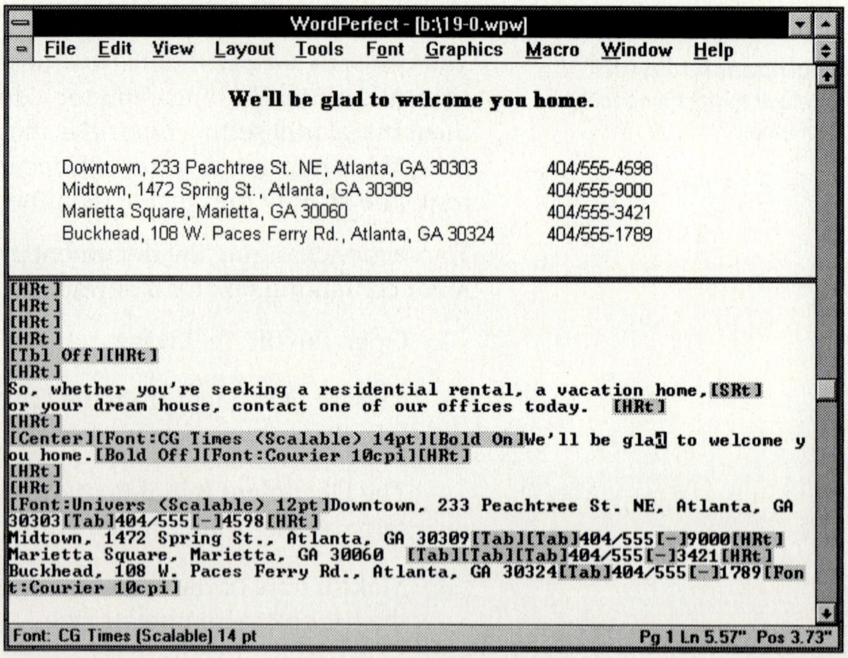

Figure 19-4
The status bar shows the font active at the insertion point.

Note: Changes made to the font, size, or attributes of text can affect the space it occupies. In some cases, tab alignment, document length, or other document formatting may be altered.

You also can choose a font for a block of selected text. WordPerfect inserts a new font code before the block and restores the old font code after the block.

Choosing Fonts Using the Font Dialog Box

The Font dialog box is available from the Font menu. You also can double-click the Font or Size buttons on the Ruler or press **F9**. The Font dialog box lists available fonts, sizes, and other character attributes.

To choose a font in a new file:

1. Open a new file.
2. Choose Font from the Font menu.

   The Font dialog box appears. In this dialog box, you can choose fonts, type sizes, and attributes. The font currently chosen is the printer initial font. See Figure 19-5 on page 19-7.

3. Choose CG Times from the Font list and 14 from the Point Size list to highlight them. Then click OK.
4. Key your name and press **Enter**.

   Notice that your name appears in the font and size you have chosen.

5. Double-click the Font button on the Ruler.

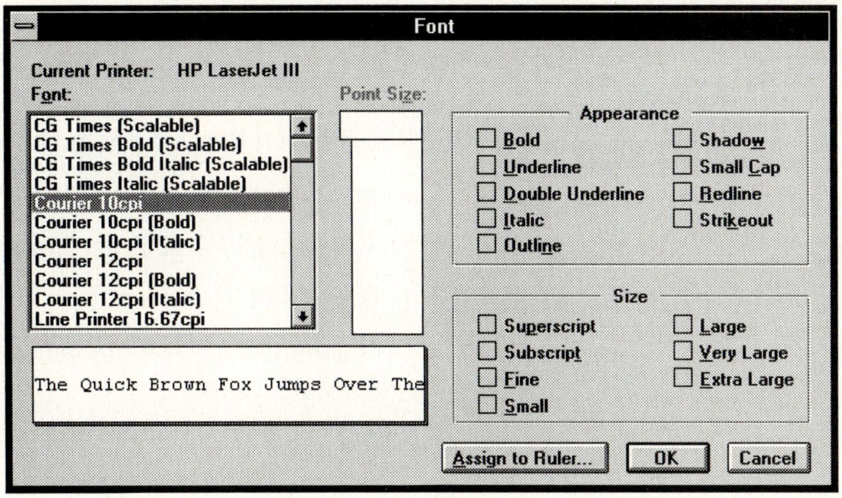

Figure 19-5
The Font dialog box (as in step 2 on page 19-6)

6. In the Font dialog box, choose 12 from the Point Size list and click OK.

7. Key an address.

   The text appears in the same font, but in a smaller size.

8. Close the document without saving it.

To practice choosing a font in an existing document:

1. Select the headline at the top of document 19-0.wpw.

2 Press **F9.**

   The Font dialog box appears.

3. Choose Univers from the Font list box. (If this font is not available, choose another sans serif font, such as Helvetica or Arial.)

   Univers is a scalable font, so the Point Size list box becomes active.

4. Choose 18.

5. Choose Bold and Italic in the Appearance group.

6. Click OK to confirm your selection and return to your document.

7. Deselect the text, and delete the period at the end of the headline.

   The text you selected becomes an attractive headline.

Assigning Fonts to the Ruler Button Bar

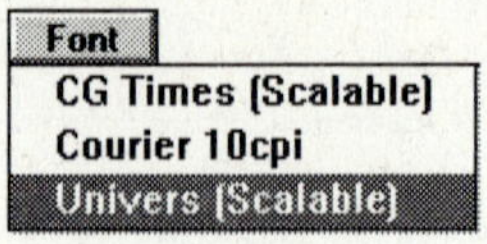

The Font pop-up list

You can choose fonts from the Ruler Button Bar, once they have been assigned there. To keep the font list brief, you can delete fonts from the Ruler Button Bar that you no longer need.

To assign a font to the Ruler Button Bar:

1. If necessary, choose Ruler from the View menu.
2. Click and hold the Font button.

   The Font pop-up box appears. The fonts in this box were assigned previously.
3. Release the Font button, and then double-click it.

   The Font dialog box appears.
4. Choose Assign to Ruler.

   The Ruler Fonts Menu dialog box appears.

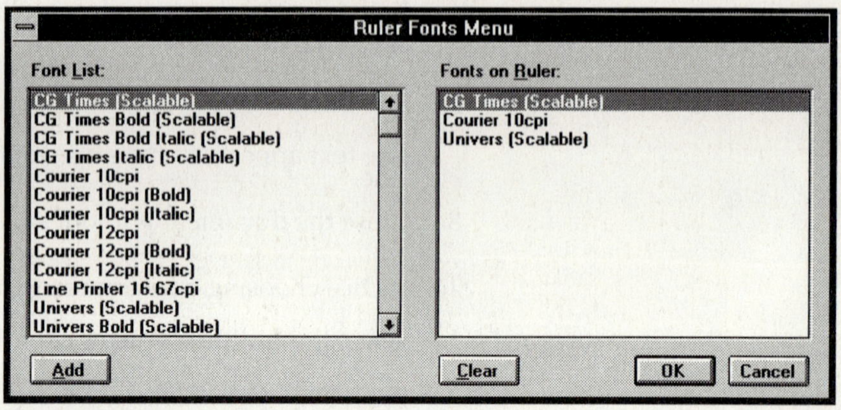

Figure 19-6
The Ruler Fonts Menu dialog box

5. In the Font list box, choose Univers Bold. Then choose Add.

   The font is added to the Fonts on Ruler list.
6. Repeat step 5 for Univers Bold Italic and Univers Italic.
7. Click OK to return to the Font dialog box.
8. Click OK again to return to the document.
9. Click and hold the Font button on the Ruler.

   The added fonts appear on the Font pop-up list.
10. Double-click the Font button. Then choose Assign to Ruler from the Font dialog box.
11. Highlight the last item in the Fonts on Ruler list box. Then choose Clear.

Adjusting Spacing with Typesetting Options

WordPerfect has several typesetting options that adjust the amount of space between words, letters, and lines of text.

Word Spacing

Words that are too close together or too far apart can be difficult to read. For scalable fonts, you can choose either WordPerfect's optimal word-spacing option (WordPerfect Optimal) or the font maker's font-spacing option (Normal). Your decision depends on how you prefer the text to look when it is printed. (A nonscalable font uses its maker's word spacing.)

In addition, you can customize the space between words from 50 percent to 250 percent of the WordPerfect optimal spacing. Values greater than 100% increase spacing; lower values decrease spacing.

To adjust word spacing:

1. Copy the headline at the top of the document, including its font code.
2. Insert a [HRt], and then paste the headline below the original. Repeat this step until you have six copies of the headline.
3. Select the first copy you pasted.
4. Choose Typesetting from the Layout menu.

   The Typesetting dialog box appears.

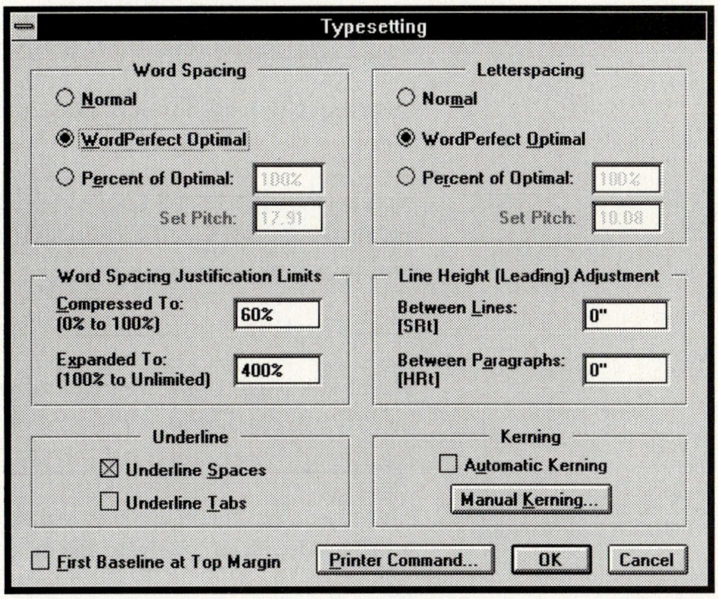

Figure 19-8
The Typesetting dialog box

5. Choose Percent of Optimal in the Word Spacing group.

   The percent text box becomes active.

6. Press the **Tab** key and key **150%**. Then click OK.

   WordPerfect inserts codes before and after the selected text. However, the word spacing is not visible in the document window.

7. Deselect the text. Then choose Print Preview from the File menu.

   The spacing between words is increased by half to 150% of the optimal spacing WordPerfect had provided. The headline now stretches beyond the others.

8. Close the Print Preview menu.

Letter Spacing

You can adjust the space between letters in much the same way you adjusted word spacing. Again, WordPerfect provides optimal spacing.

To adjust letter spacing:

1. Select the third copy of the headline.

2. Choose Typesetting from the Layout menu.

3. Choose Percent of Optimal in the Letter Spacing group.

4. Key **150%** in the percent text box and click OK.

5. Deselect the text. Then choose Print Preview from the File menu.

   Notice that the word spacing and letter spacing now appear about equal. Without capital letters, you would have trouble seeing where words end.

6. Close the Print Preview window.

7. Select the third copy again, and choose Typesetting from the Layout menu. Choose Percent of Optimal in the Letter Spacing group. Then key **110%** in the percent text box.

8. Click OK. Then deselect the text, and open the Print Preview window to view the new letter spacing in the third headline.

9. Close the Print Preview window.

Kerning

Kerning
An adjustment that reduces the spacing between certain letter pairs.

Kerning reduces the spacing between certain letter pairs to make them appear visually even. Because of their shapes, these letters appear too far apart when they are spaced normally.

To see the effect of kerning clearly:

1. Press **Ctrl+End** to move to the bottom of the document.
2. Insert a [HRt] code. Then key the following letter combinations, including the commas:

   Ta, Te, To, Tr, We, Wo, WA

3. Copy the line, and paste it below the original, so you can compare these combinations, kerned and unkerned.
4. Select the two lines, and choose 18-point CG Times.
5. Deselect the text, and then select the second line only.
6. Choose Typesetting from the Layout menu.
7. Choose Automatic Kerning in the Kerning group.
8. Click OK. Then deselect the text, and open the Print Preview window.
9. Choose 200%, and use the scroll bars to view the two lines.

   Notice that the kerned lower line is shorter. The spaces between most letters (and between letters and commas) are smaller. Furthermore, these spaces differ for the individual pairs of characters, but actually make the characters seem more evenly spaced.

10. Close the Print Preview window. Then select the fifth copy of the headline you pasted earlier.
11. Choose Typesetting from the Layout menu. Then choose Automatic Kerning in the Kerning group and click OK.
12. Deselect the text, open the Print Preview window, and choose 100%.

    The kerned line is slightly shorter than the normal lines above and below it.

13. Choose 200%. Then choose Zoom In several times until Print Preview magnification reaches its maximum (400%).
14. Click in the Preview Screen Area. When the mini-page appears, move the red location box to the last three headlines.

    A section of the last three headlines is displayed.

15. Use the horizontal scroll bar to compare the spacing of the kerned line with the normal lines above and below it.

16. Close the Print Preview window.

17. Select the fourth headline.

18. Choose Typesetting from the Layout menu.

19. Choose Percent of Optimal in the Letter Spacing group. Then key **110%** in the text box.

20. Choose Automatic Kerning and click OK.

21. Deselect the text.

22. Open the Print Preview window and choose 100%.

    The letters in the third and fourth lines are spaced at 110% of normal. The fourth and fifth lines are kerned.

23. Close Print Preview. Delete all the headlines except the fourth headline.

    The kerned line with 110% letter spacing looks best with the ad.

24. Delete the two lines of sample letter combinations at the end of the document.

Kerning makes letters appear evenly spaced, giving text a more professional, typeset look. Depending on the length of your text and the speed of your computer, however, kerning may take time. Note, also, that the ability to print customized spacing may be limited on some printers.

Leading

Baseline
The invisible line on which capital letters appear to sit.

In WordPerfect, the line height is the height of a font plus any white space included with that font. It is measured from baseline to baseline in a single-spaced document. A *baseline* is the invisible line on which the capital letters appear to sit. Parts of some lowercase letters, such as p, g, y, and q, extend below the baseline. Therefore, all fonts are designed with enough leading to keep "descenders" from looking cramped.

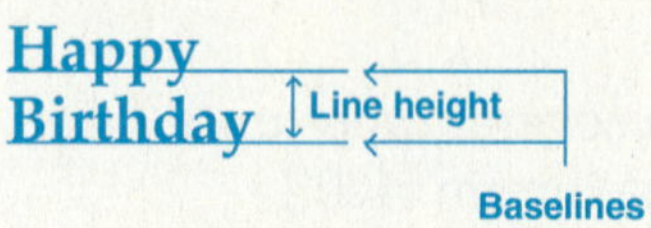

Line height

The white space between lines sometimes is called *leading* (its pronunciation rhymes with heading). This term comes to us from old printing technology that formed lines of type in lead, a soft metal. To add space between lines, a craftsman inserted thin lead strips between lines of type.

Leading
The white space between lines.

WordPerfect's Line Height Adjustment option allows you to change the amount of vertical space assigned to soft returns within a paragraph and hard returns between paragraphs. This vertical space is in addition to the white space built in to the font itself.

To make line-height adjustments:

1. Select all four cells of the table.

2. Choose Typesetting from the Layout menu.

3. Key **0.05** in the Between Lines text box.

4. Key **0.2** in the Between Paragraphs text box.

5. Click OK to return to the document window. Then deselect the text.

   WordPerfect inserted codes before and after the selected text. Within the table, the space between lines was increased by 0.05″ and by 0.2″ between paragraphs.

   These line-height adjustments altered the shape of the table, however.

6. Insert and delete [HRt] codes to make all four table cells approximately square.

7. Format the text in the lower left cell flush right.

8. Save the document as *[your three-letter identifier]*19-0.wpw.

9. Exit WordPerfect (unless you will be doing the following exercises immediately).

Fonts and Headers and Footers

WordPerfect applies the initial font to the text of headers and footers. However, a font within a document affects all text following a font code, until it reaches the next font code or the end of the document. If you place a font code before a header or footer code, the font code will affect the header or footer. However, you can place a font code within a header or footer that will affect only the text within that header or footer.

Table 19-2: Keyboard Shortcuts for Fonts

Keyboard Shortcut	Action
F9	Font dialog box
Ctrl+S	Font Size cascading menu

Key Terms

Baseline	Pitch
cpi	Point (pt)
Document initial font	Printer initial font
Font	Sans serif fonts
Initial font	Scalable font
Kerning	Serif fonts
Leading	Serifs

Exercises

Exercise 19.1

1. Start WordPerfect, if necessary.
2. Open the file 19-1.wpw.
3. Format the document initial font to 12-point CG Times (or another serif font):
   A. Choose Document from the Layout menu.
   B. Choose Initial Font.
   C. Choose CG Times from the Font list and 12 from the Point Size list. Then click OK.
4. Assign the Univers Italic font (or another sans serif italic font) to the Ruler Font button:
   A. Press **F9** to open the Font dialog box.
   B. Choose Assign to Ruler.
   C. Choose Univers Italic from the Font List.
   D. Choose Add.
   E. Click OK to accept your choices and close the Ruler Fonts Menu dialog box.
   F. Choose Cancel to close the Font dialog box.
5. Format the first three lines below the photo box in 18-point Univers:
   A. Select the text.
   B. Choose Univers from the Ruler Font pop-up list.
   C. Choose 18 from the Ruler Size pop-up list.
6. Format the next paragraph in 14-point Univers.

7. Format the next four lines (the list of amenities) in 14-point CG Times.

8. Format the last paragraph in 16-point Univers Italic.

9. Format the leading words in the list of amenities in bold:

   A. Select "Four Bedrooms:".

   B. Press **F9**.

   C. Choose Bold from the Appearance group.

   D. Click OK.

   E. Repeat steps B, C, and D for "Garden Conservatory", "Indoor Swimming Pool", and "Various outbuildings,".

10. Save the document as *[your three-letter identifier]*19-1.wpw.

11. Print the document.

12. Close the document and exit WordPerfect (unless you will be doing the following exercises immediately).

Exercise 19.2

1. Start WordPerfect, if necessary.

2. Open the file 19-2.wpw.

3. For the three lines below the photo box, adjust the letter spacing to 110% of normal and the word spacing to 150% of normal:

   A. Select the text below the photos box, which begins "2377 Brookhaven".

   B. Choose Typesetting from the Layout menu.

   C. Choose Percent of Optimal for Word Spacing. Then press the **Tab** key until the insertion point is in the text box and key **150**.

   D. Choose Percent of Optimal for Letter Spacing. Then press the **Tab** key until the insertion point is in the text box and key **110**.

   E. Click OK.

4. Increase the leading between the paragraphs in the list of amenities by 0.15":

   A. Select the text from "Four Bedrooms" to "studio space".

   B. Choose Typesetting from the Layout menu.

   C. Double-click in the Between Paragraphs text box, key **0.15**, and click OK.

5. Format the entire document with automatic kerning:
   A. Position the insertion point at the beginning of the document.
   B. Choose Typesetting from the Layout menu.
   C. Choose Automatic Kerning.
   D. Click OK.
6. Save the document as *[your three-letter identifier]*19-2.wpw.
7. Print the document.
8. Close the document and exit WordPerfect (unless you will be doing the following exercises immediately).

Exercise 19.3

1. Start WordPerfect, if necessary.
2. Open the file 19-3.wpw.
3. Edit this document as shown in Figure 19-9, which appears at the end of this exercise.
4. Define the paper size for the document as 4″ x 6″ cardstock.
5. Format narrow margins, so the announcement fits on one page.
6. Center-justify the document.
7. Format the text in 12-point CG Times.
8. Add white space between the listed tenants by adding 0.05 inches of leading between paragraphs.
9. Format the tenant list in 12-point Univers.
10. Format the quotation in italics.
11. Add 0.05 inches of white space after the line that begins "Alex Griffith".
12. Position the insertion point at the end of the quotation, press **Enter** twice, choose 10-point Univers, and key the following (the last line should be italicized):

    The exclusive lease agent for this property is [ENTER]
    Five Points Realty. For other availabilities [ENTER]
    call Bud Porter at (404) 555-4598.

13. Center the document vertically on the page.

14. Spell-check the document.
15. Save the document as *[your three-letter identifier]*19-3.wpw.
16. Print the document.
17. If you added the paper-size definition, delete it now.
18. Close the document and exit WordPerfect (unless you will be doing the following exercises immediately).

Figure 19-9

```
The owners of Ramsey Court, 45 Peachtree Street, proudly announce the
lease renewals of these four prestigious tenants Satellite Graphics, inc.
Biotechtronics, Millington, Trumble and Allard and M&A Worldwide
Consulting. These leases secure Ramsey Courts' 100% occupancy status
through 1995.

Alex Griffith, president of Satellite Graphics, Inc., said, "Ramsey Court
is the perfect location for my company. By leasing space here I'm close to
both CNN and Coca Cola, my two largest clients."
```

Exercise 19.4

1. Start WordPerfect, if necessary.
2. Open a new file, and define the paper size as 5.5″ x 8″ cardstock.
3. Set the top and bottom margins at 0.3 inches, and center-justify the document.
4. Key Document 19-4, which appears at the end of this exercise. Include the line breaks [HRt] and page breaks [HPg] shown. Format the text as described below.
5. Format the page-1 headline starting on the line at 6.8 inches in 16-point Univers Bold Italics.
6. Format the page-2 body of the invitation starting on the line at 4.5 inches in 12-point CG Times.
7. Format the RSVP line in 10-point CG Times Italics.
8. Spell-check and proofread the document.

9. Save the document as *[your three-letter identifier]*19-4.wpw.
10. Print page 1 on 5.5″ x 8″ cardstock. Then print page 2 on the opposite side, so the headline will become the bottom of the cover, and the body of the invitation will fall on the bottom of the inside page.
11. If you added the paper-size definition, delete it now.
12. Close the document and exit WordPerfect (unless you will be doing the following exercise immediately).

Document 19-4

Page one headline:

There Are Lots of Surprises in Store for You [HRt] at [HRt] The Great Southeastern Mall. [HPg]

Page two invitation:

You are cordially invited to a Gala Dinner [HRt] to celebrate the completion of [HRt] The Great Southeastern Mall at Marietta Square, [HRt] Thursday, October 15, 199- at 7:30 p.m. [HRt] [HRt]

Your host for the evening will be Bud Porter, [HRt] community developer [HRt] and president of Five Points Realty. [HRt] [HRt]

RSVP Mary Rigdon at (404) 555-3421 by October 5, 199-.

Exercise 19.5

1. Start WordPerfect, if necessary.
2. Open a new file, and define the paper size as 6″ x 4″ cardstock.
3. Set the side margins at 0.5 inches and the top and bottom margins at 0.3 inches. Full-justify the document.
4. Key Document 19-5, which appears at the end of this exercise, and format the text as described below.
5. Format the headline in 16-point Univers Italics. Make the word "Congratulations!" bold.

6. To fit it on one line, format both word spacing and letter spacing as 95 percent of optimal for the headline.
7. Center the first paragraph, which begins "You've won", and format it in 14-point CG Times.
8. Format the next paragraph in 13-point CG Times. Make "Gainesborough Pines" and "there's no lovelier vacation spot in Georgia." italic.
9. Format the line height for the first two paragraphs as follows:

   Between Lines: 0.05 inches

   Between Paragraphs: 0.1 inches
10. Format the last paragraph in 12-point Univers Italics.
11. Format the document with automatic kerning.
12. Turn hyphenation on, and set both hyphenation zones at 0 percent. Accept suggested hyphenation.
13. Spell-check and proofread the document.
14. Save the document as *[your three-letter identifier]*19-5.wpw.
15. Print the document on 6″ x 4″ cardstock.
16. If you added the paper-size definition, delete it now.
17. Close the document and exit WordPerfect.

Document 19-5

CONGRATULATIONS! Mr. and Mrs. Elliot Jackson.

You've won a free weekend at Gainesborough Pines!

Gainesborough Pines is one of the most popular vacation communities in the Atlanta area. We'd like you to spend the weekend with us and see for yourself, there's no lovelier vacation spot in Georgia.

To claim your prize, call Mary Rigdon at Five Points Realty's Marietta Square office at (404) 555-3421.

Special Characters and Attributes

Objectives

- Set special font attributes and sizes.
- Set text to different colors.
- Use WordPerfect characters.

WordPerfect characters
Characters supplied with WordPerfect that do not appear on a standard keyboard.

In WordPerfect, special font attributes, type sizes, and colors are available to meet specific character-formatting needs. In addition, WordPerfect supplies special-purpose characters, called *WordPerfect characters*, that are not available on standard keyboards. This lesson describes the use of special attributes, colors, and WordPerfect characters to enhance the appearance of documents.

Note: Color, special attributes, and special type sizes can be set within WordPerfect; however, they will not appear on the screen unless your monitor is capable of displaying them, and they will not print unless your printer is capable of printing them.

Special Attributes and Sizes

The Font dialog box contains many options for altering the appearance and size of text. Some of the commonly used options have been described in earlier lessons; however, additional options are available for use in a variety of special circumstances. These options can be used individually or combined to create different text effects.

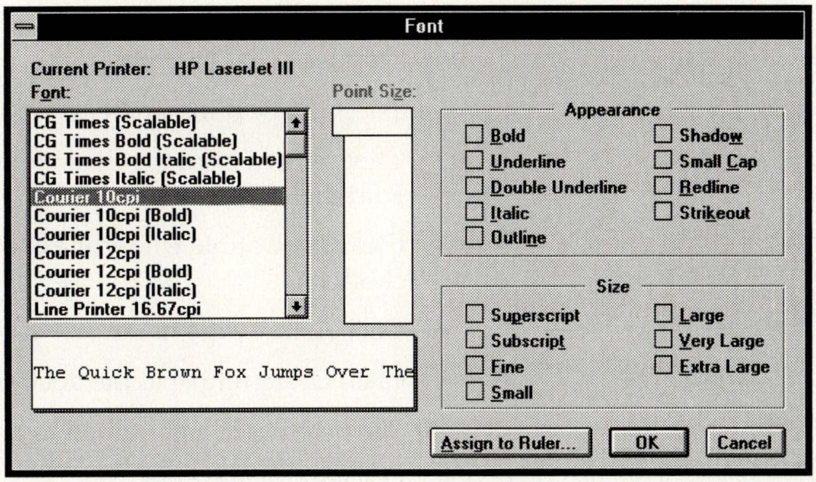

Figure 20-1
The Font dialog box

The Double Underline Option

The Double Underline option places two lines underneath each keyed or selected character. When surrounded by normal text, characters with the double-underline attribute are emphasized. Double underlining is used rarely with text keyed in all-capital letters.

To apply the double-underline attribute to existing text:

1. Start WordPerfect, and open the file 20-0.wpw.
2. Choose Ruler and Reveal Codes from the View menu, if necessary.
3. Select the heading "FOR IMMEDIATE RELEASE" at the top of the document.
4. Choose Font from the Font menu (or double-click the Ruler Font button) to open the Font dialog box.
5. Click Double Underline in the Appearance group. Then click OK to return to the document window.
6. Click once to deselect the text.

   A double underline appears beneath the heading.

The Outline Option

An outlined letter

The Outline option in the Font dialog box causes text to appear as if the characters had been drawn with two lines, one inside the other. Text that has the outline attribute appears highlighted in green (when selected) or purple (when not selected) to indicate the outline attribute. That is because the attribute does not appear on the screen. The text will print as outline characters on printers capable of printing these characters. You can use Print Preview to view outlined characters, but only in large type sizes.

To remove the double-underline attribute from and apply the outline attribute to the heading:

1. Select the heading at the top of the document again.
2. Choose Font from the Font menu (or press **F9**) to open the Font dialog box.
3. Clear the Double Underline check box. Then click the Outline check box.
4. Click Extra Large in the Size group.
5. Click OK to return to the document window.

   The heading is highlighted in green, and the text is enlarged.
6. Deselect the heading.

   The heading is highlighted in purple.

7. Open the Print Preview window and select 200%.

   The heading appears in outlined characters.

8. Close the Print Preview window.
9. Select the heading again, and choose Font from the Font menu.
10. Clear the Extra Large and Outline check boxes and click OK.

A shadow letter

The Shadow Option

The Shadow option in the Font dialog box makes a character appear to have a shadow behind it. Shadow text sometimes is used in advertisements and flyers to present text in a light-hearted manner. When used in a large block of text, shadow text can be difficult to read.

The Shadow option is available from the Font dialog box. It is applied in the same way as the Double Underline option.

Small cap
A capital letter that is shorter than the full-size capital letters in the same type size.

Normal
ALL CAPS
SMALL CAPS

The Small Cap Option

A small cap is a capital letter that is shorter than the full-size capital letters in the same type size. Small caps are used to take the place of lowercase letters to create a special look for text. They sometimes appear in formal invitations and on business cards.

In WordPerfect, Small Cap is an option in the Font dialog box. It is applied in the same way as the Double-Underline option.

Redlining
The process of marking new text to distinguish it from original text in a document.

Redline and Strikeout Options

The Redline and Strikeout options are available in the Font menu and in the Font dialog box. *Redlining* is the process of marking new text to distinguish it from the original text. Suggested revisions sometimes are keyed in redlined text before the text is altered.

On color monitors, this text appears red. On monochrome monitors, redlined text may appear the same as normal text or may appear gray.

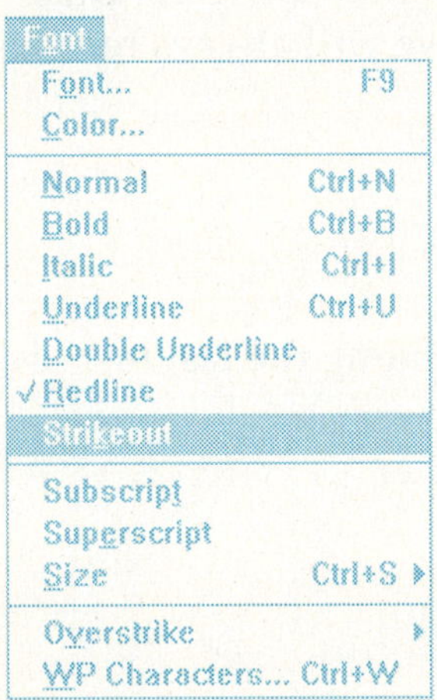

The Font menu

The print appearance of redline text can be changed in the Document Redline dialog box. You can choose from three options: Printer Dependent, Mark Left Margin, and Mark Alternating Margins. The Printer Dependent setting is the default and bases the redlined output on the capabilities of the printer. The Mark Left Margin and Mark Alternating Margins settings show redlined text with a vertical bar in the margins. The Document Redline dialog box is accessed by choosing Document from the Layout menu and choosing Redline Method from the Document cascading menu.

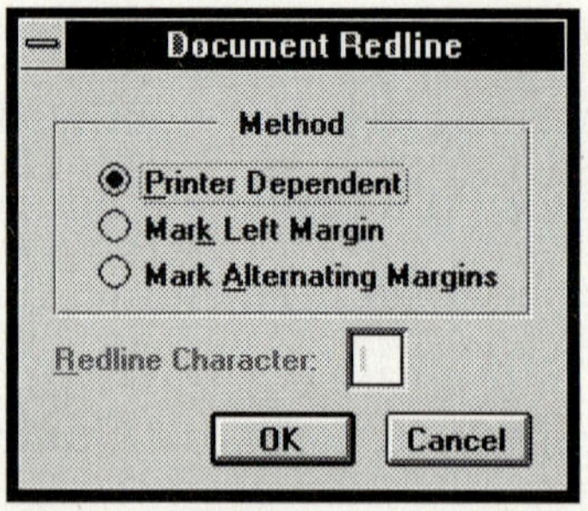

Figure 20-2
The Document Redline dialog box

Strikeout marks
Horizontal lines running through the middle of characters to mark text that is to be deleted.

Strikeout marks are horizontal lines running through the middle of characters. They generally are used to indicate text that is to be deleted from a document. The purpose of strikeout marks is to allow a person reading the document to see planned deletions

new home, the G&H Building at the corner of Techwood and Luckie Streets. Actron has just signed a five-year contract ~~with Five Points Realty~~ for the lease of this property through Five Points Realty.

Figure 20-3
Redline and strikeout options can show suggested revisions.

To apply the redline and strikeout attributes to existing text:

1. Position the insertion point at the end of the third paragraph of body text, which ends with "Renee and David." and press **Enter** twice.

2. Choose Redline from the Font menu.

   The status bar indicates a redline font.

3. Key **Barry George, Actron's Chief Executive Officer, called the evening a "tremendous welcome we will always remember."**

4. Choose Redline from the Font menu.

   This turns off redlining.

5. Key **Mr. George and his family were among the last to leave.**

6. Select the sentence keyed in step 5.

7. Choose Redline from the Font menu.

8. Select the last paragraph.

9. Choose Strikeout from the Font menu.

The paragraph shows strikeout marks, and the status bar indicates a strikeout font.

10. Choose Strikeout from the Font menu again.

    The strikeout marks disappear.

11. Select the last sentence, and choose Strikeout from the Font menu. Then deselect the text.

    The last sentence is marked with strikeout characters.

Subscript and Superscript Options

Superscript
Characters positioned above the baseline.

Subscript
Characters positioned below the baseline.

$e=mc^2$
H_2O

Superscript and subscript

Lesson 19 introduced the concept of a baseline, an imaginary line on which text appears to sit. All text in a WordPerfect document has some relation to its baseline. Most characters rest directly on the baseline. However, some special characters may be positioned above or below the baseline. When characters are positioned above the baseline, they are called *superscript* characters; when they are positioned below the baseline, they are called *subscript* characters. Superscript and subscript characters print in a smaller size than normal text. This is so they will fit in the space between the lines of text.

Superscript and subscript characters often are used in mathematics and science. Another common use of superscripting is in footnotes and references. The superscript and subscript options appear in the Font menu and in the Font dialog box.

To practice keying text using the superscript attribute:

1. Position the insertion point at the end of the first sentence in the last paragraph.

2. Key **1**.

3. Select the "1", and choose Superscript from the Font menu.

   WordPerfect has inserted [Suprscpt On] and [Suprscpt Off] codes, which can be seen in the Reveal Codes space. Most systems display the "1" smaller than other the text and positioned above the baseline.

4. Position the insertion point after the last sentence (and after the [Suprscpt Off] code) and press **Enter**.

5. Advance To the line at 9 inches. (Choose Advance from the Layout menu. Choose To Line, key **9** in the text box, and click OK.)

6. Key a 2-inch-long underscore beginning at the left margin.

7. Press **Enter**, and key **1. The telephone number at the main office is (405) 555-4598.**

Note: Colors can be set on a monochrome monitor. These colors will not be displayed on the screen, but they can be saved in a file to be printed on a color printer. If colors are printed on a black and white printer, they may print as shades of gray.

Color

WordPerfect is able to display and print text in color. Choosing the Color command in the Font menu opens the Select Text Color dialog box. In this dialog box, you can choose from several predefined colors or create custom colors for on-screen and printed text. To print in color, a color printer is necessary, and, to see colors on the screen, a color monitor is necessary.

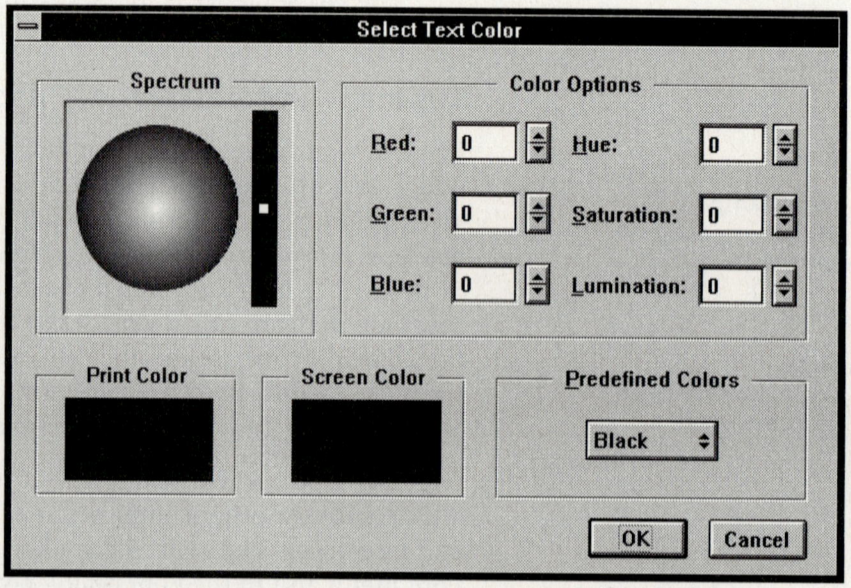

Figure 20-4
The Select Text Color dialog box

Predefined colors can be chosen from the Predefined Colors pop-up list. Custom colors can be created using either of two methods.

The first method uses a combination of three colors (red, green, and blue) to create custom colors. In this method, the amount of red, green, and blue are adjusted up or down to create a variety of other colors. Using the incrementing buttons or text boxes to the right of "Red", "Green", and "Blue", you can increase or decrease the amount of each color from 0 to 255. A "0" in the text box indicates that none of the color is present. A "255" indicates that the pure color is present.

Hue
The ratio of red, green, and blue used to make a custom color (from 0 to 360).

Saturation
The purity of a color, or the degree to which it has been diluted by white (from 0% to 100%).

Lumination
The lightness or darkness of a color (from 0% to 100%).

The second method uses a combination of three elements common to all colors—hue, saturation, and lumination—to create custom colors. Starting with the three basic colors (red, green, and blue), *hue* represents the ratio of these colors used to make the custom color (yellow, purple, etc.). It can be adjusted from 0 to 360. *Saturation* is the measure of the purity of a color, or the degree to which it has been diluted by the addition of white. It can be adjusted from 0% to 100%. A blue with 100% saturation is pure blue. *Lumination* is the lightness or darkness of the color. It is adjustable from 0% (black) to 100% (white).

Color spectrum
A representation of all the available custom colors.

The Select Text Color dialog box also contains a *color spectrum*, which represents all the custom colors. The color spectrum contains a small, box-shaped cursor that can be moved with the mouse to adjust colors.

To change colors:

1. Select the title of the press release, which begins "Five Points Realty".
2. Choose Color from the Font menu.

   The Select Text Color dialog box appears.

Note: Colors may not print exactly as they are displayed. Look at the Print Color box and Screen Color box to see any differences.

3. Choose Blue from the Predefined Colors pop-up list in the lower right corner of the box.

   The spectrum and the values in the color-options boxes change.
4. Click OK to confirm your selection and return to the document window.
5. Deselect the text.

   The title appears in blue. WordPerfect inserts a [Color:Blue] code before the selected text and a [Color:Black] code after.
6. Select the title again, but do not select the Blue code. Then choose Color from the Font menu.
7. Set the Green text box to 170. (Key **170** in the box, or use the up arrow).

   The spectrum and the hue value also change. These settings produce cyan, a color similar to turquoise.
8. Click OK to return to the document.
9. Deselect the text.

   The title now appears in cyan.
10. Select the title again, and choose Color from the Font menu.
11. Choose Black from the Predefined Colors pop-up list and click OK.
12. Deselect the title.

    The color returns to black.

WordPerfect Characters

WordPerfect supplies many characters that are not found on your keyboard. These characters are used to add mathematic and scientific symbols, foreign-language characters, typographic marks, and

Note: Printers that are capable of printing graphics can print the WordPerfect characters. Printers that cannot print graphics can print WordPerfect characters only if a font has been installed that contains those characters.

other decorative and representative symbols to documents. The WordPerfect Characters dialog box provides three ways to access these characters: by character set, by character number, and by character combination. The dialog box is accessed by choosing WP Characters from the Font menu or by pressing **Ctrl+W**.

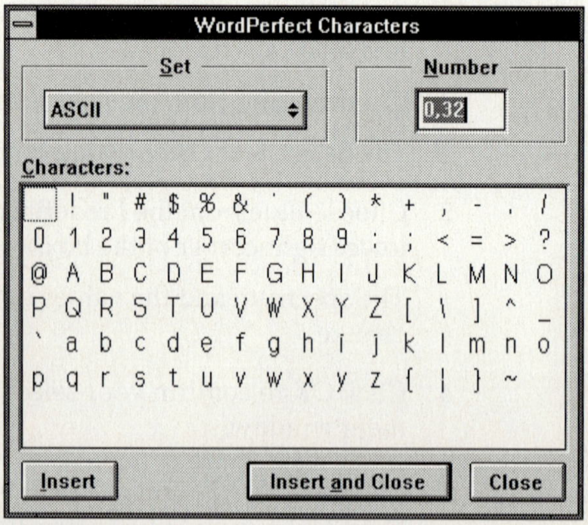

Figure 20-5
The WordPerfect Characters dialog box

Character Sets

WordPerfect provides several sets of related characters. These sets are displayed in the WordPerfect Characters dialog box and also are shown in the Appendices of the *WordPerfect for Windows Reference*.

You can choose a character set from the Set pop-up list in the WordPerfect Characters dialog box. The set appears in the Character box. To insert a character at the insertion point in a document, choose the character from the set, and then click Insert or Insert and Close.

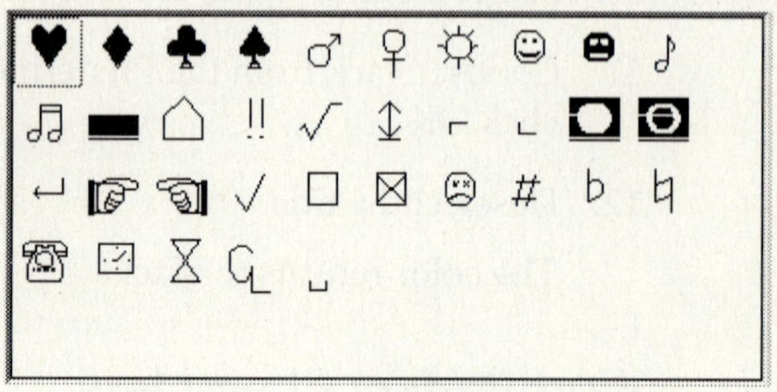

Figure 20-6
The Iconic Symbols character set

Note: The first time you select a foreign-language setting, Windows will ask you to insert one of the original setup disks, so that it can copy the foreign-language printer-driver file. Once the file has been copied from the disk, you can switch to the foreign-language setting automatically without using the setup disk again.

Foreign Language Characters

If you need to key an entire document in a foreign language, you can adapt the keyboard to the language. For example, if you change the keyboard to Spanish, when you key the semicolon (;), the character ñ appears instead. Or, when you key the plus sign (+), the character ¿ appears.

To change the keyboard to a foreign language, minimize the Word window, and choose Control Panel from the Windows Main group. In the Control Panel window, choose the International icon. In the International dialog box, choose the language in which you want to work. Select the keyboard layout that matches the language. Windows uses this setting to interpret the keys you press in the selected language. You also can specify a country. If you do this, Windows adjusts the date, time, number, and currency formats to match the particular country.

Changing the language and keyboard setting does not change the language of Windows or WordPerfect itself. If you change the setting to another language, remember to restore the settings to English if you share your computer with others.

The characters in each character set are numbered to allow quick access to specific characters. The character number is composed of its set number followed by a comma and its character number. For instance, the character 0,32 is character 32 in set 0. If you know the number of a character, you can key it in the Number box in the WordPerfect Characters dialog box to access the character quickly.

A third way to access some characters is by keying a combination of two characters in the Number box in the WordPerfect Characters dialog box. For example, the character combination "ro" produces the symbol ®. Many other symbols are possible. Table 20-1 shows a partial listing of these symbols.

Table 20-1: WordPerfect Character Combinations

Combination	Symbol
	Diacritic
'i	í
`e	è
,c	ç
_u	ū
	Other Symbols
+-	±
<=	
>=	

continued on next page

Table 20-1—Continued

Combination	Symbol
	Other Symbols
/=	
tm	™
ro	®
co	©
??	¿
!!	¡
n-	– (the en dash)
m-	— (the em dash)

Inserting WordPerfect Characters

The three methods of accessing WordPerfect characters may be used interchangeably to insert special characters into documents.

To practice inserting WordPerfect Characters using the three methods:

1. Position the insertion point after "Multimedia" in the title.
2. Choose WP Characters from the Font menu or press **Ctrl+W**.

   The WordPerfect Characters dialog box appears.

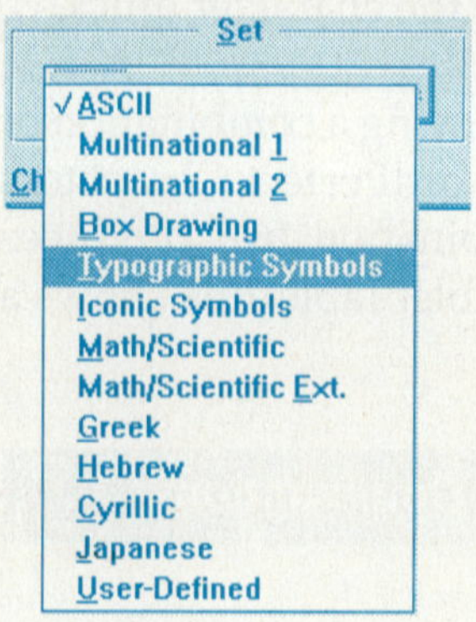

The Set pop-up list

3. Choose Typographic symbols from the Set pop-up list.
4. Click the registered trademark symbol ® in the Character box.

   A box flashes around the selected symbol.

5. Click the Insert and Close button to insert the character in the document at the insertion point and close the dialog box.

   The Insert command lets you select a sequence of characters without closing the dialog box. Click the Insert button after each selection. Then click the Insert and Close button after the last character.

6. Select the final "e" in "Renee" in the second-to-last paragraph.
7. Press **Ctrl+W**.
8. In the Number box, key **1,41**. Then click the Insert and Close button.

   The "e" receives an accent mark for the French name "Reneé".

9. In the same paragraph, position the insertion point after "Excellence".
10. Press **Ctrl+W**.
11. In the Number box, key **tm**.
12. Click Insert and Close.

    The trademark symbol ™ appears.

En and Em Dashes and Other Typographic Marks

En dash
A dash the width of a capital N.

Em dash
A dash the width of a capital M.

Many typographic symbols are available in the Typographic Symbols character set. In addition, some are available as character combinations. Two of the most frequently used typographic symbols are en dashes and em dashes. An *en dash*, which is the width of a capital N, is used to separate two items in a range of items, such as 1-5. An *em dash*, which is the width of a capital M, is used to indicate a break in thought. There are no spaces before or after an em dash.

Notice also the first four typographic symbols in the top line. These are "bullets," which can be used to call attention to listed items.

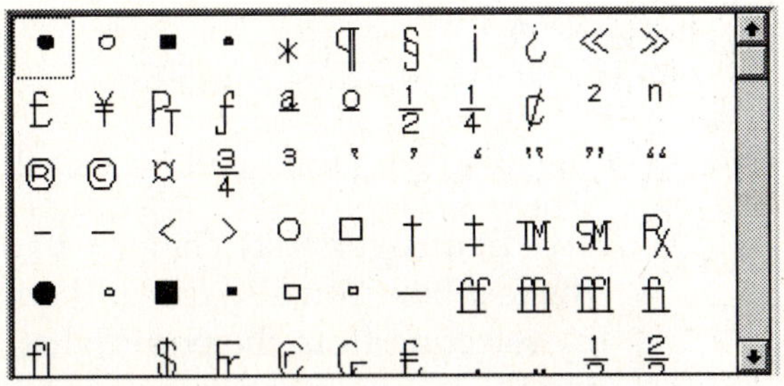

Figure 20-7
The Typographic Symbols character set

To insert an em dash:

1. Position the insertion point in the heading, after "RELEASE".
2. Open the WordPerfect Characters dialog box.
3. Choose Typographic Symbols from the Set pop-up list.
4. Click the longer dash in the fourth row of the character set.

   This is the em dash.
5. Click Insert and Close to return to the document.
6. Insert the date code after the em dash.

Overstrike Characters

An overstrike character is created by keying one character on top of another. The purpose of the overstrike feature is to create combination characters from characters on the keyboard.

To practice creating an overstrike character:

1. Delete the "0" in the area code "(404)" at the bottom of the page.

2. With the insertion point between the two 4s, choose Overstrike from the Font menu. Then choose Create.

   The Create/Edit Overstrike dialog box appears.

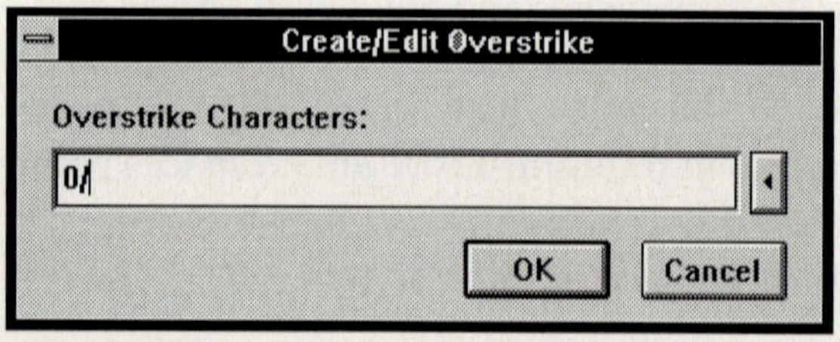

Figure 20-8
The Create/Edit Overstrike dialog box

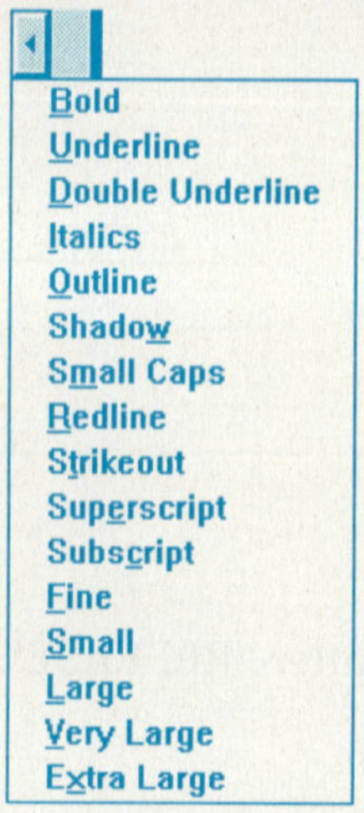

The Overstrike Attributes pop-up list

3. Key **0/** (a zero followed by a slash).

   To edit an overstrike character, add or delete any characters in the text box. You also can add attributes to the new character by selecting from the pop-up list, which is accessed by clicking the left-pointing arrowhead.

4. Click OK to exit the dialog box.

   The new overstrike character "Ø" appears between the 4s (at the insertion point).

5. To get a closer look, open the Print Preview window and choose 200%.

   You have created a character for zero that is distinctly different from a capital letter O.

6. Close the Print Preview window.

7. Save the document as *[your three-letter identifier]*20-0.wpw.

8. Print the document.

9. Close the document and exit WordPerfect (unless you will be doing the following exercises immediately).

Table 20-2: Keyboard Shortcuts for Special Characters and Attributes

Keyboard Shortcut	Action
F9	Font dialog box
Ctrl+W	WordPerfect Characters dialog box

Key Terms

Color spectrum	Saturation
Em dash	Small cap
En dash	Strikeout marks
Hue	Subscript
Lumination	Superscript
Redlining	WordPerfect characters

Exercises

Exercise 20.1

1. Start WordPerfect, if necessary.
2. Open the file 20-1.wpw. Choose Ruler from the View menu, if necessary.
3. Format all the text in 14-point CG Times, and center-justify the document.
4. Format the first three lines of text in 18-point small caps:
   A. Select the first three lines of text.
   B. Choose Font from the Font menu.
   C. Choose 18 in the Size list.
   D. Click Small Cap in the Font dialog box and click OK.
5. Replace the "(R)" in the third line with a registered trademark symbol:
   A. Select "(R)".
   B. Choose WP Characters from the Font menu.
   C. Choose Typographic Symbols from the Set pop-up list.
   D. Choose the ®, and click the Insert and Close button.
6. Increase the line height between the first three lines of text by 0.1 inches.

7. Format the "®" in the third line as superscript:

    A. Select the "®".

    B. Choose Superscript from the Font menu.

8. Change the color of the first three lines to red:

    A. Select the first three lines of text.

    B. Choose Color from the Font menu.

    C. Choose Red from the Predefined Colors pop-up list.

    D. Click OK.

9. Format the "th" in the fourth line to superscript.

10. Double-underline "RSVP (404) 555-4598":

    A. Select "RSVP (404) 555-4598".

    B. Choose Font from the Font menu.

    C. Choose Double Underline.

    D. Click OK.

11. Save the document as *[your three-letter identifier]*20-1.wpw.

12. Print the document.

13. Close the document and exit WordPerfect (unless you will be doing the following exercises immediately).

Exercise 20.2

1. Start WordPerfect, if necessary.

2. Open the file 20-2.wpw. Choose Ruler from the View menu, if necessary.

3. Change the headline "Babysitting By Gail" to shadow lettering:

    A. Select the headline.

    B. Choose Font from the Font menu.

    C. Click Shadow and click OK.

4. Change the size of the headline to Extra Large, center it, and format it in CG Times.

5. Change the color of the headline to green.

6. Change the size of the remainder of the text to Very Large, and format it in Univers (or a similar sans serif font).

7. Change the color of the text (except the headline) to purple:
   A. Position the insertion point in front of the second line of text, which begins "Attending".
   B. Choose Color from the Font menu.
   C. Set the Red text box to 150 (key **150** in the box, or use the up arrow).
   D. Set the Blue text box to 200.
   E. Click OK.
8. Replace the "(R)" in the third line with a registered trademark symbol.
9. Add diamond symbols (♦) in front of "Toys", "Games", and "Fun". Separate each symbol from the text with a tab:
   A. Position the insertion point before "Toys".
   B. Press **Ctrl+W** to open the WordPerfect Characters dialog box.
   C. Choose Iconic Symbols from the Set pop-up list.
   D. Choose the diamond.
   E. Click Insert and Close.
   F. Press the **Tab** key.
   G. Repeat steps A through F for "Games" and "Fun".
10. Format "Toys", "Games", and "Fun" to outline text:
    A. Select "Toys".
    B. Press **F9** to open the Font dialog box.
    C. Click Outline and then click OK.
    D. Repeat these steps for "Fun" and "Games".
11. Replace "to" in the line "Ages 1 to 12" with an en dash:
    A. Delete "to" and the spaces before and after it. Leave the insertion point between "1" and "12".
    B. Open the WordPerfect Characters dialog box, and choose the Typographic Symbols set.
    C. Choose the en dash (the shorter dash).
    D. Click Insert and Close.
12. Save the document as *[your three-letter identifier]*20-2.wpw.
13. Print the document.
14. Close the document and exit WordPerfect (unless you will be doing the following exercises immediately).

Exercise 20.3

1. Start WordPerfect, if necessary.
2. Open the file 20-3.wpw.
3. Format the document as an informal business report.
4. Edit the document as shown in Figure 20-9, which appears at the end of this exercise. Add format changes, including redlined text, strikeout marks, and color, as indicated. Use WordPerfect character 4,0 (the first in the typographic symbols set) as a bullet.
5. At the beginning of the document, identify the parties to the agreement in separate indented paragraphs, as marked.
6. Add a footer:

   Lucas/Horvath **pB^** **Draft [Date Code]**

7. Spell-check the document, and save it as *[your three-letter identifier]*20-3.wpw.
8. Print the document.
9. Close the document and exit WordPerfect (unless you will be doing the following exercises immediately).

Figure 20-9

AGREEMENT ← Blue, double underlined centered

Blue

This AGREEMENT, made this 6th day of July 199_ between **Gregory Lucas** of the City of Atlanta, County of Fulton and State of Georgia, **Seller**, and **Janice P. Horvath** (Blue) of the City of Alpharetta County of Fulton and State of Georgia, **Purchaser** (Blue):

Small caps

Witnesseth, that, if Purchaser shall first make the payments and perform the covenants hereinafter mentioned ~~on the part of the Purchaser to be made and performed~~ (Strikeout), Seller hereby covenants and agrees to convey or cause to be conveyed to Purchaser, ~~in fee simple, free and sufficient recordable Warranty Deed, with release of dower and homestead rights~~ (Strikeout), good title to the real estate situated in the County of Fulton and State of Georgia, known and described as follows:

Indent, Blue

Lot 23A, Block 3 of the City Subdivision, Township 2 Northeast, also known as 2398 North Harris Trail, Atlanta, Georgia.

Small caps

This conveyance shall be made subject to zoning and building laws or ordinances, building, line, and use or occupancy restrictions, conditions and covenants of record, and party wall rights or agreements, if any, roads, highways, streets and alleys, if any, and to general taxes for the year 199_ ~~and subsequent years, and to any unpaid installments of special assessments or special taxes which fall due after this date~~ and to a mortgage securing an unpaid principal balance of , which Purchaser hereby assumes and agrees to pay as a part of the purchase price hereof.

Strikeout

Small caps

¶ This conveyance combines uniform covenants for national use and non-uniform covenants with limited variations.

¶And in addition to paying the mortgage above mentioned Purchaser hereby covenants and agrees to pay to Seller at the office of Atlanta Bank, 44 Peachtree St., Atlanta or at such place as the sum of $93,000 DOLLARS, with interest at 8.50 per centum per annum, payable monthly, over the course of ten years or sooner. Minimum timely payments will be as follows:

+1l#

$18,000 cash, receipt of which is hereby acknowledged,

$18,000 on August 1, and $706.80 on the 15th day of each month thereafter for 120 months until the principal and interest on the remaining $57,000 are fully paid.

Indent and precede with bullets

Monthly installments will be applied to interest and principal according to the mortgage schedule attached.

¶ Purchaser shall promptly pay when due, the principal and interest.

Small caps

As soon as Purchaser has paid said purchase price down to the amount of unpaid balance payable on account of the mortgage at the time on said premises, the Seller shall convey said premises to Purchaser subject to said mortgage, to the matters and things hereinabove referred.

Exercise 20.4

1. Start WordPerfect, if necessary, and check your target printer.
2. Open a new file, and key document 20-4, which appears at the end of this exercise.
3. Change the initial document font to 14-point CG Times.
4. Format the first three lines in 18-point bold outline type, centered.
5. Insert an overstrike character composed of the WordPerfect Characters for the heart ♥ and the house ⌂ (in the Iconic Symbols set) before each of the four lines in the list of amenities. Adjust the attributes of these two symbols using the pop-up list, so the heart fits in the house. (Use a bold large house and a small heart.) To access the WordPerfect characters while the Create/Edit Overstrike dialog box is open, press **Ctrl+W**.
6. Insert an indent between each overstrike character and the text that follows it.
7. Strikeout the last paragraph in the flyer.
8. Add the following new paragraph after the last paragraph as redlined text: **For further information, call the Marietta office of Five Points Realty at (404) 555-1789**.
9. Spell-check the document, and save it as *[your three-letter identifier]*20-4.wpw.
10. Print the document.
11. Close the document and exit WordPerfect (unless you will be doing the following exercise immediately).

Document 20-4

2377 Brookhaven Drive

$295,000

4BR, 3BAs, FMDR, EIK

This handsome property set in 3.5 park-like acres has a wide range of amenities, which include:

Four Bedrooms: 21' X 19', 15' X 19', 12' X 17', and 9' X 12'

```
Garden Conservatory

Indoor Swimming Pool

Various outbuildings, including a converted barn suitable for work or
studio space

For further information regarding this property, contact Mary Rigdon at
Five Points Realty, (404) 555-3421.
```

Exercise 20.5

1. Start WordPerfect, if necessary.
2. Open the file 20-5.wpw.
3. Increase the line height after hard returns by 0.1 inches for the document.
4. Format the document's initial font as 18-point Univers.
5. Center-justify the first four lines.
6. Format "Open House" in blue 36-point type.
7. Format the address in blue 24-point type.
8. Insert the WordPerfect character for the right-pointing hand (☞) before each of the four features. Follow this character with an indent.
9. Replace the 1/2 with the WordPerfect character (½), and delete the space before it.
10. Format the line that begins "Come see" in bold italics.
11. Format the last line in 12-point CG Times bold, flush right.
12. Save this document as *[your three-letter identifier]*20-5.wpw.
13. Print the document.
14. Close the document and exit WordPerfect.

Module 7

Tables and Columns

Lessons

Creating Tables

Objectives

- Create a table using the menu.
- Create a table using the mouse.
- Enter text in a table.
- Use the keyboard to move within a table.
- Use Go To to move within a table.
- Select the table structure.
- Select text in a table.

The table feature makes it easy to arrange information in horizontal rows and vertical columns. It is a flexible alternative to the tab feature described in Lesson 9. Using the table feature, you can add lines and boxes to enhance a table and easily create multiple-line entries that word-wrap automatically from line to line. It also is very easy to change the order of rows and columns, insert or delete rows and columns, and change the width of columns.

Creating a Table

You can create a table anywhere in a document by first moving the insertion point to the location where you want the table to begin and then using one of the two methods for creating a table:

- Menus

  The Tables option in the Layout menu opens a cascading menu of options for working with tables. The Create option opens the Create Table dialog box. In this dialog box, you can enter the number of columns and the number of rows for a table.

- The mouse and the Ruler

  A quick way to create a table is to use the mouse to click the Tables button on the Ruler. A grid pattern appears that you can use to select the number of rows and columns for the table.

In the table that appears using either method, all the columns are the same width, a double line frames the table, and a series of single lines forms a grid that separates the rows and columns. This is the default table style.

When you insert a table directly into a document, it fills the entire width of each line it occupies, even if it is a narrow table. In other words, you cannot put two tables side by side, add text along the side of a table, or put a table in a column. You can, however, use WordPerfect's graphics features, which are described in "Lesson 31: Working with Graphics Boxes," to achieve greater flexibility in table placement.

Creating a Table Using the Menu

To create a table using the menu:

1. Start WordPerfect, if necessary.

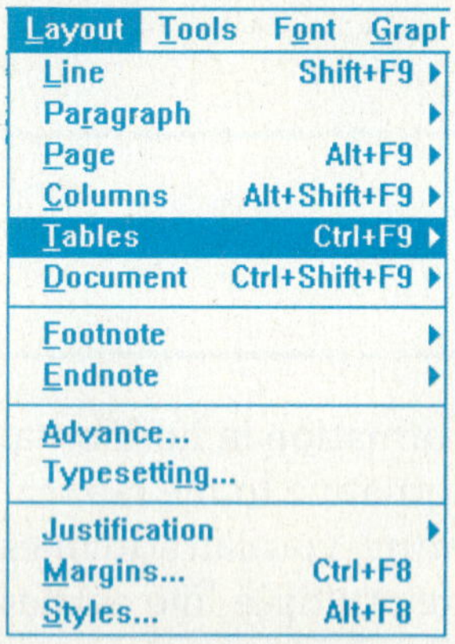

The Layout menu

2. Working in a new, untitled document window, choose Tables from the Layout menu (or press **Ctrl+F9**), and then choose Create from the Tables cascading menu.

   The Create Table dialog box appears.

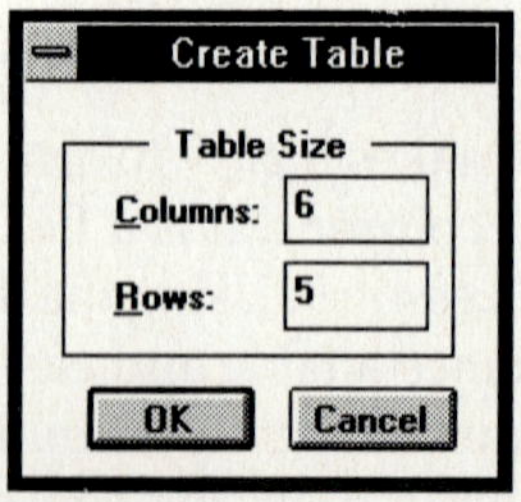

Figure 21-1
The Create Table dialog box

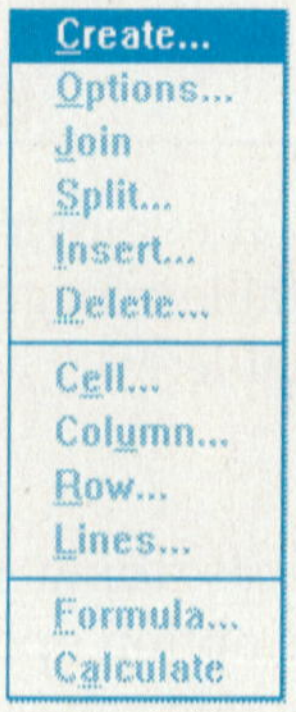

The Tables cascading menu

3. Key **6** in the Columns text box.

4. Key **5** in the Rows text box.

5. Click OK.

   A table with six vertical columns and five horizontal rows appears. Double lines indicate the outside boundaries of the table, and single lines separate the rows and columns inside the table.

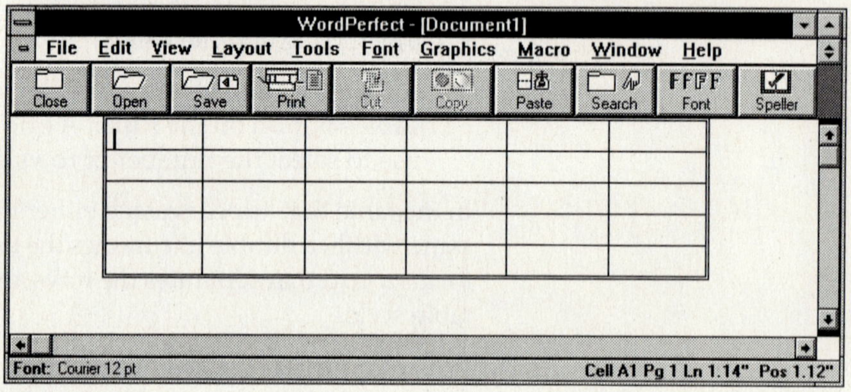

Figure 21-2
An empty table with six columns and five rows

6. Close the document without saving it.

Creating a Table Using the Mouse and the Ruler

Tables button

The Tables button

To use the mouse to create a table, you first need to display the Ruler. On the Ruler, the Tables button is the fourth button from the right (to the right of the Zoom button). It has an icon on it that looks like a grid.

To create a table using the mouse and the Ruler:

1. Open the file 21-0a.wpw.
2. Position the insertion point at the end of the document.
3. Choose Ruler from the View menu.

   The Ruler appears at the top of the document window.
4. Click the Tables button, and hold down the mouse button.

   A pop-up grid appears with the title "No Table".

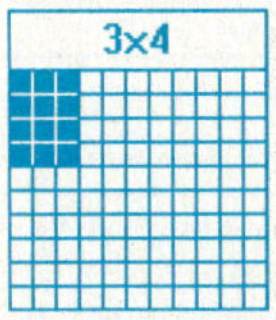

The Tables button pop-up grid

5. Drag the mouse pointer diagonally down and to the right until "3x4" appears.

   Notice that, as you move the mouse, the numbers listed at the top of the pop-up grid change. The "3x4" indicates a table that has three columns and four rows.
6. Release the mouse button.

   An empty table appears at the insertion point.

To examine the codes that define a table:

1. Choose Reveal Codes from the View menu or press **Alt+F3**.

   A table has an elaborate system of codes. You cannot delete or change codes individually, but you can delete the entire table if you delete the table definition code, [Tbl Def].

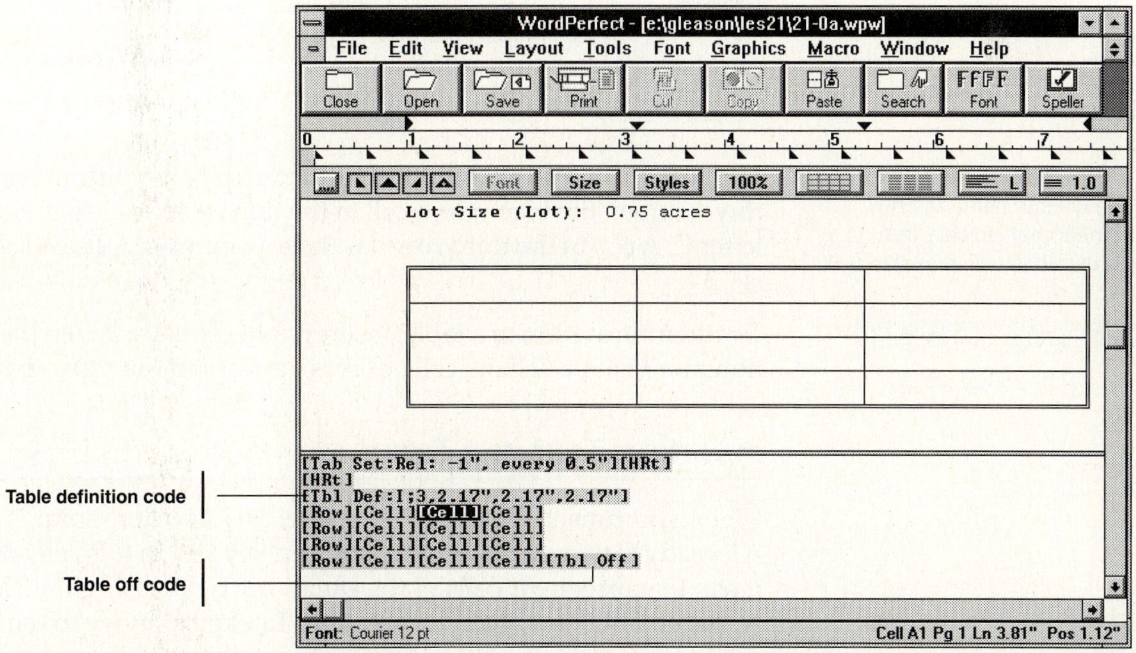

Figure 21-3
A table with the Reveal Codes space displayed

2. Choose Reveal Codes again to close the Reveal Codes space.

Parts of a Table

Cells
The boxes created by the intersections of rows and columns in a table.

In WordPerfect, a table is organized in numbered rows and lettered columns that form boxes called *cells*. Cells are easy to recognize when separated by lines, as in the default table. Cells are numbered and lettered beginning at the upper left corner of the table.

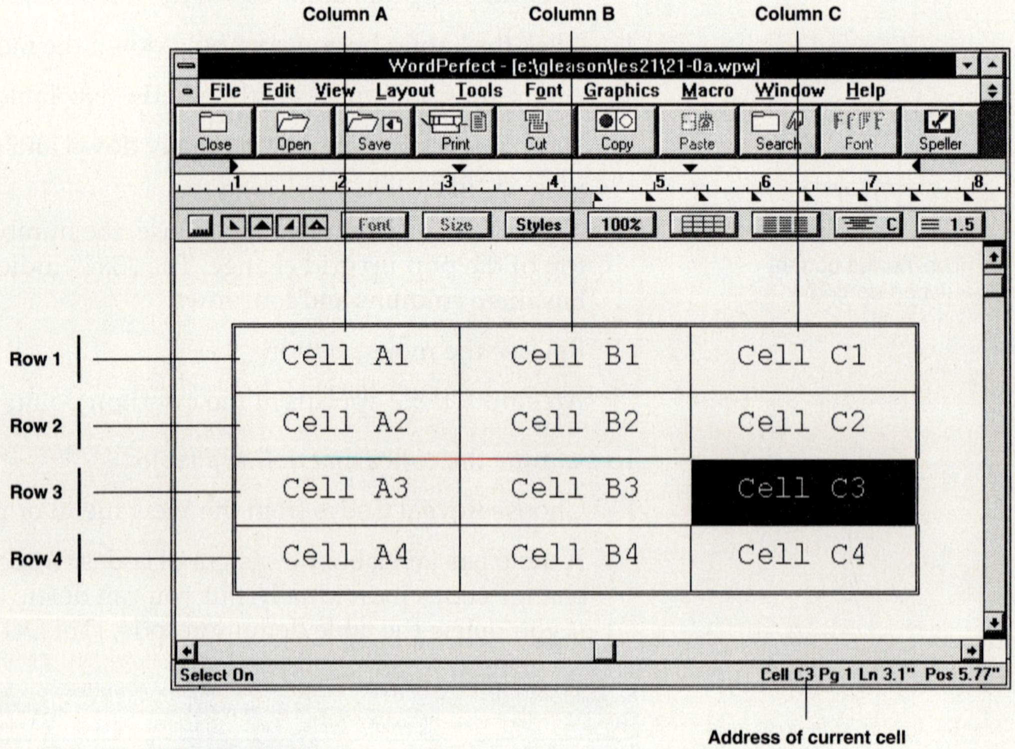

Figure 21-4
Parts of a table

Cell address
The column letter and row number that indicate the location of a cell in a table.

The status bar

Each cell has a *cell address*, which is made up of its column letter and row number. For example, a cell in the third column has the column letter C. A cell in the third row has the row number 3. Its cell address is C3.

To add information to a table, insert it into the cells. When the insertion point is in a cell, its cell address appears in the status bar.

Inserting Text in a Table

When you finish creating a new table, the insertion point is in cell A1, ready for you to insert text. You can key text in this cell and then move to subsequent cells in the same row by pressing the **Tab** key. At the end of a row, you can press the **Tab** key to move to the beginning of the next row. To go back to the previous cell, you can press **Shift+Tab**. You also can move the insertion point to a specific cell using the mouse or the Arrow keys.

To insert information in the table:

1. Position the insertion point in cell A1, if necessary.

2. Key **Address**.

3. Press the **Tab** key.

   The insertion point moves to the first row of column B. The status bar shows the cell address B1.

4. Key **Date Sold**, and press the **Tab** key.

5. Key **Price**, and press the **Tab** key.

   The first row is filled with information, and the insertion point is at the beginning of the second row.

6. Key **1278 Crique Way, Roswell**, and press the **Tab** key.

   The address is longer than the width of the cell, so it automatically word-wraps to a new line within the cell.

7. Using the table in Figure 21-5 as a guide, fill in the rest of the table.

   You can press **Shift+Tab** to go back to a previous cell, if necessary.

Address	Date Sold	Price
1278 Crique Way, Roswell	6/16/199-	$158,900
2180 Raleigh Tavern Drive, Roswell	8/24/199-	160,000
1582 Powder Ridge Road, Roswell	4/14/199-	161,000

Figure 21-5
The completed table

8. Spell-check the document.

9. Save the document as *[your three-letter identifier]*21-0a.wpw.

10. Print the document.

11. Close the document, but do not exit WordPerfect. You will open a new document for the next procedure.

Moving Within a Table

There are several methods for moving within a table using the mouse and the keyboard. For instance, you can use the mouse to move the insertion point to a specific cell, or you can use the **Tab** and **Shift+Tab** keys to move forward and backward through the table. If you are working in a very large table, you can use the scroll bar to move to a distant cell. The mouse is a convenient way to browse through a table; however, you may find it easier to keep your hands on the keyboard and use keystrokes when entering large amounts of information.

If a table is empty, you can move from cell to cell using the Arrow keys, but, if there is information in a cell, the Arrow keys will move the insertion point through the text in the cell character by character or line by line. It is more efficient to use the keystrokes listed in Table 21-1 below.

Note: If you need to insert a tab code within a cell, press **Ctrl+Tab**.

Table 21-1: Keystrokes for Moving Within a Table

Keystroke	Action
Tab	Move right to the next cell.
Shift+Tab	Move left to the previous cell.
Home, Home	Move to the first cell in a row.
End, End	Move to the last cell in a row.
Alt+Left Arrow	Move left one cell.
Alt+Right Arrow	Move right one cell.
Alt+Up Arrow	Move up one cell.
Alt+Down Arrow	Move down one cell.
Alt+Home	Move to the first line of a cell containing more than one line.
Alt+End	Move to the last line of a cell containing more than one line.

To practice the keystrokes for moving in a table:

1. Open the file 21-0b.wpw.
2. Position the insertion point anywhere in cell A1.
3. Press the **Tab** key four times.
4. Press the **Right Arrow** key several times, until the insertion point is in cell F1.

   It takes many keystrokes to move from cell to cell using this method.
5. Press the **Tab** key twice, and look at the status bar.

The insertion point should be in cell B2. This is a quicker method for moving from cell to cell.

6. Press **Shift+Tab**.

   The insertion point moves back one cell to A2.

7. Press the **Down Arrow** key six times.

   The insertion point is in cell A5.

8. Press **Alt+Up Arrow** three times.

9. Press **End, End**.

   The insertion point moves to the last column in row 2.

10. Press **Home, Home**.

    The insertion point moves to cell A2 at the beginning of the row.

Using the Go To Feature in Tables

If you have a very large table, you will want to use the Go To feature to move around in the table quickly. If the insertion point is in a table when you open the Go To dialog box, several options are available from the Position pop-up list.

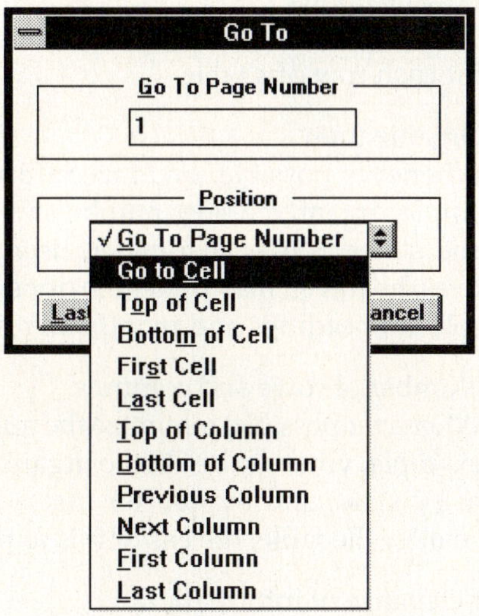

Figure 21-6
The Go To dialog box with the Position pop-up list displayed

The Top of Column and Bottom of Column options are very useful, because there are no keystroke equivalents for these movements. If you choose Go to Cell, you can key a cell address in the Go To Cell text box.

To experiment with Go To:

1. Position the insertion point anywhere in cell A1.
2. Choose Go To from the Edit menu or press **Ctrl+G**.
3. Choose Go To Cell from the Position pop-up list.

   The text on the Position pop-up button changes from "Go To Page Number" to "Go to Cell", and the text box changes to "A1".

4. Key **D3** in the Go to Cell text box.
5. Click OK.

   The insertion point moves to cell D3.

Considerations for Designing a Table

Tables are used to present information in an organized way. Often, even a small amount of information can be presented more clearly in a table than in paragraph form. When designing a table, there are several things you should consider before keying the information:

- Column headings
  Information in a table is arranged in rows and columns. The first row always should contain descriptive column headings, and the information in each column should be consistent with the heading.

- Row headings
  The leftmost column of a table often contains descriptive headings for each row of a table.

- Organization
  Whenever possible, organize information for the reader. For example, organizing sales numbers with months as column headings and states as row headings is useful to accountants. Sales executives, however, may prefer the opposite arrangement with states as column headings and months as row headings.

- Number of rows and columns
  Whenever possible, minimize the number of rows and columns. For example, you may be able to organize sales data by region instead of by state, and by quarter instead of by month. Generally, the smaller the table, the easier it is to understand.

- Relevance of information
  For example, a table that presents weather-related figures in major U.S. cities does not need a population column.

- Consistency of format
  If there is more than one table in a document, make sure the tables have a consistent format. For example, the text style in column headings should match. Titles usually appear above a table, although they can appear below instead. Whichever you choose, make sure that title placement is consistent throughout a document.

Selecting Cells and Text in a Table

When working with tables, it is important to understand the difference between selecting text and selecting the table structure. When you select the table structure, table commands are available, but some text-formatting commands are not. For example, you can change the table's column width or decimal alignment, but not the font or size of text. When you select text in a table, you can change fonts and use other text-formatting commands, but none of the table-formatting commands are available. Formatting the table structure and table text is discussed in the Lesson 22.

Selecting the Table Structure

Table structure
The rows and columns that make up a table, but not the text in it.

When you move the mouse pointer into a cell and drag across or down several cells, the selection appears as a solid highlight that completely fills the cells. This indicates that the table structure, not the text, has been selected for those cells. The *table structure* is made up of the rows and columns in the table.

Address	BR	BA	Lot	Date Sold	Price
1278 Crique Way, Roswell	4	2.5	.75	6/199-	$158,900
2180 Raleigh Tavern Drive, Roswell	4+	3.0	.50	8/199-	160,000
1582 Powder Ridge Rd., Roswell	4	2.5	1.00	4/199-	161,000
7500 Taylor Oaks Dr., Roswell	4	2.5	.75	5/199-	163,000

Figure 21-7
A table with part of the structure selected

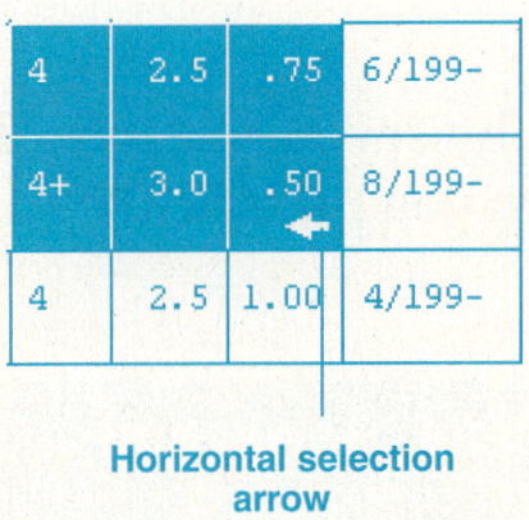

Table structure

Another way to select the table structure is to use the table selection arrows.

To use the horizontal selection arrow:

1. Move the mouse pointer into the center of cell A2, but do not click.

   The mouse pointer is an I-beam.

2. Move the pointer slowly towards the left edge of the cell, until the horizontal selection arrow appears.

3. Click the mouse button.

   Cell A2 is selected.

To select a row:

1. Move the mouse pointer to the left edge of cell C3.

   You should see the horizontal selection arrow.

2. Double-click.

   The table structure of row 3 is selected.

Note: If the table is large, or the computer is running slowly, it may take a few moments before the row selection takes place. Resist the urge to click again, or the entire table may be selected.

To select a cell using the vertical selection arrow:

1. Move the I-beam to cell B2.

2. Slowly move the I-beam to the upper edge of the cell, until the vertical selection arrow appears.

3. Click the mouse button.

   The cell is selected.

To select a column:

1. Move the I-beam to the upper edge of cell C2.

   You should see the vertical selection arrow.

2. Double-click.

   Column C is selected.

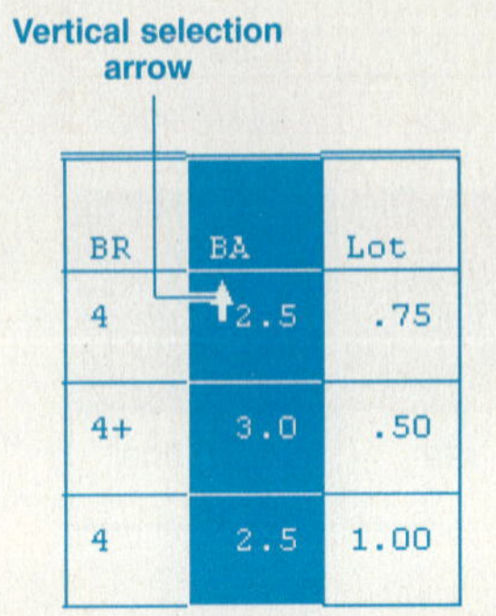

A selected table column

To select the entire table:

1. Move the I-beam in any cell, until either the horizontal or the vertical selection arrow appears.

2. Triple-click.

   The entire table is selected.

3. Click once in any cell to deselect the table.

Additionally, you can use **Shift+F8** followed by several keyboard combinations to select cells within a table. When you press **Shift+F8**, "Select On" appears on the status bar.

Table 21-2: Keystrokes for Selecting Cells, Rows, and Columns in a Table

Press:	Result
Shift+F8	Select is turned on, and a cell is selected.

continued on next page

Table 21-2—Continued

With Select on, press:	Result
Shift+Arrow	Add one cell, row, or column at a time. Can extend selection outside the table.
Shift+Alt+Arrow	Add one cell, row, or column at a time. Does not extend outside the table.
Shift+Home	Extend selection to the beginning of the current row.
Shift+End	Extend selection to the end of the current row.
Shift+Ctrl+Home	Extend selection to the beginning of the document.
Shift+Ctrl+End	Extend selection to the end of the document.
Ctrl+Up or Down Arrow	Selects the current column.
Ctrl+Left or Right Arrow	Selects the current row.

Selecting the Text in a Table

When you want to work with the text without affecting the row and column settings, you can select the text in a table without selecting the table structure. To select a small amount of text within a cell, drag the mouse pointer. If you need to select the text in more than one cell, use the selection key, **F8**. When you press **F8**, "Select Mode" appears on the status bar.

Practice selecting text in a table:

1. Move the mouse pointer to the left of "25" in cell A2.

   Make sure the mouse pointer is an I-beam and not an arrow.

2. Drag the I-beam across the address "25 Kingston Road".

   The address is highlighted, but the background of the cell is white. The white border indicates that the text, not the table structure, is selected.

3. Now, drag the I-beam across the address in cell A2 and "4+" in cell B2.

   Notice that, as you drag to the second cell, the I-beam changes into a left-pointing horizontal arrow, indicating that the table structure and not the text is being selected. Cells A2 and B2 have a solid highlight now, another indication that the table structure is selected.

To select just the text in more than one cell, use the Select key, **F8**. First, position the insertion point in a cell and press **F8**. Second, use insertion-point movement keys and table movement keys to select additional text. To select text in a table using the mouse, position the insertion point at the beginning of the selection, press **F8**, hold down the **Shift** key, position the I-beam at the end of the selection, and click.

Table 21-3: Examples of Text-Selection Keystrokes

Press:	Result
F8	Turn Select Mode on/off (toggle).
With Select Mode on, press:	Result
Arrow key	Extend text selection one character (left or right) or one line (up or down).
Tab	Extend text selection one cell to the right.
Shift+Tab	Extend text selection one cell to the left.
Alt+Arrow key	Extend text selection one cell (left or right) or one row (up or down).
Shift+left mouse button	Extend text selection to the I-beam position.

To practice selecting text across cells in a table:

1. Position the insertion point to the left of "2.5" in cell C2.
2. Press **F8**.

   "Select Mode" appears on the status bar.

3. Press **Shift+Tab** twice.

   Text from the insertion point to the beginning of the row is selected.

4. Press **F8** to turn off Select Mode.

   "Select Mode" no longer appears on the status bar, the text is no longer selected, and the insertion point is at the beginning of cell A2.

5. Press **F8** again to turn on Select Mode.
6. Use the scroll bar, if necessary, to display row 8.

   Be careful not to click on the document screen while scrolling, because doing so will reposition the insertion point and turn off Select Mode.

7. Hold down the **Shift** key, position the I-beam to the right of "158,900" in cell F8, and click.

   Now all the text in rows 2 through 8 is selected.

Address	BR	BA	Lot	Date Sold	Price
1278 Crique Way, Roswell	4	2.5	.75	6/199-	$158,900
2180 Raleigh Tavern Drive, Roswell	4+	3.0	.50	8/199-	160,000
1582 Powder Ridge Rd., Roswell	4	2.5	1.00	4/199-	161,000
7500 Taylor Oaks Dr., Roswell	4	2.5	.75	5/199-	163,000

Figure 21-8
A table with text selected

8. Click once anywhere in the table to deselect the text.

   Select Mode is turned off.

9. Position the insertion point to the right of "Roswell" in cell A4 and press **F8**.

   Select Mode is turned on.

10. Press **Home**.

    Text is selected to the beginning of the line.

11. Press the **Up Arrow** key three times.

    The text in cell A4 and all the text in row 3 is selected.

12. Close the document without saving it.

13. Exit WordPerfect (unless you will be doing the following exercises immediately).

Table 21-4: Keyboard Shortcuts for Creating and Selecting Tables

Keyboard Shortcut	Action
Ctrl+F9	Open the Create Table dialog box.
Tab	Move to the next cell.
Shift+Tab	Move to the previous cell.
Ctrl+Tab	Insert a tab within a cell.
Ctrl+G	Open the Go To dialog box.

Key Terms

Cell address
Cells
Table structure

Exercises

Exercise 21.1

1. Start WordPerfect, if necessary.
2. Open the file 21-1.wpw.
3. Position the insertion point at the end of the document and press **Enter**.
4. Create a four-column by five-row table at the insertion-point location:
   A. Choose Tables from the Layout menu or press **Ctrl+F9**, and then choose Create from the Tables cascading menu.
   B. Key **4** in the Columns text box.
   C. Key **5** in the Rows text box.
   D. Click OK to close the dialog box and create the table.

   A table four columns wide and five rows long appears at the insertion point.
5. Add column headings to the table:
   A. Position the insertion point in cell A1, if necessary.
   B. Key **Agent**, and press the **Tab** key to move to cell B1.
   C. Key **Office**, and press the **Tab** key.
   D. Key **Sales**, and press **Enter** to move to a new line in cell C1.
   E. Key **Q2 199-**, and press the **Tab** key.
   F. Key **Sales** in cell D1 and press **Enter**.
   G. Key **Year-to-Date**, and press the **Tab** key to move to the beginning of row 2.

   The column headings are entered, and the insertion point is in cell A2, ready to enter information.
6. Key the following lines of text in the remaining rows of the table, inserting each item in a separate cell:

G. Crane	**Buckhead**	**$525,000**	**$812,000**
A. Delbridge	**Buckhead**	**633,000**	**998,900**
D. Feingold	**Marietta**	**250,500**	**450,000**
E. Hemmings	**Marietta**	**450,500**	**730,900**

The numbers will not align, because there are dollar signs in the first row. Aligning numbers is discussed in Lesson 22.

7. Spell-check the document.

8. Save the document as *[your three-letter identifier]*21-1.wpw.

9. Print the document.

10. Close the document and exit WordPerfect (unless you will be doing the following exercises immediately).

Exercise 21.2

1. Start WordPerfect, if necessary.

2. Open the file 21-2.wpw.

3. Choose Ruler from the View menu to display the Ruler.

4. Create a four-column by eight-row table using the mouse method:

   A. Position the insertion point at the end of the document and press **Enter**.

   B. Move the mouse pointer to the Tables button on the Ruler.

   C. Drag the mouse pointer diagonally down and to the right until "4x8" appears on the title of the pop-up grid.

   D. Release the mouse button.

   A four-column by five-row table appears at the insertion point.

5. Fill the empty table with the text and numbers that appear in Figure 21-9 below.

Agent	Office	YTD through Q1 199-	YTD through Q2 199-
G. Crane	Buckhead	$760,000	$812,000
R. Mercer	Buckhead	675,900	998,900
W. Reston	Buckhead	n/a	450,000
M. Washington	Buckhead	760,900	959,900
R. Palmer	Marietta	625,000	1,075,900
M. Rigdon	Marietta	600,000	1,800,000
P. Silvers	Marietta	362,900	507,200

Figure 21-9
The completed table for Exercise 21.2

6. Practice selecting cells in a table with the mouse:
   A. Move the insertion point to the left edge of cell A2, until you see the horizontal selection arrow.
   B. Click the mouse button to select the cell.
   C. Move the mouse pointer to the left edge of any cell in row 3, and double-click to select the entire row.
   D. Move the mouse pointer to the top edge of cell B4, until you see the vertical selection arrow, and double-click to select the column.
7. Practice selecting cells in a table using the keyboard:
   A. Position the insertion point to left of the number in cell C5.
   B. Press **Shift+F8**.
   C. Hold down the **Shift** key, and press the **Down Arrow** key twice to select cells C5 through C7.
   D. Press **Ctrl+Right Arrow** to select all the cells in rows 5 through 7.
8. Practice selecting text in the table:
   A. Position the insertion point to the left of "YTD" in cell C1.
   B. Press **F8** to turn on Select Mode.
   C. Press the **Tab** key twice to select all the text in cells C1 and D1.
   D. Press the **Right Arrow** key four times to add some text in cell A2 to the selection.
   E. Press **F8** to turn off Select Mode and deselect the text.
9. Spell-check the document.
10. Save the document as *[your three-letter identifier]*21-2.wpw.
11. Print the document.
12. Close the document and exit WordPerfect (unless you will be doing the following exercises immediately).

Exercise 21.3

1. Start WordPerfect, if necessary.
2. Open the file 21-3.wpw.
3. Complete the table by filling the empty cells with the information appearing in Figure 21-10.

2400 Orleans Court, Dunwoody	5	3.5	.50	Apr.	247,900
12 Sharon Valley Court, Dunwoody	5	3.0	.75	Apr.	259,900
23 Fenhurst Place, Dunwoody	4+	3.0	.50	Mar.	230,900
86 Ellisbury Drive, Dunwoody	5	3.5	.50	Jun.	262,000
1 Pineridge Circle, Dunwoody	5+	3.5	1.00	Dec.	285,900

Figure 21-10
Information to complete the table in Exercise 21.3

4. Edit the table headings to match the following:

Address	Br	Ba	Lot	Month Sold	Selling Price

5. In cell A3, change "Springhouse" to "Spring House".
6. Change the price in cell F3 to 274,900.
7. Change the number of bathrooms in cell C2 to 2.5.
8. Spell-check the document.
9. Save the document as *[your three-letter identifier]*21-3.wpw and print it.
10. Exit WordPerfect (unless you will be doing the following exercises immediately).

Exercise 21.4

1. Start WordPerfect, if necessary.
2. Key Figure 21-11, which appears at the end of this exercise, including the table and the corrections indicated.
3. Format the document in the standard memo format.
4. Use the Go To feature to move to cell B5.
5. Delete "E. Hemmings" and key **D. Feingold**.
6. Change the date in cell C5 from 09/28 to **10/05**.
7. Change the information in cell A7 to **Chattahoochee River Rafting**.
8. Change the information in cell A6 to **Botanical Gardens Walk**.

9. Spell-check the document.
10. Save the document as *[your three-letter identifier]*21-4.wpw.
11. Print the document.
12. Close the document and exit WordPerfect (unless you will be doing the following exercise immediately).

Figure 21-11

MEMO TO: Bud Porter

FROM: Ann Delbridge

DATE: June 15, 199-

SUBJECT: "Things to Do in Atlanta" tour schedule

Final arrangements for tour leaders and dates are ~~finalized at last~~ now complete! The table below is a schedule of these activities:

Activity	Tour Leader	Date	Phone
CNN Center	M. Rigdon	08/24	555-0867
Ebenezer Baptist Church	G. Crane	08/10	555-1298
Atlanta Underground	W. Reston	09/14	555-3374
Johnny Mercer Room	E. Hemmings	09/28	555-9424
Chattahoochee River Rafting	M. Washington	10/12	555-1341
Botanical Gardens Walk	A. Delbridge	10/26	555-7708

Please let me know ~~ASAP~~ as soon as possible if ~~you are going to change your mind again~~ any changes will be necessary. It's ~~really tough~~ will be difficult to coordinate ~~these things~~ last minute arrangements.

Exercise 21.5

1. Start WordPerfect, if necessary.
2. Open the file 21-5.wpw.
3. Fill in the first part of the Comparable Listings form using the following information:

Date:	**July 20, 199-**
Prepared for:	**Jack and Melanie Llewelyn** **18 The Prado** **Ansley Park** **Atlanta, GA 30309** **555-9078**
Bedrooms (BR):	**3+**
Baths (BA):	**2.5**
Lot Size (Lot):	**0.25 acres**

4. Set a 2-inch top margin (or use the Advance command).
5. Set tabs for the above information, so that it is aligned as illustrated. Convert the headings "Date", "Prepared for", "Bedrooms", "Baths", and "Lot Size" to uppercase.
6. Complete the form by creating a five-column by nine-row table with the following information:

Address	**Br**	**Lot**	**Date**	**Price**
100 East Park Road	**3+**	**.50**	**4/199-**	**$278,000**
67 Avery Drive	**4**	**.25**	**4/199-**	**298,000**
65 Ansley Drive	**4+**	**.35**	**5/199-**	**338,000**
75 Walker Terrace	**3+**	**.95**	**5/199-**	**398,000**
44 Maddox Drive	**3+**	**.25**	**6/199-**	**320,000**
22 Lombary Way	**3+**	**.25**	**6/199-**	**350,000**
2 Blossom Lane	**3**	**.75**	**8/199-**	**310,000**
109 Avery Drive	**5**	**.33**	**12/199-**	**299,000**

7. Insert blank rows above the table, if necessary, so that there are two blank rows between the table and the heading information.
8. Spell-check the document.
9. Save the document as *[your three-letter identifier]*21-5.wpw.
10. Print the document.
11. Close the document and exit WordPerfect.

Lesson 22

Working with Tables

Objectives

- Use the Tables Button Bar.
- Change the table structure.
- Format and align text in tables.

Lesson 21 includes basic information about tables: How to create them, add text, move from cell to cell, select text, and select the table structure. This lesson describes how to change a table's appearance and size.

When modifying tables, you should keep in mind the difference between selecting the table structure and selecting text in the table. When you select the table structure, you can use the options on the Tables cascading menu to format the table, but you cannot use some of the text-formatting options described later in this lesson. When you select just the text in a table, you cannot use the options on the Tables cascading menu.

Changing the Table Structure

When you first create a table, it has the WordPerfect default table style: All the columns are the same size, there are single lines between rows and columns, and there is a double line bordering the table. You can change this structure by inserting or deleting rows and columns, moving or copying rows and columns, changing the width of columns, and joining or splitting cells. Also, you can change the line styles inside or outside the table, and you can remove some or all of the lines.

You access the options for changing the table structure by choosing Tables from the Layout menu and then choosing the desired option from the Tables cascading menu. The keyboard shortcut to open the Tables cascading menu is **Ctrl+F9**.

The Tables Button Bar

Another way to access options for changing the table structure is the Tables Button Bar. If you are planning to make several changes to a table, you will find the Tables Button Bar very helpful. It provides quick access to table-formatting options.

WordPerfect has several specialized Button Bars from which to choose, but allows only one to be displayed at a time. When you display the Tables Button Bar, you no longer can view or access the standard WordPerfect buttons. However, you still can access these options from the menus.

To display the Tables Button Bar:

1. Start WordPerfect, if necessary.
2. Open the file 22-0.wpw.
3. Choose Button Bar Setup from the View menu, and then choose Select from the Button Bar Setup cascading menu.

   The Select Button Bar dialog box is displayed.
4. Choose the file tables.wwb from the Files list box.
5. Click Select.

   The dialog box closes, and the Tables Button Bar replaces the default Button Bar.

Button Bar directional arrows

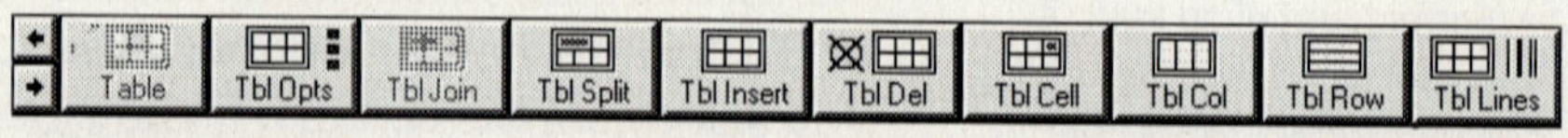

Figure 22-1
The Tables Button Bar

Another way to change Button Bars is to click the right mouse button on the Button Bar. This opens the Button Bar Quick Menu.

To return to the default Button Bar:

1. Move the mouse pointer to the Button Bar, and click the right mouse button.

   The Button Bar Quick Menu appears.
2. Choose the default Button Bar, wp{wp}.wwb (which appears at the bottom of the list).

   The default Button Bar replaces the Tables Button Bar.
3. Click the Button Bar with the right mouse button again and choose tables.wwb.

   The Tables Button Bar is displayed again.

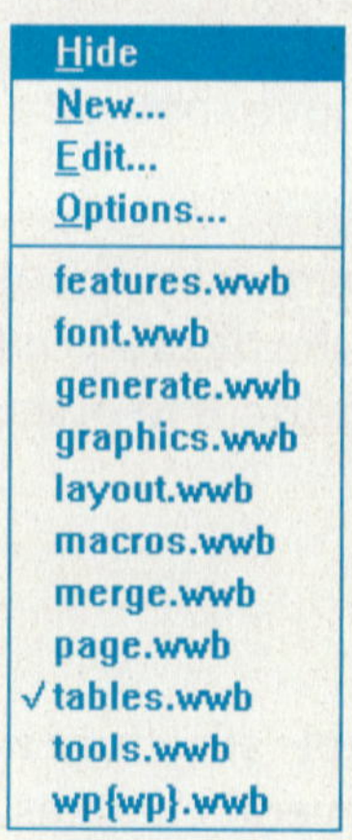

The Button Bar Quick Menu

Inserting Rows and Columns

You can change the structure of a table at any time by inserting rows or columns, using one of two methods available. You can use the Insert option on the Tables cascading menu, or, if the Tables Button Bar is displayed, you can click the Tbl Insert button. When you insert new rows or columns, they appear in the table at the current insertion-point position. New rows cause existing rows to move down, and new columns cause existing columns to move right to make room.

The keyboard shortcuts for inserting rows are **Alt+Insert** to insert a row at the insertion-point position and **Alt+Shift+Insert** to insert a row below the insertion-point row.

To insert a row:

1. Position the insertion point in cell A5.
2. Choose Tables from the Layout menu, and then choose Insert (or press **Alt+Insert**).

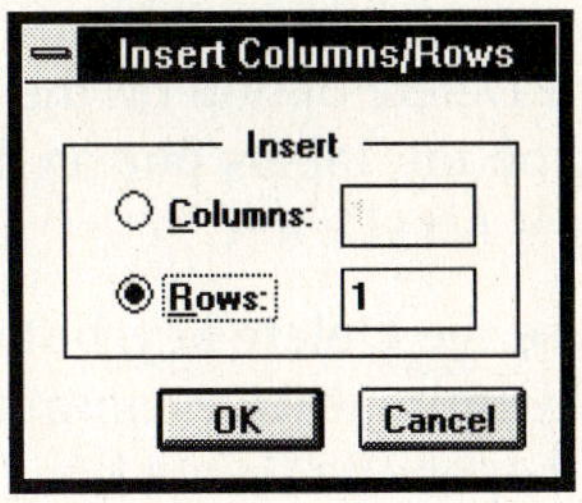

Figure 22-2
The Insert Columns/Rows dialog box

3. Select Rows from the Insert Columns/Rows dialog box and click OK.

   A new row is inserted, and the original row 5 becomes row 6.

4. Key **Subtotal** in the new cell A5.

To insert two rows at one time:

1. Position the insertion point in a cell in row 3.
2. Click Tbl Insert on the Tables Button Bar.

The Tbl Insert button

3. Choose Rows from the Insert Columns/Rows dialog box, and key **2** in the Rows text box. Click OK.

   Two blank rows are inserted between the names Mercer and Reston.

To insert columns:

1. Position the insertion point in a cell in column C.
2. Choose Tables from the Layout menu, and then choose Insert (or click the Tbl Insert button).
3. Choose Columns from the Insert Columns/Rows dialog box, and key **2** in the Columns text box. Click OK.

   Two blank columns are inserted to the left of column C.

To add a heading in column C:

1. Position the insertion point in cell C1.
2. Key **$ Change**.

   The text wraps to three lines inappropriately. This will be corrected later.

Deleting Rows and Columns

You delete rows and columns in much the same way as you insert them, using the Delete option on the Tables cascading menu or the Tbl Del button on the Tables Button Bar. The keyboard shortcut for deleting a row is **Alt+Delete**.

You also can use the **Delete** key, but only if you use a selection arrow to select an entire row or column before deleting. Pressing the **Delete** key will open the Delete Row or Delete Column dialog box. This box gives you the choice of deleting just the text or the selected rows or columns.

Note: WordPerfect does not ask you to confirm the delete action. If the row or column contains text, the text will be lost. Undelete will not bring it back. You can use Undo if it is the very next action you take, but it is always a good idea to save a table before deleting.

To delete a column:

1. Save the document as *[your three-letter identifier]*22-0.wpw.
2. Select column D by double-clicking the vertical selection arrow.
3. Choose Tables from the Layout menu, and then choose Delete (or click the Tbl Del button on the Button Bar).

The Tbl Del button

   The Delete Columns/Rows dialog box appears.

4. Choose Columns and click OK.

   Column D is deleted, and column E becomes the new column D.

Now delete multiple rows:

1. Use the Save command to update the document changes. (You saved the document previously as *[your three-letter identifier]*22-0.wpw.)
2. Scroll to the top of the table, if necessary.

3. Select rows 3 and 4 (the two blank rows you inserted).

4. Click the Tbl Del button.

5. Choose Rows from the Delete Columns/Rows dialog box and click OK.

   The two rows are deleted. Now you should have a new row with the heading "Subtotal" and a new column with the heading "$ Change".

Changing the Size of a Table

As you have seen, the Insert command always inserts rows above the current row and columns to the left of the current column. It is not possible to insert rows at the bottom of the table or columns at the right edge using the Insert command. To do this, you need to use the Table Size options found in the Table Options dialog box. The Table Size options also can be used to delete rows and columns.

If you specify a number of rows or columns that is greater than the size of the existing table, extra rows and columns will be added to the bottom and right edge of the table. If you specify a number of rows or columns that is less than the number in the existing table, rows and columns will be deleted from the bottom and right. If those rows contain text, the text will be lost without warning. (Remember, save your table before performing any step involving deletions, in case the next step deletes valuable data).

To change the size of the table:

1. Save the document.

2. Scroll to the last row of the table, so you will be able to see the new rows when they are added.

3. Position the insertion point inside the table.

The Tbl Opts button

4. Choose Tables from the Layout menu, and then choose Options (or click the Tbl Opts button).

   The Table Options dialog box appears.

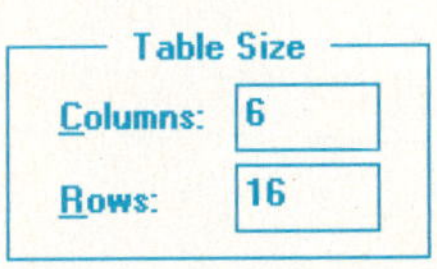

The Table Size options box

5. In the Table Size options box, key **6** in the Columns text box and **16** in the Rows text box.

6. Click OK.

   One column is added to the right side of the table, and three rows are added to the bottom of the table.

Use the Table Size options to make the table smaller:

1. Position the insertion point inside the table, if necessary.

2. Click the Tbl Opts button on the Tables Button Bar.

   The Tables Options dialog box opens.

3. Key **5** in the Columns text box.

4. Key **14** in the Rows text box and click OK.

5. Position the insertion point in cell A14 and key **Total**.

   Your table now should have 5 columns and 14 rows. You can move the insertion point to the cell in the lower right corner of the table to check this. The status bar should indicate that this is cell E14.

6. Save the document.

Moving and Copying Rows and Columns

The Cut, Copy, and Paste commands in the Edit menu can be applied to tables. Use these commands to move or copy selected columns and rows in a table.

Moving a column:

1. Scroll to the top of the table.

2. Double-click the vertical selection arrow in column D to select the column.

3. While pressing the **Shift** key, click anywhere in column E.

   The two columns are selected.

4. Choose Cut from the Edit menu (or press **Shift+Delete**).

   The Table Cut/Copy dialog box opens.

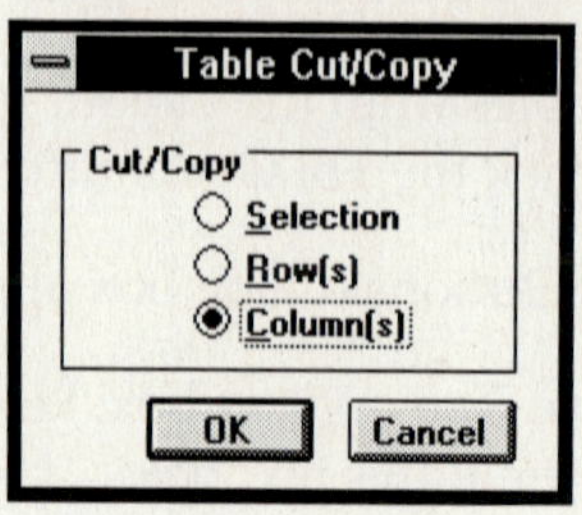

Figure 22-3
The Table Cut/Copy dialog box

5. Choose Columns and click OK.

   The columns are removed from the table.

6. Position the insertion point in column C, if necessary.
7. Choose Paste from the Edit menu (or press **Shift+Insert**).

   The move is completed. Now the "$ Change" column is at the right edge of the table.

Table lines may be formatted incorrectly after moving or copying rows or columns. Formatting table lines is discussed later in this lesson.

To copy rows:

1. Save the document.
2. Select row 5 (the Subtotal row).
3. Choose Copy from the Edit menu (or press **Ctrl+Insert**).
4. Choose Rows from the Table Cut/Copy dialog box and click OK.
5. Position the insertion point in cell A9 (the cell that contains the name "Crandon").
6. Choose Paste from the Edit menu.

   A copy of the subtotal row is inserted above the current row.
7. Position the insertion point row in 13 (the row that contains the name "Parker").
8. Choose Paste from the Edit menu.
9. Move the insertion point to the last row (the Total row) and paste another copy.

   A Subtotal row is inserted above the Total row.
10. Save the document.

Changing the Width of Columns

When you insert columns, WordPerfect sets their sizes automatically to accommodate the existing columns on the page. After inserting columns, you often will need to adjust their widths based on the information the columns will contain. You can do this by keying measurements in the Format Column dialog box or by using the Ruler.

To change the width of a column using the Format Columns dialog box:

1. Scroll to the top of the table, if necessary.
2. Position the insertion point in column B.

The Tbl Col button

3. Choose Tables from the Layout menu, and then choose Column (or click the Tbl Col button).

   The Format Column dialog box opens.

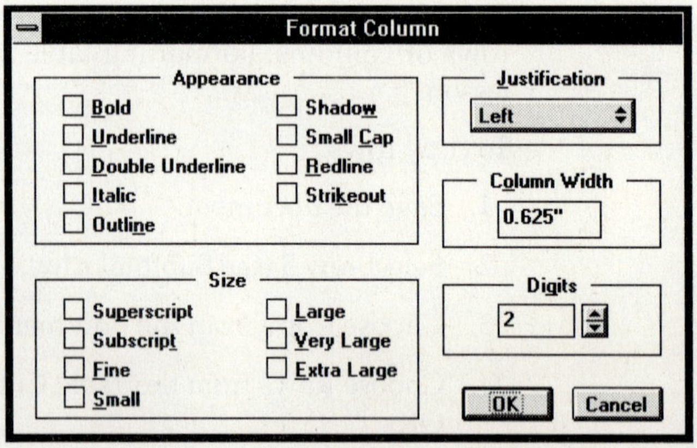

Figure 22-4
The Format Column dialog box

4. Key **5/8"** in the Column Width text box and click OK. (You can enter the decimal equivalent .625, if you prefer.)

   The column width changes to 0.625 inches.

To change the widths of two columns at the same time:

1. Select cells C2 and D2.
2. Click the Tbl Col button.
3. Key **1 1/4"** in the Column Width text box and click OK. (Be sure to key a space character after the first "1".)

   Remember, you can enter the decimal equivalent, 1.25, if you prefer.

4. Save the document.

Table-column markers
Marks on the Ruler that indicate the right edge of each column in a table.

If you display the Ruler when the insertion point is in a table, you will see *table-column markers* that show the position of the right edge of each column. These markers are the downward-pointing triangles on the upper edge of the Ruler. Margin markers indicate the left and right boundaries of the table. You can change the width of columns by dragging table-column markers or margin markers. While you are dragging a marker, a dotted vertical line will appear showing the position of the column edge in the table. Also, while you are dragging, a blue marker shows the original marker position.

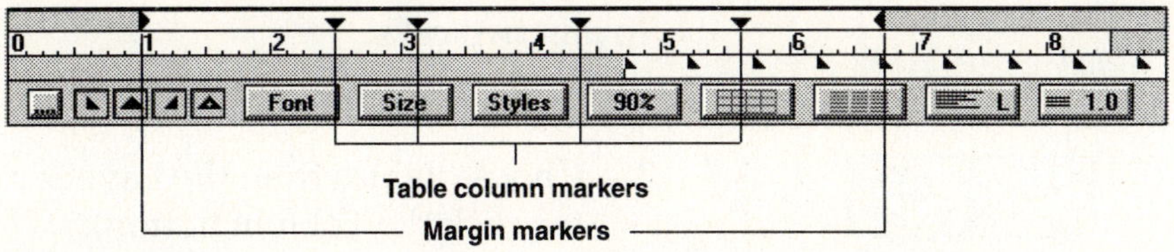

Figure 22-5
Table-column markers and margin markers on the Ruler

To change the width of columns using the Ruler:

1. Choose Ruler from the View menu, if necessary.
2. Position the insertion point inside the table.
3. Point to the table-column marker at the 2⅝-inch mark (the marker at the right edge of column A).
4. Drag the marker to the 2⅜-inch mark to make the column slightly smaller.

   While you are dragging, notice the vertical line showing the column-edge position.
5. Drag the right margin marker from the 6⅜-inch mark to the 6⅞-inch position.
6. Drag the table-column markers so that they are at these positions: 2½", 3⅛", 4⅜", and 5⅝".

Joining and Splitting Cells

A table can be made more interesting by splitting some cells into multiple cells or by joining two or more cells into a single cell. To join two or more cells, select them, and then choose Join from the Tables cascading menu. To split cells, select the cell or group of cells to be split, and then choose Split from the Tables cascading menu. Also, you can use the Tbl Join and Tbl Split buttons on the Tables Button Bar.

To split two cells:

1. Select cells C1 and D1 (the cells that contain the text "YTD").
2. Choose Tables from the Layout menu, and then choose Split (or click the Tbl Split button).
3. Choose Row from the Split Column/Row dialog box.
4. Key **2** in the Row text box and click OK.

   The selected cells are split horizontally. The resulting new cells are in row 2. The former row 2 is now row 3.

To join two cells:

The Tbl Join and Tbl Split buttons

1. Select cells C1 and D1.
2. Choose Tables from the Layout menu, and then choose Join (or click the Tbl Join button).

   Now there is one cell containing the text "YTD YTD".
3. Delete the text in the new cell C1, and key **Year to Date**.
4. Join cells A1 and A2.
5. Save the document.

Agent/Office	Year to Date		$ Change
	Q2 199-	Q2 199-	

Figure 22-6
Table cells after splitting and joining

Changing Line Style

WordPerfect offers many line-style options to enhance the appearance of a table. Change the line style by selecting the cells to be changed, opening the Table Lines dialog box, and choosing the location and type of line needed. You can specify the line-type for the left, right, top, bottom, inside, or outside of any selected section of the table.

To change the lines for the entire table:

The Tbl Lines button

1. Select the entire table by triple-clicking either the horizontal or the vertical selection arrow.
2. Choose Tables from the Layout menu, and then choose Lines (or click the Tbl Lines button).

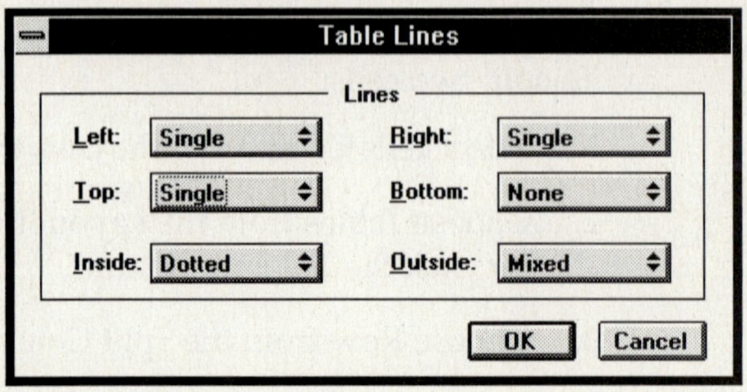

Figure 22-7
The Table Lines dialog box

3. Choose Single from the Outside pop-up list.
4. Choose Dotted from the Inside pop-up list and click OK.

5. Scroll to the top of the table, and click once to deselect the cells.

   The table has dotted grid lines and a single-line frame.

To change the lines in just one section of the table:

1. Drag the insertion point from cell A3 to cell E3.

   The first row below the heading is selected.

2. Choose Tables from the Layout menu, and then choose Lines (or click the Tbl Lines button).
3. Choose Single from the Top pop-up list.
4. Select cells A1 to E1.
5. Click the Tbl Lines button.
6. Choose None from the Inside pop-up list and click OK.
7. Deselect the cells.
8. Save the document.

Table Options

You opened the Table Options dialog box earlier in this lesson to add rows and columns to the table. The Table Options dialog box also allows you to change many other options that apply to the whole table. For instance, you can set the horizontal position of the table on the page and set the text margins inside the cells in the table.

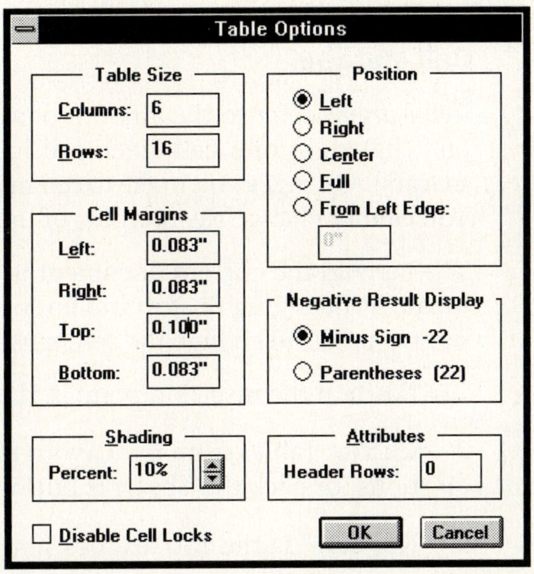

Figure 22-8
The Table Options dialog box

Positioning the Table

Note: According to *The Gregg Reference Manual*, the standard table position is centered horizontally on the page; however, there may be cases, such as in a newsletter layout, when the table must be aligned with the left or right margin.

The table on which you have been working is aligned with the left margin. Using the Table Options dialog box, you can choose to center it or to align it with the right margin. You also can key a specific measurement to indent it from the left edge of the paper.

The Full option in the Table Options dialog box will adjust the column widths, so that the table stretches from margin to margin. These column width changes are permanent, so choosing Center or Left after applying the Full option will not return the column widths to their original size. (Remember, save the table often, because there are many options that are not undone easily).

To change the table position:

1. Scroll to the top of the table, if necessary.
2. Position the insertion point inside the table.
3. Choose Tables from the Layout menu, and then choose Options (or click the Tbl Opts button).

   The Table Options dialog box appears.

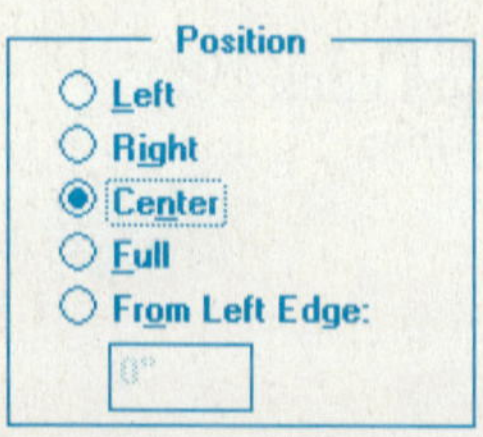

The Position options box

4. Choose Right in the Position options box and click OK.

   The table aligns with the right margin.

The Tbl Opts button

5. Click the Tbl Opts button.
6. Choose the Center option and click OK.

   The table is centered horizontally on the page.

Cell Margins

Cell margins
The amount of space between text in a cell and the edges of a cell. Each cell has top, bottom, left and right margins.

Cell margins refer to the amount of space between the text in a cell and the edges of a cell. Each cell has top, bottom, left, and right margins. Changes you make to cell margins apply to the entire table. You cannot change the margins of individual cells.

The table in the current document is long and contains a soft page break. By changing the top and bottom cell margins, more rows will fit on a page. To change the cell margins:

1. Position the insertion point in the table, if necessary.
2. Choose Tables from the Layout menu, and then choose Options (or click the Tbl Opts button).
3. Key **0.07"** in the Top text box in the Margins options box.
4. Key **0.05"** in the Bottom text box and click OK.

Note: If you key different measurements for the left and right cell margins, centered text will appear to be off-center. This is because the text is centered between the margins, not between the cell edges.

The top and bottom cell margins are slightly narrower now. As a result, the rows are narrower, and more rows fit on the page.

Formatting Text in a Table

There are two ways to format text in a table. First, you can select only the text and apply the standard formatting options used for document text. Second, you can select the cells containing the text and use table-formatting options. Because you normally format cells as a group, the table-formatting options are very useful.

Note: If you want to change the font for some of the text in your table, such as the headings, you must be sure to select the text to be changed, and not the cells themselves (the table structure). The Font dialog box is not available when the table structure is selected.

Using table-formatting commands, you can format columns or individual cells. For example, you can format a column to contain decimal-aligned text. Since decimal alignment is not appropriate for the column heading, you can use the cell-formatting options to center the text in the cell containing the heading. Column formatting applies to the entire column, but cell formatting always overrides column formatting.

Column Alignment

Like regular document text, text in table columns can be aligned along the left, right, center, or both left and right (full) cell margins. Text also can be aligned on decimals. The exact position of the text within the cells will depend on the cell margins that have been set.

To change the alignment of text in columns:

1. Select cells C3, D3, and E3.

2. Choose Tables from the Layout menu, and then choose Column (or click the Tbl Col button).

3. Choose Right from the Justification pop-up list and click OK.

   Columns C, D, and E are right-aligned. Notice that the headings also are right-aligned.

4. Save the document.

Formatting Text in Cells

When you changed the text alignment in columns, you saw the column headings align with the rest of the column. In many cases, you may want headings to be aligned differently (for example, centered over multiple columns). The Format Cell dialog box contains options for changing the alignment and appearance of text in selected cells, so you can format cells individually.

The Alignment pop-up list in the Format Cell dialog box controls the vertical position of text within a cell. According to *The Gregg Reference Manual*, the standard vertical alignment is one blank line above the text and none below. You can approximate this standard by setting the top cell margin twice as large as the bottom cell margin. When you choose a vertical-alignment option, you will not see the results on the screen, unless you choose Print Preview.

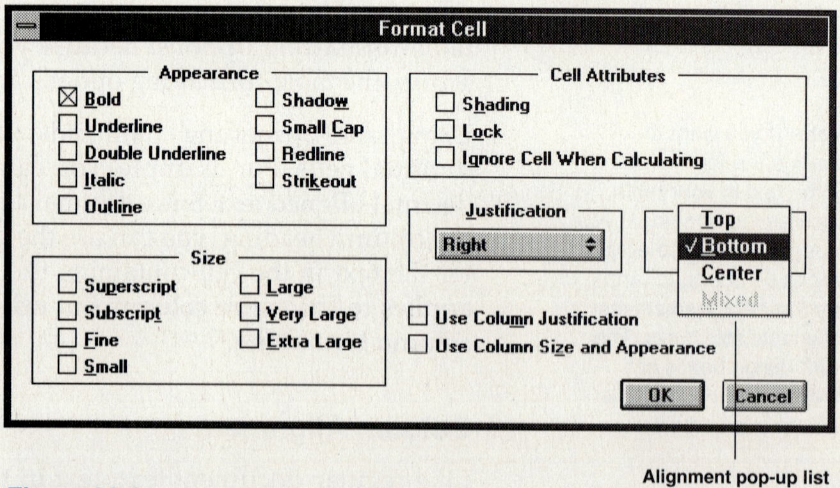

Figure 22-9
The Format Cell dialog box with the Alignment pop-up list displayed

To change the alignment and appearance of the headings:

1. Drag-select the heading area from cell A1 to cell E1.
2. Choose Tables from the Layout menu, and then choose Cell (or click the Tbl Cell button).
3. Choose Center from the Justification pop-up list.

   Notice that selecting a Justification option causes the Use Column Justification check box to become unchecked.
4. Choose Bold.
5. Choose Center from the Alignment pop-up list and click OK.

   The headings appear centered and bold. The headings do not appear to be centered vertically, however.
6. Select cell A6, and click the Tbl Cell button.
7. Choose Right from the Justification pop-up list, and choose Bold from the Appearance options box. Click OK.
8. Apply the bold attribute and right justification to cells A10, A14, A17, and A18.

9. Choose Print Preview from the File menu to view the table.

   Now you can view the heading text centered vertically in the cells.

☐ Use Column Justification
☐ Use Column Size and Appearance

Check boxes in the Format Cell dialog box

When you apply cell formatting, it overrides column formatting. If you apply column formatting, and it does not seem to have an effect on some or all of the cells in a column, cell formatting may be in effect. To cancel cell formatting so that column formatting can take effect, check the Use Column Justification and the Use Column Size and Appearance check boxes in the Format Cell dialog box.

Formatting U.S. Currency in Tables

When creating tables that contain numbers representing U.S. currency, follow these formatting rules for the currency columns:

- Right-align or decimal-align the columns. (Specify extra decimal places if you want to add space to the right edge of the column.)
- For large numbers, display currency rounded to the nearest dollar. For very large numbers, round to the nearest thousand or million, and do not key the zeros. (Be sure to add a note at the top of the table telling the reader you did this.)
- Right-align the column headings. This is not a hard and fast rule, but columns containing currency (and other types of numbers) often look best when their headings are right-aligned.
- Place dollar signs in the first row and the total row only. Intermediate subtotals do not get a dollar sign. If there is no total row for the table, dollar signs appear only in the first row.
- Dollar signs should be aligned to the left of the largest number in the column, even when the number in the first row contains fewer digits. You can insert spaces between the dollar sign and the number to accomplish this.

For examples of currency formatting, refer to corporate annual statements and financial statements, which are available in many libraries.

Shading

Shading makes selected cells, rows, columns, or the entire table appear on a darker background than the rest of the document. Shaded rows, columns, or cells within a table can emphasize particular sections of the table and make the table easier to read.

The degree of shading is adjustable and is measured in percentages. Ten percent shading, the default shading, provides the lightest shaded background; 100 percent provides the darkest (solid black). You cannot mix the percentages of shading within a table.

To apply shading to the subtotal rows:

1. Click the Tbl Opts button.

   10% appears in the Shading Percent text box.

2. Using the up arrow to the right of the text box, change the percentage of shading to 20% and click OK.

3. Select row 6 by double-clicking the horizontal selection arrow.

4. Click the Tbl Cell button.

5. Check the Shading box under Cell Attributes and click OK.

6. Following steps 3 through 5, apply shading to rows 10, 14, and 17.

7. With the right mouse button, click the Button Bar to display the Button Bar Quick Menu.

8. Choose wp{wp}.wwb to redisplay the default Button Bar.

9. Spell-check the document.

10. Save the document.

11. Print the document.

12. Close the document and exit WordPerfect (unless you will be doing the following exercises immediately).

Table 22-1: Keyboard Shortcuts for Inserting Rows

Keyboard Shortcut	Action
Alt+Insert	Inserts a row at the insertion-point position (moves the insertion-point row down).
Alt+Shift+Insert	Inserts a row below the row that contains the insertion point (keeps the insertion-point row in its current position).
Alt+Delete	Deletes the row that contains the insertion point.

Key Terms

Cell margins

Table-column markers

Exercises

Exercise 22.1

1. Start WordPerfect, if necessary.
2. Open the file 22-1.wpw.
3. Display the Tables Button Bar:
   A. Choose Button Bar Setup from the View menu and then choose Select.
   B. Double-click tables.wwb in the Files list box.
4. Insert three rows above row 6:
   A. Position the insertion point in cell A6.
   B. Click the Tbl Insert button.
   C. Choose Rows, key **3** in the Rows text box, and click OK.
   D. Key the following text in the blank rows:

M. Washington	**Buckhead**	**499,000**	**760,900**
D. Feingold	**Marietta**	**200,000**	**250,000**
E. Hemmings	**Marietta**	**280,400**	**450,500**

5. Add a row to the bottom and a column to the right edge of the table:
   A. Click the Tbl Opts button.
   B. Key **5** in the Columns text box.
   C. Key **12** in the Rows text box and click OK.
   D. Key **Total** in cell A12 and **Year to Date** in cell E1.
6. Move column E to the column C position:
   A. Double-click the vertical selection arrow anywhere in column E.
   B. Choose Cut from the Edit menu.
   C. Choose Columns from the Table Cut/Copy dialog box and click OK.
   D. Position the insertion point anywhere in column C.
   E. Choose Paste from the Edit menu.
7. Join cells in the total row:

A. Select cells A12 and B12 using the horizontal selection arrow.

B. Click the Tbl Join button.

8. Split the sales headings in row 1 into two rows:

A. Select cells C1, D1, and E1.

B. Click the Tbl Split button.

C. Choose Row, key **2** in the Row text box, and click OK.

D. Use Cut and Paste (or Drag and Drop) to move the text "Year to Date" from cell C1 to cell C2.

9. Join cells C1, D1, and E1, and then delete the extra word "Sales". Use the Reveal Codes space to delete any extra spaces or hard tab codes that may be in cell C1.

10. Right-justify columns C, D, and E:

A. Select cells C3, D3, and E3.

B. Click the Tbl Col button.

C. Choose Right from the Justification pop-up list and click OK.

11. Make the text in the heading area bold and centered horizontally and vertically:

A. Select rows 1 and 2.

B. Click the Tbl Cell button.

C. Choose Center from the Justification pop-up list.

D. Choose Center from the Alignment pop-up list.

E. Choose Bold from the Appearance option box and click OK.

12. Make the word "Total" in cell A12 bold and right-justified using the Tbl Cell button.

13. Change all the table grid lines to Single:

A. Select the entire table.

B. Click the Tbl Lines button.

C. Choose Single from the Inside pop-up list, and choose Single from the Outside pop-up list.

D. Click OK.

14. Change the font in the table:

A. Position the insertion point to the left of "Agent" in cell A1.

B. Double-click the Font button on the Ruler.

C. Choose 12-point CG Times and click OK.

15. Use Print Preview to check the formatting. (Remember, you can press **Shift+F5** to go to the preview screen and **Ctrl+F4** to get back to the document screen).

16. Spell-check the document.

17. Save the document as *[your three-letter identifier]*22-1.wpw.

18. Print the document.

19. Change the Button Bar to the WordPerfect default (wp{wp}.wwb):

    A. Using the right mouse button, click the Button Bar.

    B. Choose wp{wp}.wwb from the Button Bar Quick Menu.

20. Exit WordPerfect (unless you will be doing the following exercises immediately).

Exercise 22.2

1. Start WordPerfect, if necessary.
2. Open the file 22-2.wpw.
3. Change the Button Bar to the Tables Button Bar (table.wwb).
4. Insert a column between column A and column B.
5. Key "**Location**" in cell B1, and then key the following information in the column:

   Cell B2: **Buckhead Community College**
   Cell B3: **Central High School**
   Cell B4: **Midtown Community Center**
   Cell B5: **Downtown Continuing Education Center**

6. Adjust the widths of all the columns:

   A. Display the Ruler, if necessary.

   B. Drag the table-column marker located at 3⅛ inches to the 3-inch mark.

   C. Drag the other table-column markers to 5 inches and 6½ inches. Drag the right margin marker to 8¼ inches.

7. Save the document as *[your three-letter identifier]*22-2.wpw.

8. Make a copy of row 2:

   A. Select row 2.

   B. Choose Copy from the Edit menu.

   C. Choose Rows and click OK.

   D. Move the insertion point to row 3.

   E. Choose Paste from the Edit menu.

   F. Select cell B3, and key **Marietta Voc-Tech High School**.

   G. Change "Mon. & Wed." to **Tues. & Thurs.** in cell C3.

9. Add a title to the table:

   A. Insert a row above row 1.

   B. Join all the cells in the new row 1.

   C. With the insertion point in cell A1, key **Course Schedule Summary - Fall 199-**.

10. Horizontally center the table, and change the cell margins:

    A. Position the insertion point inside the table, if necessary.

    B. Click the Tbl Opts button.

    C. Key **0.10"** in the Top, Left, and Right text boxes, and **0.05"** in the Bottom text box.

    D. Choose Center from the Position options box and click OK.

11. Change the font in row 2 to 12-point Univers:

    A. Position the insertion point to the left of "Course" in cell A1.

    B. Press **F8**, the Select key.

    C. While pressing the **Shift** key, position the I-beam to the right of "Time", and click the left mouse button.

    D. Choose 12-point Univers from the Font dialog box.

12. Select the text in cell A1, and change the font to 14-point Univers.

13. Using the Tbl Cell button, make rows 1 and 2 bold and shaded.

14. Horizontally center the text in cell A1.

15. Change the table lines, so that there is a single line framing the table and no lines inside.

16. Put a thick line under the heading area:

    A. Select row 2.

    B. Click the Tbl Lines button.

    C. Choose Thick from the Bottom pop-up list and click OK.

17. Center the two-line heading above the table that begins "Atlanta Board", make it bold, and change the font size to 14 points.

18. Spell-check the document.

19. Save the document. (You saved it previously as *[your three-letter identifier]*22-2.wpw.)

20. Print the document.

21. Change the Button Bar to the WordPerfect default (wp{wp}.wwb).

22. Close the document and exit WordPerfect (unless you will be doing the following exercises immediately).

Exercise 22.3

1. Start WordPerfect, if necessary.

2. Open the file 22-3.wpw.

3. Change the document initial font to 12-point CG Times.

4. Insert the following text above the table, allowing two blank lines between the text and the table:

    MEMO TO: **Bud Porter**
    FROM: **Ann Delbridge**
    DATE: **June 9, 199-**
    SUBJECT: **New Properties**

    The following properties have been listed with the Buckhead office since May 1:

5. Format the document as a standard memo.

6. Key the following information at the bottom of the table:

80886	**Hillbrooke**	**G. Crane**	**179,900**
88788	**Dunwoody**	**M. Washington**	**350,000**
97558	**Alpharetta**	**A. Delbridge**	**565,000**

7. Save the document as *[your three-letter identifier]*22-3.wpw.
8. Delete row 3, which contains information for inventory number 34490.
9. Insert a new column between columns A and B. Key **Binder** in cell B1.
10. Insert a check mark in the "Binder" column for the following inventory numbers: 51234, 67890, and 76121. Use the WordPerfect character 5,23 for the check mark.
11. Center columns A and B.
12. Right-justify column E, and then left-align cell E1.
13. Use the Tbl Col button to make column B bold.
14. Change the font in row 1 to 11-point bold Univers.
15. Insert a new row at the top of the table, join the cells, and key **New Listings: May 199-**. Center the text in the cell, if necessary.
16. Format the text in the new line as bold 14-point Univers.
17. Change the column widths, so that the table-column markers on the Ruler are at the following positions: 1⅞, 2⅝, 4, and 5¼ inches. Set the right margin marker at 6¼ inches.
18. Center the table horizontally.
19. Select the entire table. Change the inside lines to None and the outside lines to Single.
20. Add a single line to the bottom of row 2.
21. Spell-check the document
22. Save the document. (You saved it previously as *[your three-letter identifier]*22-3.wpw.)
23. Print the document.
24. Change the Button Bar to the WordPerfect default, if necessary.
25. Close the document and exit WordPerfect (unless you will be doing the following exercises immediately).

Exercise 22.4

1. Start WordPerfect, if necessary.
2. Set the document initial font to 12-point CG Times.
3. Key Figure 22-10, which appears at the end of this exercise. Include the editing and formatting changes indicated.
4. Format the document as a standard memo using the following information:

MEMO TO:	**Help the Homeless Volunteers**
FROM:	**Bud Porter, Project Coordinator**
DATE:	**June 22, 199-**
SUBJECT:	**Help the Homeless Update**

5. Decimal-align column B, and set the decimal places to 2 digits.
6. Center column C.
7. Center all the cells in row 1, and make them bold. Format the text as 11-point Univers.
8. Insert a row at the top of the table, join all the cells in the first row, and key **Help the Homeless Sponsors** in cell A1.
9. Make cell A1 centered and bold, if necessary.
10. Format the text in rows 1 and 2 as 14-point Univers.
11. Set the table-column markers and the right margin marker at the following positions: 3½, 4½, and 5½ inches.
12. Center the table horizontally on the page.
13. Set all table lines to Single.
14. Remove the inside lines for rows 1 and 2, and set a thick top line for row 3.
15. Spell-check the document.
16. Save the document as *[your three-letter identifier]*22-4.wpw.
17. Print the document.
18. Change the Button Bar to the WordPerfect default, if necessary.
19. Close the document and exit WordPerfect (unless you will be doing the following exercise immediately).

Figure 22-10

The following is the list of the sponsors of the Help the Homeless fund. Sponsors are all contributors who donated $1,000 or more.

Insert gridlines on table

Name	Donation	Date
Anthony Brown, M.D. 1 Somerset Rd. Stone Mountain, GA 30331	$2,000	3/22/199-
Mr. & Mrs. Martin Jones 49 Worth St. Atlanta, GA 30302	1,000	2/25/199-
Mr. & Mrs. David Nelson 94-26 85th St. Elmhurst, NY 11422	1,000	11/15/199-
Karen D. Reynolds, Esq. 114-14 209th Street Cambria Heights, NY 11411	1,500	12/21/199-

Exercise 22.5

1. Start WordPerfect, if necessary.
2. Open a new file, and set the document initial font to 12-point Univers.
3. Insert two blank rows, and then create a 5-column by 12-row table.
4. Key the following information in the table:

Agent	Office	Extension	Shift	YTD Sales
W. Reston	Buckhead	X4454	First	$1,870,000
M. Washington	Buckhead	X4333	First	1,259,900
A. Delbridge	Buckhead	X4562	Second	998,900
G. Crane	Buckhead	X4245	First	812,000

P. Silvers	**Marietta**	**X4187**	**Second**	**507,900**
M. Rigdon	**Marietta**	**X4299**	**Second**	**2,400,000**
R. Palmer	**Marietta**	**X4477**	**Second**	**1,700,900**
E. Hemmings	**Marietta**	**X4118**	**First**	**730,900**
D. Crandon	**Downtown**	**X4343**	**First**	**3,950,000**
E. Norton	**Downtown**	**X4211**	**Second**	**1,470,000**
A. Beasley	**Downtown**	**X4549**	**First**	**1,950,000**

5. Drag the table-column markers and the right margin marker to the following positions on the Ruler: 2⅜, 3⅜, 4⅝, 5⅜, and 6⅜ inches.

6. Center the table horizontally.

7. Set the font for the text in row 1 to 11-point bold Univers.

8. Insert a new row at the top of the table, join the cells, and key **Office list - June, 199-**.

9. Center the text in the new cell A1, and format it as 14-point bold Univers.

10. Make column C centered and column E decimal-aligned with one decimal place.

11. Remove all the lines inside the table, make the outside lines Single, and then make the bottom line in row 2 Single.

12. Apply 10% shading to every other row, starting with row 4.

13. Center the page vertically.

14. Spell-check the document.

15. Save the document as *[your three-letter identifier]*22-5.wpw.

16. Print the document.

17. Change the Button Bar to the WordPerfect default.

18. Close the document and exit WordPerfect.

Lesson 23

Advanced Table Formatting and Mathematics

Objectives

- Perform advanced table formatting.
- Perform mathematical calculations.
- Convert tabbed columns into tables.

Many tables have special formatting requirements that go beyond the basic text and table-structure formatting covered in Lessons 21 and 22. To accommodate these requirements, you will use WordPerfect's advanced table-formatting features. Many tables also contain numerical values. To add, subtract, multiply, or divide them automatically, you can create mathematical formulas in WordPerfect. An additional time-saving feature that is particularly helpful in formatting an existing document is the ability to convert existing tabbed columns into a table structure.

Advanced Table Formatting

The advanced table-formatting features provide methods for modifying table structures to accommodate special table elements and formats. These features include adjusting the row height and the number of lines of text per row, repeating column headings on two or more pages, and making the contents of specific cells unavailable for editing by locking the cells.

Changing Lines Per Row and Row Height

When set to the default row-height and lines-per-row settings, rows automatically expand vertically to accommodate all the text keyed or inserted into them. For each new line of text you key into any cell in a row, the row grows one line taller to allow the new line of text to appear. In some cases, you may want to limit the height of the rows in a table. For example, to fill a specific amount of vertical space, you can calculate a specific row height by dividing the number of rows in the table by the amount of vertical space. Then you can set the height for each row, so that the table fills the space exactly.

Alternatively, you can specify the number of lines of text to appear in a row (either one line or multiple lines). In this case, only the specified number of lines appears, regardless of how many lines are contained in the cells. This feature is useful for creating abbreviated tables when vertical space is limited. For instance, you can create a table with a customer name on the first line in each row, followed by a phone extension on one additional line. To create an abbreviated table containing just the names, you can set the number of lines per row to one line. The extension line disappears from the table, but it

Note: When a table is formatted with one line per row before text is entered, only one line of text can be keyed into each row. Additional text will not be allowed or saved.

is not deleted from the document. The full text of the table is saved and can be displayed again by resetting the number of lines per row.

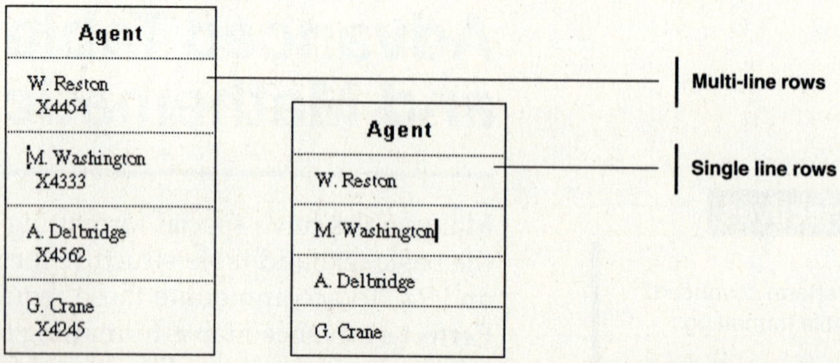

Figure 23-1
Complete rows and abbreviated rows created from the same text

To set the number of lines per row and the row height:

1. Start WordPerfect, if necessary.
2. Display the Tables Button Bar.

   Remember, to display the Tables Button Bar, click the Button Bar with the right mouse button, and then choose tables.wwb.
3. Open the file 23-0.wpw.
4. Select the entire table.
5. Choose Tables from the Layout menu, and choose Row from the Tables cascading menu (or click the Tbl Row button on the Button Bar).

The Tbl Row button

The Format Row dialog box appears.

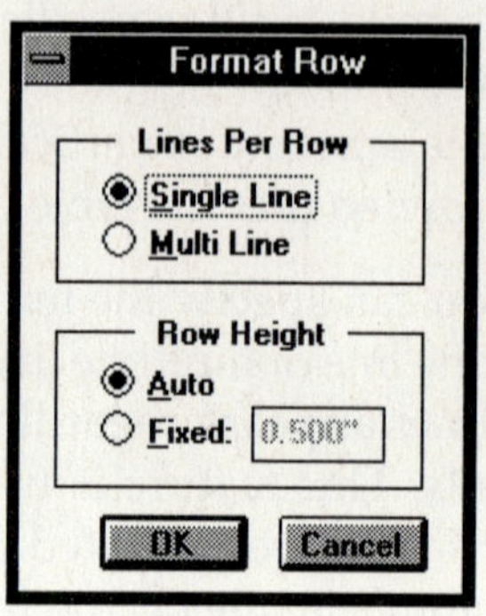

Figure 23-2
The Format Row dialog box

6. Choose Single Line and click OK.

   The second line of text (which contains the telephone extension) disappears from the cells in column A. Each row now has one line of text.

7. With the table still selected, click the Tbl Row button.

8. Choose Multi Line and click OK.

   The second line of text reappears.

9. With the table still selected, click the Tbl Row button again.

10. Choose Fixed, key **.25** in the Fixed text box, and click OK.

    The rows are all single lines again. The fixed row height is another way to limit the number of lines in a row.

11. Repeat steps 9 and 10, but set the fixed row height to .5.

12. Deselect the table cells.

13. Save the document as *[your three-letter identifier]*23-0.wpw.

Defining Header Rows

Often, columns in a table have headings that describe the contents of the column. For instance, in document 23-0.wpw, the column heading "Office" alerts the reader that the items in that column are the names of the agents' offices. When one table spans two or more pages, the column headings should appear at the top of each page of the table. The WordPerfect Header Rows option automatically places the column headings from the first page of a table onto each subsequent page that contains a continuation of the table. A row of column headings is called a *header row* when it has been defined to appear at the top of each page in a multiple-page table.

Header row
A row of column headings that is defined to appear at the top of each page in a multiple-page table.

A row that has been defined as a header row is identified by an asterisk in the status bar next to the cell address. A table may have more than one row defined as a header row. The header row appears only at the beginning of the table in a document window. To view the header row on subsequent pages, you can use Print Preview.

To define a header row:

1. Position the insertion point in the table, if necessary.

2. Click the Tbl Opt button to open the Table Options dialog box.

   The Header Rows text box identifies the number of rows (counting from the first row in the table) that are defined as header rows. The default is zero.

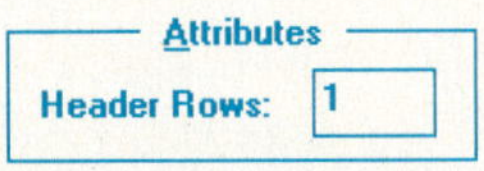

The Header Rows text box

3. Key **1** in the Header Rows text box and click OK.

4. Position the insertion point in row 1.

   Notice the asterisk immediately to the right of the cell address in the status bar.

5. Position the insertion point to the left of "D. Crandon" in cell A12.

6. Press **Ctrl+Enter** to insert a hard page break.

7. Choose Print Preview from the File menu.

8. Click the Next Page button to go to page 2, if necessary.

9. Click the 100% button, and then scroll to the top of the page, if necessary.

   Notice the header row at the top of the page.

10. Close the Print Preview window.

Setting, Removing, and Disabling Cell Locks

Note: Cell locks are useful for protecting formulas in a table.

The cell-lock function protects individual cells from inadvertent changes. When a cell is locked, you cannot key or paste anything into it. If information is already in the cell, you cannot delete or change it. If you want to change information in a locked cell, you must either remove the cell lock from the cell or temporarily disable the cell lock. When the cell lock is removed, the cell-lock function is no longer in use for that cell. When the cell lock is disabled, the cell-lock function is still in use, but it is turned off temporarily.

To set cell locks:

1. Select the cells C2 through E2.

2. Click the Tbl Cell button.

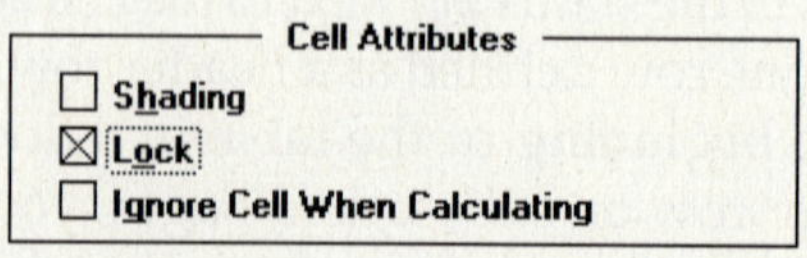

Figure 23-3
The Lock option in the Format Cell dialog box

3. Check the Lock check box in the Cell Attributes options box and click OK.

   The cells are locked.

4. Position the insertion point in cell B2, to the right of "Buckhead".

5. Press the **Right Arrow** key once.

   The insertion point jumps over the locked cells, and appears in cell A3.

6. Try to position the insertion point on the number in cell D2.

   The insertion point jumps to cell B2. You cannot position the insertion point in a locked cell.

To disable cell locks:

1. Click the Tbl Opts button.

The Disable Cell Locks option

2. Check the Disable Cell Locks check box in the lower left of the Table Options dialog box.

3. Click OK.

4. Position the insertion point in cell E2 and key **870,000**.

   With the cell lock disabled, you can edit a locked cell.

5. Click the Tbl Cell button.

   Notice that the cell lock function is still selected.

6. Click Cancel.

7. To reinstate cell locks, click the Tbl Opts button, and then click the Disable Cell Locks check box to uncheck it.

8. Click OK.

9. Try to delete the number you keyed in cell E2.

   The cell is locked again and cannot be edited.

To remove cell locks:

1. Using the horizontal selection arrow, select cells B2 through E2.

2. Click the Tbl Cell button.

3. Click the Lock check box to uncheck it and click OK.

4. Delete the number in cell E2.

   Because the cell is no longer locked, you can delete the number now.

Performing Math in a Table

Formula
A formula is a combination of cell addresses, mathematical operators (+, -, *, or /), and/or numbers, used to perform simple calculations in tables.

Simple calculations are easy to perform in WordPerfect tables using math formulas. A *formula* is made up of cell addresses, mathematical operators, and/or numbers. The mathematical operators are "+" for addition, "-" for subtraction, "*" for multiplication, and "/" for division. For example, the formula for adding the numbers in cell C3 and D3 is C3+D3. If you want to divide the number in cell D4 by 2, the formula is D4/2.

There are three symbols for totaling columns. They are "+" to calculate a subtotal, "=" to calculate a total (the sum of the results of the subtotals), and "*" to calculate a grand total (the sum of the totals).

Creating Formulas

The simplest formulas to create consist of a mathematical operator alone. These formulas automatically give a subtotal (+), a total (=), or a grand total (*) when keyed in the Tables Formula dialog box.

Directional arrows

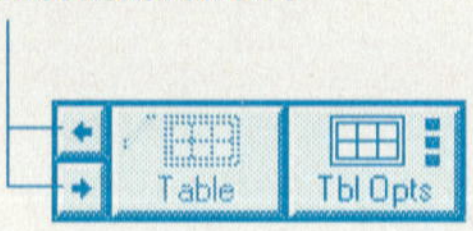

The Button Bar directional arrows

The Tbl Form button

The Tables Formula dialog box can be accessed both from the Tables cascading menu and the Tbl Form button on the Tables Button Bar. Because the Tbl Form button is at the extreme right of the Button Bar, it is not normally in view. To bring it into view, scroll to the right using the Button Bar directional arrows, which are located on the left side of the Button Bar.

To create a subtotal formula:

1. Position the insertion point in cell C6.
2. Choose Tables from the Layout menu and then choose Formula, or click the Tbl Form button on the far right end of the Button Bar.

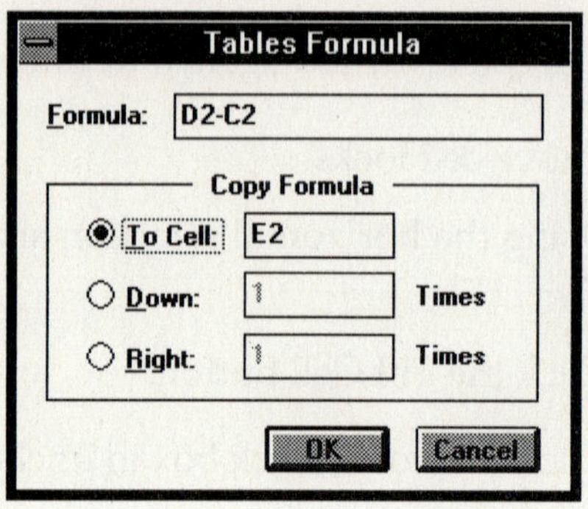

Figure 23-4
The Tables Formula dialog box

3. Key + in the Formula text box.

4. Click OK.

   The subtotal result appears in cell C6.

5. Use the above steps to enter subtotal formulas in cells C11, C15, and C18.

   The subtotal formula adds all the numbers in a column, starting with the first number following a previous subtotal formula.

To create a total formula:

1. Position the insertion point in cell C19.

2. Click the Tbl Form button.

3. Key = in the formula text box and click OK.

   The total of column C appears in cell C19. The total formula adds all the cells in the column that contain subtotal formulas, starting with the first subtotal formula after a previous total formula, if it exists.

4. Position the insertion point to the left of the total result in cell C19.

5. Key **$**, and then press the **Spacebar**.

   Characters can be inserted in formula cells without affecting the results.

Using Cell Addresses in a Formula

A second way to construct formulas is to specify the cell addresses on which to perform a mathematical operation and which operation to perform.

To find the difference between the sales figures for the first and second quarters:

1. Position the insertion point in cell E2.

2. Click the Tbl Form button.

3. Key **D2-C2** in the Formula text box.

   This will subtract the number in cell C2 from the number in cell D2.

4. Click OK.

   The difference between the two sales figures appears in cell E2.

Copying Formulas

You can copy a formula to adjacent cells that are to the right of or below a cell containing a formula. The Right and Down options in the Tables Format dialog box determine the direction for copying and the number of times to copy a formula.

Copy the formula in cell E2 to every cell in column E:

1. Position the insertion point in cell E2, if necessary.

2. Click the Tbl Form button.

3. Choose Down in the Copy Formula options box.

4. Key **17** in the Down text box.

5. Click OK.

   The formula is copied, and the cells in column E are filled with the results.

6. Save the document. (It was saved previously as *[your three-letter identifier]*23-0.wpw.)

If you want to copy formulas to non-adjacent cells, use the Copy and Paste commands. To Copy and Paste formulas:

1. Select cell C6.

   Be sure to select the cell and not just the text.

2. Choose Copy from the Edit menu.

   The Table Cut/Copy dialog box opens.

3. Choose Selection and click OK.

4. Position the insertion point in cell D6.

5. Choose Paste from the Edit menu.

   The formula is copied, but the result is incorrect. This will be corrected in the next procedure.

6. Position the insertion point in cell D11, choose Paste again, and copy the formula to cells D15 and D18.

7. Copy the total formula from cell C19 to cell D19.

8. Insert a dollar sign followed by a space character to the left of the formula result in cell E19.

Calculating Formulas

When you copy formulas using Copy and Paste or edit the numerical values in a table, the cells containing formulas do not automatically change to reflect the editing changes. You must choose Tables from the Layout Menu, and then choose Calculate (or click the Tbl Calc button on the far right end of the Button Bar) to update calculations.

The Tbl Calc button

To update calculations:

1. Position the insertion point in the table, if necessary.

2. Choose Tables from the Layout menu, and then choose Calculate (or click the Tbl Calc button).

   The calculations change to reflect any changes made to cells in the table.

3. Save the document.

Deleting Formulas

When you need to delete a formula, you simply select the cell containing the formula (not just the text) and press the **Delete** key. If you select the text in the cell and not the cell structure, the formula will appear to be deleted, but, the next time you calculate the table, the deleted number will reappear.

To delete a formula:

1. Select cell E2.

   Select the cell and not just the number in it.

2. Press the **Delete** key.

3. To see that the formula is deleted, click the Tbl Forms button.

   The Formula text box is empty.

4. Click Cancel.

5. Copy the formula in cell E3 to cell E2 and recalculate the table.

Displaying Negative Results

The results of some calculations may be negative numbers. By default, these numbers are preceded by a minus sign. For example, cell E2 contains the negative result "-290,000". You can use the Table Options dialog box to change the way WordPerfect displays negative results. If you choose the Parentheses option, negative results will appear enclosed in parentheses, without a minus sign.

To change the negative results display to parentheses:

1. Position the insertion point in the table, if necessary.

2. Click the Tbl Opts button.

The Negative Result Display options box

3. Choose Parentheses from the Negative Result Display options box and click OK.

   The results do not reflect the change until you recalculate the table.

4. Click the Tbl Calc button.

   The negative results now are enclosed in parentheses.

5. Insert a dollar sign followed by a space character to the left of the formula result in cell E2.

Ignoring Cells When Calculating

There may be times when you want to disallow certain cells from a calculation that normally would include them. For example, in the table in document 23-0.wpw, WordPerfect has included the numbers in the column headings for columns C and D in the subtotal calculation. You can format these cells so that they are ignored when the calculation is performed.

To format cells C1 and D1 so that they are not included in the table calculations:

1. Select cells C1 and D1.

2. Click the Tbl Cell button.

3. Check the Ignore Cell When Calculating check box in the Cell Attributes options box and click OK.

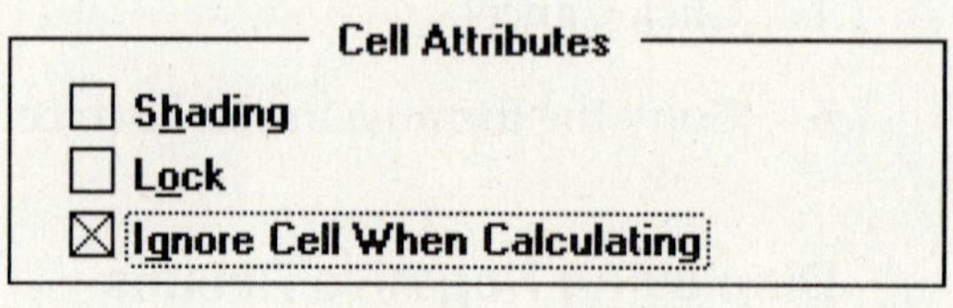

Figure 23-5
The Ignore Cell When Calculating option in the Cell Attributes options box

4. Click the Tbl Calc button.

   The values in cells C6 and D6 change.

Aligning Dollar Signs in Columns of Numbers

Aligning dollar signs in a table (and in other types of columns) can present problems when you are working with proportionally spaced fonts. The usual way to align dollar signs is to insert enough space characters between the dollar sign and the leftmost digit so that the dollar sign aligns to the left of the largest number in the column.

When working with proportionally spaced fonts, it is almost impossible to get two dollar signs in the same column to line up exactly, because the width of a space character is not the same as the width of a digit, and the digits are not all the same width. The following tips can help when aligning dollar signs:

- You can measure the horizontal position of two dollar signs in a column by positioning the insertion point to the left of each dollar sign and checking the position on the status bar. When working with proportionally spaced fonts, you can make the positions close, but rarely precisely the same.
- If you are working with tabular columns, set a right-aligned tab to the left of the column of numbers. The new tab setting will place the dollar signs precisely.
- When working with tables, you can create a separate narrow column to the left of a number column just for dollar signs. Format the column to be right-aligned. If the table has lines, remove the vertical lines between the column with numbers and the column with the dollar signs.

Converting Columns into Tables

You can easily convert information from tabbed columns into a table structure. When you select tabbed columns and open the Convert Table dialog box, you can choose to convert from tabular (tabbed) or parallel columns to a table structure. Parallel columns are covered in Lesson 24. You may need to adjust the table-column widths after converting tabular or parallel columns.

To convert tabular columns to a table:

1. Scroll to the tabular columns on page 3 of the current document.
2. Position the insertion point at the beginning of the first line of the tabular columns.
3. Drag the insertion point down to the last row of the tabular columns to select all of the columns of text.
4. Choose Tables from the Layout menu, and then choose Create from the cascading menu (or click the Tables button).

   The Convert Table dialog box appears.

The Convert Table dialog box

5. Choose Tabular Column in the Convert Table dialog box and click OK.

   The tabular information appears in a table, but the column widths need to be adjusted.

To adjust the columns:

1. Choose Ruler from the View menu, if necessary.
2. Drag the table-column markers, so that each column is 1¼ inches wide.
3. Center the table horizontally, if necessary.
4. Change to the default Button Bar.

   Remember, to return to the default Button Bar, click the Button Bar with the right mouse button and choose wp{wp}.wwb.

5. Spell-check the document.
6. Save the document. (It has been saved previously as *[your three-letter identifier]*23-0.wpw.)
7. Print the document.
8. Close the document and exit WordPerfect (unless you will be doing the following exercises immediately).

Key Terms

Formula
Header row

Exercises

Exercise 23.1

1. Start WordPerfect, if necessary.
2. Open the file 23-1.wpw.
3. Display the Tables Button Bar.
4. Define row 1 of the table as a header row:
   A. Position the insertion point in the table.
   B. Open the Table Options dialog box.
   C. Key **1** in the Header Rows text box and click OK.

5. View the header row at the top of page 2:
   A. Open the Print Preview window.
   B. Go to page 2, and scroll to the top of the page, if necessary.
   C. Change to 100% size, if necessary.
   D. Close the Print Preview window.
6. Format the table, so that only one line is displayed in each row, and so that each row has a fixed height of 0.4 inches:
   A. Select the entire table.
   B. Choose Tables from the Layout menu, and choose Row from the cascading menu (or click the Tbl Row button).
   C. Choose Single Line from the Lines Per Row options box.
   D. Choose Fixed from the Row Height options box, and key **0.4"** in the Row Height text box.
7. Set the height of row 1 to 0.60 inches.
8. Lock the cells in row 1:
   A. Select the cells A1 through D1.
   B. Choose Tables from the Layout menu, and choose Cell from the cascading menu (or click the Tbl Cell button).
   C. Check the Lock check box in the Attributes options box and click OK.
9. Change the heading text for column A to "Number":
   A. Attempt to position the insertion point in cell A1.
   B. Use the horizontal selection arrow to select cell A1.
   C. Click the Tbl Opts button.
   D. Check the Disable Cell Locks check box and click OK.
   E. Select cell A1, if necessary, and key **Number**.
10. Reset the cell locks:
    A. Position the insertion point in the table, if necessary.
    B. Open the Table Options dialog box.
    C. Click the Disable Cell Locks check box to uncheck it and click OK.
11. Using the Tbl Cell button, set the vertical alignment for the cells in row 1 to Bottom, and set the vertical alignment for all other cells in the table to Center.

    Remember, open the Print Preview window to see the results of cell-alignment changes.

12. Convert the tabular columns at the end of the document to a table:
    A. Move to the end of the document, and select the tabular columns, including the title.
    B. Click the Table button on the far left end of the Button Bar.
    C. Choose Tabular Column, if necessary, and click OK.
13. Format the new table:
    A. Display the Ruler, if necessary.
    B. Make each column 1.5 inches wide, and center the table horizontally, if necessary.
    C. Delete the empty row below the table title. If necessary, delete the empty row above the title.
    D. Make the text in the first two rows bold and centered.
    E. Make all the table lines single lines, and then remove the inside lines from the first two rows (which are the title and heading rows.)
14. Spell-check the document
15. Save the document as *[your three-letter identifier]*23-1.wpw.
16. Print the document.
17. Change the Button Bar to the WordPerfect default (wp{wp}.wwb).
18. Close the document and exit WordPerfect (unless you will be doing the following exercises immediately).

Exercise 23.2

1. Start WordPerfect, if necessary.
2. Open the file 23-2.wpw.
3. Change the Button Bar to the Tables Button Bar.
4. Create a subtotal formula:
    A. Position the insertion point in cell C8.
    B. Click the Tbl Form button at the far right end of the Button Bar.
    C. Key + in the Formula text box and click OK.
5. Copy the subtotal formula to cell D8:
    A. Position the insertion point in cell C8, if necessary.
    B. Click the Tbl Form button.

   C. Choose Right, and key **1** in the Right text box.
   D. Click OK.
6. Insert a copy of the subtotal row above the total row:
   A. Select the subtotal row (row 8).
   B. Choose Copy from the Edit menu (or press **Ctrl+Insert**).
   C. Choose Row(s) and click OK.
   D. Position the insertion point in the total row (row 14).
   E. Choose Paste from the Edit menu (or press **Shift+Insert**).
   F. Click the Tbl Calc button to update the formula results.
7. Create a formula to add the first- and second-quarter sales:
   A. Position the insertion point in cell E3.
   B. Click Tbl Form at the far right end of the Button Bar.
   C. Key **C3+D3** in the Formula text box and click OK.
8. Copy the formula to all the cells in column E:
   A. Position the insertion point in cell E3, if necessary.
   B. Click the Tbl Form button.
   C. Choose Down, and key **12** in the Down text box.
   D. Click OK.
   E. Insert a dollar sign followed by two space characters to the left of the number in cell E3.
9. Create total formulas in cells C15 and D15:
   A. Position the insertion point in cell C14.
   B. Open the Tables Formula dialog box.
   C. Key = in the formula text box and click OK.
   D. Copy the formula into cell D14.
   E. Click the Tbl Calc button to update the calculations.
   F. Insert dollar signs followed by one space character to the left of each number in the total row.
   G. If necessary, adjust the position of the dollar signs in the first row by adding spaces so that they align with the dollar signs in the total row.
10. Format cells C2 and D2 so that they cannot be included in any calculations:
   A. Select cells C2 and D2.
   B. Click the Tbl Cell button.
   C. Check the Ignore Cell When Calculating check box and click OK.
   D. Update the calculations.

11. Spell-check the document.
12. Save the document as *[your three letter-identifier]*23-2a.wpw.
13. Print the document. Do not close the document.
14. Delete the text **"Year to Date"** in cell E2, and key **$ Change**.
15. Change column E so that it displays the difference between columns D and C:
    A. Position the insertion point in cell E3.
    B. Click the Tbl Form button.
    C. Delete the formula in the Formula text box and key **D3-C3**. Click OK.
    D. Click the Tbl Form button again.
    E. Choose Down, and key **12** in the Down text box. Click OK.
16. Change the display of negative results to parentheses:
    A. Position the insertion point in the table, if necessary.
    B. Open the Table Options dialog box.
    C. Choose Parentheses and click OK.
17. Recalculate the formulas in the table.
18. Spell-check the document.
19. Save the document as *[your three-letter identifier]*23-2b.wpw.
20. Print the document.
21. Change the Button Bar to the WordPerfect default.
22. Close the document and exit WordPerfect (unless you will be doing the following exercises immediately).

Exercise 23.3

1. Start WordPerfect, if necessary.
2. Open the file 23-3.wpw.
3. Change the Button Bar to the Tables Button Bar.
4. Create a four-column by nine-row table three lines below the memo text.
5. Key the following information in the table:

Number	Location	Agent	Price
23145	N. Fulton	G. Crane	$228,300
34490	Parsons Station	G. Crane	138,900
51234	Roswell	A. Delbridge	647,800
56790	Roswell	G. Crane	288,900

67890	**Martins Landing**	**M. Washington**	**147,200**
80886	**Hillbrooke**	**G. Crane**	**172,500**
88788	**Dunwoody**	**M. Washington**	**345,100**
97558	**Alpharetta**	**A. Delbridge**	**533,400**

6. Add a column to the right edge of the table and a row to the bottom.
7. Position the insertion point in cell E1 and key **Comm.**
8. Create a formula to calculate a 6% commission in cell E2, and copy it down to the bottom of column E. (Multiply the price by 0.06. Remember, the asterisk (*) is the multiplication operator.)
9. Format column A to be center-justified and columns D and E to be right-aligned with zero decimal places. Recalculate the table.
10. Join cells A10, B10, and C10.
11. Key **Total** in cell A10, and format the cell to be right-aligned and bold.
12. Format the text in cell A10 as 12-point Univers.
13. Insert a total formula in cell D10 and E10.
14. Change the widths of the columns as follows:

Column A:	1¼ inches
Column B:	1½ inches
Column C:	1½ inches
Column D:	1¼ inches
Column E:	1 inch

15. Insert dollar signs in cells C2, D2, C10, and E10. Use space characters to align the dollar signs appropriately.
16. Change the font for the text in the first row to 12-point Univers.
17. Format the cells in row 1 to be center-justified, bottom-aligned, and bold.
18. Change the height of row 1 to .5 inches.
19. Remove the inside lines from row 1.
20. Make the top lines of the cells in row 2 and row 10 double.
21. Spell-check the document.
22. Save the document as *[your three-letter identifier]*23-3.wpw.
23. Print the document.
24. Change the Button Bar to the WordPerfect default.
25. Close the document and exit WordPerfect (unless you will be doing the following exercises immediately).

Exercise 23.4

1. Start WordPerfect, if necessary.
2. Change the Button Bar to the Tables Button Bar.
3. Open a new file, change the document font to 12-point CG Times, and format the document as a standard block-type business letter. Use the current date.
4. Address the letter to:

   Mr. and Mrs. Michael A. Cresskill
   2190 Pineridge Circle
   Dunwoody, GA 30338

   Salutation: **Dear Marcie and Mike:**

5. For the body of the letter, key Figure 23-6, which appears at the end of this exercise. Insert the purchase information in a table 3 columns wide by 7 columns long, as illustrated in the figure. Join all the cells in column A before keying the description of the home.
6. Adjust the table so that column A is 3.5 inches wide, column B is 2 inches wide, and column C is 1 inch wide.
7. Make the top, left, and right cell margins 0.01 inches wide, and the bottom cell margin 0.05 inches wide.
8. Right-align the text in cells B6 and B7.
9. Format the table lines and shading as shown in Figure 23-6. Shaded cells should have 10% shading.
10. Copy all the table rows to the clipboard.
11. Position the insertion point in cell A1, and paste the clipboard contents.
12. Select rows 8 through 14, and change the top lines to None.
13. Delete the text in cell A8, and key the following in its place:

    <u>CHARMING LIGHT-FILLED RANCH</u> (North Fulton) Well-established neighborhood close to town. Remodeled, updated, new kitchen and bath. Meticulously maintained. Amazing condition at an amazing price. $199,900.

14. Make the following changes to the numbers in column C:

Cell C8:	**189,400**
Cell C10:	**126,400**
Cell C11:	**1,976**
Cell C13:	**1,281.79**
Cell C14:	**1,026.08**

15. Insert a suitable signature block from Ronnie Palmer, Sales Associate.

16. Insert a second-page single-line continuation header.

17. Spell-check the document.

18. Save the document as *[your three-letter identifier]*23-4.wpw.

19. Print the document.

20. Change the Button Bar to the WordPerfect default.

21. Close the document and exit WordPerfect (unless you will be doing the following exercise immediately).

Figure 23-6

in which you expressed an interest

The following table shows monthly payment figures for the two homes ~~you are interested in~~. It shows the lowest mortgage rates currently available, includes real estate tax payments, and shows both 15-year and 30-year repayment options. Remember, you must reserve approximately $3,000 for closing costs.

Add lines

<u>COUNTRY FARMHOUSE COLONIAL</u>	Purchase Price	$199,900
(Roswell)	Down Payment	63,000
Remodeled with all the charm	Mortgage Amount	136,900
and warmth of the past ~~with~~ *and* all	Real Estate Taxes	2,046
the convenience of today. Open,	Monthly Pmt	
flowing, bright rooms. Country	15 yr-term (6.73%)	1,380
kitchen, extraordinary master	30 yr-term (7.24%)	1,103
suite. Picture-book home.		
$205,000.		

10% shading

Many prospective buyers have shown genuine interest in both of these homes*, so you need to make your decision as soon as possible.*

Please call if you have any further questions.

Exercise 23.5

1. Start WordPerfect, if necessary.
2. Change the Button Bar to the Tables Button Bar.
3. Open a new file, if necessary.
4. Set the document initial font as 12-point CG Times, and set the paper size to Standard 11" x 8.5" (landscape).
5. Create a 7-column by 6-row table.
6. Key the following information in the table:

	January	February	March	April	May	June
G. Crane	**5,294**	**3,228**	**8,143**	**2,401**	**2,006**	**5,481**
A. Delbridge	**4,788**	**4,581**	**7,486**	**6,001**	**5,499**	**7,034**
R. Mercer	**3,048**	**4,476**	**3,165**	**5,840**	**4,609**	**3,225**
W. Reston	**4,963**	**2,005**	**5,671**	**3,749**	**3,267**	**5,493**
M. Washington	**7,442**	**2,357**	**5,310**	**8,410**	**6,773**	**4,004**

7. Add one column to the right edge of the table and one row to the bottom.
8. Make columns B through H right-justified, 1 inch wide, and set to display zero decimal places.
9. Make column A 1½ inches wide.
10. Key **Total** in cell H1 and **Office Total** in cell A7.
11. Format cell A7 to be right-justified and bold. Format the text in cell A7 as 12-point Univers.
12. Create a formula in cell H2 to add the January through June commissions for G. Crane.
13. Copy the formula down to the end of column H.
14. Create a total formula in cell B7, and copy it across the row.
15. Make all of the cells in row 8 bold and vertically centered.
16. Insert a new row at the top of the table, join all the cells in the new row, and format the new cell A1 as center-justified, bottom-aligned, and bold.
17. Key **Buckhead Office Half-Year Totals** in cell A1.
18. Change the font for the text in the first and second rows to 12-point bold Univers.
19. Change the height of rows 1 and 8 to 0.5 inches.

20. Insert dollar signs at the top and bottom of each column of numbers and align them appropriately.
21. Remove all the inside table lines, and make the outside lines single.
22. Make a double line at the bottom of cells B2 through H2, and at the top of cells B8 through H8.
23. Center the table horizontally and vertically.
24. Recalculate the table.
25. Spell-check the document.
26. Change the Button Bar to the WordPerfect default.
27. Save the document as *[your three-letter identifier]*23-5.wpw.
28. Print the document.
29. Close the document and exit WordPerfect.

Lesson 24

Working with Columns

Objectives

- Define columns.
- Create newspaper columns.
- Force column breaks.
- Create parallel columns.
- Edit text in columns.

Newspaper columns
Text arranged on a page in two or more columns that flows continuously from the top to the bottom of one column, then to the top of the next column.

Parallel columns
Blocks of related text placed in side-by-side columns.

The WordPerfect Columns feature can be used to create newspaper columns and parallel columns. *Newspaper columns* are similar to those used in newspapers, magazines, and newsletters. Text that is arranged in newspaper columns flows continuously from the top to the bottom of one column, then to the top of the next column.

In *parallel columns*, short blocks of related text appear side by side. You can use parallel columns to create itineraries, catalogs, and information sheets. Although you also can use the Tables feature to create the same effect as parallel columns, you will find that, in most cases, parallel columns are easier to use. Also, the computer can execute parallel-column commands more quickly than table commands.

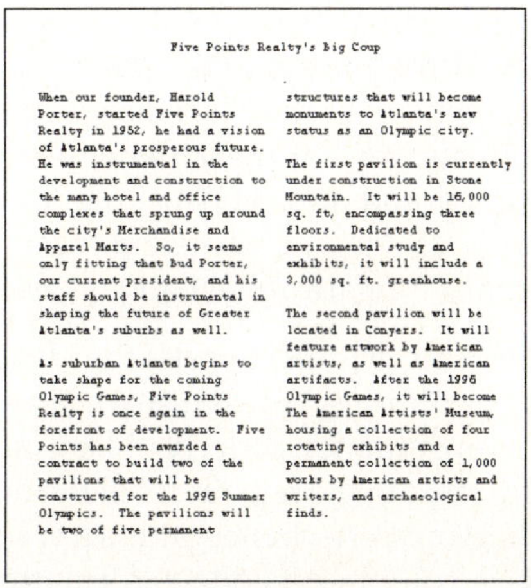
Five Points Realty's Big Coup

When our founder, Harold Porter, started Five Points Realty in 1952, he had a vision of Atlanta's prosperous future. He was instrumental in the development and construction to the many hotel and office complexes that sprung up around the city's Merchandise and Apparel Marts. So, it seems only fitting that Bud Porter, our current president, and his staff should be instrumental in shaping the future of Greater Atlanta's suburbs as well.

As suburban Atlanta begins to take shape for the coming Olympic Games, Five Points Realty is once again in the forefront of development. Five Points has been awarded a contract to build two of the pavilions that will be constructed for the 1996 Summer Olympics. The pavilions will be two of five permanent structures that will become monuments to Atlanta's new status as an Olympic city.

The first pavilion is currently under construction in Stone Mountain. It will be 16,000 sq. ft, encompassing three floors. Dedicated to environmental study and exhibits, it will include a 3,000 sq. ft. greenhouse.

The second pavilion will be located in Conyers. It will feature artwork by American artists, as well as American artifacts. After the 1996 Olympic Games, it will become The American Artists' Museum, housing a collection of four rotating exhibits and a permanent collection of 1,000 works by American artists and writers, and archaeological finds.

Newspaper columns

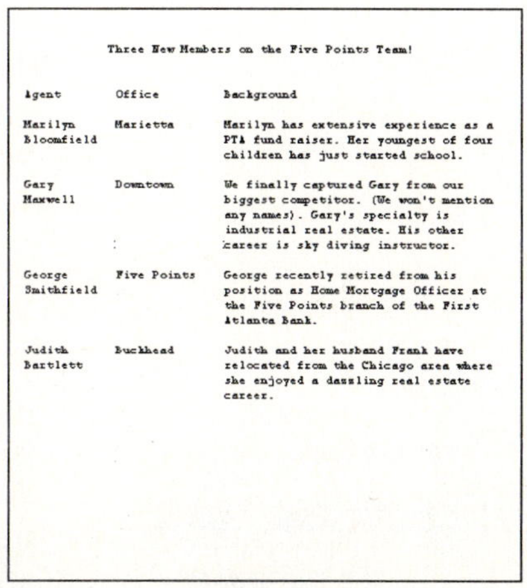
Three New Members on the Five Points Team!

Agent	Office	Background
Marilyn Bloomfield	Marietta	Marilyn has extensive experience as a PTA fund raiser. Her youngest of four children has just started school.
Gary Maxwell	Downtown	We finally captured Gary from our biggest competitor. (We won't mention any names). Gary's specialty is industrial real estate. His other career is sky diving instructor.
George Smithfield	Five Points	George recently retired from his position as Home Mortgage Officer at the Five Points branch of the First Atlanta Bank.
Judith Bartlett	Buckhead	Judith and her husband Frank have relocated from the Chicago area where she enjoyed a dazzling real estate career.

Parallel columns

Figure 24-1
Examples of newspaper and parallel columns

Defining and Turning On Columns

Gutter
The distance between columns.

Although newspaper and parallel columns are used for very different purposes, they are defined the same way, using the Define Columns dialog box. The Define Columns dialog box allows you to choose the number of columns (up to 24), the type of columns (newspaper, parallel, or parallel block protect), and the distance between columns (sometimes called the *gutter*).

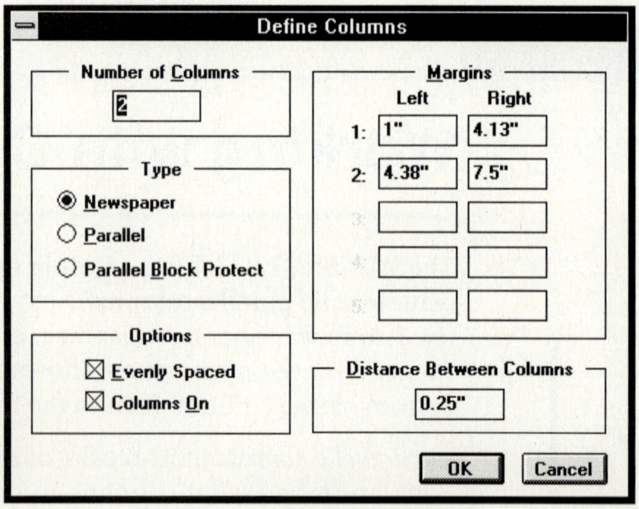

Figure 24-2
The Define Columns dialog box

Note: The default distance between columns is ½ inch. This is usually too wide. Try ¼ inch instead.

By default, columns are equal in width. WordPerfect calculates the amount of space needed for the gutters and margins and then divides the remaining space evenly by the number of columns. You can set the width of individual columns by keying the right and left margin positions in the Margins text boxes, but it can be tedious to determine just what measurements to use. It is easier to create equal columns, and then use the Ruler to adjust the column size to accommodate the text. Unequal columns are rarely used in newspaper columns, but are almost always used in parallel columns.

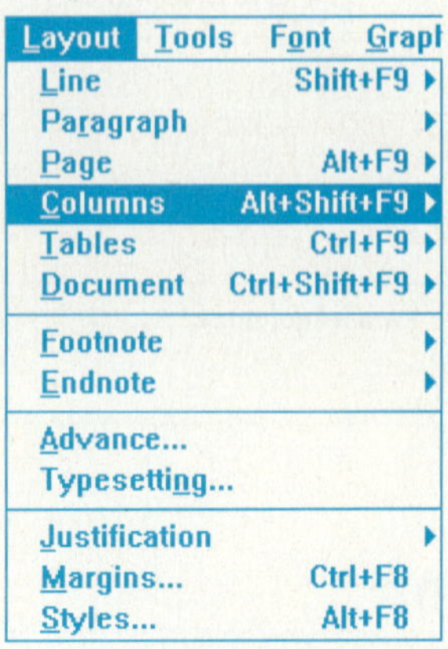

The Layout menu

When you click OK to close the Define Columns dialog box after you define columns, WordPerfect places two codes in the document: the column definition code, [Col Def], and the column on code, [Col On]. All the text in the remainder of the document is formatted as columns until WordPerfect encounters a column off code, [Col Off]. The text after a column off code is formatted as single-column text, unless another column on code is inserted.

When the Ruler is displayed, you can create newspaper columns by clicking the Columns pop-up button on the Ruler, and then choosing the number of columns desired. If you define columns this way, the distance between columns (the gutter) will be ½ inch. You also can double-click the Columns pop-up button to open the Define Columns dialog box.

The Columns cascading menu

When editing existing columns, it is very important to position the insertion point inside the column codes. For example, to add text to the end of a newspaper column after you have turned off columns, you should display the Reveal Codes space to make sure the Reveal Codes insertion point is positioned before the column off code. Otherwise, the text will not be formatted as part of the column.

Creating Newspaper Columns

When creating newspaper columns, it is best to key and edit all the text as a normal document before defining the columns. If you key the text after defining newspaper columns, the computer will respond more slowly, and it will be more difficult to move through the text to make changes.

To create newspaper columns:

1. Start WordPerfect, if necessary.
2. Open the file 24-0.wpw.
3. Position the insertion point to the left of the word "When" at the beginning of the first paragraph.
4. Choose Columns from the Layout menu and then choose Define.

   The Define Columns dialog box opens.
5. Key **2** in the Number of Columns text box, if necessary.
6. Choose Newspaper from the Type option box, if necessary.
7. Key **.25** in the Distance Between Columns text box.

   Notice that the left and right margins for each column are calculated and displayed in the Margins text boxes automatically. The difference between the second column's left-margin measurement and the first column's right-margin measurement is the Distance Between Columns measurement.
8. Click OK.
9. Open the Reveal Codes space to examine the column codes.

   The code [Col Def] indicates that two newspaper columns have been chosen. The column margin measurements are indicated as part of the code. Notice that the Reveal Codes insertion point is immediately to the right of the code [Col On].

Figure 24-3
The define column and column on codes for newspaper columns

To change the two newspaper columns back to one column, you can delete either the column on code or the define column code. If you delete the define column code, any column on and column off codes associated with it will be deleted along with it. If you delete the column on code instead, the define column code will remain in the document, but columns will be displayed as single-column text. If the define column code remains, you can turn columns on again later without redefining them.

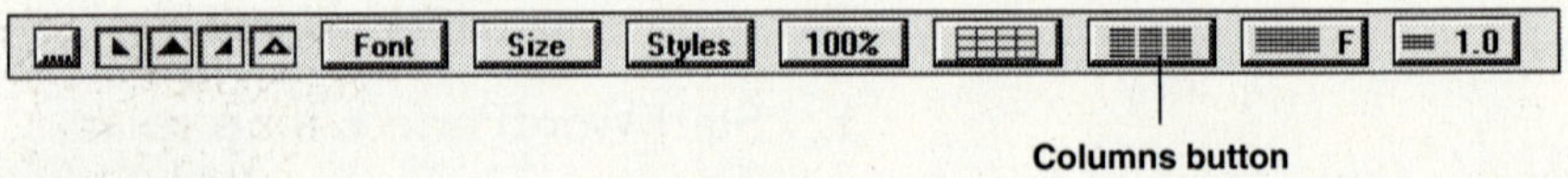

Figure 24-4
The Columns pop-up button on the Ruler

To delete the define column code, [Col Def], and redefine the columns using the Ruler:

1. Choose Ruler and Reveal Codes from the View menu, if necessary.

2. Position the Reveal Codes insertion point on the code [Col Def], and press the **Delete** key.

   The text returns to one column.

3. Position the insertion point at the beginning of the first paragraph, if necessary.

4. Choose 2 Columns from the Columns pop-up button on the Ruler.

   The text changes to two columns, and the gutter (the distance between the columns) is ½ inch. You cannot specify the gutter space when you use the Columns pop-up button to define the columns.

To change the distance between columns:

1. Double-click the Columns pop-up button.

   The Define Columns dialog box opens.

2. Key **.25** in the Distance Between Columns text box and click OK.

When you turn on columns, all the text that follows the code [Col On] is formatted as columns until a column off code, [Col Off], is encountered.

Note: If you are using the keyboard, press **Alt+Right Arrow** to move one column to the right and **Alt+Left Arrow** to move one column to the left.

To insert a [Col Off] code:

1. Position the insertion point at the beginning of the last paragraph in column 2, which begins "We know you".

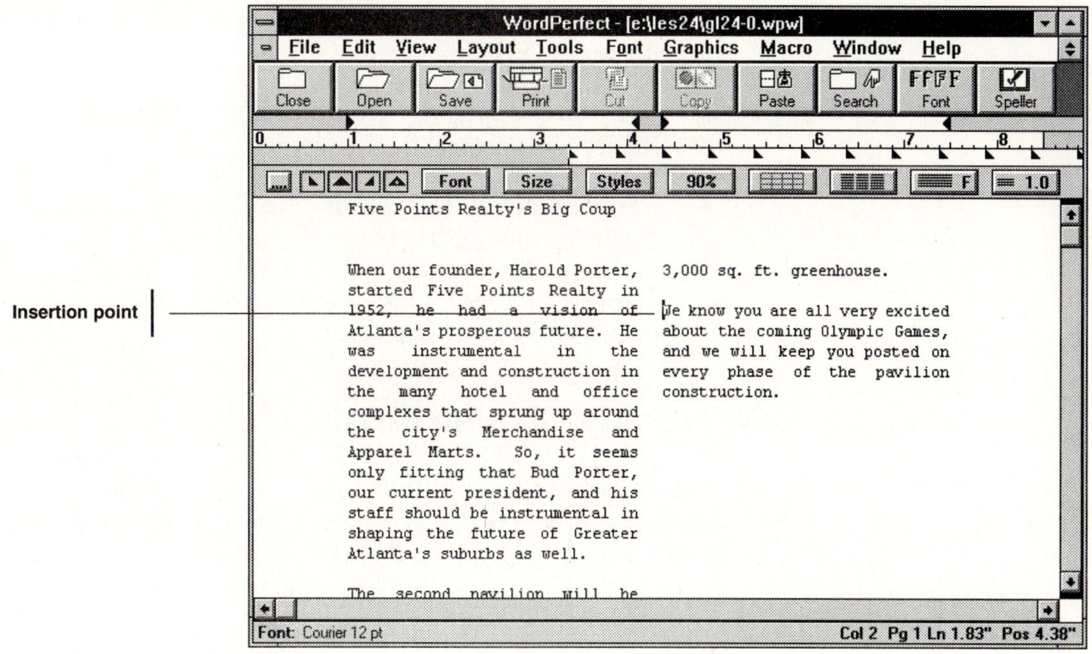

Figure 24-5
The insertion-point position for turning off columns

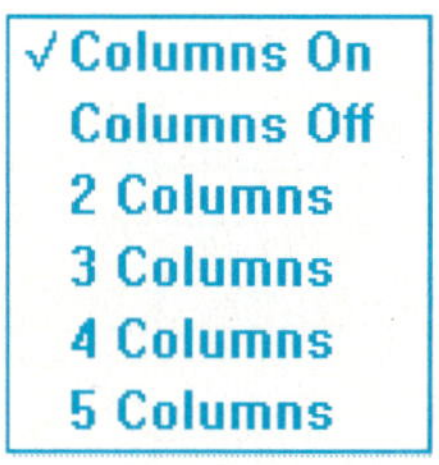

The Columns button pop-up list

2. Choose Columns from the Layout menu, and then choose Columns Off (or choose Columns Off using the Columns pop-up button on the Ruler).

3. Display the Reveal Codes space, if necessary.

   The code [Col Off] is placed at the beginning of the last paragraph, and the last paragraph is formatted as single-column text and moved to page 2.

The columns are unbalanced now. This is because the first column of text flows to the bottom of the page and then continues at the top of the next column. Forcing a column break to balance the columns is discussed later in this lesson.

The Justification pop-up button

You may have noticed the large gaps between the words in the columns. These gaps happen when text is formatted with the default full justification. This can be attractive in a one-column document, but it does not work well in multiple columns. Changing to left justification will improve the appearance of columns.

The Justification button pop-up list

You can change text justification from the Ruler. From the Justification pop-up button, you can choose Left, Right, Center, or Full.

To enhance the appearance of the columns:

1. Position the insertion point in the first paragraph of the first column.

2. Choose Left from the Justification pop-up button on the Ruler (or press **Ctrl+L**).

3. Position the insertion point on the heading "Five Points Realty's Big Coup".

4. Choose Center from the Justification pop-up button on the Ruler (or press **Ctrl+J**).

   The heading is centered across both columns, because it is positioned before the column on code.

Forcing Column Breaks

Although you created two columns, most of the text is in the first column, which creates an unattractive document. To correct the unbalanced columns, position the insertion point where you want a new column to begin, and press **Ctrl+Enter** (the hard page break) to force a new column.

To force a column break:

1. Position the insertion point at the beginning of the third paragraph, to the left of "As suburban Atlanta".

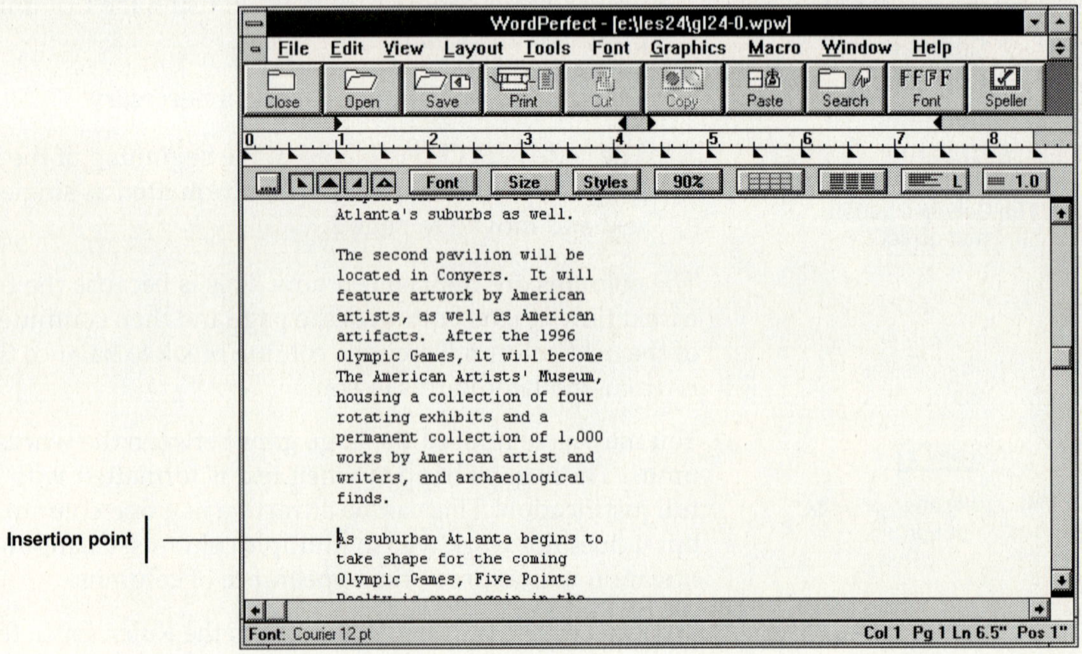

Figure 24-6
The insertion-point position for forcing a column break

2. Press **Ctrl+Enter**.

Now the columns are more balanced on the page, and the single-column text at the end of the document moves back onto page 1.

Moving Between and Editing Newspaper Columns

If you need to edit text that has been formatted in newspaper columns, you can move from column to column by positioning the insertion point with the mouse and editing just as if you were in a one-column document. If you prefer to use the keyboard, press **Alt+Right Arrow** or **Alt+Left Arrow** to move from column to column.

Experiment with moving from column to column:

1. Position the insertion point anywhere in the first paragraph of the left column.
2. Press **Alt+Right Arrow**.

   The insertion point moves to the right column. Notice that the status bar displays Col 2.
3. Press **Alt+Left Arrow**.

   The insertion point moves back to the left column, and the status bar displays Col 1.

To move a paragraph from the right column to the left column:

1. Quadruple-click the first paragraph at the top of the right column to select it.
2. Choose Cut from the Edit menu.
3. Position the insertion point at the beginning of the second paragraph in the left column, to the left of the words "The second pavilion".
4. Choose Paste from the Edit menu.

   The paragraph moves to the left column, but the column break is in the wrong place now.

To change the column break:

1. Position the insertion point at the beginning of the right column, to the left of the words "The first pavilion".
2. Open the Reveal Codes space, if necessary.
3. Position the Reveal Codes insertion point on the hard page code, [HPg], just before the words "The first pavilion", to select it.
4. Press the **Delete** key.

   The column break is deleted.

Insertion point

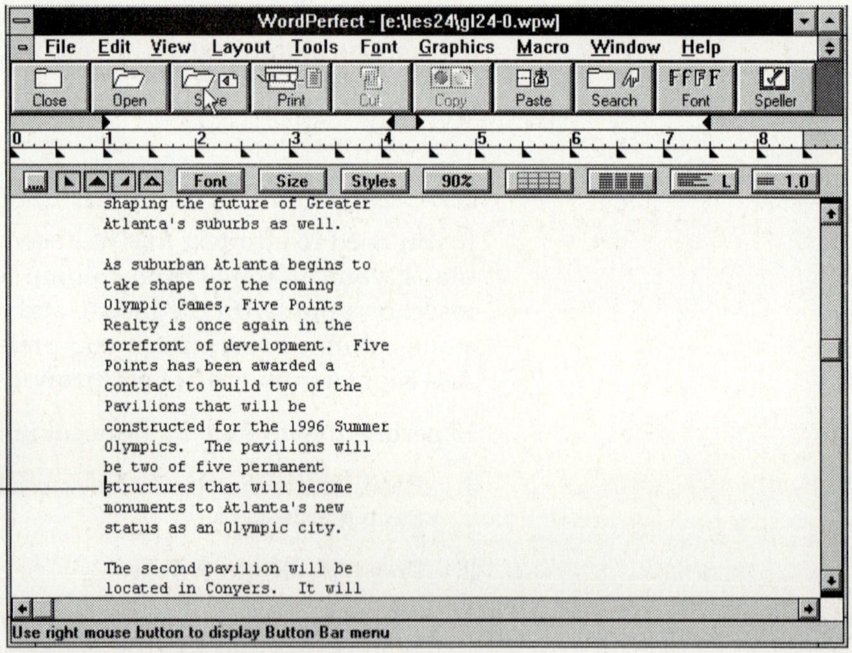

Figure 24-7
The insertion-point position for forcing the new column break

5. Position the insertion point in the second paragraph, at the beginning of the line that starts "structures that will" (three lines up from the bottom of the paragraph).

6. Press **Ctrl+Enter**.

   Now the columns are balanced again.

Another way to edit newspaper columns is to change back to one column of text temporarily. You do this by deleting the column on code, [Col On]. The column definition is still there, as long as you do not delete the column definition code. After you complete the editing, you can position the insertion point in the first paragraph of the text to be restored to columns, and reinsert the column on code. When you reinsert the code, make sure the code [Col On] is placed after the column definition code. You also will need to reinsert the column off code at the end of the text being restored to columns.

To change the columns back to single-column text temporarily:

1. Position the insertion point at the beginning of the first paragraph of columnar text.

2. Open the Reveal Codes space, if necessary.

3. Position the Reveal Codes insertion point on the [Col On] code.

4. Press the **Delete** key.

The code [Col On] is deleted, and the text reverts back to one column of text. Notice that the column definition code remains in the document.

As you scroll through the text, you will notice a hard page break at the point where you forced a column break by pressing **Ctrl+Enter**. This will be converted back to a column break when you turn columns on again.

Editing the document in single-column format:

1. Quadruple-click the third paragraph, which begins "The second pavilion".
2. Use the Cut and Paste commands to move the paragraph down below the one that begins "The first pavilion".
3. In the fourth line of the second paragraph, change the uppercase "P" in "Pavilions" to lowercase.
4. In the second line of the next-to-last paragraph, change "American artist" to "American artists".
5. Position the insertion point at the beginning of the first paragraph.
6. Choose Columns On from the Columns pop-up button on the Ruler.
7. Position the insertion point at the beginning of the last paragraph in the second column.
8. Choose Columns Off from the Columns pop-up button on the Ruler.

   The columns are restored to the format they were in before you did the editing. All the column information was retained in the column definition code.

9. Save the document as *[your three-letter identifier]*24-0.wpw. Do not close the document.

Displaying Columns One at a Time

Editing newspaper columns can be a challenge. When text breaks to form a new column, you cannot display the end of one column and the beginning of the next at the same time, making it difficult to check the continuity of the text. If you prefer the keyboard to the mouse, moving the insertion point from one column to the next requires special keystrokes.

Temporarily turning off columns when editing solves these problems, but you cannot see where column breaks will be, or how the words

continued on next page

Displaying Columns One at a Time (continued)

will flow from one line to the next. Another way to edit newspaper columns is to display them one column at a time.

When displaying one column at a time, a new page is displayed wherever there is a column break (soft or hard). With this arrangement, you can move the insertion point through columns just as you normally do when working with pages of single-column text, and you can see the bottom of one column and the top of the next at the same time. Another benefit of displaying columns one at a time is that WordPerfect can execute commands faster than when displaying side-by side columns.

To display columns one at a time:

- Choose Preferences from the File menu.
- Choose Display from the Preferences cascading menu to open the Display Settings dialog box.
- Click the Display Columns Side-by-Side check box in the Document Window options box to uncheck it.

To redisplay columns side-by-side, open the Display Settings dialog box again, and check the Display Columns Side-by Side check box.

Creating Parallel Columns

You can use parallel columns to keep blocks of related text together in a table-like fashion. Although parallel columns look very much like tables without grid lines, the structure behind them is quite different. You should use parallel columns rather than a table structure when you do not need grid lines or mathematical calculations, because parallel columns are easier to create and faster to use.

Parallel block protect
A column format that prevents a block of text from being divided by a soft page break.

Parallel block protect ensures that a soft page break will not occur within a block of text in a column. You should use parallel block protect for itineraries, inventory lists, and other types of documents where the text blocks are relatively short. Use parallel columns without block protect for columns containing long text blocks.

Parallel columns work best if you define them before you key the text. Codes are inserted between each text block as you type, and it can be tricky to insert these codes after you have keyed the text.

To define parallel columns:

1. Press **Ctrl+End** to move the insertion point to the end of the document.
2. Press **Enter** to move the insertion point to the third line below the last paragraph, if necessary.

3. Key the heading **Three New Members on the Five Points Team!** and center it.

4. Press **Enter** three times to add two blank lines before creating the parallel columns.

   When you define columns, be sure that the insertion point is not on the line that has the heading, or it will be formatted as part of the columns. (The column definition code is inserted at the beginning of the paragraph containing the insertion point.)

5. Choose Columns from the Layout menu, and then choose Define (or double-click the Columns pop-up button).

   The Define Columns dialog box opens.

6. Key **3** in the Number of Columns text box.

7. Choose Parallel Block Protect from the Type option box.

8. Key **.25** in the Distance Between Columns text box.

9. Click OK.

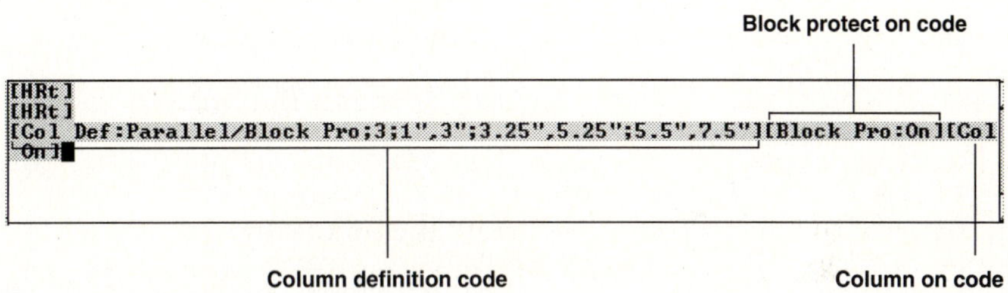

Figure 24-8
Codes for parallel columns with block protect

10. Open the Reveal Codes space, if necessary, and examine the column codes.

    The column definition code is very similar to the newspaper-column code. It indicates the type of columns, number of columns, and column margins. Notice also the block protect on code, [Block Pro:On], and the column on code, [Col On].

When you enter text in parallel columns, key the text for the first column, and press **Ctrl+Enter** (the hard page) to move to the next column. WordPerfect inserts a hard page code between each column in a row. When you reach the end of a row, press **Ctrl+Enter** again to start a new row. When you press **Ctrl+Enter** at the end of a row, WordPerfect inserts the codes [Col Off][HRt][Col On], or [Block Pro:Off][Col Off][HRt][Block Pro:On][Col On] if you are working with block protect.

To enter text in parallel columns:

1. Position the Reveal Codes insertion point immediately to the right of the [Col On] code, if necessary.
2. Key **Agent** and press **Ctrl+Enter.**

   The word "Agent" appears in the first column, and the insertion point moves to the second column. Notice the hard page code in the Reveal Codes space.

3. Key **Office** and press **Ctrl+Enter.**
4. Key **Background** and press **Ctrl+Enter.**

   The cursor moves to the beginning of the next row. The codes [Block Pro:Off][Col Off] are inserted at the end of the row, the code [HRt] is inserted to force a blank line between rows, and the codes [Block Pro:On][Col On] are inserted at the beginning of the new row.

The columns are spaced evenly now. When all the text is entered, you will change the size of the columns by dragging the column markers on the Ruler. As you enter the remainder of the text, you will see the text wrap within a column.

To complete the columns:

1. Key **Marilyn Bloomfield** and press **Ctrl+Enter.**
2. Key **Marietta** and press **Ctrl+Enter.**
3. Key the following:

   Marilyn has extensive experience as a PTA fund raiser. Her youngest of four children has just started school.

   The text wraps over several lines.

4. Press **Ctrl+Enter.**

   The insertion point is at the beginning of the next row, ready for the next group of text blocks. Notice that the insertion point moves down one line below the longest block of text in the previous row.

5. Key the information shown below for George Smithfield and Judith Bartlett, following the example for Marilyn Bloomfield.

   George Smithfield **Five Points**

   George recently retired from his position as Home Mortgage Officer at the Five Points branch of the First Atlanta Bank.

   Judith Bartlett **Buckhead**

   Judith and her husband, Frank, have relocated from the Chicago area, where she enjoyed a dazzling real estate career.

6. Display the Ruler, if necessary, and position the insertion point at the end of Judith's background paragraph, if necessary.
7. Choose Columns Off from the Columns pop-up button on the Ruler.

It is easy to forget to turn off columns. If you are not going to add text to a document containing columns, this is not a problem. However, if you decide to insert more text with a new column definition, the existing table might be altered by the new definition.

Using the Ruler to Change the Size of Columns

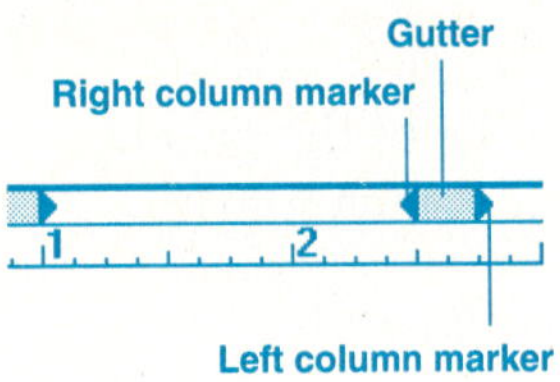

Column markers and a gutter on the Ruler

Note: Be careful not to drag the column markers below the top edge of the Ruler. If you do, the column markers will be deleted, destroying the format by merging two columns into one. To guard against this, save the document often. Undo usually is not successful.

If you display the Ruler when the insertion point is within the columns, you will see column markers that show the edges of each column and the size of the gutters. These markers consist of a pair of outward pointing triangles connected by a gray bar on the upper edge of the Ruler. The triangles represent the right margin of one column and the left margin of the next. The gray bar represents the gutter between the two columns.

You can change the width of columns by dragging these markers. If you drag the gray bar, both column markers move, and the gutter retains its original size. While you are dragging, a double line the width of the gutter drops down through the text to indicate the new column size. Also while you are dragging, blue column markers (dimmed on monochrome monitors) show the original position of the markers. If you want to change the size of the gutter, drag one or the other of the margin markers.

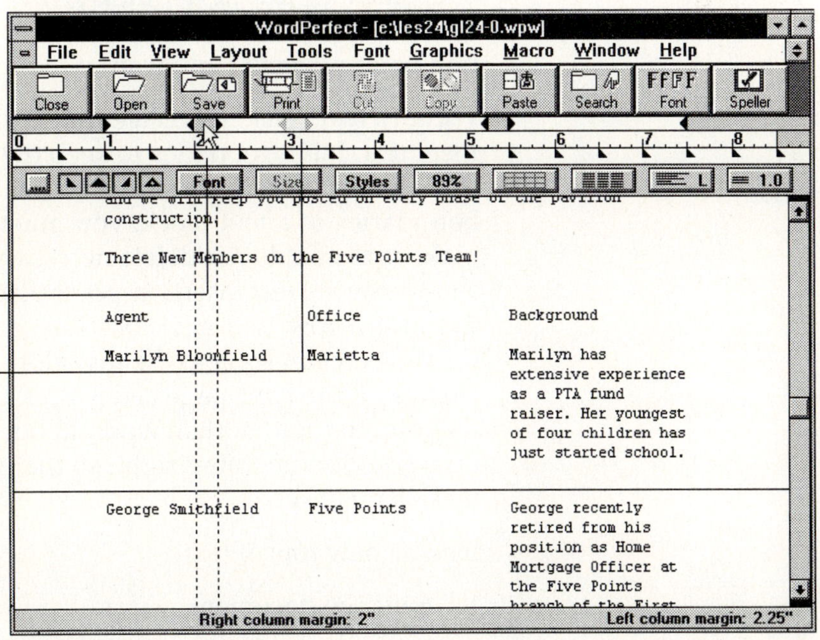

Figure 24-9
Dragging column markers

To change column widths:

1. Display the Ruler, if necessary.

2. Save the document. You saved it previously as *[your three-letter identifier]*24-0.wpw.

3. Position the insertion point on the word "Agent" in the first row of the parallel columns.

   Notice the column markers at the top edge of the Ruler.

4. Point to the gutter section of the column markers between the first and second column.

5. Drag the column marker, so that the left edge of the gutter (the right edge of the first column) is at the 2-inch mark.

   The names in the first column wrap to two lines.

6. Using steps 4 and 5 as a guide, drag the column marker between the second and third columns to the 3½-inch mark.

Moving Between and Editing Parallel Columns

Once you have inserted text into parallel columns, you can move from column to column by pressing **Alt+Left Arrow** or **Alt+Right Arrow**, just as you did with newspaper columns. Also, you can move from paragraph to paragraph (which will help you move from one text block to the next quickly) by pressing **Ctrl+Up Arrow** or **Ctrl+Down Arrow**. If you are using a mouse, just position the insertion point wherever you want it to be.

Within a text block, you can edit text just as you do in normal document text. It is a good idea to keep the Reveal Codes space open, so that you can keep track of the codes. When you move beyond the boundaries of a text block, you must exercise extreme caution to make sure you do not delete necessary codes. If you want to insert a new row, correct insertion-point placement is critical. If you want to move a row to a new location, you must be sure to bring all the codes that belong to the row along with it. One wrong step can change all the hard page codes back to hard page breaks and ruin the columns. Rather than worry about this, save the document each time you do something right, so that you can recover easily if you make a mistake.

Insert a new row of text:

1. Save the document.

2. Position the insertion point at the end of George Smithfield's background paragraph, after the words "First Atlanta Bank".

3. Open the Reveal Codes space, if necessary, and then select the code [Col Off] after "First Atlanta Bank", if necessary.

4. Press **Ctrl+Enter**.

   The insertion point is at the beginning of a new row. It is absolutely necessary that the [Col Off] code is selected when you press **Ctrl+Enter**. If the code is anywhere else, you will disturb the column structure.

5. Key **Gary Maxwell** and press **Ctrl+Enter**.

6. Key **Downtown** and press **Ctrl+Enter**.

7. Key the following:

   We finally captured Gary from our biggest competitor. (We won't mention any names.) Gary's specialty is industrial real estate. His other career is sky diving instructor.

   Gary's information is inserted between George's and Judith's. You could insert another row after Gary's by pressing **Ctrl+Enter** when you finish keying Gary's background paragraph.

To move a row of text to a new location:

1. Save the document.

2. Position the insertion point to the left of the name "George Smithfield".

3. Press **Home** twice to move to the first code on the line.

4. Check the Reveal Codes space to be sure the [Block Pro:On] code to the left of "George" is selected.

   If there is no [Block Pro:On] code, the [Col On] code should be selected.

5. While holding the **Shift** key down, press the **Down Arrow** key three times, until the insertion point is to the left of the name "Gary".

   All the text in George's row is selected. The [Block Pro:On] code to the left of "Gary" should be selected.

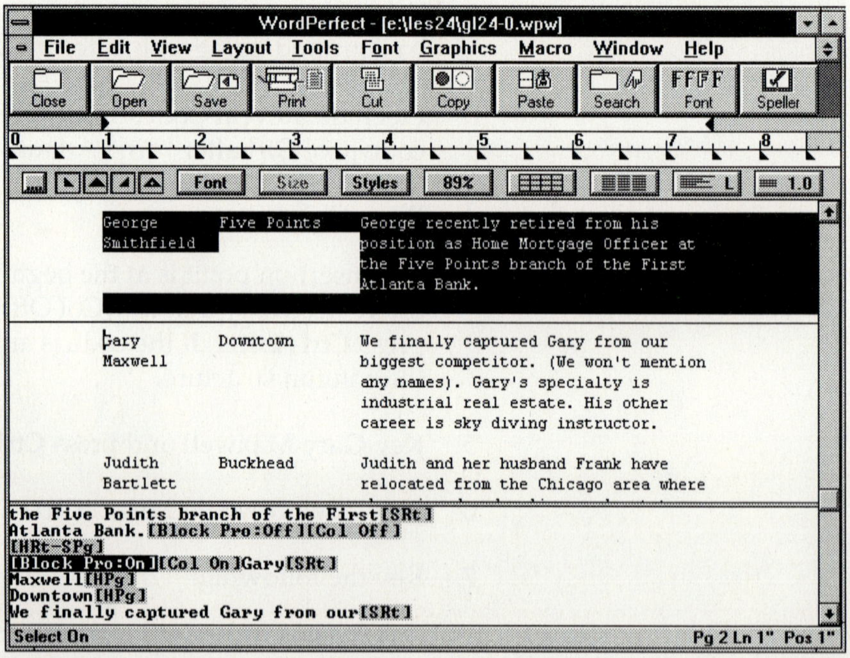

Figure 24-10
The selected text ready to be moved

6. Choose Cut from the Edit menu.

7. Position the Reveal Codes insertion point on the code [Block Pro:On], to the left of the name "Judith".

   If there is no [Block Pro:On] code, the code [Col On] should be selected.

8. Choose Paste from the Edit menu.

   George Smithfield's information has moved down below Gary Maxwell's.

   It is absolutely necessary to place the insertion point precisely on the correct codes to move a row successfully. If you are working with parallel columns without block protect, select the [Col On] code instead of the [Block Pro:On].

   Remember, always save your work before attempting this maneuver.

9. Spell-check the document.

10. Save the document.

11. Close the document and exit WordPerfect (unless you will be doing the following exercises immediately).

Table 24-1: Keyboard Shortcuts for Columns

Keyboard Shortcut	Action
Alt+Shift+F9	Displays the Columns cascading menu.
Alt+Right Arrow	Moves the cursor one column to the right.
Alt+Left Arrow	Moves the cursor one column to the left.

Key Terms

Gutter
Newspaper columns
Parallel block protect
Parallel columns

Exercises

Exercise 24.1

1. Start WordPerfect, if necessary.
2. Open the file 24-1.wpw.
3. Display the Ruler, if necessary.
4. Define three newspaper columns with ¼-inch space between columns:
   A. Position the insertion point at the beginning of the first paragraph.
   B. Double-click the Columns pop-up button on the Ruler.
   C. Key **3** in the Number of Columns text box.
   D. Choose Newspaper from the Type option box, if necessary.
   E. Key **.25** in the Distance Between Columns text box and click OK.
5. Change the text justification from full to left using the Ruler:
   A. Position the insertion point anywhere in the first paragraph, if necessary.
   B. Choose Left from the Justification pop-up button on the Ruler.
6. Force column breaks to create three columns of equal length:
   A. Position the insertion point in the first paragraph, at the beginning of the sentence "It was hot and humid."
   B. Press **Ctrl+Enter**.

C. Position the insertion point at the beginning of the second paragraph in the second column, which begins "In the end", and press **Ctrl+Enter.**

7. Insert a new paragraph before the paragraph in column 3:

   A. Position the insertion point at the beginning of the third column, before "In the end neither".

   B. Key the following:

   It wasn't until she caught up with her teammate from Five Points' midtown office, John Soloman, at the 3.5-mile mark of the 5-mile race, that she knew she was doing well. "I thought I was running at a pretty comfortable pace, but when I looked around, there was Ann right on my heels," says John. "I thought 'uh oh! I'd better pick up the pace'."

   C. Press **Enter** twice to add a blank line between the two paragraphs.

8. Delete the existing column breaks so that they can be repositioned:

   A. Display the Reveal Codes space, if necessary.

   B. Position the insertion point at the top of the third column.

   C. Delete the [HPg] code just before the insertion point. (Position the insertion point on the code, and press the **Delete** key.)

   D. Position the insertion point at the top of the second column.

   E. Delete the [HPg] code just before the insertion point.

9. Insert new column breaks, so that the columns will be of equal length:

   A. Position the insertion point in the first paragraph, at the beginning of the line that starts with the words "men and it's" (four lines from the bottom of the paragraph).

   B. Press **Ctrl+Enter**.

   C. Position the insertion point in the middle of the second paragraph, at the beginning of the line "around, there was" (six lines up from the end of the second paragraph).

   D. Press **Ctrl+Enter**.

10. Add a centered heading at the top of the document:

    A. Press **Ctrl+Home** to move to the top of the document.

    B. Key **Corporate Challenge Winners**.

C. Position the insertion point anywhere in the heading, if necessary.

D. Choose Center from the Justification pop-up button on the Ruler.

11. Spell-check the document.

12. Save the document as *[your three-letter identifier]*24-1.wpw.

13. Print the document.

14. Close the document and exit WordPerfect (unless you will be doing the following exercises immediately).

Exercise 24.2

1. Start WordPerfect, if necessary.

2. Open the file 24-2.wpw.

3. Display the Ruler, if necessary.

4. Press **Ctrl+End** to position the insertion point at the end of the document.

5. Define two parallel columns with ¼-inch space between columns:

   A. Double-click the Columns pop-up button on the Ruler.

   B. Key **2** in the Number of Columns text box.

   C. Choose Parallel Block Protect from the Type option box.

   D. Key **.25** in the Distance Between Columns text box and click OK.

6. Key the text for the first row:

   A. Key **Real Estate Principles and Practices** and press **Ctrl+Enter**.

   B. Key the following:

   Suitable for entry-level and experienced salespersons and appraisers. This course is also acceptable as a prerequisite for the realty broker's license.

   There will be 12 sessions at a cost of $75 for members and $150 for non-members. The class will be held Mondays and Wednesdays 6 p.m. - 9 p.m.

   C. Press **Ctrl+Enter**.

7. For the remaining rows, key the text in Figure 24-11, which appears at the end of this exercise.

8. Choose Columns Off from the Columns pop-up button on the Ruler.

9. Press **Enter**, and key **For more information, contact Mary Trant at 555-4931.**

10. Change the text justification to left:

    A. Position the insertion point in the first row of the columns.

    B. Choose Left from the Justification pop-up button on the Ruler.

11. Change the column width:

    A. Position the insertion point in the first row of the columns, if necessary.

    B. Drag the first column marker so that the right margin of the first column is at the 2½-inch mark.

12. Move the course "Real Estate Appraisal I" to the first row:

    A. Position the insertion point at the beginning of the third row, before the word "Real".

    B. Press **Home** twice to move to the first code in the line.

    C. Display the Reveal Codes space, if necessary, and position the Reveal Codes insertion point on the code [Block Pro:On], if necessary.

    D. While holding the **Shift** key down, press the **Down Arrow** three times.

    E. While holding the **Shift** key down, position the Reveal Codes insertion point on the code [Block Pro:On] at the beginning of the third row, if necessary.

    F. Choose Cut from the Edit menu.

    G. Position the Reveal Codes insertion point on the [Block Pro:On] code at the beginning of the first row (after the [Col Def] code).

    H. Choose Paste from the Edit menu.

13. Spell-check the document.

14. Save the document as *[your three-letter identifier]*24-2.wpw.

15. Print the document.

16. Close the document and exit WordPerfect (unless you will be doing the following exercises immediately).

Figure 24-11

Real Estate Finance	The syllabus will include mortgage loans, the basics of mortgage financing, and how to qualify for a loan. There will be 6 sessions at a cost of $75 for members and $150 for non-members. The class will be held Saturdays 9 a.m.-3 p.m.
Real Estate Appraisal I	This course encompasses the estimating, replacement, and repair costs of residential real estate. There will be 12 sessions at a cost of $75 for members and $150 for non-members. The class will be held Wednesdays 6:30 p.m.-9:30 p.m.
Review for Real Estate Exam	Intensive review for those who failed to pass the license exam and need a refresher course. Sample exams, study tips, and test-taking techniques are included. This class will meet for two sessions only. Tuesday 6 p.m.-8 p.m. and Saturday 9 a.m.-11 a.m.

Exercise 24.3

1. Start WordPerfect, if necessary.
2. Open the file 24-3.wpw.
3. Format the course descriptions in the document into two newspaper columns with a ¼-inch gutter. The columns should start with the first underlined heading.
4. Change the document's justification from full to left.

5. Force a column break, so that there are two course descriptions in each column.
6. Turn columns off at the beginning of the line that begins "See the following page".
7. Force a page break at the bottom of the document.
8. At the top of page 2, key the heading **Course Schedule Summary:** and make it bold.
9. Press **Enter** three times.
10. Define three parallel columns, and enter the text in Figure 24-12, which appears at the end of this exercise.
11. Change the column margins, so that the right margin of the first column is at the 3½-inch mark, and the right margin of the second column is at the 5¾-inch mark.
12. Spell-check the document.
13. Save the document as *[your three-letter identifier]*24-3.wpw.
14. Print the document.
15. Close the document and exit WordPerfect (unless you will be doing the following exercises immediately).

Figure 24-12

Course Schedule Summary:

Course	**Days**	**Time**
Real Estate	Wednesday	6 p.m.-9 p.m.
Appraisal I	12 Sessions	
Real Estate Principles	Monday and Wednesday	6 p.m.-9 p.m.
and Practices	12 Sessions	
Real Estate Finance	Saturday	9 a.m.-3 p.m.
	6 Sessions	
Review for Real Estate	Tuesday and Saturday	6 p.m.-8 p.m;
Exam	2 sessions only.	9 a.m.-11 a.m.

Exercise 24.4

1. Start WordPerfect, if necessary.

2. Open a new file, if necessary.

3. Change the font for the entire document to 12-point CG Times.

4. Format the document as a standard memo with the following heading information:

MEMO TO:	**Bud Porter**
FROM:	**Ann Delbridge**
DATE:	**June 24, 199-**
SUBJECT:	**New Properties**

5. Key the opening paragraph that appears in Figure 24-13 at the end of this exercise.

6. Define three parallel columns with block protect.

7. Enter the new property listings that appear in Figure 24-13 at the end of this exercise, including the corrections indicated.

8. Move the column markers on the Ruler, so that the right margin of the first column is at the 1½-inch mark, and the right margin of the second column is at the 3½-inch mark.

9. Insert the following information in a new row following property number 76121:

97558	**Alpharetta**	**BRAND NEW CONSTRUCTION 4 bedrooms, 3 1/2 baths. Almost 4 super acres. $565,000.**

10. Apply bold formatting, as shown in the sample document.

11. Format the columns to be left-justified.

12. Spell-check the document.

13. Save the document as *[your three-letter identifier]*24-4.wpw.

14. Print the document.

15. Close the document and exit WordPerfect (unless you will be doing the following exercise immediately).

Figure 24-13

The following new properties have been listed by the Buckhead office in the past week:

Number	Location	Description
80886	Hillbrooke	**GOOD STARTER HOME** Living room w/fpl. 2 bed-rooms & bath. Covered porch. Fine condition. Walk to center of town. $179,900.
34490	Parsons Station	**MINT CONDITION** 3 bed-rooms, 2 baths. Playroom w/fpl, cul-de-sac. What more could you ask for? $144,900.
76121	Dunwoody	**TWO FAMILY HOUSE** Each side 3 bed-rooms, 1 1/2 baths, bsmt. Excellent neighborhood. $240,000.
51234	Roswell	**ARCHITECT DESIGNED CONTEMPORARY** 12 rooms, 3 1/2 baths, cathedral ceilings, custom windows, professionally landscaped yard with in-ground sprinkler system. $799,000.

Exercise 24-5

1. Start WordPerfect, if necessary.
2. Open the file 24-5.wpw.
3. Assign the fonts CG Times and Univers Bold to the Font button on the Ruler, if necessary.
4. Change the base font for the entire document to 12-point CG Times.

5. Format the text starting at the heading "Atlanta Hawks" into 2 newspaper columns with a ¼-inch gutter.

6. Center the first two lines of text.

7. Change the justification of the text in columns to left.

8. Change the base font of the two heading lines "Five Points Reporter" and "Newsworthy articles for our agents" to 18-point Univers Bold.

9. Change the base font of the article headings to 12-point Univers Bold.

10. Move the article "Atlanta Hawks" to the bottom of the second column. (Check the Reveal Codes space to be sure to include the font formatting codes, but not the [Col Def], [Col On], or [Just:Left] codes.)

11. Force a column break at the beginning of the second article. Make sure that the tops of the two columns align after the column break is made.

12. Spell-check the document.

13. Save the document as *[your three-letter identifier]*24-5.wpw.

14. Print the document.

15. Close the document and exit WordPerfect.

Module 8

Styles and Macros

Lessons

25: Styles
26: Macros

Lesson 25

Styles

Many of the previous lessons presented techniques for enhancing the way your documents look, including character formatting, font and type-size selection, and setting margins. This lesson shows how you can combine those enhancements in time-saving styles. You can use styles to define the way headings and special paragraphs will look, set the formatting for a bulleted list, or specify the page layout and base font for the entire document.

Objectives

- Understand styles.
- Apply styles.
- Understand style codes.
- Create styles.
- Edit styles.
- Delete styles.
- Use the style library.

Style
A group of formatting commands that can be named and saved with a document or as part of a separate style library.

Style library
A group of styles, saved as a file, designed to be used together in a document. Style libraries ensure consistent appearance of documents.

Paired style
A style used to format small amounts of text. A paired style has a style on code and a style off code.

Open style
A style that goes into effect at the position where it is inserted, and remains in effect for the remainder of the document.

What are Styles?

A *style* is a group of formatting codes and other items, such as text or special characters, that you can define and then use over and over again to format text. Styles are useful when you need to apply identical formatting to several separate blocks of text, such as paragraph headings. They can save time and ensure a uniform appearance for all the documents you create.

A single document can have several styles for different purposes. You may want to create one style for main headings, another one for subheadings, and a third one for indented paragraphs. A group of styles can be saved in a *style library* and then used to format other documents. Many business organizations use style libraries to ensure that all the documents they produce have a consistent appearance.

Before using styles, it is important to understand the two types of styles, paired and open:

- *Paired styles*, similar to paired codes, are used to format small amounts of text. Just as bold on and bold off turn the bold character attribute on and off, a style on code turns on a style, and a style off code turns off a style.

- *Open styles* work in much the same way as open formatting codes. There is only one code, [Open Style], associated with an open style. An open style goes into effect at the position where it is inserted, and stays in effect for the remainder of the document (or until other formatting codes or other styles override it).

Applying Styles

WordPerfect has a default style library of styles to apply to documents. This style library also can be used as a starting point when creating new styles and building custom style libraries.

To apply a paired style to existing text, select the text to be formatted, choose Style from the Layout menu to open the Style dialog box, choose the desired style from the Style list box, and click the On command button.

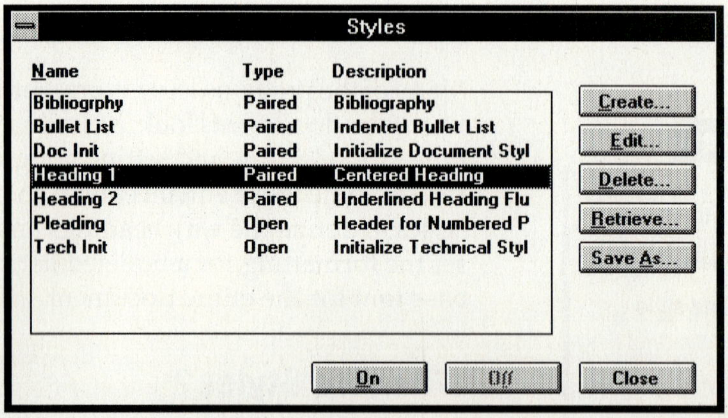

Figure 25-1
The Styles dialog box

When you open the Styles dialog box for the first time, the WordPerfect default styles are displayed in the list box. The three columns in the list box are Name, Type, and Description. The names are arranged alphabetically, the type indicates whether the style is paired or open, and the description tells you what the style will do.

The Styles dialog box allows you to:

- Choose an existing style from the Styles list box
- Create a new style, and add it to the list
- Edit an existing style to change its format
- Delete a style from the list, and delete its codes from the document
- Retrieve a different style library to change the styles used in the document
- Save the styles on the list as a new style library

To apply a paired style to existing text:

1. Start WordPerfect, if necessary.
2. Open the file 25-0.wpw.
3. Select the text "OUR RESPONSIBILITIES" on the third line.
4. Choose Styles from the Layout menu (or press **Alt+F8**) to open the Styles dialog box.

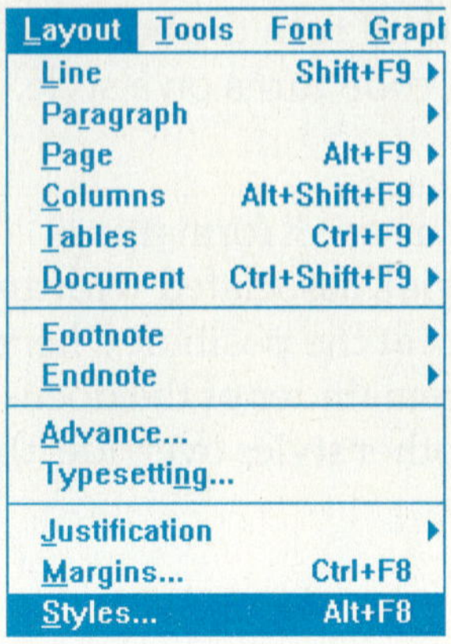

The Layout menu

The Styles dialog box opens. Standard styles supplied by WordPerfect are displayed in the list box.

5. Choose the style Heading 1 from the list box.

6. Click the On command button at the bottom of the dialog box.

   The dialog box closes. The selected text is now large, bold, and centered. Two blank lines have been inserted below the text (the blank lines are part of the style).

Figure 25-2
The Styles button on the Ruler

You can save steps when applying styles by double-clicking the Styles button on the Ruler. To apply a style using the Ruler:

1. Choose Ruler from the View menu (or press **Alt+Shift+F3**) to display the Ruler, if necessary.

2. Select the text "Investigate commercial tenants" at the beginning of the first paragraph.

3. Double-click the Styles button on the Ruler.

   The Styles dialog box opens.

4. Choose Heading 2, the fifth style in the list box, and then click the On button (or double-click Heading 2).

   The paragraph heading is underlined, appears in larger type, and has a blank line below it.

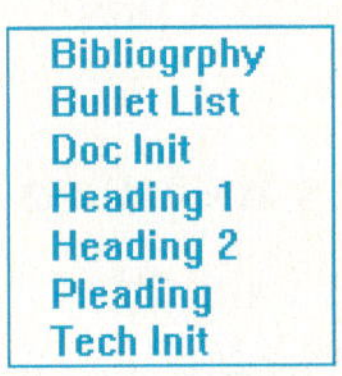

The Styles pop-up list

Another way to save steps is to use the Styles button pop-up list:

1. Select the text "Collect rents" at the beginning of the second paragraph.

2. Point to the Styles button on the Ruler, and click and hold down the mouse button.

   The Styles button pop-up list appears.

3. Choose Heading 2 from the pop-up list.

   The selected text is formatted with the Heading 2 style.

4. Using steps one through three above as a guide, apply the Heading 2 style to the remaining paragraph headings in the document.

It should be obvious by now that using styles is more convenient than applying several individual formatting codes.

To apply styles as you key text, turn on the style, key the text, and then turn off the style again. As you key text, you can turn on and off styles from the Styles button pop-up list or from the Styles dialog box. An alternate way to turn off styles as you key text is simply to press the **Right Arrow** key. This moves the insertion point to the right of the style off code.

To apply a style as you key text:

1. Press **Ctrl+End** to move the insertion point to the end of the document.
2. Choose Heading 2 from the Styles button pop-up list.
3. Press **Alt+F3** to display the Reveal Codes space.

   Notice the style on and style off codes.

4. Key **Hire and supervise employees.**

   Notice that the text is inserted between the style on and style off codes. While you are keying the text, the Reveal Codes insertion point (the highlight) remains on the style off code.

5. Choose Heading 2 from the Styles button pop-up list again.

   The style is turned off. The Reveal Codes insertion point moves to the right of the [Style Off] code.

6. Press **Enter** to insert a blank line, and then key the paragraph:

   We believe that our employees are our most valuable asset. For that reason, we train each one individually and provide a benefits package that has produced a staff with the lowest turnover in the metropolitan area.

7. Press **Enter** twice to end the paragraph and insert a blank line.

   The paragraph text is inserted after the style off code and appears as normal text.

You can save time turning off a paired style (or a paired format) simply by pressing the **Right Arrow** key to move the Reveal Codes insertion point to the right of the [Style Off] code:

1. Use the Styles button on the Ruler to turn on the Heading 2 style.
2. Key **Provide monthly reports for each property.**

   Notice that the Reveal Codes insertion point is on the style off code.

3. Press the **Right Arrow** key.

   The Reveal Codes insertion point is to the right of the [Style Off] code, and the style is turned off.

4. Press **Enter**, and then key the following paragraph:

   Again, through our networked data base we always have accurate and appropriate records. Our detailed monthly reports provide you with all the information you need to insure that your property is managed profitably and effectively.

Examining Style Codes

When many different styles are inserted in a document, it can be a challenge to remember the function of each one just by looking at its name in the Reveal Codes space. You already may have noticed that, when the insertion point is on a code, it expands. For example, if the code [Style Off: Heading 2] in the above procedure is highlighted, it expands to [Style On: Heading 2;[Large On][Und On]], indicating that the Heading 2 style applies the Large and Underline attributes.

```
Property Management Group[HRt]
[HRt]
[Style On:Heading 1;[Center][Vry Large On][Bold On]]OUR RESPONSIBILITIES[Sty
le Off:Heading 1][HRt]
[HRt]
```

Figure 25-3
An expanded style code

To examine style codes in the on-screen document:

1. Working in the document window, move the insertion point to the left of "Our Responsibilities" at the top of the document.

2. Working in the Reveal Codes space, position the Reveal Codes insertion point on the code [Style On: Heading 1].

   The code expands to [Style On: Heading 1;[Center][Vry Large On][Bold On]].

3. Press the **Right Arrow** key (or use the mouse) to position the Reveal Codes insertion point to the right of the code.

   The code returns to its condensed format, [Style On: Heading 1].

4. Using steps 2 and 3 above as a guide, examine some of the other style codes in the document.

Creating Styles

The standard styles that WordPerfect provides are samples designed to help you get started. You can create a wide variety of your own styles to enhance your documents. You also can edit existing styles, delete styles, save the list of styles as a style library to use with other documents, and retrieve a saved library to use with the current document.

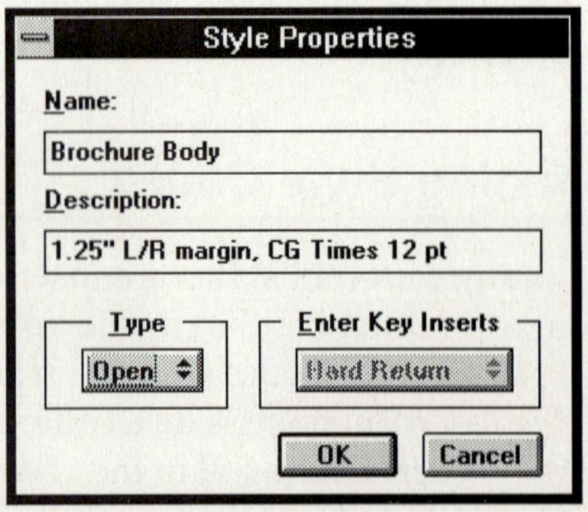

Figure 25-4
The Style Properties dialog box

Note: Although the description text box allows up to 54 characters, only the first 19 characters will be displayed in the Styles list box. The only way to see the rest of the description is by clicking the Properties button in the Style Editor window.

When you choose Create from the Styles dialog box, the Style Properties dialog box opens, prompting you to enter a name and a description for the style. The name can have up to 20 characters and can include spaces. It should describe how the style will be used, for example "Heading 1", or "Bullet list". Use the Description text box to list the formatting contained in the style, for example, "CG Times Bold 18 pt".

The Style Properties dialog box allows you to choose the type of style you are creating (paired or open). Paired is the default style type. The Enter Key Inserts pop-up button is dimmed if you choose the Open style type. It is used only for paired styles, allowing you to choose how the **Enter** key functions when the style is active.

Creating an Open Style

Use open styles when you need to format large sections of text. An open style can define the format for an entire document, setting the margins, line spacing, and base font, for example. To create a style for the body of the document:

1. Double-click the Styles button on the Ruler to open the Styles dialog box.
2. Click Create.

   The Style Properties dialog box opens.

The Properties button

3. Key **Brochure Body** in the Name text box. Do not press **Enter**.

   If you accidentally press **Enter**, the Style Properties dialog box will close. Click the Properties button to reopen the Style Properties dialog box.

4. Press the **Tab** key to move to the Description box, and key **1.25" L/R margin, CG Times 12 pt**.

5. Choose Open from the Type pop-up button.

   The Enter Key Inserts pop-up button is dimmed. This option is available only for paired styles.

6. Click OK.

   The Style Editor window opens with the Reveal Codes space displayed.

The Style Editor window looks very much like a document window, except for the added Close and Properties buttons in the upper left portion of the text area. When working in the Style Editor window, you can:

- Insert and delete codes and text, just as if you were working in a document window.
- Change properties (Name, Description, Type) by clicking the Properties button.
- Close the window by clicking the Close button.

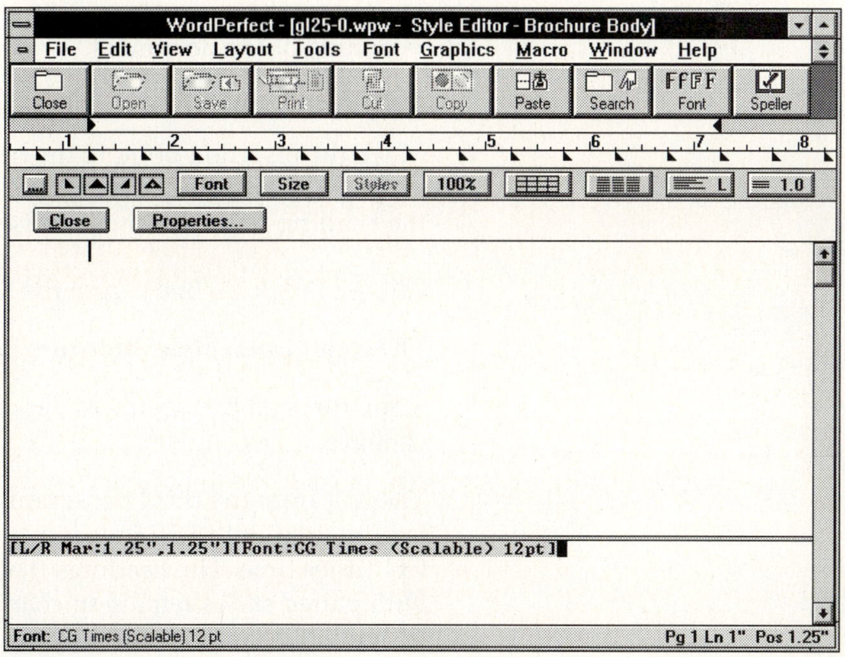

Figure 25-5
The Style Editor window

To insert formatting codes for the Brochure Body style:

1. Double-click the Font button on the Ruler to open the Font dialog box.

2. Choose CG Times (Scalable) from the Font list box.

3. Choose 12 from the Point Size list box, if necessary, and click OK.

   The Font code appears in the Reveal Codes space.

4. Choose Margins from the Layout menu.

5. Set 1.25-inch left and right margins and click OK.

   The margin code appears in the Reveal Codes space.

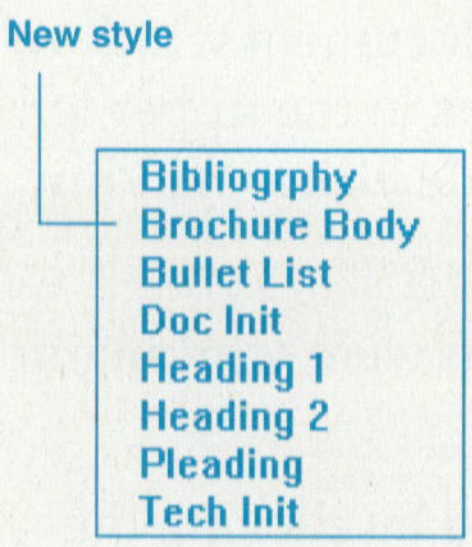

Brochure Body added to the Style pop-up list

6. Click the Close button to close the Style Editor window and return to the Styles dialog box.

   Brochure Body appears in the Style list box. (Style names are alphabetized.)

7. Click Close to close the Styles dialog box.

It is not necessary to select text before applying an open style. Just position the insertion point (usually at the top of a document), and then turn on the style the same way as for a paired style. The style is applied from the insertion point to the end of the document. If you need to format the entire document, the open style code must be at the beginning of the document.

To apply the Brochure Body style:

1. Move the insertion point to the beginning of the third paragraph, which begins "Five Points Realty employs" (just below the heading "Care for the premises").

2. Choose Brochure Body from the Styles button pop-up list.

   The code [Open Style: Brochure Body] is inserted.

3. Scroll through the document, and observe the formatting changes.

   The text from the third paragraph to the end of the document is formatted with 1.25-inch left and right margins and 12-point CG Times type. The headings that were formatted previously with paired styles remain unchanged. The beginning of the document is not formatted by the Brochure Body style.

Format the entire document with the Brochure Body style:

1. Position the Reveal Codes insertion point on the code [Open Style:Brochure Body] in the third paragraph, to the left of "Five Points Realty".

2. Press the **Delete** key to delete the code.

3. Working in the document window, position the insertion point at the beginning of the document.

4. Choose Brochure Body from the Styles button pop-up list on the Ruler.

   Now the entire document is formatted in the Brochure Body style.

Creating a Paired Style

Creating a paired style is similar to creating an open style, but there are more options to consider. When you choose Paired in the Style options box, the Enter Key Inserts options are available. These options are useful if you apply paired styles as you key text rather than to existing text. The choices are:

- Hard Return

  When a style with this option is active, pressing the **Enter** key inserts a hard return code, and the style remains active. Use this option if the style will be applied to more than one paragraph at a time.

- Style Off

  Pressing the **Enter** key inserts the [Style Off] code, and returns the text to the format that was active before the style was applied. This is a good option to use for paragraph headings, where the text that follows requires a different format.

- Style Off/On

  Pressing the **Enter** key inserts a style off code and then a style on code. Use this option for bulleted list styles.

The Style Editor window for paired styles is slightly different from the Open Styles window. A comment is displayed in the document window, and a corresponding comment code is displayed in the Reveal Codes space. (For more information on comments, see "Lesson 12: Working with Multiple Documents.")

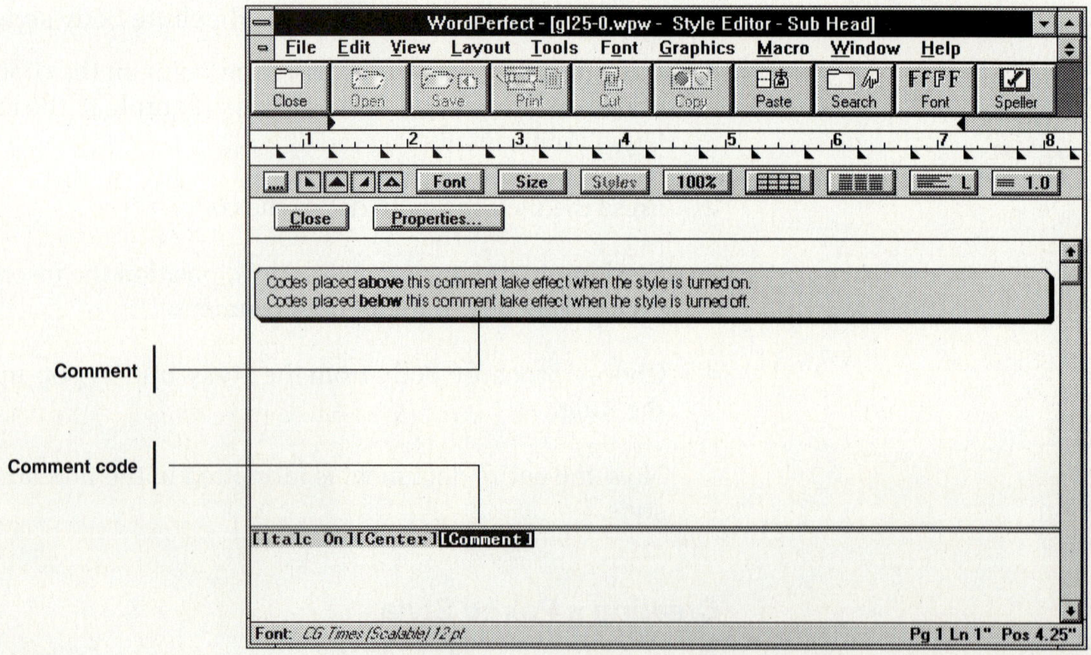

Figure 25-6
The Style Editor window for paired styles

Codes and text that should be included with the style on code are inserted before the comment. Most formatting codes are turned off automatically by the style off code. For example, if you insert a bold on code (or another paired code) before the comment, the bold off code will be inserted automatically into the style off code. When you insert an open-formatting code, such as a margin or font code, the style off code automatically contains whatever codes are necessary to return to the format that was active before the style was applied. For example, if the text before the style on code is CG Times 12, and the style on code contains Univers Bold 14, CG Times 12 will be inserted automatically in the style off code, so that text following the style will return to the original font.

Special codes and text that are placed after the comment will be inserted in the document when the style is turned off. Use the area after the comment to insert codes or text that will be inserted to the right of the text that is being formatted by the paired style. For example, insert a hard return code if you want a blank line to follow the formatted text or a hard page code if you want the text following the style to start on a new page.

To create a paired style:

1. Double-click the Styles button on the Ruler to open the Styles dialog box.

2. Click Create.

3. Key **Sub Head** in the Name text box, and key **Centered, Italics** in the Description text box.
4. Choose Paired for the Type option and Hard Return for the Enter Key Inserts option, if necessary.
5. Click OK.

   The Style Editor window opens.
6. Press **Ctrl+I** to insert the Italics On code.
7. Press **Shift+F7** to insert the Center code.
8. Click Close to close the Style Editor, and then click Close again to close the Styles dialog box.

To apply the Sub Head style:

1. Position the insertion point at the beginning of the document, if necessary.
2. Select the second line of text, "Property Management Group".
3. Choose the Sub Head style using any method.

   The selected text is centered and italicized.

Using Styles to Store Boilerplate Text

Styles can contain more than just formatting codes. They can contain text and graphics, as well. You can use a style to store standard text, a graphic, or a WordPerfect character that you use often.

To keep a closing paragraph handy, create an open style with the name Closing in the same way as if you were creating a formatting style. In the Style Editor window, key the text that is needed for the closing paragraph, but do not add formatting codes. Be sure to spell-check the text before closing the style editor. To make the closing paragraph available for future documents, save the style library after creating the new style.

To use the Closing style, position the insertion point where you want to insert the closing text, and then choose Closing from the Styles pop-up list on the Ruler. The text you keyed in the Style Editor window will appear. If you want the text to be formatted differently, select it, and apply another style on top of it. (Applying one style on top of another is called nesting.)

One drawback to using styles in this way is that you cannot edit the text in the document window. You must edit it in the Style Editor window.

When a bulleted list is needed, it is more convenient to apply a bullet style as you key text than to apply it after the fact. When creating a bullet style, use the Style Off/On option from the Enter Key Inserts pop-up list. When this option is chosen, pressing the **Enter** key automatically turns the bullet style off and then on again to start a new bullet item.

To create a bullet style:

1. Open the Styles dialog box and click Create.

   The Style Properties dialog box opens.

2. Key **Square Bullet List** in the Name text box.

3. Key **Indented bullet list** in the Description text box.

4. Choose Paired from the Type pop-up list, if necessary.

5. Choose Style On/Off from the Enter Key Inserts pop-up list.

6. Click OK.

   The Style Properties dialog box closes, and the Style Editor window opens.

7. Press the **Tab** key to insert a tab code.

8. Choose WP Characters from the Font menu (or press **Ctrl+W**) to open the WordPerfect Characters dialog box.

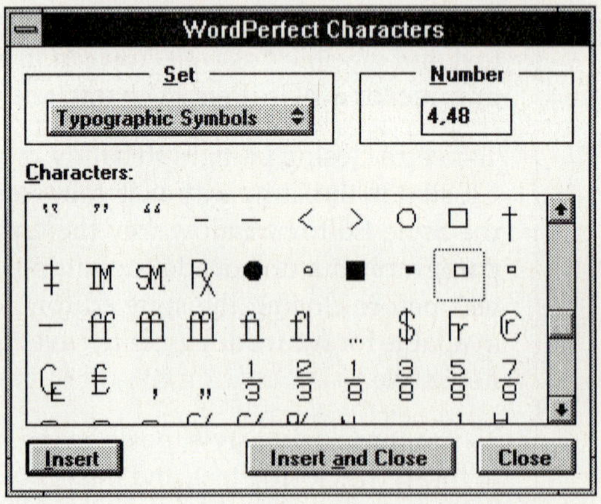

Figure 25-7
The WordPerfect Characters dialog box

9. Choose the medium-sized, hollow square character from the Typographic Symbols set (or key **4,48** in the Number text box).

10. Click the Insert and Close button.

    The WordPerfect Characters dialog box closes, and a hollow square is inserted in the Style Editor window.

11. Press **F7** to insert an [Indent] code after the square.

12. Press the **Right Arrow** key to move the insertion point below the comment.

    The Reveal Codes insertion point should be to the right of the comment code.

13. Press **Enter** twice to insert two hard return codes after the comment.

    The hard return codes insert a blank line between bullet items. (For single-spaced bullets, insert one hard return code instead of two.)

14. Click Close to close the Style Editor window, and then click Close again to close the Styles dialog box.

To use the Square Bullet style:

1. Move to the end of the last paragraph of the on-screen document.

2. To add a sentence to the last paragraph, press the **Spacebar**, and then key **Typical reports include the following information:**.

3. Press **Enter** twice to insert a blank line.

4. Choose Square Bullet List from the Styles button pop-up list on the Ruler.

   A square bullet appears, and the insertion point is at the indented position.

□ Rents collected

□ Year-to-date expenses

□ Budget variances

□ Repairs made

□ Repairs required

A bullet list formatted with a style

5. Key **Rents collected** and press **Enter**.

   The insertion point moves to a new line, and a second square bullet is inserted.

6. Key **Year-to-date expenses** and press **Enter** again.

7. Key the following list, pressing **Enter** at the end of each line:

   Budget variances
   Repairs made
   Repairs required

8. Key the last item on the list, **Annualized income forecast**, but do not press **Enter**.

   If you press **Enter**, a new, unneeded bullet will be inserted.

9. Choose Square Bullet List from the Styles button pop-up list to turn off the style (or press the **Right Arrow** key).

Special WordPerfect characters, text, or graphics can be inserted in a style. In the case of a paired style, text or graphics inserted before the comment will be inserted before the text to which the style is applied. Text or graphics inserted after the comment will be inserted after the styled text.

Create a style with WordPerfect characters:

1. Open the Styles dialog box and click Create.
2. Key **Logo** in the Name text box, and key **Univers Bold 18 pt** in the Description text box.
3. Verify that the Paired and Hard Return options are chosen.
4. Click OK.

   The Style Editor window opens.

5. Open the Font dialog box; choose Univers (Scalable), 18, Bold, and Italic; and click OK.

   The font codes are inserted.

6. Press **Shift+F7** to insert the center code.
7. Choose WP Characters from the Font menu (or press **Ctrl+W**).
8. Choose the star from the Math/Scientific set (or key **6,112** in the Number text box).
9. Click Insert three times to insert three stars and then click Close.
10. Press the **Spacebar** once to insert a space after the stars.
11. Click Close to close the Style Editor window, and then click Close again to close the Styles dialog box.

Apply the Logo style:

1. Select "Five Points Realty" at the top of the document.
2. Choose Logo from the Styles button pop-up list on the Ruler.

   Five Points Realty is now centered and formatted in 18-point Univers bold, and three stars are inserted to the left of the text.

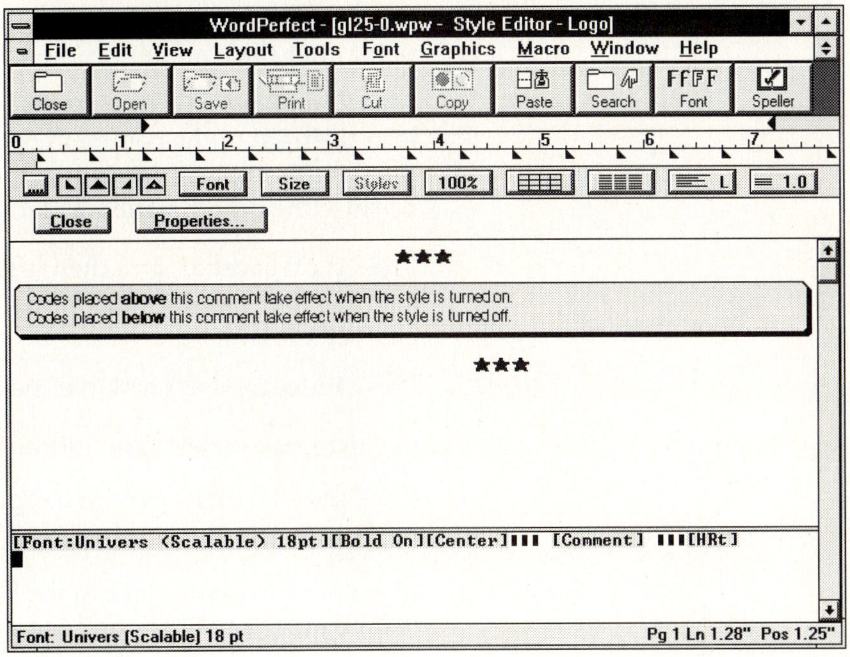

Figure 25-8
The Logo style codes after editing

Editing a Style

When a style is edited, all the text in the document formatted with the style changes to reflect the style's new attributes. Editing a style is a powerful tool, allowing you to change the look of an entire document quickly.

It is very easy to edit a style once it has been created. Select the style from the Styles list box and then click Edit. The Style Editor window appears displaying all the codes, text, and other items that are part of the style already. You can delete and insert codes and text just as you do when creating a style. Click the Properties button in the Style Editor window to change the style's Name, Description, Type, or Edit Key Inserts options.

The Logo style created in the above procedure dramatically enhanced the "Five Points Realty" text, but, with a few changes, it will look even better. Adding three stars to the right of the styled text will make the logo look balanced. Adding two blank lines below the logo will set it off from the rest of the document.

To edit the Logo style:

1. Open the Styles dialog box and choose Logo.
2. Click Edit.

   The Style Editor window opens, displaying the codes and WP characters that make up the Logo style.

3. Click the I-beam below the comment to position the insertion point after the comment code.

   Check the Reveal Codes space to make sure the insertion point is to the right of the comment code. In the document window, the insertion point appears centered, below the comment, because the center attribute is in effect.

4. Press the **Spacebar**, and then insert three stars using steps 7, 8, and 9 in the last procedure as a guide (the star is WordPerfect character 6,112).

5. Press **Enter** to insert a blank line after the Logo style.

Change the Logo style's description:

1. Click the Properties button to open the Style Properties dialog box.

2. Move the insertion point to the beginning of the Description text box and key **Stars,** and then press the **Spacebar**.

   The description now reads "Stars, Univers Bold 18 pt".

3. Click OK to close the Style Properties dialog box.

4. Close the Style Editor window, and then close the Styles dialog box.

   The changes made to the Logo style are applied automatically to "Five Points Realty".

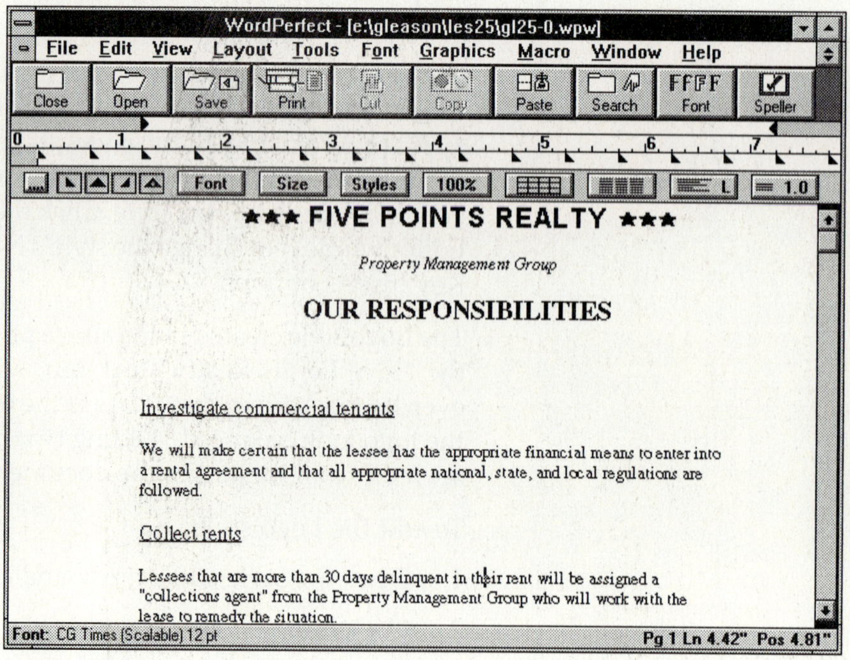

Figure 25-9
The document 25-0.wpw with styles applied

2. Click the Save As button.

   The Save Styles dialog box opens. The current directory is C:\wpwin.

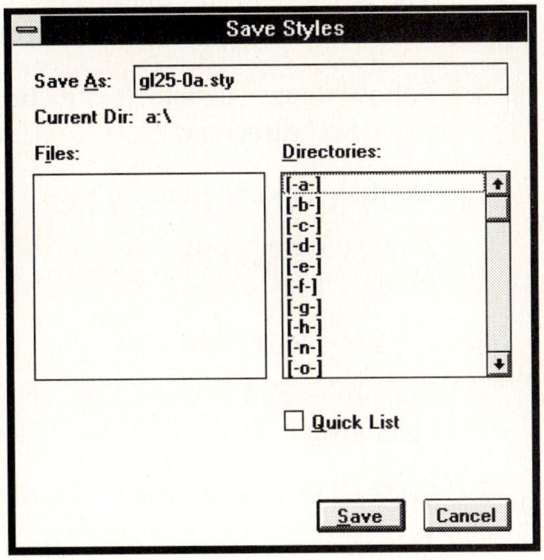

Figure 25-11
The Save Styles dialog box

3. Follow your instructor's directions to change the current drive and directory to the place where your practice files are saved.
4. Key ***[your three-letter identifier]*25-0a.sty** in the Save As text box.
5. Click the Save button.

   The styles are saved as a file on your student disk.

6. Click Close to close the Styles dialog box.

Retrieving Styles

If styles have been saved as a style library, they can be retrieved into another document. This is a powerful feature that can easily change the way a document is formatted. If the style names in the style library match the style names in the current document, the styles from the retrieved library replace the styles in the document, changing the document's format. If the style library contains names that do not match the style names in the document, they are added to the list of styles in the document.

To retrieve a style:

1. Press **Ctrl+Home** twice to position the insertion point at the beginning of the document, before any codes.

2. Double-click the Styles button on the Ruler to open the Styles dialog box.

3. Click the Retrieve button.

   The Retrieve Styles dialog box opens. It is very similar to the Open file dialog box, but the current directory is C:\wpwin.

4. Follow your instructor's directions to change to the student drive and directory.

5. Double-click the file 25-0b.sty.

   A question box pops up, warning you that the styles already exist.

6. Click Yes to replace styles with the same names.

   The Styles dialog box reappears. Notice that a new style, "Hanging Indent," is added to the Styles list box.

7. Click Close to close the Styles dialog box.

   The on-screen document is changed dramatically. Each of the Style codes in the document received a new definition from the retrieved style library.

To retrieve another style library:

1. Open the Styles dialog box and click Retrieve.

2. Move to the drive and directory where your student files are saved.

3. Double-click the file 25-0a.sty. (This is a copy of the style library you saved previously.)

4. Click Yes to replace existing styles.

5. Close the Styles dialog box.

   The on-screen document is changed to its original format.

6. Spell-check the document.

7. Save the on-screen document as *[your three-letter identifier]*25-0.wpw.

8. Exit WordPerfect (unless you will be doing the following exercises immediately).

Table 25-1: Keyboard Shortcut for Styles

Keyboard Shortcut	Action
Alt+F8	Opens the Styles dialog box

Key Terms

Open style	Style
Paired style	Style library

Exercises

Exercise 25.1

1. Start WordPerfect, if necessary.
2. Open the file 25-1.wpw.
3. Create an open style, named "Body", to format the page layout and base font for the on-screen document:
   A. Display the Ruler, if necessary.
   B. Open the Styles dialog box by double-clicking the Styles button on the Ruler.
   C. Click Create.
   D. Key **Body** in the Name text box and **Univers 12 pt** in the Description text box.
   E. Set the Type option to Open.
   F. Click OK to close the Style Properties dialog box and open the Style Editor.
   G. Insert codes to set the top margin to 2 inches and the font to 12-point Univers.
   H. Close the Style Editor and the Style dialog box.
4. Apply the Body style to the document:
   A. Position the insertion point at the beginning of the document.
   B. Choose Body from the Styles button pop-up list on the Ruler.
5. Create a paired style with the name "Title" for the document heading:
   A. Open the Styles dialog box and click Create.
   B. Key **Title** in the Name text box and **Bold, Centered, 18 pt Univers** in the Description text box.
   C. Verify that the Type option is set to Paired and the Enter Key Inserts option is set to Hard Return, and then click OK to open the Style Editor window.
   D. Enter the codes for 18-point Univers, bold, and centered above the comment.

E. Press the **Right Arrow** key to move the insertion point below the comment.

F. Enter two hard return codes below the comment.

G. Close the Style Editor and the Styles dialog box.

6. Apply the Title style:

A. Select "FALL ANNOUNCEMENT" at the beginning of the document.

B. Choose Title from the Styles button pop-up list. (Scroll to the top of the document to see the results.)

7. Create a paired style for a bullet list:

A. Open the Styles dialog box and click Create.

B. Enter the following information and options in the Style Properties dialog box:

Name:	**Arrowhead Bullet**
Description:	**Indented bullet list**
Type:	Paired
Enter Key Inserts:	Style Off/On

C. Insert the following codes in the Styles Editor window above the comment: Tab, the right-pointing arrowhead from the Math/Scientific set (WP Character 6,27), and Indent.

D. Enter a hard return code below the comment. (Entering one hard return code instead of two will create a single-spaced list.)

E. Close the Style Editor and the Styles dialog box.

8. Apply the Arrowhead Bullet List style to text as you key it:

A. Move the insertion point to the blank line below the fourth paragraph, which begins "To register, submit", and press **Enter**.

B. Choose Arrowhead Bullet from the Styles button pop-up list.

C. Key **Check** and press **Enter**.

D. Add the following items to the bullet list (remember, instead of pressing **Enter** after the last item in the list, turn the style off from the Styles button, or press the **Right Arrow** key):

Money order
MasterCard
Visa

9. Apply the Arrowhead Bullet style to the three paragraphs following the sentence "You can register in the following ways:"

   A. Select the paragraph that begins "Mail registrations".

   B. Choose the Arrowhead Bullet style from the Styles button.

   C. Select the next two paragraphs, one at a time, and apply the Arrowhead Bullet style.

10. Delete the unused styles from the Styles list:

    A. Open the Styles dialog box.

    B. Choose Bibliography and then click Delete.

    C. Click OK.

    D. Delete the following styles from the Styles list: Bullet List, Doc Init, Pleading, and Tech Init.

11. Save the remaining styles in a style library:

    A. Open the Styles dialog box, if necessary.

    B. Click Save As.

    C. Choose the drive and directory where your student files are stored.

    D. Key ***[your three-letter identifier]*****25-1.sty** in the Save As text box.

    E. Click Save.

12. Spell-check the document.

13. Save the document as *[your three-letter identifier]*25-1.wpw.

14. Print the document and close it.

15. Close the document and exit WordPerfect (unless you will be doing the following exercises immediately).

Exercise 25.2

1. Start WordPerfect, if necessary.

2. Open the file 25-2.wpw.

3. Create a paired style to format a tabular table heading:

   A. Display the Ruler, if necessary.

   B. Open the Styles dialog box and click Create.

C. Enter the following information in the Style Properties dialog box:

Name:	**Tabbed Table Heading**
Description:	**Bold, Underlined**
Type:	Paired
Enter Key Inserts:	Hard Return

D. Click OK to open the Style Editor window.

E. Position the insertion point above the comment, if necessary, clear the tabs, and set centered tabs at 1.88 inches and 3.38 inches (relative).

F. Insert a bold on code and an underline on code above the comment.

G. Close the Style Editor window and the Styles dialog box.

4. Create a paired style to format the body of a table:

   A. Following step 3, above, name the style "Tabbed Table Body," key **Normal text** in the Description text box, and verify that the type is Paired and that Enter Key Inserts is set to Hard Return.

   B. In the Style Editor window, set right-aligned tabs at 2.25 inches and 3.75 inches (relative).

   C. Close the Style Editor window and the Styles dialog box.

5. Apply the tabbed table styles:

   A. Select the text "Buckhead Qtr2 Qtr1", and then choose Tabbed Table Heading from the Styles button pop-up list.

   B. Select the body of the Buckhead tabbed table, and apply the Tabbed Table Body style using the Styles button.

   C. Apply the appropriate tabbed table styles to the heading and body of the second table in the document.

6. Format the document as a memo with the following information:

TO:	**Bud Porter**
FROM:	**John Soloman**
DATE:	**August 7, 199-**
SUBJECT:	**First Half Sales Totals for 199-**

7. Spell-check the document.

8. Save the document as *[your three-letter identifier]*25-2.wpw.

9. Print the document.

10. Close the document and exit WordPerfect (unless you will be doing the following exercises immediately).

Exercise 25.3

1. Start WordPerfect, if necessary.
2. Open the file 25-3.wpw.
3. Apply the default Heading 1 style to the line beginning "Atlanta Board of Realtors" at the top of the document.
4. Apply the default Heading 2 style to the following course titles:

   Real Estate Principles and Practices

   Real Estate Appraisal I

   Real Estate Finance

   Review for Real Estate Exam
5. Create a paired style named "Emphasized Paragraph" that will apply the bold and italics character attributes.
6. Apply the Emphasized Paragraph style to the last line in the document.
7. Create an open style named "Body" to format the entire document in 12-point CG Times with 1.25-inch left and right margins and a 2-inch top margin.
8. Apply the Body style to the entire document. (Press **Ctrl+Home** twice to be sure the insertion point is at the very beginning of the document.)
9. Edit the Heading 1 style to remove the centering and change the font to 14-point bold Univers. Change the description to reflect the formatting changes. (Be sure to delete the code [Vry Large On].)
10. Edit the Heading 2 style to remove the underlining and change the font to 12-point bold Univers. Change the description to reflect the formatting changes. (Be sure to delete the code [Large On].)
11. Delete the styles that are not used in this document.
12. Save the styles as *[your three-letter identifier]*25-3.sty.
13. Spell-check the document.
14. Save the document as *[your three-letter identifier]*25-3.wpw.
15. Print the document.
16. Close the document and exit WordPerfect (unless you will be doing the following exercises immediately.)

Exercise 25.4

1. Start WordPerfect, if necessary.
2. Open a new file, if necessary.
3. Open the Styles dialog box, and delete all the styles in the list box.
4. Retrieve the style 25-4.sty.
5. Turn on the Title style, key **Real Estate Seminars**, and then turn off the Title style.
6. Key Figure 25-12, which appears at the end of this exercise, including the corrections.
7. Position the insertion point on the blank line above "Non-Credit Enrichment Seminars" and press **Enter**.
8. Use the Arrowhead Bullet style to create a bullet list, keying the following list of seminar topics as entries:

   Fair Housing & Ethical Practices
   Property Management
   Real Estate Appraisal
   Real Estate Contracts
   Real Estate Finance
   Real Estate Law
   Real Estate Taxes

9. Apply the Title style to the heading "Non-Credit Enrichment Seminars".
10. Key the following text as a list above the last paragraph, which begins "We invite your suggestions". If necessary, insert a blank line before and after the list:

    Buyers' Brokerage
    Closing the Transaction
    Counseling the First-time Home Buyer
    Dealing with Foreign Investors
    Detecting Property Flaws
    Marketing Foreclosed Properties
    Using Your Computer for Sales Enhancement

11. Format the list with the Arrowhead Bullet style.
12. Remove the blank lines between the bullet-list items. (Position the insertion point at the end of an item, and press the **Delete** key, or use Reveal Codes to locate the hard return codes.)
13. Create a style named "Emphasized Paragraph" with the attributes Bold and Italics.
14. Apply the Emphasized Paragraph style to the last paragraph in the document.

15. Edit the Arrowhead Bullet style so that the bullet character is WP Character 6,56 (a small, right-pointing arrow in the Math/Scientific set).
16. Edit the Title style so that it is left-justified, 14-point bold Univers. Remove one of the hard return codes from the style.
17. Apply the Body style to the entire document. (Before applying this style, be sure the insertion point is at the top of the document, before any codes.)
18. Using Reveal Codes, delete or insert hard return codes where necessary, so that there is one line before and one line after the main headings and bullet lists.
19. Save the style as *[your three-letter identifier]*25-4b.sty.
20. Spell-check the document.
21. Save the document as *[your three-letter identifier]*25-4.wpw.
22. Print the document.
23. Close the document and exit WordPerfect (unless you will be doing the following exercise immediately).

Figure 25-12

```
1 Session (3 hours)

Applicable toward the state licensing requirement. Details to be announced
                 members of the Atlanta Board of Realtors
in a mailing to ~~every real estate licensee in the Chicago area~~ by November
1. See proposed list of seminar topics below.
Non-member fee: $30. Member fee: $15.

Non-Credit Enrichment Seminars
1 Session (3 hours)
For those interested in upgrading their knowledge and skill in various
                        ABR
areas of activity. ~~GCBR~~ members only.
Member fee: $15.

We invite your suggestions for additional enrichment seminars and seminar
leaders.
```

Exercise 25.5

1. Start WordPerfect, if necessary.
2. Open the file 25-5.wpw.
3. Open the Styles dialog box, and delete all the styles in the list box.
4. Create the following styles:

Body:	Open, left-justified, CG Times 12 pt, 2-inch top margin
Heading 1:	Paired, centered, Univers 18 pt, bold, italic, WP Characters 5,21 and a space character before the comment, a space character, WP Character 5,22 and a Hard Return after the comment
Heading 2:	Paired, left-justified, Univers 14 pt, bold
Sub Head:	Paired, centered, italics, two blank lines below
Column:	Open, two newspaper-style columns, ½ inch gutter

   Emphasized Paragraph: Paired, italics, bold

5. Save the styles as *[your three-letter identifier]*25-5.sty.
6. Apply the Body style to the entire document.
7. Apply the Heading 1 style to "The Five Points Reporter" at the top of the document.
8. Apply the Sub Head style to the text "Newsworthy articles for our agents" on the second line.
9. Apply the Heading 2 style to the following paragraph headings:

   Atlanta Hawks Ticket Discounts
   G&H Building Gets New Tenants
   Homes on the Rental Market for the 1996 Olympics
10. Apply the Emphasized Paragraph style to the second paragraph below the "Atlanta Hawks" heading, which begins "For more information, contact".
11. Apply the Column style at the beginning of the "Atlanta Hawks" heading line.
12. Insert a column break where necessary to make the two columns balanced.
13. Spell-check the document.
14. Save the document as *[your three-letter identifier]*25-5.wpw.
15. Print the document.
16. Close the document and exit WordPerfect.

Macros

If you use WordPerfect regularly, you soon will recognize that some word-processing procedures are repeated often during the course of your work. Macros can save time and simplify repetitive or complicated procedures. This lesson presents several macros supplied by WordPerfect and teaches you how to create simple macros of your own.

Objectives

- Understand what a macro is.
- Execute macros.
- Use WordPerfect-supplied macros.
- Understand where macros are stored.
- Create macros.
- Edit macros.

What Is a Macro?

Macro
A collection of menu commands and keystrokes that are saved as a file and can be played back exactly as saved by executing a single command.

A *macro* is a collection of menu commands and keystrokes that are saved as a file. When you play a macro, the saved commands and keystrokes are executed automatically, saving time and assuring that procedures are performed accurately.

Macros can be played over and over again and are ideal for repetitive, tedious, and complicated tasks. A simple macro, for example, can set margins, the base font, and tab settings for a standard report format that you use regularly in your work. Another macro can insert a signature block or standard closing paragraph automatically that you would otherwise key each time you create a letter.

WordPerfect allows you to create two types of macros:

- Recorded macros

  These are created by recording the commands and keystrokes that you use when performing a WordPerfect task.

- Programmed macros

  These macros are created in the same way as a computer program, by keying all the necessary commands. WordPerfect macros are, in fact, computer programs, using WordPerfect's powerful macro programming language.

This lesson deals with recorded macros. Mastering programmed macros requires knowledge of computer-programming techniques that are beyond the scope of this text.

Note: The WordPerfect-supplied macros provide good learning examples for creating programmed macros.

WordPerfect-Supplied Macros

Approximately 30 macros are supplied with the WordPerfect program. Some of them are very useful timesavers for common word-processing tasks, and others are useful only to programmers who are creating complex macros. Table 26-1 lists some of the more useful macros:

Table 26-1: Useful WordPerfect Macros

Macro	Purpose
barcode.wcm	Converts a ZIP Code into its bar-code equivalent
bullet.wcm	Converts a group of paragraphs or a list of items into a bulleted list
bulletdf.wcm	Changes the bullet character used in the bullet.wcm macro
codes.wcm	Inserts text representations of formatting codes into a copy of the current document
edit.wcm	Edits a formatting code from within the Reveal Codes space
envelope.wcm	Addresses and prints an envelope
glosedit.wcm	Allows you to define abbreviations and acronyms for use with the glossary.wcm macro
glossary.wcm	Expands an abbreviation or acronym into the text it represents
labels.wcm	Adds paper definitions for specific label styles to the list of paper types in the Paper Size dialog box
replace.wcm	Replaces a paired-code format with another paired format

Two macros, glosedit.wcm and glossary.wcm, although very worthwhile, are not used in this lesson's procedures or exercises. These macros change WordPerfect defaults, making them unsuitable for classroom purposes. They are very useful, however, and should be explored if you have a computer at home or at work. Run glosedit.wcm to define acronyms and the text they represent. To expand an acronym in a document, key the acronym, select it, and play the glossary.wcm macro to expand it.

Note: The default macro directory is c:\wpwin\macros. It usually is the current directory when you open the Play Macro dialog box. If the current directory is different, change to the correct directory using the Directories list box.

Playing Macros

WordPerfect-supplied macros are stored in the c:\wpwin\macros directory. To play one of these macros, choose Play from the Macro menu (or press **Alt+F10**) to open the Play Macro dialog box, and then double-click a macro in the Files list box (or select it and then click Play).

The Macro menu

Using the Bullet Macro

The bullet.wcm macro adds bullets to a list of items. To use it, first select the text, and then play the bullet.wcm macro.

To insert bullets:

1. Start WordPerfect.

2. Open the file 26-0.wpw.

3. Select the last five paragraphs in the document, beginning with the paragraph that starts "Improving the property:" and ending with the paragraph that starts "Adjusting the rental fee:".

4. Choose Play from the Macro menu.

   The Play Macro dialog box opens.

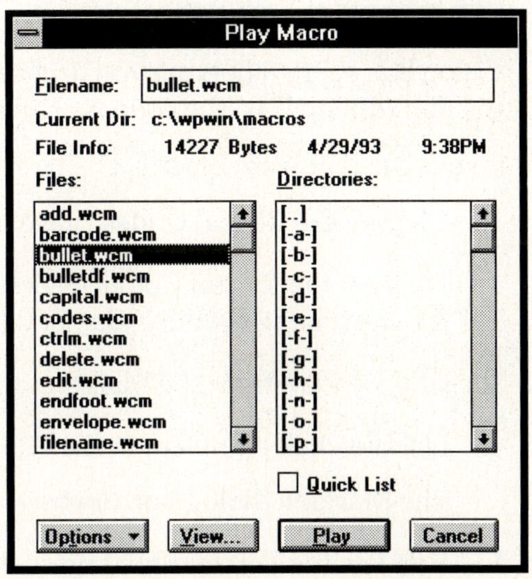

Figure 26-1
The Play Macro dialog box

5. Change the current directory to C:\wpwin\macros, if necessary.

6. Double-click the file bullet.wcm (or choose the file, and then click the Play button).

   Bullets appear to the left of each selected paragraph. While the macro is playing, the mouse pointer changes into the international "No" symbol (a circle with a slash through it), indicating that the mouse cannot be used. When the macro is finished, the mouse pointer returns to normal.

The first time the macro is played, you will see the message "Compiling macro" on the left side of the status bar. Compiling is the process of converting the macro text into a format that the computer can execute more quickly. Once a macro is compiled, it can be played as often as desired without the need to compile it again. If a macro is edited, WordPerfect will detect the changes the next time it is played and recompile it automatically.

The Undo Command and Macros

The Undo command will not undo the results of a macro. You should always save the document on which you are working before running a macro, in case you get unexpected results.

Using the Edit Macro

The edit.wcm macro allows you to change the attributes of a formatting code from within the Reveal Codes space. For example, to edit a base-font code, click it, and then run the edit.wcm macro. The Font dialog box opens, allowing you to choose a new font. When you close the Font dialog box, the code is changed.

To use the edit.wcm macro:

1. Display the Reveal Codes space, if necessary.
2. Position the Reveal Codes insertion point at the beginning of the document, on the code [L/R Mar:0.75",0.75"].
3. Choose Play from the Macro menu.
4. Double-click edit.wcm in the Files list box.

   The Margins dialog box opens.
5. Key **1** in the Left text box, press the **Tab** key, and then key **1** in the Right text box.
6. Click the OK button to close the Margins dialog box.

   The selected code is changed.

Using the Replace Macro

The replace.wcm macro allows you to replace paired formatting codes with other paired formatting codes throughout the document automatically. This macro affects the document from the insertion-point position to the end of the document.

Selecting text before running the replace.wcm macro has no effect on what text will be changed in the document. If text is selected, the macro deselects the text and then makes changes from the insertion point to the end of the document, just as if no text had been selected.

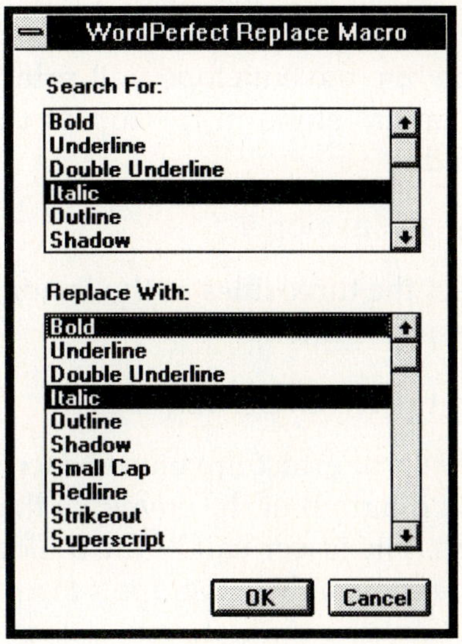

Figure 26-2
The WordPerfect Replace Macro dialog box

Replace italics with bold and italics:

1. Position the insertion point at the beginning of the document, if necessary.
2. Play replace.wcm.

   The WordPerfect Replace Macro dialog box opens.
3. Choose Italic from the Search For list box.
4. Choose Bold from the Replace With list box, and then choose Italic.

   Both attributes are selected. You can select as many attributes as needed from the Replace With list box, but only one from the Search For list box.
5. Click OK to close the dialog box.

   The international "No" symbol indicates that the macro is working.
6. When the macro is finished playing, scroll through the document.

   The text that formerly was italicized now is bold and italicized.

Using the Envelope Macro

The envelope macro automatically formats an envelope. You can choose to have it inserted at the bottom of the current document to print along with the document, or to send the envelope information directly to the printer. In either case, if your printer has a special envelope bin, the envelope will print automatically. If not, be sure to feed an envelope in the top of the printer's paper tray when prompted.

Creating an envelope:

1. Select the three lines of the inside address at the top of the on-screen document.

2. Play the envelope.wcm macro.

   The WordPerfect Envelope Macro dialog box opens, displaying a diagram of the envelope that includes the selected address. The lower half of the dialog box offers several options to customize the envelope's format.

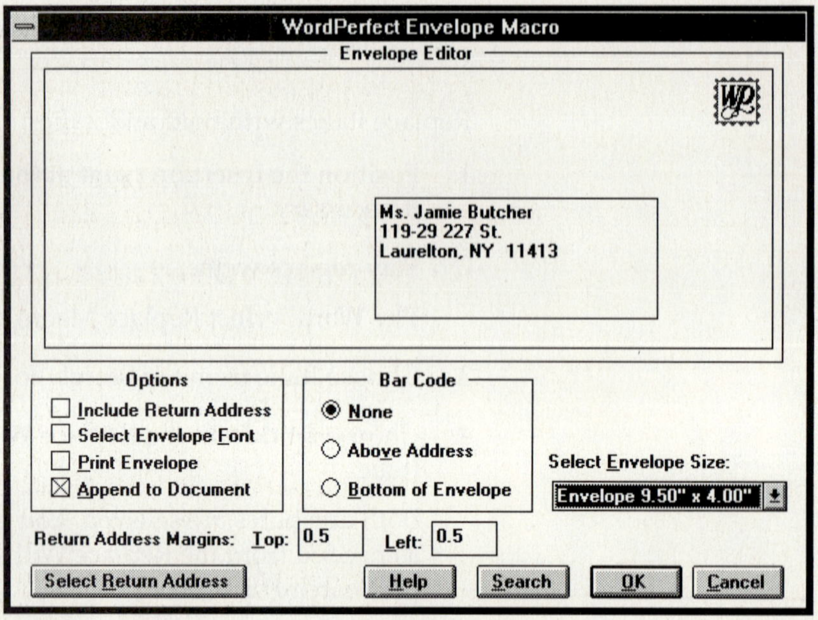

Figure 26-3
The WordPerfect Envelope Macro dialog box

3. In the Options box, check Append to Document (uncheck the other options, if necessary).

4. In the Bar Code options box, choose None.

   If you choose Above Address or Bottom of Envelope, a ZIP Code bar code conforming to postal regulations will be printed on the envelope.

5. In the Select Envelope Size list box, choose Envelope 9.50″ x 4.00″, if necessary.

6. Click OK to insert the envelope information at the end of the document.

7. Display the Reveal Codes space, if necessary, and scroll to the end of the document.

   A hard page break separates the envelope from the rest of the document, and a paper-size code indicates that the current page is an envelope.

Using the Bar Code Macro

If you prefer to create envelopes without using the envelope.wcm macro, you can use the barcode.wcm macro to insert a bar code when needed.

To insert a bar code:

1. Press **Ctrl+End** to position the insertion point at the end of the envelope text.

2. Press **Enter** four times to position the insertion point on the last line of the envelope.

3. Play the barcode.wcm macro.

   The WordPerfect Bar Code Macro dialog box opens.

Figure 26-4
The WordPerfect Bar Code Macro dialog box

Bar code on an envelope

4. Drag the dialog box out of the way, if necessary, so you can see the ZIP Code on the envelope.

5. Key **11413** in the ZIP Code text box and click OK.

   The bar code is inserted at the bottom of the envelope.

Location of Macro Files

When you play macros, WordPerfect automatically looks for the macro files in the default macro directory c:\wpwin\macros. When you record new macros, they are saved in the default directory automatically. You can change the default macro directory, so that macros relating to specific documents or specific projects can be saved together with them in the same directory. Another reason to change the location of macro files is to keep your macros separate from those created by others using the same computer.

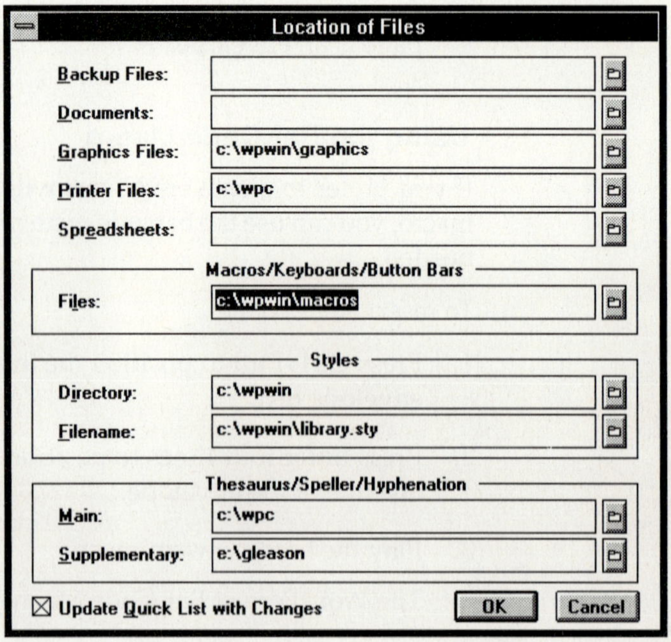

Figure 26-5
The Location of Files dialog box

To change the default macro directory, choose Preferences from the File menu, and then choose Location of Files from the Preferences cascading menu. The Location of Files dialog box lists all the default directories that can be changed. When working with this dialog box, be careful not to change the wrong text box. For example, do not change the printer files directory. If you do, your WordPerfect documents will not print. Likewise, if you change the main speller directory, the speller will not work.

In the following procedure, you will change the location of macro files to the drive and directory where your student files are stored.

To change the default macro directory:

1. Choose Preferences from the File menu, and then choose Location of Files from the Preferences cascading menu.

2. Select the text in the Files text box under the heading Macros/Keyboards/Button Bars.

3. Follow your instructor's directions, if necessary, and key the drive and directory where your student files are saved.

4. Click OK.

   The Location of Files dialog box closes, and the macro directory is changed to your student drive and directory.

When two or more users share a computer, it is important to undo changes that you make to program defaults before exiting the program. Doing so will insure that the program operates the way other users expect. At the end of this lesson, you will be instructed to change the macro directory back to the WordPerfect default.

Creating Recorded Macros

You can record macros with a few easy steps. Recorded macros can be used to create letterheads and memo headings, set formatting and fonts, and insert standard paragraphs in a document.

To begin the recording process, open a new file, and then open the Macro Record dialog box by choosing Record from the Macro menu. The Record Macro dialog box will open.

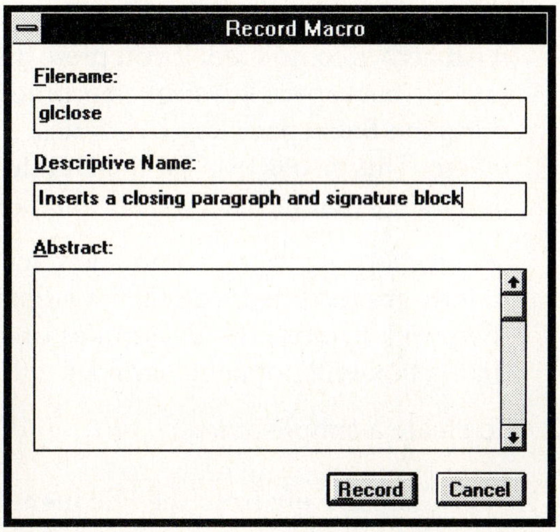

Figure 26-6
The Record Macro dialog box

The Record Macro dialog box has three text boxes:

- Filename

  The Filename is required and must follow the same rules as for document filenames. The .wcm extension is added automatically.

Note: The Descriptive Name and Abstract information can be viewed when a macro is being edited. To see it, choose Document from the Layout menu and then choose Summary. This information also can be viewed from the WordPerfect File Manager.

- Descriptive Name

  The Descriptive Name is optional. Use it to describe the purpose of the macro.

- Abstract

  The Abstract is optional. Use it to enter instructions and other useful information.

When the Record Macro dialog box is completed, click the Record button. While recording, the phrase "Recording Macro" appears on the status bar.

The Macro Recorder mouse pointer

When you key text as part of a macro, the I-beam is replaced with the international "No" symbol, reminding you that you cannot use the mouse to move the insertion point. You can, however, use either the mouse or keyboard shortcuts to choose menu commands. When you point to a menu command or a button, the pointer changes to an arrow. As the macro is being recorded, every character that you key and every menu command that you choose is recorded in sequence exactly as you press the keys.

You may find that pressing the **Backspace** key is an automatic reflex when you make a keystroke error, but you should resist the urge to correct text while recording. Keystroke errors are easily edited after the macro is completed. If you press the **Backspace** key while recording, the backspace keystroke becomes a recorded command. If you press the **Backspace** key five times, it will appear five times in the macro. This also is true for the **Delete** key, the Arrow keys, and any other keys that move the insertion point.

When choosing menu commands in a macro, only completed commands are recorded. In other words, if you open a dialog box and then click Cancel, the keystrokes or mouse clicks that opened the dialog box will not be recorded.

To create a simple macro:

1. Choose New from the File menu to open a new file. (Do not close the on-screen document.)

2. Choose Record from the Macro menu (or press **Ctrl+F10**).

   The Record Macro dialog box opens.

3. Key ***[your three-letter identifier]*****close** in the Filename text box.

4. Key **Inserts a closing paragraph and signature block** in the Descriptive Name text box.

5. Click the Record button.

   The Record Macro dialog box closes. The status bar displays "Recording Macro" in the lower left corner.

6. Key the following paragraph:

   Please review the enclosed brochure describing our property management services in detail. I will call you in one week to answer any further questions you might have.

   (Remember, try not to correct keystroke errors—but, if you do, the macro will still work.)

7. Press **Enter** twice and then key **Sincerely,**.

8. Press **Enter** four times, and then key:

   Della Crandon
   Office Manager

9. Press **Enter** twice.

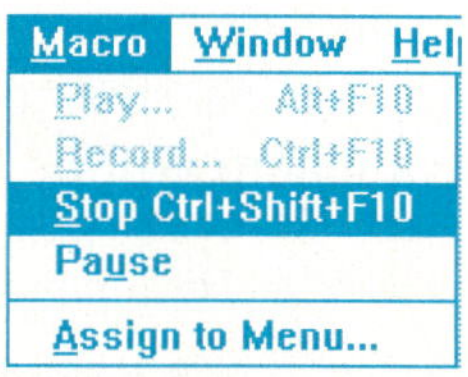

The Macro menu

10. Choose Stop from the Macro menu (or press **Ctrl+Shift+F10**) to end the recording.

    The macro is saved as a file on your student drive and directory with the name *[your three-letter identifier]*close.wcm.

11. Close the unnamed on-screen document without saving it.

    The on-screen document was used to create the macro, but it is not part of the macro and does not need to be saved. Document 26-0.wpw returns to the document window.

Always test macros before applying them to a document. To test the macro:

1. Open a new file.

2. Choose Play from the Macro menu (or press **Alt+F10**).

3. Choose *[your three-letter identifier]*close.wcm.

   The text contained in the macro appears on the screen. If you made keystroke errors, they appear in the text. These can be corrected by editing the macro.

4. Close the unnamed on-screen document without saving it.

   Document 26-0.wpw returns to the document window.

Replacing an Existing Macro

If you play a macro that you created, and it does not execute correctly, many times the easiest way to fix it is simply to rerecord it. To do this, open the Macro Record dialog box, and enter the same filename that the incorrect macro has. A question box will open, asking if you want to replace the existing macro. Choose Yes, and then proceed with the macro-recording steps.

Editing a Macro

You can open a macro file and then edit it in the same way as you edit a document file. The content of the macro file is very different from that of a document file, however. When you record a macro, WordPerfect inserts macro commands into the file. It is important to understand the structure of these commands before attempting to edit the macro.

Syntax
The structure or rules of construction for a macro command.

The structure of a macro command is called its *syntax*. You can think of the syntax as the rules that must be followed when typing or editing a macro command. If the rules are not followed exactly, the macro will not work. Although this may sound intimidating, remember that, when you record a macro, the commands are inserted correctly for you. Your main concern when editing a macro will be to correct errors made when keying text.

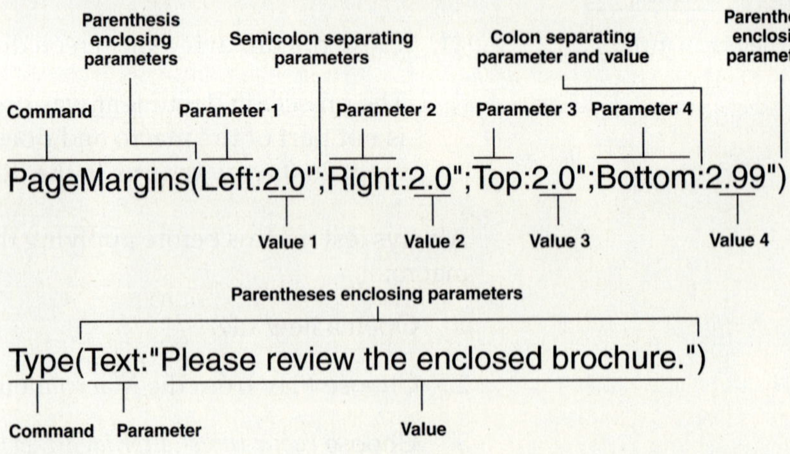

Figure 26-7
Macro-command syntax

Some examples of macro commands are:

- PageMargins(Left:2.0";Right:2.0";Top:2.0";Bottom:2.99")
- HardReturn()
- Type(Text:"Please review the enclosed brochure.")

The parts of a command are the command name, a pair of parentheses, and the parameters located inside the parentheses. Different commands have different numbers of parameters, depending on the information needed. In the above examples, the PageMargins command has four parameters, the HardReturn command has no parameters, and the Type command has one parameter. Each parameter has two parts: a parameter name and a value. A colon separates a parameter name from its value, and a semicolon separates one parameter from another. Text that you key when recording a macro is a parameter value. When a parameter value is text, it must be enclosed in quotes. This distinguishes text from commands. For example, in the command

```
Type(Text:"Please review the enclosed brochure.")
```

the text inside the quotes will be inserted in the document when the macro is played.

When you record a macro, WordPerfect inserts all the necessary parentheses, parameters, and punctuation. When you edit a macro, you can change the values for parameters. For example, you can correct the spelling of a word in a Type command or change a margin measurement in a PageMargins command. You also can delete unwanted commands and combine two or more Type commands into one. You must be careful, however, to be sure that the command syntax is correct when your editing is complete.

Individual commands can be placed on one line, with no spaces between parts, or they can have spaces and hard returns added to make them easier to read. The only formatting restriction is that all the parts of a command must be included, and that the parts must be in their proper order. For example,

```
PageMargins(Left:2.0";Right:2.0";Top:2.0";Bottom:2.99")
```

is equivalent to

```
PageMargins
(
        Left:2.0";
        Right:2.0";
        Top:2.0";
        Bottom:2.99"
)
```

In the above example, note that there is no semicolon after the last parameter. (This also is true when the entire command is on one line.) Note, also, that the required opening and closing parentheses stand alone on separate lines. Missing parentheses are a common error in macros.

Deleted word

Commands inserted by **Backspace** key

Misspelled word

```
Application (WP;WPWP;Default;"WPWPUS.WCD")
Type
(
  Text:"Please review the enclosed brochure describing the"
)
DeleteCharPrevious()
DeleteCharPrevious()
DeleteCharPrevious()
Type
(
  Text:"our property management services in detail. I willl call you"
)
Type
(
  Text:" in one week to ansner any further questions you might
havwe."
)
HardReturn()
HardReturn()
Type
(
  Text:"Sincerely,"
)
HardReturn()
HardReturn()
HardReturn()
HardReturn()
Type
(
  Text:"Della Crandon,"
)
HardReturn()
Type
(
  Text:"Office Manager"
)
```

Figure 26-8
Recorded macro illustrating a deleted word

Figure 26-8 shows a macro in a document window, ready for editing. The first line of every macro is the Application command that tells WordPerfect that this is a WordPerfect Macro. This command should not be edited.

It is easy to locate the commands in the above figure that result from deleting a word and then correcting it. The command DeleteCharPrevious() is listed three times, indicating that the three text characters (the word "the") immediately preceding were deleted by pressing the **Backspace** key three times when the macro was being recorded. The next Text parameter begins with the word "our" that was keyed to replace "the."

If you corrected text while recording a macro, you can remove the extra keystroke commands when you edit the macro. This is not a necessary step, but it will make the macro easier to read. Figure 26-9 shows selected text and command parts that will be deleted to combine two Text parameters, making the macro easier to read.

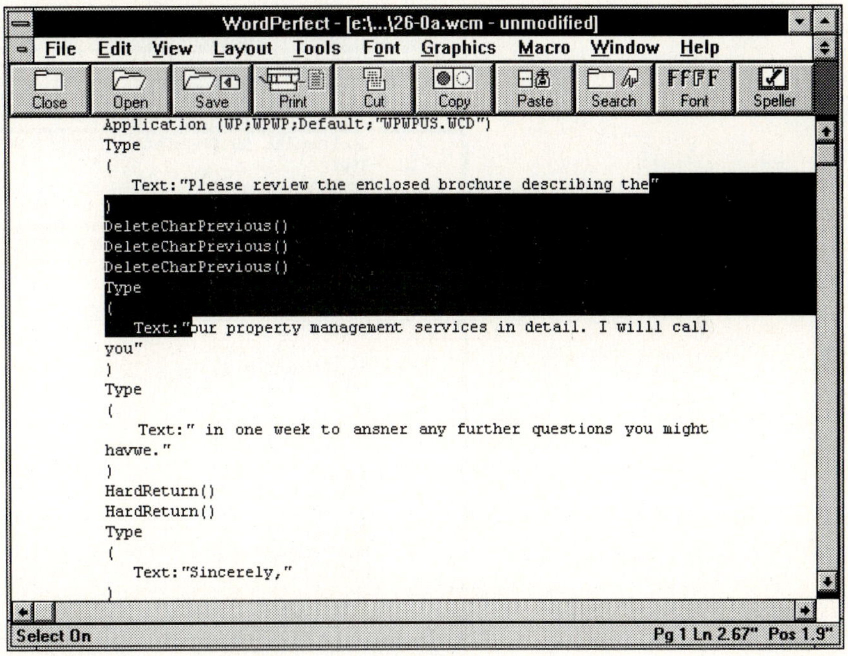

Figure 26-9
Two Text parameters to be combined

To combine two Text parameters:

1. Open the file 26-0a.wcm.

   A macro file is opened in the same way as a document file. This file is a copy of the macro created in the previous procedure.

2. Using the above figure as a guide, position the insertion point at the end of the first Text parameter, just to the left of the closing quotation mark.

3. Drag the insertion point down to the next line, which begins Text:, ending the selection just to the right of the opening quotation mark.

4. Press the **Delete** key.

   The two Text parameters now are combined into one, but the text has errors that must be corrected.

By combining two Text parameters, you eliminate all the punctuation and commands from the end of the text in the first Text parameter to the beginning of the text in the second parameter. When the text is contained completely in one parameter, it is easier to read and check for errors. You can edit the text in a Text parameter just as you edit text in a normal document. You can insert and delete words and sentences to correct keystroke errors or revise the text. Approximately 500 text characters can be included in each Text parameter.

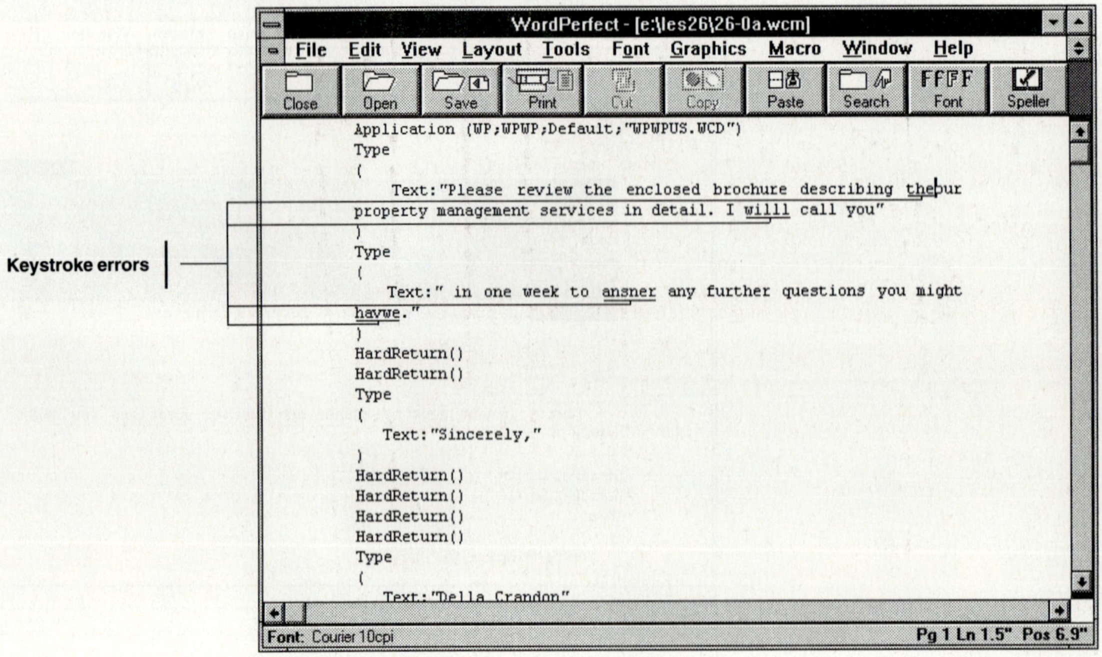

Figure 26-10
Two Text parameters after combining

To correct text errors:

1. Using the Figure 26-10, as a guide, correct the text in the Text parameters.
2. Save the macro in the same way that you save a document. Use the name *[your three-letter identifier]*close.wcm. (Be sure to use the .wcm extension.)
3. Click Yes to replace the existing macro with the same name.
4. Close the macro file.

   The macro file closes, and the document 26-0.wpw appears in the current document window.

Compiling Errors

When you play a macro that you edited, WordPerfect automatically recompiles it, converting the commands into compressed instructions that can be executed. During the compiling process, the macro is checked for syntax errors. If an error is detected, the WordPerfect Macro Facility-Syntax Error dialog box opens.

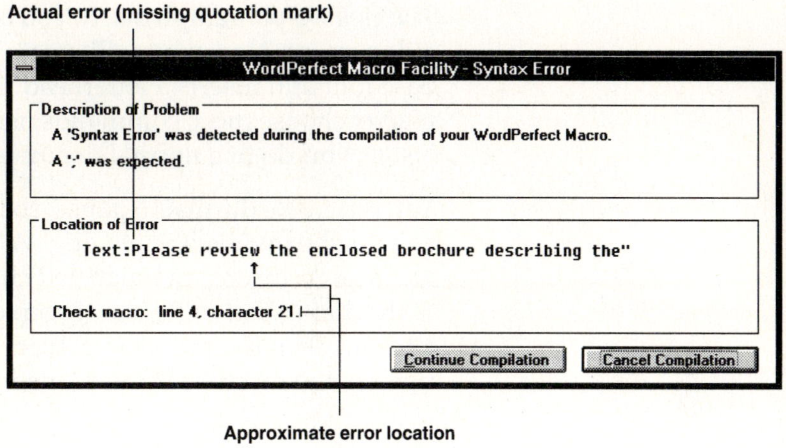

Figure 26-11
The WordPerfect Macro Facility - Syntax Error dialog box

The dialog box shows the command that contains the error and indicates the line and approximate character location of the error. If you see this dialog box, do the following:

- Click the Cancel Compilation button.
- Edit the macro to correct the problem (usually missing punctuation).
- Play the macro again.

Repeat the above process until all errors are found and corrected. Note that the WordPerfect compiler finds syntax errors only. Even if your macro passes the compiler test, it may not execute correctly because of logical errors. You will recognize the existence of logical errors if you get unexpected results when you play the macro.

Now, play the macro to insert the closing paragraph and signature block in the current document:

1. Move the insertion point to the end of the last paragraph in the current document, before the hard page break that marks the beginning of the envelope.
2. Press **Enter** twice to insert a blank line.
3. Choose Play from the Macro menu (or press **Alt+F10**).

4. Double-click the file glclose.wcm.

   The closing paragraph and signature block are inserted in the document.

Creating Macros that Use Menu Commands

The closing-paragraph macro you created and edited inserts text into a document. Now, you will create a macro that sets margins and a base font and inserts a letterhead. To insert menu commands into a macro, choose those commands using menus or keyboard shortcuts just as you do in a normal document.

You can make the macro pause, so that you can choose options from a dialog box while it is playing. When you open a dialog box while recording a macro, an unlabeled check box appears on the right side of the dialog box's title bar. If you check this box, the dialog box will appear when the macro is played, allowing the user to choose options as the macro is being played.

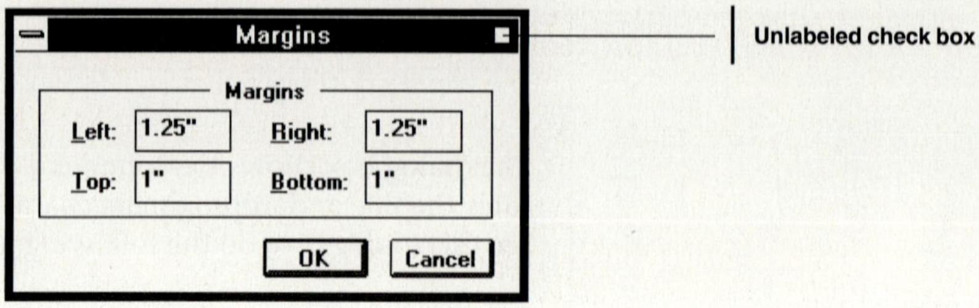

Figure 26-12
The Margins dialog box showing the unlabeled check box

To create the macro:

1. Open a new file. (Do not close the current document.)
2. Open the Record Macro dialog box.
3. Key ***[your three-letter identifier]*****lethd** in the Filename text box and **Five Points Letterhead** in the Descriptive Name text box.
4. Click the Record button.

   The status bar indicates that a macro is being recorded.

5. Choose Margins from the Layout menu, and enter 1.25″ for the left and right margins.

   Notice the check box on the right side of the Margins dialog box title bar, but do not check it.

6. Click OK to set the margins and close the dialog box.

7. Open the Font dialog box, and check the unlabeled check box on the right side of the title bar. Do not choose a font. This can be done when the macro is played.
8. Click OK to close the Font dialog box.
9. Press **Shift+F7** and then **Ctrl+B** to insert the Center and Bold codes.
10. Key **Five Points Realty**, press **Ctrl+B** to turn off the Bold attribute, and then press **Enter** to start a new line.
11. Key and center the following:

    233 Peachtree Street NE
    Atlanta, GA 30303

12. Press **Enter**, and use the Advance command to advance the insertion point to the 2-inch line position.
13. Choose Date from the Tools menu and then choose Text to make the macro insert the current date automatically (or press **Ctrl+F5**).
14. Press **Enter**, and use the Advance command to advance the insertion point to the 3-inch line position.
15. Choose Stop from the Macro menu to end recording and save the macro.
16. Close the current document window without saving it.

    The document 26-0.wpw is displayed again.

Now, play the macro to insert the letterhead in the current document:

1. Press **Ctrl+Home** twice to move the insertion point to the very beginning of the document, before the first code.
2. Play the macro *[your three-letter identifier]*lethd.wcm.

   The Font dialog box opens.
3. Choose 12-point CG Times and click OK.

   The letterhead and date appear at the top of the document. The font for the entire document changes to 12-point CG Times.
4. Block-protect the closing paragraph and signature block, so that they stay together on the same page.
5. Spell-check the document.
6. Save the document as *[your three-letter identifier]26*-0.wpw.
7. Print the document.

8. Close the document.
9. Open the macro file *[your three-letter identifier]*lethd.wcm and print it.
10. Close all open documents.

Earlier in this lesson, you changed the default drive and directory where WordPerfect macro files are stored. Before you exit WordPerfect, it is necessary to change the macro directory back to the original WordPerfect default, so that the program will operate the way other users expect. The table below shows the standard defaults if WordPerfect is installed on drive C:

Table 26-2: WordPerfect Location of Files Defaults

File Types	Location of Default
Backup Files	none
Documents	none
Graphic Files	c:\wpwin\graphics
Printer Files	c:\wpc
Spreadsheets	none
Macro Files	c:\wpwin\macros
Style Files	c:\wpwin
Style Library Name	c:\wpwin\library.sty
Main Dictionary Files	c:\wpc
Supp Dictionary Files	c:\wpc

To reset the Location of Files defaults:

1. Choose Preferences from the File menu, and then choose Location of Files.
2. Select the text in the Files text box under the heading Macros/Keyboards/Button Bars.
3. Follow your instructor's directions, if necessary, and key the drive and directory where the WordPerfect macro files are stored (in a standard installation, this is c:\wpwin\macros).
4. Click OK.
5. Exit WordPerfect (unless you will be doing the following exercises immediately).

Table 26-3: Keyboard Shortcuts for Macros

Keyboard Shortcut	Action
Alt+F10	Play a macro
Ctrl+F10	Record a macro
Ctrl+Shift+F10	Stop a macro

Key Terms

Macro
Syntax

Exercises

Exercise 26.1

1. Start WordPerfect, if necessary.
2. Change the default macro directory to the disk and drive where your student files are stored:
   A. Choose Preferences from the File menu, and then choose Location of Files.
   B. Key the drive and directory location where your student files are stored in the Files text box under the heading Macros/Keyboards/Button Bars.
   C. Click OK.
3. Start recording a macro that creates a memo form:
   A. Press **Ctrl+F10** to open the Record Macro dialog box.
   B. Key ***[your three-letter identifier]*memo** in the Filename text box and **Memo form** in the Descriptive Name text box.
   C. Click Record.
4. Set the memo's margins and base font:
   A. Open the margins dialog box, and set a 2-inch top margin. Leave all other margins at the 1-inch default.
   B. Open the Font dialog box.
   C. Check the unlabeled check box on the right side of the dialog box title bar, so that a font can be chosen while the macro is playing.
   D. Click OK to close the Font dialog box.
5. Key the memo headings:
   A. Key **MEMO TO:**, press the **Tab** key, and then press **Enter** twice.
   B. Key **FROM:**, press the **Tab** key, and then press **Enter** twice.
   C. Key **DATE:**, press the **Tab** key, press **Ctrl+F5** to insert a date, and then press **Enter** twice.
   D. Key **SUBJECT:**, press the **Tab** key, and then press **Enter** twice.

6. Choose Stop from the Macro menu (or press **Ctrl+Shift+F10**) to stop recording.

7. Close the on-screen document without saving it.

8. Create a macro that inserts an opening paragraph and creates tabular column headings:

   A. Open the Record Macro dialog box, and key ***[your three-letter identifier]*****list** in the Filename text box and **Tabular table** in the Descriptive Name text box.

   B. Click the Record button.

   C. Key the following:

   The properties in the table below have been listed since the beginning of the month:

   D. Press **Enter** twice.

   E. Open the Tab Set dialog box, clear the tabs, and set left-aligned relative tabs at 1.5 inches and 3.25 inches and a right-aligned tab at 5.5 inches.

   F. Click OK.

   G. Key the following column headings, pressing the **Tab** key between each heading, and making the headings bold and underlined:

   Number **Location** **Agent** **List Price**

   H. Press **Enter** twice to add space below the table heading.

9. Press **Ctrl+Shift+F10** to stop recording.

10. Close the on-screen document without saving it.

11. Create a memo using the memo and list macros:

   A. Open the Play Macro dialog box, and double-click *[your three-letter identifier]*memo.wcm in the files list to play the memo macro.

   B. Choose 12-point CG Times and click OK.

   C. Key the following information at the appropriate headings:

   MEMO TO: **Bud Porter**

   FROM: **Ann Delbridge**

   SUBJECT: **New Properties**

   D. Move the insertion point to the end of the memo, and play the macro *[your three-letter identifier]*list.wcm.

E. Move the insertion point to the second line below the table headings, and key:

80886	**Hillbrooke**	**G. Crane**	**$179,900**
97588	**Alpharetta**	**A. Delbridge**	**565,000**
76121	**Dunwoody**	**M. Washington**	**240,000**
51234	**Roswell**	**A. Delbridge**	**799,000**

12. Spell-check the document.
13. Save the document as *[your three-letter identifier]*26-1.wpw.
14. Print the document.
15. Print the macros *[your three-letter identifier]*memo.wcm and *[your three-letter identifier]*list.wcm.
16. Reset the Location of Files defaults for macro files:
    A. Choose Preferences from the File menu, and then choose Location of Files.
    B. Select the text in the Files text box under the heading Macros/Keyboards/Button Bars.
    C. Key the drive and directory where the WordPerfect macro files are stored (in a standard installation, this is C:\wpwin\macros).
    D. Click OK.
17. Close all open files and exit WordPerfect (unless you will be doing the following exercises immediately).

Exercise 26.2

1. Start WordPerfect, if necessary.
2. Using step 2 in Exercise 26.1 as a guide, set the default macro directory to the location of your student files.
3. Edit the macro 26-2.wcm to correct the letterhead it creates:
    A. Open the macro file 26-2.wcm.
    B. Scroll through the file to locate the text "Five Points REalty", and then correct the capitalization of "REalty".
    C. Scroll through the file to locate "108 W. Paces Ferry Road", and change "W." to "West".
    D. Save the macro as *[your three-letter identifier]*26-2.wcm and then print it.
    E. Close the macro.

4. Play the macro to insert a letterhead:
   A. Open a new file.
   B. Play the macro *[your three-letter identifier]*26-2.wcm.
   C. When the font dialog box opens, choose 12-point Univers and click OK.
   D. When the second font dialog box opens, choose 12-point CG Times and click OK.
5. With the insertion point at the end of the document, retrieve the file 26-2.wpw.
6. Using step 16 in Exercise 26.1 as a guide, reset the Location of Files default for macros to the WordPerfect default.
7. Play the WordPerfect replace.wcm macro to change the bold headings in the body of the letter to italics:
   A. Position the insertion point on the line below the salutation.
   B. Open the Play Macro dialog box, and verify that the C:\wpwin\macros directory is current.
   C. Double-click replace.wcm in the Files list box.
   D. Select Bold from the Search for list box, and then select Italic from the Replace with list box.
   E. Click OK.
8. Use the WordPerfect edit.wcm macro to change the 2-inch left and right margins in the center of the document to 1.25-inch margins:
   A. Move the insertion point to the beginning of the line that begins "Total enrollment:".
   B. Display the Reveal Codes space, and position the Reveal Codes insertion point on the code [L/R Mar:2",2"].
   C. Play the edit.wcm macro.
   D. Key **1.25** in the Left and Right text boxes and click OK.
9. Spell-check the document.
10. Save the document as *[your three-letter identifier]*26-2.wpw.
11. Print the document.
12. Close the document and exit WordPerfect (unless you will be doing the following exercises immediately).

Exercise 26.3

1. Start WordPerfect, if necessary.
2. Set the default macro directory to the location of your student files.

3. Open the Record Macro dialog box, and key ***[your three-letter identifier]*26-3** in the Files text box and **Landscape course announcement** in the Descriptive Name text box.
4. Click the Record button to start recording a macro.
5. Set the paper size to Standard 11x8.5 (landscape) and the font to 18-point Univers.
6. Set 2-inch left and right margins, a 1.5-inch top margin, and a 1-inch bottom margin.
7. Press **Shift+F7** to center the insertion point, turn on the bold and italics attributes, and key:

   Atlanta Board of Realtors
8. Turn off the bold and italics attributes, and press **Enter** twice to insert a blank line.
9. Set the font to 14-point Univers; apply the center, bold, and italics attributes; and key:

   New Course Offerings
10. Turn off the bold and italics attributes, and press **Enter** four times to add space below the heading.
11. Define two newspaper columns with a ½-inch space between, and turn on newspaper columns.
12. Set the font to 12-point CG Times.
13. Create a footer using the 14-point Univers font; apply the center, italic and bold attributes; and key the following text:

    For more information, contact Mary Trant at 555-4931
14. Choose Stop from the Macro menu to save the macro, and close the document window without saving it.
15. Play the macro *[your three-letter identifier]*26-3.wcm.
16. Move the insertion point to the end of the on-screen document, if necessary, and retrieve the file 26-3.wpw.
17. If necessary, force a column break at the beginning of the heading "Real Estate Finance".
18. Move the entire course description for "Real Estate Appraisal I" to the beginning of the first column, and correct heading underlines and spacing between paragraphs, if necessary.
19. Spell-check the document.
20. Save the document as *[your three-letter identifier]*26-3.wpw.

21. Print the document.
22. Print the macro *[your three-letter identifier]*26-3.wcm.
23. Reset the Location of Files defaults to the WordPerfect defaults.
24. Close all document windows and exit WordPerfect (unless you will be doing the following exercises immediately).

Exercise 26.4

1. Start WordPerfect, if necessary.
2. Set the default macro directory to the location of your student files.
3. Begin recording a macro with the name *[your three-letter identifier]*26-4a. Give it the descriptive name "Downtown office letterhead".
4. Set the base font to 12-point CG Times, and set 1.25-inch left and right margins, a 0.5-inch top margin, and a 1-inch bottom margin.
5. Create a centered letterhead with the following text, applying the bold and large attributes to "Five Points Realty" and the italics attribute to "Downtown Office":

   Five Points Realty
   Downtown Office
   233 Peachtree Street NE
   Atlanta, GA 30303

6. Press **Enter**, and then use the Advance command to move to the 2-inch line position.
7. Insert a date code, press **Enter**, and then use the Advance code to move to the 3-inch line position.
8. End the macro recording by pressing **Ctrl+Shift+F10**.
9. Close the current document without saving it.
10. Begin recording a new macro with the name *[your three-letter identifier]*26-4b. Give it the descriptive name "Bud Porter's signature block".
11. Key **Sincerely yours**, press **Enter** four times, and key:

    Bud Porter
    President

12. End the macro recording, and close the current document without saving it.
13. In a new file, play the macro *[your three-letter identifier]*26-4a.wcm. If there are errors, edit the macro, save it, and play it again.

14. Key Figure 26-13, which appears at the end of this exercise, including the corrections indicated.
15. Insert a blank line at the end of the document, and then play the macro *[your three-letter identifier]*26-4b.wcm.
16. Spell-check the document.
17. Save the document as *[your three-letter identifier]*26-4.wpw.
18. Print the document.
19. Print the two macros *[your three-letter identifier]*26-4a.wcm and *[your three-letter identifier]*26-4b.wcm.
20. Reset the Location of Files defaults to the WordPerfect defaults.
21. Close all document windows and exit WordPerfect (unless you will be doing the following exercise immediately).

Figure 26-13

Mr. Stephen Alvarez

My Favorite Vegetables ^Restaurant

91 Richmond Hill Drive

Ash^e ville, NC 28803

Dear Mr. Alvarez:

We were happy to hear of your plans to investigate the relocation of your restaurant to Atlanta. Your plan to establish a gourmet vegetarian restaurant at Woodruff Arts Center is quite exciting.

^As you may know, The Woodruff Arts Center, ~~you know,~~ is home to both the Atlanta Symphony and the Alliance Theatre, which has more subscribers than any other regional theater in the country. ~~Of course~~ Also, the High Museum of Art is located next door to ^the Woodruff Arts ^Center, so this is certainly a high-traffic area.

Please let us know your plans. With the recent concern for healthy food, it would seem to be a very favorable time for a restaurant such as "My Favorite Vegetable^s." ^We look forward to hearing from you.

Module 9

Merging and Sorting

Lessons

Lesson 27

Merging

The WordPerfect merge feature has many uses, including creating personalized form letters, address lists, and mailing labels; filling in forms; and completing legal contracts. Merge is used most often to create personalized form letters. The merge process uses two files: the primary file, which contains standard text, and the secondary file, which contains a list of variables.

Objectives

- Understand merging.
- Create a secondary file.
- Create a primary file.
- Merge primary and secondary files.
- Merge to an existing form.
- Use keyboard-merge and print-merge.

Merging Documents: Basic Techniques

Creating merged documents requires three procedures:

- Create a secondary file.

  A *secondary file* contains the variable information that will be inserted in the merged document. For example, if you are creating a letter for a mass mailing, the secondary file will contain a list of names and addresses. It also may contain other information about each individual on the list, such as a birthday or occupation.

- Create a primary file.

  The *primary file* contains the text of the document to be merged, but substitutes codes for the variable information found in the secondary file.

- Merge the primary and secondary files.

  Once you create the primary file and the secondary file, the merge process is very simple. First, open a new file, and choose Merge from the Tools menu. Enter the names of the primary and secondary files in the Merge dialog box and click OK. WordPerfect will create a separate document for each entry in the secondary file.

Secondary file
A file containing a list of information (usually names and addresses) to be used in a merge. The information is organized as records and fields.

Primary file
The file that contains the text for the merged documents. The primary file contains codes that indicate where the variable information from the secondary file will be inserted.

Creating a Secondary File

If you are creating a form letter, the secondary file contains the names and addresses of each person who will receive the letter. Think of this file as a *database*, having records and fields. A *record* is a group of related pieces of information. For example, the name, address, and phone number for an individual is one record. If there are ten names and addresses in the secondary file, then there are ten records in the file. A *field* is a category or a piece of information within a record. For

Database
A collection of records. A secondary file is a kind of database.

Record
A group of related pieces of information, such as the name, address, and telephone number for a person.

Field
A category or a piece of information within a record. Examples of fields are name, address, and phone number.

example, if your records contain names and addresses, the name, address, and phone number each would be a field. You can give fields any name you choose, but it is a good idea to use short, descriptive names. Field names are not case sensitive.

You can create one secondary file that can be used again and again for different letters, address lists, and mailing labels. Creating a secondary file can take some time if you have many records to enter. It is a good idea to anticipate future uses, so you can use the file without making major changes. For example, if you are creating a mass mailing, you probably do not need phone numbers. In the future, however, you may want to make up a phone list so you can follow up on the letters. If you included the phone number in the original secondary file, you can use the same file to generate a list of phone numbers.

Note: Multi-line fields simplify the merge process, but they are not compatible with other word processors or database applications. If you anticipate converting your secondary file for use in another application, design your secondary file with single-line fields.

WordPerfect allows you to create fields with more than one line of information. A good example of a multi-line field is the Address field. You can define one field to contain all the parts of an address, or you can define each part as a separate field (Address, City, State, ZIP Code). If you use separate fields for each part of an address, you may need two address field names (Address 1 and Address 2) to accommodate box numbers or building names.

Defining Field Names

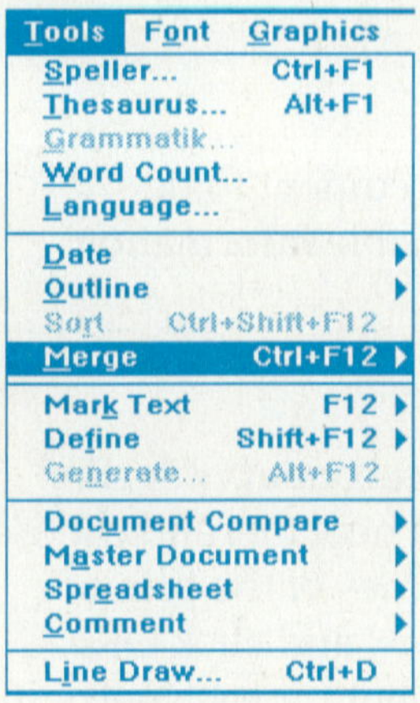

The Tools menu

WordPerfect allows you to define names for each field in your secondary file. This step is not necessary, but it helps you enter information correctly. If you do not define field names, WordPerfect will assign numbers to each field.

To define field names:

1. Start WordPerfect, if necessary.
2. In a new document, choose Merge from the Tools menu.

   The Merge menu appears.
3. Choose Merge Codes from the Merge menu.

   The Insert Merge Codes dialog box appears.

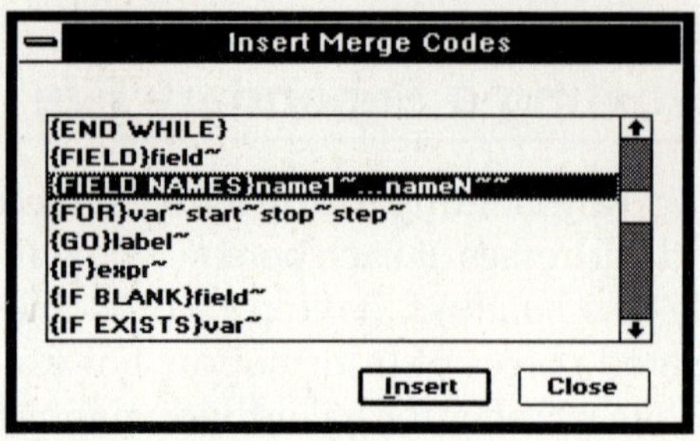

Figure 27-1
The Insert Merge Codes dialog box

Note: The Insert Merge Codes dialog box contains approximately 70 codes that can be used in primary or secondary files. These codes can be combined with macros to create very sophisticated document-assembly systems. Taking full advantage of all these codes requires a knowledge of computer programming.

4. Choose {FIELD NAMES}name1~...nameN~~ from the Insert Merge Codes list box and click Insert.

   The Merge Field Name(s) dialog box opens.

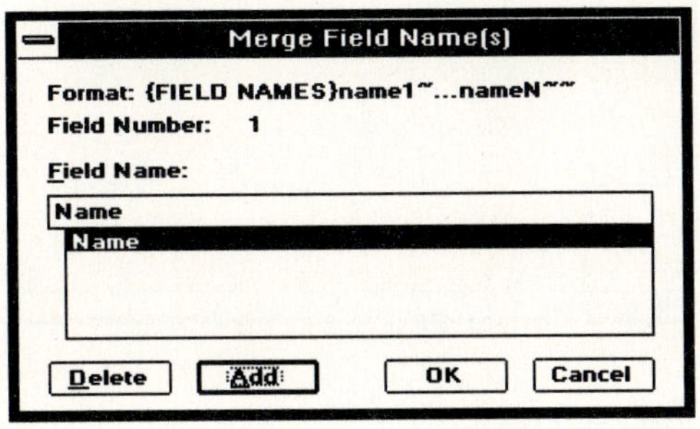

Figure 27-2
The Merge Field Name(s) dialog box

5. Key **Name** in the Field Name text box and click Add. (Do not press **Enter**.)

   "Name" is added to the Field Name list box. The names of fields are not case sensitive. You could have entered "name" instead.

6. Click "Name" in the Field Name text box to choose it.

Note: If you press **Alt+A** on the keyboard instead of clicking the Add button, you will not need to click the Field Name text box to add the next name.

7. Key **Title** and click Add (or press **Alt+A**).

   "Title" is added to the Field Name list box.

8. Add the following field names the same way you added "Title":

   Company, Address, Salutation, and Phone

9. Click OK.

   The Insert Merge Codes dialog box remains open.

10. Click Close to close the Insert Merge Codes dialog box.

    The {FIELD NAMES} code and the field names are inserted at the top of the document, and a [HPg] code (hard page) is inserted after the field names.

11. Examine the left side of the status bar (at the bottom of the screen).

    "Field: Name" appears in the status bar, indicating that you should key the Name field for the first record.

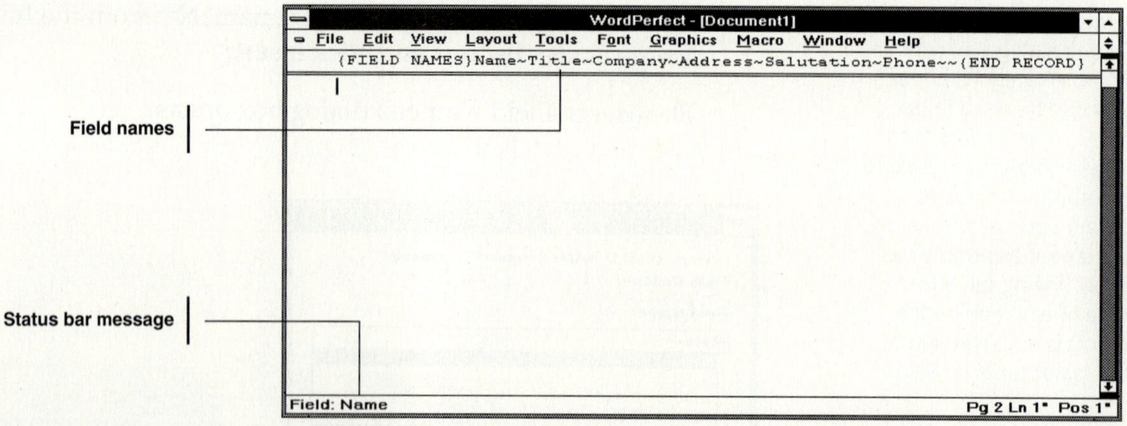

Figure 27-3
The secondary file with field names defined

Entering Information in a Secondary File

When entering information in the secondary file, you enter one record at a time, entering the information for each field in exactly the same order as the field names appear in the {FIELD NAMES} code. Each field ends with an {END FIELD} code and a hard return [HRt] code, and each record ends with an {END RECORD} code and a [HPg] code (hard page).

In the following procedure, the entire address will be one multi-line field. Since some addresses have apartment or suite numbers, the Address field will not always be the same number of lines. To enter a multi-line field, press **Enter** at the end of each line except the last one. Insert the {END FIELD} code at the end of the last address line.

To enter a record:

1. Click the insertion point immediately after the [HPg] code, if necessary.

   The status bar should display "Field: Name".

2. Key **Mr. James Barboza.**

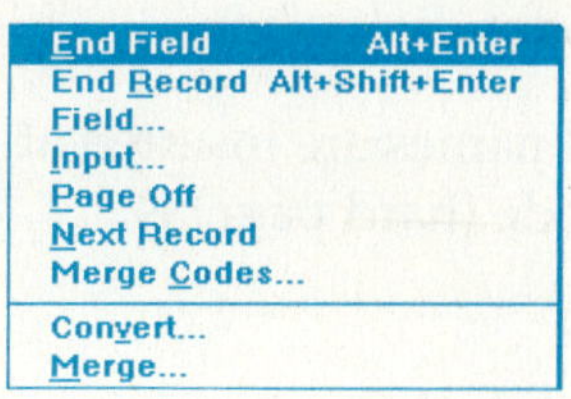

The Merge menu

3. Choose Merge from the Tools menu, and choose End Field from the Merge menu (or press **Alt+Enter**).

   An {END FIELD} code and a [HRt] code are inserted. Your insertion point is at the beginning of the next line, and the status bar displays "Field: Title".

4. Key **Director of Research** and press **Alt+Enter**.

Another set of {END FIELD} and [HRt] codes is inserted, and the insertion point is on a new line. The status bar displays "Field: Company".

5. Key **Southern Industries, Inc.** and press **Alt+Enter**.

6. Key the following, pressing **Enter** (not **Alt+Enter)** at the end of each line:

   Suite 23
   1100 Peachtree Street NE

   Notice the status bar displays "Field: Address" while you are entering this information. The status bar will not change until you press **Alt+Enter**.

7. Key **Atlanta, GA 30303** and press **Alt+Enter**.

   This is the last line of the Address field, so it needs an {END FIELD} code. Make sure there are no {END FIELD} codes at the end of the other address lines. (You can delete merge codes in the same way as any other code.) The status bar now should display "Field: Salutation".

8. Enter the following information in the next two fields, pressing **Alt+Enter** after each:

   Mr. Barboza
   (404) 555-7100

   When you complete the Phone field, you will see "Field: 7" on the status bar. This indicates that you have entered the information for all the named fields.

9. Choose Merge from the Tools menu, and choose End Record (or press **Alt+Shift+Enter**).

   An {END RECORD} code and a [HPg] code are inserted. The insertion point is at the beginning of a new line, ready for the next record to be entered.

Accounting for Blank Fields

Sometimes, you may not have information for every field that you defined. For example, you may have some names on your address list that do not have company names or titles associated with them. You must insert an {END FIELD} code, even if the field is blank. If you do not insert the {END FIELD} code for a blank field, WordPerfect will insert all the information that follows for that record in the wrong place on the merged document.

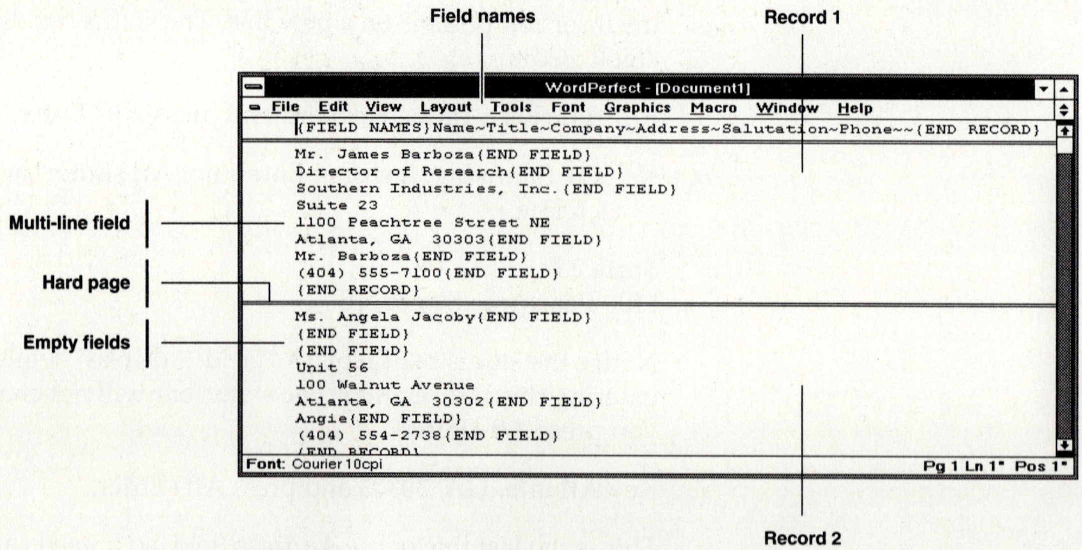

Figure 27-4
The secondary file with records entered

To enter a record with missing fields:

1. Key **Ms. Angela Jacoby** and press **Alt+Enter.**

2. Press **Alt+Enter** twice.

   This record has no information for the Title or Company fields.

3. Key the following information in the Address field (do not forget to insert the {END FIELD} code at the end of the last address line):

   Unit 56
   100 Walnut Avenue
   Atlanta, GA 30302

4. Key **Angie** and press **Alt+Enter.**

   Ms. Jacoby is a personal friend of the author of the letter, so her salutation is informal.

5. Key the phone number **(404) 554-2738,** and press **Alt+Shift+Enter** to complete this record.

6. Enter the remainder of the records using the information in Figure 27-5. Remember to insert an {END FIELD} code for fields with no information.

Figure 27-5

```
Mr. Anthony Williams
Sales Manager
Spruce Graphics, Inc.
10 Spruce Avenue
Conyers, GA  30321
Tony
(404) 555-1200

Ms. Nancy Rodriquez, Esq.
(No Title)
Johnson, Boyd, & Smith
2100 Peachtree Street NE
Atlanta, GA  30303
Ms. Rodriquez
(404) 554-8380

Mr. Andrew Andersen
(No Title)
(No Company)
2310 Dorset Rd.
Atlanta, GA  30302
Mr. Andersen
(404) 554-3021
```

Saving the Secondary File

You must save primary and secondary files before they can be used for a merge. WordPerfect uses the information from a disk file, and not the information from a document window, when it performs a merge. If you do not save a newly created secondary file, you cannot use it for a merge. Also, if you open the secondary file and make changes or additions, you must save it again before performing a merge. If you do not save it, the merged documents will reflect the information before you updated it.

It is a good idea to choose a file name that indicates the file is a merge file, not a document file. In this lesson, you will use the extension .sf for secondary files and the extension .pf for primary files.

To save the secondary file:

1. Spell-check the document.

   It is especially important to spell-check secondary and primary files, because the text in these documents may be used many times.

2. Create a document summary, and write your own abstract. List the field names in the abstract.

3. Choose Save As from the File menu.

4. Key ***[your three-letter identifier]*****27-0.sf** in the Save As text box.

   Be sure to use .sf for the file extension.

5. Click Save.

6. Close the document.

Creating Document Summaries for Merge Files

Create a document summary for all merge files. Because primary and secondary merge files contain many codes, it often is difficult to determine the use of these files, especially if you haven't worked with them for a long time, or if they were created by someone else.

To make sure you and anyone else using the files use the merge files correctly, include the following information in document summaries for merge files. Describe the purpose of the merge file in the Descriptive Name text box. State whether the file is a primary or secondary file in the Descriptive Type text box. For secondary files, list the field names in the Abstract text box. It also is helpful to list the field names in the order they appear in the {FIELD NAMES} code. For primary files, use the Abstract text box to specify any secondary files with which the primary file is to be merged (if there are dedicated secondary files for the primary file).

Creating a Primary File

A primary file contains the text of the document and field codes that indicate where the information from the secondary file will be inserted. You can place field codes anywhere in the primary file.

The field-name codes that you use in the primary file must be spelled exactly as they appear in the {FIELD NAMES} code in the secondary file. However, field names are not case sensitive. In addition, they do not need to appear in the same order as the secondary file, and you can use them more than once if you choose. You can skip codes if you do not want them to appear in the primary file. Every field does not have to be used in every primary file.

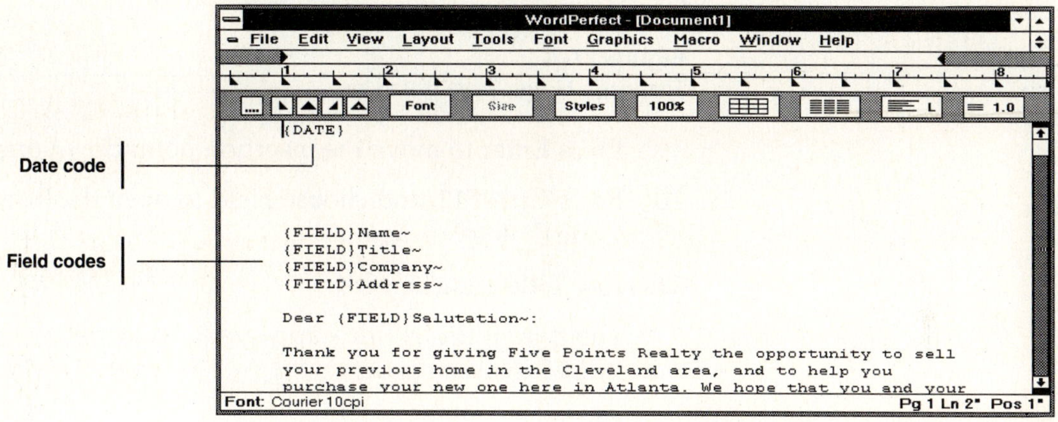

Figure 27-6
The primary file with field codes inserted

To create a primary file:

1. Open the file 27-0.wpw.

   The body of this letter has been keyed. You will add the field codes for the inside address and the salutation.

2. Advance the first line to 2 inches from the top of the page.

3. Choose Merge from the Tools menu (or press **Ctrl+F12**) and choose Merge Codes.

   The Insert Merge Codes dialog box opens.

4. Choose {DATE} from the Insert Merge Codes list box and click Insert.

   The {DATE} code will insert the date into the merged document when the merge occurs.

5. Click Close to close the Insert Merge Codes dialog box.

6. Press **Enter** six times to separate the date and inside address.

7. Press **Ctrl+F12** and choose Field.

   The Insert Merge Code dialog box opens.

8. Key **Name** in the Enter Field text box and click OK.

   The code {FIELD}Name~ appears at the insertion point.

Figure 27-7
The Insert Merge Code dialog box

9. Press **Enter** to move the insertion point down one line.
10. Press **Ctrl+F12**, and choose Field to open the Insert Merge Code dialog box again.
11. Key **Title** and click OK.

    The code {FIELD}Title~ appears one line below the {FIELD}Name~ code.

12. Press **Enter** to move down to the next line.
13. Use the above three steps as a guide to insert the {FIELD}Company~ code and the {FIELD}Address~ code on the next two lines.
14. Press **Enter** twice to move the insertion point two lines below the {FIELD}Address~ code.
15. Key **Dear** and press the **Spacebar**.
16. Open the Insert Merge Code dialog box (press **Ctrl+F12** and choose Field).
17. Key **Salutation** and click **OK**.
18. Key **:** (the colon) and press **Enter** to complete the salutation.
19. Position the insertion point in the second line of the second paragraph, to the left of "please don't hesitate".
20. Using steps 16 and 17 as a guide, insert the salutation field code again.
21. Key **,** (the comma) after the salutation field code, and press the **Spacebar** to complete the punctuation.

    The salutation field code is used a second time in the body of the letter to make it more personalized.

22. Create a document summary, and write your own abstract.
23. Spell-check the document.
24. Save the document as *[your three-letter identifier]*27-01.pf.

Be sure to use the .pf extension, not the .wpw extension.

25. Print the document and the document summary.
26. Close the document.

If you change open-code settings, such as fonts, tabs, or margins, in the body of your primary file, be sure to insert codes at the end of the primary file that return these settings to normal (the way the beginning of the document was set). Otherwise, all the merged documents following the first one will be formatted entirely in the changed settings. In addition, if you use initial document codes or initial document fonts when you create the primary file, these codes will remain in effect unless you insert open codes that override them in the body of the file. The initial codes will not be reset at the beginning of the second or subsequent merged documents.

Merging

Start with a new file when you perform a merge. Merging creates one large document containing a separate copy of the primary file for each record in the secondary file. Once the merge is complete, you can scroll through the on-screen document to make sure it is correct and then print it. There is no need to save the merged document, because it is easy to create again, if necessary, from the saved primary and secondary files.

To perform a merge:

1. Choose New from the File menu to open a new file.
2. Choose Merge from the Tools menu, and choose Merge again from the Merge menu.

   The Merge dialog box opens.
3. Key ***[your three-letter identifier]*****27-01.pf** in the Primary File text box and ***[your three-letter identifier]*****27-0.sf** in the Secondary File text box.

   These are the primary and secondary files you created in the preceding procedures.

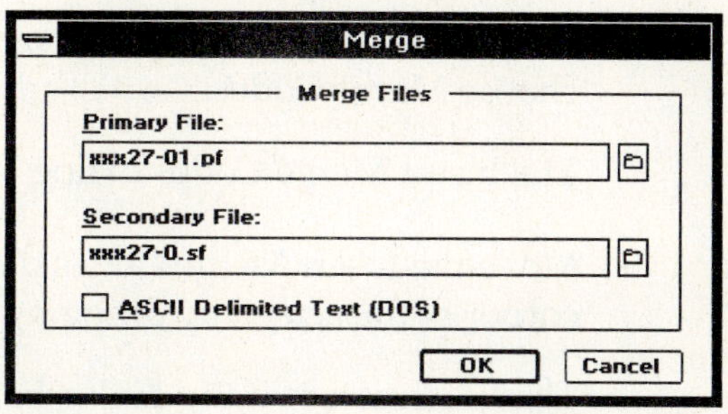

Figure 27-8
The Merge dialog box

4. Click OK.

   The merged document appears in the current document window.

Removing Blank Lines Caused By Empty Fields

When the secondary file contains records with blank fields, those fields will appear as blank lines or blank spaces in the merged document. You can eliminate those blank lines by inserting an {IF NOT BLANK} code in the primary file for any codes that sometimes have blank fields.

Examine the merged document:

1. Scroll to the second page, and locate the name "Ms. Angela Jacoby".

   Notice the blank lines between her name and the address. These blank lines are caused by the blank fields for Title and Company in the secondary file. You will learn how to eliminate these blank lines in the next procedure.

2. Scroll through the rest of the letters to see that they merged correctly.

   Notice that Ms. Rodriquez and Mr. Andersen also have blank lines in their inside addresses.

3. Close the document without saving it.

To eliminate the blank lines in the merged documents:

1. Open the file *[your three-letter identifier]*27-01.pf.

2. Click the insertion point at the beginning of the line that has the {FIELD}Title~ code in it.

3. Press **Home** twice to make sure the insertion point is at the very beginning of the line.

4. Choose Merge from the Tools menu (or press **Ctrl+F12**) and choose Merge Codes.

   The Insert Merge Codes dialog box opens.

5. Move the Insert Merge Codes dialog box to the lower right corner of the screen by dragging its title bar.

   This is necessary if the dialog box is in the way.

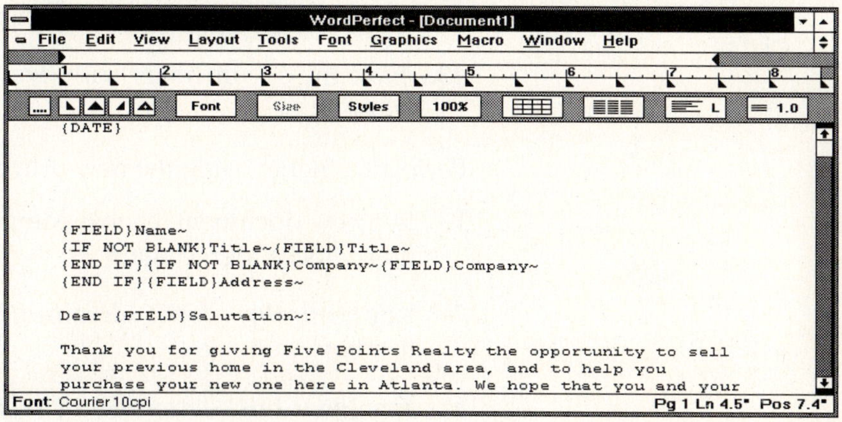

Figure 27-9
The {IF NOT BLANK} and {END IF} codes

6. Choose {IF NOT BLANK}field~ from the Insert Merge Codes list box and click Insert.

   The Insert Merge Code dialog box appears.

7. Key **Title** in the Enter Field text box and click OK.

   The code {IF NOT BLANK}Title~ appears in front of the code {FIELD}Title~. The Insert Merge Code dialog box closes, but the Insert Merge Codes dialog box remains open. Do not close it.

8. Move the insertion point to the beginning of the next line, which contains the company field code.

9. Choose {END IF} from the Insert Merge Codes dialog box, and click Insert (or double-click the code).

   The {END IF} code must be at the beginning of the line following the {IF NOT BLANK} code. All text and codes between the {IF NOT BLANK} code and the {END IF} code are ignored if the field is blank. If the [HRt] code is before the {END IF} code, it will not be inserted in the merged document when the field is blank. If the [HRt] code is after the {END IF} code, then it will be inserted, causing a blank line to appear if the field is blank.

10. Move the insertion point to the left of the company field code, if necessary.

11. Use steps 6 through 9 as a guide to insert an {IF NOT BLANK}Company~ code, and then insert an {END IF} code at the beginning of the next line. Compare your codes with those in Figure 27-9, above.

12. Click the Close button in the Insert Merge Codes dialog box.
13. Save the document as *[your three-letter identifier]*27-02.pf and close it.

Perform a merge using the new primary file:

1. In a new document, choose Merge from the Tools menu, and then choose Merge again.
2. Key ***[your three-letter identifier]*27-02.pf** in the Primary File text box.
3. Key ***[your three-letter identifier]*27-0.sf** in the Secondary File text box.
4. Click OK.
5. Scroll through the merged documents.

   This time, there are no blank lines in the inside addresses.
6. Print the document.
7. Close the document without saving it.

Merging To an Existing Form

You can design a form that will receive information stored in a secondary file. Using merge in this way requires three files: (1) the secondary file, (2) the primary file containing the field codes to be used in the form, and (3) a document that does not contain any merge codes. In the following procedure, you will use merge to insert a list of names and phone numbers into a memo.

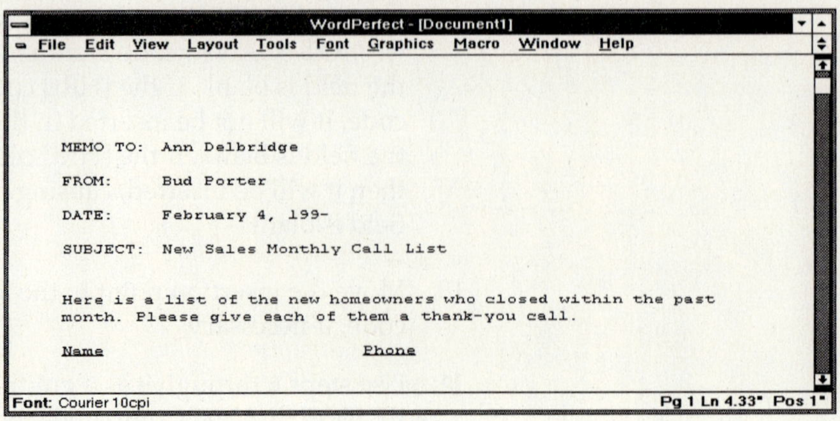

Figure 27-10
The phone list memo

First, create the memo that will contain the phone-number list:

1. In a new document, create a memo using the standard memo format, as shown in Appendix C. The memo is to Ann Delbridge from Bud Porter. The subject is "New Sales Monthly Call List".

2. Key the following first paragraph:

   The following is a list of the new homeowners who closed within the past month. Please give each of them a thank-you call.

3. Press **Enter** twice to move the insertion point down two lines.

4. Clear the tabs, and then set a left-justified tab at the 3-inch mark (relative).

5. Key **Name**, and press the **Tab** key.

6. Key **Phone** and press **Enter** twice.

   "Name" and "Phone" will be the headings for the merged list.

7. Underline the headings.

   The memo form is now set up, ready to be used in a merge.

8. Spell-check the document.

9. Save the document as *[your three-letter identifier]*27-02.wpw.

10. Close the document.

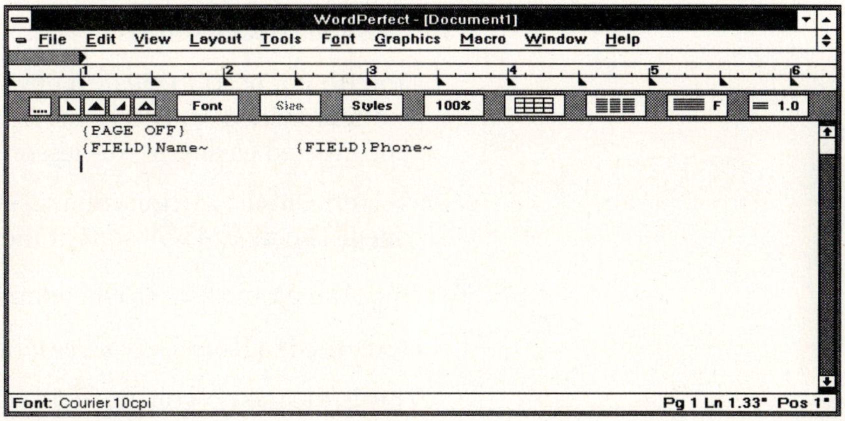

Figure 27-11
The primary file for a phone list

Create a primary file for the phone list:

1. In a new document, press **Ctrl+F12.**

2. Choose Page Off.

   Inserting the {PAGE OFF} code at the beginning of a primary file prevents page breaks from being inserted during the merge, allowing all the secondary file information to be printed on one page.

3. Press **Enter**.

   This will insert a hard return at the beginning of each record in the merged list, so each record starts on a new line.

4. Press **Ctrl+F12** and choose Field.

   The Insert Merge Code dialog box opens.

5. Key **Name** in the Enter Field text box and click OK.

   The code {FIELD}Name~ appears at the insertion point.

6. Press the **Tab** key.

   Because you want the merged data to be displayed in tabular columns, you must insert the [Tab] code in the primary file.

7. Using steps 4 and 5 as a guide, insert a field code for the Phone field.

8. Press **Enter**.

   This will make the merged list double-spaced.

9. Create a document summary, and write your own abstract.

10. Save the document as *[your three-letter identifier]*27-03.pf.

11. Close the document.

    You do not need to create a new secondary file. All the information needed for the memo is already in the secondary file you created earlier in this lesson.

    To perform the merge, you will start with the memo document open. The merge will start at the insertion point.

To merge the phone list into the memo:

1. Open the file *[your three-letter identifier]*27-02.wpw.

   This is the memo you created earlier.

2. Move the insertion point to the end of the memo (two lines below the phone-list headings).

3. Open the Merge dialog box (press **Ctrl+F12** and choose Merge).

4. Key ***[your three-letter identifier]*27-03.pf** in the Primary File text box, and key ***[your three-letter identifier]*27-0.sf** in the Secondary File text box.

5. Click OK.

   The list of names and phone numbers is inserted in the memo.

6. Save the document as *[your three-letter identifier]*27-03.wpw.

7. Print the document and close it.

Keyboard-Merge

A keyboard-merge allows you to enter variable information into a primary file from the keyboard. This is useful for form letters that you produce one or two at a time. In such cases, it may be easier to key the information as needed than to create a secondary file. Keyboard-merges are useful also for lengthy legal contracts that need information to be inserted in many different places. A keyboard-merge will assure that none of the required information is omitted.

Keyboard-merges require a primary file, but not a secondary file. You insert {KEYBOARD} or {INPUT} merge codes wherever variable information is needed. When you perform a merge, your insertion point will move to each location where information is needed. After you key the required information, press **Alt+Enter** to move the insertion point to the next {KEYBOARD} or {INPUT} code. If you use the {INPUT} code, you can key a message to remind you of the kind of information needed. In the next procedure, you will use both the {KEYBOARD} and {INPUT} codes in the primary file you create.

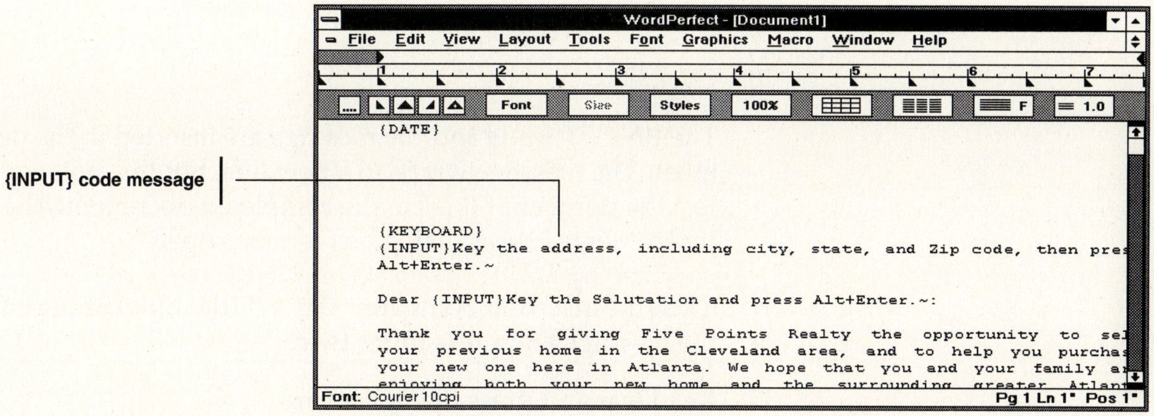

Figure 27-12
Codes inserted for a keyboard-merge

Create a primary file for a keyboard-merge:

1. Open the file 27-0.wpw.
2. Advance the first line to 2 inches from the top of the page to allow for letterhead.
3. Press **Ctrl+F12** and choose Merge Codes.
4. Choose {DATE} from the Insert Merge Codes list box and click Insert.

   The {DATE} code is inserted at the insertion point. The Insert Merge Codes dialog box remains open.

5. Position the insertion point at the end of the {DATE} code, and press **Enter** six times to insert space after the date.
6. Choose {KEYBOARD} from the Insert Merge Codes list box and click Insert.
7. Position the insertion point at the end of the {KEYBOARD} code, and press **Enter** once to move to the next line.

   You will enter a name at the {KEYBOARD} code when you perform the merge.

8. Choose {INPUT}message~ from the Insert Merge Codes list box and click Insert.

   The Insert Merge Code dialog box opens.

9. Key the following in the Enter Message text box:

   Key the address, including city, state, and ZIP Code, and then press Alt+Enter.

10. Click OK.

    The {INPUT} code and the message are inserted in the document. The message wraps to a new line, but this will not affect the number of lines in the completed document. The Insert Merge Codes dialog box remains open.

11. Click the insertion point after the "~" (the tilde) at the end of the message and press **Enter** twice.
12. Key **Dear** and press the **Spacebar.**
13. Insert the {INPUT}message~ code again.
14. Key **Key the Salutation and press Alt+Enter**. This is the input message.

15. Click OK.

    The {INPUT}message~ code is inserted.

16. Click Close from the Insert Merge Codes dialog box.

17. Key : (the colon) after the input message and press **Enter**.

18. Create a document summary, and write your own abstract.

19. Spell-check the document.

20. Save the document as *[your three-letter identifier]*27-04.pf.

21. Print the document and the document summary. Indicate that the primary file is set up for a keyboard-merge.

22. Close the document.

To perform a keyboard-merge, open the Merge dialog box just as in any other kind of merge. The difference this time is that you do not have a secondary file, so leave the Secondary File text box blank. The insertion point will move to the first {KEYBOARD} or {INPUT} merge code and wait for you to key the needed information. When you are finished entering the required information, press **Alt+Enter** to move the insertion point to the next code.

To perform a keyboard-merge:

1. In a new document, press **Ctrl+F12** and choose Merge.

   The Merge dialog box opens.

2. Key ***[your three-letter identifier]*****27-04.pf** in the Primary File text box.

3. Leave the Secondary File text box blank. If there is text in the Secondary File text box, delete it.

4. Click OK.

   The date is inserted in the document, and the insertion point is six lines below it. Notice the message "Merging" on the left side of the status bar.

5. Key **Mr. and Mrs. Steve Johnson** and press **Alt+Enter**.

   The insertion point moves to the next line, and the Merge Message dialog box opens, instructing you to key the address. There was no message box for the name, because the {KEYBOARD} code, and not the {INPUT} code, was used there.

Figure 27-13
The Merge Message dialog box

6. Key the following address:

   3041 N. Tower Way
   Conyers, GA 30207

7. Press **Alt+Enter**.

   The insertion point moves to the salutation line. The Merge Message box instructs you to key the salutation.

8. Key **Mr. & Mrs. Johnson** and press **Alt+Enter**.

   The insertion point moves to the end of the document. There are no more merge codes in the document. The message "Merging" no longer appears on the status bar.

9. Spell-check the document.

10. Save the document as *[your three-letter identifier]*27-04.wpw.

11. Print the document and close it.

Using Print-Merge

Sometimes, you may need to merge directly to the printer instead of to a document window. This is usually the case only if you are merging an extremely large number of documents, or if your computer has a limited amount of RAM memory or disk space available. Print-merging has the disadvantage that you cannot check the merged documents before sending them to the printer.

To create a print-merge, open the primary file to be merged, and insert the {PRINT} merge code at the very end of the document. To do this, press **Ctrl+F12**, choose Merge Codes, choose {PRINT} from the Insert Merge Codes list box, and then click Insert.

Before starting a large print-merge, you should run a test-merge. Create a small secondary file by copying some of the records from the larger secondary file into a new file and saving it. Perform the test-merge using the small secondary file.

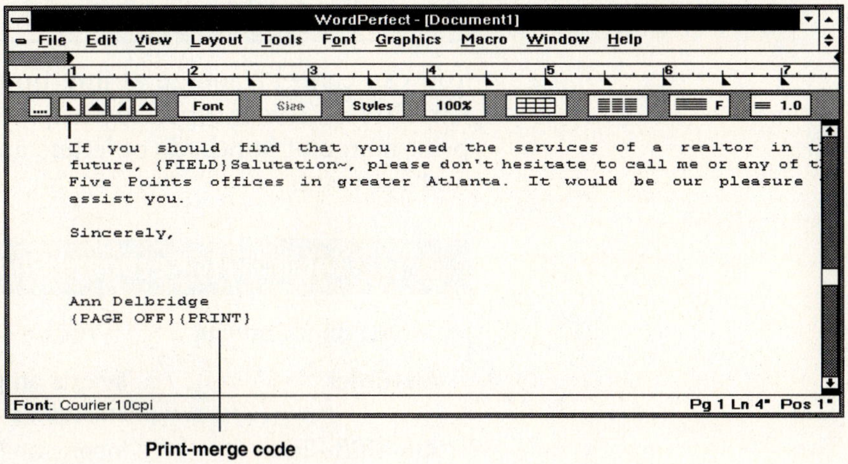

Figure 27-14
Primary file for a print-merge

To create a print-merge:

1. Open the file *[your three-letter identifier]*27-02.pf.
2. Position the insertion point at the very end of the document.
3. Press **Ctrl+F12** and choose Page Off.

   The {PAGE OFF} code is inserted at the end of the document, and the Insert Merge Codes dialog box closes.
4. Press **Ctrl+F12** again and choose Merge Codes.
5. Double-click {PRINT} in the Insert Merge Codes list box.

   The {PRINT} code is inserted to the right of the {PAGE OFF} code.
6. Create a document summary, and write your own abstract. Mention that the primary file is set up for print-merging.
7. Save the document as *[your three-letter identifier]*27-05.pf and close it.
8. Merge the files *[your three-letter identifier]*27-05.pf and *[your three-letter identifier]*27-0.sf.

   The merged documents are printed, but no document is created on-screen.
9. Exit WordPerfect (unless you will be doing the following exercises immediately).

Canceling a Merge

You can cancel a merge at any time by pressing the **Esc** key or **Ctrl+Break**. This is especially helpful to know if you have started a print-merge of hundreds of letters and discover an error when the first one prints.

Table 27-1: Keyboard Shortcuts for Merging

Keyboard Shortcut	Action
Alt+Enter	Inserts an {END FIELD} code at the insertion point.
Alt+Shift+Enter	Inserts an {END RECORD} code at the insertion point.
Ctrl+F12	Opens the Merge menu.
Esc or **Ctrl+Break**	Cancels a merge.

Key Terms

Database
Field
Primary file
Record
Secondary file

Exercises

Exercise 27.1

1. Start WordPerfect, if necessary.
2. Open a new file, and define the field names for a secondary file:
   A. Choose Merge from the Tools menu and choose Merge Codes.
   B. Choose {FIELD NAMES}name1~...nameN~~ from the Insert Merge Codes list box and click Insert.
   C. Key **Social Title** in the Field Name text box and click Add (or press **Alt+A**).
   D. Add the field names First Name, Last Name, Business Title, Company, Street Address, City, State, Zip, Salutation, and Donation.
   E. Click OK to close the Merge Field Name(s) dialog box, and click Close to close the Insert Merge Codes dialog box.

3. Enter the information for the first record in the secondary file:

   A. Key **Mrs.** (the Social Title field) and press **Alt+Enter**.

   B. Key **Dorothy** (the First Name field) and press **Alt+Enter**.

   C. Key **Harris** (the Last Name field) and press **Alt+Enter**.

   D. Key the following fields, pressing **Alt+Enter** at the end of each:

      Chairperson
      Atlanta Board of Realtors
      45 Peachtree Street
      Atlanta
      GA
      30303
      Mrs. Harris
      $10,000

   E. Press **Alt+Shift+Enter** to insert an {END RECORD} code.

4. Key the following information for the second record:

   Mrs.
   Karen
   Reynolds
   114 209th Street
   Cambria Heights
   NY
   11411
   Mrs. Reynolds
   $1,500

   Remember to insert an {END FIELD} code for the two missing fields, Title and Company.

5. Refer to Document 27-1 at the end of this exercise, and key the remaining records. Remember to include the {END FIELD} codes for missing fields.

6. Spell-check the document.

7. Create a document summary, and write your own abstract.

8. Save the document as *[your three-letter identifier]*27-1.sf.

9. Close the document and exit WordPerfect (unless you will be doing the following exercises immediately).

Document 27-1

```
Mr.

Stephen

Alvarez

My Favorite Vegetables Restaurant

91 Richmond Hill Dr.

Asheville

NC

28803

Mr. Alvarez

$5,000

Mr. & Mrs.

David

Nelson

94 85th Street

Elmhurst

NY

11422

Mr. & Mrs. Nelson

$1,000

Mr. & Mrs.

Steve

Johnson

3041 N. Tower Way

Conyers

GA

30207

Mr. & Mrs. Johnson

$1,000
```

```
Mr. & Mrs.

Anthony

Brown

1 Somerset Rd.

Stone Mountain

GA

30331

Mr. & Mrs. Brown

$2,000
```

Exercise 27.2

1. Start WordPerfect, if necessary.
2. Open the file 27-2.wpw.
3. Insert the {DATE} merge code and the codes for an inside address using standard business-letter formatting:
   A. Advance the first line to 2 inches from the top of the page.
   B. Press **Ctrl+F12** and choose Merge Codes.
   C. Choose {DATE} and click Insert.
   D. Click Close.
   E. Press **Enter** six times to insert space between the date and the inside address.
   F. Press **Ctrl+F12** and choose Field.
   G. Key **Social Title** in the Enter Field text box and click OK.
   H. Position the insertion point to the right of the social title field code and press the **Spacebar**.
   I. Press **Enter**, and insert the field codes for the First Name and Last Name fields, adding a space between the codes.
   J. Insert the code {IF NOT BLANK}Title~ and the business title field code on the next line.
   K. Insert the {END IF} code at the beginning of the next line, then insert the {IF NOT BLANK}Company~ code and the company field code.
   L. Insert the {END IF} code at the beginning of the next line, and insert the field code for the street address.
   M. On the next line, insert the field codes for the city, state, and ZIP Code. Insert punctuation and spaces as needed.
   N. Press **Enter** twice to insert a blank line.

4. Insert the field code for the salutation:
   A. Key **Dear** and press the **Spacebar**.
   B. Insert the field code for the salutation.
   C. Key **:** (colon) and press **Enter**.
5. Insert the donation amount in the body of the letter:
   A. Click the insertion point between the words "of" and "to" in the center of the first line of the letter.
   B. Insert the donation field code.
   C. Adjust the spacing and punctuation, if necessary.
6. Create a document summary, and write your own abstract.
7. Spell-check the document.
8. Save the document as *[your three-letter identifier]*27-2.pf and close it.
9. Merge the secondary file created in Exercise 27.1 with the primary file created in this exercise.
   A. Choose Merge from the Tools menu (or press **Ctrl+F12**) and choose Merge.
   B. Enter the primary and secondary file names in the Merge dialog box. Use the file *[your three-letter identifier]*27-2.pf as the primary file and the file *[your three-letter identifier]*27-1.sf as the secondary file.
   C. Click OK.
   D. Scroll through the document to make sure the merge worked correctly.
10. Save the document as *[your three-letter identifier]*27-2.wpw.
11. Print the document.
12. Close the document and exit WordPerfect (unless you will be doing the following exercises immediately).

Exercise 27.3

1. Start WordPerfect, if necessary.
2. In a new file, create a primary file that will be used to insert a list in a memo.
3. Insert the {PAGE OFF} code and press **Enter**.
4. Insert the field codes for License, Location, Agent, and SS#, pressing the **Tab** key after all but SS#.
5. Create a document summary, and write your own abstract.
6. Save the document as *[your three-letter identifier]*27-3.pf and close it.

7. Open the file 27-3.wpw.
8. At the end of the document, clear all the tabs, and set left relative tabs at the 1.25-inch, 3-inch, and 5-inch marks.
9. Key the following headings, inserting one tab between each heading and pressing **Enter** at the end of the heading line:

   **License #	Location	Agent	SS#**

10. At the end of the document, merge the primary file *[your three-letter identifier]*27-3.pf and the secondary file 27-3.sf.
11. Spell-check the document.
12. Save the document as *[your three-letter identifier]*27-3.wpw.
13. Print the document.
14. Close the document and exit WordPerfect (unless you will be doing the following exercises immediately).

Exercise 27.4

1. Start WordPerfect, if necessary.
2. Open the file 27-4.wpw.
3. Insert an {INPUT} code in the third line, where the date should be placed. Key the message **Key the date here**.
4. Insert an {INPUT} code to the right of "The" at the beginning of the first paragraph. Key the message **Key the number of potential new members**.
5. Insert an {INPUT} code at the end of the document. Key the following message:

   Key the name, company (if any), address, and type for each prospective member

6. Create a document summary, and write your own abstract.
7. Save the document as *[your three-letter identifier]*27-4.pf and close it.
8. In a new document, perform a keyboard-merge using the primary file you just created. Use the information in Figure 27-15, which appears at the end of this exercise, to key the information required at the {INPUT} codes. Remember to press **Alt+Enter** to move to the next {INPUT} code.
9. Spell-check the document.
10. Save the document as *[your three-letter identifier]*27-4.wpw.
11. Close the document and exit WordPerfect (unless you will be doing the following exercise immediately).

Figure 27-15

```
Name:       Mr.Yves Deblois
Company:
Address:    21 210th Srteet
            New York, NY  10221
Type:       3-br contemporaries

Name:       Ms. Robert Walker
Company:    The Walker Foundation
Address:    3600 Maple Ave.
            Syracuse, NY  13201
Type:       1800 sq. ft.

Name:       Ms. Butcher Jamie
Company:
Address:    119-29 227th Street
            Laurelton, N Y  11413
Type:       2-BR condominiums

Name:       Mr. David Riley
Company:
Address:    3610 Maple Ave.
            Syracuse, NY
Type:       four-BR raised ranches

Name:       Mr Christian Knight
Company:
Address:    1992 Kingston
            Atlanta, ga  30301
Type:       1-BR condominiums
```

Lesson 28

Sorting

The WordPerfect Sort feature allows you to arrange a list of items alphabetically or numerically. You can sort a list of names, paragraphs, rows in a table, or records in a secondary merge file. The Sort feature allows you to sort a selected block of text or the entire document.

Objectives

- Understand what sorting can do.
- Understand the parts of the Sort dialog box.
- Define a Sort key.
- Sort with multiple keys.
- Sort secondary merge records.
- Sort rows in a table.

Sort
To arrange a list of items in alphabetical or numerical order.

What Is Sorting?

A *sort* can be as simple as arranging a list of names in a memo in alphabetical order, or as involved as arranging addresses in a secondary merge file numerically by ZIP Code and alphabetically by last name within each ZIP Code.

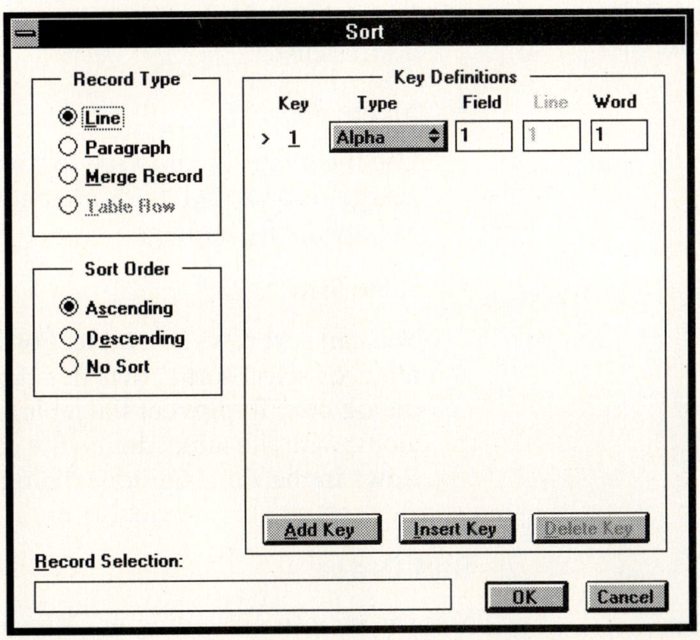

Figure 28-1
The Sort dialog box

Parts of the Sort Dialog Box

The Sort dialog box has three areas for defining the way information is to be sorted: Record Type, Sort Order, and Key Definitions.

Record Type

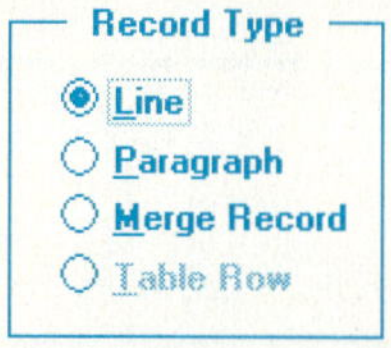

The Record Type options box

Use the Record Type option box to define the type of information you are sorting. Each record type uses a different series of codes to define the end of a record. You can choose from the following record types:

- Line

  A line record type sorts each line of the selected text. When you choose Line as the record type, each record is defined as any text ending with a soft return or a hard return. Line sort is used to sort a list of names or objects. Each item in a line sort can be only one line long.

- Paragraph

  A paragraph record type is a group of lines that ends with two or more hard returns. Each line within the paragraph can end with either a soft return or a single hard return. A three-line address is an example of a paragraph record. Each line ends with a hard return, and there are two or more hard returns at the end of the address. Paragraph sort can be used to sort a list of defined terms and numbered paragraphs, as well as an address list.

Note: The paragraph record type in the sort procedure is an exception to the general definition for a paragraph. In most word-processing procedures, a paragraph is defined as any text that ends with one or more hard returns.

- Merge Record

  Use the merge record type to sort a secondary merge file. Merge records and fields are defined the same way for a sort as they are for a merge.

- Table Row

  You can sort rows in a table. Position the insertion point in the table, or select some rows in a table, before opening the Sort dialog box. To prevent the table headings from being sorted along with the table, define the column headings as Header Rows in the Table Options dialog box.

Sort Order

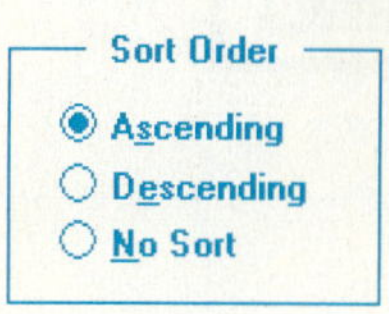

The Sort Order options box

You can choose Ascending or Descending from the Sort Order options box. Ascending sorts letters from A to Z and numbers from lowest to highest. Descending sorts in the opposite order.

Record Selection

The Record Selection text box allows you to select records meeting certain criteria from the information being sorted. For example, you can select the records for addresses in Atlanta or the records for ZIP Codes greater than 30300 and less than 30400. Record selection is an advanced topic and is beyond the scope of this text. Refer to the WordPerfect reference manual for more information on record selection.

Key Definitions

Use the Key Definitions options box to define by what words, lines, or fields within a record to sort. For example, if you have a list of first and last names, you can choose to sort them by either the first or the last names. The name by which you choose to sort is called the *key*.

Key
The category of information by which text is sorted.

To start a sort, select the text that you want to sort, and then choose Sort from the Tools menu to open the Sort dialog box. In the following procedure, you will sort a simple list of items alphabetically.

To open the Sort dialog box:

1. Start WordPerfect.
2. Open the file 28-0.wpw.

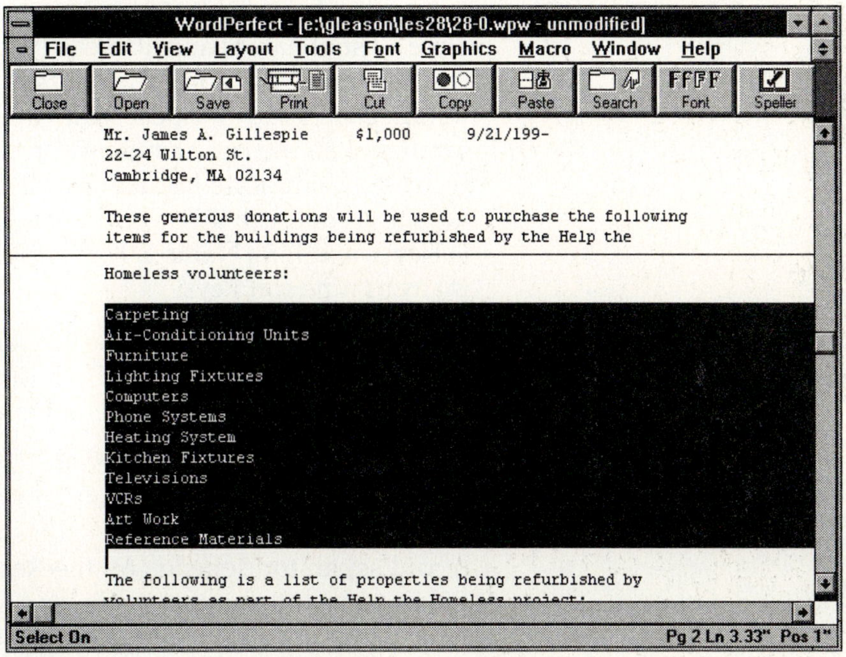

Figure 28-2
A list of items selected for sorting

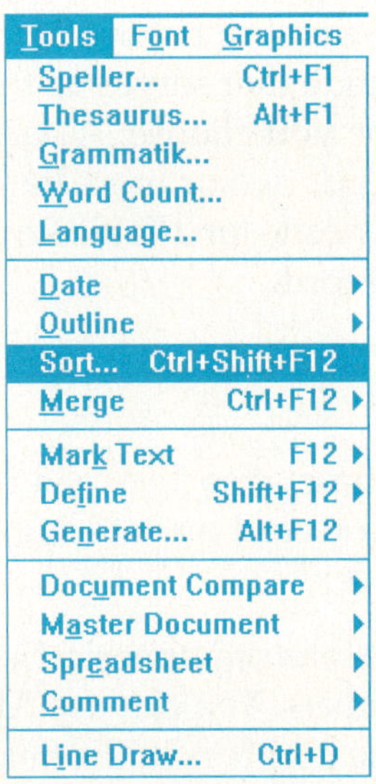

The Tools menu

3. Select the list on the second page that begins with "Carpeting" and ends with "Reference Materials".
4. Choose Sort from the Tools menu.

   The Sort dialog box opens.
5. Choose Line from the Record Type options box, if necessary.
6. Choose Alpha from the Type pop-up button, if necessary, to sort alphabetically.

7. Choose Ascending from the Sort Order options box, if necessary, to sort from A to Z (descending sorts from Z to A).

8. Key **1** in the Field text box and **1** in the Word text box, if necessary.

   This simple list has only one field and one word. If you are sorting tabbed columns, the number in the Field text box specifies which column is sorted. If the list has more than one word on a line, such as first and last names, then the number in the Word text box specifies which word on the line to use as the sort key.

9. Click OK.

   The list is sorted alphabetically.

Sorting with Multiple Keys

In the simple line sort above, you sorted by one key. Suppose you have a list of names and addresses that you want to sort, so that all the information is sorted by state, and all cities are alphabetized within each state. Suppose you want to refine the sort further by arranging all the last names within each city alphabetically and, in the case of duplicate last names, all the first names. You need four keys to accomplish this task: State is Key 1, City is Key 2, Last Name is Key 3, and First Name is Key 4. WordPerfect allows you to use as many as nine sort keys.

When you open the Sort dialog box, only one key is displayed in the Key Definitions options box. To add additional keys to the bottom of the list, click the Add Key command button.

A record, as previously defined in "Lesson 27: Merging," is a collection of related items, such as the name, address, and telephone number for one person. When you sort, the code that serves as the record separator depends on the Record Type you choose: A hard return code or soft return code for a Line record, two or more hard return codes for a Paragraph record, a table row code for a Table Row record, and an end record code for a Merge record.

Key Type, Field, Line, and Word

For each key definition, you can specify the type of sort (Alpha or Numeric) and the location of the key within a record by entering a number in the Field, Line, and Word text boxes.

The Type pop-up button allows you to choose Alpha or Numeric. Use Alpha to sort words and Numeric to sort numbers. You can use Alpha to sort numbers alphanumerically, if all the numbers in the field have the same number of digits (for example, telephone numbers,

ID numbers, or social-security numbers). Always remember to choose Numeric if you are sorting numbers with a varying number of digits, such as dollar amounts, quantities, and ages.

If you are performing a line or paragraph sort, fields are separated by tab codes or indent codes. If you are sorting a merge record, the field separator is the end field code. Many times, the text you want to sort does not contain tabs or indents. In this case, you can break down records even further by words. The space, hyphen, and slash are recognized as word separators when performing a sort.

Line, Field, and Word Numbers

Specify which line, field, and word to use as a key by entering its number in the Key Definitions text boxes. The lines, fields, and words are numbered from left to right and top to bottom within a record.

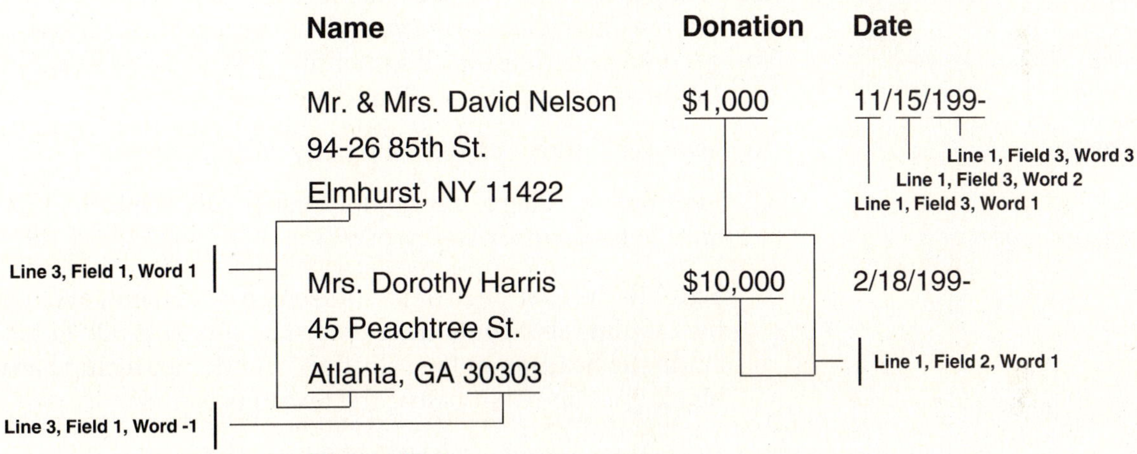

Figure 28-3
Key definitions for a paragraph record with tabular columns

In Figure 28-3, each record is several lines long and has the structure of a paragraph record type. The first line of each record contains the name, donation, and the date the donation, was made. The donations and dates are separated by tab codes. Since the tab code is a field separator, the name is field 1, the donation is field 2, and the date is field 3.

Negative Numbers for Lines, Fields, and Words

If you need to sort an address list by ZIP Code, the ZIP Code usually will be word 3 on line 3, but, if the city is Los Angeles, then the Zip Code is word 4. If you define the sort key as word 3, all the addresses in Los Angeles will sort incorrectly. Fortunately, WordPerfect allows you to use negative numbers to count from right to left and bottom to top. Counting from right to left, the ZIP Code is word -1, the state is word -2, Angeles is word -3, and Los is word -4. If you use negative numbers to specify the ZIP Code key, it does not matter if the city is Los Angeles or Atlanta. In both cases, the ZIP Code is word -1.

```
Mr. Carl Andersen{END FIELD}
2100 Peachtree St. NE
Atlanta, GA  30303{END FIELD}
{END RECORD}
```

Line 1, Field 1, Word -1 (or Word 3)

Line 2, Field 2, Word 1

Line 2, Field 2, Word -1 (or Word 3)

Figure 28-4
Line, field, and word numbers for a merge record sort

Note: Negative numbers cannot always be used for all the parts of a key. When you are performing a paragraph sort, you can use negative numbers for fields and words, but not for lines. When you are performing a merge record sort, however, you can use negative numbers for lines and words, but not for fields.

Undoing a Sort

Choosing Undo from the Edit menu does not always work to undo a sort. It is a good idea to save your document before you sort, in case you get unexpected results. If something goes wrong, close the document without saving it, and then open it again.

To perform a paragraph record sort by ZIP Code:

1. Save the document, but do not close it. Use the format *[your three-letter identifier]*28-0.wpw.
2. Scroll to the first page of the on-screen document, and select the tabular table containing the list of sponsors. Do not include the heading in the selection, and do not include any blank lines above or below the text to be sorted.

   Remember, when you are sorting, a paragraph is any group of information that ends with two or more hard returns. The first line of each selected paragraph contains tabs, separating the first line into three fields.

3. Choose Sort from the Tools menu.
4. Choose Paragraph from the Record Type options box.
5. Choose Ascending from the Sort Order options box to sort from lowest to highest.
6. Choose Numeric from the Type pop-up button for Key 1.

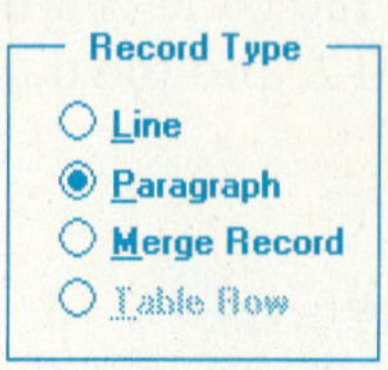

The Record Type options box

Figure 28-5
Key definitions for sorting by ZIP Code

7. Key **3** in the Line text box, **1** in the Field text box, and **-1** in the Word text box.

   The ZIP Code is on the third line of each paragraph. Since the third line contains no tabs, it has only one field, making the ZIP Code in field 1. The ZIP Code is the last word in the line, making it word -1.

8. Click OK.

9. Scroll through the document, and verify that the addresses are sorted by ZIP Code.

Now, sort the information by last name:

1. Save the document, but do not close it (you saved it previously as *[your three-letter identifier]*28-0.wpw).

2. Select the list of sponsors (not including the heading).

3. Choose Sort from the Tools menu.

   The Sort dialog box opens. Notice that the settings you chose for the ZIP Code sort still are displayed in the dialog box.

4. Choose Paragraph and Ascending, if necessary.

5. Change Type for Key 1 to Alpha.

6. Set Line to 1, Field to 1, and Word to -1 to specify Last Name as the first sort key.

7. Click OK.

   The information is sorted, but not exactly as you might have expected. The last names are not alphabetized.

8. Scroll through the sorted information, and notice that there are several names sorted incorrectly.

   Reynolds, Jones, and Brown are sorted by their suffixes, M.D. and Esq. You will correct this problem in the next procedure.

Hard Spaces

When sorting, the hard space (**Ctrl+Spacebar**), the hard hyphen (**Ctrl+-**), and the backslash (\) are considered as regular characters and not as word separators. If you have two words that should be considered as one sort key, they should be separated by a hard space and not a regular space. For example, if a last name ends with Jr. or Esq., those names may sort incorrectly unless you use a hard space between the name and the suffix. Also, first names and middle initials should be separated by a hard space if you plan to sort by first name, because sometimes there is no middle initial.

Add hard spaces, and re-sort the addresses by last name:

1. Scroll to the first address, and position the insertion point to the left of the space between "Reynolds," and "Esq."
2. Press the **Delete** key, and then press **Ctrl+Spacebar**.

   The space between the last name and the suffix is replaced with a hard space.

3. In the next record, replace the space between "Jones," and "Esq." with a hard space.
4. Scroll to "Anthony Brown" near the bottom of the list, and replace the space to the left of "M.D." with a hard space.
5. Scroll to "James A. Gillespie", and insert a hard space between "James" and "A."
6. Save the document.
7. Select the list of sponsors (not including the heading).
8. Choose Sort from the Tools dialog box.
9. Verify that Type is set to Alpha, Line is set to 1, Field is set to 1, and Word is set to -1.
10. Click OK.

    The information is re-sorted. Notice that "Anthony Brown, M.D." is now at the top of the list.

11. Scroll through the names, and verify that they now are sorted correctly.

In the following procedure, you will sort the addresses by state, city within each state, last name within each city, and first name to further sort duplicate last names. To perform a paragraph sort with multiple keys:

1. Save the document, but do not close it.
2. Select the list of sponsors in the document (not including the heading).
3. Open the Sort dialog box.
4. Choose Paragraph and Ascending, if necessary.
5. Click the Add Key button three times to add three keys.

The Add Key button

Four keys are displayed in the Key Definitions options box.

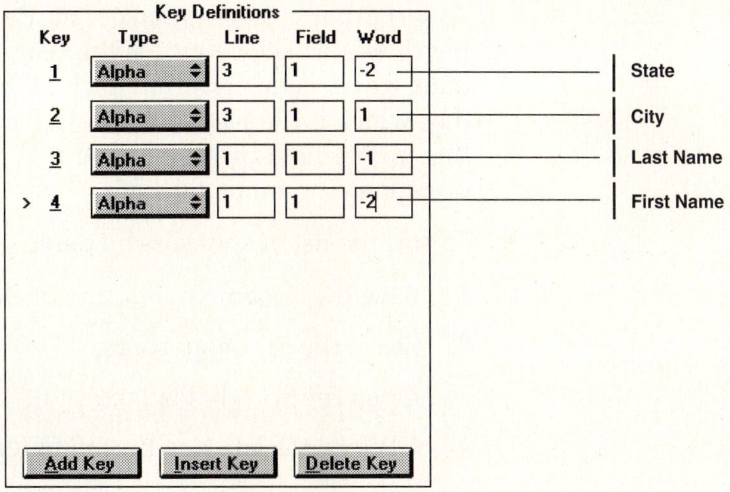

Figure 28-6
The Key Definitions options box with four keys defined

6. For Key 1, set Type to Alpha, Line to 3, Field to 1, and Word to -2 to specify the state as the first sort key.
7. For Key 2, set Type to Alpha, Line to 3, Field to 1, and Word to 1 to specify the city as the second sort key.
8. For Key 3, set Type to Alpha, Line to 1, Field to 1, and Word to -1 to specify the last name as the third sort key.
9. For Key 4, set Type to Alpha, Line to 1, Field to 1, and Word to -2 to specify the first name as the fourth sort key.

   Specifying Word as -2 takes care of the problem that the prefix is sometimes "Mr." (one word) and sometimes "Mr. & Mrs." (three words). Remember that, in order for the first name to be Word -2, there must be a hard space between the first name and the middle name or initial if it exists.

Note: If you insert hard spaces between "Mr.", "and", and "Mrs.", you can count the prefix as one word, however, this does not account for missing prefixes, for example, when a name ends in "M.D." or "Esq."

10. Click OK, and then scroll through the addresses to verify that they are sorted by (1) state, (2) city, (3) last name, and (4) first name.

Sorting Dates

Note: Be sure not to confuse the backslash (\) with the standard slash (/). The backslash is treated as a character, in the same way as a hard space; the standard slash is treated as a word separator, in the same way as a normal space.

When sorting dates, use the date format m/d/yy or mm-dd-yy in the text to be sorted, and choose Numeric for the type. If you spell out the months, your text will be alphabetized by month and will not be in month order (April will sort before January). If you use the hyphen as the separator, you must use a two-digit month and two-digit day, such as 04-02-92 rather than 4-2-92. If you use the slash as the separator, however, it is not necessary to add the leading zeros (for example, 3/24/92).

To sort a date correctly, think of the date as being three words requiring three sort keys. Key 1 is the year, which is the third word in the date. Key 2 is the month, which is the first word, and Key 3 is the day, which is the second word. In the list of sponsors, the date is on line one in field three, because it is separated from the name and donation amount by tab codes.

To sort the list of sponsors by date:

1. Save the document, but do not close it.
2. Select the list of sponsors.
3. Open the Sort dialog box.
4. Click the Delete Key button to remove one of the keys.

   Three sort keys remain in the Key Definitions options box.

The Delete Key button

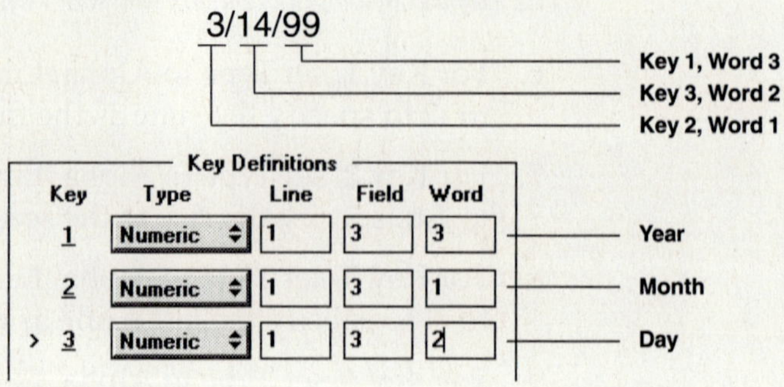

Figure 28-7
Key Definitions for sorting dates

5. For Key 1, set Type to Numeric, Line to 1, Field to 3, and Word to 3 to specify the year.
6. For Key 2, set Type to Numeric, Line to 1, Field to 3, and Word to 1 to specify the month.
7. For Key 3, set Type to Numeric, Line to 1, Field to 3, and Word to 2 to specify the day.
8. Click OK to perform the sort.
9. Scroll through the list, and verify that it is sorted by the date of the donation.

Sorting Secondary Merge Records

You can sort the records in secondary merge files in much the same way as a paragraph sort. In a secondary merge sort, the field separator is the end field code and the record separator is the end record code. Each field can contain multiple lines and multiple words that you can specify as separate keys.

> **Sorting a Secondary Merge File Two Ways**
>
> Often, a secondary merge file is used to store names and addresses for personalizing form letters. When you edit an address file, it is convenient to have the file alphabetized by last name or company. When it is time to create a mailing, however, you may want to sort the file by ZIP Code to take advantage of postage savings.
>
> You may be tempted to keep two secondary merge files, one arranged by last name and another arranged by ZIP Code. This is dangerous, because you may make revisions to the alphabetized list but forget to make the same revisions to the list arranged by ZIP Code.
>
> A better way is to record one macro to sort alphabetically and another macro to sort by ZIP Code. In this way, it is easy to switch from one arrangement to the other simply by playing the macro. Remember, always save a file before sorting just in case something goes wrong.

Sorting Rows in a Table

You also can sort rows in a table. To sort a table, first position the insertion point in the table, and then open the Sort dialog box. If the insertion point is in a table when you open the Sort dialog box, Table Row is selected automatically in the Record Type options box, and all the other record types are dimmed and not available.

Most tables have headings in one or more rows at the top. You can define these rows as header rows in the Table Options dialog box. When you sort a table, the header rows will remain at the top of the table after the sort. If you do not define them as header rows, they most likely will appear somewhere in the middle of the table after the sort.

To sort a table by number of units with the largest number first:

1. Save the on-screen document, but do not close it.
2. Position the insertion point anywhere in the table at the end of the document.
3. Choose Tables from the Layout menu and then choose Options.
4. Key **1** in the Header Rows text box to define the first row of the table as a header row.
5. Click OK to close the Table Options dialog box.
6. Open the Sort dialog box.

   The Table Row record type is highlighted.

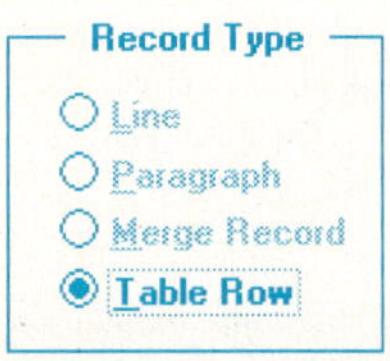

The Record Type options box

7. Click the Delete Key button twice, so that only one sort key remains in the dialog box.

8. Set the Type to Numeric, Cell to 3, Line to 1, and Word to 1 to specify "# Units" as the sort key.

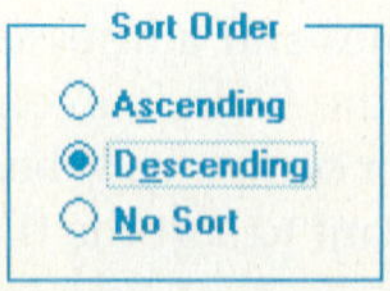

The Sort Order options box

9. Choose Descending from the Sort Order options box to sort from highest to lowest.

10. Click OK.

    The rows are sorted in descending order by number of units, but the screen may appear to be jumbled.

11. Press **Ctrl+F3** to redisplay the screen.

    The table rows are in the correct sort order now, but the table lines are not correct. Table lines always need to be redefined after a sort.

12. Triple-click the horizontal selection arrow to select the entire table.

13. Choose Tables from the Layout menu and then choose Lines.

14. Choose Single from the Inside pop-up list and Single from the Outside pop-up list.

15. Click OK.

16. Spell-check the document.

17. Save the document (you saved it previously as *[your three-letter identifier]*28-0.wpw).

18. Print the document.

19. Close the document and exit WordPerfect (unless you will be doing the following exercises immediately).

Table 28-1: Keyboard Shortcut for Sorting

Keyboard Shortcut	Action
Ctrl+Shift+F12	Opens the Sort dialog box

Key Terms

Key
Sort

Exercises

Exercise 28.1

1. Start WordPerfect, if necessary.
2. Open the file 28-1.sf.

   This is a secondary merge file.
3. Sort the file by last name:

   A. Choose Sort from the Tools Menu.

   B. Choose Merge Record from the Record Type options box.

   C. Choose Ascending from the Sort Order options box, if necessary.
4. Define the last word in the name field as the sort key:

   A. Choose Alpha from the Type pop-up list in the Key Definitions options box, if necessary.

   B. Key **1** in the Field text box, **1** in the Line text box, and **-1** in the Word text box to select the last word in the field.
5. Click OK to perform the sort.
6. When the sort is completed, press **Ctrl+F3** to redisplay the screen, if necessary.
7. Check the results, and make corrections so the records sort correctly:

   A. Scroll through the records, and notice that the fourth and sixth records ("Nancy Rodriquez, Esq." and "Thomas R. White, III") are not in the correct sort order.

   B. Delete the space before "Esq." in the fourth record, and replace it with a hard space (**Ctrl+Spacebar**).

   C. Delete the space before "III" in the sixth record, and replace it with a hard space (**Ctrl+Spacebar**).

   D. Open the Sort dialog box again and click OK.

   E. Scroll through the records, and notice that the last names are sorted correctly now, but the three Jones records are not sorted by first name.
8. Sort the merge file again, by ZIP Code, then by last name, and then by first name:

   A. Open the Sort dialog box.

   B. Change the Key type to Numeric.

C. Key **2** in the Field text box, **-1** in the Line text box, and **-1** in the Word text box to define the ZIP Code as the first key.

D. Click the Add Key button twice to add Keys 2 and 3.

E. Change Key 2 to Type Alpha, Field 1, Line 1, and Word -1 to specify the last name.

F. Change Key 3 to Type Alpha, Field 1, Line 1, and Word 2 to specify the first name.

G. Click OK.

9. Scroll through the resulting file and observe the following:

A. All the records with ZIP Code 30302 are sorted first, and those with 30303 are sorted second.

B. There are three Jones records in ZIP Code 30302. They are sorted correctly by first name.

10. Save the document as *[your three-letter identifier]*28-1.sf.

11. Close all open documents.

12. Perform a merge using the primary file 28-1.pf and the secondary file *[your three-letter identifier]*28-1.sf.

13. Spell-check the resulting document, and save it as *[your three-letter identifier]*28-1.wpw.

14. Print the document.

15. Close the document and exit WordPerfect (unless you will be doing the following exercises immediately).

Exercise 28.2

1. Start WordPerfect, if necessary.

2. Open the file 28-2.wpw.

3. Select the entire list of terms and the definitions that accompany them, starting with "Agreement" and ending with the paragraph that follows the term "Management Fee".

4. Use the paragraph sort to alphabetize the selected list of terms:

A. Open the Sort dialog box.

B. Choose Paragraph from the Record Type options box.

C. If there is more than one key listed in the Key Definitions options box, use the Delete Key button to delete the extra keys.

D. Set the Key Type to Alpha, if necessary.

E. Key **1** in the Line text box, **1** in the Field text box, and **1** in the Word text box.

F. Click OK.

5. Perform a line sort to alphabetize the distribution list at the end of the memo:

   A. Scroll to the end of the memo.

   B. Select the names in the distribution list. (Do not select the heading or the blank line below it.)

   C. Open the Sort dialog box.

   D. Choose Line in the Record Type options box.

   E. Choose Alpha for the Key type, key **1** in the Field text box, and key **-1** in the Word text box.

   F. Add a second Alpha key and set the field to 1 and the word to 1 to define the first initial as the second key.

   G. Click OK.

6. Spell-check the document.

7. Save the document as *[your three-letter identifier]*28-2.wpw.

8. Print the document.

9. Close the document and exit WordPerfect (unless you will be doing the following exercises immediately).

Exercise 28.3

1. Start WordPerfect, if necessary.

2. Open the file 28-3.wpw.

3. Define the first row of the table as a header row.

4. Perform a descending numeric sort by the third column of the table (Cell 3).

5. Redisplay the screen by pressing **Ctrl+F3**.

6. Sort the table in ascending order by office, and by agent within office. (Hint: Use Word -1 for the agent cell to work around the fact that some names have a first initial and some do not.)

7. Redisplay the screen.

8. Save the document as *[your three-letter identifier]*28-3.wpw, but do not close it.

9. Insert a new row below the last listing for each office, and insert one more row at the bottom of the table. (There should be two blank rows at the bottom of the table).

10. Join the first and second cells in each blank row, and then format the joined cells as right-justified and bold.

11. Key **Subtotal** in the first cell of all the blank rows except the last row. Key **Total** in the first cell of the last row.

12. Enter subtotal and total formulas in the appropriate cells and calculate the table.
13. Make the third and fourth columns 1.5 inches wide.
14. Insert dollar signs at the top and bottom of the third and fourth columns.
15. Apply 10% shading to the subtotal rows.
16. Redraw the table lines. Make all the lines single.
17. Spell-check the document.
18. Save the document (you saved it previously as *[your three-letter identifier]*28-3.wpw).
19. Print the document.
20. Close the document and exit WordPerfect (unless you will be doing the following exercises immediately).

Exercise 28.4

1. Start WordPerfect, if necessary.
2. Open a new document window.
3. Create a secondary merge file using the information in Figure 28-8, which appears at the end of this exercise. Use the field names Number, Location, Agent, and List Price.
4. Save the file as *[your three-letter identifier]*28-4.sf, but do not close it.
5. Sort the file by agent's last name and then by location.
6. Save the secondary merge file again and close it.
7. Create a primary merge file containing a page off code on the first line, and field codes separated by tabs on the second line with the field names in the following order: Number, Agent, Location, List Price. End the second line with a hard return.
8. Save the primary merge file as *[your three-letter identifier]*28-4.pf.
9. Close the primary merge file.
10. Open the file 28-4.wpw.
11. Position the insertion point at the end of the document.
12. Perform a merge using the primary file *[your three-letter identifier]*28-4.pf and the secondary file *[your three-letter identifier]*28-4.sf.
13. Spell-check the document.
14. Save the document as *[your three-letter identifier]*28-4.wpw.

15. Print the document.

16. Close the document and exit WordPerfect (unless you will be doing the following exercise immediately).

Figure 28-8

Number ~~ID #~~	Location	Agent	List Price
80886	Hillbrooke	G. Crane	179,900
97558	Alpharetta	A. Delbridge	565,000
34490	Parsons Station	G. Crane	144,900
76121	Dunwoody	M. Washington	238,900 ~~240,000~~
67890	Martins Landing	M. Washington	152,900
512~~3~~64	Roswell	A. Delbridge	799,000
67540	Litchfield	G. Crane ~~A. Delbridge~~	524,900
23145	Parsons Station ~~N. Fulton~~	G. Crane	340,800 ~~229,000~~
56790	Roswell	G. Crane	298,900
88788	Dunwoody	M. Washington	350,000

Exercise 28.5

1. Start WordPerfect, if necessary.
2. Open the file 28-5.wpw.
3. Use the Table Options dialog box to define the first table row as a header row.
4. Sort the table by the second line of the second column (the business type).
5. Redisplay the screen by pressing **Ctrl+F3**.
6. Scroll through the sorted table, and notice that there are some business types with more than one business listed, such as law firm and restaurant.
7. Resort the table by the second column. Make Key 1 the business type and Key 2 the last name.
8. Select the entire table, and change the lines to single for both the inside and the outside.
9. Save the document as *[your three-letter identifier]*28-5a.wpw, but do not close it.

10. Re-sort the table by the first column, by ZIP Code, then by last name within ZIP Code and by first name within last name. (Some names appear more than one time, because they sponsored more than one recruit.)

    (Hint: Drag the sort dialog box out of the way to see the table.)

11. Redisplay the screen.

12. Re-sort the table, keeping the first three keys as they were. Add a fourth key to sort the second column by business.

13. Redisplay the screen.

14. Change the table lines, so that the inside and the outside lines are single.

15. Spell-check the document.

16. Save the document as *[your three-letter identifier]*28-5b.wpw.

17. Print the document.

18. Close the document and exit WordPerfect.

Module 10

Lines and Graphics

Lessons

Lesson 29

Working With Lines

Lines can separate or call attention to text, making a document clearer and more attractive. For instance, columns of text can be separated with a vertical line, and headings can be boxed for emphasis. WordPerfect for Windows provides two types of lines: *character-based lines* and *graphics lines*. Character-based lines are useful for modifying lines created in character-based word processors, like WordPerfect 5.1 for DOS. Graphics lines are easier to use in WordPerfect for Windows.

Objectives

- Create character-based lines.
- Create graphics lines.
- Customize graphics lines.

Character-based lines
Lines made of a series of individual characters, such as line segments, WordPerfect characters, letters, or other symbols.

Graphics lines
Lines created in a graphic format and defined in terms of thickness, length, shading, and position.

The Line Draw Command

Line Draw allows you to draw lines in a document using any of the WordPerfect character sets. The Line Draw dialog box offers several drawing characters that also are available from the Box Drawing character set. You may define any other character for drawing, in addition to those provided.

In the Line Draw workspace, the direction keys insert the selected character to form lines, boxes, and other shapes. You also can erase existing Line Draw characters and move the cursor without drawing or erasing anything.

Note: Because Line Draw inserts blank spaces as you move or draw, you should use only monospace fonts with this feature. (In a monospace font, every character has the same width, so a "w", "i", and blank space occupy the same amount of horizontal space.) Choose a font measured in characters per inch (such as Courier 10cpi or 12cpi) for the section of a document where Line Draw will be used.

Follow these steps when you want to use Line Draw:

- Position the insertion point.
- Choose Line Draw from the Tools menu (or press **Ctrl+D**).
- Choose a mode (Draw, Erase, or Move).
- Choose a Line Draw character (or choose Character, and specify a character for drawing).
- Use the Arrow keys to draw, erase, or move (depending on the mode you selected), or use the quick-draw keystrokes listed in Table 29-1, on page 29-2.
- Choose Close.

When you enter the Line Draw workspace, the WordPerfect screen switches to *Draft Mode*. (The screen will resemble WordPerfect 5.1 for DOS.) Also, Line Draw mode automatically puts you in Insert mode (although this is not reflected in the status bar). The lines you draw will overwrite any text they cross.

Draft Mode
A screen mode available from the View menu that displays characters with uniform (monospace) spacing.

Table 29-1: Quick-Draw Keystrokes for Line Draw

Keystroke	Result
Home or **Ctrl+Left Arrow**	Extends line to the left margin.
End or **Ctrl+Right Arrow**	Extends line to the right margin.
Ctrl+Up Arrow	Extends line to the top margin.
Ctrl+Down Arrow	Extends line to the bottom margin.

If a line is extended using the **Ctrl** key, it will stop at any intervening line before the margin. Line extension with the **Home** and **End** keys, however, will cross intervening lines and continue to the margin.

To use Line Draw:

1. Start WordPerfect, if necessary, and choose Reveal Codes from the View menu.
2. Open the file 29-0a.wpw.
3. Press **Ctrl+Home** to move to the beginning of the file, if necessary. Then choose a monospaced font (such as Courier 10cpi).
4. Choose Line Draw from the Tools menu, or press **Ctrl+D**.

   The screen changes to the Line Draw workspace, including the Line Draw dialog box.

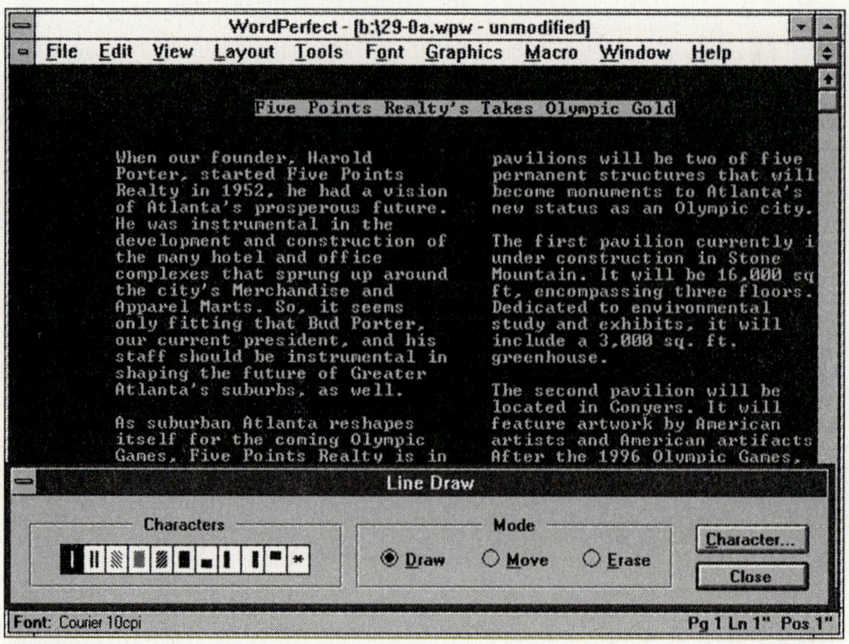

Figure 29-1
The Line Draw workspace and dialog box

5. Click on the third Line Draw character from the group on the left (a wide, shaded character) to choose it.

6. Choose Draw Mode, if necessary.

7. Press the **Right Arrow** key a few times.

   The character you chose is inserted each time the Arrow key is pressed.

8. Move the Line Draw dialog box up by dragging its title bar until the Reveal Codes space is visible.

   The codes for the selected Line Draw characters (Box Drawing character 3,0) are inserted.

9. Press **End**.

   The line is filled to the right margin with the selected character.

10. Click Move Mode.

11. Press the **Down Arrow** key three times to move past the heading.

    The heading changes position, since WordPerfect inserted blank spaces in that center-aligned paragraph.

12. Press **End** to move to the right margin.

13. Choose Draw Mode and press **Home**.

    A line of the chosen character is inserted from the right to the left margin.

14. Choose Close.

15. Delete the blank spaces at the end of the heading.

    The alignment appears centered again.

16. Position the insertion point at the end of the document.

17. Turn off columns by choosing Columns from the Layout menu and then choosing Columns Off.

18. Press **Ctrl+D** to open the Line Draw workspace.

19. Click the Character button.

    The Line Draw Character dialog box appears with the default asterisk character in the text box. (The text box will accept any character.)

Figure 29-2
The Line Draw Character dialog box

20. Press **Ctrl+W** to open the WordPerfect Characters dialog box, choose the Iconic Symbols character set, and choose the house symbol (number 5,12). Then choose Insert and Close.

    The house icon appears in the Line Draw Character text box.

21. Click OK.

22. If necessary, move the Line Draw dialog box to see the insertion point at the bottom of the document.

23. Choose Draw mode, if necessary. Then press and hold the **Right Arrow** key (or press **End**).

    A line of houses extends to the right margin.

24. Choose Close.

25. Select the line of house characters. Then apply the Large font attribute by choosing Font from the Font menu, choosing Large, and clicking OK.

    The characters are larger, and the sequence of characters now takes more than one line.

26. Delete the house characters on the second line.

27. View the document in Print Preview at 100 percent magnification.

    The heading is framed by wide, horizontal lines. The document ends with a decorative row of houses.

28. Print the document, and save it as *[your three-letter identifier]*29-0a.wpw.

29. Close the document.

Line Draw is a convenient way to create vertical and horizontal lines using any element in the WordPerfect character set, including Box Drawing characters. Graphics lines, however, are easier to create, modify, and move.

Creating Graphics Lines

The Graphics Line feature lets you place horizontal and vertical lines in your document. A line is actually a very narrow rectangle, and you define it by specifying its size (length and thickness), starting point, and gray shading (black = 100%).

Follow these steps when you create a graphics line:

- Position the insertion point where the top left corner of the line will be.
- Choose Line from the Graphics menu. Then choose Horizontal or Vertical to open the appropriate dialog box.
- Make adjustments and click OK.

Unlike character-based lines, graphics lines do not erase material that they cross, and they do not insert extra hard returns or blank spaces. Instead, they overlap other elements on the page. Furthermore, graphics lines work well with both proportional and monospace fonts.

To insert a graphics line:

1. Open the file 29-0b.wpw, and choose Reveal Codes from the View menu, if necessary.
2. Position the insertion point on the blank line above the heading.
3. Choose Line from the Graphics menu, and then choose Horizontal.

   The Create Horizontal Line dialog box appears.

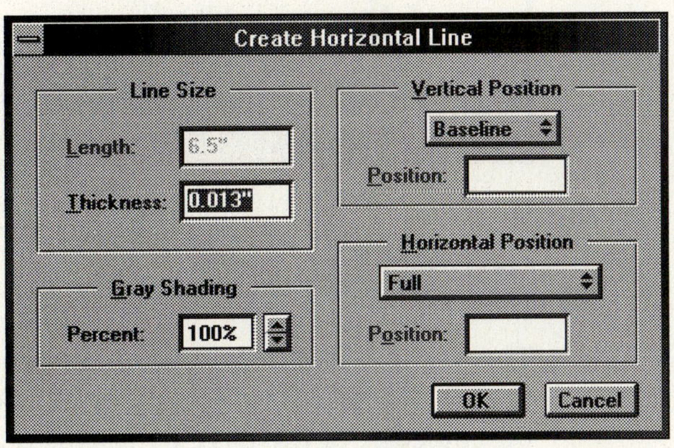

Figure 29-3
The Create Horizontal Line dialog box

4. Click OK.

   A thin line extends from the left to the right margin at the vertical position of the insertion point.

   A [HLine:Full, Baseline, 6.5", 0.013", 100%] code is inserted at the beginning of the blank line.

Editing Horizontal Graphics Lines

Note: Before choosing an Edit option from the Graphics Line cascading menu, position the insertion point immediately after the line you want to edit. WordPerfect searches backwards (and then forwards) until it finds a line.

Graphics lines can be edited from either the dialog box or the mouse. Using a dialog box, you can specify choices exactly. Using the mouse, you can see the effects of your editing as you work. You may combine these methods, roughly adjusting a line with the mouse, and then fine-tuning your choices with a dialog box. (Gray shading must be done in a dialog box, however.)

Changing Position in the Dialog Box

The position of a graphics line is its starting point (its topmost and leftmost position). Baseline and Full are the defaults. The baseline is the invisible line on which letters sit. Figure 29-4 shows text keyed over a default horizontal line. Notice that the tails of the letters p, y, and g descend below the default line. Its horizontal position is full, starting at the left margin and extending to the right margin.

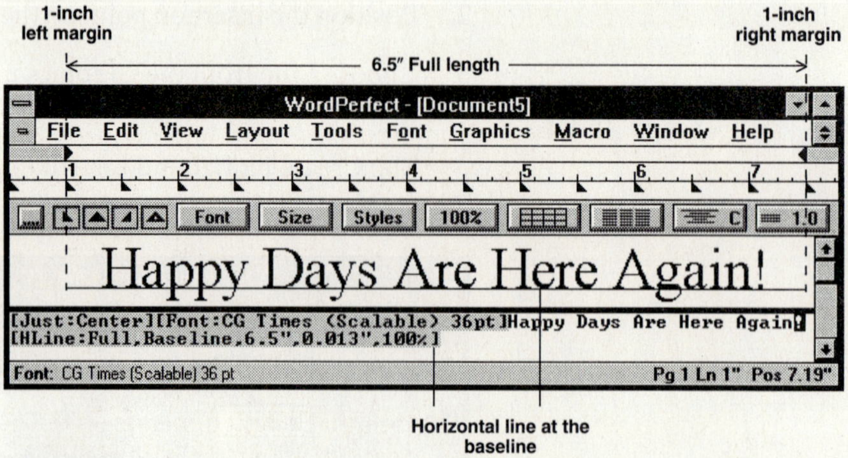

Figure 29-4
A horizontal line with default settings

The Horizontal Line Vertical Position pop-up list

The Vertical Position pop-up list offers two choices: Baseline and Specify. If you choose Specify, you can change the starting point from the top edge of the page by keying a distance in inches in the Position text box.

The Horizontal Position pop-up list offers five choices: Left, Right, Center, Full, and Specify. If you choose Specify, you can change the starting point from the left edge of the page by keying a distance in the Position text box. Otherwise, choose Left or Right to position the

The Horizontal Line Horizontal Position pop-up list

line against either margin, choose Center to position the line exactly between the margins, or choose Full to extend the line from the left to the right margin.

To change the horizontal line position:

1. Choose Line from the Graphics menu and then choose Edit Horizontal.

   The line is selected, and the Edit Horizontal dialog box (which is identical to the Create dialog box) appears.

2. Choose Specify from the Vertical Position pop-up list.

   The Position text box shows the vertical distance from the top of the page to the baseline of the current line.

3. Tab to the Position text box and key **1.1**.

4. Choose Center from the Horizontal Position pop-up list.

   The Length text box in the Line Size group becomes active, showing 6.5 inches.

5. Click OK.

   The vertical position of the line shifts up. The horizontal position does not change, because the default line length fills the space between the left and right margins.

Changing Line Size in the Dialog Box

Since a line is actually a thin rectangle, its size has two dimensions: length and thickness. The default line thickness is 0.013 inches. This is about one typesetting "point." (Remember, in typesetting, distance can be expressed in inches or points. A point is 1/72 inches, or 0.01388".) To change the thickness or length of a line, key a new value in inches in the Thickness text box.

The Length text box is active whenever Horizontal Position is not Full.

The default Length depends on the margin settings, since a horizontal line originally is defined as Full. Using standard paper and 1-inch left and right margins, the default length is 6.5 inches, extending from the left to the right margin (8.5" standard page width – 1" left margin – 1" right margin = 6.5").

To change the line size:

1. Open the Edit Horizontal Line dialog box.

2. Key **5.5** in the Length text box.

3. Key **0.13** (not 0.013) in the Thickness text box.

   The line will be ten times thicker than before.

4. Click OK.

   A thick, solid line 5.5 inches long is centered 1.1 inches from the top edge of the paper.

Editing Graphics Lines with the Mouse

To change the position and size of a line using the mouse, click on the line to select it. Sizing handles appear around the line.

To move the line, position the mouse pointer over the selected line until it becomes a four-directional arrow. Then drag the line to a new position.

To resize the line, position the mouse pointer on a sizing handle until it becomes a two-directional arrow. Then drag the handle to change the line's length or thickness. (You can drag a corner handle diagonally to change both dimensions at once.)

To edit a line with the mouse:

1. Click on the horizontal line to select it.

   Eight sizing handles appear. (Very thin lines display only six sizing handles).

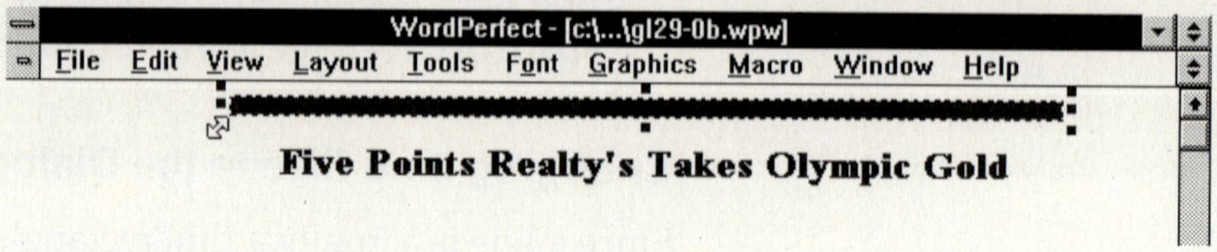

Figure 29-5
The pointer becomes a two-directional arrow over any sizing handle of a selected graphics line.

2. Position the mouse pointer over the line, until it becomes a four-directional arrow. Then drag the line toward the heading about the distance of the line's width.

   As you drag, a dotted shape represents the changing position of the line. The original line remains in place as a point of reference, until you release the mouse button.

3. Release the mouse button.

   The line is moved down and remains selected.

4. Position the mouse pointer over the left center sizing handle. When the two-directional arrow appears, drag the handle to the right. Stop before you reach the left edge of the heading.

5. Repeat step 3 for the right edge of the line.

   The line now extends just beyond the heading on the left and the right.

6. Drag the top center sizing handle toward the heading, until the line is about half its original thickness.
7. Click outside the line.

   The line is deselected.

Opening the Edit Horizontal Line Dialog Box with the Mouse

When you click the right mouse button on a graphics line, an Edit menu option appears. Click that pop-up menu option (or press **Enter**), and the Edit Horizontal Line dialog box appears.

Gray Shading

In the Edit Horizontal Line dialog box, the Gray Shading text box lets you specify the intensity of shading of a graphics line (100% is black).

To change the shading of a line:

1. Click the right mouse button on the line.

   The Edit Horizontal Line pop-up menu option appears.
2. Click that option.

   The Edit Horizontal Line dialog box appears.
3. Key **75** in the Gray Shading Percent text box. Then click OK.

   The line changes from black to dark gray.

Deleting, Copying, Cutting, and Pasting Lines

You can delete, copy, cut, and paste a graphics line as you would with any other code. To paste a line, first select the code (or click on the line itself), and then delete, copy, or cut the line. You then may move the insertion point and undelete or paste.

To copy a graphics line:

1. Click on the horizontal line to select it.
2. Choose Copy from the Edit menu (or press **Ctrl+Insert**).
3. Move the insertion point to the blank line under the heading.
4. Choose Paste from the Edit menu (or press **Shift+Insert**).

   Identical lines now frame the heading.
5. Open the Edit Horizontal Line dialog box.
6. Key **50** in the Gray Shading text box and click OK.

   The lower line is now medium gray.

Designing Styles with Graphics Lines

In WordPerfect, styles provide a convenient way to produce a document with consistent design elements (see Lesson 24). Styles commonly include horizontal graphics lines, and you only have to format a line once in a heading, header, footer, or title. Applying the style will always produce the same look.

When designing styles that includes graphics lines, however, consider both the look of each style itself and how these design elements will work together.

Tips for Spacing Graphics Lines Within a Style

You can add white space within a style by inserting hard returns and by adjusting the line height (see Lesson 19).

- Sometimes, horizontal lines separate text elements. When you position a line below a heading, you can reduce the white space before the text that follows it. Otherwise, the heading may seem to "float" away from the material it introduces.

- Sometimes, horizontal lines can link text elements. When you position a line above a heading, you might need to increase the white space above the line. Otherwise, the line may seem to underscore the preceding material.

Tips for Making Styles with Graphics Lines Work Together

With some planning, you can add variety to a document while limiting the number of horizontal lines in it.

- Use different line dimensions to identify different levels of headings. Titles and first-level headings might use full-length heavy lines. Second-level headings might use lighter, shorter lines. Third-level headings might include no lines at all.

- If a document includes several headings on a single page, avoid full-length lines. They will make the text look choppy.

- Avoid "bumping" horizontal lines. For instance, a caption may be followed by a horizontal line, and a heading may be preceded by one. If the heading follows the caption, the two lines "bump." You can design two styles for captions to solve this problem: one without a line for use before the heading.

Editing Vertical Graphics Lines

You create and edit vertical graphics lines in much the same way as horizontal lines, using the mouse or the dialog box. In the Create (Edit) Vertical Line dialog box, however, there are some differences worth noting. Figure 29-6 shows the default values.

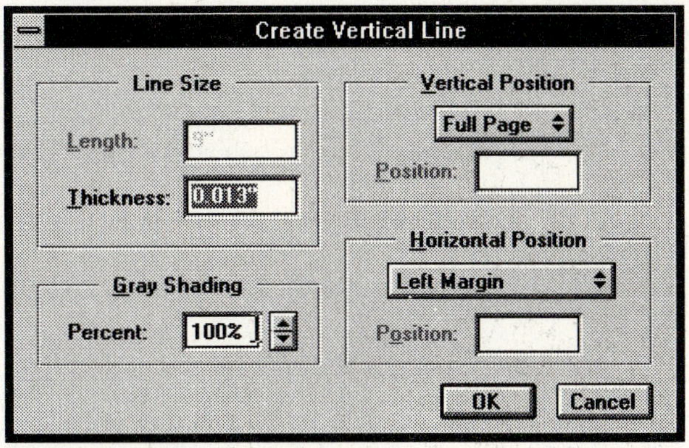

Figure 29-6
The Create Vertical Line dialog box

Vertical Position

The Vertical Line Vertical Position pop-up list

If you choose Full, the line will extend from the top to the bottom margin. Otherwise, choose Top or Bottom to position the line against that margin, choose Center to position the line exactly between the top and bottom margins, or choose Specify to specify a distance from the top edge of the page in the Position text box.

Horizontal Position

If you choose Left Margin, the line will be positioned slightly to the left of the left margin. Right Margin positions the line slightly to the right of the right margin.

Note: Position the insertion point after the Column On code before specifying Between Columns as the horizontal position. Otherwise, WordPerfect will treat the text set in columns as a single block and position the vertical line to its right.

You can choose Between Columns and specify a column number to position the line to the right of that column.

Choose Specify to specify a distance for the line from the left edge of the page.

Line Size

If the Vertical Position of the line is Top or Bottom, the default line length is calculated from the insertion point to the specified margin. For instance, with default margins and the insertion point at 1.93″, choosing Top will create a line Length of 0.93″ (the distance from the insertion point to the top margin: 1.93″ – 1″ = 0.93″).

The Vertical Line Horizontal Position pop-up list

If the Vertical Position of the line is Center, the default length is the distance between the top and bottom margins. (For a standard page without headers or footers using default 1-inch margins, the length would be 9 inches: 11″ – 1″ – 1″ = 9″.)

Note: WordPerfect will not extend a vertical line from the document body into a header or footer automatically. Of course, you can specify such a line.

To position a vertical line:

1. Move the insertion point to the beginning of the first line of the article, before the word "When".
2. Choose Line from the Graphics menu and then choose Vertical.

   The Create Vertical Line dialog box appears.
3. Choose Specify from the Vertical Position pop-up list.

   The current vertical position appears in the Position text box.
4. Choose Between Columns from the Horizontal Position pop-up list. Then key **1** in the Right of Column text box, if necessary.
5. Key **4.5** in the Length text box.
6. Click OK.

   A thin, vertical line is positioned between the two columns, extending from the insertion point down 4.5 inches.

Note: The position of a line may move slightly when it is shortened or lengthened with the mouse. Use the dialog box to specify exact length and positioning.

7. Use the mouse to shorten the bottom end of the line to stop at the end of the text. Then open the Edit Vertical Line dialog box by pressing **Alt, G, L, E**.

   The Length should be about 3.8 inches.

   Notice that both Vertical and Horizontal Positions become specified after editing with the mouse.
8. Adjust the settings in the Edit Vertical Line dialog box as follows:

Length: 3.8	Vertical Position: 1.92
	Horizontal Position: 4.25
9. Check the document in Print Preview.

   The position of graphics appears more accurately in Print Preview than in the document window.
10. Print the document, and save it as *[your three-letter identifier]*29-0b.wpw.
11. Close the document.
12. Exit WordPerfect (unless you will be doing the following exercises immediately).

Table 29-2: Keyboard Shortcuts	
Keyboard Shortcut	Action
Ctrl+D	Open the Line Draw workspace/dialog box
Alt, G, L, H	Open the Create Horizontal Line dialog box
Alt, G, L, O	Open the Edit Horizontal Line dialog box
Alt, G, L, V	Open the Create Vertical Line dialog box
Alt, G, L, E	Open the Edit Vertical Line dialog box

Key Terms

Character-based lines
Draft Mode
Graphics lines

Exercises

Exercise 29.1

1. Start WordPerfect, if necessary.
2. Open the file 29-1.wpw.
3. Choose Ruler and Reveal Codes from the View menu, if necessary.
4. Move the insertion point to the top of the document.
5. Select a monospace font, such as Courier 10cpi, if necessary.
6. Use the Line Draw feature to create a double-lined box above the article, between the 2.5-inch and 5.5-inch measures on the Ruler and four lines deep:
   A. Press **Ctrl+D** to open the Line Draw workspace.
   B. Choose Move Mode. Then press the **Right Arrow** key until the insertion point reaches the 2.5-inch measure.
   C. Choose the double-line character (the second from the left) and choose Draw Mode.
   D. Draw the top of the box by pressing the **Right Arrow** key until the double line reaches the 5.5-inch measure.
   E. Press the **Down Arrow** key four times to draw the left side of the box.

F. Draw the bottom of the box by pressing the **Left Arrow** key until the double line reaches the 2.5-inch measure.

G. Press the **Up Arrow** key to draw the right side of the box.

H. Choose Close.

7. Key a heading in the box:

A. Press **Insert**.

B. Press the **Down Arrow** key once and the **Right Arrow** key twice to move the insertion point within the box.

C. Key **NEW CORPORATE CHALLENGE**.

D. Move the insertion point to the next line, and key **HAS AGENTS ON THE RUN**.

8. Make the box and its contents bold:

A. Select all text and spaces from the beginning of the document to the end of the box.

B. Press **Ctrl+B**.

9. Adjust spacing:

A. Turn off Insert mode.

B. Delete and insert spaces to center and align the contents of the heading box.

10. Spell-check the document.

11. Print the document and save it as *[your three-letter identifier]*29-1.wpw.

12. Close the document.

13. Exit WordPerfect (unless you will be doing the following exercises immediately).

Exercise 29.2

1. Start WordPerfect, if necessary.

2. Open the file 29-2.wpw.

3. Make a frame around the four margins of the page by creating two horizontal and two vertical lines:

A. Choose Line from the Graphics menu, and then choose Horizontal. Specify the following, and then close the dialog box:

Length: 6.7 Vertical Position: 0.9
Thickness: 0.013 (default) Horizontal Position: 0.9

B. Repeat step A, specifying the following:

Length: 6.7 Vertical Position: 10.1
Thickness: 0.013 (default) Horizontal Position: 0.9

C. Press **Alt, G, L, V**. Specify the following, and then close the dialog box:

Length: 9.2 Vertical Position: 0.9
Thickness: 0.013 (default) Horizontal Position: 0.9

D. Repeat step C, specifying the following:

Length: 9.2 Vertical Position: 0.9
Thickness: 0.013 (default) Horizontal Position: 7.6

E. Change all the margins to 1.1 inches to allow adequate space between the frame and the text.

F. Check the page in the Print Preview window. All corners should meet.

4. At the top of the document, choose a 12-point serif font (such as CG Times Scalable) for the document.
5. Select and format the heading as centered in a 16-point sans serif font (such as Univers), bold, small caps.
6. Format each course title in the same sans serif font in 12-point size, bold, small caps.
7. Keep course titles at the left margin, and add another blank line above each.
8. Above the heading, create a full horizontal line with 0.15 inch thickness and 40% shading. Specify 1 inch as the vertical position.
9. Select and copy that line. Paste it below the heading.
10. Using the mouse, shorten the line below the heading to about half its original length:

    A. Click on the line.

    B. Drag the left center (or right center) sizing handle toward the middle of the line.
11. Center the line.

    A. Click the line with the right mouse button, and choose the pop-up menu option.

    B. In the dialog box, choose Center as the Horizontal position and click OK.
12. Move the insertion point to the bottom of the page, and paste the full-length line.
13. Check the page in Print Preview.
14. Print the document, and save it as *[your three-letter identifier]*29-2.wpw.
15. Close the document.
16. Exit WordPerfect (unless you will be doing the following exercises immediately).

Exercise 29.3

1. Start WordPerfect, if necessary.
2. Open the file 29-3.wpw.
3. Edit the document as shown in Figure 29-7 (which appears at the end of this exercise), and spell-check the document.
4. Format the article in a 12-point serif font (such as CG Times).
5. Make the heading centered, bold, italic, and extra large.
6. Select the body of the article, and define it in two newspaper columns, full-justified. (Remember, Columns is a Layout command.)
7. Break the columns at the quotation that begins "Being close".
8. Adjust typesetting in the first column to add 0.01 inches of leading between lines.
9. Delete the extra hard returns after each paragraph in the second column. Then adjust leading in the second column to add 0.05 inches between paragraphs. (This should balance the columns.)
10. Use the Graphics Line feature to create a box around the article and its heading. Use default line thickness.
11. Separate the two columns with a graphics line.
12. Print the document, and save it as *[your three-letter identifier]*29-3.wpw.
13. Close the document.
14. Exit WordPerfect (unless you will be doing the following exercises immediately).

Figure 29-7

```
Headline: G&H Building Gets New Tenant

Five Points Realty today announced that they have rented the G&H building
to Actron Multimedia, Inc., one of the national leaders in producing
sophisticated computer graphics for television. In a press conference, the
```

president of Actron, Sharon Acquilar, said that her decision to move from the company's former headquarters in Doraville was based on the need for more space. ¶ ~~She~~ *Acquilar* said that Actron had grown by more than 200 percent in the past two years. "Being closer to CNN didn't hurt, either," she added.

Market analysts estimate that the CNN account, Actron's largest, amounted to between $35 and $45 million in annual billings for ~~Actron~~ *the company*, roughly half of ~~the company's billings~~ *Actron's business*.

The G&H Building at the corner of Techwood and Luckie Street ~~is a~~ *was constructed at a cost of* $7.2 million ~~building~~ *in 1989*. The space was vacant for more than six months.

Exercise 29.4

1. Start WordPerfect, if necessary.
2. In a new file, key the press release in document 29-4, which appears at the end of this exercise.
3. Create a header as follows, making the text uppercase and bold and using the date code. Above this text, insert a full-length horizontal line 0.1 inches thick with 50% gray shading:

   FOR IMMEDIATE RELEASE [date code]

4. Create a footer as follows, making the text upper and lowercase in italic. Insert a full-length black horizontal line of default thickness above the text. Be sure the line does not overlap the text:

   Five Points Realty 555-1234

5. Spell-check the document.
6. Print the document, and save it as *[your three-letter identifier]*29-4.wpw.
7. Close the document.
8. Exit WordPerfect (unless you will be doing the following exercise immediately).

Document 29.4

Headline: Homes on the Rental Market for the 1996 Olympics

The 1996 Olympic Games may be a few years away, but people in the Greater Atlanta area already have started to capitalize on the event. Five Points Realty has begun to book homes in the Marietta Square, Stone Mountain and Conyers communities for the two-weeks-long Games. "A lot of people already have decided that they'll take their vacations out of town during the Olympics and are renting their homes. Others are opening up their homes and B&Bs, says Mary Rigdon, of the Five Points Marietta Square office.

Some of the prices on the market currently are $2,500 per week for a three-bedroom house in Stone Mountain and $75 per night for a Bed and Breakfast arrangement.

Lesson 30

Creating Graphics Boxes

Objectives

- Create and edit figure boxes.
- Create and edit text, table, and user boxes.
- Create and edit equation boxes.

Graphics box
A rectangle that can hold text, a table, or an illustration, and can be positioned as a unit anywhere in a document.

Graphics box type
The WordPerfect category for a graphics box: Figure, Text, Equation, Table, or User.

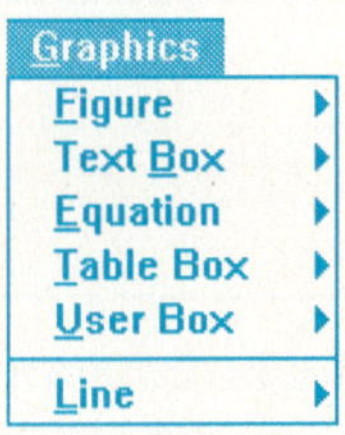

The Graphics menu

Illustrations add interest to documents and also help convey meaning. Clear explanations often include text, pictures, diagrams, and tables. In WordPerfect, any of these elements can be placed in a *graphics box*, a rectangle that can be positioned anywhere in a document.

This Lesson describes how to create graphics boxes and edit their contents. In Lesson 31, you will adjust box position, size, captions, and appearance.

Types of Graphics Boxes

The Graphics menu lists the five different *graphics box types*: Figure, Text, Equation, Table, and User. You can put any content into each type of box, but boxes generally are used as shown in Table 30-1.

Table 30-1: Suggested Use of Graphics Boxes

Box Type	Suggested Use
Figure	Graphics images, diagrams, charts
Text	Quotations, sidebars, text set off from the body of the document
Equation	Mathematical and scientific equations
Table	WordPerfect tables, statistical tables, maps
User	Any image, text, or table

Each type of box in a document is numbered by WordPerfect in a separate list. For instance, the third figure box is "Figure 3," and the second table box is "Table 2." You may create captions for any type of box and, using the List feature, generate a separate list of each type of box.

To improve their visual effect, graphics boxes may be given borders and shading. Each of the five types of graphics boxes has a default border and shading.

Table 30-2: Default Appearance of Graphics Boxes

Box Type	Border	Shading
Figure	thin lines on four sides	none
Text	thick top and bottom lines	10% (light gray)
Equation	none	none
Table	thick top and bottom lines	none
User	none	none

Graphics Box Editors

Figure Editor
An editor for retrieving and manipulating graphics images in a graphics box.

Text Box Editor
An editor for retrieving, entering, and manipulating text and tables in a graphics box.

Equation Editor
An editor for creating complex mathematical and scientific equations in a graphics box.

WordPerfect provides three environments for creating and editing graphics boxes: the Figure Editor, the Text Box Editor, and the Equation Editor. Once a box is created, its editor cannot be changed.

Graphics images can be manipulated only in the *Figure Editor.* The *Text Box Editor* can be used to create text or tables. The *Equation Editor* provides a convenient work space for creating complex symbolic expressions.

Figure 1 Optional figure box caption.

Text Designed to Stand Out

1 Optional text box caption.

Table I
Optional table box caption.

YR	$ million	Units (000)
92	$1.2	120
93	$1.1	175

Figure 30-1
Sample figure, text, and table boxes

Note: You can change the Box Type of any graphics box, regardless of the editor used to create its contents. For instance, a graphics image may be contained within a table box; it will be numbered with other table boxes and have the appearance of a table box. When you edit the image in that box, however, you will use the Figure Editor.

Retrieving Graphics Images

Graphics image
A picture stored as a pattern of dots.

A *graphics image* is a picture stored as a pattern of dots. When you choose Figure from the Graphics menu, the Figure cascading menu

The Graphics Figure cascading menu

appears. There, you may choose Retrieve to get a graphics image from a file and put it into a graphics box in the document. (You may choose Create to open the Figure Editor and retrieve the file to manipulate there, instead.)

When a file is retrieved, it is converted to the WordPerfect Graphics format automatically.

To retrieve a graphics file:

1. Start WordPerfect, if necessary.

2. Open the file 30-0.wpw.

3. Move the insertion point to the beginning of the document, if necessary.

4. Choose Figure from the Graphics menu and then Choose Retrieve (or press **F11**).

   The Retrieve Figure dialog box appears. The current directory should list all files with the .wpg extension (indicating WordPerfect Graphics format).

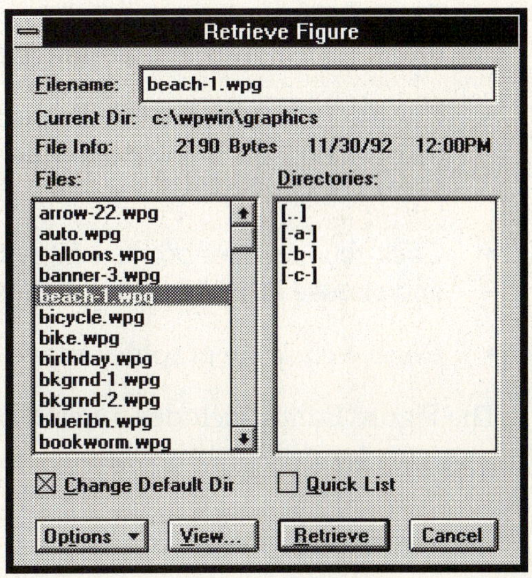

Figure 30-2
The Retrieve Figure dialog box

Note: If the file is not currently listed in the Retrieve Figure dialog box, select Find Files from the Options pop-up list. Use the Find Files dialog box to locate beach-1.wpg.

5. Scroll through the list and highlight beach-1.wpg. Then choose Retrieve.

The image (which includes a beach umbrella) is inserted in a graphics figure box and appears in the document on the right margin. The width of the box is half the distance between margins.

> **Using Graphics in Other Formats and Programs**
>
> Various business and illustration programs produce graphics files, and most programs give you a choice of formats in which to save them. You can convert a file into .wpg (WordPerfect Graphics) format simply by retrieving it into a graphics box. Furthermore, if you want to convert several graphics files into .wpg format at once, you can use the Graphics Conversion Program that comes with WordPerfect (if it has been installed).
>
> Some of the common formats that can be retrieved by WordPerfect for Windows are .bmp (Windows Bitmap Format), .eps (Encapsulated PostScript), .msp (Microsoft Windows Paint Format), .pcx (PC Paintbrush Format), .pic (Lotus 1-2-3 PIC Format), and .tif (Tagged Image File Format).

Using the Figure Editor

In the Figure Editor, you can retrieve and manipulate WordPerfect graphics. You can select a portion of the image, enlarge it, display its mirror image, rotate it, and move it within the graphics box.

You can open the Figure Editor in four ways:

- Choose Create from the Graphics Figure cascading menu. (You then can retrieve an image to create a new box.)
- Choose Edit from the Figure cascading menu (or press **Shift+F11**), and then specify the figure number in the Edit Figure dialog box.
- Click the graphics box to edit with the right mouse button, and choose Edit Figure from the short menu.
- Double-click the graphics box to edit.

The Figure Editor includes a menu bar and a Button Bar of mouse shortcuts for most manipulations.

Editing Figures with the Button Bar and the Mouse

The Figure Editor Button Bar provides mouse tools to manipulate graphics images. You also may choose these options from the Figure Editor menus. Table 30-3 on page 30-5 lists some of the functions available from the Button Bar.

The Edit Figure dialog box

To use the Figure Editor with the mouse:

1. Choose Edit from the Figure cascading menu (or press **Shift+F11**).

   The Edit Figure dialog box appears, with Figure Number 2 highlighted in the text box.

Table 30-3: Functions of the Figure Editor Button Bar

Button	Function	Menu
Close	Close the Figure Editor	File
Retrieve	Insert an image	File
Fig Pos	Open the Box Position and Size dialog box (see Lesson 31)	File (Box Position)
Move	Enable the mouse to move the image within the box	Edit
Rotate	Enable the mouse to rotate the image within the box	Edit
Enlarge	Enable the mouse to select a portion of the image and enlarge it	Edit (Scale)
Reset Size	Reset the original size of the image	Edit (Scale)
Mirror	Reverse the left/right direction of the image	Edit
Outline	Change a color image into a black-and-white outline. All colors become white.	Edit
Reset All	Reset the image to its original state.	Edit
Edit All	Open the Edit All dialog Box.	Edit

2. Key **1** in the text box and click OK.
3. The Figure Editor opens with the beach-1 image in the workspace.

Figure 30-3
The Figure Editor

4. Click the Retrieve Button to open the Retrieve Figure dialog box.
5. Highlight sail-bt.wpg and click Retrieve.

   The image in the workspace is replaced with sailboats.

6. Close the Figure Editor to return to the document.

   The new image is longer and extends into the descriptive paragraph. Notice that, by default, text wraps around a graphics box.

7. Click with the right mouse button in the sailboat graphics box.

   The Graphics Figure short menu appears.

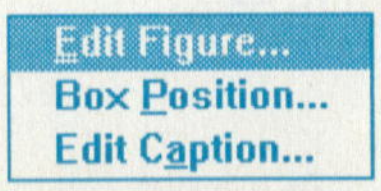

The Graphics Figure short menu

8. Choose Edit Figure to open the Figure Editor for the selected figure.
9. Click the Move button. Then move the mouse pointer to the graphics box in the workspace, and drag the image to the left. Release the mouse button when the left number in the status bar reads between -0.5 and -0.6 inches.

   The pointer becomes a four-headed arrow as you drag. When you release the mouse button, the image is moved. Notice that the position change in inches is reflected in the status bar at the bottom of the workspace. (A move to the left or down is reported as a negative number.)

10. Click the Rotate button.

    A rotation angle appears on the figure.

11. Drag the right axis up slightly. Release the mouse button when the Rotate number in the status bar reads 5.

    The image is tilted up 5 degrees (and the water seems a little rough).

12. Click the Enlarge button, and drag over half the image to open a dotted rectangle. Then release the mouse button.

    The part of the image included in your rectangle now fills the graphics box.

13. Click the Reset Size button.

    The image is reset to its original size.

14. Click the Mirror button.

    The image now faces the opposite direction.

15. Click the Mirror button again. The image is back in its original direction.

16. Click the Reset All button.

    The image is returned to its original state. Rotation, position, direction, and size are the same as when the image was created.

17. Click the Edit All Button.

    The Edit All dialog box appears.

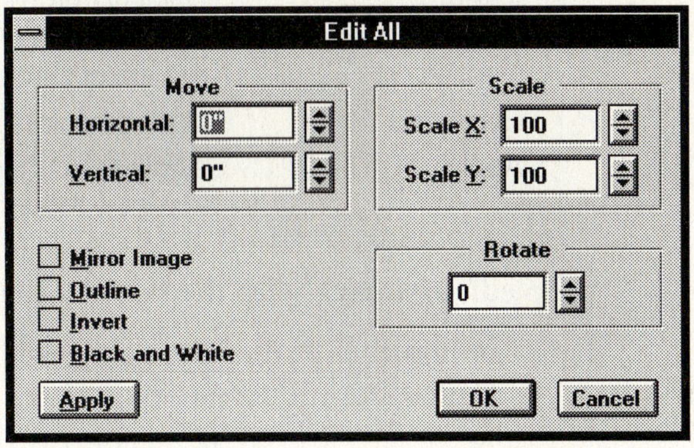

Figure 30-4
The Edit All dialog box

Editing Figures with the Edit All Dialog Box

The Edit All dialog box lets you move, scale, rotate, and otherwise adjust the graphics image in the Figure Editor. You can choose Apply to see the change in the image without closing the dialog box. You then may change the image further.

When the image is satisfactory, click OK to accept all the changes. (You may edit the image further before closing the Figure Editor.)

Table 30-4: Edit All Options

Option	Effect
Move, Horizontal	Move the image within the box the specified distance in inches. Positive values move right, negative values move left.
Move, Vertical	Move the image within the box the specified distance in inches. Positive values move up, negative values move down.
Scale X	Widen (>100%) or narrow (<100%) the image within the box.
Scale Y	Lengthen (>100%) or shorten (<100%) the image within the box.
Rotate	Turn the image within the box the specified number of degrees (between 0 and 360).

continued on next page

Table 30-4—Continued

Option	Effect
Mirror	Flip the image left or right.
Outline	Change color image to a line drawing. Color becomes white. Does not affect black-and-white images.
Invert	Display complementary colors of color image (like a photograph negative). Does not affect black-and-white images.
Black and White	Change colors in a color image to black.
Apply	Apply the current Edit All settings to the image without closing the dialog box.

To edit an image with the Edit All dialog box:

1. In Figure Editor, choose Edit All from the Edit menu (or the Button Bar), if necessary.

   The image is partially visible behind the dialog box. The settings show that the image is displayed as it originally was created.

2. Check Mirror and then click Apply.

   The image is flipped along the vertical axis. (The boat in the foreground now faces left.)

3. Key **0.5** in the Horizontal Move text box and click Apply.

   The image is moved ½ inch to the right.

4. Key **110** in the Scale X text box, key **90** in the Scale Y text box, and click Apply.

   The image becomes wider (110% of its original) and shorter (90% of its original).

5. Key **5** in the Rotate text box and click Apply.

   The image tilts 5 degrees.

6. Drag the title bar of the dialog box to the upper left of the screen, and look at the image.

   The boat in the foreground will now appear to be sailing into the page. Its angle conveys more speed.

7. Click OK to close the dialog box, and close the Figure Editor.

Editing Around and Deleting Graphics Boxes

Of course, you can edit the text of a document that contains graphics boxes. A graphics box stays in place unless it is deleted or moved (see Lesson 31). If text in the document bumps into a box, it will wrap around it by default.

To delete a graphics box, you can delete its code. You also can select a graphics box by clicking it once. The selected box can be deleted, cut, or copied.

To edit the document:

1. Change the years in the document. Give the August date the current year, and the May date the following year.

2. Select the paragraphs that begin "location" and "phone".

   Notice that the selected paragraphs appear to run behind the graphics box.

3. Delete these paragraphs. Then key **Marietta Square**, press **Enter**, and key **404/555-3421**.

   The box is not disturbed. The text flows around the box as editing changes are made.

4. Move the insertion point to the beginning of the paragraph that begins "Exclusive agents". Choose Advance from the Layout menu, and then specify To Line 6.43". (This is the position of the first line that wraps at the right margin after the box.) Click OK.

   The text moves past the box and now wraps normally at the right margin.

Note: To find the vertical position of a point on a page, click in the text near that point. Then read the "Ln" value in the status bar.

5. Click the box once to select it and press **Delete**.

   The box is deleted. The text stretches across the page where the box once was.

6. Choose Undelete from the Edit menu and then choose Restore.

   The box is restored.

Using the Text Box Editor

The Text Box Editor is used to create or edit text or tables in a graphics box. You may use this editor to create text boxes, table boxes, or user boxes. When you create a text box, the Text Box Editor opens automatically. When you create a table box or user box, however, you first must pick an editor in the Select Editor dialog box.

The techniques described for opening the Figure Editor apply to the other graphics editors, as well: Double-click the box, right-click the box and choose Edit, or choose Edit from the cascading menu of any box type and specify the box number.

To edit a text box, you also may press **Alt+Shift+F11** and specify the text box number.

You may key any text, insert WordPerfect codes, or retrieve a document into the Text Box Editor. The contents of the editor cannot be longer than one document page, however. You may define columns; key merge codes; and import and export spreadsheets, DDE files, or other files.

Any features not available in the Text Box Editor are dimmed in the menus.

The Text Box Editor Button Bar

The Button Bar in the Text Box Editor lets you close the editor and accept the current changes, cancel current changes and close the editor, open the Box Position and Size dialog box (see Lesson 31), and rotate the text.

In order to print rotated text, your printer must be able to print rotated fonts. When you select Rotate, the Rotate Text dialog box opens. There, you can select an option (Rotate none, 90, 180, or 270 degrees). Rotated text appears in Print Preview, but not in the document window.

Creating a Text Box

You can create a text box by choosing Text Box from the Graphics menu and then choosing Create (or by pressing **Alt+F11**). When you close the Text Box editor, the text box code is inserted in the document at the insertion point, and the box appears nearby.

To create a text box:

1. Position the insertion point at the beginning of the paragraph that begins "Exclusive agents".

2. Press **Alt+F11** (or choose Text Box from the Graphics menu and then choose Create).

   The Text Box Editor opens.

3. Turn on the Ruler.

   Notice that the margin limits the width of the box to half the distance between margins in the document.

4. Choose the font that matches the rest of the document (Univers, or another sans serif font), and choose 14-point (or Large) type size, bold, and italic.

   Since the box will have gray shading, large, bold type will stand out better.

5. Key **Offering by prospectus only.** Then close the editor.

   The text box appears beside the "Exclusive Agents" notice.

Creating a Table Box

A table box can contain text, one or more WordPerfect tables, or a graphics image. Normally, however, it contains a single table (and, sometimes, related text).

There are several advantages to using a table box, rather than inserting a table in text:

- The table-box caption can serve as a title (see Figure 30-1).
- The table can be kept together with related text.
- The table box can be positioned in the document as a unit.
- Text will flow normally around the box.
- The box can have borders and shading.
- The box can be numbered automatically, and a list of all table boxes can be generated.

To create a table box:

1. Move the insertion point to the beginning of the paragraph that begins "Five Points Realty announces".
2. Press **Ctrl+Enter** to insert a hard page break.
3. Choose Table Box from the Graphics menu and then choose Create.
4. Press **Enter** to accept the Text Editor (the default) in the Select Editor dialog box.

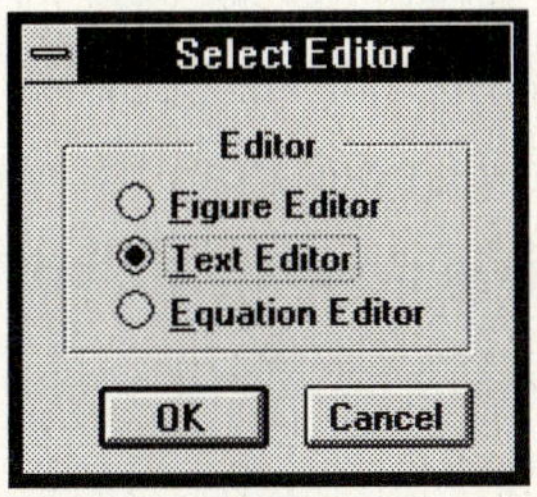

Figure 30-5
The Select Editor dialog box

5. In the Text Box Editor, select Retrieve from the File menu. Then select file 30-0.tbl from your student disk. Choose Retrieve, and confirm that choice in the next dialog box.

   A table appears in the Text Box Editor.

6. Close the Editor.

   The table box appears beside the descriptive paragraph in the document.

User Boxes

User boxes are created in the same way as table boxes. Choose User Box, choose an editor, create the box contents, and close the editor.

User boxes have no borders or shading by default, so they sometimes are used to represent photographs or other illustrations that will be physically pasted on a hard copy of a document.

Creating A Box Caption

Any graphics box can have a caption. The box and caption are positioned as a unit (see Lesson 31), and WordPerfect can generate a list of the captions of each type of box.

Each box type places its captions in a default position (see Figure 30-1). The Caption Editor automatically inserts the appropriate box number code, which you may delete. You can apply any available fonts and character attributes to caption text.

The Caption Editor for a box can be opened from any place in the document using the Graphics menu. Choose the box type, and then choose Caption from the cascading menu. Specify the box number in the Edit Caption dialog box. You also can right-click any graphics box and choose Edit Caption from the short menu.

To create a caption:

1. Right-click the table box.
2. Choose Edit Caption from the short menu.

   The Caption Editor for Table 1 opens. "Table 1" begins the caption.
3. Choose Reveal Codes from the View menu, if necessary.

   "Table 1" was generated by a box number code.
4. Delete this code.
5. Choose a font to match the document. Choose 18 point or Very Large, small caps, and bold. Then key **The Tides**.
6. Close the caption editor.

   The caption appears above the table box.
7. Choose Reveal Codes from the View menu, if necessary.
8. If necessary, position the insertion point immediately after the [Tbl Box:I...] code.
9. Press **Enter** to insert a hard return and align the paragraph with the table box.

Using the Equation Editor

WordPerfect includes an Equation Editor designed for creating mathematical or scientific equations. This editor uses the initial font for the document. You can change this font in the document window by choosing Document from the Layout menu, and then choosing Initial Font.

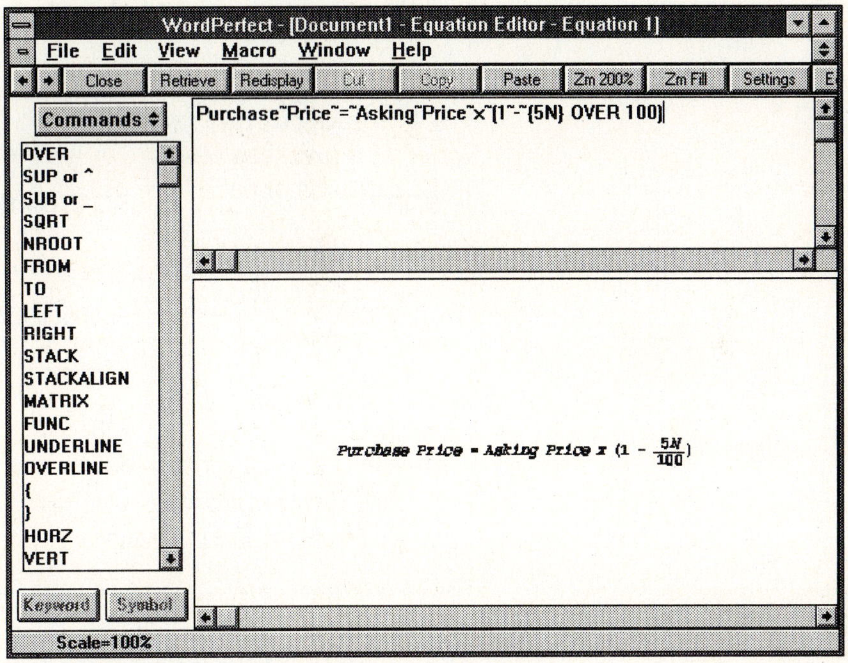

Figure 30-6
The Equation Editor

The Equation Editor includes an equation pane, an editing pane, and a display pane. To move between panes, use the Next Pane (**F6**) or Previous Pane (**Shift+F6**) function keys.

To create an equation in the Equation Editor, choose Equation from the Graphics menu. Then choose Create to open the Equation Editor. Create the equation text in the editing pane, using the equation palettes as needed. Choose Redisplay from the View menu or the Button Bar to view your equation in the display pane. When you are satisfied with the appearance of the equation, close the Equation Editor.

The Equation Palette pop-up list

You may choose any equation palette from the Equation Palette pop-up list. The default palette is "Commands." These palettes provide shortcuts for entering specialized symbols and for formatting equation text.

Commands and symbols may be keyed normally or selected from a palette. Table 30-4 describes the effect of some of the keywords and symbols.

Table 30-5: Selected Equation Editor Keywords and Symbols

Keyword or Symbol	Use	Effect
{ }	Group elements together	Treat symbols within curly brackets as a group
OVER	xOVER{y+1}	Create a fraction $\frac{x}{y+1}$
~ (tilde)	y~+~1	Insert a space y + 1
SQRT	SQRT{x+1}	Put the symbol or group under a square-root symbol
LONGDIV	3LONGDIV{197}	Put the symbol or group under a long-division symbol
SUP or ^ SUB or _	x^3 x_{3y}	Superscript (or subscript) the following symbol or group x^3 x_{3y}

The Equation Editor is useful for complex formatting. For instance, it automatically sizes a fraction bar, square-root symbol, or long-division symbol to accommodate the factors involved. However, in the Equation Editor, character attributes must be specified with keywords. For instance, you must key **BOLD{always}** to produce "**always**".

To create an equation box:

1. Position the insertion point at the end of the paragraph that begins "As a special incentive for early buyers".

2. Insert two hard returns.

3. Choose Equation from the Graphics menu and then choose Create.

   The Equation Editor opens.

4. Key the following in the editing pane, using the tilde (~) character to insert spaces:

   Purchase~Price~=~Asking~Price~x~(1~-~

5. Key **{5N}**, using curly brackets to group the expression "5N".

6. Choose OVER from the Command list in the equation palette and then click Keyword.

   The word is inserted in the equation you are creating. You could have just keyed "OVER".

7. Key **100)**.

8. Choose 100% from the View menu, if necessary.

9. Click the Settings button.

   The Equation Settings dialog box appears.

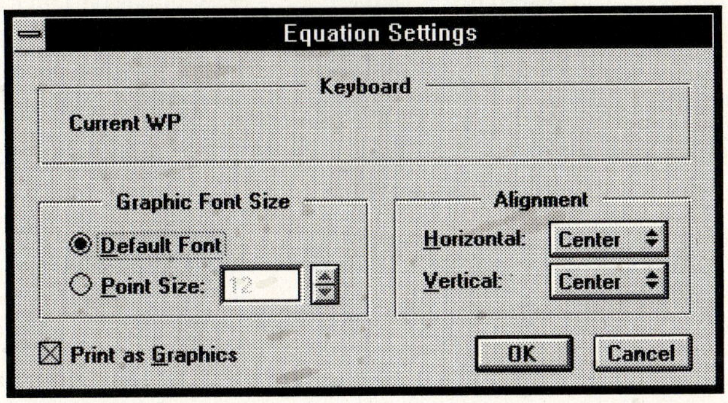

Figure 30-7
The Equation Settings dialog box

10. Click Point Size, key **16** in the Point Size text box, and click OK.

11. Click the Redisplay button, or choose Redisplay from the View menu.

    The equation appears in the display palette. Notice that the expression *"5N"* is set over *"100"* as a built-up fraction. The keyword OVER caused that effect.

12. Close the editor.

    The equation appears in the document.

13. Spell-check the document.

14. Print the document. Then save it as *[your three-letter identifier]*30-0.wpw.

15. Close the document and exit WordPerfect (unless you will be doing the following exercises immediately).

Table 30-6: Keyboard Shortcuts

Keyboard Shortcut	Action
F11	Open the Retrieve Figure dialog box
Shift+F11	Open the Edit Figure dialog box
Alt+Shift+F11	Open the Edit Text Box dialog box
Alt+F11	Create a text box (open the Text Box Editor)

Key Terms

Equation Editor
Figure Editor
Graphics box
Graphics box type
Graphics image
Text Box Editor

Exercises

Exercise 30.1

1. Start WordPerfect, if necessary.
2. Open the file 30-1.wpw.
3. Format the initial font for this flier in 12-point Univers (or a similar sans serif font) by choosing Document from the Layout menu and then choosing Initial Font.
4. Format the text as follows:
   A. Format the title (the first three lines) in 16-point type, bold, and centered.
   B. Format the next two lines of text in 14-point type. Format the first of these lines as bold, and format the second as italic.
   C. Format the next paragraph in 14-point normal type, centered, and double-spaced.
   D. Format the word "Featuring:" and the following blank line in 14-point type. Leave the rest of the text in 12-point normal type, single-spaced.
5. Change the top and bottom margins to 0.3 inches.
6. Position the insertion point on the blank line after the title. Then create a figure box including the image sail-bt.wpg. Edit the image as follows:
   A. Choose Figure from the Graphics menu and then choose Create.
   B. Choose Retrieve from the File menu, highlight sail-bt.wpg in the Retrieve Figure text box, and click Retrieve.

C. Click Edit All, and click OK after making the following changes:

Move, Horizontal: 0.5	Scale X: 120
Move, Vertical: 0.5	Scale Y: 90
Mirror Image	Rotate: 3

D. Click Close.

7. Create a caption:

   A. Right-click the box. Then choose Edit Caption from the short menu.

   B. Delete the box number, choose 12-point italic, choose center justification, and key ***where vacations are smooth sailing . . .***

   C. Close the Caption Editor.

8. Position the type around the box:

   A. Advance the centered text down 1.5 inches.

   B. Advance the "Featuring:" heading and list 0.75 inches, so it is below the figure box.

9. Move the list of advantages and its lead-in to a text box beside the Features list:

   A. Cut (do not delete) the rest of the text in the document, beginning with "The Tides Vacation Condominiums offer".

   B. Position the insertion point in the blank line after "Featuring:".

   C. Press **Alt+F11** to create a text box.

   D. Paste the text you cut.

   E. Close the Text Box Editor.

10. Edit the text box to format the text:

    A. Double-click the box.

    B. Center-justify the text.

    C. Format the first line in bold small caps.

    D. Format the next two lines in normal small caps.

    E. Close the Text Box Editor.

11. View the document in Print Preview.

12. Adjust the document, so it fits on one page. Spell-check and proofread the document.

13. Print the document, and save it as *[your three-letter identifier]*30-1.wpw.

14. Close the document and exit WordPerfect (unless you will be the following exercises immediately).

Exercise 30.2

1. Start WordPerfect, if necessary.
2. Open the file 30-2.wpw.
3. In the first line, change "199-" to next year.
4. Insert two hard returns after the second line, and double-space the paragraph that begins "Optional additional".
5. Full-justify the text, starting at "Optional additional".
6. Create a table box beside that paragraph:
   A. Position the insertion point at the beginning of the paragraph that begins "Optional".
   B. Choose Table Box from the Graphics menu and then choose Create.
   C. Choose Text Editor in the Select Editor dialog box and then click OK.
   D. Retrieve the file 30-2.tbl.
   E. Move the right table margin ⅛ inch to the right, so each price fits on one line.
   F. Move the left table box margin ¼ inch to the right to center the table.
   G. Close the Text Box Editor.
7. Insert hard returns to move the paragraph that begins "Bonus" below the table box.
8. Insert an equation box on the blank line after the label "Discount Formula":
   A. Choose Equation from the Graphics menu and then choose Create.
   B. Key the following in the editing pane:
      Discount~Package~Price~=~Price~x~(1~-~{1.5N}
   C. Choose OVER from the Commands palette and click Keyword.
   D. Key the rest of the equation: **100)**.
9. Close the Equation Editor.
10. Spell-check and proofread the document.
11. Print the document, and save it as *[your three-letter identifier]*30-2.wpw.
12. Close the document and exit WordPerfect (unless you will be doing the following exercises immediately).

Exercise 30.3

1. Start WordPerfect, if necessary.
2. Open the file 30-3.wpw.
3. Format this memo according to Appendix C, using 1-inch side margins.
4. Make the editing changes shown in Figure 30-8, which appears at the end of this exercise, including the current year.
5. Insert a table box beside the first paragraph of the body of the memo. Use the table in the file 30-3.tbl.
6. Format the table in 10-point text. Adjust the column markers so that the table fits in the box.
7. Apply right alignment to the table cells with dollar amounts.
8. Spell-check and proofread the document.
9. Print the document, and save it as *[your three-letter identifier]*30-3.wpw.
10. Close the document and exit WordPerfect (unless you will be doing the following exercises immediately).

Figure 30-8

MEMO TO: Office Managers

FROM: Bud Porter

DATE: August 7, 199- Current Year

ds Full Justify

SUBJECT: Financial Information on The Tides

In response to numerous requests for a summary of important financials handouts on The Tides, I have prepared the table below of prices and costs for various units at The Tides. Bear in mind that these prices are for the basic units. Most buyers will want to purchase a package of options as well for their units. A separate document detailing these options packages will be sent to you soon.

At the right is a table showing the base price, monthly maintenance, and estimated property taxes for each of the four units at The Tides. For more details, please consult the prospectus.

Exercise 30.4

1. Start WordPerfect, if necessary.
2. Using the style shown in Appendix C, create a memo on the subject of "Grand Opening at The Tides" from Bud Porter to his Office Managers, dated August 6 of the current year. Key the text in Figure 30-9, which appears at the end of this exercise, as the body of the memo.
3. On the blank line before the first body paragraph, create a figure box containing the file beach-1.wpg.
4. Position the insertion point in the blank line before the second paragraph. Advance to line 7" to move the paragraph below the figure box.
5. Position the insertion point on the first line of the second paragraph, and create a text box with the following message formatted as bold, italic, and center-justified. Break the message in two lines as shown:

   I hope to see you all

   at the Tides on the 10th!
6. Spell-check and proofread the document.
7. Print the document, and save it as *[your three-letter identifier]*30-4.wpw.
8. Close the document and exit WordPerfect (unless you will be doing the following exercise immediately).

Figure 30-9

The grand opening at The Tides is scheduled for August 10 at 2 p.m. All office managers are expected to attend. After the opening ceremonies and a guided tour of the site, there will be an opportunity for you to ask questions of the developers and to consult with the representatives from the financial institutions that will be offering mortgages to prospective buyers.

After the meeting, which is expected to last until 5 p.m., we hope that you will stay to be our guests at a barbecue on the beachfront at The Tides.

Working with Graphics Boxes

Objectives

- Change box position and size.
- Change box type.
- Overlay graphics images with text.
- Change box borders and shading.
- Change caption numbering style.
- Change box number.

WordPerfect graphics boxes can be positioned and sized within a document. Also, a box's appearance can be modified by changing its border and shading. These features allow you to enhance the appearance of newsletters, flyers, reports, and other documents.

Box Position and Size

You can use the mouse or the Box Position and Size dialog box to change the location and dimensions of a graphics box. The dialog box will give you more exact results, but the mouse lets you see the results as you work. In either case, you can check the appearance of your layout in Print Preview and make necessary adjustments.

To access the dialog box from the document window, first choose the box type (Figure, Text Box, Equation, Table Box, or User Box). Then choose Position from the cascading menu, and specify the box number. You may, instead, click the right mouse button in any box, and choose Box Position from the short menu.

The Box Position and Size dialog box also is available from any of the three graphics box editors through a button or menu command, as shown in Table 31-1.

Table 31-1: Accessing the Box Position and Size Dialog Box

From	Shortcut	Menu Item
Document	Box Position from short menu (click the right mouse button in the box)	Position (from the Graphics box type cascading menu); specify box number
Figure Editor	Fig Pos button	Box Position (from the File menu)
Text Editor	Box Position button	Position (from the Graphics Text Box cascading menu)
Equation Editor	Equ Pos button	Box Position (from the File menu)

To open the Box Position and Size dialog box:

1. Start WordPerfect, if necessary.

2. Open the file 31-0a.wpw.

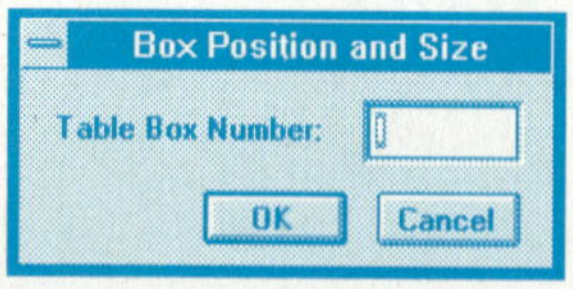

The Table Box Number dialog box

3. Choose Table Box from the Graphics menu and then choose Position.

   The Table Box Number dialog box appears.

4. Key **1** in the text box and click OK.

   The table box is selected, and the Box Position and Size dialog box appears. The settings reflect the default values for a table box. The Width depends on the margin settings, and Height depends on the content of the box when it was created.

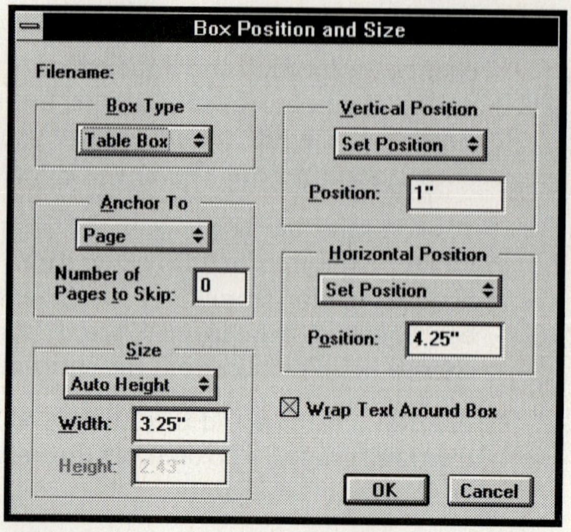

Figure 31-1
The Box Position and Size dialog box

5. Choose Cancel to close the dialog box.

6. Double-click the equation box, which includes the "Discount Price = Asking Price" formula.

   The Equation Editor opens.

7. Click the Equ Pos button above the Editing Pane.

   The Box Position and Size dialog box opens with the default settings for an equation box. (Here, the Width is the distance between paragraph margins, and the Height depends on the content.)

8. Choose Cancel to close the dialog box.

9. Close the Equation Editor.

Box Type

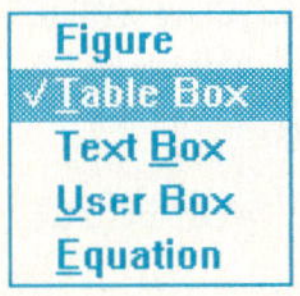

The Box Type pop-up list

The Box Type pop-up list lets you assign any graphics box to any box type. Choosing a different type does not change the position, size, contents, or editor of the box. Rather, boxes of a type are listed together and share the same box appearance (see the section titled "Box Appearance Options" later in this lesson).

Anchor To

The Anchor To pop-up list

This option lets you determine whether the graphics box moves with the text that wraps around it (Paragraph), remains placed at a fixed position on a page (Page), or is treated as part of the text on a line (Character).

Paragraph anchors the box to the paragraph where the insertion point was located at the time of creation. The code is placed at the beginning of the paragraph. Do not add text in front of the graphics-box code; it should appear at the beginning of the paragraph.

Page anchors the box to a specified page. In long documents, make sure the insertion point is at the top of the page when you choose this option. If you want the box on a later page, type a number in the Number of Pages to Skip text box.

Character anchors the box to a line of text. The box is treated as a single character in the line.

Size

The default width of all graphics boxes (except equation boxes) is one half the space between the side margins of the page. (An equation box fills the entire space between its paragraph's side margins.) For instance, the standard line length is 6.5 inches (based on paper 8.5 inches wide with 1-inch side margins). The default width, then, is 3.25 inches, or half the line length.

The default height depends on the content of the box. WordPerfect allows enough room to show all the content. If you make the box shorter, some of its content may not appear. (The contents of a box are not altered by the box size, however. When you make the box big enough, the contents are displayed in the document. The contents are always visible in the graphics box editor.)

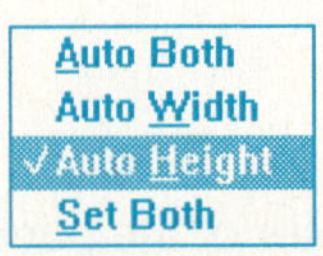

The Size pop-up list

The Size pop-up list offers the options shown in Table 31-2.

Table 31-2: Graphics Box Size Options

Option	Use
Auto Both	Restore the dimensions that an image or equation had when it originally was created (rather than when the graphics box was created).
Auto Width	Specify a height for the box only (WordPerfect calculates the proportional width).
Auto Height	Specify a width for the box only (WordPerfect calculates the proportional height).
Set Both	Specify your own measurements for both height and width.

Note: The allowable width and height of a box depends partly on its vertical and horizontal position. WordPerfect automatically resets improper box dimensions to allowable limits.

Vertical Position

The default vertical position of a box depends on the anchor type. Initially, when a box is anchored to a page, its top aligns with the vertical position of the insertion point. When a box is anchored to a paragraph, its top aligns at the top of the paragraph. When a box is anchored to a character, its top is placed at the baseline of the text containing the graphics-box code.

The vertical-position options also depend on the anchor type:

- When Paragraph is the anchor type of the box, you may key an offset distance from the top of the paragraph to the top of the box. For instance, key **.5** to align the top of the box ½ inch below the top of the paragraph.

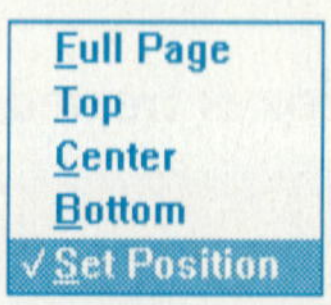

Vertical Position pop-up list (Page Anchored)

- When Page is the anchor of a graphics box, the box's vertical position is set in relation to page elements, such as margins, headers, footers, and page numbers. The Set Position option lets you specify an absolute distance from the top edge of the page that will not change even if you later change margins.

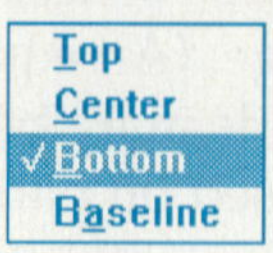

Vertical Position pop-up list (Character Anchored)

- When Character is the anchor of a graphics box, the box's vertical position is set in relation to the baseline for the anchoring text. (Remember, the baseline is the invisible line on which letters sit.)

Table 31-3: Vertical Position Options When Anchored to a Page

Options	Vertical Position of the Box
Full Page	From the top to bottom margins
Top	Below the header, page number, or top margin
Center	Center of the box at the vertical center of the page
Bottom	Above the footer, page number, or bottom margin
Set Position	Specified distance from the top edge of page

Table 31-4: Vertical Position Options When Anchored to a Character

Options	Vertical Position of the Box
Top	Top of the box at the baseline
Center	Vertical center of the box at the baseline
Bottom	Bottom of the box at the baseline
Baseline	Bottom baseline in the box at the baseline of the anchoring text

Horizontal Position

The default horizontal position of graphics boxes (except equation boxes) is the middle of the line. In other words, the box takes up half the distance between page or column margins, starting in the middle. (Equation boxes initially are positioned at the left paragraph margin and take up the full width of the paragraph.)

The horizontal-position options depend on the anchor type:

- When Character is the anchor of a graphics box, the box moves with that character; Horizontal Position is dimmed.

Horizontal Position pop-up list (Paragraph Anchored)

- When Paragraph is the anchor type, horizontal-position options depend on the paragraph's margins. For instance, Margin, Left aligns the left edge of the box at the left margin of the paragraph. Margin, Full causes the box width to fill the space between the paragraph's side margins. (Tab and indent codes act as temporary margins, which do affect horizontal positioning.) The Set Position option lets you specify a distance from the left margin of the paragraph to the left edge of the box.

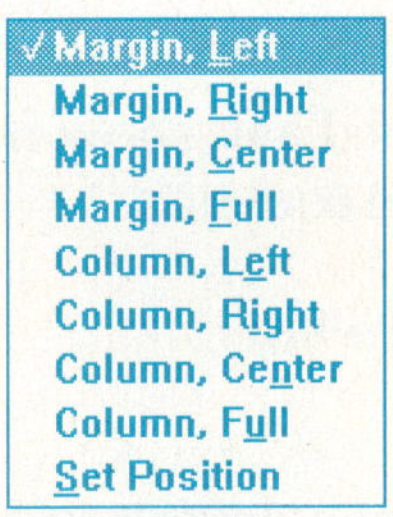

Horizontal Position pop-up list (Page Anchored)

- When Page is the anchor type, you can choose horizontal-position options related to the page margins or to column margins within the page. The Set Position option lets you specify an absolute distance from the left edge of the page that will not change, even if you later change margins.

When you choose a Columns option for a page-anchored box, you must specify one or more column numbers. For instance, choosing Columns, Center and specifying 2-3 will center the box between the left margin of column 2 and the right margin of column 3. See Figure 31-2 on page 31-6.

To change box size and position using the dialog box:

1. Click the right mouse button in the table box, and then choose Box Position from the short menu.

2. Choose Top from the Vertical Position pop-up list.

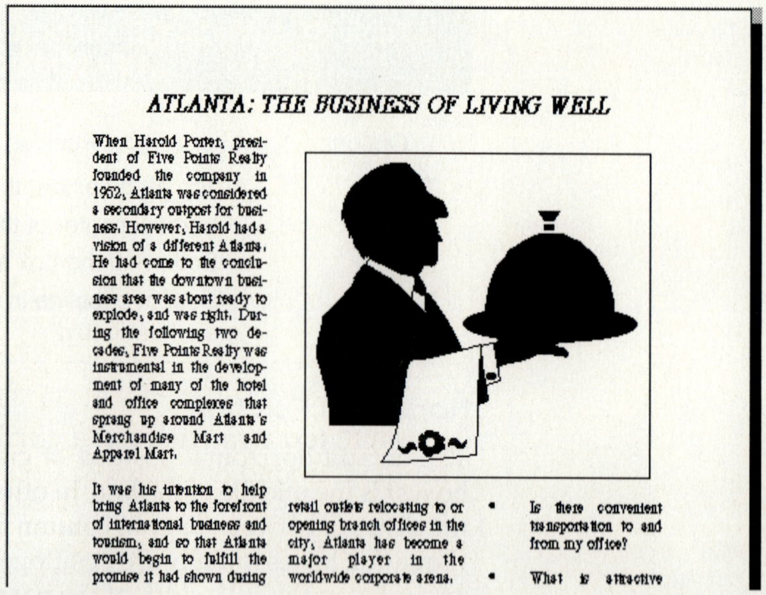

ATLANTA: THE BUSINESS OF LIVING WELL

When Harold Porter, president of Five Points Realty founded the company in 1952, Atlanta was considered a secondary outpost for business. However, Harold had a vision of a different Atlanta. He had come to the conclusion that the downtown business area was about ready to explode, and was right. During the following two decades, Five Points Realty was instrumental in the development of many of the hotel and office complexes that sprang up around Atlanta's Merchandise Mart and Apparel Mart.

It was his intention to help bring Atlanta to the forefront of international business and tourism, and so that Atlanta would begin to fulfill the promise it had shown during retail outlets relocating to or opening branch offices in the city, Atlanta has become a major player in the worldwide corporate arena.

- Is there convenient transportation to and from my office?
- What is attractive

Figure 31-2
Figure box centered between columns 2 and 3

3. Choose Margin, Left from the Horizontal Position pop-up list.
4. Click OK.

   The table box moves to the left margin and to the top margin of the page.

5. Click the right mouse button in the equation box, and then choose Box Position.
6. Choose Margin, Center from the Horizontal Position pop-up list.
7. Choose Auto Both from the Size pop-up list.

   The Width and Height text boxes are dimmed and show new dimensions based on the original size of the equation.

8. Choose Text Box from the Box Type pop-up list.
9. Click OK.

   The equation box takes on the appearance of a default text box (notice the borders and shading). It is sized to match the width and height of the equation.

   The increased box height causes the box to bump into some text, which now flows around it.

10. Position the insertion point before "N=Number". Advance down 1 inch to move the text below the equation.

    Notice that the vertical position of the box is too close to the preceding paragraph.

11. Position the insertion point before the text-box code (choose Reveal Codes from the View menu, if necessary). Press **Enter** to insert a blank line.

    The text box moves down, since it is anchored to a paragraph.

12. Print the document, and save it as *[your three-letter identifier]*31-0a.wpw.

13. Close the document.

Wrap Text Around Box

By default, text wraps around a graphics box. When you clear the Wrap Text Around Box check box, text will overlay a graphics box. You then can annotate illustrations or fill in decorative graphics with text. If you use hard returns and tabs to position text, be aware that they may affect the position of other text in the document. You can position text without disturbing other text using the Advance feature, which was discussed in Lesson 14.

Note: When the Wrap Text Around Box option is not selected, the left mouse button does not select the box. Instead, click the right mouse button in the box, and choose Select Box (which is added to the short menu).

You may align text over a graphics image by changing the margins, if you use the Set Position options (which do not depend on margins to position the box).

To overlay text on a graphics image:

1. Choose New from the File menu.

2. Choose a landscape paper size by choosing Page from the Layout menu, and then choosing Paper Size. Select a Paper Type with 11″ x 8.5″ dimensions and then choose Select.

3. Retrieve bord-2.wpg by pressing **F11**, selecting bord-2.wpg, and choosing Retrieve.

4. Click the right mouse button in the box, and choose Box Position from the short menu.

5. Make the following changes:

Box Type: **User Box**	Vertical Position: **Set Position**
Size: **Set Both**	Position: **1"**
Width: **9"**	Horizontal Position: **Set Position**
Height: **6.5"**	Position: **1"**

6. Clear the Wrap Text Around Box check box and click OK.

    The bord-2.wpg graphic appears without a box border as a default style User Box. It is anchored to an absolute position on the page using vertical and horizontal Set Position options. The box dimensions are 9 x 6.5 inches.

7. Choose Advance from the Layout menu. Then check To Line, key **3.5** in the Advance text box, and click OK.

8. Choose Justification from the Layout menu and then choose Center.

9. Choose an Extra Large (or 48 point) font in bold italic. Then key ***Sales,*** press **Enter,** key ***Achievement,*** press **Enter,** and key ***Award***.

   The text overlays the box.

10. Choose Print Preview (press **Shift+F5**), view the document as a Full Page, and close the Print Preview window.

11. Spell-check the document, print, and save it as *[your three-letter identifier]*31-0b.wpw.

12. Close the document.

Changing Box Position and Size with the Mouse

You can click and drag to reposition or resize any graphics box. First, select the box by clicking within the box boundaries. Sizing handles appear. If Wrap Text Around Box is not selected, click the right mouse button in the box. Then choose Select Box from the short menu. When the mouse arrow changes to a four-headed arrow, you can drag to reposition the box.

To resize the box, move the mouse arrow over any sizing handle, and it becomes a two-headed arrow. Drag a side handle to extend or reduce the width. Drag a top or bottom handle to extend or reduce the height. Drag a corner handle to change two dimensions at one time.

To move and resize boxes using the mouse:

1. Open the file 31-0c.wpw, and choose the Ruler from the View menu.

2. Scroll down until the top of the box is near the Ruler, so you can judge the position of the side borders.

3. Click the sailboat to select the figure box.

   The sizing handles appear.

4. Drag the left, center side handle toward the left margin to the 3-inch measure on the Ruler.

   The box widens, and the text beside it wraps.

5. Click in the text to the left of the box, above the paragraph that begins "Just 15 of these".

   The box is deselected.

6. Open the Print Preview window, and choose Full Page, if necessary. Examine the page and then choose Close.

   The text beside the figure box extends too far down the page.

7. Delete four hard returns above the centered text.

   The text beside the sailboat box now ends near the bottom of the box.

8. Scroll down until the text box is near the Ruler.

9. Click the text box, and hold down the left mouse button.

   The four-headed arrow appears.

10. Drag the text box to the left margin, and then deselect the box.

    The Features list wraps to the right of the box, but part of it is forced to the next page.

11. Choose Reveal Codes from the View menu.

Note: You may Undelete a graphics box, if necessary.

12. Delete hard returns as necessary to bring the entire Features list back to page 1. Be careful not to delete the box code.

13. Right-justify the Features list.

14. Check the document in Print Preview.

15. Print the document, and save it as *[your three-letter identifier]*31-0c.wpw.

16. Close the document.

Box Appearance Options

You can change the appearance of any type of graphics box, including the borders, gray shading, and caption numbering style and position. WordPerfect inserts a [(Box Type) Opt] code, and all boxes of that type are affected from the insertion point forward.

Each box type in the Graphics menu has a command in its cascading menu that opens its Options dialog box. The title bar identifies the box type, since the options are identical for every box type.

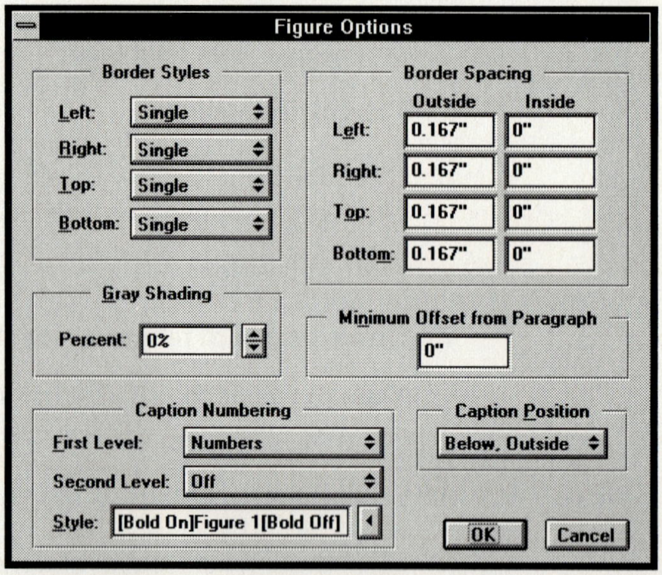

Figure 31-3
The Figure Options dialog box offers the same choices as those for other box types.

Border Style

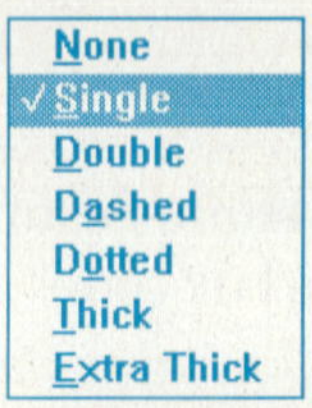

The Border Style Pop-up List

Border Style determines the styles for each box border (left, right, top, and bottom) from a pop-up list. Each border can have its own style. For instance, you can create a three-dimensional effect by choosing Thick for left and bottom borders, and Single for top and right borders.

Border Spacing

Border Spacing determines the amount of space between a box border and the content outside and inside the box. (Settings for outside border spacing are ignored for boxes that are anchored to a character.)

Dropped capital letter
The first letter of a paragraph that is enlarged and set off from the rest of the paragraph.

Creating Dropped Capital Letters

In books and periodicals, the first paragraph of a chapter or section often begins with a dropped capital letter, such as the one that begins this paragraph. A *dropped capital letter* is the first letter of a paragraph that is enlarged and set off from the rest of the paragraph, generally extending two or more lines into the paragraph and calling attention to the text.

To create a dropped capital, create a graphics box using the Text Editor. In the Text Editor, key the capital letter, and choose the font, size, and other attributes you want. In the Box Position and Size dialog box, anchor the box to a paragraph, and set the size to Auto Both (note the automatic width and height settings for future reference). Then format

continued on next page

Creating Dropped Capital Letters—continued

the box options. If you choose "none" for border styles, format all border spacing to 0 (zero). You also may adjust gray shading.

In the document, key or paste a paragraph beside the dropped capital. Then look at the effect in print preview. Adjust the size to eliminate unwanted white space. (Set Size to Set Both, and experiment to get the look you want.)

Minimum Offset from Paragraph

When you anchor a box to a paragraph, you can specify an offset that positions the box a distance from the top of the paragraph (see the section titled "Vertical Position" earlier in this lesson). Of course, that box will move with its anchoring paragraph. When the box gets close to the bottom of a page or column, WordPerfect automatically adjusts its position by reducing this offset to keep the box at the beginning of the paragraph.

The Minimum Offset from Paragraph option lets you limit this adjustment. For instance, if you key **1"**, the box can move up to 1 inch below the top of the paragraph before moving to the next page or column.

Gray Shading

Gray shading determines the background shading intensity (100% is black). Dark shading can mask the contents of a box, so you may need to use large and bold fonts within a shaded box to achieve a desirable contrast.

To change box-appearance options:

1. Open the file 31-0d.wpw, and choose Reveal Codes from the View menu.

   The first page includes two text boxes.

2. Choose Text Box from the Graphics menu, and then choose Position. Specify text box 1 and click OK.

   In the Box Position and Size dialog box, notice that the box is anchored to the paragraph. The vertical position is 0.5 inches from the top of the paragraph, and the horizontal position is Margin, Left. (Text box 2 has the same position in its paragraph.)

3. Click Cancel. Position the insertion point at the beginning of the document.

4. Choose Text Box from the Graphics menu and then choose Options.

   The Text Box Options dialog box appears.

5. Change the border styles and gray shading options as follows and click OK:

   Left: Thick

   Right: Single

   Top: Single

   Bottom: Thick

   Gray Shading: 0%

   WordPerfect inserts a [Txt Opt] code. The borders and shading for both text boxes are changed.

To see the effect of a minimum offset for a paragraph-anchored box:

1. At the bottom of the first page in the left column, position the insertion point on the blank line before the last paragraph.

2. Press **Enter** six times, and notice the change in the box position after each hard return is entered.

   The box begins 0.5 inches (two lines) from the top of its anchoring paragraph. It moves down the page this way, until it reaches the bottom. WordPerfect then adjusts the position, moving the box back toward the top of its paragraph. Finally, the box is forced to the second column.

3. Delete the six hard returns.

4. Position the insertion point to the immediate right of the [Txt Opt] code at the beginning of the page. Then choose Graphics Text Box Options.

   The Text Box Options dialog box opens with your last settings.

5. Key **0.5** in the Minimum Offset from Paragraph text box and click OK.

6. Repeat steps 1 through 3, inserting hard returns and observing the box position. Then delete the hard returns.

   The box moves down as before, but, at the bottom of the page, it is forced immediately to the next column. WordPerfect respects the 0.5-inch minimum offset option.

To create a figure box, customize its appearance, and position it between two columns:

1. Choose Reveal Codes from the View menu, if necessary. Position the insertion point immediately after the [Col On] code at the top of the first column.

2. Choose Figure from the Graphics menu and then choose Create.

3. In the Figure Editor, click Retrieve. Highlight waiter.wpg in the Retrieve Figure dialog box and then click Retrieve.

4. In the Figure Editor, click Mirror.

5. Click Fig Pos, and make the following changes in the Box Position and Size dialog box:
   - Horizontal Position: Column, Center
   - Columns: 2-3
   - Size: Set Both
   - Width: 4 inches
   - Height: 2.5 inches

6. Click OK.

   The box is centered between the second and third columns at the vertical position of the insertion point.

7. Click the right mouse button in the figure box and choose Box Position.

8. Examine the settings, and close the dialog box.

   The width was reduced to 3.92 inches automatically to fit between the specified columns.

9. Print the document, and save it as *[your three-letter identifier]*31-0d.wpw.

10. Close the document.

Caption Position

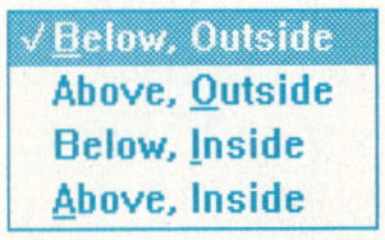

The Caption Position pop-up list for figures

Caption Position lets you place captions below or above the box, and outside or inside the border. For equation boxes, you can position captions below, above, on the left, or on the right side of the equation (inside the box). If you choose Left or Right, and the equation is too wide for the caption to fit inside the box, the caption is placed below the equation.

Caption Numbering

You can adjust the appearance of box numbering in captions. WordPerfect automatically numbers graphics boxes of each type. For example, the third figure box may be numbered "Figure 3" or "Figure III". As discussed in Lesson 30, the box number appears when you open the Caption Editor for that box and whenever you choose Box Number in the Caption Editor.

You can choose one or two levels of numbering, and each numbering level may use numbers, letters, or Roman numerals. For instance, table boxes could be numbered I, II, III; 1-a, 1-b, 1-c; or 1.1, 1.2, 1.3. If you choose Letters or Roman Numerals, the first-level number is always uppercase, and the second-level number is lowercase (Table I-ii, for instance). Just choose an option from either Caption Numbering Level pop-up list. (If you choose Off, no number appears for that level.)

The Caption Numbering pop-up list

To create a two-level caption number, you also must adjust the Caption Numbering Style text box.

Caption Style

Edit or key text in the Caption Numbering Style text box to change the numbering style for boxes of that type. To apply font attributes to the text, choose from the Style pop-up list. Then, when you choose the Box Number command in the Caption Editor, text, numbering, and attributes will appear as you specified.

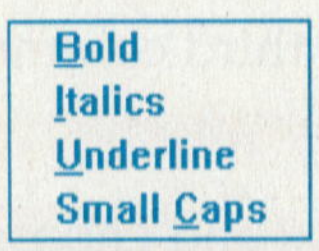

The Caption Numbering Style Pop-up List

For instance, "[Ital On]Exhibit 1[Ital Off]" in the Style text box will produce *Exhibit 1*, *Exhibit 2*, *Exhibit 3* in the Caption Editor for the first three boxes.

Creating a Two-Level Caption Number

Figures, tables, and exhibits sometimes are numbered consecutively within chapters using a two-level format. For instance, the second figure in Chapter 5 might be Figure 5-2.

To specify a two-level caption number, position the insertion point where the format is to begin. Choose Options from the Graphics cascading menu for the box type you want. Choose a style from the First Level pop-up list and one from the Second Level pop-up list. In the Style text box, edit the text before the 1, if necessary. Change the 1 to the first-level number. (For Chapter V, key **v** or **V**. For Chapter 5, key **5**.) Key a decimal point or hyphen, as needed. Key the numeral **2**. This numeral represents the second-level number, which will be assigned consecutively to boxes. Click OK to close the dialog box.

To create a two-level caption style:

1. Open the file 31-0e.wpw.
2. At the beginning of the document, choose Figure from the Graphics menu and then choose Options.
3. Choose Roman Numeral from the Caption Numbering First Level pop-up list.
4. Choose Numbers from the Second Level pop-up list.

5. In the Caption Numbering Style text box, delete the content of the box, including the bold on and bold off codes, and key **Fig. III-2**. Then, with the insertion point at the beginning of the text box, choose Small Caps from the Style pop-up list.

6. Choose Above, Inside from the Caption Position pop-up list and click OK.

   The captions in both figure boxes reflect your changes. The next figure box will be numbered FIG. III-3.

7. Save the document as *[your three-letter identifier]* 31-0e.wpw.

8. Close the document and exit WordPerfect (unless you will be doing the following exercises immediately).

Changing a Box Number

Graphics boxes are numbered consecutively in a document according to the box type. You can start numbering with a new number at any point in the document.

The New Box Number dialog box

When you renumber a box type, position the insertion point immediately before the box you want to renumber. Choose the appropriate graphics type from the Graphics menu. Choose New Number to open the New Box Number dialog box. Key a number in the New Number text box and click OK.

You only can specify a new number for the first-level number of a caption number.

Key Term

Dropped capital letter

Exercises

Exercise 31.1

1. Start WordPerfect, if necessary.
2. Open the file 31-1.wpw.
3. Anchor the table box to a character, so it can be positioned like text:
   A. Select the table box by clicking the right mouse button within its borders.
   B. Choose Box Position from the short menu.
   C. Choose Character from the Anchor To pop-up list and click OK.

4. Cut the box, and paste it after the second paragraph.
5. Move the insertion point before the box, and press **Shift+F7** to center the box on the line. Then press **Enter** before and after the line containing the box.
6. Change the caption to include only the figure number code, set in the font currently used in the caption:
   A. Click the right mouse button in the box and choose Edit Caption.
   B. Choose Reveal Codes from the View menu, and then delete "The Tides" without deleting the font code.
   C. Choose Box Number. Then close the Caption Editor.
7. At the beginning of the document, create a figure box containing device-2.wpg (an image of a heralding trumpet appropriate for an announcement, which is available on your student disk):
   A. Move the insertion point to the beginning of the document.
   B. Choose Figure from the Graphics menu and then choose Create.
   C. Choose Retrieve from the File menu (or click the Retrieve button).
   D. Double-click the drive containing your student disk. Then highlight device-2.wpg, and click Retrieve.
8. Adjust the position and size of the figure, so it can serve as a decorative banner introducing this flier:
   A. Click the Fig Pos button (or choose Box Position from the File menu).
   B. Make the following changes in the Box Position and Size dialog box:

Box Type: User Box	Vertical Position:
	Set Position 1.5″
Size: Auto Width	Horizontal Position:
Height: 2″	Margin, Full

9. Change the appearance of the figure:
   A. Choose the Edit All button.
   B. Key **250** in the Scale X text box.
   C. Click the Mirror Image and the Black and White check boxes and click OK.
   D. Close the Figure Editor.

10. Key the following headlines. Then select them, and apply bold, italic, 24 point (or very large) attributes:

    Announcing (flush left)

    THE TIDES (centered)

    ("Announcing" should precede the graphics box, and "THE TIDES" should follow the box.)

11. Press **Enter** after the second headline. Then full-justify the rest of the text.
12. View the document in Print Preview. Adjust it so it fits on one page, if necessary.
13. Spell-check the document.
14. Print the document, and save it as *[your three-letter identifier]*31-1.wpw.
15. Close the document and exit WordPerfect (unless you will be doing the following exercises immediately).

Exercise 31.2

1. Start WordPerfect, if necessary.
2. Open the file 31-2.wpw.
3. Create dropped capital letters to begin the first paragraph after each heading:
    A. In the first paragraph, delete the "A" in "Atlanta".

    B. Choose User Box from the Graphics menu, and then choose Create. Click OK to accept the Text Box Editor.

    C. In the Text Box Editor, choose 36-point CG Times. Then key an uppercase **A**.

    D. Click Box Position, and choose Paragraph from the Anchor To pop-up list. Then choose Auto Both from the Size pop-up list, note the width and height, and click OK.

    E. Close the Text Box Editor.

    F. Position the insertion point at the top of the document. Choose User Box from the Graphics menu and then choose Options.

    G. Key **0** (zero) in Border Spacing text boxes and click OK.

    H. Look at the text in Print Preview.

    I. Open the Box Position and Size dialog box, and choose Set Both from the Size pop-up list. Key **0.361** (or the auto-sized width) in the Width text box and **0.4** in the Height text box.

J. Create dropped capitals for the "A" in "As a tourist" and the "B" in "Beautiful plants". (You do not have to change the User Box Options.)

4. Create an empty figure box to represent a photograph 4 inches wide and 3 inches high, positioned at the beginning of the text between the first two columns:

   A. Position the insertion point between the [Col On] and [Usr Box:1] codes.

   B. Choose Figure from the Graphics menu and then choose Create.

   C. Click Fig Pos to open the Box Position and Size dialog box.

   D. Choose Column, Center from the Horizontal Position pop-up list.

   E. Choose Set Both from the Size pop-up list. Then key **4** in the Width text box and **3** in the Height text box.

   F. Click OK. Then close the Figure Editor.

5. Create a caption for the figure box in 10-point Univers:

   A. Click the right mouse button in the figure box, and then choose Edit Caption.

   B. Position the insertion point before the [Fig Num] code, and format the caption in 10-point Univers.

   C. Key this caption after the [Fig Num] code:

   Floating up a lazy river on a spring afternoon is a perfect prelude to a night on the town.

   D. Close the Caption Editor.

6. Change the caption numbering for figures:

   A. Position the insertion point at the beginning of the document. Choose Figure from the Graphics menu and then choose Options.

   B. Choose Numbers from both the First Level and Second Level pop-up lists.

   C. Delete the content of the Style text box. Then key **Figure 3-2.**

   D. Select this text, and choose Italics from the style attributes pop-up list.

   E. Click OK.

7. Spell-check the document.

8. Print the document, and save it as *[your three-letter identifier]*31-2.wpw.

9. Close the document and exit WordPerfect (unless you will be doing the following exercises immediately).

Exercise 31.3

1. Start WordPerfect, if necessary.
2. Open the file 31-3.wpw.
3. Format this document in modified block style as a form letter to potential buyers, which will be printed on letterhead. Use 12-point CG Times font and 1.5-inch side margins. Use a date code to represent the date. Use field codes to represent the client name (field 1), address (field 2), and name for the salutation (field 3). Close the letter with Bud Porter's signature line, and add your reference initials. Also note the enclosure of the "Windward Options Package Flier". Insert a hard return before the last paragraph, if the letter extends to two pages.
4. Create a table box using file 31-3.tbl as its contents. Make the box size 3.75 x 2.13 inches. Format the table in 10-point Univers bold, and adjust its size to fit centered in the box. Anchor this box to the second body paragraph, which begins "Model units", positioned 0.5 inches from the top of this paragraph at the right margin.
5. Key a caption for the box, **BASIC PRICES**, formatted in 12-point Univers bold.
6. Apply 10% gray shading to the table box.
7. Full-justify the letter, and check the document in Print Preview.
8. Spell-check and proofread the document.
9. Print the document, and save it as *[your three-letter identifier]*31-3.wpw.
10. Close the document and exit WordPerfect (unless you will be doing the following exercises immediately).

Exercise 31.4

1. Start WordPerfect, if necessary.
2. In a new document, format document initial codes to full-justified, double-spaced, with 1-inch margins. Format the document initial font to 14-point CG Times.
3. At the beginning of the document, create a user box with the Text Editor. Advance down 0.75 inches, and key **QUALITY OPTION PACKAGES** centered in 36-point Univers bold italic. Rotate the text 90 degrees. Anchor the box to the page, and set both vertical and horizontal positions to 0. Choose Set Both from the Size pop-up list, and specify 2 inches for width

and 11 inches for height. (WordPerfect will reset the minimum positions and maximum length allowed by your printer.) Apply 10 percent gray shading to the user box.

4. After the user box, key the heading **WINDWARD at THE TIDES.** Select the heading, and format it in 24-point Univers bold italic. Insert a full-length horizontal line 0.04 inches thick, positioned 1.4 inches from the top edge of the page.

5. Press **Enter** twice, and key the text shown in Figure 31-4, which appears at the end of this exercise, using the document initial formatting.

6. Using the Text Editor, create a table box anchored to the paragraph you keyed. Set the horizontal position to Margin, Center, and the vertical position to 1 inch. Set the size to Auto Height and the width to 4.5 inches. Retrieve the file 31-4.tbl into the table box, and adjust the table margins so that only the longest line of text in the table wraps. Center the table within the box. Choose single lines for the top and bottom border styles of the box.

7. Spell-check and proofread the document.

8. Print the document, and save it as *[your three-letter identifier]*31-4.wpw.

9. Close the document and exit WordPerfect (unless you will be doing the following exercise immediately).

Figure 31-4

(bf)

Optional additional features may be added to The Windward, making it a truly unique vacation home. These packages cost substantially less than you would pay for each of the options if purchased separately. See the table above for some sample packages.

Appendices

Appendices

- **A: Proofreaders' Marks**
- **B: Standard Forms for Business Letters**
- **C: Standard Form for a Memorandum**
- **D: Standard Form for a Business Envelope**

Appendix A

Proofreaders' Marks

PROOFREADERS' MARK	DRAFT	FINAL COPY
ss [Single-space	ss [I have heard he is leaving	I have heard he is leaving
ds [Double-space	ds [When will you have a decision?	When will you have a decision?
+1ℓ# → Insert 1 line space	Percent of Change +1ℓ# 16.25	Percent of Change 16.25
−1ℓ# → Delete (remove) 1 line space	Northeastern −1ℓ# → regional sales	Northeastern regional sales
⁀‿ Delete space	to gether	together
∧# Insert space	Itmay be	It may not be
Move as shown	it is not true	it is true
∽ Transpose	beleivable	believable
	is it so	it is so
○ Spell out	2 years ago	two years ago
	16 Elm St.	16 Elm Street
∧ Insert a word	How much ∧ it? (is)	How much is it?
ℓ OR — Delete a word	it may not be true	it may be true
∧ OR ʎ Insert a letter	temperture (a)	temperature
ℓ OR ℓ Delete a letter and close up	committment to buy	commitment to buy
⁀‿ Add on to a word	a real good day (ly)	a really good day
ℓ OR / Change a letter	this supercedes (s)	this supersedes
∧ OR — Change a word	and if you won't (but, can't)	but if you can't
····· Stet (don't delete)	I was very glad	I was very glad
/ Lowercase a letter (make it a small letter)	Federal Government	federal government

PROOFREADERS' MARK	DRAFT	FINAL COPY
Capitalize	Janet L. greyston	Janet L. Greyston
Raise above the line	in her new book*	in her new book[*]
Drop below the line	H2S04	H_2S0_4
Insert a period	Mr Henry Grenada	Mr. Henry Grenada
Insert a comma	a large old house	a large, old house
Insert an apostrophe	my childrens car	my children's car
Insert quotation marks	he wants a loan	he wants a "loan"
Insert a hyphen	a first rate job	a first-rate job
	ask the co owner	ask the co-owner
-- OR $\frac{1}{M}$ Insert a dash or change a hyphen to a dash	Success at last! Here it is cash!	Success—at last! Here it is—cash!
Insert underscore	an issue of Time	an issue of <u>Time</u>
Delete underscore	a very long day	a very long day
Set in italic	The New York Times	*The New York Times*
Set in boldface	the Enter key	the **Enter** key
Set in roman	the *most* likely	the most likely
Insert parentheses	left today May 3	left today (May 3)
Start a new paragraph	¶ If that is so	If that is so
Indent 2 spaces	Net investment in tangible assets	Net investment in tangible assets
Move to the right	$38,367,000	$38,367,000
Move to the left	Anyone can win!	Anyone can win!
Align horizontally	TO Bob Mueller	TO: Bob Mueller
Align vertically	Jon Peters Ellen March	Jon Peters Ellen March

Standard Forms for Business Letters

Two frequently used formats for business letters are the Block Style and the Modified Block Style. Individual businesses and offices usually have a style preference.

Block Style

In the Block Style, text begins at the left margin. Nothing is indented except for quotations, tables, and other displayed material. (See page B-2 for an example of the Block Style using paper with a letterhead.)

Modified-Block Style

In the Modified-Block Style, all text begins at the left margin except for the return address (if there is one), the date line, the complimentary closing, and the writer's identification, all of which begin at the center. A variation of the Modified Block Style indents the first line of each paragraph five spaces. (See page B-3 for an example of the Modified Block Style using paper without a letterhead.)

Using Paper with a Letterhead

The first page of a business letter typically is written on paper with a letterhead. The letterhead usually consists of at least the following components: the company's name, its street address, its city, state, and ZIP code. Most letterheads indicate the area code and telephone number. Some letterheads also contain a graphic element (such as a logo) and a facsimile (fax) number.

Most large businesses have printed letterhead paper. However, with the increasing sophistication of word-processing programs, many businesses have also developed letterhead files that can be added to a letter and provide a professional-looking letterhead on a laser printer.

When not using a letterhead, a return address is required. A return address is also used when writing a personal-business letter (that is, a letter you write as an individual, unrelated to business). The return address usually consists of your street address; your city, state, and

(Continued on page B-4)

Business Letter—Block Style

Heading

Opening

Body

Closing

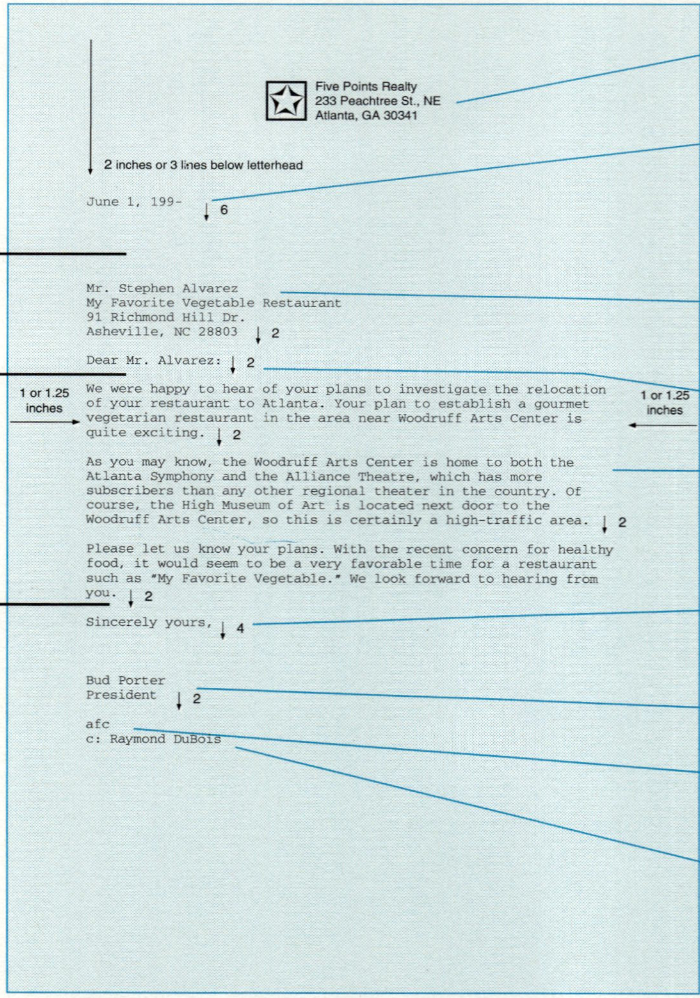

Five Points Realty
233 Peachtree St., NE
Atlanta, GA 30341

June 1, 199-

Mr. Stephen Alvarez
My Favorite Vegetable Restaurant
91 Richmond Hill Dr.
Asheville, NC 28803

Dear Mr. Alvarez:

We were happy to hear of your plans to investigate the relocation of your restaurant to Atlanta. Your plan to establish a gourmet vegetarian restaurant in the area near Woodruff Arts Center is quite exciting.

As you may know, the Woodruff Arts Center is home to both the Atlanta Symphony and the Alliance Theatre, which has more subscribers than any other regional theater in the country. Of course, the High Museum of Art is located next door to the Woodruff Arts Center, so this is certainly a high-traffic area.

Please let us know your plans. With the recent concern for healthy food, it would seem to be a very favorable time for a restaurant such as "My Favorite Vegetable." We look forward to hearing from you.

Sincerely yours,

Bud Porter
President

afc
c: Raymond DuBois

Letterhead: The company's name and address, along with other information (such as a telephone number).

Date Line: The date (month, day, and year) on which the letter is typed; starts at center on the third line below the letterhead, 2 inches from the top of the page, or immediately below the return address.

Inside Address: The name and address of the to whom person you are writing.

Salutation: An opening greeting, such as "Dear Ms. Morales:".

Message: The text of the letter; all paragraphs are typed single-spaced with no indentions; leave one blank line between paragraphs.

Complimentary Closing: A parting phrase, such as "Sincerely", or "Sincerely yours", starts at center.

Writer's Identification: The signer's name and title.

Reference Initials: The initials of the typist and sometimes those of the writer as well.

Copy Notation: The names of those who will receive copies of this letter.

Business Letter—Modified-Block Style

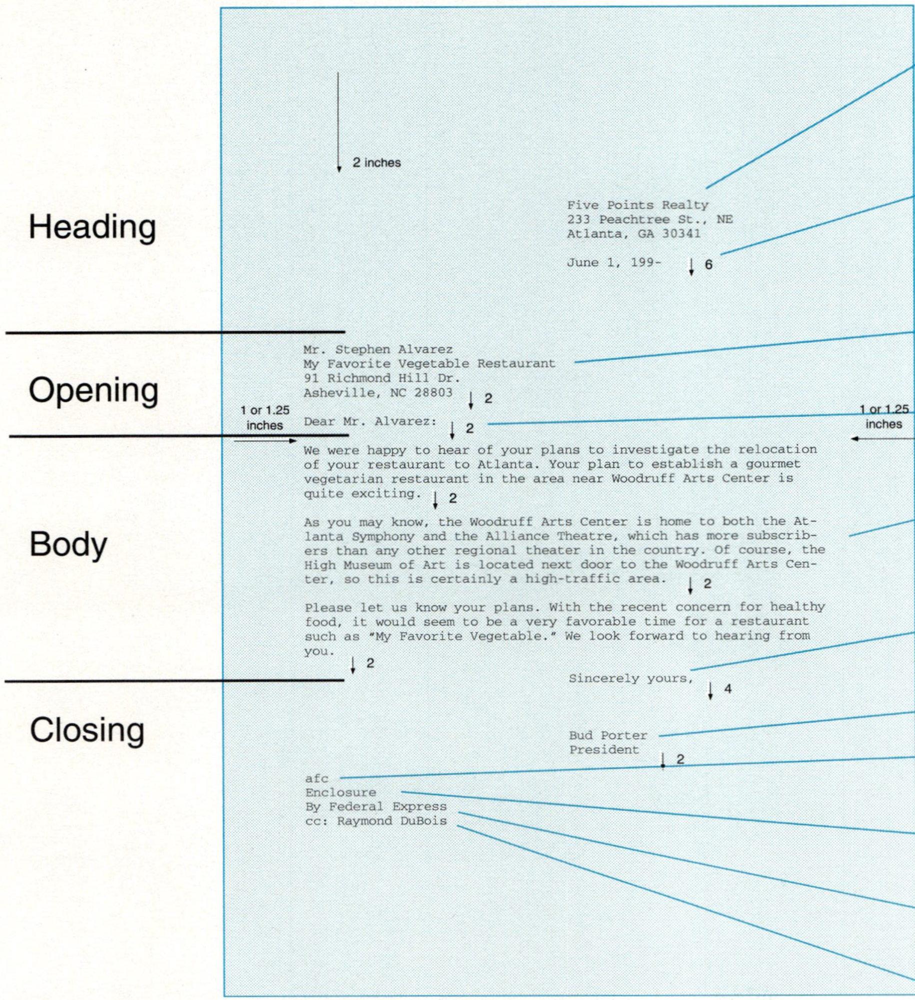

Return Address: When not using letterhead paper, a return address is needed. A return address consists of the company's name and address. In a personal-business letter, the company's name is optional.

Date Line: The date (month, day, and year) on which the letter is typed; starts at center on the third line below the letterhead, 2 inches from the top of the page, or immediately below the return address.

Inside Address: The name and address of the person to whom you are writing.

Salutation: An opening greeting, such as "Dear Ms. Morales:".

Message: The text of the letter; all paragraphs are typed single-spaced with no indentions; leave one blank line between paragraphs.

Complimentary Closing: A parting phrase, such as "Sincerely", or "Sincerely yours", starts at center.

Writer's Identification: The signer's name and title.

Reference Initials: The initials of the typist and sometimes those of the writer as well.

Enclosure Notation: A reminder that the letter is accompanied by an enclosure.

Delivery Notation: An indication that the letter has been sent a special way.

Copy Notation: The names of those who will receive copies of this letter.

(Continued from page B-1)

ZIP Code; your phone number (if appropriate); and the date. A business letter using a return address often includes the business name as well.

Continuation Pages

For letters that are two or more pages, use plain paper without letterhead for the continuation pages. Insert a header on the continuation pages that consists of the name of the addressee, the page number, and the date, using either of the following styles:

```
Mr. Steven Alvarez
Page 2
June 1, 199-


Mr. Steven Alvarez        2       June 1, 199-
```

Place the header 1 inch from the edge of the page. Insert two blank lines between the header and the continuation text.

Standard Form for a Memorandum

Many businesses use preprinted memorandum forms that standardize the key information required by the business. When a business does not use a preprinted memo form, you can use paper with a letterhead or, if the company does not use a letterhead, you can use plain paper.

There isn't a single correct form for memos typed on letterhead or plain paper. However, the memo form shown on page C-2 illustrates the elements of a good memo: "Memo To," "From," "Date," and "Subject".

For memos that are two or more pages, insert a header on the continuation pages that consists of the name of the addressee, the page number, and the date, using either of the following styles:

```
Ms. Susan Allen
Page 2
November 15, 199-
```

```
Ms. Susan Allen        2        November 15, 199-
```

Place the header 1 inch from the edge of the page. Insert two blank lines between the header and the continuation text.

2 inches

↓ Tab 10

MEMO TO: Atlanta Board of Realtors Membership ↓ 2

FROM: Bud Porter ↓ 2

DATE: August 15, 199- ↓ 2

SUBJECT: Fall Course Announcement ↓ 3

The Atlanta Board of Realtors is happy to announce the fall schedule of real estate courses offered to members at discount rates. The curriculum is designed to meet state requirements for obtaining and maintaining a Geogia real estate license. ↓ 2

1 or 1.25 inches → ← 1 or 1.25 inches

Our faculty consists of outstanding professionals with at least 10 years' experience in real estate. Five convenient class sites and varying class times have been selected. In addition, arrangements may be made to teach any class at your business location if there are enough sign-ups. Minimum class enrollment is 20. ↓ 2

To register, submit a completed registration form with full payment via check, money order, MasterCard, or Visa. Mail registrations must be received at least 5 business days prior to the first class. ↓ 2

In-person registration many be completed any business day from 9:00 a.m. - 6:00 p.m. at the ABR offices up to 48 hours prior to the first class. Make checks payable to Atlanta Board of Realtors, 245 Peachtree Center Ave., Atlanta, GA 30303.
For additional information contact Sheila Baldwin at the Board office, 555-2323. ↓ 2

BP ↓ 2

afc

Standard Form for a Business Envelope

Many businesses use envelopes with preprinted return addresses for all correspondence. When the envelope contains a preprinted return address, you can key the name of the writer so that it prints above the preprinted return address. (However, some printers are not able to print a name that is too close to the edge of the envelope. In these cases, you will have to use a typewriter, insert the name by hand, or omit the name altogether.)

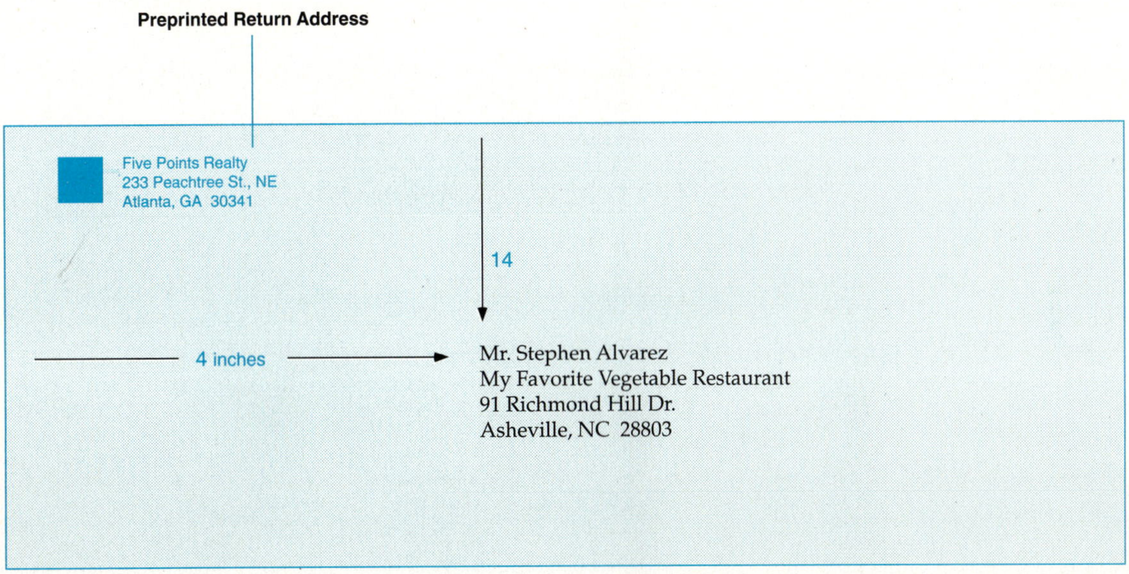

Glossary

The number following the definition of a glossary term indicates the Lesson in which the term is first used.

Absolute tab A tab measured from the left edge of the paper. (9)

Abstract A narrative summary of a document. (8)

Active window The window currently in use on the computer screen. (1)

Append To add text or graphics to the contents of the Clipboard. (11)

Application A computer program used to do a particular kind of work, such as word processing. (3)

Application window A window that contains a running application and has a menu bar. (1)

Auto Code Placement The automatic placement of codes in their proper place in a page or paragraph. (8)

Baseline The invisible line on which capital letters appear to sit. (19)

Bullet A character (such as a bold dot) that calls attention to an item. (10)

Bulleted list A series of bulleted items treated as separate paragraphs. (10)

Cascading menu A menu that opens from a command on another menu. (2)

Cascading windows Open windows that are arranged in layers with the title bar of each window visible. (1)

Cell address The column letter and row number that indicate the location of a cell in a table. (21)

Cell margins The amount of space between text in a cell and the edges of a cell. Each cell has top, bottom, left, and right margins. (22)

Cells The boxes created by the intersections of rows and columns in a table. (21)

Center To align text with equal distance from the left and right margins. (8)

Character attribute A formatting option, such as bold, italic, or underline, that determines the appearance of text. (6)

Character-based lines Lines made of a series of individual characters, such as line segments, WordPerfect characters, letters, or other symbols. (29)

Character format The combined character attributes of text. (6)

Check box A small box offering you the chance to switch an option off or on. An "X" in the box indicates a yes response. (2)

Click To press the mouse button and then quickly release it. (1)

Clipboard A temporary electronic holding area, or buffer, in the computer memory that stores text or graphics for later use. (11)

Color spectrum A representation of all the available custom colors. (20)

Command button A small rectangle, sometimes with rounded corners, that you click to choose an option. (2)

Control Panel A Windows application with controls for adjusting the screen and mouse and for choosing the printer. (2)

Control-menu box The box in the upper left corner of the window. Clicking this box displays the Control menu, which contains options for manipulating windows. (1)

Copy To store a copy of selected text or graphics on the Clipboard for future use. (11)

cpi Abbreviation for characters per inch. (19)

Cut To delete selected text or graphics and store it on the clipboard. (11)

Database A collection of records. A secondary file is a kind of database. (27)

Default settings Settings predefined by WordPerfect. The user can change default settings to customize documents. (4)

Desktop The area of the computer screen outside the window borders. (1)

Dialog box A box that displays a question or presents options and asks you to respond. (2)

Document comment A note within a document that is displayed on the screen, but that does not print. (12)

Document initial font A default font for a specific document. (19)

Document summary A formal document description including reference information. (8)

Document window A window without a menu bar, appearing in the workspace of an application window. (1)

Dot leader A series of periods before a tab or text. (9)

Double-click To quickly press and release the mouse button twice. (1)

Draft Mode A screen mode available from the View menu that displays characters with uniform (monospace) spacing. (29)

Drag To point to an object, hold down the mouse button, move the mouse to a new position, and then release the mouse button. (1)

Drag and Drop To move selected text by dragging it with the mouse. (11)

Drag-select To select text by holding down the mouse button while moving the mouse. (5)

Drop-down list box A list box that contains additional choices that appear when an arrow on the right side of the list box is clicked. (2)

Drop-down menus Menus that drop down to display a list of options when the name of the menu is clicked. (Also called *Pull-down menus.*) (2)

Dropped capital letter The first letter of a paragraph that is enlarged and set off from the rest of the paragraph. (31)

Em dash A dash the width of a capital M. (20)

En dash A dash the width of a capital N. (20)

Equation Editor An editor for creating complex mathematical and scientific equations in a graphics box. (30)

Field A category or a piece of information within a record. Examples of fields are name, address, and phone number. (27)

Figure Editor An editor for retrieving and manipulating graphics images in a graphics box. (30)

File A document that has been created and saved under a unique filename. (4)

Filename The unique name given to a document that is saved in WordPerfect. (4)

Flush right To align text at the right margin. (8)

Font A set of letters, numbers, and special characters with a consistent design. (19)

Footer Text that is repeated at the bottom of a series of document pages. (16)

Formula A combination of cell addresses, mathematical operators (+, -, *, or /), and/or numbers, used to perform simple calculations in tables. (23)

Graphics box A rectangle that can hold text, a table, or an illustration, and can be positioned as a unit anywhere in a document. (30)

Graphics box type The WordPerfect category for a graphics box: Figure, Text, Equation, Table, or User. (30)

Graphics Image A picture stored as a pattern of dots. (30)

Graphics lines Lines created in a graphic format and defined in terms of thickness, length, shading, and position. (29)

Gutter The distance between columns. (24)

Hard page break A page break that is inserted manually and does not move, regardless of changes in the document. (14)

Hard return A non-printing character, created by pressing the **Enter** key, that creates a new line. (5)

Header Text that is repeated at the top of a series of document pages. (16)

Header row A row of column headings that is defined specially to appear at the top of each page in a multiple-page table. (23)

Headword A word that can be looked up in the Thesaurus. (7)

Highlighting To position the pointer on a menu option, causing the option to change to light type on a dark background. (2)

Hue The ratio of red, green, and blue used to make a custom color (from 0 to 360). (20)

Hyphenation The division of words, usually with a hyphen (-). (8)

Icons Small pictures or symbols on the computer screen representing programs or tools. (1)

Indent The distance between the sides of a paragraph and the margins. (10)

Initial font A font that is set as the default for a printer or document. (19)

Insertion point A vertical blinking bar on the WordPerfect screen that shows the current location and determines where an action will begin. (4)

Jump term A Help topic that is linked to other Help topics or to more information, usually identified by an underline and a color. (4)

Justification The alignment of text in relation to the side margins. (8)

Kerning An adjustment that reduces the spacing between certain letter pairs. (19)

Key The category of information by which text is sorted. (28)

Landscape orientation Printing parallel to the long edge of the paper. (18)

Leading The white space between lines. (19)

Line spacing The amount of space from the bottom of one line to the bottom of the next line. (8)

List box A box that contains a list of available choices. (2)

Logical page A single label within a paper-size definition. (18)

Lumination The lightness or darkness of a color (from 0% to 100%). (20)

Macro A collection of menu commands and keystrokes that are saved as a file and can be played back exactly as saved by executing a single command. (26)

Margin The white space between the text and the edge of the printed page. (8)

Margin marker A Ruler icon that marks and sets the boundary between the text and the margin. (8)

Maximize button The box in the upper right corner containing an up arrow. Clicking this button enlarges the window to fill the entire screen. (1)

Menu bar The area under the title bar that displays the words File, Options, Window, and Help. (1)

Minimize button The box in the upper right corner containing a down arrow. Clicking this button shrinks the window to its icon. (1)

Mouse pad A small mat on which a mouse may be rolled. (1)

Newspaper columns Text arranged on a page in two or more columns that flows continuously from the top to the bottom of one column, then to the top of the next column. (24)

Numbered list A series of numbered items treated as separate paragraphs. (10)

Open style A style that goes into effect at the position where it is inserted, and remains in effect for the remainder of the document. (25)

Option button A small circle that indicates a list of mutually exclusive items. You can select only one item from the list at a time. (2)

Orphan A line that appears by itself at the bottom of a page of text. (14)

Paired codes A set of codes to turn an attribute on and off. (6)

Paired style A style used to format small amounts of text. A paired style has a style on code and a style off code. (25)

Paper definition A description, including paper dimensions and orientation, used to format and print documents. (18)

Paper location The source of the paper being fed into the printer: Continuous, Bin #, or Manual. (18)

Paragraph Any part of a document that ends with a hard return, and the blank lines that follow it. (5)

Parallel block protect A column format that prevents a block of text from being divided by a soft page break. (24)

Parallel columns Blocks of related text placed in side-by-side columns. (24)

Paste To insert a copy of the Clipboard's contents at the insertion point. (11)

Physical page A sheet to be fed into the printer. A physical page may contain one or more labels (logical pages). (18)

Pitch The horizontal measurement of a font in characters per inch. (19)

Point To move the mouse until the on-screen pointer is on top of an item on the computer screen. (1)

Point (pt) A measure of type height equal to 1/72 of an inch. (19)

Pointer A small symbol on the screen that shows the position of the mouse. (1)

Portrait orientation Printing parallel to the short edge of the paper. (18)

Primary file The file that contains the text for the merged documents. The primary file contains codes that indicate where the variable information from the secondary file will be inserted. (27)

Printer definition A technical definition of a printer, including its driver and connections. (17)

Printer driver A file that contains codes to control a printer. (17)

Printer initial font The default font for a particular printer. (19)

Pull-down menus Menus that pull down to display a list of options when the name of the menu is clicked. (Also called *Drop-down menus*.) (2)

Quick List In the Open File dialog box, a list of descriptive names that allow you to move quickly to frequently used paths and filenames. (5)

Ragged Uneven, as the edge of text that is not aligned with a margin. (8)

Record A group of related pieces of information, such as the name, address, and telephone number for a person. (27)

Redlining The process of marking new text to distinguish it from original text in a document. (20)

References The synonyms and antonyms that are found for a particular headword in the Thesaurus. (7)

Relative tab A tab measured from the left margin. (9)

Restore button The box at the right of the title bar containing a double arrow that, when clicked, returns the window to its original size. The restore box appears after a window has been maximized. (1)

Sans serif fonts Fonts without serifs. (19)

Saturation The purity of a color, or the degree to which it has been diluted by white (from 0% to 100%). (20)

Scalable font A font that is defined mathematically, so its size can be changed. (19)

Scroll arrow The arrow at either end of the scroll bar that, when clicked, causes the workspace to move a short distance in the opposite direction of the arrow. (2)

Scroll bar A bar appearing at the right and bottom edge when the contents of the window are not entirely visible. (2)

Scroll box The box in a scroll bar that represents your approximate position in the window. (2)

Secondary file A file containing a list of information (usually names and addresses) to be used in a merge. The information is organized as records and fields. (27)

Selection The selected portion of a document (or the whole document) that appears highlighted on the screen. (5)

Sentence Any text ending with a period or other end-of-sentence punctuation and at least one space. (5)

Serif fonts Fonts with serifs. (19)

Serifs Small projections at the top and bottom of a letter. (19)

Small cap A capital letter that is shorter than the full-size capital letters in the same type size. (20)

Soft page break A page break automatically placed by WordPerfect, which is adjusted automatically to reflect changes in the document. (14)

Sort To arrange a list of items in alphabetical or numerical order. (28)

Strikeout marks Horizontal lines running through the middle of characters to mark text that is to be deleted. (20)

String A series of any combination of characters, punctuation marks, spaces, format codes, or wildcards. (13)

Style A group of formatting commands that can be named and saved with a document or as part of a separate style library. (25)

Style library A group of styles, saved as a file, designed to be used together in a document. Style libraries ensure consistent appearance of documents. (25)

Subscript Characters positioned below the baseline. (20)

Superscript Characters positioned above the baseline. (20)

Syntax The structure or rules of construction for a macro command. (26)

Tab A code that advances the insertion point a set distance from the left. (9)

Tab buttons Ruler buttons for setting left, center, right, and decimal tabs. (9)

Tab marker A triangle that marks a tab setting on the Ruler. (9)

Tab setting The set distance where a tab stops. (9)

Table-column markers Marks on the Ruler that indicate the right edge of each column in a table. (22)

Table structure The rows and columns that make up a table, but not the text in it. (21)

Text box A rectangle in which you can type information. (2)

Text Box Editor An editor for retrieving, entering, and manipulating text and tables in a graphics box. (30)

Tiled windows Open windows that are resized and arranged side by side on the screen. (1)

Title bar The shaded bar at the top of the window that displays the name of the window. (1)

Widow A line that appears by itself at the top of a page of text. (14)

Wildcard A character or code representing an unknown character. In WordPerfect, the code [Any Char] represents one unknown character in a search string. (13)

Window A rectangular area on the computer screen with borders that separate it from the rest of the screen. (1)

Window borders The boundary lines surrounding the window. (1)

Window corners The four corners of the window border, which are used to adjust the size of the window. (1)

Word The characters that make up a word, plus any spaces that follow it. (5)

WordPerfect characters Characters supplied with WordPerfect that do not appear on a standard keyboard. (20)

Wordwrap The automatic placement of text on the next line. (4)

Workspace The area in the window that displays the contents of the window. (1)

Index